Al-Kafi

Volume 3 of 8

(Fru‘ al-Kafi)

English Translation

Second Edition

Compiled by
Thiqatu al-Islam, Abu Ja’far Muhammad
ibn Ya’qub al-Kulayni

Translated by
Muhammad Sarwar

Published by
The Islamic Seminary Inc.
www.theislamicseminary.org

The Islamic Seminary Inc., New York

Second Edition 2015
Printed in the United States of America.

ISBN: 978-0-9914308-2-6

Al-Kafi, Volume 3 of 8. English Translation – 2nd ed.
Rabi' al-Thani 1436
February 2015

Al-Kafi

Volume 3 of 8

English Translation

Note to Readers

Dear respected readers, please note the following:

The English translation of this volume from Kitab al-Kafi is now, by the will of Allah, in your hands. It was only because of the beauty of the words of Ahl al-Bayt *'Alayhim al-Salam* that made it all possible. The magnitude of this project had become quite large and complex due to two language texts and it was sometimes difficult to handle.

All comments, suggestions and corrections will be very much appreciated. In fact it will be your participation in the good cause and rewarding in the sight of Allah, most Majestic, most Glorious. Please e-mail your comments, suggestions or corrections to: info@theislamicseminary.org.

With thanks,

The Islamic Seminary
www.theislamicseminary.org

Contents

Part Two: The Book of Hayd (Menses)

Part Three: The Book on Dying People

Part Four: The Book of Prayer

Part Five: The Book of al-Zakat

An Outline of the Number of Volumes, Sections and Sub-divisions of Kitab al-Kafi

Part 1 - Al-'Usul (Principles)

Volume 1

This part of the book consists of *Ahadith* on the principles of beliefs and it is called 'Usul (principles) in *al-Kafi.*

The sections or chapters in volume 1 are as follows:

1. The Book of Intelligence and Ignorance (*Kitab al-'Aql wa al-Jahl*)
2. The Book of the Excellence of Knowledge (*Kitabu Fad al-'Ilm*)
3. The Book on Oneness of Allah (*Kitab al-Tawhid*)
4. The Book about the people who possess Divine Authority (*Kitab al-Hujja*)

Volume 2

Sections or Chapters in Volume 2:

5. The Book on Belief and Disbelief (*Kitab al-'Iman wa al-Kufr*)
6. The Book on Prayers (*Kitab al-Du'a'*)
7. The Book on the Excellence of the Holy Quran (*Kitabu Fadl al-Quran*)
8. The Book of Social Discipline (*Kitab al-'Ishra*)

PART 2 - Al-*Furu'* (Branches)

Volumes 3-7

This part consists of *Ahadith* on Islamic practical laws such as:

The acts of worship (*'Ibadat*)

Business transactions (*mu'amalat*)

Judicial laws (*al-Qada'*)

Furu' al-Kafi (volume 3 – 7): The rules of conduct, the practical laws of the Islamic system, consists of the following:

9. The Book of Laws of Cleanliness (*Kitab al-Tahara*)
10. The Book of Laws of Menstruation (*Kitab al-Hayd*)
11. The Book of Laws about the dying people and their burials (*Kitab al-Jana'iz*)
12. The Book of Laws of Prayer (*Kitab al-Salat*)
13. The Book of Laws of Charities, Taxes (*Kitab al-Zakat*)
14. The Book of Laws of Fasting (*Kitab al-Siyam*)

15. The Book of Laws of Pilgrimage (*Kitab al- Hajj*)
16. The Book of Laws of Defense (*Kitab al-Jihad*)
17. The Book of Laws of Business (*Kitab al-Ma'ishah*)
18. The Book of Laws of Marriage (*Kitab al-Nikah*)
19. The Book of Laws about New-born (*Kitab al-'Aqiqa*)
20. The Book of Laws of Divorce (*Kitab al-Talaq*)
21. The Book of Laws of Emancipation of Slaves (*Kitab al-'Itq wa al-Tadbir wa al-Mukataba*)
22. The Book of Laws of Hunting (*Kitab al-Sayd*)
23. The Book of Laws of Slaughtering Animals for food (*Kitab al-Dhaba'ih*)
24. The Book of Laws of Foods (*Kitab al-At'imah*)
25. The Book of Laws of Drinks (*Kitab al-Ashriba*)
26. The Book of Laws of Dresses, Beautifying and the Ideal of Manhood (*Kitab al-Zay wa al-Tajammul*)
27. The Book of Laws of Animal Farming and Poultry (*Kitab al-Dawajin*)
28. The Book of Laws of Wills (*Kitab al-Wasaya'*)
29. The Book of Laws of Inheritances (*Kitab al-Mawarith*)
30. The Book of Laws of Penalties (*Kitab al-Hudud*)
31. The Book of Laws of Restitution for Bodily Injuries (*Kitab al-Diyat*)
32. The Book of Laws of Testimony and Witnessing (*Kitab al-Shahadat*)
33. The Book of Judicial Laws (*Kitab al-Qada' wa al-Ahkam*)
34. The Book of Laws of Oaths, Vows and Expiation (*Kitab al-'Ayman wa al-Nudbur wa al-Kaffarat*)

PART 3 - Al-Rawdah (Garden of Flowers (Hadith))

Volume 8

This part consists of miscellaneous *Ahadith* of both the *'Usul* and *Furu'* of *al-Kafi*. The topics are not arranged and organized as in the other volumes. The chapters are not in alphabetical order of *Ahadith* or narrators.

This volume comprises about six hundred *Hadith* on various topics and is a treasure of knowledge of the matters of belief, spiritual discipline, interpretations of many verses of the Holy Quran, accounts of the noble manners of the Holy Prophet and infallible members of his family and information about the system of this and the next life.

In the Name of Allah, the Beneficient, the Merciful

Part One: The Book of Taharat (Cleansing)

Chapter 1 - The Cleansing Quality of Water

H 3783, Ch. 1, h 1

Abu Ja'far, Muhammad ibn Ya'qub al-Kulayniy (rh) has said that narrated to me Ali ibn Ibrahim ibn Hashim from his father from al-Nawfaliy from al-Sakuniy, who has said the following:

"Abu 'Abd Allah, Ja'far ibn Muhammad, *'Alayhim al-Salam*, has said, that the Messenger of Allah, O Allah grant compensation to Muhammad and his family worthy of their services to Your cause, has said, 'Water cleanses but it is not cleanable.'"

H 3784, Ch. 1, h 2

Muhammad ibn Yahya and others have narrated from Muhammad ibn Ahmad from al-Hassan ibn al-Hassan al-Lu'lu'iy through his chain of narrators has said the following:

"Abu 'Abd Allah, *'Alayhi al-Salam*, has said, 'All water is clean until it is found out that it is not clean.'"

H 3785, Ch. 1, h 3

Muhammad ibn Yahya has narrated from Muhammad ibn al-Hassan from abu Dawud al-Munshid from Ja'far ibn Muhammad from Yunus from Hammad ibn 'Uthman who has said the following:

"Abu 'Abd Allah, *'Alayhi al-Salam*, has said, that all water (from source) is clean until it is found out that it is not clean."

H 3786, Ch. 1, h 4

Ali ibn Ibrahim has narrated from Muhammad ibn 'Isa from Yunus ibn 'Abd al-Rahman from 'Abd Allah ibn Sinan who has said the following:

"I once asked abu 'Abd Allah, *'Alayhi al-Salam*, 'Is sea water clean?' He (the Imam) replied, 'Yes, it is clean.'"

H 3787, Ch. 1, h 5

Muhammad ibn Yahya has narrated from Ahmad ibn Muhammad ibn 'Isa from 'Uthman ibn 'Isa from abu Bakr al-Hadramiy who has said the following:

"I once asked abu 'Abd Allah, *'Alayhi al-Salam*, 'Is sea water clean?' He (the Imam) replied, 'Yes, it is clean.'"

Chapter 2 - The Quantity of Water that Always Remains Clean

H 3788, Ch. 2, h 1

Muhammad ibn 'Isma'il has narrated from al-Fadl ibn Shadhan from Safwan ibn Yahya and Ali ibn Ibrahim has narrated from his father from Hammad ibn 'Isa all from Mu'awiyah ibn 'Ammar who has said the following:

"I heard abu 'Abd Allah, *'Alayhi al-Salam*, say, 'If the quantity of water is one Kur, then things do not make it unclean.'"

H 3789, Ch. 2, h 2

A number of our people have narrated from Ahmad ibn Muhammad ibn 'Isa from Ali ibn al-Hakam from abu Ayyub al-Khazzaz from Muhammad ibn Muslim who has said the following:

"I once asked abu 'Abd Allah, *'Alayhi al-Salam*, about a water which dogs lick and in which animals urinate and people take baths after sexual activities. He (the Imam) said, 'If its quantity is one Kur, then such things cannot make it unclean.'"

H 3790, Ch. 2, h 3

Ali ibn Ibrahim has narrated from his father and Muhammad ibn 'Isma'il from al-Fadl ibn Shadhan from Hammad ibn 'Isa from Hariz from Zurarah who has said the following:

"If the quantity of water is more than a Rawiyah, then it does not become unclean because of things falling in it, regardless of whether they have disintegrated or not, unless the smell of such things overwhelms the smell of water."

H 3791, Ch. 2, h 4

Muhammad ibn Yahya has narrated from Ahmad ibn Muhammad from ibn Mahbub from al-Hassan ibn Salih al-Thawriy who has said the following:

"Abu 'Abd Allah, *'Alayhi al-Salam*, has said, 'If a quantity of water measures one Kur it does not become unclean.' I then asked, 'How much is the quantity of Kur?' He (the Imam) replied, 'Three and a half shibr in depth and three and a half in width.'"(A Shibr is from the tip of thumb to the tip of the small finger with the palm spread open)

H 3792, Ch. 2, h 5

Muhammad ibn Yahya has narrated from Ahmad ibn Muhammad from 'Uthman ibn 'Isa form ibn Muskan from abu Basir who has said the following:

"I asked abu 'Abd Allah, *'Alayhi al-Salam*, 'How much is the quantity of one Kur of water?' He (the Imam) replied, 'If the size of water is three and a half shibr by three and a half shibr, and three and a half shibr in its depth in the ground, then it is one Kur.'"

H 3793, Ch. 2, h 6

Ahmad ibn Idris has narrated from Muhammad ibn Ahmad from Ya'qub ibn Yazid from ibn abu 'Umayr from certain persons of our people who has said the following:

"Abu 'Abd Allah, *'Alayhi al-Salam*, has said that the quantity of one Kur of water is one thousand and two hundred ritl (a certain measurement)."

H 3794, Ch. 2, h 7

Muhammad ibn Yahya has narrated from Ahmad ibn Muhammad from al-Barqiy from ibn Sinan from 'Isma'il ibn Jabir who has said the following:

"I asked abu 'Abd Allah, *'Alayhi al-Salam*, about the water which does not become unclean by anything. He (the Imam) replied, 'It is one Kur.' I then asked, 'How much is one Kur?' He (the Imam) replied, 'It is three shibr by three shibr in size.'"

H 3795, Ch. 2, h 8

Ali ibn Ibrahim has narrated from his father from 'Abd Allah ibn al-Mughirah from certain persons of our people who has said the following:

"Abu 'Abd Allah, *'Alayhi al-Salam*, has said, 'The quantity of one Kur of water is of the size of this Hubb (a water container).' He pointed with his hand to one of those Hubb which are used in al-Madinah."

Chapter 3 - The Case of a Small Quantity of Water, the Water with a Dead Body in it and its use by a Man to Wash His Dirty Hand in it

H 3796, Ch. 3, h 1

A number of our people have narrated from Ahmad ibn Muhammad from Ali ibn al-Hakam from 'Abd Allah ibn Yahya al-Kahiliy who has said the following:

"I heard abu 'Abd Allah, *'Alayhi al-Salam*, say, 'If you find a small quantity of water, then take away some water from the right, left and in front of you, then take a Wudu'.'"

H 3797, Ch. 3, h 2

Ali ibn Ibrahim has narrated from his father from 'Abd Allah ibn al-Mughirah from ibn Muskan who has said that Muhammad ibn al-Muyassir has said the following:

"I asked abu 'Abd Allah, *'Alayhi al-Salam*, 'A man, after a sexual activity finds water on the way which is less than a Kur in quantity. He wants to take a bath but he does not have a bowl to pick up water with. His hands are dirty (but they are clean). What should he do?' He (the Imam) said, 'He may place his hand in it to take Wudu' (to wash) then he takes a bath. Allah, the most Majestic, the most Glorious, has said, "He (Allah) has not made in religion anything that causes you hardships."' (22:78)

H 3798, Ch. 3, h 3

Ali ibn Ibrahim has narrated from his father and Muhammad ibn 'Isma'il from al-Fadl ibn Shadhan from Hammad from Hariz from those who reported to him who has said the following:

"Abu 'Abd Allah, *'Alayhi al-Salam*, has said that as long as water overwhelms the smell of a dead animal you can take Wudu' with it and drink it, but when the smell changes as well as its taste, then do not take Wudu' with it and do not drink it."

H 3799, Ch. 3, h 4

Ali ibn Ibrahim has narrated from Muhammad ibn 'Isa ibn 'Ubayd from Yunus ibn 'Abd al-Rahman from 'Abd Allah ibn Sinan who has said the following:

"A man asked abu 'Abd Allah, *'Alayhi al-Salam*, when I was present, about a pond of water where a dead animal was found. He (the Imam) said, 'If water is overwhelming and there is no smell in it, then you can take Wudu' with it.'"

H 3800, Ch. 3, h 5

A number of our people have narrated from Ahmad ibn Muhammad from al-Husayn ibn Sa'id from al-Qasim ibn Muhammad from Ali ibn abu Hamzah who has said the following:

"I asked abu 'Abd Allah, *'Alayhi al-Salam*, about a (pond of) water which is not running and has a dead animal in it. 'How can one cleanse oneself with such water?' He (the Imam) said, 'You can take Wudu' from the other side and not from the side of the dead animal.'"

H 3801, Ch. 3, h 6

Ali ibn Ibrahim has narrated from his father from ibn abu 'Umayr from Hammad from al-Halabiy who has said the following:

"I asked abu 'Abd Allah, *'Alayhi al-Salam*, 'Is it permissible to take Wudu' with water which is discolored?' He (the Imam) said, 'You can do so but if you find other water cleanse yourself with it.'"

H 3802, Ch. 3, h 7

Ali ibn Muhammad has narrated from Sahl from Ahmad ibn Muhammad ibn abu Nasr from Safwan al-Jammal who has said the following:

"I once asked abu 'Abd Allah, *'Alayhi al-Salam*, 'There are ponds between al-Madinah and Makkah where beasts come and dogs lick, people take baths because of sexual activities or take Wudu' with it.' He (the Imam) asked, 'How much water is it?' I replied, 'It is up to the leg or up to half of the leg or up to the knees or less.' He (the Imam) said, 'You can take Wudu' with such water.'"

Chapter 4 - The Case of a Well and Things that May Fall in It

H 3803, Ch. 4, h 1

A number of our people have narrated from Ahmad ibn Muhammad from Muhammad ibn 'Isma'il ibn Bazi' who has said the following:

"I once wrote to a person to write to abu al-Hassan al-Rida, *'Alayhi al-Salam*, to ask him about a well in one's house for Wudu'. If some drops of urine, or blood, or animal dung and so forth fall in it, then how can it be cleansed so one can take Wudu' with water from such a well for Salat (prayer). He (the Imam) sent the answer with his signature that said, 'Draw a few buckets of water from it and dispose such water away.'"

H 3804, Ch 4, h 2

Through the same chain of narrators as the previous Hadith the following is stated:

"He (the Imam) *'Alayhi al-Salam*, said, 'Well water is vast. It does not become polluted until it is changed.'"

H 3805, Ch. 4, h 3

Ali ibn Ibrahim has narrated from his father from ibn abu 'Umayr from Jamil ibn Darraj from abu 'Usamah who has said the following:

"This is about the case of a rat, cat, chicken, bird and dog in a well. Abu 'Abd Allah, *'Alayhi al-Salam*, has said, 'As long as they have not disintegrated or water's taste is not changed, take out five buckets of water thereof, but if there is a change in the water then continue drawing out the water until the smell is gone.'"

H 3806, Ch. 4, h 4

Muhammad ibn Yahya in a marfu' manner has narrated the following:

"Abu 'Abd Allah, *'Alayhi al-Salam*, has said, 'Water does not become polluted because of the living things which do not have spurting blood when a cut is made in its body.'"

H 3807, Ch. 4, h 5

Ahmad ibn Idris has narrated from Muhammad ibn Salim from Ahmad ibn al-Nadr from 'Amr ibn Shimr from Jabir who has said the following:

"This is about the case of al-Sam al-Abras (a poisonous snake) that falls in the well. Abu Ja'far, *'Alayhi al-Salam*, has said, 'It is not harmful. Just stir the water with the bucket.'"

H 3808, Ch. 4, h 6

A number of our people have narrated from Ahmad ibn Muhammad from al-Husayn ibn Sa'id from ibn Sinan from ibn Muskan from abu Basir who has said the following:

"I once asked abu 'Abd Allah, *'Alayhi al-Salam*, about things that fall into the wells. He (the Imam) said, 'Because of rats and similar things, seven buckets of water must be drawn out, unless the water is changed, in which case drawing water out must continue until it becomes clean. If a dog falls in it, if you can, draw all of the water out. Falling in a well of anything without blood like a scorpion or beetle and similar things is not harmful.'"

H 3809, Ch. 4, h 7

Ahmad ibn Idris has narrated from Muhammad 'Abd al-Jabbar from Safwan from ibn Muskan from al-Halabiy who has said the following:

"Abu 'Abd Allah, *'Alayhi al-Salam*, has said, 'If something small falls in a well and dies, then take a few buckets of water out. If a person involved in sexual activities (because of which Ghusl (bath) is obligatory) falls in it, you must draw seven buckets of water out thereof. If a camel dies in it or wine is poured in it then you must draw out all of the water.'"

H 3810, Ch. 4, h 8

Muhammad ibn Yahya has narrated from al-'Amrakiy ibn Ali from Ali ibn Ja'far who has said the following:

"I once asked abu al-Hassan, *'Alayhi al-Salam*, about a man who slaughters a sheep and due to the shock it falls into the water well with blood gushing from its veins. Can one take Wudu' from such well? He (the Imam) said, 'One must draw out thirty to forty buckets of water, then one can take Wudu' with its water and it is not harmful.' I then asked about a man who slaughters a chicken or pigeon and it falls into the well. Can one take Wudu' with water from such well? He (the Imam) said, 'A few buckets of water must be taken out, then one can take Wudu'.' I then asked about someone from whose nostril blood falls into the well can one then take Wudu' with water from such well? He (the Imam) said, 'A few buckets of water must be taken out.'"

H 3811, Ch. 4, h 9

Ali ibn Ibrahim has narrated from his father from ibn abu 'Umayr from 'Abd Allah ibn al-Mughirah from those whom he has mentioned who have said the following:

"I once said to abu 'Abd Allah, *'Alayhi al-Salam*, that there is a water-well and with its water pieces of skin come out. He (the Imam) said, 'It is not anything. Perhaps a frog sheds its skin.' He (the Imam) said that one bucket of water is sufficient for you.'"

H 3812, Ch. 4, h 10

Muhammad ibn Yahya has narrated from Ahmad ibn Muhammad from ibn Mahbub from ibn Ri'ab from Zurarah who has said the following:

"I once asked abu 'Abd Allah, *'Alayhi al-Salam*, about a rope made of the hairs of hogs which is used to take out water from the well. Can Wudu' be made with such water? He (the Imam) said, 'It is not harmful.'"

H 3813, Ch. 4, h 11

Muhammad ibn Yahya has narrated from Ahmad ibn Muhammad from al-Husayn ibn Sa'id from al-Qasim ibn Muhammad from Ali ibn abu Hamzah who has said the following:

"I once asked abu 'Abd Allah, *'Alayhi al-Salam*, about the falling of feces into a well. He (the Imam) said, 'Ten buckets of water must be taken out and if it has disintegrated then forty or fifty buckets of water must be taken out.'"

H 3814, Ch. 4, h 12

Ali ibn Muhammad has narrated from Sahl from Ahmad ibn Muhammad from ibn abu Nasr from 'Abd al-Karim from abu Basir who has said the following:

"I once said to abu 'Abd Allah, *'Alayhi al-Salam*, that there was a well from which people drank, took Wudu', washed their clothes and flour was made into dough with its water, and then a dead body was found in it. He (the Imam) said, 'It does not matter, there is no need to wash clothes or perform Salat (prayer) again.'"

(Fatwa best explains Ahadith 2-12 as well as the following chapter.)

Chapter 5 - A Well near a Cesspool

H 3815, Ch. 5, h 1

A number of our people have narrated from Ahmad ibn Muhammad from Muhammad ibn Sinan from al-Hassan ibn Ribat who has said the following:

"I once asked abu 'Abd Allah, *'Alayhi al-Salam*, about a cesspool which is above a well. He (the Imam) said, 'If it is above the well, the distance in between must be seven yards, but if it is below the well, the distance must be five yards from all sides, and that is a large area.'"

H 3816, Ch. 5, h 2

Ali ibn Ibrahim has narrated from his father from Hammad ibn 'Isa from Hariz from Zurarah, Muhammad ibn Muslim and abu Basir who have said the following:

"We once asked him (abu 'Abd Allah, *'Alayhi al-Salam*) about a well which is used for Wudu' and nearby urine flows. 'Is such a well Najis (unclean)? He (the Imam) replied, 'If the well is above the place where urine flows below the well and there is a distance of three or four yards in between, it does not make anything of the well Najis (unclean) but if the distance is less than this, the well becomes Najis (unclean). If the well is below the place where water (urine) flows and there is a distance of nine yards between them it does not make the well Najis (unclean). If the distance is less than this then it cannot be used for Wudu'.' Zurarah then asked, 'What happens if the place is steep and urine flows fast and is not stationary on the ground?' He (the Imam) said, 'If it is not stationary it is not harmful, and even if a little of it is stationary, it does not make a deep hole in the ground to reach the well and it is not harmful to the well, thus it can be used for Wudu'. It is harmful to the well only when all of it (urine) is absorbed in the ground.'"

H 3817, Ch. 5, h 3

Muhammad ibn Yahya has narrated from Ahmad ibn Muhammad from Muhammad ibn `Isma'il from abu `Isma'il from al-Sarraj from 'Abd Allah ibn 'Uthman from Qudamah ibn abu Yazid al-Hammar from certain persons of our people who have said the following:

"I once asked abu 'Abd Allah, *'Alayhi al-Salam*, about the distance needed between a well and a cesspool. He (the Imam) replied, 'If the ground is plain, the distance must be seven yards; and if it is a hillside the distance must be five yards.' He (the Imam) then said, 'Water flows forward in direction, to the right or to the left or from its left side to its right side (in) forward direction but it does not flow backward.'"

H 3818, Ch. 5, h 4

Ahmad ibn Idris has narrated from Muhammad ibn Ahmad from 'Abbad ibn Sulayman from Sa'd ibn Sa'd from Muhammad ibn al-Qasim who has said the following:

"I once asked abu al-Hassan, *'Alayhi al-Salam*, about a well which is five yards or more or less away from a cesspool. Can it be used for Wudu'? He (the Imam) said, 'Shortness or length of distance does not matter. It can be used for Wudu' or Ghusl (bath) if the water has not changed.'"

Chapter 6 - Taking Wudu' With Water from Which Animals, Beasts and Birds Have Drunk

H 3819, Ch. 6, h 1

Ali ibn Ibrahim has narrated from Muhammad ibn 'Isa from Yunus from 'Abd Allah ibn Sinan who has said the following:

"Abu 'Abd Allah, *'Alayhi al-Salam*, has said that it is permissible to use for Wudu' the water from which edible animals have drunk."

H 3820, Ch. 6, h 2

Muhammad ibn Yahya has narrated from Ahmad ibn Muhammad ibn Khalid and Al-Husayn ibn Sa'id from al-Qasim ibn Muhammad from Ali ibn abu Hamzah from abu Basir who has said the following:

"Abu 'Abd Allah, *'Alayhi al-Salam*, has said that it is permissible to use for Wudu' the water from which pigeons, chickens or birds have drunk."

H 3821, Ch. 6, h 3

Abu Dawud has narrated from al-Husayn ibn Sa'id from his brother al-Hassan from Zur'ah, from Sama'ah who has said the following:

"I once asked him (the Imam), *'Alayhi al-Salam*, 'Is it permissible to use for Wudu' the leftover water from which animals have drunk?' He (the Imam) replied, 'As far as the camel, cow and sheep are concerned, it is permissible.'"

H 3822, Ch. 6, h 4

Ali ibn Ibrahim has narrated from his father from ibn abu 'Umayr from 'Umar ibn 'Udhaynah from Zurarah who has said the following:

"Abu 'Abd Allah, *'Alayhi al-Salam,* has said that it is in the book of Ali, *'Alayhi al-Salam*, that cats are beasts but there is no offense in using the leftover of what they eat. I feel embarrassed before Allah to throw away a food from which a cat has eaten.'"

H 3823, Ch. 6, h 5

Ahmad ibn Idris and Muhammad ibn Yahya have narrated from Ahmad ibn al-Hassan from 'Arm ibn Sa'id from Musaddiq ibn Sadaqah from 'Ammar ibn Musa who has said the following:

"Once abu 'Abd Allah, *'Alayhi al-Salam,* was asked about the leftover of the water from which pigeons have drunk. He (the Imam) said, 'It is permissible for you to use the leftover from which edible animals have used. You can use it for Wudu' or drink the leftover of the water from which they have drunk, like a falcon or a hawk or an eagle.' He (the Imam) then said, 'You can use for Wudu' the water from which birds have drunk, unless you see blood on their beaks. If so then do not use it for Wudu' or drinking.'"

H 3824, Ch. 6, h 6

Muhammad ibn Yahya has narrated from Ahmad ibn Muhammad from 'Uthman ibn 'Isa from Sama'ah who has said the following:

"I once asked abu 'Abd Allah, *'Alayhi al-Salam,* about a jar in which a beetle is found dead. He (the Imam) said, 'Throw it away then use the water for Wudu'; but if it is a scorpion, then throw the water away and use some other water for Wudu'.' I then asked him (the Imam) about a man who has two water containers of which he knows one is unclean but does not know exactly which one and he is not able to find other water. He (the Imam) said, 'He must throw away the water in both containers and take a Tayammum instead of Wudu'.'"

H 3825, Ch. 6, h 7

Ahmad ibn Idris has narrated from Muhammad ibn Ahmad from Ayyub ibn Nuh from al-Washsha' from those whom he has mentioned who have said the following:

"Abu 'Abd Allah, *'Alayhi al-Salam,* disliked using the leftover of the water from which inedible animals have drunk."

Chapter 7 - Taking Wudu' with the Water from Which a Woman during Her Hayd (menses), People After Having Carnal Relations, a Jew, a Christian or a Person Hostile toward `A'immah Has Drunk

H 3826, Ch. 7, h 1

Muhammad ibn Yahya has narrated from Muhammad ibn al-Husayn and Muhammad ibn `Isma'il from al-Fadl ibn Shadhan all from Safwan ibn Yahya from Mansur ibn Hazim from 'Anbasah who has said the following:

"Abu 'Abd Allah, *'Alayhi al-Salam,* has said that it is permissible for you to drink the leftover water from which a woman during her Hayd (menses) has drunk but do not take Wudu' with it."

H 3827, Ch. 7, h 2

Muhammad ibn `Isma'il has narrated from al-Fadl ibn Shadhan from Safwan ibn Yahya from al-'Is ibn al-Qasim who has said the following:

"I once asked abu 'Abd Allah, *'Alayhi al-Salam*, 'Can a man and a woman take a Ghusl (bath) from the same water container?' He (the Imam) replied, 'Yes, they can do so. They first must pour water on their hands and then place their hands in the water container.' I (the narrator) then asked, about the leftover water from which a woman during her Hayd (menses) has drunk. He (the Imam) said, 'Do not use it for Wudu' but it is permissible to use for Wudu' the leftover water from which a person after sexual relations has drank if such person is trustworthy (in matters of cleanliness). She then must wash her hands before placing them in the water container. The Messenger of Allah and 'A'isha would take Ghusl (bath) together from one water container.'"

H 3828, Ch. 7, h 3

Muhammad ibn Yahya has narrated from Ahmad ibn Muhammad from Ali ibn al-Hakam from al-Husayn ibn abu al-'Ala' who has said the following:

"I once asked abu 'Abd Allah, *'Alayhi al-Salam*, 'Can a woman during her Hayd (menses) drink water which is her own leftover?' He (the Imam) replied, 'It is permissible for her to do so but she must not use it for Wudu'.'"

H 3829, Ch. 7, h 4

Al-Husayn ibn Muhammad has narrated from Mu'alla' ibn Muhammad al-Washsha' from Hammad ibn 'Uthaman from ibn abu Ya'fur who has said the following:

"I once asked abu 'Abd Allah, *'Alayhi al-Salam*, if a man can take Wudu' with the water from which a woman has drunk. He (the Imam) said, '(Yes, he can do so) if she knows Wudu', but one cannot take Wudu' with water which is left over of a woman who experiences Hayd (menses).'"

H 3830, Ch. 7, h 5

Ali ibn Ibrahim has narrated from his father from 'Abd Allah ibn al-Mughirah from Sa'id al-'Araj who has said the following:

"I once asked abu 'Abd Allah, *'Alayhi al-Salam*, about the leftover of Jews and Christians. He (the Imam) said, 'No.'"

H 3831, Ch. 7, h 6

Ahmad ibn Idris has narrated from Muhammad ibn Ahmad from Ayyub ibn Nuh from al-Washsha' from those whom he has mentioned who have said the following:

"Abu 'Abd Allah, *'Alayhi al-Salam*, did not like the leftover of a person born out of wedlock, Jews, Christians and pagans and whoever opposed Islam and most serious to him was the leftover of one hostile to `A'immah, *'Alayhim al-Salam*."

(Fatwa best explains Ahadith 4-6 of this chapter.)

Chapter 8 - A Man Places His Hand in the Water before Washing, the Limit of Washing Hands Because of Carnal Relations, Urination, Feces and Sleeping

H 3832, Ch. 8, h 1

Ali ibn Ibrahim has narrated from his father from 'Abd Allah ibn al-Mughirah from Sama'ah from abu Basir the following:

"('A'immah), *'Alayhim al-Salam*, have said that it is permissible to place one's hand in a water container before washing them, provided, urine or things from semen discharge has not reached them; otherwise, one must throw away such water."

H 3833, Ch. 8, h 2

A number of our people have narrated from Ahmad ibn Muhammad from al-Husayn ibn Sa'id from Muhammad ibn Sinan from ibn Muskan from abu Basir from 'Abd al-Karim ibn 'Utbah who has said the following:

"I once asked the Shaykh, 'Is it permissible for a man who wakes up to place his hand in the water container before urinating?' He (the Imam) replied, 'No, he cannot do so because he does not know where his hands may have been. He must wash them first.'"

H 3834, Ch. 8, h 3

Muhammad ibn Yahya has narrated from Muhammad ibn 'Isma'il from Ali ibn al-Hakam from Shihab ibn 'Abd Rabbihi who has said the following:

"I once asked abu 'Abd Allah, *'Alayhi al-Salam*, 'Can a man immerse his hands in the water container before washing them?' He (the Imam) replied, 'Yes, he can do so, provided they have not touched any unclean substance.'"

H 3835, Ch. 8, h 4

Muhammad ibn Yahya has narrated from Muhammad ibn al-Husayn, from Ali ibn al-Hakam, from 'Ala' ibn Razin, from Muhammad ibn Muslim who has said the following:

"I once asked one of the two Imam, *'Alayhim al-Salam*, about a man who urinates but does not touch anything, must he wash it with water? He (the Imam) said, 'Yes, if he has experienced sexual relation.'"

H 3836, Ch. 8, h 5

Ali ibn Ibrahim has narrated from his father from ibn abu 'Umayr from Hammad from al-Halabiy who has said the following:

"Abu 'Abd Allah, *'Alayhi al-Salam*, was asked about how many times one must wash his hands before immersing them in the water container. He (the Imam) said, 'Once, because of urination, twice because of defecation and three times because of sexual relation.'"

H 3837, Ch. 8, h 6

Ali ibn Muhammad has narrated from Sahl from those whom he has mentioned from Yunus from Bakkar ibn abu Bakr who has said the following:

"I once asked abu 'Abd Allah, *'Alayhi al-Salam*, about the case of a mug with which one takes water from a large water container but one places it on a dirty place, then immerses it in the large water container. He (the Imam) said, 'He must pour water on the mug three times and rub it.'"

Chapter 9 - Mixing of Rain Water with Urine, with Water Used for Taking Ghusl (bath) Because of Carnal Relations, Touching of One's Cloth with Water Used for Washing Because of Urine

H 3838 Ch. 9, h 1

Ali ibn Ibrahim has narrated from his father from ibn abu 'Umayr from Hisham ibn al-Hakam who has said the following:

"I once asked abu 'Abd Allah, *'Alayhi al-Salam*, about two drain-shoots; one is rain water and the other urine which mix with each other and drops thereof sprinkle over one's clothes. He (the Imam) said, 'It is not harmful (when it still is raining).'"

H 3839, Ch. 9, h 2

A number of our people have narrated from Ahmad ibn Muhammad from al-Haytham ibn abu Masruq from al-Hakam ibn Miskin from Muhammad ibn Marwan who has said the following:

"Abu 'Abd Allah, *'Alayhi al-Salam*, has said that if two drain-shoots, one with rain water and the other with urine mix, and drops thereof sprinkle over one's clothes, it is not harmful for him."

H 3840, Ch. 9, h 3

Ahmad ibn Muhammad from has narrated from Ali ibn al-Hakam from al-Kahiliy from a man who has said the following:

"I once asked abu 'Abd Allah, *'Alayhi al-Salam*, 'I sometimes, pass by and water from a drain-shoot falls on me. At such time, I know, people take Wudu'. He (the Imam) said, 'It is not harmful. You do not need to ask (inquire).' I (the narrator) then asked, 'What happens if rain water falls on me and I see its color is changed; there are signs of dirt with it and several drops sprinkle and fall on me, while on the roof of the house people take Wudu'. Should we keep our clothes on us in such condition?' He (the Imam) said, 'It is not harmful. You do not need to wash your clothes. Everything and substance which has become unclean turns clean when rain falls on it.'"

H 3841, Ch. 9, h 4

Muhammad ibn Yahya has narrated from Ahmad ibn Muhammad from Muhammad ibn 'Isma'il from certain persons of our people who have said the following:

"I once asked abu al-Hassan, *'Alayhi al-Salam*, about soil which is found with rain water. He (the Imam) said, 'It is not harmful up to three days unless it is found out to have become Najis (unclean) by something after rainfall. If such drops sprinkle after three days, then you must wash, but if the road is clean, then you do not need to wash.'"

H 3842, Ch. 9, h 5

Ali ibn Ibrahim has narrated from his father from ibn abu 'Umayr from ibn 'Udhaynah from al-Ahwal who has said the following:

"I once asked abu 'Abd Allah, *'Alayhi al-Salam*, 'I may use the toilet and then wash to clean myself but my clothes touch the water which was used for cleaning. He (the Imam) said, 'It is not harmful.'"

H 3843, Ch. 9, h 6

Muhammad ibn Yahya has narrated from Ahmad ibn Muhammad from Muhammad ibn `Isma'il from Ali ibn al-Hakam from Shihab ibn 'Abd Rabbihi who has said the following:

"It is about the case of a man who takes Ghusl (bath) and water-drops from his body sprinkle into the water container and from the ground. Abu 'Abd Allah, *'Alayhi al-Salam*, has said, 'It is not harmful.'"

H 3844, Ch. 9, h 7

Muhammad ibn `Isma'il has narrated from al-Fadl ibn Shadhan from Hammad ibn 'Isa from Rib'iy ibn 'Abd Allah from al-Fudayl ibn Yasar who has said the following:

"It is about a man who takes Ghusl (bath) due to sexual matters and water drops sprinkle into the water container. Abu 'Abd Allah, *'Alayhi al-Salam*, has said, 'It is not harmful. Allah has not sanctioned anything in religion which causes hardships for you.'"

H 3845, Ch. 9, h 8

Al-Husayn ibn Muhammad has narrated from Mu'alla' ibn Muhammad, from al-Washsha', from Hammad ibn 'Uthman, from 'Umar ibn Yazid who has said the following:

"I once asked abu 'Abd Allah, *'Alayhi al-Salam*, 'I may take Ghusl (bath) in a place which is used for taking Ghusl (bath) due to sexual matters, and urination and water-drops sprinkle from the ground into the water container.' He (the Imam) said, 'It is not harmful.'"

Chapter 10 - Water of Bath Houses and Water Heated by the Sun's Rays

H 3846, Ch. 10, h 1

Certain persons of our people have narrated from ibn Jumhur from Muhammad ibn al-Qasim from ibn abu Ya'fur who has said the following:

"Abu 'Abd Allah, *'Alayhi al-Salam*, has said, 'Do not take Ghusl (bath) from a well in which water from bath houses accumulate, because in it there is water which is used by one born out of wedlock and it does not become clean for seven generations. In it there is water used by one hostile to `A'immah, *'Alayhim al-Salam*. One who is hostile to `A'immah, *'Alayhim al-Salam*, is the worse than the two others. Allah has not created a creature more evil than the dog but one hostile to `A'immah is more worthless than a dog.' I then asked him (the Imam) about the water of bathhouses from which one involved in sexual activities, children, Jews, Christians and Zoroastrians take Ghusl (bath). He (the Imam) said, 'It is like canals in which one part of water cleanses the other part.'"

H 3847, Ch. 10, h 2

A number of our people have narrated from Ahmad ibn Muhammad from al-Husayn ibn Sa'id from Safwan ibn Yahya from Mansur ibn Hazim from Bakr ibn Habib who has said the following:

"Abu Ja'far, *'Alayhi al-Salam*, has said, 'Water of bathhouses does not have problems if it is water from a large source; like a fountain.'"

H 3848, Ch. 10, h 3

Al-Husayn ibn Muhammad has narrated from 'Abd Allah ibn 'Amir from Ali ibn Mahziyar from Muhammad ibn `Isma'il from Hanan who has said the following:

"I once heard a man saying to abu 'Abd Allah, *'Alayhi al-Salam*, 'In the morning I enter the bathhouse and there is one who has experienced sexual relation and so on. I then stand up and take Ghusl (bath) and water from them sprinkles on me after I finish.' He (the Imam) asked, 'Is it not running water?' He replied, 'Yes, it is running water.' He (the Imam) said, 'It is not harmful.'"

H 3849, Ch. 10, h 4

Muhammad ibn Yahya has narrated from Ahmad ibn Muhammad from abu Yahya al-Wasitiy from certain persons of our people who have said the following:

"Abu al-Hassan, the one before, *'Alayhi al-Salam*, was asked about accumulated water in bathhouses used by people which pollutes clothes. He (the Imam) said, 'It is not harmful.'"

H 3850, Ch. 10, h 5

Ali ibn Ibrahim has narrated from his father, from al-Hassan ibn abu al-Husayn al-Farisiy, from Sulayman ibn Ja'far, from 'Isma'il ibn abu Ziyad who has said the following:

"Abu 'Abd Allah, *'Alayhi al-Salam*, has said that the Messenger of Allah has said, 'Do not use water which is heated by sun rays for Wudu', Ghusl (bath) or to turn flour into dough with it; it causes leprosy.'"

Chapter 11 - Places Not Desirable to Use as a Lavatory

H 3851, Ch. 11, h 1

Ali ibn Ibrahim has narrated from his father from al-Nawfaliy from al-Sakuniy who has said the following:

"Abu 'Abd Allah, *'Alayhi al-Salam*, has said that the Messenger of Allah has said, 'It is of proper understanding (of law) for a man to search for and prepare a place for urination.'"

H 3852, Ch. 11, h 2

Ahmad ibn Idris has narrated from Muhammad ibn 'Abd al-Jabbar from Safwan ibn Yahya from 'Asim ibn Humayd who has said the following:

"Abu 'Abd Allah, *'Alayhi al-Salam*, has said that once a man asked Ali ibn Al-Husayn, *'Alayhi al-Salam*, 'Where should outsiders take Wudu'?' He (the Imam) said, 'They should avoid places like the banks of the canals, open roads, under fruit-bearing trees and places that may subject one to public condemnation.' Someone asked, 'What kind of places are such?' He (the Imam) said, 'One example is the front portions of the doors of houses.'"

H 3853, Ch. 11, h 3

Muhammad ibn Yahya through the chain of his narrators in a marfu' manner has said the following:

"Abu al-Hassan, *'Alayhi al-Salam*, was asked about (one's condition) when defecating. He (the Imam) said, 'One should not face the direction of al-Ka'bah, turn one's back toward al-Ka'bah, face the direction from which wind blows or turn one's back to such direction.'"

"It is narrated in another Hadith that one should not face toward the sun or moon (when using the toilet)."

H 3854, Ch. 11, h 4

Ali ibn Ibrahim has narrated from his father from al-Nawfaliy from al-Sakuniy who has said the following:

"Abu 'Abd Allah, *'Alayhi al-Salam*, has said that the Holy prophet prohibited one's allowing his urine to sprinkle from rooftops or high places in the air."

H 3855, Ch. 11, h 5

Ali ibn Ibrahim has narrated in a marfu' manner the following:

"Once, abu Hanifah came out of a meeting with abu 'Abd Allah, *'Alayhi al-Salam*. Abu al-Hassan, Musa, a young boy at that time, was standing in the meeting place. Abu Hanifah asked him, 'O young man, where does an outsider relieve himself of nature's demand in your town?' He (the Imam) replied, 'You must avoid the courtyard of a Masjid, banks of canals, places where fruits fall from trees and people's rest areas. Do not face the direction of al-Ka'bah, when defecating or urinating and keep your clothes away (from pollution). Thereafter relieve yourself wherever you like.'"

H 3856, Ch. 11, h 6

Muhammad ibn Yahya has narrated from Muhammad ibn al-Husayn from Muhammad ibn 'Isma'il from Salih ibn 'Uqbah from Ibrahim al-Karkhiy who has said the following:

"Abu 'Abd Allah, *'Alayhi al-Salam*, has said that the Messenger of Allah has said, 'Three characteristics subject one to condemnation: Defecating in the shadows which are used as rest areas, obstructing people from reaching water for public use or public road."

Chapter 12 - Expressions to Say When Entering a Lavatory and When Coming Out

H 3857, Ch. 12, h 1

Ali ibn Ibrahim has narrated from Muhammad ibn 'Isa from Yunus from Mu'awiyah ibn 'Ammar who has said the following:

"I heard abu 'Abd Allah, *'Alayhi al-Salam*, say, 'When going to a restroom say, "In the name of Allah, O Lord, I seek protection with You against filth and the filthy, unclean Satan, condemned to be stoned." When coming out of a restroom say, "In the name of Allah, all praise belongs to Allah who has saved me from filth and filthy materials and has removed from me hardship." When taking Wudu' say, "I testify that no one, other than Allah, deserves to be worshipped. O Lord, make me of those who repent and of those who cleanse themselves. All praise belongs to Allah, the Cherisher of the worlds."'"

H 3858, Ch. 12, h 2

A number of our people have narrated from Ahmad ibn Muhammad from al-Husayn ibn Sa'id from ibn abu 'Umayr from certain individuals of our people who has said the following:

"Abu 'Abd Allah, *'Alayhi al-Salam*, has said that when you mention the name of Allah in your Wudu', the whole of your body is cleansed, but if you do not mention the name of Allah only the parts of your body over which water has passed are cleansed."

H 3859, Ch. 12, h 3

Muhammad ibn Yahya has narrated from Ahmad ibn Muhammad from Ibrahim ibn abu Mahmud who has said the following:

"I heard abu al-Hassan, al-Rida, *'Alayhi al-Salam*, say, 'One should get rid of remaining feces and urine by washing what is outside of the buttocks and there is no need to enter one's fingers inside.'"

H 3860, Ch. 12, h 4

Ahmad ibn Idris has narrated from Ahmad ibn Muhammad from Ahmad ibn al-Hassan ibn Ali from 'Amr ibn Sa'id from Musaddiq ibn Sadaqah from 'Ammar al-Sabatiy who has said the following:

"I once asked abu 'Abd Allah, *'Alayhi al-Salam*, 'Should a man after using the toilet first wash his buttocks or his urethra?' He (the Imam) said, 'It is buttocks, then urethra.'"

H 3861, Ch. 12, h 5

Ali ibn Ibrahim has narrated from Muhammad ibn 'Isa from Yunus from certain persons of our people who has said the following:

"Abu 'Abd Allah, *'Alayhi al-Salam*, has said that the Holy Prophet prohibited using one's right hand to wash one's buttocks and urethra."

H 3862, Ch. 12, h 6

Muhammad ibn Yahya has narrated from Muhammad ibn Ahmad from Muhammad ibn 'Isa from Ali ibn al-Husayn ibn 'Abd Rabbihi who has said the following:

"I once asked him (the Imam), 'Is it permissible to wear a ring with a stone of Emerald?' He (the Imam) replied, 'It is not harmful but during washing one's self after using the toilet, one should remove it.'"

H 3863, Ch. 12, h 7

Ali ibn Ibrahim has narrated from his father from al-Nawfaliy from al-Sakuniy who has said the following:

"Abu 'Abd Allah, *'Alayhi al-Salam*, has said that washing one's self with the right hand after using toilet is of injustice."

"It is narrated in another Hadith that it is permissible if there something is wrong with the left hand."

H 3864, Ch. 12, h 8

Ali ibn Ibrahim has narrated from his father and Muhammad ibn 'Isma'il from al-Fadl ibn Shadhan all from ibn abu 'Umayr from Jamil who has said the following:

"Abu 'Abd Allah, *'Alayhi al-Salam*, has said that when the gushing out of urine stops, you can pour water to wash it clean."

H 3865, Ch. 12, h 9

Ali ibn Ibrahim has narrated from his father from ibn al-Mughirah who has said the following:

"I once asked abu al-Hassan, *'Alayhi al-Salam*, 'How is washing oneself after using the toilet done?' He (the Imam) said, 'It is not clean as long as something is there.' I then asked, 'What happens if everything there is washed clean but smell is there?' He (the Imam) said, 'Smell is not a thing that can be seen.'"

H 3866, Ch. 12, h 10

Ali ibn Muhammad has narrated from Sahl from Ahmad ibn Muhammad ibn abu Nasr from 'Abd al-Karim ibn 'Amr from al-Hassan ibn Ziyad who has said the following:

"Once abu 'Abd Allah, *'Alayhi al-Salam*, was asked about a man whose thigh and knee come in contact with a small drop of urine. He performs Salat (prayer) then remembers that he had not washed it clean? He (the Imam) said, 'He must perform his Salat (prayer) again.'"

H 3867, Ch. 12, h 11

Muhammad ibn al-Hassan has narrated from Sahl from Musa ibn al-Qasim from 'Amr ibn Sa'id from Musaddiq ibn Sadaqah from 'Ammar who has said the following:

"I once asked abu 'Abd Allah, *'Alayhi al-Salam*, 'A man wants to wash himself clean after using toilet. How should he sit?' He (the Imam) said, 'He sits just as he does when defecating.' He (the Imam) then said, 'He only needs to wash the outside and not the inside.'"

H 3868, Ch. 12, h 12

Ali ibn Ibrahim has narrated from Harun ibn Muslim from Mas'adah ibn Ziyad who has said the following:

"Abu 'Abd Allah, *'Alayhi al-Salam*, has said that the Holy prophet once said to a certain one of his wives, 'Instruct the believing women to wash themselves clean with water thoroughly; it cleanses the surrounding areas and removes the hemorrhoids.'"

H 3869, Ch. 12, h 13

Muhammad ibn 'Isma'il has narrated from al-Fadl ibn Shadhan and Ali ibn Ibrahim has narrated from his father from ibn abu 'Umayr from Jamil ibn Darraj who has said the following:

"Abu 'Abd Allah, *'Alayhi al-Salam*, about the words of Allah, most Majestic, most Glorious, 'Allah loves those who repent and cleanse themselves', said, 'People would cleanse themselves after using the toilet with cotton and stones. Thereafter, He (Allah) sanctioned Wudu' and it is of the noble characteristics. The Messenger of Allah commanded people to take Wudu' and himself performed it. Thereafter Allah revealed in His book, "Allah loves those who repent and those who cleanse themselves. (2:222)'"

H 3870, Ch. 12, h 14

Ali ibn Ibrahim has narrated from his father from ibn abu 'Umayr from ibn 'Udhaynah from Zurarah who has said the following:

"One day I took Wudu' but forgot to wash my urethra clean; then I performed Salat (prayer). I asked abu 'Abd Allah, *'Alayhi al-Salam*, about it. He (the Imam) said, 'Wash your urethra clean and perform your Salat (prayer) again.'"

H 3871, Ch. 12, h 15

Muhammad ibn Yahya has narrated from Ahmad ibn Muhammad ibn 'Isa from al-Hassan ibn Ali ibn Yaqtin from his brother, Al-Husayn, from Ali ibn Yaqtin who has said the following:

"I once asked abu al-Hassan, *'Alayhi al-Salam*, about a man who forgets to wash clean his urethra but he takes Wudu' and performs Salat (prayer). He (the Imam) said, 'He must wash his urethra clean and perform his Salat (prayer) again, but he does not have to take Wudu' again.'"

H 3872, Ch. 12, h 16

It is a narration from him (narrator of previous Hadith) by Ahmad from ibn Faddal from ibn Bukayr from certain persons of our people who have said the following:

"I once asked abu 'Abd Allah, *'Alayhi al-Salam*, about a man who takes Wudu' but forgets to wash his urethra clean and then performs Salat (prayer). He (the Imam) said, 'He must wash his urethra clean and perform his Salat (prayer) again but he does not have to take Wudu' again.'"

H 3873, Ch. 12, h 17

Ali ibn Ibrahim has narrated from Muhammad ibn 'Isa from Yunus from Zur'ah, from Sama'ah who has said the following:

"Abu 'Abd Allah, *'Alayhi al-Salam*, has said, 'After using toilet if you forget to wash clean your buttocks (because of feces) and take Wudu', then remember after performing Salat (prayer), you must perform your Salat (prayer) again. If you wash your buttocks clean but forget washing your urethra clean and perform Salat (prayer), you must take Wudu', wash your urethra and perform your Salat (prayer) again. It is because urine is not like feces.'"

Chapter 13 - Draining Urine, Washing and If One Does Not Find Water

H 3874, Ch. 13, h 1

Ali ibn Ibrahim has narrated from his father, from Hammad, from Hariz, from Muhammad ibn Muslim who has said the following:

"I once asked Abu Ja'far, *'Alayhi al-Salam*, about a man who urinates but does not have water to wash it clean. He (the Imam) said, 'He must drain his urine passageway by pressing (with his fingers), against the bones underneath, beginning from his buttocks and move upward, three times, to where the passageway separates from the bones. Then hold it (the passageway) between his two fingers (the thumb, forefinger) and middle finger, press and pull to the end of his penis three times. Then press its end three times. Thereafter if any moisture comes out it is not urine. Instead such moistures are considered of the moisture associated with the veins (and activities) of sexual organs.'"

H 3875, Ch. 13, h 2

A number of our people have narrated from Ahmad ibn Muhammad from and abu Dawud all al-Husayn ibn Sa'id from Safwan ibn Yahya from al-'Ala' ibn abu Ya'fur who has said the following:

"I once asked abu 'Abd Allah, *'Alayhi al-Salam*, about a man who urinates, then takes Wudu'. He then stands up for Salat (prayer) and finds a certain moisture. He (the Imam) said, 'He does not need Wudu'; it is of Haba'il (passageways, veins).'"

H 3876, Ch. 13, h 3

Muhammad ibn Yahya has narrated from Ahmad ibn Muhammad from Ali ibn Ahmad ibn 'Ushaym from Safwan who has said the following:

"Once a man asked al-Rida', *'Alayhi al-Salam*, when I was present, saying, 'There is a wound in my anus. I take Wudu' and wash clean; but then I find wetness and yellowness there. Do I need to take Wudu' again?' He (the Imam) said, 'Had you cleaned it?' he replied, 'Yes, I did so.' He (the Imam) said, 'No, but pour water on it and you do not need to take Wudu' again.'"

Ahmad ibn abu Nasr has said that a man asked al-Rida', *'Alayhi al-Salam*, a question like that in Hadith of Safwan.

H 3877, Ch. 13, h 4

Ali ibn Ibrahim has narrated from his father from Hanan ibn Sadir who has said the following:

"Once a man asked abu 'Abd Allah, *'Alayhi al-Salam*, saying, 'At times when I urinate, I cannot find water and it becomes severe for me.' He (the Imam) said, 'When you urinate and wipe it clean, you can then wipe your penis with saliva; and if you find something then say it is of that (moisture from passageways and veins).'"

H 3878, Ch. 13, h 5

Ali ibn Ibrahim has narrated from his father from 'Abd Allah ibn al-Mughirah from Mansur ibn Hazim who has said the following:

"I once asked abu 'Abd Allah, *'Alayhi al-Salam*, about a man who has the urge to urinate and cannot hold it any longer. He (the Imam) said to me, 'If he is not able to hold, Allah is the foremost to accept apologies, he can allow it to come out in a bag.'"

H 3879, Ch. 13, h 6

Al-Husayn from Muhammad has narrated from Ahmad ibn Muhammad from Ahmad ibn Ishaq from Sa'dan from 'Abd al-Rahman who has said the following:

"I once wrote to abu al-Hassan, *'Alayhi al-Salam*, about a castrated man who when urinating feels great pain and finds wetness time after time. He (the Imam) said, 'He must take Wudu' and pour water on it once during the day.'"

H 3880, Ch. 13, h 7

Muhammad ibn Yahya has narrated from Ahmad ibn Muhammad from Ali ibn al-Hakam from Al-Husayn ibn abu al-'Ala' who has said the following:

"I once asked abu 'Abd Allah, *'Alayhi al-Salam*, about urine which pollutes the body. He (the Imam) said, 'Pour water on it twice.' It is a narration that one can wash it with the same amount of water if it is on the tip of the penis or on something else. It also is a narration that it is water and not dirt and it needs to be dropped down.'"

H 3881, Ch. 13, h 8

Muhammad ibn Yahya has narrated from Muhammad ibn al-Husayn from ibn Faddal from Ghalib ibn 'Uthman from Rawh ibn 'Abd al-Rahim who has said the following:

"Once, abu 'Abd Allah, *'Alayhi al-Salam*, urinated. I was standing nearby with a water container or a jug. When the jet of urine stopped, he (the Imam) made a gesture with his hand for water and I gave it to him and he (the Imam) made Wudu' at the same place."

Chapter 14 - The Quantity of Water Required for Wudu', Showers and One Who Is Excessive in the Use of Water for Wudu'

H 3882, Ch. 14, h 1

Ali ibn Ibrahim has narrated from Muhammad ibn 'Isa from Yunus from al-'Ala' from Muhammad ibn Muslim who has said the following:

"Abu Ja'far, *'Alayhi al-Salam*, has said, 'One of you in order to rub oil on his body covers his whole body with an amount of oil on his palm. Water, however, is more plentiful than this.'"

H 3883, Ch. 14, h 2

Ali ibn Ibrahim has narrated from his father and Muhammad ibn 'Isma'il from al-Fadl ibn Shadhan from Hammad from Hariz from Zurarah and Muhammad ibn Muslim who has said the following:

"Abu Ja'far, *'Alayhi al-Salam*, has said, 'Wudu' is one of the boundaries Allah has established so that He finds out who obeys or disobeys Him. The believing people do not allow it (their body) to remain unclean. It is sufficient to use a small amount of water like rubbing oil on one's body.'"

H 3884, Ch. 14, h 3

A number of our people have narrated from Ahmad ibn Muhammad and abu Dawud all from al-Husayn ibn Sa'id from Fadalah ibn Dawud ibn Farqad who has said the following:

"I once heard abu 'Abd Allah, *'Alayhi al-Salam*, say, 'My father would say, "Wudu' has certain limits. If one trespasses such limits, he will not receive any reward." My father would also say, "(Certain people) only make it perplexed."' A man then asked, 'What then are the limits of Wudu'?' He (the Imam) said, 'Wash your face and hands and wipe your head and feet.'"

H 3885, Ch. 14, h 4

Ali ibn Ibrahim has narrated from his father from ibn abu 'Umayr from Jamil from Zurarah who has said the following:

"Abu Ja'far, *'Alayhi al-Salam*, has said, 'In taking a Ghusl (bath) because of sexual relations it is sufficient to allow water flow, a small or plenty of water over one's body. This is sufficient for such Ghusl (bath).'"

H 3886, Ch. 14, h 5

Muhammad ibn Yahya has narrated from Muhammad ibn al-Husayn, from Safwan, from 'Ala' ibn Razin, from Muhammad ibn Muslim who has said the following:

"I once asked abu 'Abd Allah or abu Ja'far, *'Alayhim al-Salam*, about how much water is needed for Ghusl (bath) because of sexual relations. He (the Imam) said, 'The Messenger of Allah would use five handfuls of water, share it with his partner, and both of them would take Ghusl (bath) from the same water container.'"

H 3887, Ch. 14, h 6

Muhammad ibn Yahya has narrated from Muhammad ibn al-Husayn from Yazid ibn Ishaq from Harun ibn Hamzah who has said the following:

"Abu 'Abd Allah, *'Alayhi al-Salam*, has said, 'An amount of water which can fill up your right hand is sufficient for your Ghusl (bath) and washing clean your urethra.'"

H 3888, Ch. 14, h 7
A number of our people have narrated from Ahmad ibn Muhammad from al-Husayn ibn Sa'id from Fadalah ibn Ayyub from Jamil from Zurarah who has said the following:
"Abu Ja'far, *'Alayhi al-Salam*, has said, 'It is sufficient for Wudu' to allow water to touch your skin (of the parts to be washed for Wudu').'"

H 3889, Ch. 14, h 8
Ali has narrated from his father from al-Nawfaliy from al-Sakuniy who has said the following:
"I once asked abu 'Abd Allah, *'Alayhi al-Salam*, about a man who after sexual relations immerses his whole body in water at once and comes out. 'Is this sufficient for Ghusl (bath)?' He (the Imam) replied, 'Yes, it is sufficient.'"

H 3890, Ch. 14, h 9
Ali ibn Muhammad and others have narrated from Sahl ibn Ziyad from Muhammad ibn al-Hassan ibn Shammun from Hammad ibn 'Isa from Hariz who has said the following:
"Abu 'Abd Allah, *'Alayhi al-Salam*, has said, 'Allah has an angel who writes down one's acting excessively or transgressing limits.'"

Chapter 15 - Brushing One's Teeth

H 3891, Ch. 15, h 1
Ali ibn Muhammad has narrated from Sahl and Ali ibn Ibrahim has narrated from his father all from Ja'far ibn Muhammad al-Ash'ariy from 'Abd Allah ibn Maymun from al-Qaddah who has said the following:
"Abu 'Abd Allah, *'Alayhi al-Salam*, has said, 'Performing two Rak'at Salat (prayer) with one's teeth brushed is better than seventy Rak'at without one's teeth brushed. The Messenger of Allah has said, 'Were it not to cause hardships to my followers, I would command them to brush their teeth for every Salat (prayer).'"

H 3892, Ch. 15, h 2
A number of our people have narrated from Ahmad ibn Muhammad from ibn Mahbub from Yunus ibn Ya'qub from abu 'Usamah who has said the following:
"Abu 'Abd Allah, *'Alayhi al-Salam*, has said, 'Brushing one's teeth is of the traditions of the messengers (of Allah)."

H 3893, Ch. 15, h 3
Ahmad ibn Muhammad has narrated from ibn Mahbub form al-'Ala' from Muhammad ibn Muslim who has said the following:
"Abu Ja'far, *'Alayhi al-Salam*, has said, 'The Holy Prophet has said, "Jibril continued urging me to brush my teeth, until I became fearful of the falling off of my teeth."'"

H 3894, Ch. 15, h 4
Ali ibn Ibrahim has narrated from his father from ibn abu 'Umayr from ibn Bukayr from those whom he has mentioned has said the following:

"Abu Ja'far, *'Alayhi al-Salam*, has said, 'You must not neglect brushing after every third (Salat (prayer)) even though it is a light one (brushing).'"

H 3895, Ch. 15, h 5

Ali through his chain of narrators has narrated the following:

"He (the Imam), *'Alayhi al-Salam*, has said, 'The least for brushing is using one's fingers as a tooth brush."

H 3896, Ch. 15, h 6

Ahmad ibn Idris has narrated from Muhammad ibn 'Abd al-Jabbar from Safwan from al-Mu'alla' abu 'Uthman from Mu'alla' ibn Khunays who has said the following:

"I once asked abu 'Abd Allah, *'Alayhi al-Salam*, about brushing one's teeth after Wudu'. He (the Imam) said, 'Brushing is before Wudu'.' I then asked, 'What should one do if he forgets and remembers only after Wudu'?' He (the Imam) said, 'In such case he should brush and then rinse his mouth three times.'"

It is narrated that the time for brushing according to Sunnah is at the time of al-Sahar (near dawn).

H 3897, Ch. 15, h 7

Ali ibn Muhammad ibn Bundar has narrated from Ibrahim ibn Ishaq al-Ahmar from 'Abd Allah ibn Hammad from abu Bakr ibn abu Sammak who has said the following:

"Abu 'Abd Allah, *'Alayhi al-Salam*, has said, 'When you wake up during the night (for Salat (prayer)) you should brush your teeth; the angel comes and places his mouth over your mouth. Every word you say, he climbs with it to the heaven. Your mouth should have a pleasant smell.'"

Chapter 16 - Rinsing One's Mouth and Nostrils

H 3898, Ch. 16, h 1

Al-Husayn ibn Muhammad has narrated from Mu'alla' ibn Muhammad from al-Washsha' from Hammad ibn 'Uthman from Hakam ibn Hukaym who has said the following:

"I once asked abu 'Abd Allah, *'Alayhi al-Salam*, 'Is rinsing one's mouth and nostrils part of Wudu'?' He (the Imam) said, 'No, they are not part of Wudu'.'"

H 3899, Ch. 16, h 2

Muhammad ibn Yahya has narrated from Ahmad ibn Muhammad from Shadhan ibn al-Khalil from Yunus ibn 'Abd al-Rahman from Hammad from abu Basir who has said the following:

"I once asked abu 'Abd Allah, *'Alayhi al-Salam*, about rinsing one's mouth and nostrils. He (the Imam) said, 'They are not part of Wudu'.'"

H 3900, Ch. 16, h 3

Muhammad ibn Yahya has narrated from Ahmad ibn Muhammad from Ali ibn al-Hakam from Sayf ibn 'Amirah from abu Bakr al-Hadramiy who has said the following:

"Abu 'Abd Allah, *'Alayhi al-Salam*, has said, 'You do not have to rinse your mouth and nostril (for Wudu'); they are of the inside parts of the body.'"

Chapter 17 - Description of Wudu'

H 3901, Ch. 17, h 1

Ali ibn Ibrahim has narrated from Muhammad ibn 'Isa from Yunus ibn 'Abd al-Rahman from Aban and Jamil from Zurarah who has said the following:

"Abu Ja'far, *'Alayhi al-Salam*, once demonstrated for us how the Messenger of Allah would take Wudu'. He asked for a glass of water. He (the Imam) then with some water in the palm of his hand allowed it to flow down his face and wiped both sides of his face. He (the Imam) then with some water in the palm of his left hand allowed it to flow down his right hand and then wiped both sides. He (the Imam) with some water in the palm of his right hand allowed it to flow over his left and did as he had done to his right hand. Thereafter he, with whatever was left on his hand, wiped his head and feet but he did not place his hands in the water container (again)."

H 3902, Ch. 17, h 2

A number of our people have narrated from Ahmad ibn Muhammad from Ali ibn al-Hakam from Dawud ibn al-Nu'man from abu Ayyub from Bukayr ibn `A'yan who has said the following:

"Abu Ja'far, *'Alayhi al-Salam*, once said, 'Allow me to demonstrate before you how the Messenger of Allah would take Wudu'. He (the Imam) then with some water in the palm of his right hand washed his face. He (the Imam) then with some water in the palm of his left hand washed his right hand. He (the Imam) then with some water in the palm of his right hand washed his left hand. He (the Imam) then with whatever water left in his hands wiped his head and feet."

H 3903, Ch. 17, h 3

Ali ibn Ibrahim has narrated from Muhammad ibn 'Isa from Yunus from al-'Ala' ibn Razin from Muhammad ibn Muslim who has said the following:

"Abu Ja'far, *'Alayhi al-Salam*, once said, 'When one of you wants to rub oil over his body, he does so only with some oil in the palm of his hand and covers his whole body. Water, however, is more plentiful. Do you want me to demonstrate how the Messenger of Allah would take Wudu'?' I said, 'Please do so.' He (the Imam) then placed his hand in the water but did not wash his hand. He (the Imam) then with some water in the palm of his hand, allowed it to flow down his face and then wiped both sides of his face until he wiped it all. He (the Imam) then with some water in the palm of his right hand, poured it on the palm of his left hand and with it he washed his right forearm. He (the Imam) with some water in the palm of his right hand, washed his left forearm. He (the Imam) then with whatever water was left on his hands, wiped his head and feet."

H 3904, Ch. 17, h 4

Ali has narrated from his father and Muhammad ibn `Isma'il from al-Fadl ibn Shadhan all from Hammad ibn 'Isa from Hariz from Zurarah who has said the following:

"Abu Ja'far, *'Alayhi al-Salam*, once said to us, 'Should I demonstrate for you how the Messenger of Allah would take Wudu'?' We replied, 'Yes, please do so.' He (the Imam) then asked for a bowl with a quantity of water in it. He (the Imam) placed it in front of him and uncovered both his forearms. He (the Imam) then immersed the palm of his right hand in the water, saying, 'This is when the palm is clean and free of Najis (unclean) substances. He (the Imam) then filled the palm of his hand, placed on his forehead, saying 'In the name of Allah', allowed it to flow over the sides of his beard. He (the Imam) then passed his hand over his face and the apparent parts of his forehead only once. He (the Imam) then immersed his left hand in the water, filled his palm and placed it over his right elbow. He (the Imam) passed his palm over his forearm until water flowed toward the ends of his fingers. He (the Imam) then filled the palm of his right hand, placed it over his left elbow and passed it over his left forearm until water flowed over the ends of his fingers. He (the Imam) then wiped the front portion of his head and the back of his feet with whatever water was left in his left and right hands. Abu Ja'far, *'Alayhi al-Salam*, said, 'Allah is odd. He loves odd numbers. Three handfuls of water is sufficient for Wudu'. One handful is for the face, one for the right forearm and one for the left forearm. With moisture in your right hand, wipe the front portion of your head, and with the remaining moisture on it wipe the back of your right foot and with the moisture in your left hand wipe the back of your left foot.' Zurarah has said that Abu Ja'far, *'Alayhi al-Salam*, said, 'Once a man asked 'Amir al-Mu'minin about the Wudu' of the Messenger of Allah and he ('Amir al-Mu'minin) demonstrated like this.'"

H 3905, Ch. 17, h 5

Ali ibn Ibrahim has narrated from his father from ibn abu 'Umayr from 'Umar ibn 'Udhaynah from Zurarah from and Bukayr who have said the following:

"Once we asked abu Ja'far, *'Alayhi al-Salam*, about the manner the Messenger of Allah would take Wudu' He (the Imam) then asked for a washbasin or a pail with some water in it. He then immersed his right hand in it, took some water in the palm of his hand and poured it on his face. He washed his face with it. He then immersed his left hand in the water and took some water, which he poured on his right forearm, washed therewith his right hand from his elbow to his palm and did not rub it backward to his elbow. He then immersed the palm of his right hand in the water, poured water over his left forearm from the elbow and worked with it as he did with his right hand. He then wiped his head and his feet with moisture in his palm. He did not take new water in his hands. He did not push his hand under his shoelace. He then said, 'Allah, the most Majestic, most Glorious, says, "Believers, when you rise for Salat (prayer) wash your faces and hands." He must not have left any part of his face without being washed. He commanded him to wash his hands upto (from) the elbows. He must not have left his hands without being washed upto (from) the elbows. It is because Allah says, "Wash your faces and hands upto (from) the elbows." He (Allah) then says, "Wipe your heads and feet up to your ankles." If one wipes a part of his head and a part of the backs of his feet between his ankles, it is sufficient.' We then asked, 'What part of the feet is between ankles to the ends of fingers?' He (the Imam) said, 'It is here, the joint below the bones of the leg.' We then asked, 'What exactly is this?' He (the Imam) replied, 'This is of the bones of the leg. The ankle is below this.' We then said, 'May Allah keep you well, is one handful of water sufficient for washing the face and another to wash the forearm?' He (the Imam) said, 'The most you can do is two (washing; washing the face and forearms) which does it all.'"

H 3906, Ch. 17, h 6

Muhammad ibn al-Hassan and others have narrated from Sahl ibn Ziyad from ibn Mahbub from ibn Ribat from Yunus ibn 'Ammar who has said the following:

"I once asked abu 'Abd Allah, *'Alayhi al-Salam*, about Wudu' for Salat (prayer). He (the Imam) said, 'It is (washing the face) once and (hands) once.'"

H 3907, Ch. 17, h 7

A number of our people have narrated from Ahmad ibn Muhammad and abu Dawud all from al-Husayn ibn Sa'id from Fadalah ibn Ayyub from Hammad ibn 'Uthaman from Ali ibn al-Mughirah from Maysarah who has said the following:

"Abu Ja'far, *'Alayhi al-Salam*, has said, 'Wudu' is one (washing of the face and hands) and one (wiping of the head and feet).' He (the Imam) then explained about the ankle in the back of the foot.'"

H 3908, Ch. 17, h 8

Al-Husayn ibn Muhammad has narrated from 'Abd Allah ibn 'Amir from Ali ibn Mahziyar from Muhammad ibn Yahya from Hammad ibn 'Uthaman who has said the following:

"Once I was in the presence of abu 'Abd Allah, *'Alayhi al-Salam*. He (the Imam) asked for water. He then filled up his hand with water and allowed it to flow over all of his face. He then filled the palm of his hand with water and washed therewith his right hand. He then filled the palm of his right hand with water, washed therewith his left hand and thereafter wiped his head and feet saying, 'This is a Wudu' of one who does not invent anything in it, meaning thereby transgression against the limits of Wudu'.'"

H 3909, Ch. 17, h 9

Ali ibn Muhammad and Muhammad ibn al-Hassan have narrated from Sahl ibn Ziyad and Ali ibn Ibrahim has narrated from his father and Muhammad ibn Yahya has narrated from Ahmad ibn Muhammad all from Ahmad ibn Muhammad ibn abu Nasr from 'Abd al-Karim who has said the following:

"I once asked abu 'Abd Allah, *'Alayhi al-Salam*, about Wudu'. He (the Imam) said, 'Wudu' of Ali, *'Alayhi al-Salam*, was once (washing of face and hands) and once (wiping of head and feet).'"

"This is proof that Wudu' is once (washing of face and hands) and once (wiping of the head and feet). Had he (the Holy prophet) received commandments for two, he would obey both, to ascertain that he has obeyed the commandment, even though it required him more labor. The report that says, "'A'immah, *'Alayhim al-Salam*, have said that twice (washing of face and hands) is for those who are not satisfied with once.' He then increased it and said, 'It is twice.' He (the Imam) then said, 'Those who do it (washing) more than twice will not receive any reward. This is the maximum of the limits of Wudu'. Whoever transgresses it has committed a sin and his Wudu' is invalid. It is like performing five Rak'at for al-Zuhr Salat (prayer).' If he (the Imam) were not to leave the expression "twice" unconditional, it would lead to the same path as three times.

"It is also narrated about a man who had only one handful of water and it was time for Salat (prayer). He (the Imam) said, 'He must divide it into three portions; one for washing his face, one for washing his right hand and one for washing his left hand, then wipe his head and feet with the moisture in his hands." (al-Kulayniy)

Chapter 18 - The Area of the Face and Hands to be Washed for Wudu'

H 3910, Ch. 18, h 1

Ali ibn Ibrahim has narrated from his father and Muhammad ibn `Isma'il from al-Fadl ibn Shadhan all from Hammad ibn 'Isa from Hariz from Zurarah who has said the following:

"I once asked him (the Imam) about the limits of the face that must be washed for Wudu' about which Allah, most Majestic, most Glorious, has also spoken. He (the Imam) said, 'The face which Allah, most High, has commanded to wash to the limits of which no one has permission for addition or reduction; for addition one cannot receive any reward and for reduction one commits a sin. That limit is the area of the face which one's forefinger, middle finger and thumb cover in width and in depth from the hairline on the forehead down to one's chin and the area of the face over which the two fingers (middle finger and thumb) pass downward is of the face, besides this is not of the face.' I (the narrator) then said, 'Is the temple not of the face?' He (the Imam) said, 'No, it is not (part) of the face.'"

H 3911, Ch. 18, h 2

Muhammad ibn Yahya has narrated from Ahmad ibn Muhammad and Muhammad ibn al-Husayn from Safwan from al-'Ala' from Muhammad ibn Muslim who has said the following:

"I asked one of the two Imam, *'Alayhim al-Salam*, about a man who takes Wudu', 'Is he required to wash inside his beard?' He (the Imam) replied, 'No, he is not required to do so.'"

H 3912, Ch. 18, h 3

Muhammad ibn Yahya has narrated from 'Abd Allah ibn Muhammad ibn 'Isa from his father from ibn al-Mughirah from al-Sakuniy who has said the following:

"Abu 'Abd Allah, *'Alayhi al-Salam*, has said, 'The Messenger of Allah has said, "Do not strike water against your face when taking Wudu'. Allow the water to flow over your face.'"

H 3913, Ch. 18, h 4

Ali ibn Muhammad has narrated from Sahl ibn Ziyad from `Isma'il ibn Mehran who has said the following:

"I wrote to al-Rida, *'Alayhi al-Salam*, and asked him about the limits of the area of the face. He wrote this back to me, 'It is from the hairline down to the end and (beginning of) both brows.'"

H 3914, Ch. 18, h 5

Muhammad ibn al-Hassan and others have narrated from Sahl ibn Ziyad from Ali ibn al-Hakam from al-Haytham ibn 'Urwah al-Tamimiy who has said the following:

"I once asked abu 'Abd Allah, *'Alayhi al-Salam*, about the words of Allah, the most Majestic, most Glorious, '. . . wash your faces and hands to the elbow. . .' and I passed my hand over my hand to my elbow asking, 'Should I wash in this manner?' He (the Imam) said, 'It is not revealed for that manner. It is only "wash your faces and hands to the elbow"' He (the Imam) passed his hand over his elbow toward his fingers."

H 3915, Ch. 18, h 6

Ali ibn Ibrahim has narrated from his brother Ishaq ibn Ibrahim from Muhammad ibn 'Isma'il ibn Bazi' who has said the following:

"Abu al-Hassan, al-Rida, *'Alayhi al-Salam*, has said, 'In the case of women about Wudu' for Salat (prayer), Allah has made it obligatory in washing their hands to pour water over the interior side of their forearm and for men to pour water over the exterior side of their forearms.'"

H 3916, Ch. 18, h 7

Ali ibn Ibrahim has narrated from his father from ibn abu Najran from 'Asim ibn Humayd from Muhammad ibn Muslim who has said the following:

"I once, asked Abu Ja'far, *'Alayhi al-Salam*, about rules of Wudu' in the case of a cut-off hand or leg. He (the Imam) said, 'One must wash them.'"

H 3917, Ch. 18, h 8

It is a narration from him (narrator of the previous Hadith) by his father from ibn abu 'Umayr from Rifa'ah and Muhammad ibn Yahya from Ahmad ibn Muhammad from al-Hassan ibn Ali from Rifa'ah, who has said the following:

"I once asked abu 'Abd Allah, *'Alayhi al-Salam*, about a cut-off hand for Wudu'. He (the Imam) said, 'One must wash the cut-off part.'"

H 3918, Ch. 18, h 9

Muhammad ibn Yahya has narrated from al-'Amrakiy from Ali ibn Ja'far who has said the following:

"I asked my brother, Musa ibn Ja'far, *'Alayhi al-Salam*, about a man whose hand is cut off from the elbow. How he should take Wudu'? He (the Imam) said, 'He must wash what is left of his arm.'"

H 3919, Ch. 18, h 10

Muhammad ibn Yahya has narrated from Ahmad ibn Muhammad from ibn Faddal from ibn Bukayr from Zurarah who has said the following:

"I once said to abu Ja'far, *'Alayhi al-Salam*, 'There are people who say that the inside of ears is (part) of the face and their outside is (part) of the head.' He (the Imam) said, 'There is no washing or wiping for them.'"

Chapter 19 - Wiping of Head and Feet

H 3920, Ch. 19, h 1

A number of our people have narrated from Ahmad ibn Muhammad from Shadhan ibn Khalil al-Naysaburiy from Mu'ammar ibn 'Umar who has said the following:

"Abu Ja'far, *'Alayhi al-Salam*, has said, 'For wiping the head it is sufficient to wipe a portion of it the size of three fingers and so also is the case of the feet.'"

H 3921, Ch. 19, h 2

Ali ibn Ibrahim has narrated from his father from ibn abu 'Umayr from abu Ayyub from Muhammad ibn Muslim who has said the following:

"Abu 'Abd Allah, *'Alayhi al-Salam*, has said, 'Ears are not (part) of the face or of the head.' Muhammad ibn Muslim has said that wiping was mentioned before the Imam who said, 'You must wipe the front portion of your head and feet. You must first wipe the right side (foot).'"

H 3922, Ch. 19, h 3

Muhammad ibn Yahya has narrated from Ahmad ibn Muhammad, from Shadhan ibn al-Khalil, from Yunus, from Hammad, from Al-Husayn who has said the following:

"I once asked abu 'Abd Allah, *'Alayhi al-Salam*, about a man who wears a turban and it is difficult for him to remove it because of the cold. He (the Imam) said, 'He can push his finger under the turban.'"

H 3923, Ch. 19, h 4

Ali ibn Ibrahim has narrated from his father and Muhammad ibn 'Isma'il from al-Fadl ibn Shadhan all from Hammad ibn 'Isa from Hariz from Zurarah who has said the following:

"I once said to abu Ja'far, *'Alayhi al-Salam*, 'Please teach me on what basis you say that wiping is only on certain portions of the head and feet.' He (the Imam) smiled and then said, 'O Zurarah, the Messenger of Allah has said so and the book from Allah is revealed about it. It is because Allah, most Majestic, most Glorious, says, "Wash your faces." From this we learn that one must wash the whole face. He (Allah) then has said, "And (wash) your hands upto (from) the elbows." He (Allah) then has placed a disjointing in the statement saying, "You must wipe with/of your heads." From His saying, "With/of your heads" we learn that wiping is only for a portion of the head because of His use of (Arabic letter) al-Ba' (which means, "with" or "of"). He then has joined (the case of) the feet with that of the head. He has joined the rule of hands with the face, saying, ". . . and your feet up to the ankles" from which we learn that since He has joined it (wiping of feet) with the case of the head, wiping (of the feet) is also for certain portions of it. The Messenger of Allah explained it to people but they lost it. He (Allah) then says, "If you cannot find water, take a Tayammum with clean soil. Wipe your faces and hands therewith." (5:6) Since He (Allah) has set aside Wudu' in case you cannot find water He has established wiping (of face partially) as substitute for washing. He has said, "Wipe with/of your faces" and then has joined it with the expression, "and (wipe) your hands" and thereafter has said, "therewith" that is the soil. It is because He (Allah) knows that all of it (soil) does not go to the face. Some of the soil remains attached to certain parts of the palm and not to the other parts. He (Allah) then says, "Allah does not want to sanction in religion such matters that cause you hardships." Hardships are difficulties.'"

H 3924, Ch. 19, h 5

Ali has narrated from his father from Hammad from Hariz from Zurarah who has said the following:

"Abu Ja'far, *'Alayhi al-Salam*, has said, 'In the case of women it is sufficient for them to wipe the front portion of their head the size of three fingers without removing their head scarf.'"

H 3925, Ch. 19, h 6

A number of our people have narrated from Ahmad ibn Muhammad from Ahmad ibn Muhammad ibn abu Nasr who has said the following:

"I once asked abu al-Hassan, al-Rida, *'Alayhi al-Salam*, about wiping the backs of the feet as to how they must be wiped. He (the Imam) placed the palm of his hand over his toes add wiped to the ankles over the back of the feet. I then said, 'I pray to Allah to keep my soul in service for your cause, what happens if one places two fingers and wipes up to the ankle?' He (the Imam) said, 'No, it must be done with one's palm.'"

H 3926, Ch. 19, h 7

Ahmad ibn Idris has narrated from Muhammad ibn Ahmad from Muhammad ibn 'Isa from Yunus who has said the following:

"One who had seen abu al-Hassan, *'Alayhi al-Salam*, in Mina narrated to me that he (the Imam) wiped over his feet to the ankles and from the ankles toward the backs of his feet and said that the matter about wiping the feet is simple. One may wipe forward or backward; it is one of the matters in which ease is granted by the will of Allah.'" (Fatwa best explains this Hadith.)

H 3927, Ch. 19, h 8

Ali ibn Ibrahim has narrated from his father from Hammad from Hariz from Zurarah who has said the following:

"He (the Imam) has said, 'If you take Wudu' and instead of wiping your feet wash them, thinking that this is what is obligatory, it is not considered Wudu'.' He (the Imam) then said, 'First you must wipe your feet. Then if you like to wash them and you did so thereafter wipe them to make it the last obligatory act (of Wudu').'"

H 3928, Ch. 19, h 9

Muhammad ibn Yahya has narrated from Muhammad ibn al-Husayn from al-Hakam ibn Miskin from Muhammad ibn Marwan who has said the following:

"Abu 'Abd Allah, *'Alayhi al-Salam*, has said, 'One may live for sixty or seventy years while Allah has not accepted not even one of his Salat (prayer).' I (the narrator) then asked, 'How can that happen?' He (the Imam) said, 'It is because he washes what Allah has commanded to wipe.'"

H 3929, Ch. 19, h 10

Muhammad ibn Yahya has narrated from Ali ibn 'Isma'il from Ali ibn al-Nu'man from al-Qasim ibn Muhammad from Ja'far ibn Sulayman, his uncle who has said the following:

"I once asked abu al-Hassan, Musa, *'Alayhi al-Salam*, saying, 'I pray to Allah to keep my soul in service for your cause, if the back of one's slipper is torn and he pushes his hand through the torn portion to wipe the back of his feet, is this acceptable?' He (the Imam) said, 'Yes, it is sufficient.'"

H 3930, Ch. 19, h 11

Al-Husayn ibn Muhammad has narrated from Mu'alla' ibn Muhammad from al-Washsha' from Aban from Zurarah who has said the following:

"Abu Ja'far, *'Alayhi al-Salam*, has said, 'Ali, *'Alayhi al-Salam*, once took Wudu'. He washed his face and forearms, then wiped on top of his head and over his shoes but he did not push his hand under his shoelaces.'" (Fatwa best explains this Hadith.)

H 3931, Ch. 19, h 12
Muhammad ibn Yahya in a marfu' manner has narrated from the following:
"About a man who dyes his head with henna and notices it during Wudu', abu 'Abd Allah, *'Alayhi al-Salam*, has said, 'It is not permissible until water reaches the skin of his head.'"

Chapter 20 - Wiping Over the Shoes

H 3932, Ch. 20, h 1
A number of our people have narrated from Ahmad ibn Muhammad from al-Husayn ibn Sa'id from Fadalah ibn Ayyub from Aban from Ishaq ibn 'Ammar who has said the following:
"I once asked abu 'Abd Allah, *'Alayhi al-Salam*, about the case of one suffering from illness if it is permissible for him to wipe for Wudu'. He (the Imam) said, 'No, it is not permissible.'"

H 3933, Ch. 20, h 2
Ali ibn Ibrahim has narrated from his father from Hammad from Hariz from Zurarah who has said the following:
"I once asked him (the Imam), *'Alayhi al-Salam*, about wiping for Wudu' over one's shoes because of Taqiyyah (fear). He (the Imam) said, 'I do not practice Taqiyyah before anyone in three things: Drinking intoxicating liquor, wiping for Wudu' over the shoes and in Mut'ah during Hajj.' Zurarah has said that he (the Imam) did not say, 'It is obligatory on you to disregard Taqiyyah before anyone.'"

Chapter 21- Bandages and Wounds

H 3934, Ch. 21, h 1
Muhammad ibn Yahya has narrated from Muhammad ibn al-Husayn and Muhammad ibn 'Isma'il from al-Fadl ibn Shadhan from Safwan ibn Yahya from 'Abd al-Rahman ibn al-Hajjaj who has said the following:
"I once asked abu al-Hassan, al-Rida, *'Alayhi al-Salam*, about how to go about for Wudu' on a broken part (to be washed or wiped for Wudu') with bandage or a wound on them, or when taking a Ghusl (bath) due to sexual relation or Friday Ghusl (bath). He (the Imam) said, 'One must wash the parts that are not covered by the bandage and leave the parts that are not accessible because of it, one must not remove the bandage and must not play around with the wound.'"

H 3935, Ch. 21, h 2
Ali ibn Ibrahim has narrated from Muhammad ibn 'Isa from Yunus from' Abd Allah ibn Sinan who has said the following:
"I once asked abu 'Abd Allah, *'Alayhi al-Salam*, about how one should take Wudu' with a wound. He (the Imam) said, 'He must wash the area around it.'"

H 3936, Ch. 21, h 3
Ali ibn Ibrahim has narrated from his father from ibn abu 'Umayr from Hammad from al-Halabiy who has said the following:

"Abu 'Abd Allah, *'Alayhi al-Salam*, was asked about a man in whose forearm there is a wound or such part to wash or wipe for Wudu' which is bandaged with a piece of fabric, he takes Wudu' and wipes on it when taking Wudu'. He (the Imam) said, 'If water hurts him he must wipe over the fabric, but if water does not hurt, he must remove the fabric, then wash it.' I (the narrator) then asked about the case of a wound, how to deal with it for a Ghusl (bath). He (the Imam) said, 'One must wash the area around it.'"

H 3937, Ch. 21, h 4

A number of our people have narrated from Ahmad ibn Muhammad from ibn Mahbub from Ali ibn al-Hassan ibn Ribat from 'Abd al-A'la', Mawla' Ale Sam who has said the following:

"I once said to abu 'Abd Allah, *'Alayhi al-Salam*, 'I slipped and my toe nail suffered a cut. I have placed a bitter ointment on my toe. How should I take Wudu'?' He (the Imam) said, 'This and such matters are learned from the book of Allah, most Majestic, most Glorious, which says, "Allah has not sanctioned anything in religion which may cause you hardships." You must wipe over the bandage.''''"

Chapter 22 - Facing Doubts about Wudu', Forgetting or Mixing Proper Order

H 3938, Ch. 22, h 1

A number of our people have narrated from Ahmad ibn Muhammad from al-'Abbass ibn 'Amir from 'Abd Allah ibn Bukayr from his father who has said the following:

"Abu 'Abd Allah, *'Alayhi al-Salam*, once said to me, 'When you are certain that your Wudu' has become invalid you must take Wudu'. You must never invent a Wudu' until you are certain that your Wudu' has become invalid.'"

H 3939, Ch. 22, h 2

Ali ibn Ibrahim has narrated from his father and Muhammad ibn 'Isma'il from al-Fadl ibn Shadhan all from Hammad ibn 'Isa from Hariz from Zurarah who has said the following:

"Abu Ja'far, *'Alayhi al-Salam*, has said, 'While taking Wudu' if you are not certain of washing your forearm, you must go back to wash it and repeat all of the acts of Wudu' that you doubt about its being washed or wiped which Allah has commanded to be done. This applies when you are still taking Wudu', but when you complete Wudu', stand up and move to another condition such as Salat (prayer) or something else, and then doubt about something which Allah, most High has mentioned or has made obligatory on you as part of Wudu', then there is nothing necessary for you to do. If during Wudu' you doubt about wiping your head and you can find moisture in your beard, you must use such moisture to wipe your head and feet and if you do not find such moisture, you must not consider your Wudu' invalid because of such doubt but you must proceed to your Salat (prayer). If you become certain that your Wudu' is left incomplete, you must return to complete that which you are certain is left incomplete.' Hammad has said that Hariz said that Zurarah has said, 'I asked him (the Imam) about a man who has left out a certain part of his forearm or a certain part of his body for Ghusl (bath) because of sexual relation.' He (the Imam) said, 'If one doubts so and there is still moisture on him when he is in his

Salat (prayer), he must wipe that part. If he becomes certain of a part being left incomplete, he must go back to complete it by pouring water on the part which is left dry and is without moisture. If one doubts while he has already assumed another condition, he must proceed to his Salat (prayer). There is nothing necessary for him to do about it. However, if it is discovered to have been left incomplete, he must go back to pour water on it; but if he finds moisture on it he only must wipe it and perform his Salat (prayer) again with certainty. If he has doubt about it there is nothing necessary for him to do because of such doubt and he must proceed to his Salat (prayer).'"

H 3940, Ch. 22, h 3

Ali ibn Ibrahim has narrated from his father from ibn abu 'Umayr from Hammad from al-Halabiy who has said the following:

"Abu 'Abd Allah, *'Alayhi al-Salam*, has said, 'If during Salat (prayer) you remember that you have left certain obligatory acts of your Wudu' incomplete, you must go back to complete what you forgot to do out of the acts of Wudu' and perform your Salat (prayer) again. For wiping your head and feet, it is sufficient to get moisture from your beard, when you forget to wipe the front portion of your head.'"

H 3941, Ch. 22, h 4

Ali ibn Ibrahim has narrated from his father from ibn abu 'Umayr from Hammad from al-Halabiy who has said the following:

"Abu 'Abd Allah, *'Alayhi al-Salam*, has said, 'If one forgets to wash his right (forearm) but washes his left (forearm), wipes his head and feet and then remembers, he must wash his right (forearm), his left (forearm), wipe his head and feet. If one forgets to wash his left (forearm), he must wash his left (forearm) and he does not have to wash what is washed before it (left forearm).' He (the Imam) said, 'You must maintain the prescribed order for Wudu'.'"

H 3942, Ch. 22, h 5

Ali has narrated from his father and Muhammad ibn 'Isma'il from al-Fadl ibn Shadhan all from Hammad from Hariz from Zurarah who has said the following:

"Abu Ja'far, *'Alayhi al-Salam*, has said, 'You must maintain the sequence in the acts of Wudu' as Allah, most Majestic, most Glorious, has said. You must begin to wash your face, then wash your hands (forearms), then wipe your head and feet. You must not do any of such acts before what is next in the sequential order, which (is what) the command requires to maintain. If you wash your forearms before your face, you must begin with your face and wash your forearms again. If you wipe your feet before your head, you must wipe your head and then wipe your feet again. Begin with what Allah has said to begin with.'"

H 3943, Ch. 22, h 6

A number of our people have narrated from Ahmad ibn Muhammad and abu Dawud all from al-Husayn ibn Sa'id from Fadalah ibn Ayyub from al-Husayn ibn 'Uthman from Sama'ah from abu Basir who has said the following:

"Abu 'Abd Allah, *'Alayhi al-Salam*, has said, 'If you forget and wash your forearm before your face, you must go back to wash your face, then wash your forearms, after washing your face. If you begin to wash your left forearm before washing your right forearm you must wash your right forearm, then wash you left forearm. If you forget wiping your head until you wash your feet, you must wipe your head, then wash your feet (in the case of Taqiyah).'"

H 3944, Ch. 22, h 7

Through the chain of narrators as that of the previous Hadith is the following narration:

"Abu 'Abd Allah, *'Alayhi al-Salam*, has said, 'If while taking Wudu' something happens that keeps you busy and your Wudu' dries up, you must do your Wudu' again; it is not permissible to divide Wudu'.'"

H 3945, Ch. 22, h 8

Ali ibn Ibrahim has narrated from Salih ibn al-Sindiy from Ja'far ibn Bashir from Muhammad ibn abu Hamzah from Mu'awiyah ibn 'Ammar who has said the following:

"I once said to abu 'Abd Allah, *'Alayhi al-Salam*, 'I may sometimes begin to take Wudu' but water is finished before Wudu' is complete and I ask the slave-girl for more water; but she delays and my Wudu' dries up. He (the Imam) said, 'You must do your Wudu' again.'"

H 3946, Ch. 22, h 9

Al-Husayn ibn Muhammad has narrated from Mu'alla' ibn Muhammad from al-Hassan ibn Ali al-Washsha' from Hammad ibn 'Uthaman from Hakam ibn Hukaym who has said the following:

"I once asked abu 'Abd Allah, *'Alayhi al-Salam*, about a man who forgets in his Wudu' to wash his forearm and head. He (the Imam) said, 'He must do it again; it is necessary to maintain the prescribed sequence in the acts of Wudu'.'"

Chapter 23 - Matters that Invalidate or Do not Invalidate Wudu'

H 3947, Ch. 23, h 1

Muhammad ibn 'Isma'il has narrated from al-Fadl ibn Shadhan and Ahmad ibn Idris from Muhammad ibn 'Abd al-Jabbar all from Safwan ibn Yahya from Salim abu al-Fadl who has said the following:

"Abu 'Abd Allah, *'Alayhi al-Salam*, has said, 'Wudu' does not become invalid unless something from your two passages of lower end, which Allah has granted you, comes out.'"

H 3948, Ch. 23, h 2

Muhammad ibn Yahya has narrated from Ahmad ibn Muhammad from Muhammad ibn Sahl from Zakariya ibn Adam who has said the following:

"I once asked abu al-Hassan, al-Rida, *'Alayhi al-Salam*, about a fistula (a bad wound) if it invalidates Wudu' or not. He (the Imam) said, 'Only three things invalidate Wudu': urine, feces and gas.'"

H 3949, Ch. 23, h 3

Ali ibn Ibrahim has narrated from his father from ibn abu 'Umayr from Mu'awiyah ibn 'Ammar who has said the following:

"Abu 'Abd Allah, *'Alayhi al-Salam*, has said, 'Satan blows in the man's buttocks to make him feel as if gas comes out. This does not invalidate Wudu' unless one hears gas coming out or senses its smell.'"

H 3950, Ch. 23, h 4

A number of our people have narrated from Ahmad ibn Muhammad from Muhammad ibn `Isma'il from Zarif from Tha'labah ibn Maymun from 'Abd Allah ibn Yazid who has said the following:

"Abu 'Abd Allah, *'Alayhi al-Salam*, has said, 'It is not necessary to take Wudu' because of the coming out of one's buttock, such things as pumpkin seeds or small worms; they are like lice.'"

H 3951, Ch. 23, h 5

Ali ibn Ibrahim has narrated from his father from ibn abu 'Umayr from al-Hassan ibn Akhiy Fudayl from Fudayl who has said the following:

"It is about the case of a man from whose buttocks such things like pumpkin seed may come out. Abu 'Abd Allah, *'Alayhi al-Salam*, once said, 'It is not necessary for him to take Wudu'.'"

It is narrated that if such things are stained with feces, then it is necessary to take Wudu'."

H 3952, Ch. 23, h 6

Ali ibn Ibrahim has narrated from his father from Hammad from Hariz from Zurarah who has said the following:

"I asked abu Ja'far, and abu 'Abd Allah, *'Alayhim al-Salam*, about things that invalidate Wudu'. They said, 'Of such things are that which come out of one's two bottom outlets, buttocks and urethra, in the form of urine or feces, semen or gas; as well as sleeping which stops understanding and all kinds of sleep is undesirable unless one is still able to hear.'"

H 3953, Ch. 23, h 7

Muhammad ibn Yahya has narrated from al-'Amrakiy from Ali ibn Ja'far from his brother, Musa, *'Alayhi al-Salam*, who has said the following:

"I once asked him (the Imam), 'Does the medicine that one may keep inside his body during Salat (prayer), invalidate his Wudu'?' He (the Imam) said, 'It does not invalidate his Wudu' but he must not perform Salat (prayer) before taking it away.'"

H 3954, Ch. 23, h 8

A number of our people have narrated from Ahmad ibn Muhammad from Ali ibn al-Hakam from al-Husayn ibn abu al-'Ala' who has said the following:

"I once asked abu 'Abd Allah, *'Alayhi al-Salam*, about a man who belches and something comes out in his mouth. Is he required to take Wudu' again?' He (the Imam) said, 'No, it is not necessary for him to take Wudu'.'"

H 3955, Ch. 23, h 9

Ali ibn Ibrahim has narrated from his father from ibn abu 'Umayr from Ibn `Udhaynah from abu 'Usamah who has said the following:

"I once asked abu 'Abd Allah, *'Alayhi al-Salam*, about vomiting if it invalidates Wudu' or not. He (the Imam) said, 'No, it does not invalidate one's Wudu'.'"

H 3956, Ch. 23, h 10

A number of our people have narrated from Ahmad ibn Muhammad and abu Dawud from al-Husayn ibn Sa'id from Fadalah from Aban from 'Ubayd ibn Zurarah who has said the following:

"Abu 'Abd Allah, *'Alayhi al-Salam*, has said, 'If one vomits while his Wudu' is valid, he should only rinse his mouth.'"

H 3957, Ch. 23, 11

Muhammad ibn 'Isma'il has narrated from al-Fadl ibn Shadhan from Safwan ibn Yahya from ibn Muskan from Muhammad al-Halabiy who has said the following:

"I once asked abu 'Abd Allah, *'Alayhi al-Salam*, about a man whose Wudu' is valid but he shaves his head or cuts his nails; is it necessary for him to take Wudu'?' He (the Imam) said, 'No, but he should wipe his head and nails with water.' I then said, 'They say that there is Wudu' for it.' He (the Imam) said, 'If they argue with you do not argue against them. Say to them, 'This is according to the Sunnah.'"

H 3958, Ch. 23, h 12

Ali ibn Ibrahim has narrated from his father from ibn abu 'Umayr from Jamil from Zurarah who has said the following:

"Abu Ja'far, *'Alayhi al-Salam*, has said, 'It is not necessary to take Wudu' for kissing, touching private parts or because of contact.'"

H 3959, Ch. 23, h 13

Muhammad ibn al-Hassan has narrated from Sahl ibn Ziyad from Muhammad ibn Sinan from ibn Muskan from abu Basir who has said the following:

"I once asked abu 'Abd Allah, *'Alayhi al-Salam*, about bleeding of nostrils and cupping and all other kinds of bleeding. He (the Imam) said, 'It is not necessary to take Wudu' for such things. It is necessary to take Wudu' only when something comes out of the two outlets of the bottom that Allah has granted you.'"

H 3960, Ch. 23, h 14

Muhammad ibn Yahya has narrated from Ahmad ibn Muhammad from Mu'ammar ibn Khallad who has said the following:

"I once asked abu al-Hassan, *'Alayhi al-Salam*, about a man who suffers from a certain illness because of which he is not able to lie down. It is difficult for him to take Wudu' in a sitting position and leaning against something. He may also slumber when he is sitting. He (the Imam) said, 'He must take Wudu'.' I then said, 'Taking Wudu' is difficult for him with such condition.' He (the Imam) said, 'When he cannot hear any sound Wudu' becomes necessary on him.' He (the Imam) said, 'It is permissible for him to delay al-Zuhr Salat (prayer) to perform it along with al-'Asr Salat (prayer) and al-Maghrib Salat (prayer) with al-'Isha' Salat (prayer).'"

H 3961, Ch. 23, h 15

Muhammad ibn 'Isma'il has narrated from al-Fadl ibn Shadhan and Muhammad ibn Yahya from Muhammad ibn al-Husayn from Safwan ibn Yahya from 'Abd al-Rahman ibn al-Hajjaj who has said the following:

"I once asked abu 'Abd Allah, *'Alayhi al-Salam*, about slumbering once or twice. He (the Imam) said, 'I do not know what slumbering once or twice is;

however Allah says, "Man is well aware of his soul." Ali, *'Alayhi al-Salam*, would say, "If one feels the taste of sleep when standing or sitting, it then becomes necessary for him to take Wudu'.""""

H 3962, Ch. 23, h 16

Ali ibn Muhammad has narrated from ibn Jumhur from those whom he has mentioned from Ahmad ibn Muhammad from Sa'd who has said the following:

"Abu 'Abd Allah, *'Alayhi al-Salam*, has said, 'There are ears and eyes. Eyes may sleep but not yet the ears. This does not invalidate Wudu'. When both eyes and ears sleep, Wudu' becomes invalid.'"

H 3963, Ch. 23, h 17

Ahmad ibn Idris and Muhammad ibn Yahya have narrated from Muhammad ibn Ahmad from Ahmad ibn al-al-Hassan from 'Amr ibn Sa'id from Musaddiq ibn Sadaqah from 'Ammar al-Sabatiy who has said the following:

"I once asked abu 'Abd Allah, *'Alayhi al-Salam*, about a man who cuts some of his hairs with his teeth. Should he wipe it with water before Salat (prayer)? He (the Imam) said, 'It is not harmful. This (wiping) applies only when it is with iron.'"

Chapter 24 - One's Stepping over Feces or Other Such Things

H 3964, Ch. 24, h 1

Muhammad ibn Yahya has narrated from Ahmad ibn Muhammad from ibn abu 'Umayr from Jamil ibn Salih from al-Ahwal who has said the following:

"Abu 'Abd Allah, *'Alayhi al-Salam*, has said, 'If one steps on a spot which is unclean, then steps on a clean spot, it is not harmful after walking a distance of fifteen yards or so.'"

H 3965, Ch. 24, h 2

Ali ibn Ibrahim has narrated from his father, from Hammad, from Hariz from Muhammad ibn Muslim who has said the following:

"Once I was in the company of abu Ja'far, *'Alayhi al-Salam*, and on passing (stepping on) some dried up human feces, certain pieces came in contact with his clothes. I informed him about it and he (the Imam) asked, 'Was it not dried up?' I said, 'Yes, it was dried up.' He (the Imam) said, 'It (touching) then is not harmful. Certain parts of earth cleanse other parts.'"

H 3966, Ch. 24, h 3

Muhammad ibn 'Isma'il has narrated from al-Fadl ibn Shadhan from Safwan from Ishaq ibn 'Ammar from Muhammad al-Halabiy who has said the following:

"Once we found lodging in a place. Between this place and the Masjid there were dirty passageways. I visited abu 'Abd Allah, *'Alayhi al-Salam*. He (the Imam) asked, 'Where have you found lodging?' I replied, 'It is the house of so and so.' He (the Imam) or we said, 'Between that house and Masjid there are unclean passageways.' He (the Imam) said, 'It is not harmful, certain parts of earth cleanse other parts.' I (the narrator) asked, 'What happens if I step on wet dung?' He (the Imam) said, 'Such things are not harmful.'"

H 3967, Ch. 24, h 4

Ali ibn Muhammad has narrated from Sahl ibn Ziyad from Muhammad ibn Sinan from ibn Muskan from al-Halabiy who has said the following:

"I once asked abu 'Abd Allah, *'Alayhi al-Salam*, about the case of one who steps on feces or urine whether he must take Wudu' again?' He (the Imam) replied, 'No, but one must wash the polluted area clean.'"

In another Hadith the statement says that washing is not necessary if it is dry.

H 3968, Ch. 24, h 5

Ali ibn Ibrahim has narrated from his father from ibn abu 'Umayr from Jamil ibn Darraj from al-Mu'alla' ibn Khunays who has said the following:

"I once asked abu 'Abd Allah, *'Alayhi al-Salam*, about the swine which comes out of water and passes on the road while water falls from it. What happens if I walk bare foot over such areas? He (the Imam) asked. 'Are not there certain dry spots behind it?' I replied, 'Yes, there are such spots.' He (the Imam) said, 'It is not harmful. Certain parts of earth cleanse other parts.'"

Chapter 25 - Certain Fluid, Which Is Other than Urine and Semen

H 3969, Ch. 25, h 1

Ali ibn Ibrahim has narrated from his father from Hammad from Hariz from Zurarah who has said the following:

"Once abu 'Abd Allah, *'Alayhi al-Salam*, said, 'If certain fluids (called al-Madhiy or Wadiy) other than semen and urine come out of your urethra during Salat (prayer), you do not have to wash them or discontinue your Salat (prayer); nor do they invalidate Wudu' even if such fluids reach up to your backside. It is like nasal mucus. Everything like this that may come out from you after Wudu' is of secreted lubricants or Hemorrhoids, and they do not matter and it is not necessary to wash unless they are dirty.'"

H 3970, Ch. 25, h 2

Muhammad ibn Yahya has narrated from Ahmad ibn Muhammad from ibn Faddal from ibn Bukayr from 'Umar ibn Hanzalah who has said the following:

"I once asked abu 'Abd Allah, *'Alayhi al-Salam*, about al-Madhiy. He (the Imam) said, 'It is only like nasal mucus. They are very similar.'"

H 3971, Ch. 25, h 3

Ali ibn Ibrahim has narrated from his father from ibn abu 'Umayr from 'Umar ibn 'Udhaynah from Burayd ibn Mu'awiyah who has said the following:

"I once asked one of the two Imams, *'Alayhim al-Salam*, about al-Madhiy (certain secreted lubricant from urethra). He (the Imam) said, 'It does not invalidate Wudu' and it is not necessary to wash one's clothes or body. It is only like nasal mucus and saliva.'"

H 3972, Ch. 25, h 4

Ali ibn Ibrahim has narrated from his father, from Hammad, from Hariz, from Muhammad ibn Muslim who has said the following:

"I once asked Abu Ja'far, *'Alayhi al-Salam*, about al-Madhiy which flows all the way to one's thigh. He (the Imam) said, 'It is not necessary for one to discontinue one's Salat (prayer) to wash it from one's thigh. It does not come out of the passage from which semen comes. It is only like nasal mucus.'"

Chapter 26 - Kinds of Ghusl (bath)

H 3973, Ch. 26, h 1

Muhammad ibn 'Isma'il has narrated from al-Fadl ibn Shadhan from Safwan ibn Yahya and ibn abu 'Umayr from Mu'awiyah ibn 'Ammar who has said the following:

"I heard abu 'Abd Allah, *'Alayhi al-Salam*, state this Hadith: 'There is Ghusl (bath) because of sexual relations, there is Ghusl (bath) on Friday, on the two 'Ids, at the time of assuming the state of 'Ihram, there is Ghusl (bath) when entering Makkah and al-Madinah. There is Ghusl (bath) on the day of 'Arafah, (9th of the month of Dhu al-Hajjah) on the day of one's visiting the House (al-Ka'bah) for entering al-Ka'bah, in the nineteenth, twenty first, twenty-third nights of the month of Ramadan and for touching a dead body.'"

H 3974, Ch. 26, h 2

Muhammad ibn Yahya has narrated from Ahmad ibn Muhammad from Muhammad ibn 'Uthman ibn 'Isa from Sama'ah who has said the following:

"I once asked abu 'Abd Allah, *'Alayhi al-Salam*, about Ghusl (bath) on Friday. He (the Imam) said, 'It is obligatory, regardless, if one is on a journey or at home except that women are exempt on a journey due to scarcity of water.' He (the Imam) said, 'Ghusl (bath) because of sexual relation is obligatory as well as because of Hayd (menses) when bleeding stops. It is obligatory for al-Mustahazah (irregular Hayd (menses)) if blood passes through the piece of cotton, which (she has) placed in her urethra. In such case she must take Ghusl (bath) for every two Salat (prayer) and for the morning Salat (prayer). If blood does not pass through the piece of cotton, there is once Ghusl (bath) only every day and Wudu' for every Salat (prayer). Ghusl (bath) is obligatory because of al-Nifas (childbirth). Ghusl (bath) of newborn is obligatory. Ghusl (bath) of a dead body is obligatory. There is Ghusl (bath) for visiting (al-Ka'bah), for entering the House, and for pleading for rainfall. It is preferable to take Ghusl (bath) in the first night of the month of Ramadan. Ghusl (bath) in twenty-first and twenty-third nights of the month of Ramadan is Sunnah that one should not ignore because one of them is the night of al-Qadr. Ghusl (bath) on the day of al-Fitr (the first day of the month of Shawwal), on the day of al-Adha' (tenth of the month of Dhul Hajjah) is of the Sunnah. I do not like to ignore it. There is Ghusl (bath) for Istikharah. It is preferable to take Ghusl (bath) to perform acts of worship during the three nights of the month of Ramadan; the nineteenth, twenty-first and twenty-third nights.'"

Chapter 27 - Matters Covered by Ghusl (bath)

H 3975, Ch. 27, h 1

Ali ibn Ibrahim has narrated from his father from Hammad ibn 'Isa from Hariz from Zurarah who has said the following:

"He (the Imam) has said, 'If you take a Ghusl (bath) after dawn, it is sufficient for Ghusl (bath) because of sexual relations, for Friday, the day of 'Arafah, (ninth of Dhul Hajjah), tenth of Dhul Hajjah, for shaving (during Hajj), offering sacrifice and visiting the House (al-Ka'bah). One Ghusl (bath) suffices many reasons for it.' He (the narrator) has said that he (the Imam) then said, 'So also is the case with women. One Ghusl (bath) suffices for sexual relation, assuming the state of 'Ihram, Friday, Hayd (menses) and for her 'Id.'"

H 3976, Ch. 27, h 2

Muhammad ibn Yahya has narrated from Ahmad ibn Muhammad from Ali ibn Hadid from Jamil ibn Darraj from certain persons of our people who have said the following:

"One of the two Imam, *'Alayhim al-Salam*, has said, 'If one, because of sexual relation, takes a Ghusl (bath) after dawn, it is sufficient for all the Ghusl (bath) that he is required to have on that day.'"

Chapter 28 - Necessity of Ghusl (bath) on Friday

H 3977, Ch. 28, h 1

Ali ibn Ibrahim has narrated from his father from 'Abd Allah ibn al-Mughirah who has said the following:

"I once asked abu al-Hassan, al-Rida, *'Alayhi al-Salam*, about Ghusl (bath) on Friday. He (the Imam) said, 'It is obligatory on every male, female, slave or free.'"

H 3978, Ch. 28, h 2

Ali ibn Muhammad has narrated from Sahl ibn Ziyad and Muhammad ibn Yahya from Ahmad ibn Muhammad ibn abu Nasr from Muhammad ibn 'Abd Allah who has said the following:

"I once asked al-Rida', *'Alayhi al-Salam*, about Ghusl (bath) on Friday. He (the Imam) said, 'It is obligatory on every male, female, slave or free.'"

H 3979, Ch. 28, h 3

Muhammad ibn Yahya has narrated from Muhammad ibn al-Husayn from Safwan from Mansur ibn Hazim who has said the following:

"Abu 'Abd Allah, *'Alayhi al-Salam*, has said, 'On Friday Ghusl (bath) is obligatory on men and women at home, and on men also on a journey; but it is not obligatory on women on a journey.' In another Hadith it is said that women have exemption while on a journey, due to scarcity of water."

H 3980, Ch. 28, h 4

A number of our people have narrated from Ahmad ibn Muhammad from Ali ibn Sayf from his father Sayf ibn 'Amirah from al-Husayn ibn Khalid who has said the following:

"I asked abu al-Hassan, al-Awwal, *'Alayhi al-Salam*, how did Ghusl (bath) for Friday become obligatory? He (the Imam) said, 'Allah, most Blessed, most High, has completed obligatory Salat (prayer) with optional ones. He has completed obligatory fasting with optional fast. He has completed obligatory Wudu' with Ghusl (bath) on Friday in case a mistake, shortcoming, forgetfulness or flaws may take place (in such Wudu').'"

H 3981, Ch. 28, h 5

A number of our people have narrated from Ibrahim ibn Ishaq al-Ahmar from 'Abd Allah ibn Hammad al-Ansariy from Sabbah al-Muzniy from al-Harith ibn Hasirah from al-Asbagh who has said the following:

"When `Amir al-Mu'minin, *'Alayhi al-Salam*, wanted to reprimand a person he (the Imam) would say, 'By Allah, your failure is greater than one who fails to take Ghusl (bath) on Friday. It certainly is Tahur (cleansing) until next Friday.'"

H 3982, Ch. 28, h 6

A number of our people have narrated from Ahmad ibn Muhammad from al-Husayn ibn Musa from his mother, mother of Ahmad daughter of Musa who have said the following:

"We were with abu al-Hassan, *'Alayhi al-Salam*, in the desert on our way to Baghdad. He (the Imam) said to us, 'Today is Thursday, take Ghusl (bath) for Friday, tomorrow water will be scarce.' We took Ghusl (bath) on Thursday for Friday.'"

H 3983, Ch. 28, h 7

Ali ibn Ibrahim has narrated from his father from Hammad from Hariz from certain persons of our people who has said the following:

"Abu Ja'far, *'Alayhi al-Salam*, has said, 'It is necessary to take Ghusl (bath) on Friday, on a journey or at home. If one forgets it, one must do it again next day.' It is narrated that one suffering from illness is excused.'"

Chapter 29 - Description of Ghusl (bath), Wudu' Before or Thereafter and a Man's Ghusl (bath) in an Improper Place, Expressions to Say During Taking Ghusl (bath) and Moving a Ring During Ghusl (bath)

H 3984, Ch. 29, h 1

Muhammad ibn Yahya has narrated from Muhammad ibn al-Husayn and Muhammad ibn `Isma'il from al-Fadl ibn Shadhan all from Safwan ibn Yahya from 'Ala' ibn Razin from Muhammad ibn Muslim who has said the following:

"I asked one of the two Imam, *'Alayhim al-Salam*, about Ghusl (bath) because of sexual relation. He (the Imam) said, 'Begin with your palms (hands) and wash them. Thereafter wash your private parts, then pour water over your head three times, then pour water over the rest of your body twice; over whatever parts water flows, they become clean.'"

H 3985, Ch. 29, h 2

Muhammad ibn `Isma'il has narrated from al-Fadl ibn Shadhan from Hammad ibn 'Isa from Rib'iy ibn 'Abd Allah who has said the following:

"Abu 'Abd Allah, *'Alayhi al-Salam*, has said, 'One, because of sexual relation, must pour water on one's head three times. Less than this is not sufficient.'"

H 3986, Ch. 29, h 3

Ali ibn Ibrahim has narrated from his father from Hammad ibn 'Isa from Hariz from Zurarah who has said the following:

"I asked him (the Imam), 'How must a person take Ghusl (bath) because of sexual relation?' He (the Imam) said, 'If one's hand is not polluted, one should immerse it in water. One then should begin with one's private parts and wash them clean with three handfuls of water, then pour three handfuls of water on one's head, then pour water twice on one's right shoulder, then on one's left shoulder and over whatever parts water flows: it is sufficient.'"

H 3987, Ch. 29, h 4

A number of our people have narrated from Ahmad ibn Muhammad from Ali ibn al-Hakam from certain persons of our people who has said the following:

"He (the Imam) has said, 'When taking Ghusl (bath) for Friday, you should say the following: "O Lord, cleanse my heart of all afflictions which destroy my religion and invalidate my deeds." "When taking Ghusl (bath) because of sexual relation say the following: 'O Lord, cleanse my heart, purify my deeds, accept my efforts and make what is with You for me to be good.'"'"

H 3988, Ch. 29, h 5

Ali ibn Ibrahim has narrated from his father from ibn abu 'Umayr from Hammad from al-Halabiy who has said the following:

"I heard abu 'Abd Allah, *'Alayhi al-Salam*, say, 'If one, for Ghusl (bath) because of sexual relation, immerses oneself in water once, it is sufficient.'"

H 3989, Ch. 29, h 6

Muhammad ibn Yahya has narrated from al-'Amrakiy from Ali ibn Ja'far from his brother, Musa ibn Ja'far, *'Alayhi al-Salam*, who has said the following:

"I once asked him (the Imam) about a woman who wears a bracelet and there is bangle on her forearm and does not know if water reaches (her skin) under the bracelet, what should she do for Wudu' or taking Ghusl (bath)? He (the Imam) said, 'She must move them so that water reaches beneath or remove them.' I then asked about a tight ring about which one is not certain if water reaches beneath when taking Wudu'. He (the Imam) said, 'If one knows that water does not reach beneath, one must remove it when taking Wudu'.'"

H 3990, Ch. 29, h 7

A number of our people have narrated from Ahmad ibn Muhammad ibn 'Isa and abu Dawud all from al-Husayn ibn Sa'id from Muhammad ibn abu Hamzah from a man who has said the following:

"I once asked abu 'Abd Allah, *'Alayhi al-Salam*, about a man who has had sexual relation after which he stands in the rain until water flows over his body. 'Is this sufficient for Ghusl (bath)?' He (the Imam) said, 'Yes, it is sufficient.'"

H 3991, Ch. 29, h 8

Ali ibn Ibrahim has narrated from his father and Muhammad ibn 'Isma'il from al-Fadl ibn Shadhan all from Hammad ibn 'Isa from Ibrahim ibn 'Umar al-Yamaniy who has said the following:

"Abu 'Abd Allah, *'Alayhi al-Salam*, has said that 'Ali, *'Alayhi al-Salam*, would not consider it harmful if one washes his head earlier for Ghusl (bath) because of sexual relation and the rest of his body at the time of Salat (prayer).'"

H 3992, Ch. 29, h 9

Ali ibn Ibrahim has narrated from his father from Hammad from Hariz from Zurarah who has said the following:

"Abu 'Abd Allah, *'Alayhi al-Salam*, has said, 'When taking Ghusl (bath) because of sexual relation, if one does not wash one's head, then finds out that the head is not washed, he must take Ghusl (bath) again.'"

H 3993, Ch. 29, h 10

Muhammad ibn Yahya has narrated from Muhammad ibn al-Husayn from Hammad from Bakr ibn Karib who has said the following:

"I once asked abu 'Abd Allah, *'Alayhi al-Salam*, about a man who takes Ghusl (bath) because of sexual relation; must he wash his feet after Ghusl (bath)? He (the Imam) said, 'It is not necessary for him to wash if he stands during taking Ghusl (bath) at such a place where water flows over his feet, but he must wash them if, while taking Ghusl (bath) he stands in a place where his feet are in stagnant water.'"

H 3994, Ch. 29, h 11

Muhammad ibn Yahya has narrated from Ahmad ibn Muhammad from abu Yahya al-Wasitiy from Hisham ibn Salim who has said the following:

"I once said to abu 'Abd Allah, *'Alayhi al-Salam*, 'I pray to Allah to keep my soul in service for your cause, I may take Ghusl (bath) in the toilet area which is for urinating and I wear sandals which are made in Sind.' He (the Imam) said, 'If the water which flows over your body reaches the bottom of your feet then it is not necessary to wash your feet.'"

H 3995, Ch. 29, h 12

A number of our people have narrated from Ahmad ibn Muhammad from Shadhan ibn al-Khalil from Yunus from Yahya ibn Talhah from his father from 'Abd Allah ibn Sulayman who has said the following:

"I heard abu 'Abd Allah, *'Alayhi al-Salam*, say, 'Wudu' after Ghusl (bath) is heresy.'"

H 3996, Ch. 29, h 13

Muhammad ibn Yahya and others have narrated from Muhammad ibn Ahmad from Ya'qub ibn Yazid from ibn abu 'Umayr from a man who has said the following:

"Abu 'Abd Allah, *'Alayhi al-Salam*, has said, 'There is Wudu' before every Ghusl (bath) except the Ghusl (bath) because of sexual relation.'"

"It is narrated that Wudu' is not (prescribed) necessary with Ghusl (bath) except Ghusl (bath) for Friday before which there is Wudu'. It is narrated that there is no Wudu' more cleansing than Ghusl (bath).

(The above Ahadith are best explained in the form of fatwa.)

H 3997, Ch. 29, h 14

A number of our people have narrated from Ahmad ibn Muhammad from Ali ibn al-Hakam from Al-Husayn ibn abu al-'Ala' who has said the following:

"I once asked abu 'Abd Allah, *'Alayhi al-Salam*, about the ring during taking Ghusl (bath). He (the Imam) said, '(You must) change its place.' He (the Imam) said, 'You can turn the ring during Wudu' but if you forget until you are in your Salat (prayer); I do not command you to perform your Salat (prayer) again.'"

H 3998, Ch. 29, 15

A number of our people have narrated from Ahmad ibn Muhammad from al-Husayn ibn Sa'id from Fadalah from 'Abd Allah ibn Sinan who has said the following:

"Abu 'Abd Allah, *'Alayhi al-Salam*, has said, 'Once my father took Ghusl (bath) because of sexual relation. Someone said to him that water has not reached to a spot on his back. He said, "It was not necessary for you to inform me. (I wish) you sought to have remained quiet." He then wiped that spot with his hand.'"

H 3999, Ch. 29, h 16

Ali ibn Ibrahim has narrated from his father from 'Abd Allah ibn al-Mughirah from ibn Muskan from Muhammad al-Halabiy who has said the following:

"Abu 'Abd Allah, *'Alayhi al-Salam*, has said, 'It is not necessary for a woman to open up her hairs when taking Ghusl (bath) because of sexual relation.'"

H 4000, Ch. 29, h 17

Ali ibn Ibrahim has narrated from his father from ibn abu 'Umayr from Jamil who has said the following:

"I once asked abu 'Abd Allah, *'Alayhi al-Salam*, about the way women form their hairs. He (the Imam) said, 'Combs were not available. They would only tie their hairs together.' He (the Imam) mentioned four places and he (the Imam) said, 'Women should make an effort in Ghusl (bath).'"

Chapter 30 - Reason Necessitating Ghusl (bath) for Men and Women

H 4001, Ch. 30, h 1

Muhammad ibn Yahya has narrated from Muhammad ibn al-Husayn, from Safwan ibn Yahya, from al-'Ala' ibn Razin, from Muhammad ibn Muslim who has said the following:

"I once asked one of the two Imam, *'Alayhim al-Salam*, 'When does Ghusl (bath) become necessary for man and woman?' He (the Imam) said, 'After consummating sexual relation, Ghusl (bath), payment of al-Mahr (payment agreed upon during marriage) and stoning (if it is fornication) become necessary.'"

H 4002, Ch. 20, h 2

A number of our people have narrated from Ahmad ibn Muhammad ibn 'Isa from Muhammad ibn 'Isma'il who has said the following:

"I once asked al-Rida, *'Alayhi al-Salam*, about a man who performs sexual relation with woman near her vagina but does not discharge, if Ghusl (bath) becomes necessary. He (the Imam) said, 'When private parts touch each other Ghusl (bath) becomes necessary.' I (the narrator) then asked, 'Is touching of private parts disappearance of glans penis?' He (the Imam) replied, 'Yes, it is such.'"

H 4003, Ch. 30, h 3

Through the same chain of narrators as that of the previous Hadith the narrator has narrated from Ahmad ibn Muhammad from al-Hassan ibn Ali ibn Yaqtin from his brother al-Husayn from Ali ibn Yaqtin who has said the following:

"I once asked abu al-Hassan, *'Alayhi al-Salam,* about a man who pollutes a virgin girl who does not lose her virginity and does not discharge semen on her. Is Ghusl (bath) necessary on her or if she is not a virgin and he is exposed to her but intercourse does not take place, if Ghusl (bath) is obligatory on her? He (the Imam) said, 'When private part falls on private part, Ghusl (bath) becomes necessary - virgin or not virgin.'"

H 4004, Ch. 30, h 4

Ali ibn Ibrahim has narrated from his father from ibn abu 'Umayr from Hammad ibn 'Uthman from 'Ubayd Allah al-Halabiy who has said the following:

"I once asked abu 'Abd Allah, *'Alayhi al-Salam,* about one's foreplay and Ghusl (bath). He (the Imam) said, 'There is Ghusl (bath) obligatory if semen discharge takes place.'"

H 4005, Ch. 30, h 5

A number of our people have narrated from Ahmad ibn Muhammad from 'Isma'il ibn Sa'd al-Ash'ariy who has said the following:

"I once asked al-Rida, *'Alayhi al-Salam,* about a man who touches and plays by his hand with the private parts of his slave-girl without contact of his private part until she feels discharge, is Ghusl (bath) necessary on her? He (the Imam) said, 'Ghusl (bath) is necessary if discharge is accompanied by orgasm.'"

H 4006, Ch. 30, h 6

Muhammad ibn Yahya has narrated from Ahmad ibn Muhammad from Muhammad ibn 'Isma'il ibn Bazi' who has said the following:

"I once asked al-Rida, *'Alayhi al-Salam,* about a man who allows intercourse with a woman to take place but not in vagina, and she feels discharges, is Ghusl (bath) necessary on her? He (the Imam) said, 'Yes, Ghusl (bath) is necessary for her.'"

H 4007, Ch. 30, h 7

Al-Husayn ibn Muhammad has narrated from 'Abd Allah ibn 'Amir from Ali ibn Mahziyar from al-Husayn ibn Sa'id from Muhammad ibn al-Fudayl who has said the following:

"I once asked abu al-Hassan, *'Alayhi al-Salam,* about the case of a woman who hugs her husband from his backside. She moves and experiences orgasm and discharge, is Ghusl (bath) necessary on her? He (the Imam) said, 'If she experiences orgasm and discharge, Ghusl (bath) becomes necessary.'"

H 4008, Ch. 30, h 8

Muhammad ibn Yahya has narrated from Ahmad ibn Muhammad from al-Barqiy in a marfu' manner who has said the following:

"Abu 'Abd Allah, *'Alayhi al-Salam,* has said, 'If a man allows intercourse to take place in a woman's anus without discharge of semen, Ghusl (bath) is not necessary on neither one of them, but if he discharges, Ghusl (bath) is necessary on him but it is not necessary on the woman.'"

Chapter 31 - Wet Dreams of Men and Women

H 4009, Ch. 31, h 1

Muhammad ibn Yahya has narrated from Ahmad ibn Muhammad ibn 'Isa from Ali ibn al-Hakam from al-Husayn ibn abu al-'Ala' who has said the following:

"I once asked abu 'Abd Allah, *'Alayhi al-Salam*, about a man who experiences a wet dream and orgasm but when he wakes up, does not find any sign of discharge in his clothes or body. He (the Imam) said, 'Ghusl (bath) is not necessary on him.' He (the Imam) said, 'Ali, *'Alayhi al-Salam*, would say, "Ghusl (bath) becomes necessary because of major (semen) discharge. If one experiences a wet dream but does not find any sign of semen, Ghusl (bath) is not necessary on him."'"

H 4010, Ch. 31, h 2

Muhammad ibn 'Isma'il has narrated from al-Fadl ibn Shadhan from ibn abu 'Umayr from Mu'awiyah ibn 'Ammar who has said the following:

"I once asked abu 'Abd Allah, *'Alayhi al-Salam*, about a man who dreams and when he wakes up finds moisture and wet spots. He (the Imam) said, 'It is not necessary to do anything unless he suffers from an illness in which case he must take Ghusl (bath).'" (Fatwa best explains this Hadith.)

H 4011, Ch. 31, h 3

Ali ibn Ibrahim has narrated from his father from Hammad ibn 'Isa from Hariz from Zurarah who has said the following:

"He (the Imam) has said, 'When you suffer from an illness and experience orgasm, it may take place with excitement, but if it takes place in a weak manner with less force because of your illness, in intervals little by little, in such case Ghusl (bath) is obligatory.'"

H 4012, Ch. 31, h 4

Ali ibn Ibrahim has narrated from his father from ibn abu 'Umayr from ibn al-Mughirah from Hariz from ibn abu Ya'fur who has said the following:

"I once said to abu 'Abd Allah, *'Alayhi al-Salam*, there is a man who experiences wet dream and orgasm. He then wakes up and does not find anything, but after a while discharge takes place. He (the Imam) said, 'If he suffers from an illness, he must take Ghusl (bath), but if he does not suffer from any illness he is not obligated for Ghusl (bath).' I then asked him (the Imam), 'What is the difference between the two cases?' He (the Imam) said, 'It is because in the case of one without illness, it comes spurting and with force, but in the case of one suffering from an illness it comes later.'"

H 4013, Ch. 31, h 5

A number of our people have narrated from Ahmad ibn Muhammad from ibn abu 'Umayr from Hammad ibn 'Uthman from al-Halabiy who has said the following:

"I once asked abu 'Abd Allah, *'Alayhi al-Salam*, about a woman who experiences in her dream what a man does. He (the Imam) said, 'If she experiences discharge Ghusl (bath) is necessary on her; if there is no discharge, Ghusl (bath) is not necessary.'"

H 4014, Ch. 31, h 6
Muhammad ibn Yahya has narrated from Ahmad ibn Muhammad from ibn Mahbub from 'Abd Allah ibn Sinan who has said the following:
"I once asked abu 'Abd Allah, *'Alayhi al-Salam*, about a woman who in her dream finds a man who engages in an intercourse with her until she experiences orgasm. He (the Imam) said, 'She must take Ghusl (bath).'"

According to another Hadith, she must take Ghusl (bath) but must not inform others to avoid ridicule.

H 4015, Ch. 31, h 7
Muhammad ibn Yahya has narrated from Ahmad ibn Muhammad from 'Uthman ibn 'Isa from Sama'ah who has said the following:
"I once asked abu 'Abd Allah, *'Alayhi al-Salam*, about a man who does not experience any wet dream but he finds wet spots on his thigh and his clothes. Is Ghusl (bath) necessary for him? He (the Imam) said, 'Yes, Ghusl (bath) is necessary."

Chapter 32 - Finding Fluid Coming Out after Ghusl (bath)

H 4016, Ch. 32, h 1
Muhammad ibn Yahya has narrated from Ahmad ibn Muhammad from 'Uthman ibn 'Isa from 'Abd Allah ibn Muskan from Sulayman ibn Khalid who has said the following:
"I once asked abu 'Abd Allah, *'Alayhi al-Salam*, about a man who experiences a wet dream and takes Ghusl (bath) before urinating then something comes out. He (the Imam) said, 'He must take Ghusl (bath) again.' I then asked what happens if such thing happens to a woman. He (the Imam) said, 'She does not need a Ghusl (bath) again.' I then asked, 'What is the difference?' He (the Imam) said, 'A discharge from a woman is because of man's discharge.'"

H 4017, Ch. 32, h 2
Ali ibn Ibrahim has narrated from his father from ibn abu 'Umayr from Hammad from al-Halabiy who has said the following:
"Abu 'Abd Allah, *'Alayhi al-Salam*, once was asked about a man who after Ghusl (bath) finds wet spots and he had urinated before Ghusl (bath). He (the Imam) said, 'If he had urinated before Ghusl (bath), it (Ghusl (bath)) is not necessary again.'"

H 4018, Ch. 32, h 3
Al-Husayn ibn Muhammad has narrated from Mu'alla' ibn Muhammad from al-Washsha' from Aban ibn 'Uthman from 'Abd al-Rahman ibn abu 'Abd Allah who has said the following:
"I once asked abu 'Abd Allah, *'Alayhi al-Salam*, about the case of a woman who takes Ghusl (bath) because of sexual relation; then she finds man's semen after Ghusl (bath). He (the Imam) said, 'No, Ghusl (bath) is not necessary again.'"

H 4019, Ch. 32, h 4
Abu Dawud has narrated from al-Husayn ibn Sa'id from his brother, al-Hassan from Zur'ah from Sama'ah who has said the following:
"I once asked the Imam about a man who experiences sexual relation; then takes Ghusl (bath) before urinating and finds wet spots after Ghusl (bath). He (the

Imam) said, 'He must take Ghusl (bath) again. Had he urinated before Ghusl (bath), he did not have to take Ghusl (bath) again; but he must take Wudu' and cleanse himself properly.'"

Chapter 33 - One after Carnal Relations Eats, Drinks, Reads, Enters a Masjid, Dyes Hair, Uses Fragrance and So On

H 4020, Ch. 33, h 1

Ali ibn Ibrahim has narrated from his father and Muhammad ibn 'Isma'il from al-Fadl ibn Shadhan all from Hammad ibn 'Isa from Hariz from Zurarah who has said the following:

"Abu Ja'far, *'Alayhi al-Salam*, has said, 'If one after experiencing sexual relation likes to eat or drink, one must wash one's hand, rinse one's mouth, wash one's face, then eat and drink.'"

H 4021, Ch. 33, h 2

A number of our people have narrated from Ahmad ibn Muhammad from ibn Faddal from ibn Bukayr who has said the following:

"I once asked abu 'Abd Allah, *'Alayhi al-Salam*, about the case of one who after sexual relation eats, drinks or reads. He (the Imam) said, 'Yes, one can eat, drink, read and speak of Allah, most Majestic, most Glorious, as much as one likes.'"

H 4022, Ch. 33, h 3

Ali ibn Muhammad and Muhammad ibn al-Hassan have narrated from Sahl ibn Ziyad from ibn abu Nasr from Jamil ibn Darraj who has said the following:

"Abu 'Abd Allah, *'Alayhi al-Salam*, has said, 'It is permissible for one after experiencing sexual relation to walk in all kinds of Masjid but he must not sit in them. This does not apply to Masjid al-Haram and Masjid of the Messenger of Allah.'"

H 4023, Ch. 33, h 4

Ali ibn Ibrahim has narrated from his father from ibn abu 'Umayr from Jamil who has said the following:

"I once asked abu 'Abd Allah, *'Alayhi al-Salam*, about one's sitting in Masjid after experiencing sexual relation. He (the Imam) said, 'No, it is not permissible but one can pass through all kinds of Masjid except Masjid al-Haram and Masjid of the Messenger of Allah.'"

H 4024, Ch. 33, h 5

Muhammad ibn Yahya has narrated from Ahmad ibn Muhammad from al-Husayn ibn Sa'id from Hammad ibn 'Isa from al-Husayn ibn al-Mukhtar from abu Basir who has said the following:

"I once asked abu 'Abd Allah, *'Alayhi al-Salam*, about one who reads from a copy of al-Mushaf (the book) without Wudu'. He (the Imam) said, 'It is not harmful, but one must not touch the book in such condition.'"

H 4025, Ch. 33, h 6

Muhammad ibn Yahya has narrated from Ahmad ibn Muhammad from al-Husayn ibn Sa'id from 'Abd Allah ibn Bahr from Hariz who has said the following:

"I once asked abu 'Abd Allah, *'Alayhi al-Salam*, 'Can one after experiencing sexual relation, rub oil, then take Ghusl (bath). He (the Imam) said, 'No, (it is not permissible).'"

H 4026, Ch. 33, h 7

Muhammad ibn Yahya has narrated from Ahmad ibn Muhammad from Ibrahim ibn abu Mahmud who has said the following:

"I once asked al-Rida, *'Alayhi al-Salam*, 'Is it permissible for one after experiencing sexual relation to come in contact with perfume, oils or such things as chewing-gum or freshener, then take Ghusl (bath)? What happens if such one afterwards finds pieces left on one's body or marks of rubbing oil or perfumes and so on?' He (the Imam) said, 'It is not harmful.'"

H 4027, Ch. 33, h 8

Abu Dawud has narrated from al-Husayn ibn Sa'id from Fadalah ibn Ayyub from 'Abd Allah ibn Sinan who has said the following:

"I once asked abu 'Abd Allah, *'Alayhi al-Salam*, about one, who experiencing sexual relation or Hayd (menses), picks up something from Masjid. He (the Imam) said, 'It is permissible but they must not leave something in Masjid.'"

H 4028, Ch. 33, h 9

Muhammad ibn Yahya has narrated from Ahmad ibn Muhammad from ibn abu Nasr from abu Jamilah who has said the following:

"Abu al-Hassan, al-Awwal, *'Alayhi al-Salam*, has said, 'It is permissible for one who has experienced sexual relation to apply dye to one's hairs and one who has already applied dye to one's hair to experience sexual relation or apply lime.'"

It is also narrated that one who has applied dye to one's hair must not experience sexual relation until one has removed it, but in the beginning of the application one does not have to do so."

H 4029, Ch. 33, h 10

A number of our people have narrated from Ahmad ibn Muhammad from al-Husayn ibn Sa'id from his brother al-Hassan from Zur'ah, from Sama'ah who has said the following:

"I once asked him (the Imam) about a man who experiences sexual relation and wants to sleep. He (the Imam) said, 'If he likes he can take Wudu'. However, Ghusl (bath) is more desirable to me and I prefer it; and it is better than that, however, if he has gone to sleep without Wudu' and without Ghusl (bath) there is nothing obligatory for him to do, by the will of Allah, most High.'"

H 4030, Ch. 33, h 11

Ali ibn Ibrahim has narrated from his father from ibn abu 'Umayr from Hammad from al-Halabiy who has said the following:

"Abu 'Abd Allah, *'Alayhi al-Salam*, has said, 'It is permissible for one who has experienced sexual relation to draw blood from his body by means of cupping.'"

H 4031, Ch. 33, h 12

Ali ibn Ibrahim has narrated from his father from al-Nawfaliy from al-Sakuniy who has said the following:

"Abu 'Abd Allah, *'Alayhi al-Salam,* has said, 'It is permissible for a man to apply dye to his hairs and experience sexual relation with dye applied. It is permissible for a man to apply lime to his hairs and experience sexual relation or draw blood from his body by means of cupping or slaughter (an animal for food). He should not taste anything before washing his hands and rinsing his mouth because of fear of the appearance of abnormal whiteness in his skin.'"

Chapter 34 - One after Carnal Relation Sweats in His Clothes, Clothes Touch His Wet Body

H 4032, Ch. 34, h 1

Ali ibn Ibrahim has narrated from his father from ibn abu 'Umayr from ibn 'Udhaynah from abu 'Usamah who has said the following:

"I once asked abu 'Abd Allah, *'Alayhi al-Salam,* about one who has experienced sexual relation who perspires in his clothes or takes Ghusl (bath), then hugs his wife or sleeps next to her during her Hayd (menses) or has experienced sexual relation and her perspiration touches his body. He (the Imam) said, 'All of such things are not harmful.'"

H 4033, Ch. 34, h 2

Ali ibn Ibrahim has narrated from his father from ibn abu 'Umayr from Jamil ibn Darraj from abu 'Usamah who has said the following:

"I once asked abu 'Abd Allah, *'Alayhi al-Salam,* about my exposure in the open, under the sky because of which my clothes become wet, while I have experienced sexual relation, and such clothes reach the part of my body which is polluted with semen, can I perform Salat (prayer) in such clothes? He (the Imam) said, 'Yes, you can do so.'"

H 4034, Ch. 34, h 3

A number of our people have narrated from Ahmad ibn Muhammad from al-Husayn ibn Sa'id from al-Qasim ibn Muhammad from Ali ibn abu Hamzah who has said the following:

"Abu 'Abd Allah, *'Alayhi al-Salam,* once was asked, when I was present, about a man who has experienced sexual relation and perspires in his clothes. He (the Imam) said, 'I do not find anything harmful in it.' Someone then said, 'His perspiration is so much that he can wring it out.' He (the narrator) said that abu 'Abd Allah, *'Alayhi al-Salam,* then glared at the man's face and said, 'If you do not mind, in such case, he can use some water to wash it away.'""

H 4035, Ch. 34, h 4

Muhammad ibn Yahya has narrated from Ahmad ibn Muhammad from ibn Faddal from ibn Bukayr from Hamzah ibn Humran who has said the following:

"Abu 'Abd Allah, *'Alayhi al-Salam,* has said, 'Clothes do not cause one to become as one who has experienced sexual relation and one experiencing sexual relation does not affect his clothes.'"

H 4036, Ch. 34, h 5

Muhammad ibn Ahmad has narrated from Ahmad ibn Muhammad from ibn Faddal from ibn Bukayr from abu 'Usamah who has said the following:

"I once asked abu 'Abd Allah, *'Alayhi al-Salam*, about clothes in which one has experienced sexual relation and then under the open sky it becomes wet with dew. He (the Imam) said, 'It is not harmful.'"

H 4037, Ch. 34, h 6
Ali ibn Ibrahim has narrated from Muhammad ibn 'Isa from Yunus from Mu'awiyah ibn 'Ammar who has said the following:
"I once asked abu 'Abd Allah, *'Alayhi al-Salam*, about a man who urinates while he has experienced sexual relation. He then cleanses himself and his clothes touch his body while it is wet. He (the Imam) said, 'It is not harmful.'"

Chapter 35 - Semen or Al-Madhiy Comes in Contact with One's Clothes or Body

H 4038, Ch. 35, h 1
Al-Husayn ibn Muhammad has narrated from Mu'alla' ibn Muhammad from al-Washsha' from Hammad ibn 'Uthman from ibn abu Ya'fur who has said the following:
"I once asked abu 'Abd Allah, *'Alayhi al-Salam*, about the case of semen's coming in contact with one's clothes. He (the Imam) said, 'If you know the place of contact wash it clean; but if you do not know, wash all of it clean.'"

H 4039, Ch. 35, h 2
Ali ibn Ibrahim has narrated from his father from ibn abu 'Umayr from Mu'awiyah ibn 'Ammar from Muyassir who has said the following:
"I once said to abu 'Abd Allah, *'Alayhi al-Salam*, 'I instruct the slave-girl to wash my clothes because of semen, but she does not pay proper attention to washing and I perform Salat (prayer) in them and it (semen) is dry. He (the Imam) said, 'You must do your Salat (prayer) again. Had you yourself washed it, you would not have been required to perform your Salat (prayer) again.'"

H 4040, Ch. 35, h 3
Muhammad ibn Yahya has narrated from Ahmad ibn Muhammad from 'Uthman ibn 'Isa from Sama'ah who has said the following:
"I once asked him (the Imam), *'Alayhi al-Salam*, about the case of semen that pollutes one's clothes. He (the Imam) said, 'You must wash all of your clothes when you do not know exactly the polluted spot, regardless, if it is a little or large area.'"

H 4041, Ch. 35, h 4
Ali ibn Ibrahim has narrated from his father from ibn abu 'Umayr from Hammad from al-Halabiy who has said the following:
"Abu 'Abd Allah, *'Alayhi al-Salam*, has said, 'If a man experiences wet dream and his clothes come in contact with semen, he must wash the polluted area. If he thinks, but is not certain and has not seen the polluted area, he must pour water on it. If he is certain that semen has come in contact with his clothes but he has not seen the polluted spot, he must wash all of his clothes; it is better.'"

H 4042, Ch. 35, h 5

Muhammad ibn Yahya has narrated from Ahmad ibn Muhammad ibn Khalid from al-Husayn ibn Sa'id from al-Qasim ibn Muhammad from Ali ibn abu Hamzah from abu Basir who has said the following:

"I once asked abu 'Abd Allah, *'Alayhi al-Salam*, about al-Madhiy (the pre-seminal fluid) which pollutes one's clothes. He (the Imam) said, 'It is not harmful.'"

H 4043, Ch. 35, h 6

Al-Husayn ibn Muhammad has narrated from Mu'alla' ibn Muhammad from al-Washsha' from Aban from 'Anbasah ibn Mus'ab who has said the following:

"I heard abu 'Abd Allah, *'Alayhi al-Salam*, say, 'Wudu' is not necessary because of al-Madhiy (the pre-seminal fluid) nor is washing clothes which may have come in contact with it unless it is the major discharge of (semen).'"

Chapter 36 - Urine Comes in Contact with One's Clothes or Body

H 4044, Ch. 36, h 1

Muhammad ibn Yahya has narrated from Ahmad ibn Muhammad from Ali ibn al-Hakam from al-Husayn ibn abu al-'Ala' who has said the following:

"I once asked abu 'Abd Allah, *'Alayhi al-Salam*, about urine that pollutes one's body. He (the Imam) said, 'Pour water on it twice; it is water.' I then asked about urine, which pollutes one's clothes. He (the Imam) said, 'Wash it twice.' I then asked him about the urine of a child that pollutes one's clothes. He (the Imam) said, 'After pouring a small amount of water on it you must also wring it.'"

H 4045, Ch. 36, h 2

Ahmad ibn Muhammad has narrated from Ibrahim ibn abu Mahmud who has said the following:

"I once asked al-Rida, *'Alayhi al-Salam*, about how one should deal with velvet-like carpet and the beds that come in contact with urine, which are thick and bulky. He (the Imam) said, 'Whatever is on the surface of such items must be washed clean.'"

H 4046, Ch. 36, h 3

Ahmad ibn Musa has narrated from al-Qasim from Ibrahim ibn 'Abd al-Hamid who has said the following:

"I once asked abu al-Hassan, *'Alayhi al-Salam*, about clothes that come in contact with urine and it passes to the other side through its fillings. He (the Imam) said, 'You must wash the polluted area, feel the other side and wash it clean, if you found something; otherwise, pour water on it to wash it clean.'"

H 4047, Ch. 36, h 4

Ali ibn Ibrahim has narrated from his father from ibn abu 'Umayr from Hisham ibn Salim from Hakam ibn Hukaym al-Sayrafiy who has said the following:

"I once said to abu 'Abd Allah, *'Alayhi al-Salam*, 'I may urinate but do not find water, my hands have come in contact with urine and I wipe it against the wall or soil. Then it perspires and I wipe my face with it or other parts of my body or my clothes. He (the Imam) said, 'It is not harmful.'"

H 4048, Ch. 36, h 5

Ali ibn Ibrahim has narrated from his father from 'Abd Allah ibn al-Mughirah who has said that it is in the book of Sama'ah who in a marfu' manner has narrated the following:

"Abu 'Abd Allah, *'Alayhi al-Salam*, has said, 'If clothes come in contact with the urine of cats, performing Salat (prayer) with such clothes is not valid until they are washed.'"

H 4049, Ch. 36, h 6

Ali ibn Ibrahim has narrated from his father from ibn abu 'Umayr from Hammad from al-Halabiy who has said the following:

"I once asked abu 'Abd Allah, *'Alayhi al-Salam*, about the urine of a child. He (the Imam) said, 'You must just pour water on it but if the child eats food, wash it clean, and a baby boy or baby girl are the same.'"

H 4050, Ch. 36, h 7

A number of our people have narrated from Ahmad ibn Muhammad from Ali ibn al-Hakam from al-Fadl ibn Ghazwan from al-Hakam ibn Hukaym who has said the following:

"I once said to abu 'Abd Allah, *'Alayhi al-Salam*, 'I may go to market place and need to urinate but do not find water. I then wipe it dry, then wipe my hand against the wall or ground, and scratch with it my body afterwards. He (the Imam) said, 'It is not harmful.'"

H 4051, Ch. 36, h 8

A number of our people have narrated from Ahmad ibn Muhammad from ibn Faddal from al-Muthanna from abu Ayyub who has said the following:

"I once said to abu 'Abd Allah, *'Alayhi al-Salam*, 'I enter the toilet area and there is a ring on my hand with a name of the names of Allah, most High. He (the Imam) said, 'No, do not go there with it and do not perform sexual intercourse when you are wearing it.'" It also is narrated that when washing because of using a toilet one must remove such ring from the hand with which one is washing.

Chapter 37 - Urine of Animals and Their Dung

H 4052, Ch. 37, h 1

Ali ibn Ibrahim has narrated from his father from Hammad ibn 'Isa from Hariz from Zurarah who has said the following:

"The two Imam, *'Alayhi al-Salam*, have said, 'It is not necessary for you to wash your clothes because of urine of the edible animals.'"

H 4053, Ch. 37, h 2

Hammad has narrated from Hariz from Muhammad ibn Muslim who has said the following:

"I once asked abu 'Abd Allah, *'Alayhi al-Salam*, about the milk of camels, sheep and cows and their urine and their meat. He (the Imam) said, 'You must not take Wudu' with the water which is mixed with any of such items. You do not need to wash if your clothes come in contact with such items unless it is for removing stains.' He (the narrator) said that I then asked about the urine of animals, such as mules and donkeys. He (the Imam) said, 'You must wash it clean but if you do not know the polluted area, wash all of the clothes, and if you have doubts then just pour water to wash it clean.'"

H 4054, Ch. 37, h 3

Ali ibn Ibrahim has narrated from his father from 'Abd Allah ibn al-Mughirah 'Abd Allah ibn Sinan who has said the following:

"Abu 'Abd Allah, *'Alayhi al-Salam*, has said, 'Wash your clothes because of the urine of inedible animals.'"

H 4055, Ch. 37, h 4

Muhammad ibn Yahya has narrated from Ahmad ibn Muhammad from Muhammad ibn Khalid from al-Qasim ibn Muhammad ibn 'Urwah from Bukayr ibn 'A'yan from Zurarah who has said the following:

"One of the two Imam, *'Alayhim al-Salam*, about the urine of edible animals that pollutes clothes, expressed dislike. I said, 'It is from an edible animal.' He (the Imam) said, 'It is true but Allah has not made it for eating.'"

H 4056, Ch. 37, h 5

Al-Husayn ibn Muhammad has narrated from Mu'alla' ibn Muhammad from al-Washsha' from Aban ibn 'Uthman from abu Maryam who has said the following:

"I once said to abu 'Abd Allah, *'Alayhi al-Salam*, 'What do you say about the urine of animals and their dung?' He (the Imam) said, 'Because of their urine you must wash and their dung is more than that.'"

H 4057, Ch. 37, h 6

Muhammad ibn Yahya has narrated from Ahmad ibn Muhammad from al-Barqiy from Aban from al-Halabiy who has said the following:

"Abu 'Abd Allah, *'Alayhi al-Salam*, has said, 'Dung of donkeys is not harmful but you must wash clean their urine.'"

H 4058, Ch. 37, h 7

Muhammad ibn Yahya has narrated from Ahmad ibn Muhammad from Muhammad ibn Sinan from ibn Muskan from Malik al-Juhaniy who has said the following:

"I once asked abu 'Abd Allah, *'Alayhi al-Salam*, about things that come out of the nostrils of animals. He (the Imam) said, 'It is not harmful.'"

H 4059, Ch. 37, h 8

Ali ibn Ibrahim has narrated from his father from 'Abd Allah ibn al-Mughirah from Sama'ah who has said the following:

"Abu 'Abd Allah, *'Alayhi al-Salam*, has said, 'It is not proper to perform Salat (prayer) with clothes that have come in contact with the urine of cat.'"

H 4060, Ch. 37, h 9

Ali ibn Ibrahim has narrated from his father from 'Abd Allah ibn al-Mughirah from Jamil ibn Darraj from abu Basir who has said the following:

"Abu 'Abd Allah, *'Alayhi al-Salam*, has said, 'Urine and droppings of the things that fly are not harmful.'"

H 4061, Ch. 37, h 10

Muhammad ibn Yahya has narrated from Muhammad ibn al-Husayn from Ali ibn al-Hakam from abu al-'Aziz al-Nakhkhas who has said the following:

"I once said to abu 'Abd Allah, *'Alayhi al-Salam*, 'I deal with animals. Some times I go out during the night, and animals may have urinated and dunged and they spread it with their legs which pollutes my clothes; and in the morning I find the marks.' He (the Imam) said, 'You are not required to do anything.'"

Chapter 38 - Clothes Come in Contact with Blood and Pus

H 4062, Ch. 38, h 1

Muhammad ibn Yahya has narrated from Ahmad ibn Muhammad from Mu'awiyah ibn al-Hukaym from al-Mu'alla' abu 'Uthman from abu Basir who has said the following:

"I once visited abu Ja'far, *'Alayhi al-Salam*, when he was performing Salat (prayer). My guide informed me that there was blood on the clothes of the Imam. When he completed his Salat (prayer), I said that my guide has told me that there is blood on your clothes. He (the Imam) said, 'I have pimples and I did not want to wash my clothes until they are cured.'"

H 4063, Ch. 38, h 2

Ahmad has narrated from 'Uthman ibn 'Isa from Sama'ah who has said the following:

"I once asked him (the Imam), *'Alayhi al-Salam*, about a man on whose body there are sores or wounds which he cannot bandage or wash the blood. He (the Imam) said, 'He can perform his Salat (prayer) without washing his clothes except once a day; he cannot wash his clothes every hour.'"

H 4064, Ch. 38, h 3

Ali ibn Ibrahim has narrated from his father, from Hammad, from Hariz, from Muhammad ibn Muslim who has said the following:

"I once said to him (the Imam), 'I may find blood on my clothes when I am performing Salat (prayer).' He (the Imam) said, 'If you find blood and you have other clothes on you, you must remove it and complete your Salat (prayer). However, if you do not have other clothes on you besides that one, you must complete your Salat (prayer). You do not have to perform that Salat (prayer) again if the area covered by that blood is not more than the size of a dirham, and an area of smaller size does not matter, regardless if you have seen it before or not. If you have seen it before and it is bigger than the size of a dirham, but you have missed to wash it and have performed with it many Salat (prayer), you must perform again the Salat (prayers) you have performed with it.'"

H 4065, Ch. 38, h 4

Ali ibn Ibrahim has narrated from his father from al-Nawfaliy from al-Sakuniy who has said the following:

"Abu 'Abd Allah, *'Alayhi al-Salam*, has said, 'Ali, *'Alayhi al-Salam*, would not consider the blood of things that did not require slaughtering as harmful to one's Salat (prayer). That is, the blood of fish.'"

H 4066, Ch. 38, h 5

Ahmad ibn Idris has narrated from Muhammad ibn Ahmad from Ahmad ibn al-Hassan ibn Ali from 'Amr ibn Sa'id from Musaddiq ibn Sadaqah from 'Ammar al-Sabatiy who has said the following:

"Abu 'Abd Allah, *'Alayhi al-Salam*, was asked about a man from whose nostril blood flows. 'Is he required to wash inside of his nostril?' He (the Imam) said, 'He only needs to wash what is apparent.'"

H 4067, Ch. 38, h 6

Muhammad ibn Yahya has narrated from Ahmad ibn Muhammad from al-Husayn ibn Sa'id from al-Qasim ibn Muhammad from Ali ibn abu Hamzah from the virtuous servant of Allah who has said the following:

"Once a mother of the child of his father asked him (the Imam), *'Alayhi al-Salam*, saying, 'I pray to Allah to keep my soul in service for your cause, I like to ask you a question but I feel shy.' He (the Imam) said, 'Ask and do not feel shy.' She said, 'There was blood from Hayd (menses) on my clothes and I washed it, but the stain does not go away.' He (the Imam) said, 'Color it with russet color so that it is mixed and does not show.'"

H 4068, Ch. 38, h 7

Ali ibn Ibrahim has narrated from Ahmad ibn abu 'Abd Allah from his father in a marfu' manner who has said the following:

"Abu 'Abd Allah, *'Alayhi al-Salam*, has said that your blood to you is less unclean than other people's blood. If you find like sprinkles of your blood on you, it is not harmful; but if it is other people's blood, regardless of its being of a small or large quantity, you must wash it clean.'"

H 4069, Ch. 38, h 8

Muhammad ibn Yahya has narrated from Ahmad ibn Muhammad from ibn Sinan from ibn Muskan from al-Halabiy who has said the following:

"I once asked abu 'Abd Allah, *'Alayhi al-Salam*, about the blood of fleas on one's clothes - if it is harmful to his Salat (prayer). He (the Imam) said, 'It is not harmful even if they are many. So also is the case with similar things, like sprinkled nostril blood which one does not have to wash.'" "It is narrated also that things cannot be washed with saliva except blood (inside one's mouth).'"

H 4070, Ch. 38, h 9

Ali ibn Muhammad has narrated from Sahl ibn Ziyad from Muhammad ibn al-Rayyan who has said the following:

"I once wrote to the man, *'Alayhi al-Salam*, asking, 'Is the blood of bugs like the blood of fleas? Is it permissible for one to consider blood of bugs like that of fleas, perform Salat (prayer) with it and analogize to act upon such analogy?' He (the Imam) wrote with his signature, 'It is permissible to perform Salat (prayer) with it, but washing is better.'"

Chapter 39 - Dogs Touching Clothes, Body and So On

H 4071, Ch. 39, h 1

Ali ibn Ibrahim has narrated from his father from Hammad ibn 'Isa from Hariz from Muhammad from whom he has mentioned who has said the following:

"Abu 'Abd Allah, *'Alayhi al-Salam*, has said, 'If a dog pollutes your clothes, and if it is dry, just pour water on your clothes; but if it is wet, then wash them clean.'"

H 4072, Ch. 39, h 2

Hammad ibn 'Isa has narrated from Hariz from Muhammad ibn Muslim who has said the following:

"I once asked abu 'Abd Allah, *'Alayhi al-Salam*, about a man whose body is polluted because of a dog. He (the Imam) said, 'He must wash clean the area which has come in contact with a dog.'"

H 4073, Ch. 39, h 3

Muhammad ibn Yahya has narrated from al-'Amrakiy ibn Ali al-Naysaburiy from Ali ibn Ja'far from his brother, Musa, *'Alayhi al-Salam*, has said the following:

"I once asked him (the Imam), *'Alayhi al-Salam*, about a mouse that has fallen in water and then walks on clothes. Can one perform Salat (prayer) in such clothes? He (the Imam) said, 'Wash to clean the marks that you find and what you do not find just pour water on them.'"

H 4074, Ch. 39, h 4

Ali ibn Ibrahim has narrated from Muhammad ibn 'Isa from Yunus from certain persons of his people who has said the following:

"I once asked abu 'Abd Allah, *'Alayhi al-Salam*, if it is permissible to touch a fox, jackal or such other beasts dead or alive. He (the Imam) said, 'It is not harmful but he must wash his hand.'"

H 4075, Ch. 39, h 5

Muhammad ibn Yahya has narrated from Ahmad ibn Muhammad from ibn Mahbub from ibn Ri'ab from Ibrahim ibn al-Maymun who has said the following:

"I once asked abu 'Abd Allah, *'Alayhi al-Salam*, about a man whose clothes fall on a dead body. He (the Imam) said, 'If the dead body is given Ghusl (bath), then it is not necessary to wash such clothes, but if it is not given Ghusl (bath) yet, one must wash such clothes - and that is, when the dead body has become cold.'"

H 4076, Ch. 39, h 6

Muhammad ibn Yahya has narrated from al-'Amrakiy ibn Ali from Ali ibn Ja'far from Musa ibn Ja'far, *'Alayhi al-Salam*, who has said the following:

"I once asked him (the Imam), *'Alayhi al-Salam*, about a man whose clothes come in contact with pigs which he forgets to wash, but he remembers it when he is performing Salat (prayer), what he must do. He (the Imam) said, 'If he has already begun his Salat (prayer) he must continue; but if he has not yet began his Salat (prayer), he must pour water on the area which has come in contact with the pig. If there are marks on such clothes, then one must wash them clean.'"

Chapter 40 - Description of Tayammum

H 4077, Ch. 40, h 1

Ali ibn Ibrahim has narrated from his father and Ali ibn Muhammad from Sahl all from Ahmad ibn Muhammad ibn abu Nasr from ibn Bukayr from Zurarah who has said the following:

"I once asked Abu Ja'far, *'Alayhi al-Salam*, about Tayammum. He (the Imam) thumped his hands on the ground then raised them, and allowed loose soil to fall off them. He (the Imam) then wiped both (sections of) his forehead (the parts above both eyebrows) and (the back of) his palms (hands) only once."

H 4078, Ch. 40, h 2
Ali ibn Ibrahim has narrated from his father from Hammad ibn 'Isa from certain persons of our people who has said the following:
"Abu 'Abd Allah, *'Alayhi al-Salam*, was once asked about Tayammum. He (the Imam) read this verse of the Holy Quran: 'You must cut off the hands of male and female thieves.' (5:38) He (the Imam) mentioned this verse of the Holy Quran. 'Wash your faces and hands upto (from) your elbows' (5:6) and said, 'Wipe on (the back of that part of) your palms which must be cut in case of theft and your Lord is not to forget.'"

H 4079, Ch. 40, h 3
Muhammad ibn Yahya has narrated from Muhammad ibn al-Husayn from Safwan from al-Kahiliy who has said the following:
"I once asked him (the Imam) about Tayammum. He (the Imam), *'Alayhi al-Salam*, thumped his hand on the furnishing, then wiped with it his face and then the backs of his both hands one with the other."

H 4080, Ch. 40, h 4
Ali ibn Ibrahim has narrated from Muhammad ibn 'Isa from Yunus from ibn abu Ayyub al-Khazzaz who has said the following:
"I once asked abu 'Abd Allah, *'Alayhi al-Salam*, about Tayammum. He (the Imam) said, "Ammar ibn Yasir once had experienced sexual relation and he rolled himself on the ground as certain animals do. The Messenger of Allah said, 'O 'Ammar, you rolled yourself on the ground as certain animals do.' I (the narrator) then asked him (the Imam), 'How is Tayammum done?' He (the Imam) placed his hand on the sackcloth, then raised it and wiped his face, then the backs of his hands slightly."

"He (the narrator) has narrated it (the previous Hadith) from his father from ibn abu 'Umayr from abu Ayyub also.

H 4081, Ch. 40, h 5
Muhammad ibn Yahya has narrated from al-Husayn ibn Ali al-Kufiy from al-Nawfaliy from Ghiyath ibn Ibrahim who has said the following:
"Abu 'Abd Allah, *'Alayhi al-Salam*, has said that 'Amir al-Mu'minin, *'Alayhi al-Salam*, has said, 'Wudu' is not valid from the place you walk on.' Al-Nawfaliy has said, 'It means the place on which one steps.'"

H 4082, Ch. 40, h 6
Al-Hassan ibn Ali al-'Alawiy has narrated from Sahl ibn Jumhur from 'Abd al-'Azim ibn 'Abd Allah al-Hassaniy from al-Hassan ibn al-Husayn al-'Uraniy from Ghiyath ibn Ibrahim who has said the following:
"Abu 'Abd Allah, *'Alayhi al-Salam*, has said, "Amir al-Mu'minin, *'Alayhi al-Salam*, has prohibited that a man take Tayammum with the soil of the road.'"

Chapter 41 - When Tayammum Is Necessary and Finding Water Thereafter

H 4083, Ch. 41, h 1

Muhammad ibn Yahya has narrated from Muhammad ibn al-Husayn from Safwan from al-'Ala' from Muhammad ibn Muslim who has said the following:

"I heard him (the Imam), *'Alayhi al-Salam*, say, 'If you cannot find water and you decide for Tayammum, you must wait until the time (for Salat (prayer)) is about to end. If water is still not available, you do not miss the soil and the ground.'"

H 4084, Ch. 41, h 2

Ali ibn Ibrahim has narrated from his father from ibn abu 'Umayr from ibn `Udhaynah from Zurarah who has said the following:

"One of the two Imam, *'Alayhim al-Salam*, has said, 'If during a journey water cannot be found, one must search for water as long as there is time; but when there is fear for losing time, one must then take Tayammum to perform Salat (prayer) during the end of time just before it totally ends. If later water is found, then one is not required to perform Salat (prayer) again; however, Wudu' is necessary for future.'"

H 4085, Ch. 41, h 3

Ali ibn Ibrahim has narrated from his father from ibn abu 'Umayr from Hammad from al-Halabiy who has said the following:

"I once heard abu 'Abd Allah, *'Alayhi al-Salam*, say, 'If means of cleansing (water for Ghusl (bath)) cannot be found after experiencing sexual relation, one must wipe one's face with (soil for Tayammum) earth, then perform Salat (prayer). When water is found, Ghusl (bath) must be taken and Salat (prayer) so performed is sufficient.'"

H 4086, Ch. 41, h 4

Muhammad ibn `Isma'il has narrated from al-Fadl ibn Shadhan and Ali ibn Ibrahim has narrated from his father all from Hammad ibn 'Isa from Hariz from Zurarah who has said the following:

"I once asked abu Ja'far, *'Alayhi al-Salam*, 'Can one perform with a single Wudu' the Salat (prayer) of a whole day and night? He (the Imam) said, 'It is permissible as long as one has a valid Wudu'.' I then asked, 'Is it permissible in the case of one Tayammum also? He (the Imam) said, 'Yes, it is permissible as long as one has a valid Wudu' and still has not found water.' I then asked, 'What is one's duty if water is found or has hopes to be able to find other water and has a greater hope to find water when one would want but it then becomes difficult?' He (the Imam) said, 'In such case Wudu' becomes invalid therefore; Tayammum must be taken again.' I then asked, 'What is the obligation if water is found when one is performing Salat (prayer)?' He (the Imam) said, 'It must be discontinued to take Wudu' if one has not yet assumed the position of Ruku'; once already in the position of Ruku', Salat (prayer) must be continued; Tayammum is one of the two forms of Taharat (cleansing).'"

H 4087, Ch. 41, h 5

Al-Husayn ibn Muhammad has narrated from Mu'alla' ibn Muhammad from al-Washsha' from Aban ibn 'Uthman from 'Abd Allah ibn 'Asim who has said the following:

"I once asked abu 'Abd Allah, *'Alayhi al-Salam*, about a man who cannot find water and with Tayammum begins to perform Salat (prayer); then the boy brings water for him. He (the Imam) said, 'If he has not yet assumed the position of Ruku', he must discontinue his Salat (prayer) for Wudu', but if he has already assumed Ruku' position, he must continue with his Salat (prayer).'"

H 4088, Ch. 41, h 6

A number of our people have narrated from Ahmad ibn Muhammad from ibn Mahbub from Dawud al-Riqqiy who has said the following:

"I once said to abu 'Abd Allah, *'Alayhi al-Salam*. 'During a journey if I cannot find water when it is time of Salat (prayer); but it is said that water is nearby. Must I then search in the right and left directions when it is time for Salat (prayer)?' He (the Imam) said, 'Do not search for water, instead take Tayammum; I fear you may remain behind your companions and you may get lost or be eaten by the beasts.'"

H 4089, Ch. 41, h 7

Ahmad ibn Muhammad has narrated from Ali ibn al-Hakam from al-Husayn ibn abu al-'Ala' who has said the following:

"I once asked abu 'Abd Allah, *'Alayhi al-Salam*, about a man who passes by a well but does not have a bucket (to draw water). He (the Imam) said, 'It is not necessary for him to climb down the well; the Lord of water is the Lord the earth; he must take Tayammum.'"

H 4090, Ch. 41, h 8

Al-Husayn ibn Muhammad has narrated from Mu'alla' ibn Muhammad from al-Washsha' from Hammad ibn 'Uthman from Ya'qub ibn Salim who has said the following:

"I once asked abu 'Abd Allah, *'Alayhi al-Salam*, about a man who does not have any water (for Wudu') during a journey, but there is water on the right or left side of the road at a distance of once or twice throwing of an arrow or so. He (the Imam) said, 'I do not command him to mislead himself and then be endangered by the beasts or thieves.'"

H 4091, Ch. 41, h 9

Muhammad ibn 'Isma'il has narrated from al-Fadl ibn Shadhan from Safwan from Mansur ibn Hazim from ibn abu Ya'qub and 'Anbasah ibn Mus'ab who has said the following:

"Abu 'Abd Allah, *'Alayhi al-Salam*, has said, 'When you come to a well when you have experienced sexual relation and cannot find a bucket or other means to draw water, you must take Tayammum with soil; the Lord of water and the Lord of the soil is one. Do not climb down the well and destroy people's water.'"

H 4092, Ch. 41, h 10

Muhammad ibn Yahya has narrated from Ahmad ibn Muhammad from 'Uthman ibn 'Isa from ibn Muskan from abu Basir who has said the following:

"I once asked him (the Imam), *'Alayhi al-Salam*, about a man who during a journey had a certain amount of water but forgot all about it, and with Tayammum performed Salat (prayer). Then he remembered that there was water with him and still there is time for Salat (prayer). He (the Imam) said, 'He must take Wudu' and perform Salat (prayer) again.' I (the narrator) then asked him (the Imam) if Tayammum for one experiencing Hayd (menses) and sexual relation who cannot find water is the same. He (the Imam) said, 'Yes, it is the same.'"

Chapter 42 - One's having Little Water on a Journey but Is Afraid of Facing Thirst

H 4093, Ch. 42, h 1

Ali ibn Ibrahim has narrated from his father from 'Abd Allah ibn al-Mughirah from ibn Sinan who has said the following:

"I once asked abu 'Abd Allah, *'Alayhi al-Salam*, about a man who, during a journey, experiences sexual relation but does not have any water with him except very little and is afraid of facing thirst if it is used for Ghusl (bath). He (the Imam) said, 'If he is afraid of facing thirst, he must spill not even one drop; he must take Tayammum with soil; soil is more dear to me.'"

H 4094, Ch. 42, h 2

Al-Husayn ibn Muhammad has narrated from Mu'alla' ibn Muhammad from al-Hassan ibn Ali al-Washsha' from Hammad ibn 'Uthman from ibn abu Ya'fur who has said the following:

"I once asked abu 'Abd Allah, *'Alayhi al-Salam*, about a man who experiences sexual relation and has enough water only for his drinking needs; must he take Tayammum or Wudu'? He (the Imam) said, 'Tayammum is better. You should understand the fact that the task of cleansing is made only half as much in his favor.'"

H 4095, Ch. 42, h 3

Ali ibn Ibrahim has narrated from his father from ibn abu 'Umayr from Muhammad ibn Humran and Jamil who have said the following:

"Once we asked abu 'Abd Allah, *'Alayhi al-Salam*, about the case of the Imam of a people during a journey who experiences sexual relation and does not have enough water for Ghusl (bath). Can another person from among them take Wudu' and lead them in Salat (prayer)? He (the Imam) said, 'No, they cannot do so; however, he must take Tayammum and lead them in Salat (prayer); Allah, most Majestic, most Glorious, has made the soil purifying.'"

H 4096, Ch. 42, h 4

Ali ibn Ibrahim has narrated from his father from 'Abd Allah ibn al-Mughirah who has said the following:

"(Abu 'Abd Allah, *'Alayhi al-Salam*) has said, 'If the ground is wet and dry soil or water is not available you must look for an area which is the most dry of the others, take Tayammum with dust thereof or something with dust on it. If you can find nothing else other than clay, then it is not harmful to take Tayammum therewith.'"

Chapter 43 - One's Experiencing Carnal Relations and Having Only Ice

H 4097, Ch. 43, h 1

Ali ibn Ibrahim has narrated from his father and Muhammad ibn Yahya from Ahmad ibn Muhammad all from Hammad ibn 'Isa from Hariz from Muhammad ibn Muslim who has said the following:

"I once asked abu 'Abd Allah, *'Alayhi al-Salam*, about a man who experiences sexual relation during a journey and cannot find anything other than snow or ice. He (the Imam) said, 'This is like an emergency case and he must take Tayammum. I do not consider it proper for him to return to such land which ruins his religion.'"

H 4098, Ch. 43, h 2

Ali ibn Ibrahim has narrated from his father in a marfu' manner the following:

"(He (the Imam), *'Alayhi al-Salam*, has said, 'If he experiences sexual relation, he must take Ghusl (bath), but if it is a wet dream, he must take Tayammum.'"

H 4099, Ch. 43, h 3

Muhammad ibn Yahya has narrated from al-Husayn from Ja'far ibn Bashir from those whom he has mentioned who has said the following:

"I once asked abu 'Abd Allah, *'Alayhi al-Salam*, about the case of one who experiences sexual relation during a cold night and is afraid for his life due to Ghusl (bath) because of cold. He (the Imam) said, 'One must take Tayammum to perform Salat (prayer) and when safe from cold, take Ghusl (bath) and perform such Salat (prayer) again.'"

Chapter 44 - Taking Tayammum with Clay

H 4100, Ch. 44, h 1

Muhammad ibn Yahya has narrated from Ahmad ibn Muhammad from ibn Mahbub from ibn Ri'ab from abu Basir who has said the following:

"Abu 'Abd Allah, *'Alayhi al-Salam*, has said, 'In a condition where you cannot find anything other than clay, take Tayammum with it; Allah accepts one's inabilities. So also is the case if you do not have any dry clothes or bricks from which dust can be collected for Tayammum.'"

"In another Hadith it is said that soil is fine and water is purifying."

Chapter 45 - Bandages, Injuries, One's Suffering from Smallpox and or Experiencing Carnal Relations

H 4101, Ch. 45, h 1

Muhammad ibn Yahya has narrated from Ahmad ibn Muhammad from ibn Mahbub from abu Ayyub al-Khazzaz from Muhammad ibn Muslim who has said the following:

"I once asked Abu Ja'far, *'Alayhi al-Salam*, about a man on whose body there are dimples or wounds and experiences sexual relation. He (the Imam) said, 'It is not harmful if one does not take Ghusl (bath) in such condition, instead takes Tayammum.'"

H 4102, Ch. 45, h 2

Ali ibn Ibrahim has narrated from his father from ibn abu 'Umayr from certain persons of his people who has said the following:

"Abu 'Abd Allah, *'Alayhi al-Salam*, has said, 'One with smallpox or broken bones has permission to take Tayammum with soil after experiencing sexual relation.'"

H 4103, Ch. 45, h 3

A number of our people have narrated from Ahmad ibn Muhammad from Muhammad ibn Ali from Ahmad who in a marfu' manner has said the following:

"I once asked abu 'Abd Allah, *'Alayhi al-Salam*, about one with a condition of smallpox who experiences sexual relation. He (the Imam) said, 'If one has experienced sexual relation, he must take Ghusl (bath), but if it is wet dream, there is Tayammum for it.'"

H 4104, Ch. 45, h 4

Ahmad ibn Muhammad has narrated from Bakr ibn Salih and ibn Faddal from 'Abd Allah ibn Ibrahim al-Ghifariy from Ja'far ibn Ibrahim al-Ja'fariy who has said the following:

"Abu 'Abd Allah, *'Alayhi al-Salam*, has said that once the case of a man on whose body there was a wound and had experienced sexual relation was mentioned before the Holy prophet and that they compelled him to take Ghusl (bath). It shriveled him with complications, which caused his death. The Messenger of Allah said, 'They killed him, may Allah cause them to die. Only asking is medicine for ignorance.'"

H 4105, Ch. 45, h 5

Ali ibn Ibrahim has narrated from his father from ibn abu 'Umayr from Muhammad ibn Sukayn and others who has said the following:

"It was said to abu 'Abd Allah, *'Alayhi al-Salam*, that so and so had smallpox and had experienced sexual relation. They gave him Ghusl (bath) which caused him to die. He (the Imam) said, 'They killed him. Why did they not ask about giving him Tayammum? Only asking is medicine for ignorance.'" It applies also to one with broken bones and internal illness (causing discharge from the buttocks) who must do Tayammum instead of Ghusl (bath).

Chapter 46 - Rare Ahadith about Wudu'

H 4106, Ch. 46, h 1

Ali ibn Muhammad ibn 'Abd Allah has narrated from Ibrahim ibn Ishaq al-Ahmar from al-Hassan ibn Ali al-Washsha' who has said the following:

"Once I visited Ali al-Rida, *'Alayhi al-Salam*. There was a water jug in front of him and he was about to take Wudu' for Salat (prayer). I went closer to pour water to help him to take Wudu'. He said, 'Hold it, O Hassan.' I then asked, 'Why do you stop me from pouring water so you take Wudu' and I can receive rewards for it?' He replied, 'You will receive rewards, but I will be burdened.' I then asked, 'How can that happen?' He replied, 'Have you not heard the words of Allah, the Most Majestic, the Most Glorious, "Those who wish to meet (receive mercy from) their Lord should do good deeds and not allow anyone else to share in (their) worshipping their Lord." (18:110) I am about to take Wudu' for Salat (prayer). I do not want anyone to share with me my act of worship.'"

H 4107, Ch. 46, h 2

Ali ibn Muhammad has narrated from Sahl ibn Ziyad from Ja'far ibn Muhammad al-Ash'ariy from al-Qaddah from abu 'Abd Allah, who has said the following:

"The Messenger of Allah has said, 'Wudu' is the opening of Salat (prayer), Takbir marks the field of Salat (prayer) and Taslim marks the end of the field of Salat (prayer).'"

H 4108, Ch. 46, h 3

Ali ibn Ibrahim has narrated from Salih ibn al-Sindiy from Ja'far ibn Bashir from Sabah al-Hadhdh'a from abu 'Usamah who has said the following:

"Once I was in the presence of abu 'Abd Allah, *'Alayhi al-Salam*, when a man of the followers of al-Mughirah asked him about matters of tradition (the Sunnah). The Imam replied, 'There a tradition is set about everything that a son of Adam may need from Allah and His Messenger. There are those who have recognized such traditions and there are those who have rejected them.' The man then asked, 'What is the tradition about using the restroom?' The Imam replied, 'Speak of Allah and seek protection with Allah against Satan, the one condemned to be stoned. When you finish using a restroom you should say this. "All praise belongs to Allah who has relieved me of the discomfort with ease and good health."' The man then asked, 'Should one say such expressions in such a condition before looking back at what has come out?' The Imam replied, 'To every man on earth there are two angels assigned. When he is in such a condition, they bend his neck down saying, "O son of Adam, look down to the thing for which you have been struggling, into what kind of thing it has turned."'"

H 4109, Ch. 46, h 4

Muhammad ibn Yahya has narrated from Salmah ibn al-Khattab from Ibrahim ibn Muhammad al-Thaqafiy from Ali ibn al-Mu'alla' from Ibrahim ibn Muhammad ibn Humran who has said the following:

"Abu 'Abd Allah, *'Alayhi al-Salam*, has said, 'For taking Wudu', then using a towel, one gains a good deed. Instead of using a towel if one allows the moisture from Wudu' to dry up, one gains thirty good deeds."

H 4110, Ch. 46, h 5

Ali ibn Ibrahim has narrated from his father from 'Amr ibn 'Uthman from Jarrah al-Hadhdha' from Sama'ah ibn Mehran who has said the following.

"Abu al-Hassan, Musa, *'Alayhi al-Salam*, has said, 'If one takes Wudu' for Maghrib Salat (prayer), this Wudu' is expiation for the sins committed during the day that has just passed, except the major sins. If one takes Wudu' for morning Salat (prayer), this Wudu' is expiation for the sins committed during the night that has just passed, except the major sins.'"

H 4111, Ch. 46, h 6

Ali ibn Ibrahim has narrated from his father from Qasim al-Khazzaz, from 'Abd al-Rahman ibn Kathir who has said the following:

"Abu 'Abd Allah, *'Alayhi al-Salam*, has said that once, `Amir al-Mu'minin, *'Alayhi al-Salam*, while Muhammad, his son was present, asked him to bring water for Wudu'. He brought water and he (`Amir al-Mu'minin) poured with his right hand onto his left hand and said, 'All praise belongs to Allah who has made water purifying and has not made it impure.' He then used water to clean his private parts and said, 'O Lord, protect my private parts and keep them chaste, cover the parts of my body to be concealed and save them from the fire.' He then cleansed his nostrils and said, 'O Lord, do not deprive me of the fragrance of paradise; make me of those who enjoy the fragrance, goodness and delight of paradise.' He then rinsed his mouth and said, 'O Lord, allow my tongue to speak of You and make me of those with whom You are happy.' He then washed his face and said, 'O Lord, make my face white on the Day when faces turn black and do not make my face black on the Day when faces turn white.' He then washed his right hand and said, 'O Lord, please give the book of the record of my deeds in my right hand and eternity in my left hand.' He then washed his left hand and said, 'O Lord, do not give the book of the record of my deeds in my left hand and do not chain it to my neck. I seek protection with You against the cutting sections of hell.' He then wiped his head and said, 'O Lord, cover me up with Your mercy, blessings and forgiveness.' He then wiped his feet and said, 'O Lord, keep my foot firm on the bridge on the Day when feet slip and make my deeds gain Your happiness in my favor.' He then turned to Muhammad and said, 'O Muhammad, if one takes Wudu' the way I did and says what I said, Allah creates from every drop of water an angel who glorifies, says Tasbih, Takbir and Tahlil of Allah and the reward for this is written in favor of the person taking Wudu'.'"

H 4112, Ch. 46, h 7

A number of our people have narrated from Ahmad ibn Muhammad from ibn Mahbub from ibn Ri'ab from Muhammad ibn Qays who has said the following:

"I heard abu Ja'far, *'Alayhi al-Salam*, say while speaking to people in Makkah, 'One day the Messenger of Allah completed his Salat (prayer) of the morning and sat in the Masjid with his companions until sunrise. Thereafter, people one by one left the Masjid except two men, one from the people of Ansar and the other from Thaqif. The Messenger of Allah then said to them, "I understand you need to ask me questions. You may ask if you like and I will answer. If you like, I can tell you what your questions are before you ask. If you wish, you may ask me." They said, "Please inform us before we ask you our questions; it is more enlightening, frees us from doubts and strengthens our belief more." The Messenger of Allah then said, "You, gentleman from Thaqif, have come to ask me about your Wudu' and Salat (prayer) regarding what is good for you in them. You should keep in mind that when you place your hand in your water container and say 'In the name of Allah' the sins that your hands may have committed scatter away from you. The sins that your eyes and mouth may have committed scatter away from you when you wash your face. When you wash your arms to your elbows, the sins from your left and right scatter away from you. When you wipe your head and feet the sins into which you may have walked scatter away from you. This is what you gain from your Wudu'.""""

(The answer to the question of the man from Thaqif about Salat (prayer) is in the book of Salat (prayer) and the question of the man from Ansar about Hajj is in the book of Hajj Hadith No 34.)

H 4113, Ch. 46, h 8

Ali ibn Ibrahim has narrated from his father from al-Nawfaliy from al-Sakuniy who has said the following:

"Abu 'Abd Allah, *'Alayhi al-Salam*, has said, 'Wudu' is part of belief.'"

H 4114, Ch. 46, h 9

Abu Ali al-Ash'ariy has narrated from certain persons of our people from 'Isma'il ibn Mehran from Sabbah al-Hadhdha' from Sama'ah who has said the following:

"I once was in the presence of abu al-Hassan, *'Alayhi al-Salam*, and he (the Imam) performed al-Zuhr and al-'Asr Salat (prayer) before me. I remained in his presence until al-Maghrib. He (the Imam) asked for Wudu' (water) and he took Wudu' for al-Maghrib Salat (prayer), then said to me, 'You need to take Wudu'.' I said, 'I pray to Allah to keep my soul in service for your cause, my Wudu' is still valid.' He (the Imam) said, 'Even so you should take Wudu'; to those who take Wudu' for al-Maghrib it serves as expiation for the sins that they may have done during that day except the major sins. Taking Wudu' in the morning serves as expiation for the sins that one had committed during the night before except the major sins.'"

H 4115, Ch. 46, h 10

Muhammad ibn Yahya and Ahmad ibn Idris have narrated from Ahmad ibn Ishaq from Sa'dan from certain persons of his people who have said the following:

"Abu 'Abd Allah, *'Alayhi al-Salam*, has said, 'For having al-Tuhr (cleansing) over al-Tuhr one receives a reward for ten good deeds.'"

H 4116, Ch. 46, h 11

Muhammad ibn al-Hassan and others have narrated from Sahl ibn Ziyad through the chain of his narrators who has said the following:

"Abu 'Abd Allah, *'Alayhi al-Salam*, has said, 'When anyone of you completes his Wudu', he must take water in his palm and wipe with it his back; it will free his neck from the fire.'" (This perhaps is because of Taqiyah)

H 4117, Ch. 46, h 12

Ali ibn Muhammad has narrated from Sahl ibn Ziyad from Muhammad ibn 'Isa from Yunus who has said the following:

"I once asked abu al-Hassan, *'Alayhi al-Salam*, about a man who takes Wudu' with water of roses for Salat (prayer). He (the Imam) said, 'It is not harmful.'" (Fatwa best explains this Hadith.)

H 4118, Ch. 46, h 13

Abu Ali al-Ash'ariy has narrated from Muhammad ibn 'Abd al-Jabbar from Safwan from 'Abd al-Wahhab from Muhammad ibn abu Hamzah from Hisham ibn Salim from 'Isma'il al-Ju'fiy who has said the following:

"I once asked abu 'Abd Allah, *'Alayhi al-Salam*, about touching the bones of a dead person. He (the Imam) said, 'If it is after one year, it is not harmful.'"

H 4119, Ch. 46, h 14

Muhammad ibn Yahya has narrated in a marfu‘ manner from abu Hamzah who has said the following:

“Abu Ja‘far, *'Alayhi al-Salam*, has said, ‘If one sleeps in Masjid al-Haram or Masjid of the Messenger of Allah and experiences wet dream, one must take Tayammum and must not pass through the Masjid without Tayammum until one is out of the Masjid, then take Ghusl (bath). This applies to one experiencing Hayd (menses) also and she must take Tayammum as mentioned. In the case of other Masjid, passing through them in such conditions is permissible but such people must not sit in them with such conditions.’”

H 4120, Ch. 46, h 15

Muhammad ibn Yahya has narrated from Muhammad ibn al-Husayn from Wuhayb ibn Hafs from abu Basir who has said the following:

“I once asked him (the Imam), *'Alayhi al-Salam*, about the case of a snake that enters in a *Hub* (large water container) which has water in it and then comes out. He (the Imam) said, ‘If one can find other water it should be spilled away.’”

H 4121, Ch. 46, h 16

Muhammad ibn Yahya has narrated from al-‘Amrakiy ibn Ali from Ali ibn Ja‘far from his brother abu al-Hassan, *'Alayhi al-Salam* has said the following:

“I once asked abu al-Hassan, *'Alayhi al-Salam*, about the case of one who had a nosebleed; then he blew his nose and parts of it became small segments which came in contact with his water container. Can he take Wudu’ with such water? He (the Imam) said, ‘If nothing is visible in the water container it is not harmful. However, if things show in it he must not use it for Wudu’.’ I (the narrator) then asked him (the Imam) about a man who has nosebleed while taking Wudu’ and a drop falls in his water container. Can he take Wudu’ with such water? He (the Imam) said, ‘No, he cannot take Wudu’ with such water.’”

H 4122, Ch. 46, h 17

Muhammad ibn Yahya has narrated from Ahmad ibn Muhammad from al-Barqiy from Sa‘d ibn Sa‘d from Safwan who has said the following:

“I once asked abu al-Hassan, *'Alayhi al-Salam*, about a man who needs to take Wudu’ for Salat (prayer). However, he is not able to find water. He finds a certain amount of water which is enough for his Wudu’ but it costs one hundred dirham or one thousand dirham. He has that much dirham to buy and take Wudu’, should he buy the water or instead take Tayammum? He (the Imam) said, ‘No, he must buy. This kind of thing has happened to me and I bought water to take Wudu’. What is bought (in this case) is a great deal.’”

(For such Ahadith about an act or issue of the five categories of deeds the qualities such as Wujub, (Obligatory), Hurmat (Prohibited), Istihbab (Preference), Kirahat (Detestability) or Ibahah (Permissibility) one must consult fatwas of one’s Mujtahid.)

In the Name of Allah, the Beneficient, the Merciful

Part Two:
The Book of Hayd (Menses)

Chapters on Hayd (Menses)

H 4123, Ch. 1, h 1

Al-Husayn ibn Muhammad has narrated from Mu'alla' ibn Muhammad from al-Hassan ibn Ali al-Washsha' from Hammad ibn 'Uthman from 'Udaym ibn al-Hurr who has said the following:

"I once heard abu 'Abd Allah, *'Alayhi al-Salam*, say, 'Allah, most Blessed, most High, has established a certain limit for women every month.'"

H 4124, Ch. 1, h 2

Ali ibn Ibrahim has narrated from his father from ibn abu 'Umayr from Hammad from al-Halabiy who has said the following:

"I once asked abu 'Abd Allah, *'Alayhi al-Salam*, about the words of Allah, most Majestic, most Glorious, '. . . if you doubt . . .' (65:4) He (the Imam) said, 'Whatever takes place after a month is doubtful.'"

Chapter 1 - Minimum and Maximum Duration of Hayd

H 4125, Ch. 1, h 1

A number of our people have narrated from Ahmad ibn Muhammad ibn 'Isa from Ali ibn Ahmad ibn 'Ushaym from Ahmad ibn Muhammad ibn abu Nasr who has said the following:

"I once asked abu al-Hassan, *'Alayhi al-Salam*, about the minimum and maximum period of time of Hayd (menses). He (the Imam) said, 'It is three days and its maximum is not more than ten days.'"

H 4126, Ch. 1, h 2

Muhammad ibn 'Isma'il has narrated from al-Fadl ibn Shadhan and Ali ibn Ibrahim has narrated from his father all from ibn abu 'Umayr from Mu'awiyah ibn 'Ammar who has said the following:

"Abu 'Abd Allah, *'Alayhi al-Salam*, has said, 'The minimum duration of Hayd (menses) is three days and its maximum is ten days.'"

H 4127, Ch. 1, h 3

Muhammad ibn 'Isma'il has narrated from al-Fadl ibn Shadhan and Ali ibn Ibrahim has narrated from his father all from Safwan ibn Yahya who has said the following:

"I once asked abu al-Hassan, *'Alayhi al-Salam*, about the minimum duration of Hayd (menses). He (the Imam) said, 'Its minimum is three days and the longest is ten days.'"

H 4128, Ch. 1, h 4

Muhammad ibn Yahya has narrated from Ahmad ibn Muhammad from Safwan from al-'Ala' from, Muhammad ibn Muslim who has said the following:

"Abu Ja'far, *'Alayhi al-Salam*, has said, 'The minimum Hayd (menses) free period is ten days, that is, the time from the end of one period of Hayd (menses) to the beginning of the second one.'"

H 4129, Ch. 1, h 5

Ali ibn Ibrahim has narrated from his father from 'Isma'il ibn Marrar from Yunus from certain persons of his people who has said the following:

"Abu 'Abd Allah, *'Alayhi al-Salam*, has said, 'The minimum duration of Hayd (menses) free period is ten days. This is because when a woman experiences Hayd (menses) it is of a greater amount and it takes ten days. It continues and as time passes and she grows older, the duration of her Hayd (menses) reduces to three days. In this condition it does not go higher and it is not less than three days.

"During her experiencing Hayd (menses) within the date of her Hayd (menses) she must stop performing Salat (prayer). If blood discharge continues for three days it counts as her period of Hayd (menses); but if blood discharge stops within a day or two, she must take Ghusl (bath) and perform her Salat (prayer). She then waits for ten days from the first day blood discharge had started. If she experiences blood discharge within that period of ten days for one or two days to complete three days, then what she had experienced before along with this one within ten days all are of her Hayd (menses). If however, for ten days after the first day she experienced blood discharge she does not experience any blood discharge, then one or two days of blood discharge is not of Hayd (menses). Such discharge can happen because of her internal problems, such as an injury or from internal problems. She must redo her Salat (prayer) missed during such one or two days in which she had stopped performing Salat (prayer). If blood discharge continues for three days, it then is Hayd (menses), which is the minimum duration of Hayd (menses). It is not necessary to perform Salat (prayer) as remedy for those missed during experiencing menses. The duration of the period free of menses is not less than ten days. If she experiences blood discharge for five days then blood discharge stops, she must take Ghusl (bath) and perform her Salat (prayer). If she experiences blood discharge after this and before ten days from the day blood discharge had stopped this as well is of her menses, and during such time she stops performing her Salat (prayer). If she experiences blood discharge which begins from the end of ten days that she had already experienced and it continues for several more days above the first ten days and the second discharge it (that which is above ten days) is of Istihadah (irregular menses) during which she follows the rules about Istihadah (irregular menses).' He (the Imam) said, 'Blood discharge, during her established period of menses, of yellow or red color is of menses and whatever discharge takes place after the duration of her menses is not of Hayd (menses).'"

Chapter 2 - Women's Experiencing Hayd After or Before Their Date of Hayd

H 4130, Ch. 2, h 1

Ali ibn Ibrahim has narrated from his father from ibn abu 'Umayr from Jamil from Muhammad ibn Muslim who has said the following:

"Abu Ja'far, *'Alayhi al-Salam*, has stated this Hadith. 'If a woman experiences blood discharge before the passing of ten days from the end of a period of her

Hayd (menses), it is part of the first period of Hayd (menses); but if it is after ten days from the end of a period of her menses, it then is of her future period of her Hayd (menses).'"

H 4131, Ch. 2, h 2

Al-Husayn ibn Muhammad has narrated from 'Abd Allah ibn 'Amir from Ali ibn Mahziyar from al-Hassan ibn Sa'id from Zur'ah, from Sama'ah who has said the following:

"I once asked him (the Imam), *'Alayhi al-Salam*, about the case of a woman who experiences blood discharge before the time of her Hayd (menses) period. He (the Imam) said, 'If she experiences blood discharge before the time of her Hayd (menses) she must stop performing Salat (prayer). Perhaps it has started earlier. If blood discharge continues for more than the period of time she normally experiences, she must wait for three days above the normal period of time and if it did not stop after three days she then must follow the procedure for one experiencing Istihadah (irregular menses).'"

H 4132, Ch. 2, h 3

Ali ibn Ibrahim has narrated from his father from 'Abd Allah ibn al-Mughirah from those who narrated to him who have said the following:

"Abu 'Abd Allah, *'Alayhi al-Salam*, has said, 'If normal duration of a woman's blood discharge due to Hayd (menses) is ten days, she does not need to perform an examination but if it is less, she must perform an examination.'"

Chapter 3 - Women Observe Yellowish Blood Before or After Hayd (menses)

H 4133, Ch. 3, h 1

Ali ibn Ibrahim has narrated from his father and Muhammad ibn 'Isma'il from al-Fadl ibn Shadhan from Hammad ibn 'Isa from Hariz from Muhammad ibn Muslim who has said the following:

"I once asked abu 'Abd Allah, *'Alayhi al-Salam*, about the case of a woman who finds a discharge of yellow color during the time of her normal period of Hayd (menses). He (the Imam) said, 'She must not perform Salat (prayer) during the time of her normal blood discharge due to Hayd (menses). If she experiences blood discharge of yellow color in a time, which is other than the time for her normal period of blood discharge due to Hayd (menses), she must take Wudu' and perform Salat (prayer).'"

H 4134, Ch. 3, h 2

Ali ibn Ibrahim has narrated from his father from 'Abd Allah ibn al-Mughirah from Ishaq ibn 'Ammar from abu Basir who has said the following:

"Abu 'Abd Allah, *'Alayhi al-Salam*, about a woman who experiences a blood discharge of yellow color two days before her normal time for her Hayd (menses), has said that she must not perform Salat (prayer). It is Hayd (menses). If such discharge is two days after the time of her Hayd (menses) free period, she must perform Salat (prayer). It is not Hayd (menses)."

H 4135, Ch. 3, h 3

Al-Husayn ibn Muhammad has narrated from Mu'alla' ibn Muhammad from al-Washsha' from Aban from 'Isma'il al-Ju'fiy who has said the following:

"Abu 'Abd Allah, *'Alayhi al-Salam*, has said, 'If a woman experiences a discharge of yellowish color within the (normal) time period of her Hayd (menses), she must not perform Salat (prayer); but if it is after the period of Hayd-free time she must perform Salat (prayer).'"

H 4136, Ch. 3, h 4

Muhammad ibn Yahya has narrated from Ahmad ibn Muhammad from Muhammad ibn Khalid from al-Qasim ibn Muhammad from Ali ibn abu Hamzah who has said the following:

"Abu 'Abd Allah, *'Alayhi al-Salam*, was asked, when I was in his presence, about the case of a woman who experiences a discharge of yellowish color. He (the Imam) said, 'What is before Hayd (menses) is of Hayd (menses) and what is after Hayd (menses) is not Hayd (menses).'"

H 4137, Ch. 3, h 5

Muhammad ibn abu 'Abd Allah, has narrated from Mu'awiyah ibn Hukaym who has said the following:

"He (the Imam), *'Alayhi al-Salam*, has said, 'A discharge of yellowish color for two days before Hayd (menses) is of Hayd (menses) and after the days of Hayd (menses) is not of Hayd (menses); however such (discharge) during the days of Hayd (menses) is Hayd (menses).'"

Chapter 4 - First Time Hayd (menses)

H 4138, Ch. 4, h 1

Muhammad ibn Yahya has narrated from Ahmad ibn Muhammad from 'Uthman ibn 'Isa from Sama'ah ibn Mehran who has said the following:

"I once asked him (the Imam), *'Alayhi al-Salam*, about the case of a young girl who experiences Hayd (menses) for the first time. In one month she experiences for two days and in the second month for three days and so they are not certain days of known duration every month. He (the Imam) said, 'She must deal with it like Hayd (menses) and stop performing Salat (prayer) as long as there is discharge which is not more than ten days. If the duration of her Hayd (menses) in two months remains the same, this establishes a pattern for her Hayd (menses).'"

H 4139, Ch. 4, h 2

Ali ibn Ibrahim has narrated from his father from ibn abu 'Umayr from Yunus ibn Ya'qub who has said the following:

"I once said to abu 'Abd Allah, *'Alayhi al-Salam*, that a woman may experience blood discharge for three or four days. He (the Imam) said, 'She must stop performing Salat (prayer).' I then said that she might experience Hayd-free time for three or four days. He (the Imam) said, 'She must perform Salat (prayer).' I then said that she might experience blood discharge for three or four days. He (the Imam) said, 'She must stop performing Salat (prayer).' I then said that she might experience blood-discharge-free time for three or four days. He (the Imam) said, 'She must perform Salat (prayer).' I then said that she might experience blood discharge for three or four days. He (the Imam) said, 'She must stop performing Salat (prayer) and continue as such for one month and if blood discharge did not stop she must deal with it according to the rules for Istihadah (irregular menses).'"

H 4140, Ch. 4, h 3
Muhammad ibn Yahya has narrated from Ahmad ibn Muhammad in a marfu' manner from Zur'ah, from Sama'ah who has said the following:
"I once asked him (the Imam), *'Alayhi al-Salam*, about the case of a girl who experiences blood discharge for the first time. It continues for three months and she does not know the duration the discharge-free time of her Hayd (menses). He (the Imam) said, 'Her discharge-free time is like those of the women from her relatives. If the case with the women of her relatives is different, then the maximum for her is ten days and the minimum is three days.'"

Chapter 5 - Examining if Hayd (menses) has Ended or Not

H 4141, Ch. 5, h 1
Ali ibn Ibrahim has narrated from his father from 'Isma'il ibn Marrar and others from Yunus from those whom he has mentioned, has said the following:
"Abu 'Abd Allah, *'Alayhi al-Salam*, was asked about the case of a woman who experiences her blood discharge to have stopped but does not know if she is Hayd-free or not. He (the Imam) said, 'She must stand up with her belly leaned against a wall, place a piece of white cotton in her urethra and raise her right leg. Thereafter she examines the piece of cotton. If there is thick dark color blood, even of the size of the head of a fly, on the tip of the piece of cotton, her Hayd (menses) has not stopped; and if there is no blood on the tip of cotton, she must take Ghusl (bath) and perform Salat (prayer).'"

H 4142, Ch. 5, h 2
Muhammad ibn Yahya has narrated from Ahmad ibn Muhammad from ibn Mahbub from abu Ayyub from Muhammad ibn Muslim who has said the following:
"Abu Ja'far, *'Alayhi al-Salam*, has stated this Hadith. 'If a woman wants Ghusl (bath), she should place a piece of cotton in her urethra. If blood is found on it, she cannot take Ghusl (bath); but if blood is not found on it, she must take Ghusl (bath) and if thereafter she finds yellowish discharge she must take Wudu' to perform Salat (prayer).'"

H 4143, Ch. 5, h 3
Muhammad ibn Yahya has narrated from Salmah ibn al-Khattab, from Ali ibn al-Hassan al-Tatariy, from Muhammad ibn abu Hamzah, from ibn Muskan, from Shurahbil al-Kindiy who has said the following:
"I once asked abu 'Abd Allah, *'Alayhi al-Salam*, about how a woman experiencing Hayd (menses) can find out if her Hayd (menses) has ended. He (the Imam), said, 'She can find out by leaning against a wall on her left leg and place a piece of cotton in her urethra with her right hand. If there is blood even of the size of fly's head on the tip of the piece of cotton (it has not ended).'"

H 4144, Ch. 5, h 4
Muhammad ibn Yahya has narrated from Ahmad ibn Muhammad from ibn Mahbub from abu Hamzah who has said the following:

"Once it was mentioned before Abu Ja'far, *'Alayhi al-Salam*, that women, during the night, asked for a lantern to examine if blood discharge has stopped or not; and it was considered laughable. He (the Imam) said, 'When did women do this?'" (Meaning the proper test is with a piece of cotton)

H 4145, Ch. 5, h 5

Ali ibn Ibrahim has narrated from his father from ibn abu 'Umayr from Tha'labah who has said the following:

"Abu 'Abd Allah, *'Alayhi al-Salam*, would prohibit women to examine themselves at night during their Hayd (menses), saying that it can be a discharge of a yellowish color fluid or some kind of dirt.'"

H 4146, Ch. 5, h 6

Ali ibn Muhammad has narrated from certain persons of our people from Muhammad ibn Ali al-Basriy who has said the following:

"I once said to abu al-Hassan, the last, *'Alayhi al-Salam*, that the daughter of Shihab during her Hayd-free times, after taking Ghusl (bath), finds drops after drops of discharge. He (the Imam) said, 'Instruct her to stand up against a wall, then instruct a woman to press hard between her hips, because it is something which has remained in her womb that is called shedding, and this takes all of it out.' He (the Imam) then said, 'Do not tell this and similar things to them (women). Rather leave them alone with their unclean ailment.' He (the narrator) has said that he gave the woman that instruction and such discharge did not take place (thereafter) until she died."

Chapter 6 - Taking Ghusl (bath) Because of Hayd and the Kind of Water Needed

H 4147, Ch. 6, h 1

Muhammad ibn Yahya has narrated from Ahmad ibn Muhammad from Ali ibn al-Hakam and Ali ibn Ibrahim has narrated from his father from ibn abu 'Umayr all from 'Abd Allah ibn Yahya al-Kahiliy who has said the following:

"I once said to abu 'Abd Allah, *'Alayhi al-Salam*, that today women have found a certain manner of hair dressing. One of them can find a certain device made of wool which a hair dresser uses along with certain fragrance, then places in a thin piece of fabric, then ties it up with a pin and places it over her head and then she may experience sexual relation. He (the Imam), *'Alayhi al-Salam*, said, 'Women of earlier times would only decorate their hairs at the front of their head. If they may need to take Ghusl (bath), instruct them to allow water to reach their head and wring the decorated hair so water reaches it; when water reaches it then it is not harmful.' I then asked about Hayd (menses) and he (the Imam) said, 'Women experiencing Hayd (menses) must reduce it (such decoration of hairs) a great deal.'"

H 4148, Ch. 6, h 2

Muhammad ibn Yahya has narrated from Ahmad ibn Muhammad ibn abu Nasr from Muthanna' al-Hannat from Hasan al-Sayqal who has said the following:

"Abu 'Abd Allah, *'Alayhi al-Salam*, has said, 'A woman for her Ghusl (bath) due to Hayd (menses) must use nine Artal of water.'" (One Ritl is about 449.28gms).

H 4149, Ch. 6, h 3

Ali ibn Muhammad and others have narrated from Sahl ibn Ziyad from ibn Mahbub from ibn Ri'ab from abu 'Ubaydah who has said the following:

"I once asked abu 'Abd Allah, *'Alayhi al-Salam*, about the case of a woman who after Hayd (menses) experiences a Hayd-free condition during a journey and cannot find water enough for Ghusl (bath) when it is time for Salat (prayer). He (the Imam) said, 'If she has enough water to wash clean her private parts, she must do so and take Tayammum instead of Ghusl (bath); then perform Salat (prayer).' I then asked, 'What happens if her husband comes?' He (the Imam) said, 'After her washing clean her private parts and Tayammum it is not harmful.'"

H 4150, Ch. 6, h 4

Muhammad ibn Yahya has narrated from Ahmad ibn Muhammad from ibn Mahbub from abu Ayyub al-Khazzaz from Muhammad ibn Muslim who has said the following:

"Abu Ja'far, *'Alayhi al-Salam*, has said, 'For Ghusl (bath) because of Hayd (menses) if wetness and moisture reaches (the skin) from hairs it is sufficient.'"

H 4151, Ch. 6, h 5

Abu Ali al-Ash'ariy has narrated from Muhammad ibn Ahmad from Ahmad ibn al-Hassan ibn Ali from 'Amr ibn Sa'id from Musaddiq ibn Sadaqah from 'Ammar ibn Musa who has said the following:

"Abu 'Abd Allah, *'Alayhi al-Salam*, about a woman who takes Ghusl (bath) because of Hayd (menses) and there is saffron on her body which is not removed with Ghusl (bath), has said, 'It is not harmful.'"

Chapter 7 - Women Find Blood after Sexual Relation

H 4152, Ch. 7, h 1

Muhammad ibn Yahya has narrated from Ahmad ibn Muhammad from Ali ibn al-Hakam from 'Abd Allah ibn Yahya al-Kahiliy who has said the following:

"I once asked abu 'Abd Allah, *'Alayhi al-Salam*, about a woman who after sexual relation with her husband experiences Hayd (menses) and she is already in the bath area. Must she take Ghusl (bath) or not? He (the Imam) said, 'Something which invalidates Salat (prayer) has come with her. She does not need Ghusl (bath).'"

H 4153, Ch. 7, h 2

Ali ibn Ibrahim has narrated from Muhammad ibn 'Isa from Yunus from 'Abd Allah ibn Sinan who has said the following:

"I once asked abu 'Abd Allah, *'Alayhi al-Salam*, about a woman who experiences Hayd (menses) when she has had sexual relation if she needed Ghusl (bath) because of sexual relation. He (the Imam) said, 'Ghusl (bath) for Hayd (menses) and sexual relation is one.'"

H 4154, Ch. 7, h 3

Ali ibn Ibrahim has narrated from his father from 'Isma'il ibn Marrar from Yunus from Sa'id ibn Yasar who has said the following:

"I once asked abu 'Abd Allah, *'Alayhi al-Salam*, about the case of a woman who experiences blood discharge because of Hayd (menses) when she has had sexual relation if she needs Ghusl (bath) because of sexual relation or Ghusl (bath) because of the sexual relation and Hayd (menses). He (the Imam) said, 'She has experienced something bigger than that (sexual relation).'"

Chapter 8 - Comprehensive Instructions About Hayd (menses) and Istihadah (irregular menses)

H 4155, Ch. 8, h 1

Ali ibn Ibrahim has narrated from Muhammad ibn 'Isa have narrated from Yunus from more than one person who have said the following:

"They asked abu 'Abd Allah, *'Alayhi al-Salam*, about women experiencing Hayd (menses) and the tradition in his time. He (the Imam) said, 'The Messenger of Allah has established three traditions in which he has explained every difficulty for those who hear and understand them so that no one can say anything of his own opinion about it.

1. "One tradition is about one who experiences Hayd (menses) on certain dates for a known period of time without mix and confusion, but she experiences Istihadah (irregular menses) and blood discharge continues. She knows the dates and number of days of the cycle of her Hayd (menses). A woman called Fatimah bint abu Hubaysh experienced Istihadah (irregular menses) and blood discharge continued. She came to 'Umm Salamah. She asked the Messenger of Allah about it and he said that she must stop performing Salat (prayer) for a number of days, which is equal to the number of days of her Hayd-free period or the days of her Hayd (menses). He (the Messenger of Allah) said it is a (bleeding) vein. He (the Messenger of Allah) commanded her to take Ghusl (bath) (after passing either one of the two above mentioned number of days, namely, the Hayd (menses) free days or the number of days of her Hayd (menses)) and cover herself by passing her clothes between her legs to the other side and perform Salat (prayer).

"Abu 'Abd Allah, *'Alayhi al-Salam*, said, 'This is one tradition that the Holy prophet has established for women who know the date of their Hayd (menses) free period without mix and confusion. It is because he (the Messenger of Allah) did not ask how many days. He (the Messenger of Allah) did not say that if it increases above such number of days you are in the state of experiencing Istihadah (irregular menses). He (the Messenger of Allah) established a tradition for her in the case of known dates of more or less number after her knowing it (dates) exactly. In the same way my father gave the fatwa when he was asked about a woman experiencing Istihadah (irregular menses). He (the Imam) said, 'It is only a (bleeding) vein or a kick of Satan.'

"She must stop performing Salat (prayer) for number of the days which is equal to the days of her Hayd (menses)-free period, then take Ghusl (bath) and Wudu' for every Salat (prayer). It then was asked, 'Even if it (blood discharge) is flowing?' He (the Imam) said, 'Yes even if it is like flowing.'

"Abu 'Abd Allah, *'Alayhi al-Salam*, said, 'This is an explanation of Hadith of the Messenger of Allah, it (the explanation) agrees with the Hadith of the Messenger of Allah. This is the tradition about the one who knows the number of days of her Hayd (menses), not the date but only the number, less or more.

2. "This tradition is for one who experiences Hayd (menses) for a number of days but it becomes confused in terms of the number of days due to increase or decrease in such numbers as well as the exact date every month. The tradition for this kind of case is different from the previous one in which one experiences Hayd (menses) during a known number of days and date of every cycle of menses. It is because Fatimah bint abu Hubaysh came to the Holy prophet saying, 'I continuously experience Hayd (menses) and do not have any menses-free time.' The Holy prophet, said, 'That is not Hayd (menses). It is a (bleeding) vein. When Hayd (menses) comes with greater quantity of blood discharge, you must stop performing Salat (prayer); and when it comes with diminished quantity of bleeding, you must take Ghusl (bath), wash the blood clean and perform Salat (prayer).'

"She would sit in a tub that belonged to her sister and yellowish color would rise over the water. Abu 'Abd Allah, *'Alayhi al-Salam*, has said, 'Do you not hear that the Messenger of Allah commanded this woman to do something other than what he (the Messenger of Allah) had commanded the other woman to do.? Do you not see that he (the Messenger of Allah) did not say to her, 'Stop performing Salat (prayer) during the days of your Hayd (menses) free period,' but he (the Messenger of Allah) told her, 'When it comes with increased quantity stop performing Salat (prayer) and when it comes with diminished quantity, take Ghusl (bath) and perform Salat (prayer).' This explains that the case of this woman is confused in terms of number of days in which she experiences Hayd (menses). She does not know the exact number of days as well as the exact date. Do you not hear her saying, 'I continuously experience Hayd (menses) and I do not have any Hayd (menses) free condition.' My father would say that she experienced Hayd (menses) for seven years, so in a lesser time it is a confused condition and mixed one.

"For this reason she needed to know the condition of the quantity of blood discharge and its quality in terms of color and so on. Blood discharge because of Hayd (menses) is of distinguishable black color. If she had known the days of her experiencing Hayd (menses) she would not need to know the color of blood discharge; the tradition about Hayd (menses) is that yellowness and thickness and things above this are during the days of Hayd (menses). When such signs are found it is then all Hayd (menses). If the color of blood is black and so on, it all explains that blood discharge of lesser or greater quantity in the days of Hayd (menses) is all Hayd (menses) when the days are exactly known to her. However, if she does not know the exact date and number of days she then needs to know the quantity of blood discharge and changes in its color, and then she stops performing Salat (prayer) accordingly. I do not find the Holy prophet, saying, 'Sit (wait) for so and so many days and above such days is Istihadah (irregular menses). He (the Messenger of Allah) did not command the other woman in the first case like this. So also my father gave fatwa in a likewise case. Once a woman in our family experienced Hayd (menses) and she asked my father about it. He (my father) said, 'If you experience a flooding blood discharge, stop performing Salat (prayer). If you experience bleeding-free time even for an hour, take Ghusl (bath) and perform Salat (prayer).' Abu 'Abd Allah, *'Alayhi al-Salam*, has said, 'I find my father's answer in this case different from his answer in the case of one experiencing Istihadah (irregular menses) mentioned in the first tradition. Consider his saying, 'Stop performing Salat (prayer) for a period equal to the days of your discharge free period.' This is because of the number of days. In this case he has said, 'If you experience flooding blood discharge' then stop performing Salat (prayer). In this case he commanded to see the quantity in terms of increase and decrease and changes in its color and his saying, 'flooding discharge' is similar to the statement of the Holy prophet, 'Blood discharge because of Hayd (menses) is of distinguishable black color.' My father has called it flooding discharge because of its greater quantity and color.

"This is the tradition the Holy prophet has established for the case of women whose habit is confused in terms of number of days. The way for such women to know is by learning about the quantity and quality of blood discharge.

3. "He (the Imam) said, 'The third tradition established for Istihadah (irregular menses) and Hayd (menses) is about women who do not have a set pattern for their Hayd (menses); it is a confused pattern and habit. The tradition in such case is different from the first and second traditions. This is because once a woman called Hamnah bint Jahsh came to the Messenger of Allah and said, 'I have experienced an intense Hayd (menses).' He (the Messenger of Allah) said, 'Fill up with cotton.' She said, 'It is more intense than can be controlled with cotton. It is flooding.' He (the Messenger of Allah) said, 'Harness it tightly and follow the rules for Hayd (menses), according to the knowledge of Allah, for six or seven days. Thereafter, you must take Ghusl (bath) and fast twenty-three days or twenty-four days, then take Ghusl (bath) for the time of dawn (morning Salat (prayer)), one Ghusl (bath) for al-Zuhr, then perform al-'Asr Salat (prayer) quickly and another for al-Maghrib and perform al-'Isha' prayer quickly thereafter and take one more Ghusl (bath).' Abu 'Abd Allah, *'Alayhi al-Salam*, has said, 'I can see that he (the Messenger of Allah) has established in this case a tradition which is different from the traditions for the first and second case of Hayd (menses). It is because the commandment of the Messenger of Allah to her is different from those to the other two women. Consider that if the number of days in her case were less than seven and were it five or less the Messenger of Allah would not command her to consider it Hayd (menses) for seven days.

Therefore, he (the Messenger of Allah) would end up commanding her to stop performing Salat (prayer) for certain days when she experienced Istihadah (irregular menses) and not Hayd (menses). So also is the case if her Hayd (menses) was for more than seven days like being ten days or more, he (the Messenger of Allah) would end up commanding her to perform Salat (prayer) when she experienced Hayd (menses). Furthermore what it explains is his words to her, "Follow rules of Hayd (menses) in your condition." "Following rules of Hayd (menses)" is only for a woman who in fact experiences Hayd (menses). Do you not see that he (the Messenger of Allah) did not say to her to follow the rule of Hayd (menses) for a certain number of days. One more fact that explains this is his words, "according to knowledge of Allah" because it was for her, although all things are in the knowledge of Allah, most High. This explains it clearly that she did not have a pattern in the form of known days before, at all. This is the tradition for one who experiences blood discharge for the first time without stop. The maximum for such Hayd (menses) is seven days and the maximum Hayd-free period is twenty-three days until the pattern of her experiencing Hayd (menses) is established which then is followed. All cases of Istihadah (irregular menses) fall under these three traditions. It all falls under these traditions. If the number of days, more or less, are known, she follows the rules for Hayd (menses) and her habits accordingly when there is no other number and dates other than her days.

"That her days become confused because of coming earlier or later and the changes of conditions. The tradition in her case is to find about the quantity and quality, like color of blood and so on, follow that she had no experience in terms of days before and she experiences Hayd (menses) for the first time in which case it (Hayd (menses)) is seven days and the Hayd-free period is twenty-three days. If blood discharge continues for several months, she follows the rule every month as explained for her. If blood discharge stops before the seven days or after more than seven days, she then takes Ghusl (bath) as soon as she finds a Hayd-free time and performs Salat (prayer). She continues to follow such rule until the second month to see if it is in the same pattern and habit as the month before and up to two or three cycles of Hayd (menses), then it means that a distinguishable pattern and habit is established for her. She can follow the rules of Hayd (menses) accordingly. She can now ignore other conditions and this becomes her tradition for future if she experiences Istihadah (irregular menses).

"Basing establishment of pattern and habit on the grounds of two or three Hayd (menses) cycle is because of the words of the Messenger of Allah to the one who had known the number of her days that said, 'Stop performing Salat (prayer) in the days (dates) of your Hayd-free days.' This explains that one Hayd-free period is not enough to establish a pattern and habit. He (the Messenger of Allah) did not say one Hayd-free period. He set it for her to be three Hayd-free periods. The minimum is two cycles of Hayd-free periods or more.

"When days and her pattern and habit are confused because of increase or decrease in number of days and the pattern is lost even in terms of quality and color, she then follows the rules according to the quantity of blood discharge. She does not have other traditions to follow except this because of the words of the Messenger of Allah, 'When blood discharge is increased, stop performing Salat (prayer), and when it decreases take Ghusl (bath).' Also because of the words of the Messenger of Allah, 'Blood of Hayd (menses) is distinguishably of black color.' It is like the statement of my father, 'When you experience flooding blood discharge.' If this is not applicable and blood discharge continues, it is Istihadah (irregular menses) when the color of blood is of one kind and one condition, in this case the tradition to follow is seven days (of Hayd (menses)) and twenty-three days of Hayd-free period. It is because her case is like the case of Hamnah who said, 'Blood discharge from me is flooding.'"

H 4156, Ch. 8, h 2

Muhammad ibn `Isma'il has narrated from al-Fadl ibn Shadhan from Hammad ibn 'Isa and ibn abu 'Umayr from Mu'awiyah ibn 'Ammar who has said the following:

"Abu 'Abd Allah, *'Alayhi al-Salam*, has said, 'One experiencing Istihadah (irregular menses) must wait to complete the number of days of the pattern of her habit of experiencing Hayd (menses) and in such times she must not perform Salat (prayer) or go close to her husband. When such days are passed but blood discharge continues, she then must place a piece of cotton inside urethra. She must take Ghusl (bath) for al-Zuhr and al-'Asr Salat (prayer) with sometimes delay in that (al-Zuhr) and earlier in this (al-'Asr) and another Ghusl (bath) for al-Maghrib and al-'Isha' with sometimes delay for that and earlier for this. She must take a Ghusl (bath) for morning with urethra filled with cotton; she must not bend down and must keep her thighs close to each other when sitting, with other parts of her body kept out. Her husband must not go close to her during her time of Hayd (menses) free period. If blood discharge penetrates through the piece of cotton, she must take one Wudu' to enter Masjid, and take Wudu' for each Salat (prayer). In this case her husband can go close to her except in the days of her Hayd (menses).'"

H 4157, Ch. 8, h 3

Muhammad has narrated from al-Fadl from Safwan from Muhammad al-Halabiy who has said the following:

"I once asked abu 'Abd Allah, *'Alayhi al-Salam*, about the case of a woman who experiences Istihadah. He (the Imam) said that the Messenger of Allah was asked about a woman who experienced Istihadah. He (the Messenger of Allah) told her to wait for a number of days equal to the days of her Hayd (menses) in which she must not perform Salat (prayer). She then must take Ghusl (bath) and place cotton, then secure it in place with a piece of cloth; then perform Salat (prayer) until blood comes out from the other side of the cloth.' He (the Imam) then said, 'A bleeding woman must take Ghusl (bath) between every two Salat (prayer) and replace cotton and cloth, use perfume and burn incense. The piece of cloth must be like a belt to harness animals.'"

H 4158, Ch. 8, h 4

Muhammad ibn Yahya has narrated from Muhammad ibn al-Husayn from 'Uthman ibn 'Isa from Sama'ah who has said the following:

"He (the Imam), *'Alayhi al-Salam*, has said, 'In the case of Istihadah, if blood finds its way out through the cotton, she must take Ghusl (bath) for every two Salat (prayer) and one more Ghusl (bath) for the morning Salat (prayer). If blood does not come out through the cotton, then she must take one Ghusl (bath) every day and Wudu' for every Salat (prayer). If her husband wants to come to her, he must do so after her Ghusl (bath). This is when blood is of black color but if it is yellow, then she must take Wudu'.'"

H 4159, Ch. 8, h 5

Ali ibn Ibrahim has narrated from his father from 'Abd Allah ibn al-Mughirah from 'Abd Allah ibn Sinan who has said the following:

"Abu 'Abd Allah, *'Alayhi al-Salam*, has said, 'A woman experiencing Istihadah must take Ghusl (bath) for Salat (prayer) of al-Zuhr to perform Salat (prayer) of al-Zuhr and al-'Asr, then take Ghusl (bath) near al-Maghrib to perform Salat (prayer) of al-Maghrib and al-'Isha', then take Ghusl (bath) near the morning for Salat (prayer) of the morning. It is not harmful if her husband comes to her if he likes. Only in the days when she experiences Hayd (menses) he must stay away from her.' He (the Imam), said, 'Any woman who follows this instruction for the sake of reward from Allah enjoys good health.'"

H 4160, Ch. 8, h 6

Muhammad ibn 'Isma'il has narrated from al-Fadl ibn Shadhan from Safwan ibn Yahya who has said the following:

"I once asked abu al-Hassan, *'Alayhi al-Salam*, saying, 'I pray to Allah to keep my soul in service for your cause, if a woman waits for ten days experiencing blood discharge, then she becomes clean; and after three discharge-free days experiences blood discharge again, is she required to stop performing Salat (prayer)? He (the Imam) said, 'No, she is Mustahadah. She must place cotton one piece after the other piece, perform two Salat (prayer) together one after the other with one Ghusl (bath) and her husband can come to her if he wants.'"

H 4161, Ch. 8, h 7

A number of our people have narrated from Ahmad ibn Muhammad from Ali ibn al-Hakam from Dawud Mawla' abu al-Mighra' al-'Ijliy from those who narrated to him who have said the following:

"I once asked abu 'Abd Allah, *'Alayhi al-Salam*, about the case of a woman who experiences Hayd (menses), then the time for her al-Zuhr Salat (prayer) comes when she finds bleeding. He (the Imam) said, 'She must examine by means of the day to see if it stops before ten days. If it continued after ten days it, then is because of Istihadah (not Hayd (menses). If bleeding stops (before ten days) she must take Ghusl (bath) and perform Salat (prayer).' I then asked, 'If a woman whose Hayd (menses) is seven days or eight days all the time and straight then she experiences Hayd (menses) for three days, then bleeding stops, then she finds white discharge not yellow, nor blood.' He (the Imam) said, 'She must take Ghusl (bath) and perform Salat (prayer)' I then said that she performs Salat (prayer) and fasts but bleeding comes again. He (the Imam) said, 'When she finds blood she must stop Salat (prayer) and fasting.' I then said that she finds blood one day and one day finds no blood. He (the Imam) said, 'When she finds blood she must stop Salat (prayer) and fasting and when she does not find blood, she performs Salat (prayer) and when the number of the days of her Hayd (menses) are complete and bleeding stops, she must perform Salat (prayer). If she finds blood it is then because of Istihadah. I have organized all of her affairs for you.'"

Chapter 9 - Signs for Differentiating Between Blood of Hayd and Istihazah

H 4162, Ch. 9, h 1

Ali ibn Ibrahim has narrated from his father from ibn abu 'Umayr from Hafs ibn al-Bakhtariy who has said the following:

"Once a woman came to abu 'Abd Allah, *'Alayhi al-Salam*, and asked about the case of a woman who experiences blood discharge which does not stop and she does not know whether it is Hayd (menses) or something else. He (the narrator) has said that he (the Imam) then said, 'Blood discharged because of Hayd (menses) is hot, thick and of black color. It comes with pressure and hotness. Blood discharge because of Istihadah (irregular menses) is of yellow color and cold. If blood discharged is hot, comes with pressure and it is of black color, she must stop performing Salat (prayer).' He (the narrator) said that she left saying, 'By Allah, were it a woman she could not explain it any better than what he (the Imam) did.'"

H 4163, Ch. 9, h 2

Muhammad ibn 'Isma'il has narrated from al-Fadl ibn Shadhan from Hammad ibn 'Isa and ibn abu 'Umayr all from Mu'awiyah ibn 'Ammar who has said the following:

"Abu 'Abd Allah, *'Alayhi al-Salam*, has said, 'Blood discharge because of Istihadah (irregular menses) and Hayd (menses) does not come from the same place. Blood discharge because of Istihadah (irregular menses) is cold, and because of Hayd (menses) it is hot.'"

H 4164, Ch. 9, h 3

A number of our people have narrated from Ahmad ibn Muhammad from Ali ibn al-Hakam from Ishaq ibn Jarir who has said the following:

"Once, a woman of our family asked me to take her to abu 'Abd Allah, *'Alayhi al-Salam*. I asked for permission for her and permission was granted. She went to visit abu 'Abd Allah, *'Alayhi al-Salam*, along with her slave-girl. She asked, 'O abu 'Abd Allah, what is the meaning of the words of Allah, ". . . an olive tree which is not eastern or western."' (24:35) He (the Imam) said, 'Dear lady, what Allah, most High, has referred to is only a tree and nothing else and it refers only to children of Adam and no one else. Now you can ask whatever you like.' She said, 'Please tell me about the case of women sleeping with women (lesbians). What is the punishment for it?' He (the Imam) said, 'Punishment for it is like that for fornication. On the Day of Judgment they will be brought wearing cutting elements of fire, harnessed with harnesses of fire and bars of fire inserted into her inside up to her head and they are thrown into the fire. Dear woman, of the people who first committed this (sin) were the people of Lot. Men of those people began to practice sexual relation with other men and women were left without men; so they also began to practice sexual relation with other women.' She then said, 'May Allah keep you well, what do you say about the case of a woman who experiences Hayd (menses) but blood discharge does not stop when it normally would stop?' He (the Imam) said, 'If duration of her Hayd (menses) is less than ten days, after one day from such time (end of her normal habit) she must examine, and after this it is Istihadah (irregular menses).' She then said, 'What is the rule for her Salat (prayer) if blood discharge continues for one or two or three months?' He (the Imam) said, 'She must stop Salat (prayer) during the days that she experiences Hayd (menses), then take Ghusl (bath) for every two Salat (prayer).' She then said, 'What must she do if the days of her Hayd (menses) are different and it comes one or two or three days before or it comes later in the same way?' He (the Imam) said, 'Blood discharge is not confusing. It is hot and comes with burning sensation. Blood discharge because of Istihadah (irregular menses) is spoiled and cold.' She then turned to her slave-girl saying, 'Do you think he has lived as a woman before?'"

Chapter 10 - Differentiating Among Blood of Hayd, Virginity or a Wound

H 4165, Ch. 10, h 1

Ali ibn Ibrahim has narrated from his father and a number of our people have narrated from Ahmad ibn Muhammad ibn Khalid all from Muhammad ibn Khalid from Khalaf ibn Hammad and Ahmad has also narrated from Muhammad ibn Aslam from Khalaf ibn Hammad al-Kufiy who has said the following:

"A certain person of our people married a girl who had not experienced menstruation. Blood discharge started after sexual relation and it did not stop for about ten days. Nurses were called to examine and they had different opinions. Certain ones of them said that it is because of Hayd (menses) and others said that it is because of virginity. They then asked scholars of their Fiqh (law), like abu Hanifah and other of their scholars of Fiqh. They said that it is a difficult issue because Salat (prayer) is an obligatory duty. She must take Wudu', perform Salat (prayer) and keep her husband away until blood discharge stops. If in fact it is because of Hayd (menses), performing Salat (prayer) is not harmful, and if it is because of virginity, she has fulfilled her duty. She followed their instruction. I went that year for Hajj. When we were in Mina I sent someone to abu al-Hassan, Musa ibn Ja'far, *'Alayhi al-Salam*, and said, 'I pray to Allah to keep my soul in service for your cause, we have an issue which is giving us a difficult time. If you will kindly grant us an appointment, we like to present it before you for an answer.' He (the Imam) sent a message that said, 'When it becomes quiet, there are less feet walking, and roads become free, you can come by the will of Allah.' Khalaf has said that at night when people's coming and going reduced in Mina, I walked to his tent. When I was near his tent, I saw a black figure on the road who asked, 'Who are you?' I said, 'I am one of the pilgrims.' He asked, 'What is your name?' I replied, 'I am Khalaf ibn Hammad.' He said, 'You can go inside and you do not need any more permission, because he (the Imam) had instructed me to wait here to allow you to go inside.' I then went inside, expressed my greeting of peace to him and he (the Imam) responded to my expressing greeting of peace. He (the Imam) was sitting on the furnishing alone and there was no one in the tent beside him (the Imam). When I was in his presence I asked how he felt and he (the Imam) asked about my conditions and I said, 'A man who is of your followers has married a girl who had not experienced Hayd (menses). After sexual relation she experienced blood discharge, which did not stop for up to ten days. Nurses examined her and they had different opinions about it. Certain ones among them said that it is because of Hayd (menses) and others said that it is because of virginity. What must she do in such condition?' He (the Imam) said, 'She must observe piety before Allah. If it is because of Hayd (menses), she must stop performing Salat (prayer) until she is clean from Hayd (menses) and she must keep her husband away. If it is because of virginity, she must observe piety before Allah, must take Wudu', perform Salat (prayer) and allow her husband to come to her if she so pleases.' I (the narrator) then asked, 'How can she find out what it is so they can follow their duty?' He (the narrator) has that he (the Imam) looked to the left and right sides in the tent for fear of someone hearing his words. He (the narrator) has said that he (the Imam) then leaned toward me and said, 'O Khalaf, it is the secret of Allah, it is the secret of Allah, you must not publicize it and do not tell it to these people the principles of the religion of Allah. Just agree with what Allah has agreed that they follow their straying. He (the Imam) then formed the figure ninety with his left hand and said, 'She must place a piece of cotton in her urethra and allow it gently there for a while, then gently take it out. If blood is found as a circle around the piece of cotton, it is because of her virginity; and if blood is found as penetrating (in the center) inside the cotton it is because of Hayd (menses).' Khalaf has said, 'I cried because of happiness and when my weeping calmed down, he (the Imam) asked, "What made you weep?"' I replied, 'I pray to Allah to keep my soul in service for your cause, no one can give an answer better than your answer.' He (the narrator) has said that he (the Imam) raised his hand to the sky and said, 'By Allah, I only answered you from the Messenger of Allah, from Jibril from Allah, most Majestic, most Glorious.'"

H 4166, Ch. 10, h 2

Muhammad ibn Yahya has narrated from Ahmad ibn Muhammad ibn 'Isa from ibn Mahbub from ibn Ri'ab from Ziyad ibn Suqah who has said the following:

"Abu Ja'far, *'Alayhi al-Salam*, was asked about a man who experiences sexual relation with his wife or slave-girl and she finds a great deal of blood discharge that does not stop, not even for one day. What must she do for her Salat (prayer)? He (the Imam) said, 'She must keep a piece of cotton, if blood is found in the form of a circle around it, it is blood because of virginity. She must take Ghusl (bath), keep the piece of cotton and perform Salat (prayer). If blood is found to have dipped into the piece of cotton, it is because of Hayd (menses), in which case she must stop performing Salat (prayer) during the days of her Hayd (menses).'"

H 4167, Ch. 10, h 3

Muhammad ibn Yahya in a marfu' manner has narrated from Aban who has said the following:

"I once said to abu 'Abd Allah, *'Alayhi al-Salam*, a young woman of our people has a wound in her vagina. She finds bleeding but does not know if it is because of Hayd (menses) or because of the wound and blood flows. He (the Imam) said, 'Instruct her to lie down on her back, raise her legs and place her middle finger inside. If blood comes from the right side, it is because of Hayd (menses); if it comes from the left side, it is because of the wound.'"

Chapter 11 - Pregnant Woman Finds Blood

H 4168, Ch. 11, h 1

Muhammad ibn Yahya has narrated from Ahmad ibn Muhammad from al-Hassan ibn Mahbub from al-Husayn ibn Nu'aym al-Sahhaf who has said the following:

"I once said to abu 'Abd Allah, *'Alayhi al-Salam*, that the mother of my child finds bleeding and she is pregnant. What must she do for her Salat (prayer)? He (the narrator) has said that he (the Imam) said to me, 'If a pregnant woman finds bleeding after twenty days from the date in which her Hayd (menses) would begin in the month when she experienced Hayd (menses), then it is not from the womb and but because of Hayd (menses). She must take Wudu', fill herself with cotton and perform Salat (prayer). If a pregnant woman finds bleeding during a short time before the date during which she would experience Hayd (menses) or during the date of her Hayd (menses) in that month, it then is because of Hayd (menses). She must stop Salat (prayer) during a time, which is equal to the duration of her Hayd (menses). If bleeding stops before the (duration of her Hayd (menses)), she must take Ghusl (bath), and perform Salat (prayer). If bleeding did not stop before one or two days after the end of such duration in which she used to experience Hayd (menses) she then must take Ghusl (bath) then fill with cotton and tie down herself by passing her clothes between her legs to the other side, perform al-Zuhr and al-'Asr Salat (prayer). She then must wait and examine if no bleeding from behind the cotton is found after al-Zuhr and al-'Asr Salat (prayers) until al-Maghrib, she must take Wudu' and perform Salat (prayer) in each time of Salat (prayer) as long as the piece of cotton is not disposed. If cotton is disposed and bleeding is found, she must take Ghusl (bath), but if cotton is disposed and no bleeding is found, she must take Wudu' and perform Salat (prayer). She is not required to take Ghusl (bath).' He (the Imam) said, 'If bleeding emerges outside of the cotton placed inside, like perspiration and does not cease, she must take Ghusl (bath) every day and night three times and fill with cotton, then perform Salat (prayer). She must take Ghusl (bath) for the morning Salat (prayer), then take Ghusl (bath) for al-Zuhr and al-'Asr, and then take Ghusl (bath) for al-Maghrib and al-'Isha' Salat (prayers).' He (the Imam) said, 'A woman experiencing Istihadah (irregular menses) must also follow this procedure. If she did so Allah removes bleeding from her.'"

H 4169, Ch. 11, h 2

Ali ibn Ibrahim has narrated from his father from certain persons of his narrators from Muhammad ibn Muslim who has said the following:

"I once asked one of the Imam, *'Alayhim al-Salam*, about the case of the pregnant woman whose pregnancy has become apparent, but finds what a woman experiences because of Hayd (menses) of blood discharge. He (the Imam) said, 'It is a spilling of blood; if the discharge is a great deal and of red color, she must not perform Salat (prayer). She then needs to take Wudu' only if it is of a small amount and of yellow color.'"

H 4170, Ch. 11, h 3

A number of our people have narrated from Ahmad ibn Muhammad from Ali ibn al-Hakam from al-'Ala' from Muhammad ibn Muslim who has said the following:

"I once asked one of the two Imam, (abu Ja'far or abu 'Abd Allah), *'Alayhim al-Salam*, about the case of a pregnant woman who experiences blood discharge like the days of her Hayd (menses) every month as a straight habit. He (the Imam) said, 'She must hold herself back from Salat (prayer) like in days of her Hayd (menses), and when she is clean then perform Salat (prayer).'"

H 4171, Ch. 11, h 4

Muhammad ibn 'Isma'il has narrated from al-Fadl ibn Shadhan from Muhammad ibn al-Husayn all from Safwan ibn Yahya from 'Abd al-Rahman ibn al-Hajjaj who has said the following:

"I once asked abu al-Hassan, *'Alayhi al-Salam*, about the case of a pregnant woman who experiences blood discharge even when she is pregnant, like before every month, should she stop performing Salat (prayer)? He (the Imam) said, 'She must stop Salat if it continues.'"

H 4172, Ch. 11, h 5

A number of our people have narrated from Ahmad ibn Muhammad from and Abu Dawud all from al-Husayn ibn Sa'id from al-Nadr ibn Suwayd and Fadalah ibn Ayyub who has said the following:

"Abu 'Abd Allah, *'Alayhi al-Salam*, was asked about a pregnant woman who experiences blood discharge whether she must stop performing Salat (prayer)? He (the Imam) said, 'Yes, she must stop performing Salat (prayer). Sometimes pregnant women also discharge blood.'"

H 4173, Ch. 11, h 6

Ali ibn Ibrahim has narrated from his father from ibn abu 'Umayr from Sulayman ibn Khalid who has said the following:

"I once asked abu 'Abd Allah, *'Alayhi al-Salam*, about the case of a pregnant woman, saying, 'I pray to Allah to keep my soul in service for your cause, can such woman experience Hayd (menses)? He (the Imam) said, 'Yes, because the child's food in mother's womb is blood. It (blood) may exceed the amount of food for the child. It (the excess) is then repelled. When this happens, Salat (prayer) becomes unlawful for her.'"

In another Hadith it is said that it causes a birth delay.

Chapter 12 - Blood Because of Childbirth

H 4174, Ch. 12, h 1

Ali ibn Ibrahim has narrated from his father from ibn abu 'Umayr from 'Umar ibn 'Udhaynah from al-Fudayl ibn Yasar from Zurarah who has said the following:

"One of the two Imam, *'Alayhim al-Salam*, concerning how many days of Salat (prayer), a woman during her childbirth, does not need to perform, has said, 'She must not perform Salat (prayer) for a number of days which is equal to the number of her Hayd (menses) free days (10 days). Thereafter she must take Ghusl (bath) and follow the rules for Istihadah (irregular menses).'"

H 4175, Ch. 12, h 2

A number of our people have narrated from Ahmad ibn Muhammad from Ali ibn al-Hakam from 'Abd Allah ibn Bukayr from 'Abd al-Rahman ibn `A'yan who has said the following:

"I once said to him (the Imam), *'Alayhi al-Salam*, that the wife of 'Abd al-Malik gave birth. He instructed her to wait for the number of days of her Hayd (menses), then instructed her to take Ghusl (bath), fill up, wear two clean clothes and perform Salat (prayer). She said, 'My soul does not feel happy to enter the Masjid; so allow me to stay out of the Masjid and prostrate in it.' He (the Imam) said, 'The Messenger of Allah had issued such commandments and said, 'Bleeding stops and she finds cleanliness,' and Ali, *'Alayhi al-Salam*, before you had issued such commandments; once bleeding stops the woman finds herself clean. What did the woman (of your companion) do?' I replied, 'I do not know.'"

('Abd al-Malik mentioned is perhaps 'Abd al-Malik ibn `A'yan, according to al-Dhakhirah).

H 4176, Ch. 12, h 3

Ali ibn Ibrahim has narrated from his father in a marfu' the following:

"A woman once asked abu 'Abd Allah, *'Alayhi al-Salam*, saying, 'I would, because of childbirth, wait for twenty days and they gave a fatwa to wait for eighteen days. Abu 'Abd Allah, *'Alayhi al-Salam*, asked, 'Why did they give a fatwa for eighteen days?' A man then said it is because of the Hadith from the Messenger of Allah who said to Asma' bint 'Umays for the birth of Muhammad ibn abu Bakr. Abu 'Abd Allah, *'Alayhi al-Salam*, then said, 'Asma' asked the Messenger of Allah after eighteen days. Had she asked before, the Messenger of Allah would ask her to take Ghusl (bath) and do what a Mustahadah is required to do.'"

H 4177, Ch. 12, h 4

A number of our people have narrated from Ahmad ibn Muhammad and Ali ibn Ibrahim has narrated from his father and Muhammad ibn `Isma'il has narrated from al-Fadl ibn Shadhan from all from Hammad ibn 'Isa from Hariz from Zurarah who has said the following:

"I once asked him (the Imam), *'Alayhi al-Salam*, about the case of a woman who has given birth and as to when she must perform Salat (prayer). He (the Imam) said, 'She must wait for the number of days that are equal to those of her Hayd (menses). She then must examine in two days if bleeding has stopped, otherwise, she must take Ghusl (bath), fill up herself, secure it with a belt of cloths. She must perform the morning Salat (prayer) with one Ghusl (bath), Salat (prayer) of al-Zuhr and al-'Asr with one Ghusl (bath) and Salat (prayer) of al-Maghrib and al-'Isha' with one Ghusl (bath). If blood does not pass through the cotton, she can perform Salat (prayer) with one Ghusl (bath) (everyday).' I then asked about a woman experiencing Hayd (menses). He (the Imam) said, 'It is the same. If bleeding stops, otherwise, it is Istihadah and she must do what the woman after childbirth does. She must perform Salat (prayer) in all conditions; the Holy prophet, has said, 'Salat (prayer) is the pillar of your religion.'"

H 4178, Ch. 12, h 5

A number of our people have narrated from Ahmad ibn Muhammad from and abu Dawud from al-Husayn ibn Sa'id from al-Nadr ibn Suwayd from Muhammad ibn abu Hamzah from Yunus ibn Ya'qub who has said the following:

"I heard abu 'Abd Allah, *'Alayhi al-Salam*, say, 'A woman after giving birth waits for a number of days equal to those of her Hayd (menses). She then must examine, take Ghusl (bath) and perform Salat (prayer).'"

H 4179, Ch. 12, h 6

Muhammad ibn Yahya has narrated from Ahmad ibn Muhammad from ibn Faddal from ibn Bukayr from Zurarah who has said the following:

"Abu 'Abd Allah, *'Alayhi al-Salam*, has said, 'A woman for giving birth waits for the number of days of her Hayd (menses); then she must examine in two days.'"

Chapter 13 - Blood Discharge after a Woman's Experiencing Discharge-Free Period after Childbirth and Blood Discharge before Birth or after Childbirth

H 4180, Ch. 13, h 1

Muhammad ibn abu 'Abd Allah has narrated from Mu'awiyah ibn Hukaym from 'Abd Allah ibn al-Mughirah who has said the following:

"Abu al-Hassan, al-Awwal, *'Alayhi al-Salam*, was asked about a woman who after childbirth stops performing Salat (prayer) for thirty days, then finds a discharge-free period and finds blood discharge thereafter again. He (the Imam) said, 'She must stop performing Salat (prayer) because her days are those of Hayd (menses)-free period and the number of days of period of childbirth has already passed.'"

H 4181, Ch. 13, h 2

Muhammad ibn 'Isma'il has narrated from al-Fadl ibn Shadhan from and Muhammad ibn Yahya has narrated from Muhammad ibn al-Husayn all from Safwan ibn Yahya from 'Abd al-Rahman ibn al-Hajjaj who has said the following:

"I once asked abu Ibrahim, *'Alayhi al-Salam*, about the case of a woman who after giving birth waited for thirty days or more, then she becomes clean and performs Salat (prayer), then experiences blood discharge or yellowish things. He (the Imam) said, 'If it is yellowish she must take Ghusl (bath), perform Salat (prayer) and must not avoid Salat (prayer).'"

H 4182, Ch. 13, h 3

Abu Ali al-Ash'ariy has narrated from Ahmad ibn Muhammad from Ahmad ibn al-Hassan ibn Ali form 'Amr ibn Sa'id from Musaddiq ibn Sadaqah from 'Ammar ibn Musa, who has said the following:

"About the case of a woman who experiences pain of childbirth for several days or two days, then she finds yellowish discharge or blood, abu 'Abd Allah, *'Alayhi al-Salam*, has said, 'She must perform Salat (prayer) until she gives birth. If because of pain she misses Salat (prayer) and is not able to perform there is Qada' (compensatory prayer) of what is missed after she becomes clean.'"

Chapter 14 - Matters Necessary for Women during Hayd at the Times of Salat (prayer)

H 4183, Ch. 14, h 1

Ali ibn Ibrahim has narrated from his father from Hammad ibn 'Isa from Hariz from Zurarah from Muhammad ibn Muslim who has said the following:

"I once asked abu 'Abd Allah, *'Alayhi al-Salam*, about a woman experiencing Hayd (menses) who takes Ghusl (bath) on Friday and speaks of Allah. He (the Imam) said, 'Ghusl (bath) is unhelpful but she can take Wudu' at the time for Salat (prayer), then face the direction of Makkah and speak of Allah.'"

H 4184, Ch. 14, h 2

Muhammad ibn 'Isma'il has narrated from al-Fadl ibn Shadhan from ibn abu 'Umayr and Hammad from Mu'awiyah ibn 'Ammar who has said the following:

"Abu 'Abd Allah, *'Alayhi al-Salam*, has said, 'A woman experiencing Hayd (menses) can take Wudu' when she wants to eat, and when it is time for Salat (prayer) take Wudu', face the direction of Ka'bah say Tahlil, (no one deserves worship except Allah). Takbir (Allah is great beyond description) and recite from al-Quran and speak of Allah, most Majestic, most Glorious.'"

H 4185, Ch. 14, h 3

Ali ibn Ibrahim has narrated from his father from ibn abu 'Umayr from 'Ammar ibn Marwan from Zayd al-Shahham who has said the following:

"I once heard abu 'Abd Allah, *'Alayhi al-Salam*, say, 'A woman experiencing Hayd (menses) should take Wudu' at the time of each Salat (prayer), face the direction of Ka'bah and speak of Allah for a period of time equal to a period of time Salat (prayer) is performed.'"

H 4186, Ch. 14, h 4

Ali ibn Ibrahim has narrated from his father and Muhammad ibn 'Isma'il from al-Fadl ibn Shadhan all from Hammad ibn 'Isa from Hariz from Zurarah who has said the following:

"Abu Ja'far, *'Alayhi al-Salam*, has said, 'Performing Salat (prayer) during a woman's experiencing Hayd (menses) is not permissible. However, she should take Wudu' as it is taken for Salat (prayer) at the time of each Salat (prayer), sit in clean place and speak of Allah, most Majestic, most Glorious, glorify Him, praise Him and say Tahlil, (no one deserves worship except Allah) for a period of time to perform Salat (prayer), and then go for her other needs.'"

Chapter 15 - Women Find Hayd Blood after the Coming of the Time for a Salat (Prayer) Before Performing It Or Become

Clean Before the Coming of the Time for a Salat (Prayer) But Are Too Lazy for Ghusl (bath)

H 4187, Ch. 15, h 1

Muhammad ibn Yahya has narrated from Ahmad ibn Muhammad from ibn Mahbub from al-Fadl ibn Yunus who has said the following:

"I once asked abu al-Hassan, al-Awwal, *'Alayhi al-Salam*, about the case of a woman who finds herself Hayd (menses) free just before sunset. What must she do for Salat (prayer)? He (the Imam) said, 'If she finds herself Hayd (menses) free after four steps have passed from noon-time, she only performs al-'Asr Salat (prayer). It is because the time for al-Zuhr Salat (prayer) arrived when she was not Hayd (menses) free and it passed when she still was not Hayd (menses) free so it is not obligatory for her to perform al-Zuhr Salat (prayer). It is because Allah has exempted her from Salat (prayer) when she was most of the time bleeding.' He (the Imam) then said, 'If a woman finds blood discharge after four steps from the time for al-Zuhr passed, she must stop performing Salat (prayer). However, when she becomes Hayd (menses) free she must compensatory prayer that al-Zuhr Salat (prayer) because it was time for al-Zuhr when she was Hayd (menses)-free. It (time) passed while she was Hayd (menses)-free, so she lost al-Zuhr Salat (prayer). Therefore she must compensatory prayer it.'"

H 4188, Ch. 15, h 2

Muhammad ibn Yahya has narrated from Ahmad ibn Muhammad from al-Hajjal from Tha'labah from Mu'ammar ibn Yahya who has said the following:

"I once asked abu Ja'far, *'Alayhi al-Salam*, about the case of a woman experiencing Hayd (menses) becomes clean at the time of al-'Asr must she perform al-Salat (prayer) before (al-'Asr)? He (the Imam) said, 'No, she is required to perform only al-Salat (prayer) in the time of which she has become clean.'"

H 4189, Ch. 15, h 3

Ali ibn Ibrahim has narrated from his father from ibn Mahbub from ibn Ri'ab from abu 'Ubaydah who has said the following:

"He (the Imam), *'Alayhi al-Salam*, has said, 'If a woman finds herself clean when it has become time for a Salat (prayer) but she delays Ghusl (bath) until it become time for another Salat (prayer), she owes Qada' (compensatory prayer) of Salat (prayer) that is so missed. If she is clean in the time of a Salat (prayer) and delays to perform it until it becomes time of another Salat (prayer), then she experiences Hayd (menses) she owes Qada' (compensatory prayer) of Salat (prayer) that is missed due to her neglect.'"

H 4190, Ch. 15, h 4

Ibn Mahbub has narrated from ibn Ri'ab from 'Ubayd ibn Zurarah who has said the following:

"Abu 'Abd Allah, *'Alayhi al-Salam*, has said, 'Any woman who finds herself clean and is able to take Ghusl (bath) in time for Salat (prayer) but neglects it until it becomes time for another Salat (prayer), she owes Qada' (compensatory prayer) of Salat (prayer) she has neglected. If she finds herself clean in the time of a Salat (prayer), begins to prepare, but the time for that Salat (prayer) expires and it becomes time for another Salat (prayer), Qada' (compensatory prayer) of such Salat (prayer) is not obligatory on her. She must perform only that Salat (prayer) for which it has become time.'"

H 4191, Ch. 15, h 5
Ibn Mahbub has narrated from ibn Ri'ab from abu Dawud who has said the following:
"I once asked abu Ja'far, *'Alayhi al-Salam*, about the case of a woman who is in Salat (prayer) of al-Zuhr, of which two Rak'at are complete, and finds blood of Hayd (menses). He (the Imam) said, 'She must stop and move away from Masjid without performing the remaining two Rak'at. If she finds blood during her performing al-Maghrib when two Rak'at are complete, she must move away from Masjid, and when she becomes clean, she must perform Qada' (compensatory prayer) of one Rak'at missed of that Salat (prayer) of al-Maghrib.'"

Chapter 16 - Women Feel Hayd during Salat (Prayer)

H 4192, Ch. 16, h 1
Muhammad ibn Yahya has narrated from Muhammad ibn Ahmad from Ahmad ibn al-Hassan ibn Ali from 'Amr ibn Sa'id from Musaddiq ibn Sadaqah from 'Ammar ibn Musa who has said the following:
"I once asked abu 'Abd Allah, *'Alayhi al-Salam*, about the case of a woman who thinks it is blood discharge during performing Salat (prayer). He (the Imam) said, 'She must feel with her hand. If it is blood discharge, she must discontinue, and if she does not find anything, she must complete her Salat (prayer).'"

(The above Hadith is best explained in the form of fatwa.)

Chapter 17 - Women Must Make-up-for Fasting Because of Hayd but Not Salat (Prayer)

H 4193, Ch. 17, h 1
Al-Husayn ibn Muhammad al-Ash'ariy has narrated from Mu'alla' ibn Muhammad from al-Washsha' from Aban from those who narrated to him has said the following:
"Abu Ja'far, and abu 'Abd Allah, *'Alayhim al-Salam*, have said, 'Woman experiencing Hayd (menses) must compensatory prayer fasting but not for Salat (prayer).'"

H 4194, Ch. 17, h 2
Ali ibn Ibrahim has narrated from his father from ibn abu 'Umayr from al-Hassan ibn Rashid who has said the following:
"I once asked abu 'Abd Allah, *'Alayhi al-Salam*, about the case of a woman who experiences Hayd (menses) if she is required to perform Qada' (compensatory prayer) of Salat (prayer) she has missed. He (the Imam) said, 'No, she is not required.' I asked if she is required to do Qada' (compensatory prayer) of fasting. He (the Imam) said, 'Yes, she is required to fast.' I then asked, 'From where has this come?' He (the Imam) said, 'The first one who used analogy was Iblis (Satan).'"

H 4195, Ch. 17, h 3

Ali ibn Ibrahim has narrated from his father from ibn abu 'Umayr from ibn 'Udhaynah from Zurarah who has said the following:

"I once asked abu Ja'far, *'Alayhi al-Salam*, about a woman who experiences Hayd (menses). I asked about Qada' (compensatory prayer) of Salat (prayer) she has missed and that of fast. He (the Imam) said, 'She is not required to perform Qada' (compensatory prayer) of Salat (prayer) but she is required to do Qada' (compensatory prayer) of fast of the month of Ramadan.' He (the Imam) then turned to me and said that the Messenger of Allah would give such instructions to Fatimah, *'Alayha al-Salam*, and she would instruct the believing women so.'"

H 4196, Ch. 17, h 4

Al-Husayn ibn Muhammad has narrated from Mu'alla' from al-Washsha' from Aban ibn 'Uthman from 'Isma'il al- -Ju'fiy who has said the following:

"I once said to abu Ja'far, *'Alayhi al-Salam*, that al-Mughirah ibn Sa'id has narrated from you that you have said, 'A woman is required to perform Qada' (compensatory prayer) of Salat (prayer) she has missed when experiencing Hayd (menses). He (the Imam) said, 'What has happened to him, may Allah not accord him. The wife of 'Imran made a vow about what was in her belly to be dedicated. What is dedicated to Masjid enters it then does not come out whereof forever. When she gave birth she said, 'My Cherisher, I have given birth to a female. . . . and male is not like a female.' When she gave birth she entered the Masjid, prophets cooperated with her and the raffle came out in the name of Zakariya' who took charge of her upbringing. She did not come out of the Masjid until she was an adult. When she became what women become, she moved out. Was she able to perform Qada' (compensatory prayer) of the days of Salat (prayer) she was out of the Masjid while she must have remained in the Masjid forever?'" (The terms of dedication may not allow her to perform the form of Salat (prayer) Qada' (compensatory prayer) required from her).

Chapter 18 - Women's Reading the Holy Quran During Hayd or Child-birth

H 4197, Ch. 18, h 1

Muhammad ibn 'Isma'il has narrated from al-Fadl ibn Shadhan from ibn abu 'Umayr and Hammad from Mu'awiyah ibn 'Ammar who has said the following:

"Abu 'Abd Allah, *'Alayhi al-Salam*, has said, 'Women while experiencing Hayd (menses) have permission to recite al-Quran and praise Allah.'"

H 4198, Ch. 18, h 2

Ali ibn Ibrahim has narrated from his father from ibn abu 'Umayr from Zayd al-Shahham who has said the following:

"Abu 'Abd Allah, *'Alayhi al-Salam*, has said, 'Women experiencing Hayd (menses), childbirth and one involved in sexual activities (because of which Ghusl (bath) is obligatory) can read al-Quran.'"

H 4199, Ch. 18, h 3

Muhammad ibn Yahya has narrated from Ahmad ibn Muhammad from al-Hassan ibn Mahbub from ibn Ri'ab from abu 'Ubaydah who has said the following:

"I once asked abu 'Abd Allah, *'Alayhi al-Salam*, about the case of a woman who experiences Hayd (menses) whether she can listen to recitation of the verses of al-Quran that requires prostration. He (the Imam) said, 'If it is of al-'Aza'im kind, she must prostrate when she listens to it.'"

H 4200, Ch. 18, h 4

Muhammad ibn 'Isma'il has narrated from al-Fadl ibn Shadhan from Safwan ibn Yahya from Mansur ibn Hazim who has said the following:

"I once asked abu 'Abd Allah, *'Alayhi al-Salam*, about the case of al-Ta'widh (protective talisman) which women hang on themselves. He (the Imam) said, 'Yes, they can do so if it is incased with leather, silver, tube or iron.'"

H 4201, Ch. 18, h 5

Ali ibn Ibrahim has narrated from his father from ibn abu 'Umayr from Dawud ibn Farqad who has said the following:

"I once asked abu 'Abd Allah, *'Alayhi al-Salam*, about the case of al-Ta'widh (protective sacred expressions from Quran or names of Allah) which women hang on themselves. He (the Imam) said, 'Yes, it is not harmful.' He (the Imam) said, 'She can read, write but must not touch.' It is narrated that she cannot write al-Quran.'"

Chapter 19 - Women during Hayd Can Pick up Things from a Masjid but Must Not Leave Anything Therein

H 4202, Ch, 19, h 1

Muhammad ibn Yahya has narrated from Ahmad ibn Muhammad from Hammad ibn 'Isa from Hariz from Zurarah who has said the following:

"I once asked Abu Ja'far, *'Alayhi al-Salam*, 'How is it that women during their experiencing Hayd (menses) can pick up things from Masjid, but cannot leave anything therein?' He (the Imam) said, 'It is because such women can leave what is in their hands in other places and cannot take what is there (in the Masjid) except from it (Masjid).'"

(The above Hadith is best explained in the form of fatwa.)

Chapter 20 - Women's Hayd (menses) Stops, Comes Again and the Time of Menopause

H 4203, Ch. 20, h 1

Abu Ali al-Ash'ariy has narrated from Muhammad ibn 'Abd al-Jabbar from Safwan ibn Yahya from al-'Is ibn al-Qasim who has said the following:

"I once asked abu 'Abd Allah, *'Alayhi al-Salam*, about the case of a woman whose Hayd (menses) stops for years and it comes back again. He (the Imam) said, 'She must not perform Salat (prayer) until she is Hayd (menses) free.'"

H 4204, Ch. 20, h 2

Ali has narrated from Muhammad from Sahl ibn Ziyad from Ahmad ibn Muhammad from ibn abu Nasr from certain persons of our people who has said the following:

"Abu 'Abd Allah, *'Alayhi al-Salam*, has said, 'Menopause happens at the age of fifty.' It is also narrated that it is at the age of sixty."

H 4205, Ch. 20, h 3

A number of our people have narrated from Ahmad ibn Muhammad from al-Hassan ibn Tarif from ibn abu 'Umayr from certain persons of our people who has said the following:

"Abu 'Abd Allah, *'Alayhi al-Salam*, has said, 'When a woman becomes fifty years old, she does not see anything red (experience Hayd (menses)) unless she is from Quraysh.'"

H 4206, Ch. 20, h 4

Muhammad ibn 'Isma'il has narrated from al-Fadl ibn Shadhan from Safwan ibn Yahya from 'Abd al-Rahman ibn al-Hajjaj who has said the following:

"Abu 'Abd Allah, *'Alayhi al-Salam*, has said, 'Menopause happens at the age of fifty years.'"

Chapter 21 - Women's Using Medicine to Have Hayd (menses) after It Stops

H 4207, Ch. 21, h 1

A number of our people have narrated from Ahmad ibn Muhammad from ibn Mahbub from Rifa'ah ibn Musa al-Nakhkhas who has said the following:

"I once asked Musa ibn Ja'far, *'Alayhi al-Salam*, about the case of a slave-girl I purchased. She lives with me for several months without experiencing Hayd (menses) but not because of old age. Other women examine her and tell me that she is not pregnant. Can I have intercourse with her? He (the Imam) said, 'Hayd (menses) is sometimes blocked by air without pregnancy. It is not harmful if you touch her vagina.' I then asked if she is pregnant what then? He (the Imam) said, 'If you like you can benefit from other than vagina.'"

H 4208, Ch. 21, h 2

Ibn Mahbub has narrated from Rifa'ah who has said the following:

"I once said to abu 'Abd Allah, *'Alayhi al-Salam*, that I may purchase a slave-girl. Her Hayd (menses) stops because of spoiled blood or some kind of air in her womb, and she uses medicine for cure and her Hayd (menses) begins on the same day. I do not know if it is because of pregnancy or for other reasons, is it (use of medicine) permissible? He (the Imam) said, 'You must not (allow to) do so.' I then said that her Hayd (menses) has stopped for a month. Were it because of pregnancy, it would be a seed like the seed of man for which he may use contraceptives. He (the Imam) said, 'If the seed falls inside the womb, it changes into a lump, then into flesh, then into what Allah wills. If the seed (semen) falls in places other than the womb nothing is created thereof. You must not give her medicine, when her Hayd (menses) stops, for a month and her time of Hayd (menses) passes.'" (Fatwa best explains the above Hadith; it deals with several issues such as contraceptives, liability for abortion and the stages of fetuses.)

H 4209, Ch. 21, h 3

Muhammad ibn Yahya has narrated from Ahmad ibn Muhammad from ibn Mahbub from 'Abd Malik ibn 'Atiyyah from Dawud ibn Farqad who has said the following:

"I once asked abu 'Abd Allah, *'Alayhi al-Salam*, about a man who buys a slave-girl who possesses awareness but does not experience Hayd (menses) while in his possession until six months and she is not pregnant. He (the Imam) said, 'If slave-girls similar to her experience Hayd (menses) and it is not because of old age, it is a defect and a reason to revoke the contract of sale.'"

Chapter 22 - Using Dye during Hayd (menses)

H 4210, Ch. 22, h 1

A number of our people have narrated from Ahmad ibn Muhammad from Muhammad ibn Sahl ibn al-Yasa' from his father who has said the following:

"I once asked abu al-Hassan, *'Alayhi al-Salam*, about the case of a woman who uses dye during her Hayd (menses). He (the Imam) said, 'It is not harmful.'"

H 4211, Ch. 22, h 2

Ahmad ibn Muhammad has narrated from al-Husayn ibn Sa'id from al-Nadr ibn Suwayd from Muhammad ibn abu Hamzah who has said the following:

"I once asked abu Ibrahim, *'Alayhi al-Salam*, if a woman experiencing Hayd (menses) can use dyes. He (the Imam) said, 'Yes, she can do so.'"

Chapter 23 - Washing Clothes of Women during Hayd

H 4212, Ch. 23, h 1

Muhammad ibn Yahya has narrated from Ahmad ibn Muhammad from ibn Mahbub from Hisham ibn Salim from Sawrah ibn Kulayb who has said the following:

"I once asked abu 'Abd Allah, *'Alayhi al-Salam*, about the case of a woman experiencing Hayd (menses) if she must wash her clothes which she has used during her Hayd (menses). He (the Imam) said, 'She must wash only what has come in contact with blood, and leave the rest alone.' I then said, 'What happens if she perspires?' He (the Imam) said, 'Perspiration is not of Hayd (menses).'"

H 4213, Ch. 23, h 2

Ali ibn Ibrahim has narrated from his father from ibn abu 'Umayr from 'Uqbah ibn Muhriz from Ishaq ibn 'Ammar who has said the following:

"Abu 'Abd Allah, *'Alayhi al-Salam*, has said, 'Women experiencing Hayd (menses) can perform Salat (prayer) in their clothes if they have not come in contact with blood.'"

H 4214, Ch. 23, h 3

Muhammad ibn Yahya has narrated from Ahmad ibn Muhammad from al-Husayn ibn Sa'id from al-Qasim ibn Muhammad from Ali ibn abu Hamzah from virtuous servant (of Allah) who has said the following:

"Once a mother of the child of his father asked him (the Imam), *'Alayhi al-Salam*, saying, 'I pray to Allah to keep my soul in service for your cause, I like to ask you a question but I feel shy. He (the Imam) said, 'Ask and do not feel shy.' She said, 'My clothes have come in contact with blood of Hayd (menses) and I wash them, but its marks do not go away. He (the Imam) said, 'Dye them with Mishq (a kind of dye) to mix its color and it will go away.'"

Chapter 24 - Women During Hayd Pick up Prayer Rug or Water

H 4215, Ch. 24, h 1

Muhammad ibn `Isma'il has narrated from al-Fadl ibn Shadhan from ibn abu 'Umayr from Mu'awiyah ibn 'Ammar who has said the following:

"I once asked abu 'Abd Allah, *'Alayhi al-Salam*, about the woman who during her Hayd (menses) brings water for the man. He (the Imam) said, 'Wives of the Holy prophet, would pour water on him during their experiencing Hayd (menses) and furnish for him prayer mat.'"

End of the book of Hayd (menses) of al-Kafi, all praise belongs to Allah, Lord of the worlds, O Allah grant compensation to Muhammad and his family worthy of their services to Your cause

In the Name of Allah, the Beneficient, the Merciful

Part Three: The Book on Dying People

Chapter 1 - Causes of Death and that Believing People May Die by any Manner of Dying

H 4216, Ch. 1, h 1

Ali ibn Ibrahim has narrated from his father from ibn Faddal from those who narrated to him from Sa'd ibn Tarif who has said the following:

"Abu Ja'far, *'Alayhi al-Salam*, has said, 'People would just drop dead. Ibrahim (Abraham), *'Alayhi al-Salam*, in his time pleaded before Allah to create a cause for death so the dying person receives rewards and the grieving people find solace. Allah, the Majestic, the Glorious, then sent al-Mum, which is a kind of fever causing hallucination and thereafter He sent medicine.'"

H 4217, Ch. 1, h 2

Muhammad ibn Yahya has narrated from Ahmad ibn Muhammad ibn 'Isa from ibn Faddal from 'Asim ibn Humayd from Sa'd ibn Tarif who has said the following:

"Abu Ja'far, *'Alayhi al-Salam*, has said, 'People would just drop dead. Ibrahim (Abraham), *'Alayhi al-Salam*, pleaded before Allah, 'Would that You had created a cause for death to be recognized thereby and for grieving people to receive condolence.' Allah, the Majestic, the Glorious, then sent al-Mum, which is a kind of fever causing hallucination and thereafter He sent medicine."

H 4218, Ch. 1, h 3

Muhammad has narrated from Ahmad ibn Muhammad from Muhammad ibn Isma'il from Sa'dan ibn Abd Allah ibn Sinan who has said the following: *'Alayhi al-Salam*, saying:

"I heard abu 'Abd Allah, *'Alayhi al-Salam*, say that fever is the harbinger of death; it is the prison of Allah on earth and the share of a believing person from the fire."

H 4219, Ch. 1, h 4

Ali ibn Ibrahim has narrated from his father from ibn Faddal, from Muhammad ibn al-Husayn from Muhammad ibn al-Fudayl, from Abd al-Rahman ibn Yazid who has said the following:

"Abu 'Abd Allah, *'Alayhi al-Salam*, has said that the Messenger of Allah has said, 'Prophet David died suddenly on a Saturday and birds provided shadow over his body. Moses died in the wilderness where he had lost his way. A voice cried from the sky, "Moses has died! Who is he that does not die?"'"

H 4220, Ch. 1, h 5

A number of our people have narrated from Sahl ibn Ziyad from Ahmad ibn Muhammad ibn abu Nasr and al-Hassan ibn Mahbub from abu Jamilah from Jabir who has said the following:

"Abu Ja'far, *'Alayhi al-Salam*, has said, 'The Messenger of Allah has said, 'A sudden death compensates (for the short comings) of a believing person but it is a regrettable grip for an unbeliever.'"

H 4221, Ch. 1, h 6

Muhammad ibn Yahya has narrated from Ahmad ibn Muhammad or someone other than him from Ali ibn Hadid from who has said the following:

"Al-Rida, *'Alayhi al-Salam*, has said that most of our followers die from widespread stomach (internal) illness."

H 4222, Ch. 1, h 7

Muhammad ibn Yahya has narrated from Musa ibn al-Hassan from al-Haytham ibn al-Masruq from a shaykh of our people called abu 'Abd Allah from a man who has said the following:

"Abu 'Abd Allah, *'Alayhi al-Salam*, has said that the Messenger of Allah has said, 'Fever is a harbinger of death and a prison of Allah on earth. Its heat is from hell and that is the share of a believing person (instead) of hellfire.'"

H 4223, Ch. 1, h 8

Muhammad ibn Yahya has narrated from Muhammad ibn al-Husayn from Safwan from Mu'awiyah ibn 'Ammar from Najiyah who has said the following:

"Abu Ja'far, *'Alayhi al-Salam* has said, 'A believing person may die by any form of death and suffer from any form of suffering; however, he does not kill himself.'"

H 4224, Ch. 1, h 9

Humayd ibn Ziyad has narrated from al-Hassan ibn Muhammad from Wuhayb ibn Hafs from abu Basir who has said the following:

"Once I asked abu 'Abd Allah, *'Alayhi al-Salam*, about the death of a believing person. The Imam said, 'A believing person may die by any form of death, such as by drowning, or collapse of a house, by beasts or thunderous lightening but not when speaking of Allah.'"

H 4225, Ch. 1, h 10

A number of our people have narrated from Sahl ibn Ziyad from Muhammad ibn Sinan from 'Uthman al-Nawwa' from those whom he has mentioned (in his book) who has said the following:

"Abu 'Abd Allah, *'Alayhi al-Salam*, has said that Allah, the Majestic, the Glorious, places a believing person under any kind of test and trial and causes him or her to die by any form of death but He does not cause him or her to suffer the loss of reason. Consider the case of prophet Ayyub, how Satan controlled his property, children and family and all things that were his, but not his reason. It remained with him so he could worship thereby and maintain his belief in Allah, the Majestic, the Glorious."

Chapter 2 - The Reward for a Person Suffering from Illness

H 4226, Ch. 2, h 1

A number of our people have narrated from Ahmad ibn Muhammad from ibn Mahbub from 'Abd Allah ibn Sinan who has said the following:

"Abu 'Abd Allah, *'Alayhi al-Salam*, has said that once the Messenger of Allah raised his head to the heaven and smiled. He was asked, 'O Messenger of Allah, we saw you. Why did you raise your head to the heaven and smile?' He then replied, 'I was amazed when I saw two angels come down from the heaven looking for a believing, virtuous servant (of Allah) in the place he performs his prayers, so they can record his deeds of that day and night but they could not find him there. They then ascended to the heaven saying, "Lord, we looked for Your so and so believing servant in the place of his prayer to record the deeds of his day and night, but could not find him there. However, we found him (tied down) with Your ropes."' Allah, the Majestic, the Glorious, said, "Write down for My servant (a reward) equal to that of his good deeds that he normally did in his day and night when free of (illness due to) My ropes. Do so as long as he is tied down with My ropes; I must write down for him when tied down with My ropes (suffering from illness) a reward equal to the reward of the good deeds that he did when in good health.""'"

H 4227, Ch. 2, h 2

Ali ibn Ibrahim has narrated from his father from 'Amr ibn 'Uthman from al-Mufaddal ibn Salih from Jabir who has said the following:

"Abu Ja'far, *'Alayhi al-Salam*, has said that the Holy Prophet has said, 'When a Muslim is weakened due to old age, Allah, the Majestic, the Glorious, commands an angel to write down for him of good deeds equal to what he did when young, vigorous and in good health. Similarly, when he becomes ill, Allah commands an angel to write down for him during his illness of good deeds equal to what he performed in good health up to the time Allah raises him and takes him (away) from this life. In the case of an unbeliever, in his illness Allah writes down against him of evil deeds equal to what he would commit when in good health.'"

H 4228, Ch. 2, h 3

Ali ibn Ibrahim has narrated from his father from 'Abd Allah ibn al-Mughirah from 'Abd Allah ibn Sinan who has said the following:

"This is a narration of abu 'Abd Allah, *'Alayhi al-Salam*, from the Messenger of Allah. He (the Messenger of Allah) has said, 'Allah, the Majestic, the Glorious, says to the angel guarding a believing person in his illness, "Write down for him (of good deeds) what you would write down for him of good deeds in his good health; it is I who have tied him down with My rope."'"

H 4229, Ch. 2, h 4

Ali has narrated from his father from 'Abd Allah ibn al-Mughirah from abu al-Sabbah who has said the following:

"Abu Ja'far, *'Alayhi al-Salam*, has said, 'Passing a sleepless night due to an illness is more rewarding than a whole year worshipping.'"

H 4230, Ch. 2, h 5

A number of our people have narrated from Sahl ibn Ziyad from ibn Mahbub from 'Abd al-Hamid who has said the following:

"Abu 'Abd Allah, *'Alayhi al-Salam*, has said that when the two guard angels of a person suffering from illness ascend to heavens every evening, the Lord, Most Holy, Most Blessed, asks them, 'What did you write down for My servant in his illness?' They will say, 'We wrote down his complaints.' The Lord will say, 'It is not fair on My part to imprison one of My servants in a prison of My prisons without allowing him to complain.' He will then say, 'Write down for My servant of good deeds equal to what he performed when in good health and do not write down against him any bad deeds until I release him from My prison; he is in one of my prisons.'"

H 4231, Ch. 2, h 6

Muhammad ibn Yahya has narrated from Ahmad ibn Muhammad ibn 'Isa from al-Husayn ibn Sa'id from al-Nadr ibn Suwayd from Durust from Zurarah who has said the following:

"One of the two Imam, *'Alayhim al-Salam,* has said that passing a sleepless night due to an illness or pain is more excellent and of greater reward than worshipping for a whole year."

H 4232, Ch. 2, h 7

It is narrated from the narrator above from Ahmad from Ahmad ibn Muhammad ibn abu Nasr from Durust who has said the following:

"I heard abu Ibrahim, *'Alayhi al-Salam,* say, 'When a believing person becomes ill, Allah, the Majestic, the Glorious, sends revelation to the guard angel on his left side that says, "Do not write any evil thing against My servant until he is in My prison and is tied down in My heavy impediment." He then sends revelation to the guard angel on his right side that says, "Write down for My servant of good deeds equal to what he would perform when in good health."'"

H 4233, Ch. 2, h 8

A number of our people have narrated from Ahmad ibn Muhammad, from ibn Mahbub from Hafs ibn Ghiyath from Hajjaj who has said the following:

"Abu Ja'far, *'Alayhi al-Salam*, has said, 'If one's body does not become ill, he is vigorously happy. There is nothing good in a body that never becomes ill even by a strong (reason for) illness.'"

H 4234, Ch. 2, h 9

Abu Ali al-Ash'ariy has narrated from Muhammad ibn Hassan from Muhammad ibn Ali from Muhammad ibn al-Fudayl from abu Hamzah who has said the following:

"Abu Ja'far, *'Alayhi al-Salam*, has said, 'One night's suffering from fever is equal in reward to worshipping for a whole year, suffering from a fever for two nights is more rewarding than worshipping for two years, and the reward for suffering from fever for three nights is greater than the reward for worshipping up to seventy years. I then asked, 'What happens if one does not live for seventy years?' The Imam said, 'Then it is for his mother and father.' I then asked, 'What happens if they do not live for seventy years?' The Imam said, 'Then it is for his relatives.' I then asked, 'What happens if they do not live for seventy years?' The Imam said, 'Then it is for his neighbors.'"

H 4235, Ch. 2, h 10

Muhammad ibn Yahya has narrated from Muhammad ibn al-Husayn from al-Hakam ibn Miskin from Muhammad ibn Marwan who has said the following:

"Abu 'Abd Allah, *'Alayhi al-Salam*, has said that suffering from fever for one night is expiation (for the sins) before and thereafter."

Chapter 3 - Another Chapter on the Same Subject

H 4236, Ch. 3, h 1

Abu Ali al-Ash'ariy has narrated from Muhammad ibn Salim from Ahmad ibn al-Nadr from 'Amr ibn Shamir from Jabir who has said the following:

"Abu Ja'far, *'Alayhi al-Salam*, has said, 'The Messenger of Allah has said, 'Allah, the Majestic, the Glorious, says, "If one remains ill for three days and does not complain about it to anyone of his visitors, I change his flesh into a better flesh and his blood into a better blood. If I give him good health, I give him a good health free from sin. If I take him (away) from this life, I take him into My mercy.""""

H 4237, Ch. 3, h 2

Ali ibn Ibrahim has narrated from his father from certain persons of his people from abu Hamzah who has said the following:

"Abu Ja'far, *'Alayhi al-Salam*, has said, 'Allah, Most Holy, Most blessed, says, "Any servant whom I test by an affliction and who does not complain about it before any of his visitors, I most certainly change his flesh into a better flesh and his blood into a better blood. If, however, I take him (away) from this life, I take him into My mercy but if he lives he lives free of sin.""""

H 4238, Ch. 3, h 3

Al-Husayn ibn Muhammad has narrated from 'Abd Allah ibn 'Amir from Ali ibn Mahziyar from al-Hassan ibn Fadl from Ghalib ibn 'Uthman from Bashir al-Dahhan who has said the following:

"This a narration of abu 'Abd Allah, *'Alayhi al-Salam*. He (the Imam) has said that Allah, the Majestic, the Glorious, says, 'Any one of my servants whom I put to test with an affliction and who does not complain about it before any of his visitors for three days, I change his flesh into a better flesh. I change his blood into a better blood and his skin into a better skin. If I keep him living he does so free from sin and if he dies he does so in My mercy.'"

H 4239, Ch. 3, h 4

Humayd ibn Ziyad has narrated from al-Hassan ibn Ali al-Kindiy from Ahmad ibn al-Hassan al-Mithamiy from a man who has said the following:

"Abu 'Abd Allah, *'Alayhi al-Salam*, has said that if one becomes ill in a night and accepts it in the way it has come, Allah, the Majestic, the Glorious, on the other hand, writes down for him the reward for sixty years of worship. I (the narrator) then asked, 'What is the meaning of "accepts it?"' The Imam said, 'He does not complain before any of his visitors against his illness.'"

H 4240, Ch. 3, h 5

A number of our people have narrated from Ahmad ibn abu 'Abd Allah from al-'Arzamiy from his father who has said the following:

"Abu 'Abd Allah, *'Alayhi al-Salam*, has said that if a person becomes ill in a night, welcomes the night with whatever it has brought and gives thanks to Allah for that, it will be equal in reward to sixty years of worshipping.'

"I then asked, 'What is the meaning of "whatever it has brought?" He (the Imam) said, 'The patient exercises patience and does not complain about what he has experienced in that night and in the morning thanks and praises Allah for everything that happened to him that night.'"

H 4241, Ch. 3, h 6

Ali ibn Ibrahim has narrated from his father from ibn abu 'Umayr from certain persons of his people who have said the following:

"Abu 'Abd Allah, *'Alayhi al-Salam*, has said, 'If one becomes ill for three days and does not inform anyone about it, Allah, the Majestic, the Glorious, changes his flesh into a better flesh, his blood into a better blood, his skin into a better skin and his hair into better hair.' I then asked, 'May Allah keep my soul in the service of your cause, how does He do it?' He said, 'He changes it into flesh, blood, hair and skin which has not committed any sin.'"

Chapter 4 - The Limits of Complaints

H 4242, Ch. 4, h 1

Ali ibn Ibrahim has narrated from his father from ibn abu 'Umayr from Jamil ibn Salih who has said the following:

"Abu 'Abd Allah, *'Alayhi al-Salam*, on being asked about the limits of (negative) complaints against an illness by the patient, the Imam said that if a man says, 'I have fever today and last night I did not sleep restfully' and what he says is true, it is not a complaint. A (negative) complaint is if one says, 'I have suffered like no other person has suffered and I am placed in trial as no other person is.' Just saying that one could not sleep restfully last night and that he has fever today is not complaining against an illness."

Chapter 5 - A Patient's Giving Permission to His Visitors

H 4243, Ch. 5, h 1

Ali ibn Ibrahim has narrated from his father from ibn Mahbub from abu Wallad al-Hannat from 'Abd Allah ibn Sinan who has said the following:

"I heard abu 'Abd Allah, *'Alayhi al-Salam*, say, 'If one among you becomes ill, he should allow his brothers in belief to visit him during his illness, so that he may receive reward for it (for giving permission to visitors) and they may also receive reward for their visit.' He (the Imam) was asked, 'Their receiving reward for their visit is understandable, but how can he receive reward?' The Imam then said, 'He is rewarded because of giving them an opportunity to visit him. For this ten good deeds are written for him, ten degrees promoted and ten of his bad deeds are deleted.'"

H 4244, Ch. 5, h 2

Muhammad ibn Yahya has narrated from Ahmad ibn Muhammad ibn 'Isa from 'Abd al-'Aziz al-Muhtadiy from Yunus who has said the following:

"Abu al-Hassan, *'Alayhi al-Salam*, has said, 'If one of you becomes ill he should allow people to visit him; everyone's prayer has a chance to receive acceptance.'"

H 4245, Ch. 5, h 3

Muhammad ibn Yahya has narrated from Ahmad ibn Muhammad ibn Khalid, who has narrated from al-Qasim ibn Muhammad, from 'Abd al-Rahman ibn Muhammad, from Sayf ibn 'Amirah, who has said the following:

"Abu 'Abd Allah, *'Alayhi al-Salam*, has said, 'If one of you visits his brother in belief during his illness, he should ask him (the patient) to pray for him; a patient's prayer is like the prayer of the angels.'"

Chapter 6 - How Often a Patient Should Be Visited, How Long the Duration of Visitation Should Be and Complete Visit

H 4246, Ch. 6, h 1

A number of our people have narrated from Sahl ibn Ziyad from Ali ibn Asbat from certain persons of his people who have said the following:

"Abu 'Abd Allah, *'Alayhi al-Salam*, has said that visit is not necessary for one's illness of eyes, also not before every three days, unless needed in which case it should take place with a one-day interval in between. If an illness prolongs, then the patient is left in the care of his family."

H 4247, Ch. 6, h 2

Ali ibn Ibrahim has narrated from his father from 'Abd Allah ibn al-Mughirah from 'Abd Allah ibn Sinan who has said the following:

"Abu 'Abd Allah, *'Alayhi al-Salam*, has said that duration of visiting a patient is as long as a baby-camel is given the chance to suckle the mother during milking the camel or as long as it takes to milk a camel."

H 4248, Ch. 6, h 3

Muhammad ibn Yahya has narrated from Musa ibn al-Hassan from al-Fadl ibn 'Amir abu al-'Abbass from Musa ibn al-Qasim who has said that abu Zayd said to me the following:

"A servant of Ja'far ibn Muhammad, *'Alayhi al-Salam*, informed me that once one of the followers of the Imam became ill and we went to visit him. We were a group of the followers of Ja'far ibn Muhammad, *'Alayhi al-Salam*. He (the Imam) met us at a distance on the way and asked, 'Where are you going?' We replied, 'We like to visit so and so patient.' He said, 'Wait.' We waited. He asked, 'Is there with any of you some apple, pears, peaches or a measure of perfumes or fragrance like 'Ud or bakhur?' We replied, 'We do not have any such things with us.' The Imam then said, 'You should know that a patient feels relieved when something is presented to him.'"

H 4249, Ch. 6, h 4

A number of our people have narrated from Sahl ibn Ziyad from Muhammad ibn Sulayman from Musa ibn Qadim from a man who has said the following:

"Abu 'Abd Allah, *'Alayhi al-Salam*, has said that visiting of a patient is complete upon placing your hand over his arm (praying) and standing up quickly to leave; an unwise visiting of a patient is harder for him than the pain due to illness."

H 4250, Ch. 6, h 5
Humayd ibn Ziyad narrated from al-Hassan ibn Muhammad from Sama'ah from more than one person from Aban from abu Yahya who has said the following:
"Abu 'Abd Allah, *'Alayhi al-Salam*, has said, 'Visit of a patient is complete when you place your hand on him when you meet him.'"

H 4251, Ch. 6, h 6
Ali ibn Ibrahim has narrated from Harun ibn Muslim from Mas'adah ibn Sadaqah who has said the following:
"Abu 'Abd Allah, *'Alayhi al-Salam*, has said that `Amir al-Mu'minin, *'Alayhi al-Salam*, has said, 'Of the visitors who receive the greatest reward from Allah, the Majestic, the Glorious, is one whose visiting time is short, unless the patient likes otherwise and asks him to stay for a longer time.' He has also said, 'A visit is complete when one places his hand over the other hand or upon his forehead (as an expression of concern).'"

Chapter 7 - The Limit of a Sudden Death

H 4252, Ch. 7, h 1
Muhammad ibn Yahya has narrated from Musa ibn al-Hassan from abu al-Hassan al-Nahdi in a mafu' manner who has said the following:
"Abu Ja'far, *'Alayhi al-Salam*, has said, 'If one dies before the age of forty, his life is cut short, and if one dies before fourteen days from the day of his falling ill, such death is a sudden death.'"

H 4253, Ch. 7, h 2
It is narrated from the narrator of the above Hadith from Ya'qub ibn Yazid from Yahya ibn Mubarak from Buhlul ibn Muslim from Hafs who has said the following:
"Abu 'Abd Allah, *'Alayhi al-Salam*, has said that if one dies from an illness within fourteen days, such death is a sudden death."

Chapter 8 - The Virtue (Reward) of Visiting a Patient

H 4254, Ch. 8, h 1
A number of our people have narrated from Sahl ibn Ziyad from ibn Faddal from Ali ibn 'Uqbah from Muyassir who has said the following:
"I heard abu Ja'far, *'Alayhi al-Salam*, say, 'If one visits a Muslim patient, that day seventy thousand angels pray for him from morning until night, if the visit is in the morning and until morning, if the visit takes place in the evening, and such visitor will have a house in paradise.'"

H 4255, Ch. 8, h 2
Muhammad ibn Yahya has narrated from Ahmad ibn Muhammad ibn 'Isa from ibn Faddal from 'Abd Allah ibn Bukayr from Fudayl ibn Yasar who has said the following:
"Abu 'Abd Allah, *'Alayhi al-Salam*, has said that if one visits a patient, seventy thousand angels escort him and ask Allah to forgive his sins until he returns back home."

H 4256, Ch. 8, h 3

It is a narration from him (narrator of previous Hadith) by Ahmad ibn Muhammad from ibn Faddal from Muhammad ibn al-Fudayl from abu Hamzah who has said the following:

"Abu Ja'far, *'Alayhi al-Salam*, has said, 'If a believing person visits a believing patient, he enters deep into mercy, and when he sits down, mercy covers him altogether. When he returns, Allah assigns seventy thousand angels to ask forgiveness and mercy for him saying, "You did a good deed, may paradise become your dwelling," until such hour of the next day. For him, O abu Hamzah, there is a Kharif in paradise.' I then asked, 'What is a Kharif, I pray to Allah to keep my soul in service for your cause?' The Imam said, 'A Kharif is a corner in paradise with a diameter of forty years journey on horseback.'"

H 4257, Ch. 8, h 4

Ali ibn Ibrahim has narrated from his father from ibn Mahbub from Dawud al-Riqqiy from a man of the companions of abu 'Abd Allah, who has said the following:

"Abu 'Abd Allah, *'Alayhi al-Salam*, has said, 'If a believing person visits a believing patient just for the sake of Allah, the Most Majestic, the Most Glorious, Allah assigns an angel of the visiting angels to visit him in his grave and ask forgiveness for him up to the Day of Judgment.'"

H 4258, Ch. 8, h 5

A number of our people have narrated from Ahmad ibn abu 'Abd Allah from 'Abd al-Rahman ibn abu Najran from Safwan al-Jammal who has said the following:

"Abu 'Abd Allah, *'Alayhi al-Salam*, has said that if one visits a Muslim patient, Allah assigns seventy thousand angels who come to his house saying Tasbih, Taqdis, Tahlil and Takbir up to the Day of Judgment. Half of their Salat (prayer) is for the visitor of the patient."

H 4259, Ch. 8, h 6

A number of our people have narrated from Sahl ibn Ziyad from ibn Mahbub from Wahab ibn 'Abdu Rabbi hi who has said the following:

"I heard abu 'Abd Allah, *'Alayhi al-Salam*, say, 'If a believing person visits a believing patient in his illness in the morning, seventy thousand angels escort him, and when he sits down, mercy covers him altogether and they ask Allah, the Most Majestic, the Most Glorious, until nightfall to forgive him. If his visit takes place in the evening, similar things happen for him until the next morning.'"

H 4260, Ch. 8, h 7

Abu Ali al-Ash'ariy has narrated from al-Hassan ibn Ali from 'Abd Allah ibn al-Mughirah from 'Ubays ibn Hisham from Ibrahim ibn Mihzam from certain individuals of his people who has said the following:

"Abu 'Abd Allah, *'Alayhi al-Salam*, has said that if one visits a patient, Allah, the Most Majestic, the Most Glorious, assigns an angel to visit him in his grave."

H 4261, Ch. 8, h 8

Muhammad ibn Yahya has narrated from Ahmad ibn Muhammad from ibn Mahbub from Mu'awiyah ibn Wahab who has said the following:

"Abu 'Abd Allah, *'Alayhi al-Salam*, has said that if a believing person visits a believing patient in the morning, seventy thousand angels escort him. When he sits down, mercy covers him altogether until nightfall. If he visits in the evening, similar things happen for him until the next morning."

H 4262, Ch. 8, h 9

Muhammad ibn Yahya has narrated from Ahmad ibn Muhammad from ibn Sinan from abu al-Jarud who has said the following:

"Abu Ja'far, *'Alayhi al-Salam*, has said, 'One of the conversations of Moses with his Lord was this, "O Lord, what is the reward for one who visits a person during his illness?' Allah, the Most Majestic, the Most Glorious, replied, 'I assign an angel to visit him in his grave until the Day of Judgment.'"

H 4263, Ch. 8, h 10

Ali ibn Ibrahim has narrated from Harun ibn Muslim from Mas'adah ibn Sadaqah who has said the following:

"Abu 'Abd Allah, *'Alayhi al-Salam*, has said that the Messenger of Allah has said, 'If one visits a patient, a caller from the heaven calls, "O so and so, you have done a good deed. I congratulate you for your walking to paradise."'"

Chapter 9 - Dictations to a Dying Person

H 4264, Ch. 9, h 1

Ali ibn Ibrahim has narrated from his father from ibn abu 'Umayr from Hammad from al-Halabiy who has said the following:

"Abu 'Abd Allah, *'Alayhi al-Salam*, has said that when one is about to die, before he dies, you should dictate to him the two testimonies: 'No one, other than Allah who has no partners, deserves to be worshipped and Muhammad is His servant and Messenger.'"

H 4265, Ch. 9, h 2

It is narrated from the narrator of the previous Hadith from his father from ibn abu 'Umayr from abu Ayyub from Muhammad ibn Muslim from Abu Ja'far, and from Hafs ibn al-Bakhtariy who said the following:

"Abu 'Abd Allah, *'Alayhi al-Salam*, has said that you should dictate to your dying people, 'Only Allah is the Lord to be worshipped.' We, however, (in addition) dictate to our dying people, 'Muhammad is the Messenger of Allah.'"

H 4266, Ch. 9, h 3

Ali has narrated from his father from Hammad ibn 'Isa from Hariz from Zurarah who has said the following:

"Abu Ja'far, *'Alayhi al-Salam*, has said, 'If you find a man in dying condition, dictate to him the relieving words: 'Allah, the Most Forbearing, the Most Honorable, is the only Lord who must be worshipped. Allah, the Most High, the Most Great, is the only Lord who must be worshipped. It is Allah, Lord of seven heavens and seven earths, all that is between them and beneath them, Lord of the great Throne who is free of all defects, and it is only Allah, Lord of the worlds who deserves all praise.' Abu Ja'far, *'Alayhi al-Salam*, then said, 'Had you met 'Ikrimah in his dying condition you could have benefited him.' He was asked,

'In what way he could benefit him?' The Imam replied, 'By dictating to him the matters of your belief.'"

H 4267, Ch. 9, h 4

Muhammad ibn Yahya has narrated from Ahmad ibn Muhammad from al-Husayn ibn Sa'id from al-Nadr ibn Suwayd from Dawud ibn Sulayman al-Kufiy, from abu Bakr al-Hadramiy who has said the following:

"A man from my family fell ill and I went to visit him and told him, 'Son of my brother, I have an advice for you and I hope you accept it.' He said, 'I accept it.' I then asked him to say, 'It is only Allah who must be worshipped and He has no partner.' He then testified to this fact. I then said, 'This will not be of any benefit unless you are certain about it.' He said that he is certain about it. I then asked him to say, 'I testify that Muhammad is His servant and messenger.' He then testified to this fact also. I then said that this would not benefit you unless you are certain about it. He said that he is certain about it. I then asked him to say, 'I testify that Ali is the executor of the will of the Messenger of Allah, his successor and the Imam who after the Messenger of Allah must be obeyed.' He testified to such facts. I then said that this would not benefit you unless you are certain about it. He said that he was certain about it. I then mentioned all `A'immah one by one. He testified and said that he is certain about them. Not very long thereafter, he passed away. His family began to cry intensely and mourn for him. I then left them and after a while visited, offered them my condolences, inquired as how they have been and asked the woman (of the house) how she was. She said, 'His death was a great loss for us and very difficult to bear – may Allah grant him mercy – of things that provided relief for me was that one night I saw a dream.' I then asked, 'What did you see in your dream?' She said, 'I saw him – the deceased - living and sound. I asked him, "Did you not die?" He replied, 'Yes, I died but I was saved by the words that abu Bakr dictated to me. Were it not for those words I would have (most certainly) been destroyed.'""

H 4268, Ch. 9, h 5

It is narrated from him (narrator of the above Hadith) from Ahmad ibn Muhammad from al-Husayn ibn Sa'id from Qasim ibn Muhammad from Ali ibn abu Hamzah from abu Basir who has said the following:

"Humran and we were present before abu Ja'far, *'Alayhi al-Salam*, when a servant came in. He said, 'I pray to Allah to keep my soul in service for your cause, 'Ikrimah is in dying condition and he believes in the point of view of the al-Khawarij. However, he is (also) inclined to abu Ja'far, *'Alayhi al-Salam*.' The Imam then said to us, 'Wait until I return to you.' We agreed and after a while the Imam returned and said, 'Had I met 'Ikrimah before the soul reached where it was to reach, I could have taught him the words that would have benefitted him but I met him when the soul had already reached where it was to reach.' I then asked, 'May Allah keep my soul in service for your cause, what are those words?' The Imam said, 'They, by Allah, are the (testimonies) of your belief. You must dictate to those in dying condition the testimony, "It is Allah alone who must be worshipped, and al-Walayah" (belief in the fact that `A'immah possess Divine Authority).'"

H 4269, Ch. 9, h 6

Ali ibn Muhammad ibn Bandar has narrated from Ahmad ibn abu 'Abd Allah from Muhammad ibn Ali from 'Abd al-Rahman ibn abu Hashim from abu Khadijah who has said the following:

"Abu 'Abd Allah, *'Alayhi al-Salam*, has said that at the time of everyone's death, Satan assigns one of his devils to urge the dying person to disbelief and tries to make him doubt his religion until the time his soul departs. The devil is not able to control a believing person. When you find one of you in dying condition you should dictate him the testimony of belief, 'It is only Allah who must be worshipped, and that Muhammad is Allah's Messenger' until he passes away.'"

"In another Hadith it states, 'The Imam said, "You should dictate to him the words of relief, the two testimonies and explain to him to profess the Divine Authority of `A'immah one by one until he passes away."'"

H 4270, Ch. 9, h 7

A number of our people has narrated from Sahl ibn Ziyad from Ja'far ibn Muhammad al-Ash'ariy from 'Abd Allah ibn Maymun al-Qaddah who has said the following:

"Abu 'Abd Allah, *'Alayhi al-Salam*, has said that when `Amir al-Mu'minin, *'Alayhi al-Salam*, would find any member of his family in dying condition, he would ask him to say, 'It is Allah, the Most High, the Most Great, alone who must be worshipped. It is Allah, Lord of seven heavens and the Lord of seven earths, all that is between them and the Lord of the great Throne who is free of all defects. All praise belongs to Allah, Lord of the worlds.' Upon the patient's saying this, he (the Imam) then would say, 'Go on. You do not have to worry about anything.'"

H 4271, Ch. 9, h 8

Sahl ibn Ziyad has narrated from Muhammad ibn al-Hassan ibn Shammun, from 'Abd al-Rahman from 'Abd Allah ibn Qasim from abu Bakr al-Hadramiy who has said the following:

"Abu 'Abd Allah, *'Alayhi al-Salam*, has said, 'By Allah, even if a worshipper of an idol, in his dying condition, says what you say, fire will never consume anything from his body.'"

H 4272, Ch. 9, h 9

Ali ibn Ibrahim has narrated from his father from ibn abu 'Umayr from Hammad from al-Halabiy who has said the following:

"Abu 'Abd Allah, *'Alayhi al-Salam*, has said that the Messenger of Allah once visited a man from the tribe of Hashim in his dying condition. The Messenger of Allah told him to say, 'Allah, the Most Forbearing, the Most Honorable, is the only Lord who must be worshipped, Allah, the Most High, the Most Great is the only Lord who must be worshipped. It is Allah, Lord of seven heavens and seven earths, all that is between them and beneath them, Lord of the great Throne who is free of all defects, and it is only Allah, Lord of the worlds who deserves all praise.' He said those words. The Messenger of Allah then said, 'All praise belongs to Allah who saved him from the fire.'"

H 4273, Ch. 9, h 10

Muhammad ibn Yahya has narrated from Muhammad ibn al-Husayn, from 'Abd al-Rahman ibn abu Hashim from Salim ibn abu Salmah who has said the following:

"Abu 'Abd Allah, *'Alayhi al-Salam*, has said that a man was in a dying condition and the Messenger of Allah was informed about it. The Messenger of Allah decided to visit him along with a group of his companions and they found him fainted. The Messenger of Allah said, 'O angel of death, do not do anything to him; I want to ask him a question.' The man regained consciousness and the Holy Prophet asked, 'What did you see?' He replied, 'I saw a great deal of white things and a great deal of black things.' The Holy Prophet asked, 'Which kind was closer?' He replied, 'The black things were closer.' The Holy Prophet asked him to say, 'O Allah, forgive me for the great deal of my disobedience to You and accept from me the small amount of good deeds of obedience to You.' The man then fainted again. The Holy Prophet said, 'O angel of death, relieve him so I can ask him a question.' The man gained consciousness again. The Holy Prophet asked, 'What did you see?' He replied, 'I saw a great deal of white things and great deal of black things.' The Holy Prophet asked, 'Which kind was closer?' He replied, 'The white kind was closer.' The Messenger of Allah then said to his companions, 'Allah has granted forgiveness to your friend.' The narrator has said that abu 'Abd Allah, *'Alayhi al-Salam*, said, 'If you find a person in dying condition tell him to say the above words.'"

Chapter 10 - Difficulty in Dying

(If Dying Becomes Difficult and the Agony of Death Intense)

H 4274, Ch. 10, h 1

Ali has narrated from his father from ibn abu 'Umayr from al-Husayn ibn 'Uthman from Darih who has said the following:

"I heard abu 'Abd Allah, *'Alayhi al-Salam*, say, 'Ali ibn al-Husayn, *'Alayhi al-Salam*, has said, "Abu Sa'id al-Khudriy, one of the companions of the Messenger of Allah, was a straightforward person. He remained in dying condition for three days. His people gave him a bath and carried him to the place where he would say his prayers; then he died."'"

H 4275, Ch. 10, h 2

Muhammad ibn Yahya has narrated from Ahmad ibn Muhammad from al-Husayn ibn Sa'id from al-Nadr ibn Suwayd from 'Abd Allah ibn Sinan who has said the following:

"Abu 'Abd Allah, *'Alayhi al-Salam*, has said that if dying and separation of body and soul becomes difficult for one, he should be placed where he would perform his Salat (prayer)."

H 4276, Ch. 10, h 3

Ali has narrated from his father from Hammad from Hariz from Zurarah who has said the following:

"He (the Imam), *'Alayhi al-Salam*, has said, 'If dying becomes difficult for a person, you should place him in the place where he would perform his prayer.'"

H 4277, Ch. 10, h 4
Al-Husayn ibn Muhammad has narrated from Mu'alla' ibn Muhammad from al-Washsha' from Aban from Layth al-Muradiy who has said the following:
"Abu 'Abd Allah, *'Alayhi al-Salam*, has said that abu Sa'id al-Khudriy, a person of God-given good point, faced difficulties when dying. He asked his people to place him where he would perform his prayers and when they did as they were told, he died shortly thereafter."

H 4278, Ch. 10, h 5
Muhammad ibn Yahya has narrated from Musa ibn al-Hassan from Sulayman al-Jafariy who has said the following:
"I heard abu al-Hassan, *'Alayhi al-Salam*, say to his son al-Qasim, 'Son, stand up and recite Chapter thirty-seven (of the Holy Quran), near the head of your brother, to the end.' Al-Qasim began to recite, when he reached the passage, 'Is their creation more powerful or those whom We have created' (37:11) the young man passed away. When his body was prepared for burial they came out and Ya'qub ibn Ja'far turned to him (the Imam) saying, 'We would rather recite Chapter 36 and now you command us to recite Chapter 37.' The Imam said, 'Son, if one facing distress in dying condition recites it, Allah expedites relief for him.'"

Chapter 11 - Facing the Dying Person Toward Qiblah

H 4279, Ch. 11, h 1
Ali ibn Ibrahim has narrated from his father from ibn abu 'Umayr from Ibrahim al-Shu'ayriy and more than one person who has said the following:
"Abu 'Abd Allah, *'Alayhi al-Salam*, has said that facing a dying person toward Qiblah is turning his face in that direction such that the undersides of his feet point toward Qiblah."

H 4280, Ch. 11, h 2
Humayd ibn Ziyad has narrated from al-Hassan ibn Muhammad from Muhammad ibn abu Hamzah from Mu'awiyah ibn 'Ammar who has said the following:
"I asked abu 'Abd Allah, *'Alayhi al-Salam*, about a dying person. He said, 'Make the undersides of his feet face toward Qiblah.'"

H 4281, Ch. 11, h 3
Ali ibn Ibrahim has narrated from his father from ibn abu 'Umayr from Hisham ibn Salim from Sulayman ibn Khalid who has said the following:
"I heard abu 'Abd Allah, *'Alayhi al-Salam*, say, 'When any of you dies prepare his body (facing) toward Qiblah. Also, when giving the body a bath a place should be prepared for this purpose where the bottoms of his feet face the direction of Qiblah.'"

Chapter 12 - A Believing Person Is Not Caused to Die Against His Will

H 4282, Ch. 12, h 1

Abu Ali al-Ash'ariy has narrated from Muhammad ibn 'Abd al-Jabbar from abu Muhammad al-Ansariy who – a good person – has narrated from abu Yaqdan 'Ammar al-Asadiy who said the following:

"Abu 'Abd Allah, *'Alayhi al-Salam*, has said that the Messenger of Allah has said, 'If a believing person appeals before his Lord for a guarantee not to cause him to die He will never cause him to die. However, when it is the time for him to die Allah, the Majestic, the Glorious, sends two fragrances; one is called causing forgetfulness and the other is called generous. The forgetfulness-causing fragrance makes him to forget his family and property. The generous one causes him to give up all worldly issues and choose what is with Allah.'"

H 4283, Ch. 12, h 2

A number of our people have narrated from Sahl ibn Ziyad from Muhammad ibn Sulayman from his father from Sadir al-Sayrafiy who has said the following:

"Once I said to abu 'Abd Allah, *'Alayhi al-Salam*, 'May Allah keep my soul in the service of your cause, O child of the Messenger of Allah, is a believing person forced to die?' He said, 'No, by Allah, but when the angel of death comes to take his soul away, he is frightened; and the angel of death then says to him, "O friend of Allah, do not be frightened. I swear by the One who has sent Muhammad, O Allah grant compensation to Muhammad and his family worthy of their services to Your cause, I am more kind and caring to you than a kind-hearted father ready (to help). Open your eyes and look."' He said, 'Figures of the Messenger of Allah, `Amir al-Mu'minin, Fatimah, al-Hassan and al-Husayn, *'Alayhim al-Salam*, and all `A'immah, from their descendents appear before him, and it is said to him, "There are the Messenger of Allah, `Amir al-Mu'minin, Ali, Fatimah, al-Hassan, al-Husayn and all `A'immah, *'Alayhim al-Salam*, your friends."' He (the Imam) then said, 'He then opens his eyes, and looks and his soul is called by a caller from the Lord of Majesty saying, "O peaceful soul, [in the company of Muhammad and his family] come back to your Lord with pleasure [under the guardianship of Muhammad and his family] and pleased [with the rewards from your Lord]. Enter in the company of My servants [Muhammad and his family] in paradise." There is then nothing more beloved to him than allowing his soul to go and join the caller.'"

Chapter 13 - Things that Believers and Unbelievers See in Dying Conditions

H 4284, Ch. 13, h 1

A number of our people have narrated from Sahl ibn Ziyad from ibn Faddal from Ali ibn 'Uqbah from his father who has said the following:

"Abu 'Abd Allah, *'Alayhi al-Salam*, once said, 'O 'Uqbah, Allah, on the Day of Judgment, will not accept anything other than what you believe in (following Ahl al-Bayt). No other thing stands between anyone of you, and the delight of the hearts, other than the time when one's soul reaches this' (He (the Imam) pointed his hand toward his jugular vein). He then leaned against a pillow. Mu'alla' was with me and he made a gesture to ask the Imam more questions. I then said, 'O child of the Messenger of Allah, when the soul reaches here, then what is it that the patient sees?' I said it about ten times, 'What?' Every time he replied, 'He sees' and would not add anything more. At last he sat straight and said, 'O 'Uqbah.' I replied, 'Yes, here I am paying full attention.' He said, 'Is it necessary for you to know?' I said, 'Yes, O child of the Messenger of Allah, I must know. My religion is with your religion. If my religion is gone, how can I then live every hour?' I wept and he sympathized and said, 'He will see both of them.' I then asked, 'May Allah keep my soul in the service of your cause, who are the two of them?' He replied, 'The two are the Messenger of Allah and Ali, *'Alayhim al-Salam*, O 'Uqbah, there is never a believing soul who does not see them.' I then asked, 'When a believing person sees them, does he then come back to the worldly life?' He replied, 'No, but he moves forward, when he sees them he moves forward.' I then asked, 'Do they say anything?' He replied, 'Yes, they both come to the believing person. The Messenger of Allah sits near his head and Ali near his feet. The Messenger of Allah leans over him and says, "O friend of Allah, good news for you. I am the Messenger of Allah and I am better for you than all that you have left in the world." The Messenger of Allah then stands up and Ali, *'Alayhi al-Salam*, leans over him saying, "O friend of Allah, good news for you. I am Ali, ibn abu Talib, whom you loved. I am certainly to benefit you." The Imam then said, 'This is in the book of Allah, the Majestic, the Glorious.' I then asked, 'May Allah keep my soul in the service of your cause, is this from the book of Allah?' He said, 'It is in Yunus Chapter ten where the words of Allah, the Majestic, the Glorious, say, "Those who have believed and have observed rules of faithfulness, there is good news for them in the worldly life and in the hereafter, there is no change in the words of Allah and this is the great success."""(10:64)

H 4285, Ch. 13, h 2

Ali ibn Ibrahim has narrated from Muhammad 'Isa from Yunus from Khalid ibn 'Umarah from abu Basir who has said the following:

"Abu 'Abd Allah, *'Alayhi al-Salam*, has said that when a dying person loses the ability to speak, the Messenger of Allah comes to him along with whomever Allah wants. The Messenger of Allah sits near his right side and the other on his left side. The Messenger of Allah then says, 'What you hoped for is in front of you, you are safe from that of which you were afraid.' Then he opens for him a door to paradise saying, 'This is your dwelling place in paradise. However, if you like I can send you back to the worldly life where you can have gold and silver.' He will then say, 'I do not want the worldly things.' At this time his color whitens, his forehead sweats, his lips shrink, his nostrils expand and his left eye tears up (moistons with tears). Whichever of these signs you see is enough. When the soul departs the body, it is given the choice again as when in the body but it chooses the life hereafter. He is then washed among those who wash him and is turned side to side among those who turn him side to side. When he is wrapped up in the shroud and is placed on the stretcher, his spirit comes out and begins to walk before the people. The spirits of believing people meet him with greetings of peace and good news of whatever bounties Allah, to whom belongs the Glorious praise, has prepared for him. When he is placed in his grave his spirit is returned to him down to his thighs and is asked of what he knows. If he then comes up with what he knows, that door which the Messenger of Allah had shown to him is opened, light, brightness, coolness, goodness and sweet smelling fragrance comes to him from there.' The narrator has said that I then asked, 'What about the strong pressure that grave applies?' The Imam replied, 'Never, a thing as such ever happens to believing people. By Allah, this earth feels proud of him saying, "Look, a believing person walks upon me but no believing person walks upon you." The earth says to him, "I loved you when you walked upon my back and when I love, you can see what I will do for you." It opens up as far and wide as his eyes can see.'"

H 4286, Ch. 13, h 3

Muhammad ibn Yahya has narrated from Ahmad ibn Muhammad ibn 'Isa from ibn Faddal from Yunus ibn Ya'qub from Sa'id ibn Yasar who has said the following:

"I was present at the time of the death of one of the sons of Sabur – both being people of merits, piety and great sincerity in their belief. One of them became ill and I think he was Zachariah ibn Sabur. I visited him in his dying condition. He stretched his hand and then said, 'O Ali, my hands have become white.' I then visited abu 'Abd Allah, *'Alayhi al-Salam*, when Muhammad ibn Muslim was also there. When I stood up to leave, thinking that Muhammad would inform him about the case of the man (Zachariah ibn Sabur), he sent someone after me and I returned. He said, 'Tell me about the man in whose dying condition you were present. What did you hear from him?' I replied, 'He stretched his hand and then said, "O Ali, my hands have become white!" Abu 'Abd Allah, *'Alayhi al-Salam*, then said, 'By Allah he saw him, by Allah he saw him, by Allah he saw him!'"

H 4287, Ch. 13, h 4

Muhammad ibn Yahya has narrated from Ahmad ibn Muhammad from Muhammad ibn Sinan from 'Ammar ibn Marwan from a person who had who has said the following:

"I heard abu 'Abd Allah, *'Alayhi al-Salam* say, 'Only from you, by Allah, it (good deeds) is accepted and only your sins are forgiven. There is nothing between any one of you and bliss, joy and the delight of heart, except the time when the soul reaches here' - pointing to his throat he continued – 'and when that time comes the Messenger of Allah, Ali, Gabriel and the angel of death come to visit him. Ali comes near him and says, 'O Messenger of Allah, this person loved us (Ahl al-Bayt), thus please, love him.' The Messenger of Allah, then says, 'O Gabriel, this person loved Allah, His Messenger, and the family of His Messenger, thus please love him.' Gabriel then says, 'O angel of death, this person loved Allah, His Messenger, and the family of His Messenger, thus please love him and be kind to him.' The angel of death then comes near him and says, 'O servant of Allah, have you freed your neck (from punishment), acquired the certificate of exoneration (from sins) and established your hold to the greatest source of protection in the worldly life?'" The Imam then said, 'Allah, the Majestic, the Glorious, then grants him power to say, "Yes, I have done so."' The angel asks, "What is it?" He replies, "It is (my accepting) the guardianship, the Divine Authority of Ali ibn abu Talib, *'Alayhi al-Salam*." The angel then says, "You have spoken the truth. Allah has now granted you safety from whatever you feared and all of your wishes that you wanted have come true. There is good news for you along with the virtuous ancestors to be in the company of the Messenger of Allah, Ali and Fatimah, *'Alayhim al-Salam*." Then he gently separates his soul from his body. Then his shroud is brought from paradise and a special (hunut) perfume in the form of Adhfar Musk. He then is dressed up with that shroud, and that hunut is used. In addition, he is dressed up with a yellow dress of the dresses of paradise. When he is placed in the grave, a door from paradise is opened, through which breeze and fragrance come to him. Thereafter, a space of the distance of one month's journey is opened in front and on both of his sides. Then it is said to him, "Rest like a bridegroom in his bed with good news of the delightful breeze, fragrance, bountiful paradise and the pleasure of the Lord." He then visits the family of Muhammad in Rizwan paradise, and is served food and drink with them. He speaks to them in their gatherings until the reappearance of al-Qa'im from Ahl al-Bayt. When al-Qa'im reappears, Allah resurrects them and they come along with him wholeheartedly in groups and formations. The unbelievers at this time become worthless, and disrespectful ones are destroyed but they are very few. People who want the reappearance of Al-Qa'im very quickly vanish and those who believe it (reappearance) is near gain their salvation. For this reason the Messenger of Allah said to Ali, *'Alayhi al-Salam*, "You are my brother and the place for us to meet is the valley of Peace."' The Imam then said, 'When it is time for an unbeliever to die, the Messenger of Allah, Ali, Gabriel and the angel of death visit him. Ali comes closer to him and says, "O Messenger of Allah, this person disliked us (Ahl al-Bayt), thus dislike him." The Messenger of Allah then says, "O Gabriel, this person disliked Allah, His Messenger and the family of His Messenger (Ahl al-Bayt), thus please, dislike him." Gabriel then says, "O angel of death, this person disliked Allah, His Messenger, and the family of His Messenger, thus you should also dislike him and be firm with him." The angel of death then comes near him and says, "O servant of Allah, have you freed your neck from punishment, acquired the certificate of exoneration from sins and established a secure hold to the source of safety in the worldly life?" He then says, "No." The angel then says, "O enemy of Allah, the Majestic, the Glorious, His anger, punishment and hell await you. Whatever you were afraid of has come upon you"; and then he separates his soul from his body in a very harsh manner. Three hundred devils are then assigned over his soul who spit on his face and torture his soul. When he is placed in his grave a door of the doors of hell, whereby pus and flames enter in his grave, is opened.'"

H 4288, Ch. 13, h 5

Muhammad ibn Yahya has narrated from Ahmad ibn Muhammad from al-Husayn ibn Sa'id from al-Nadr ibn Suwayd, from Yahya al-Halabiy from ibn Muskan from 'Abd al-Rahim who has said the following:

"Once I said to abu Ja'far, *'Alayhi al-Salam*, that Salih ibn Mitham narrated to me from 'Abayah al-Asadi who had heard Ali, *'Alayhi al-Salam*, say the following: 'By Allah, everyone who dislikes me and dies in such condition, can see me at the time of his death but with dislike. Everyone who loves me and dies in such condition, can see me at the time of his death with love.' Abu Ja'far, *'Alayhi al-Salam,* then said, 'Yes, and the Messenger of Allah on his right side.'"

H 4289, Ch. 13, h 6

Muhammad ibn Yahya has narrated from Ahmad ibn Muhammad from Ali ibn al-Hakam from Mu'awiyah ibn Wahab from Yahya ibn Sabur who has said the following:

"I heard abu 'Abd Allah, *'Alayhi al-Salam,* say about a dying person, 'His eye tears up (moistens with tears) at the time of his death.' He then said, 'This happens upon seeing the Messenger of Allah. He sees what makes him happy.' He then said, 'Is it not a fact that when a person sees someone whom he loves his eye tears up (moistens with tears) and he laughs?'"

H 4290, Ch. 13, h 7

Humayd ibn Ziyad has narrated from al-Hassan ibn Muhammad al-Kindiy from more than one person from Aban ibn 'Uthman from 'Amir ibn 'Abd Allah ibn Judha'ah who has said the following:

"I heard abu 'Abd Allah, *'Alayhi al-Salam,* say, 'When a soul reaches the throat, an angel comes and says to him, "O you, - or so and so – what you had hoped for, be certain, is of no avail to you, meaning returning to the worldly life, but you have become safe from whatever you were afraid of."'"

H 4291, Ch. 13, h 8

Aban ibn 'Uthman has narrated from 'Uqbah who had heard abu 'Abd Allah, *'Alayhi al-Salam,* saying the following:

"I heard abu 'Abd Allah, *'Alayhi al-Salam,* say, 'When a man's soul reaches his chest he then sees.' I then asked, 'May Allah keep my soul in the service of your cause, what does he see?' The Imam said, 'He sees the Messenger of Allah and he says, "I am the Messenger of Allah. I have good news for you." He then sees Ali ibn abu Talib, *'Alayhi al-Salam,* who says, "I am Ali ibn abu Talib, whom you loved. He loves to benefit you today."' I then asked, 'Can anyone who sees them come back to this life?' He said, 'No, when one sees them, he then can never return back to this life.' He considered it a great thing. He said this is in the Quran in the words of Allah, the Majestic, the Glorious, 'Those who believe, who were faithful to their belief, receive good news in this world and in the next life and there is no change in the words of Allah.'" (10:64)

H 4292, Ch. 13, h 9

A number of our people have narrated from Sahl ibn Ziyad from ibn Mahbub from 'Abd al-'Aziz al-'Abdiy from ibn abu Ya'fur who has said the following:

"Khattab al-Juhniy was one of our associates and he was a hardheaded adversary of the family of Muhammad, *'Alayhim al-Salam.* He was a companion of Najdah al-Harawriyyah. I once went to visit him to maintain social relations and due to fear. I found him fainted in dying condition and heard him say, 'What did I have to do against you, O Ali?' I informed abu 'Abd Allah, *'Alayhi al-Salam,* about it and he said, 'By the Lord of al-Ka'bah, he saw him! By the Lord of al-Ka'bah, he saw him.'"

H 4293, Ch. 13, h 10

Sahl ibn Ziyad has narrated from Ahmad ibn Muhammad ibn abu Nasr from Hammad ibn 'Uthman from 'Abd al-'Aziz ibn 'Awwad who has said the following:

"I heard abu 'Abd Allah, *'Alayhi al-Salam*, say, 'When the soul of any one of you reaches this point, he is told, "You are now safe from the anxiety and sadness of the worldly matters."' It is also said to him, 'The Messenger of Allah, Ali and Fatimah, *'Alayhim al-Salam*, are in front of you.'"

H 4294, Ch. 13, h 11

A number of our people have narrated from Sahl ibn Ziyad from Muhammad ibn Ali from Muhammad ibn al-Fudayl from abu Hamzah who has said the following:

"I heard abu Ja'far, *'Alayhi al-Salam*, say, 'One of the signs of belief in a person is that at the time of his death his face turns more white than normal, his forehead sweats, something like tears flow from his eyes and that is the time for coming out of his soul from his body. The soul of an unbeliever comes out of his body as if forced out of his mouth with bubbles like the coming out of the soul of a camel.'"

H 4295, Ch. 13, h 12

Muhammad ibn Yahya has narrated from Ahmad ibn Muhammad ibn Khalid and al-Husayn ibn Sa'id all from al-Qasim ibn Muhammad from 'Abd al-Samad ibn Bashir from certain persons of his people who has said the following:

"I once asked abu 'Abd Allah, *'Alayhi al-Salam*, saying, 'May Allah grant you wellbeing, is it true that whoever loves to meet Allah, He loves to meet him, and whoever dislikes to meet Allah He dislikes to meet him?' He said, 'Yes, that is true.' I then said, 'By Allah, we dislike death.' The Imam then said, 'It is not the way you think it is. That happens upon observation. When one sees what he loves, then there is nothing more beloved to him than to advance forward and Allah, the Most High, loves to meet him and he loves to meet Allah at such time. When one sees things that he does not like, then there is nothing more to his dislike than meeting Allah and Allah dislikes meeting him.'"

H 4296, Ch. 13, h 13

Abu Ali al-Ash'ariy has narrated from Muhammad ibn 'Abd al-Jabbar from Safwan ibn Yahya from abu al-Mustahal from Muhammad ibn Hanzalah who has said the following:

"Once I said to abu 'Abd Allah, *'Alayhi al-Salam*, 'May Allah keep my soul in the service of your cause, I have heard a Hadith from your followers and servants who narrate from your father.' He then asked, 'What is it?' I replied, 'They think that he said, "One should be proud of his affairs being as what we believe in when his soul reaches here."' He (the Imam) said, 'Yes, when that happens, the Holy Prophet of Allah comes, Ali comes, Gabriel comes and the angel of death comes. That angel then asks Ali, *'Alayhi al-Salam*, "O Ali, did so and so love you and your family?" He says, "Yes, he loved us and denounced our enemies." Then the Holy Prophet says this to Gabriel and Gabriel raises this to Allah, the Majestic, the Glorious.'"

H 4297, Ch. 13, h 14

It is narrated from him (narrator of the above Hadith) from Safwan from Jarud ibn al-Mundhir who has said the following:

"I heard abu 'Abd Allah, *'Alayhi al-Salam,* say, 'When the soul of one of you reaches here' – pointing to his throat – 'his eyes become delightful.'"

H 4298, Ch. 13, h 15

Muhammad ibn Yahya has narrated from Ahmad ibn Muhammad ibn 'Isa from al-Husayn ibn Sa'id from al-Nadr ibn Suwayd from Yahya al-Halabiy from Sulayman ibn Dawud from abu Basir who has said the following:

"Once I said to abu 'Abd Allah, *'Alayhi al-Salam,* 'These are the words of Allah, the Majestic, the Glorious, "When it (the soul) reaches the throat. . . . if you are truthful."' (56: 82- 87) The Imam said, 'When it reaches the throat then it sees its dwelling in paradise and says, "Return me to the worldly life so I can inform my family of what I have seen."' It then is said, 'There is no way for that to happen.'"

H 4299, Ch. 13, h 16

Sahl ibn Ziyad has narrated from more than one person of our people who has said the following:

"He (the Imam) has said, 'If you see a dying person's eyes fixed upon something and tears come out of the left eye, his forehead sweats, his lips shrink and his nostrils expand, then whatever of such things you find with him is sufficient (proof of his salvation).' In another Hadith it says, 'And if he laughs also it then is proof.' He also said, 'If you find his face frowning and his right eye tear up (shed tears) then you should note that it is (otherwise).'"

Chapter 14 - Taking out of the Souls of Believing and Unbelievers

H 4300, Ch. 14, h 1

Ali ibn Ibrahim has narrated from his father from Muhammad ibn 'Isa from Yunus from Idris al-Qummiy who has said the following:

"I heard abu 'Abd Allah, *'Alayhi al-Salam,* say, 'Allah, the Majestic, the Glorious, commands the angel of death to return the soul of a believing person, make it easy for him, and then take it out in the most comfortable way. People then say, "It (dying) was very difficult for so and so." In fact it is the way Allah, the Majestic, the Glorious, provides him comfort.' He then said, 'It (comfort) is denied him if he is of those with whom Allah is angry, or Allah dislikes him. He commands him (the angel) to pull out his soul just as frying-bar is pulled out of wool soaked in water and people say, "Allah has made dying very easy for him."'"

H 4301, Ch. 14, h 2

It is narrated from him (narrator of the above Hadith) from Yunus from al-Haytham ibn Waqid from a man who has said the following:

"Abu 'Abd Allah, *'Alayhi al-Salam,* has said that the Messenger of Allah once visited a man of his companions in dying condition. He then said, 'O angel of death, make it easy for my companion; he is a believing person.' He then said, 'O Muhammad, I am a friend of every believing person. O Muhammad, please note that when I take away the soul of the sons of Adam, his family then cries and mourns. I stand on the side of their room and say, "What is this crying and mourning! By Allah, we have not done it before the due time and we have not done anything wrong. If you consider and bear patience, you will be rewarded but if you cry and howl, you sin and transgress. You should know that we come to you repeatedly; you should be on your guard and beware! There is no household in the East, West, urban, or countryside whose faces I do not study five times every day. I know their grownups and the young ones better than they themselves do. Even if I decide to take away the soul of a bug, I cannot do so without permission from its Lord."' The Messenger of Allah has said, 'He studies their faces at the times of Salat (prayer). If they observe proper times of performing their prayers, he dictates them the testimony of belief: "No one deserves to be worshipped except Allah and that Muhammad is the Messenger of Allah" and the angel of death drives Satan away from him.'"

H 4302, Ch. 14, h 3

Ali ibn Ibrahim has narrated from his father from ibn Mahbub from al-Mufaddal ibn Salih from Jabir who has said the following:

"Abu Ja'far, *'Alayhi al-Salam*, has said, 'The Messenger of Allah once visited a man from Ansar (people of Madinah) and he was of a good status before the Messenger of Allah. He visited him in his dying condition and looked at the angel of death near his head. The Messenger of Allah said, 'Be kind to my companion; he is a believing person.' The angel of death then said, 'O Muhammad, be pleased and delighted; I am a very kind friend of every believer. O Muhammad, please consider that I visit the sons of Adam in their dying conditions and when I take their souls away, their families cry at that time. I then move away to the side of the room, with his spirit with me, and say to them, "By Allah, we have not done any injustice to him or come before the due time or rushed his measures. It is not our fault. If you agree with what Allah has done to him and bear patience, you will be rewarded and admired. If you howl and become angry, you sin and transgress; and you will not have any credit with us. Our work about you is not yet finished. So be on your guard, and beware! There is no household in urban or countryside, on land or water whose faces I do not study five times every day at the time of Salat (prayer), so much so that I know them better than they themselves do. If I, O Muhammad, decide to take away the soul of a bug, I cannot do so without the command of Allah, the Majestic, the Glorious, to do so. I dictate to a believer the testimony of belief at the time of his death: "No one deserves to be worshipped except Allah and Muhammad is the Messenger of Allah."'"'

Chapter 15 - Burial Should Take Place Immediately

H 4303, Ch. 15, h 1

Abu Ali al-Ash'ariy has narrated from Muhammad ibn Salim from Ahmad ibn al-Nadr from 'Amr ibn Shimr from Jabir who has said the following:

"Abu Ja'far, *'Alayhi al-Salam*, has said that the Messenger of Allah has said, 'O people, a man in whose home a death takes place, should not wait for burial until morning or wait until night, if it takes place during the day. Do not wait for the burial of your dead people until sunrise or until sunset. Expedite their burial, may Allah grant you blessings, and people said, "May Allah grant you blessings, O Messenger of Allah.'"

H 4304, Ch. 15, h 2

Muhammad ibn Yahya has narrated from Muhammad ibn Ahmad from al-'Abbas ibn Ma'ruf from al-Ya'qubiy from Musa ibn 'Isa from Muhammad ibn Muyassir from Harun ibn al-Jahm from al-Sakuniy who has said the following:

"Abu 'Abd Allah, *'Alayhi al-Salam*, has said that if one dies in the beginning of the day, he cannot have a nap anywhere other than his grave."

Chapter 16 - Rare Ahadith

H 4305, Ch. 16, h 1

Ali ibn Muhammad has narrated from Salih ibn abu Hammad and al-Husayn ibn Muhammad from Mu'alla' ibn Muhammad all from al- -Washsha' from Ahmad ibn al-'A'idh from abu Khadijah who has said the following:

"Abu 'Abd Allah, *'Alayhi al-Salam*, has said that Satan plays inside every dead person who is left alone."

(The following chapters are about rules of washing a dead body for burial, shrouding and other matters of burial, and are best explained in the form of fatwa. Consult current fatwa about them.)

Chapter 17 - Women during Hayd Nurse a Patient

H 4306, Ch. 17, h 1

Ali ibn Ibrahim has narrated from his father from and a number of our people have narrated from Sahl ibn Ziyad from ibn Mahbub Ali ibn abu Hamzah who has said the following:

"I once asked abu al-Hassan, *'Alayhi al-Salam*, about a woman who during her Hayd (menses) sits near the head of one who is about to die. He (the Imam) said, 'It is not harmful if she is nursing. However, when death approaches, she must move away from places nearby; angels suffer thereby (Hayd (menses)).'"

Chapter 18 - Washing a Dead Body

H 4307, Ch. 18, h 1

Ali ibn Ibrahim has narrated from his father from ibn abu 'Umayr from Hammad from al-Halabiy who has said the following:

"Abu 'Abd Allah, *'Alayhi al-Salam*, has said, 'When you decide to give Ghusl (bath) to a dead body, you must keep a piece of cloth between yourself and the private parts of the dead body, like a shirt or similar. You should begin to wash the palms (hands) and the head of the dead body three times with water mixed with Sidr (berry leaves), then the rest of the body, first the right side. When you decide to wash the private parts, you must take a clean piece of fabric, wrap your left hand with it, then enter your hand under the piece of cloth with which it is covered, then wash the private parts of the dead body without seeing them. When you complete Ghusl (bath) with water mixed with Sidr (berry leaves), wash it a second time with water mixed with camphor and something with which Hunut is done; and thereafter wash the dead body with pure water. After completing all three Ghusl (baths) place the dead body on a piece of fabric and dry it up.'"

(Ahadith 2-3 are best explained in the form of fatwa.)

H 4308, Ch. 18, h 2

Muhammad ibn Yahya has narrated from Ahmad ibn Muhammad from Al-Husayn ibn Sa'id and Muhammad ibn Khalid from al-Nadr ibn Suwayd from ibn Muskan who has narrated the following:

"I once asked abu 'Abd Allah, *'Alayhi al-Salam*, about Ghusl (bath) for a dead body. He (the Imam) said, 'You must give it a Ghusl (bath) with water mixed with Sidr, (Lotus tree leaves), thereafter one more Ghusl (bath) with water mixed with camphor and Dharirah (a certain herb or incense from India), if available, then you must give it one Ghusl (bath) with pure water.' I (the narrator) then asked, 'Is it necessary to give three Ghusl (baths) to all of the body?' He (the Imam) said, 'Yes, that is correct.' I (the narrator) then asked, 'Is it necessary to keep a piece of cloth on it during Ghusl (bath)?' He (the Imam) said, 'Yes, it is necessary; if possible, there must be a shirt on it so you can give it Ghusl (bath) under the shirt. He (the Imam) said, 'I would like that one who gives Ghusl (bath) wrap his or her hand with a piece of fabric when giving Ghusl (bath) to a dead body.'"

H 4309, Ch. 18, h 3

A number of our people have narrated from Sahl ibn Ziyad from al-Hassan ibn Mahbub from ibn Ri'ab from al-Halabiy who has narrated the following:

"'Abu 'Abd Allah, *'Alayhi al-Salam*, has said that a dead body must be given three Ghusl (baths). One Ghusl (bath) with water mixed with Lotus tree leaves, one Ghusl (bath) with water mixed with camphor, and one Ghusl (bath) with pure water. Thereafter, the dead body must be wrapped in the shroud. He (the Imam) said, 'My father made a will that required me to shroud him with three pieces of cloth. One piece was a gown which was made in Hibrah, one more piece of cloth, and a shirt.' I then asked, 'Why did he say it in his will?' He (the Imam) said that he (the Imam) did it so that people will have no objection. We then prepared a turban for him. We then dug the soil like a cut in the earth for him because his body was of a large frame. He had commanded me to raise the surface of his grave from the ground by about four inches.' He (the Imam) mentioned that it is good to sprinkle water on the grave.'"

H 4310, Ch. 18, h 4

It is a narration from him (narrator of previous Hadith) by Muhammad ibn Sinan from 'Abd Allah al-Kahiliy who has said the following:

"I once asked abu 'Abd Allah, *'Alayhi al-Salam*, about Ghusl (bath) for a dead body. He (the Imam) said, 'Turn the bottom of the sole of the dead body's feet toward al-Qiblah (al-Ka'bah) which makes the dead body facing al-Qiblah (al-Ka'bah). Thereafter, soften the joints of the bones of the dead body if possible; if not then leave them alone. First wash the private parts with water mixed with Sidr (berry leaves) and al-Huruz. (saltwort), You must give it three Ghusl (baths). Use plenty of water. Rub the belly of the dead body gently. Turn to the head. Begin with the right side of the beard and head, then the left side of the head, beard and face gently and avoid roughing it up. Wash with softness. Then make it lie down on the left side, so the right side is exposed to you. Wash it from head to the toes and rub gently the back and belly, wash it three times; then turn it on its right side to expose the left side to wash it from the head to the toes; rub its back and belly gently and wash it three times. Reach out to its underarms, arms and shoulder with your hand and make its side clean. Whenever you wash, reach with your hand under his shoulders and the inside of his arms. Thereafter make the dead body lie down on its back; then begin with the private parts with water mixed with camphor and do as you did before. Wash it three times with water mixed with camphor and al-Huruz (saltwort) and rub the belly of the dead body gently. You must then turn to the head and face and do as you did before on both sides, the head and face with water mixed with camphor three times. You must then turn it on its left side, so its right side is exposed. You must then wash it from head to the toes three times. Thereafter you must turn it on its right side to expose its left side. You must then wash it from its head to its toes three times, and push your hand under the shoulder bones of the dead body and arms. The arms and hands must be cleansed along with the sides. Whenever you wash anything, push your hand under the shoulder bones of the dead body and inside of the arms. You must then turn it on its back. You must then wash it with pure water as you did before. You must begin with the private parts, then turn to the head, beard and face to do what you did before with pure water. You must then wrap it with a piece of fabric from the waist down with a great deal of cotton underneath. You must then tie the thighs with a piece of fabric tightly, so nothing can come out. You must not make the dead body sit up or press its belly. You must not fill up the ears with something but if you are afraid of something coming out of the nostrils, you may fill it with cotton; but if you are not afraid do not fill it up with anything. Do not clean underneath the nails of the dead body: and so also is Ghusl (bath) for women.'"

H 4311, Ch. 18, h 5

Ali ibn Ibrahim has narrated from his father from his people from Yunus from `A'immah, *'Alayhim al-Salam*, who have said the following:

"When you decide to give Ghusl (bath) to a dead body, place it on the platform for Ghusl (bath), facing al-Qiblah (al-Ka'bah). Remove his hands from the shirt if any, and pull it down over the private parts. Pull it up above his knees. If shirt is not there, cover his private parts with a piece of fabric. Find Sidr (berry leaves). Place them in a pail and pour water on them. Stir with your hand until foam rises. Remove the foam in something and pour the rest in a container with water. Wash his hands three times, half way up to the elbows, just as one washes them because of sexual relation. Then wash his private parts and clean them. Then wash his head with foam thoroughly and do not allow water to enter his nostrils or ears. Then place him on the platform for Ghusl (bath) on his left side, and pour water on one half of his head down to his toes three times. Rub his body gently as well as his back and belly. Then place him on his right side on the platform for Ghusl (bath). Do as you did with the left side. You must then throw away the water from the water container. You must wash it with pure water and wash your hands up to your elbows. You must then pour water in the pail and place a piece of camphor in it and do as you did before with Sidr (berry leaves). Begin with his hands, then his private parts, then rub his belly gently, and if something comes out, clean it. Then wash his head. Then place him on his left side and wash his right side, his back and belly. Then place him on his right side and wash his left side as you did before. Then wash your hands up to the elbows and the water pail with pure water. Give him Ghusl (bath) with pure water just as you did in the other two Ghusl (bath). Then dry him up with a piece of clean cloth. Then find cotton, spread a certain amount of Hunut (camphor) on it and fill it in his private parts front and back. Fill his buttocks with cotton so that nothing can come out. Then find a long piece of fabric about a foot wide and tie it tightly around him from waist down to his knees by sending one end underneath to the right side, wrapping it around tightly, and push its end underneath the end where it had started tight.'"

H 4312, Ch. 18, h 6

Muhammad ibn Yahya has narrated from al-'Amrakiy from Ali ibn Ali ibn Ja'far from his brother, abu al-Hassan, *'Alayhi al-Salam*, who has said the following:

"I once asked abu al-Hassan, *'Alayhi al-Salam*, 'Is it permissible to give Ghusl (bath) to a dead body in the open? He (the Imam) said, 'It is not harmful, but I prefer that it is covered with a covering.'"

Chapter 19 - Hunut (Rubbing Camphor) on a Dead Body and Shrouding

H 4313, Ch. 19, h 1

Ali ibn Ibrahim has narrated from his father from his people from Yunus from 'A'immah, *'Alayhim al-Salam*, who has said the following:

"About Hunut and shrouding a deceased, he (the Imam) has said, 'Spread al-Hibrah (the large sheet of fabric), then spread the loincloth over which you then spread the shirt. Then turn back upward the front side of the shirt. Then find the ground camphor, place a certain amount of it over his forehead on the place for sajdah and then rub camphor over all of his joints from his head down to his toes, on his head, neck, shoulders, and elbows and on all of joints of his hands and legs and on the middle of his palms. Then pick him up and place him on the shirt, then turn the front of the shirt over his front side. The shirt must not have any collar or buttons. Two fresh al-Jaridah (twigs of palm tree), one yard in length are placed with him. One is placed between his knees parallel with his leg and one-half of it parallel with his thigh and the other one under his right armpit. No cotton or camphor is placed in his nostril, eyes, and ears or on his forehead. Then a turban is made for him. The center of the turban is placed on his head and then turned around his head, then the remaining is thrown on his shoulders in opposite sides by throwing the right to the left and the left to the right. Then the remaining is pulled over his chest.'"

H 4314, Ch. 19, h 2

Ali ibn Ibrahim has narrated from his father from 'Amr ibn 'Uthman from Mufaddal ibn Salih from Zayd al-Shahham who has said the following:

"Abu 'Abd Allah, *'Alayhi al-Salam*, was asked about the shroud of the Messenger of Allah. He (the Imam) said, 'There were three pieces of fabric to shroud him. They were two pieces of Suhariyayn fabric and one piece of large sheet made in Hibarah.'"

H 4315, Ch. 19, h 3

A number of our people have narrated from Ahmad ibn Muhammad from 'Uthman ibn 'Isa from Sama'ah who has said the following:

"Abu 'Abd Allah, *'Alayhi al-Salam*, has said, 'When you shroud a deceased, scatter fragrant powder and camphor on every piece of the shroud.'"

H 4316, Ch. 19, h 4

Ali ibn Ibrahim has narrated from his father from ibn abu 'Umayr from Hammad from al-Halabiy who has said the following:

"Abu 'Abd Allah, *'Alayhi al-Salam*, has said, 'When applying camphor on a deceased person, apply it on the seven parts of the body which are placed on the ground during Sujud (prostrations), and all of the joints of the body, his head, beard and on his chest.' He (the Imam) said that hunut of man and woman is the same.' He (the Imam) said, 'I dislike following a dead body with burning incense.'"

H 4317, Ch. 19, h 5

Ali ibn Ibrahim has narrated from his father from Hammad ibn 'Uthaman from Hariz from Zurarah and Muhammad ibn Muslim who have said the following:

"Once we asked abu Ja'far, *'Alayhi al-Salam*, if turban is part of shroud for a deceased. He (the Imam) said, 'No, it is not part of it. The obligatory shroud consist of three pieces of cloths, one over all; the minimum of which must be large enough to cover the whole body and any extra is of the Sunnah up to five pieces and more than this is contrived.' He (the Imam) said, 'The Holy prophet commanded to prepare turban and it was prepared for the Holy prophet.' The truthful shaykh, *'Alayhi al-Salam*, sent for us one dinar, when we were in al-Madinah at the time of the death of abu 'Ubaydah al-Hadhdha'. He (the Imam) commanded us to buy for him hunut and turban which we did.'"

H 4318, Ch. 19, h 6

A number of our people have narrated from Sahl ibn Ziyad Ahmad ibn Muhammad from ibn abu Nasr from 'Abd Allah ibn Sinan who has said the following:

"Abu 'Abd Allah, *'Alayhi al-Salam*, has said, 'A deceased must be shrouded with three pieces of cloth besides turban, and one piece which is wrapped around the hips, so that nothing is exposed. The piece of cloth and turban are necessary but they are not part of shroud.'"

H 4319, Ch. 19, h 7

Ali ibn Ibrahim has narrated from his father from ibn abu 'Umayr from Hammad from al-Halabiy who has said the following:

"Abu 'Abd Allah, *'Alayhi al-Salam*, has said, 'My father, *'Alayhi al-Salam*, wrote in his will to me to shroud him with three pieces of cloth, one was a gown made in Hibarah with which he performed Salat (prayer) on Fridays and another piece of cloth, and a shirt. I asked my father, *'Alayhi al-Salam*, "Why do you write these things?" He (the Imam) replied, "I am afraid people will overpower you. If they said to use four or five pieces, do not do so. Prepare a turban for me but turban is not counted as part of shroud. It is prepared to wrap the body therewith.""""

H 4320, Ch. 19, h 8

Ali ibn Ibrahim has narrated from his father from ibn abu 'Umayr from abu Ayyub al-Khazzaz from 'Uthman al-Nawwa' who has said the following:

"I once said to abu 'Abd Allah, *'Alayhi al-Salam*, that I give Ghusl (bath) to the deceased. He (the Imam) said, 'Treat it very gently, do not pinch his body, do not touch his ears with camphor and when preparing turban for him, do not wrap it like the turban of an Arab.' I then asked, 'How must I do it?' He (the Imam) said, 'Hold it from its center and spread it on his head turn it to the back of the head and allow the rest to hang down his chest.'"

H 4321, Ch. 19, h 9

Muhammad ibn Yahya has narrated from Ahmad ibn Muhammad from al-Husayn ibn Sa'id from al-Nadr ibn Suwayd from 'Abd Allah ibn Sinan who has said the following:

"I once asked abu 'Abd Allah, *'Alayhi al-Salam*, about how shroud is prepared. He (the Imam) said, 'Take one piece of cloth to wrap around his hips and legs.' I asked about loincloth. He (the Imam) said, 'It does not count for anything. It is only to hold that area so that nothing is exposed. The cotton that is use is better than this. The shirt is torn and is taken out from the side of his legs when Ghusl (bath) is given.' He (the Imam) then said, 'Part of shroud is the shirt without buttons and borders, and a turban that is wrapped around his head and the extra is allowed to hang down to his legs.'"

H 4322, Ch. 19, h 10

Ali ibn Ibrahim has narrated from his father from ibn abu 'Umayr from certain persons of our people who has said the following:

"I once asked abu 'Abd Allah, *'Alayhi al-Salam*, about the turban for a deceased. He (the Imam) said, 'Wrap it around his head.'"

H 4323, Ch. 19, h 11

A number of our people have narrated from Sahl ibn Ziyad ibn Mahbub from Mu'awiyah ibn Wahab who has said the following:

"Abu 'Abd Allah, *'Alayhi al-Salam*, has said, 'Five pieces of cloth are used to shroud a deceased: a shirt without button, a loincloth, a piece to wrap therewith his midsection, an overall sheet to wrap him in it, a turban that is wrapped around his head and the extra is allowed to hang down his chest.'"

H 4324, Ch. 19, h 12

Ali ibn Ibrahim has narrated from his father from 'Abd Allah ibn al-Mughirah from more than one person who has said the following:

"Abu 'Abd Allah, *'Alayhi al-Salam*, has said, 'Camphor is for hunut."

H 4325, Ch. 19, h 13

Ali ibn Ibrahim has narrated from his father from Salih al-Sindiy from Ja'far ibn Bashir from Dawud ibn Sarhan who has said the following:

"Abu 'Abd Allah, *'Alayhi al-Salam*, once said to me about the shroud of abu 'Ubaydah al-Hadhdha', 'Camphor is for hunut; however, go and do what people do.'"

H 4326, Ch. 19, h 14

Muhammad ibn Yahya has narrated from Ahmad ibn Muhammad from Muhammad ibn Sinan from Dawud ibn Sarhan who has said the following:

"Abu 'Ubaydah al-Hadhdha' died and I was in al-Madinah. Abu 'Abd Allah, *'Alayhi al-Salam*, sent a dinar and said, 'Buy with it hunut and take notice that hunut is camphor; however, do as people do.' When I went, he (the Imam) sent a dinar and said, 'Buy camphor with it.'"

H 4327, Ch. 19, h 15

Humayd ibn Ziyad has narrated from al-Hassan ibn Muhammad al-Kindiy from Ahmad ibn al-Hassan al-Mithamiy from Aban ibn 'Uthman from 'Abd al-Rahman ibn abu 'Abd Allah who has said the following:

"I once asked abu 'Abd Allah, *'Alayhi al-Salam*, about hunut for a deceased. He (the Imam) said, 'Apply it on the parts of his body used during prostration.'"

H 4328, Ch. 19, h 16

Ali ibn Ibrahim has narrated from his father from al-Nawfaliy from al-Sakuniy who has said the following:

"Abu 'Abd Allah, *'Alayhi al-Salam*, has said that the Holy prophet prohibited placing of hunut on a coffin.'"

Chapter 20 - Shrouding a Deceased Women

H 4329, Ch. 20, h 1

Humayd ibn Ziyad has narrated from al-Hassan ibn Muhammad al-Kindiy from more than one person from Aban ibn 'Uthman from 'Abd al-Rahman ibn abu 'Abd Allah who has said the following:

"I once asked abu 'Abd Allah, *'Alayhi al-Salam*, about how many pieces of fabric must be used for shrouding a woman. He (the Imam) said, 'Five pieces of fabric must be used for shrouding a woman, of which one is al-Khimar (veil).'"

H 4330, Ch. 20, h 2

A number of our people have narrated from Sahl ibn Ziyad from certain persons of our people in a marfu' manner who has said the following:

"I once asked abu 'Abd Allah, *'Alayhi al-Salam*, about how must a woman be shrouded. He (the Imam) said, 'A deceased woman is shrouded just like a deceased man, except that a piece of fabric is used to tie down her breasts to her chest, with the other end tied down behind her back. More cotton and camphor is used for hunut and to fill her back and front private parts and the piece of fabric is very tightly tied down around lower part of her body (as mentioned in the case of a deceased man).'"

H 4331, Ch. 20, h 3

Al-Husayn ibn Muhammad has narrated from 'Abd Allah ibn 'Amir from Fadalah from al-Qasim ibn Yazid from Muhammad ibn Muslim who has said the following:

"Abu Ja'far, *'Alayhi al-Salam*, has said, 'A deceased man is shrouded in three pieces of fabrics. A deceased woman of greatness is shrouded with five pieces of fabrics, the shirt, loincloth, veil and the two pieces of fabric (to tie down around her chest and the lower part of her body from the waist down to her knees).'"

Chapter 21- Undesirability of Perfuming the Shroud or Warming Water for Washing Dead Bodies

H 4332, Ch. 21, h 1

Ali ibn Ibrahim has narrated from his father from ibn abu 'Umayr from certain persons of his people who has said the following:

"Abu 'Abd Allah, *'Alayhi al-Salam*, has said, 'A shroud is not perfumed.'"

H 4333, Ch. 21, h 2

A number of our people have narrated from Sahl ibn Ziyad, from Ya'qub ibn Yazid from a number of our people who have said the following:

"Abu 'Abd Allah, *'Alayhi al-Salam*, has said, 'There is no need for warming up of water for Ghusl (bath) of a deceased, starting up a fire and perfuming the shroud.'"

H 4334, Ch. 21, h 3

Ahmad ibn Muhammad al-Kufiy has narrated from ibn al-Jumhur from his father from Muhammad ibn Sinan from al-Mufaddal ibn 'Umar who has said that 'Abd Allah ibn 'Abd al-Rahman has narrated from Hariz from Muhammad ibn Muslim who has said the following:

"Abu 'Abd Allah, *'Alayhi al-Salam*, has said that `Amir al-Mu'minin, *'Alayhi al-Salam*, has said, 'You must not perfume shrouds and your deceased one's except with camphor; a deceased person is like one in the state of 'Ihram.'"

H 4335, Ch. 21, h 4

Ali ibn Ibrahim has narrated from his father from al-Nawfaliy from al-Sakuniy who has said the following:

"Abu 'Abd Allah, *'Alayhi al-Salam*, has said that the Holy prophet, has said, 'You must not walk behind the procession for a deceased with a brazier, censer.'"

Chapter 22 - The Desirable Pieces of Shroud and the Undesirable Ones

H 4336, Ch. 22, h 1

Ali ibn Ibrahim has narrated from his father from ibn abu 'Umayr from certain persons of our people who has said the following:

"Abu 'Abd Allah, *'Alayhi al-Salam*, has said, 'Prepare good quality shroud for your deceased ones; it is beautification for them.'"

H 4337, Ch. 22, h 2

A number of our people have narrated from Sahl ibn Ziyad from Ahmad ibn Muhammad from ibn abu Nasr from abu Jamilah from Jabir who has said the following:

"Abu Ja'far, *'Alayhi al-Salam*, has said, 'The Messenger of Allah has said, 'In your dresses the best is white. Dress up with them your deceased ones also.'"

H 4338, Ch. 22, h 3

A number of our people have narrated from Ahmad ibn Muhammad ibn Khalid from 'Amr ibn 'Uthman and others from al-Mufaddal ibn Salih from Jabir who has said the following:

"Abu Ja'far, *'Alayhi al-Salam*, has said that the Holy prophet has said, 'No other clothes in your clothes is better than white, so dress up and shroud your deceased ones in white."

H 4339, Ch. 22, h 4

Ali ibn Ibrahim has narrated from his father from 'Abd Allah ibn al-Mughirah from certain persons of his people who has said the following:

"He (the Imam), *'Alayhi al-Salam*, has said, 'It is desirable to keep for shroud a piece which one has used in Salat (prayer). It should be clean; it is desirable.'"

H 4340, Ch. 22, h 5

Abu Ali al-Ash'ariy has narrated from certain persons of our people from ibn Faddal from Marwan from "Abd al-Malik who has said the following:

"I once asked abu al-Hassan, *'Alayhi al-Salam*, about a man who has purchased a certain amount of the covering of al-Ka'bah of which he has used a certain amount for his needs, and a certain amount is left with him. Can he sell? He (the Imam) said, 'He can sell whatever he wants or give it as gift or benefit thereby and seek blessings.' I (the narrator) then asked, 'Can it be used for shrouding a deceased person?' He (the Imam) replied, 'No, it cannot be used for this purpose.'"

H 4341, Ch. 22, h 6

Muhammad ibn Yahya has narrated from Ahmad ibn Muhammad ibn 'Isa from Muhammad ibn al-Husayn from 'Abd al-Rahman ibn abu Hashim from abu Khadijah who has said the following:

"Abu 'Abd Allah, *'Alayhi al-Salam*, has said, 'Try to make your shrouds look beautiful; you will be raised with your shrouds.'"

H 4342, Ch. 22, h 7

Muhammad ibn Yahya has narrated from Muhammad ibn al-Husayn from 'Abd al-Rahman ibn abu Hashim from abu Khadijah who has said the following:

"Abu 'Abd Allah, *'Alayhi al-Salam*, has said, 'The Israelites used silk for shroud; and cotton is for the followers of the Holy prophet, Muhammad, O Allah grant compensation to Muhammad and his family worthy of their services to Your cause.'"

H 4343, Ch. 22, h 8

A number of our people have narrated from Sahl ibn Ziyad from Muhammad ibn 'Amr ibn Sa'id from Yunus ibn Ya'qub who has said the following:

"I once, heard abu al-Hassan al-Awwal, *'Alayhi al-Salam*, say, 'I shrouded my father with two pieces of Shatawiyayn (name of a place in Egypt) fabric. He (the Imam) had used them for 'Ihram, and with a shirt of his shirts, a turban which Ali ibn al-Husayn, *'Alayhi al-Salam*, had used, and in a large sheet, which I purchased for forty dinars. Today it costs four hundred dinars.'"

H 4344, Ch. 22, h 9

Sahl ibn Ziyad has narrated from Ayyub ibn Nuh from those whom he has mentioned from abu Maryam al-Ansariy who has said the following:

"Abu Ja'far, *'Alayhi al-Salam*, has said that abu al-Hassan, *'Alayhi al-Salam*, shrouded 'Usamah ibn Zayd with a red Burd which was made in Hibarah and Ali, *'Alayhi al-Salam*, shrouded Sahl ibn Hunayf with a red Burd which was made in Hibarah."

H 4345, Ch. 22, 10

Muhammad ibn Yahya has narrated from Ahmad ibn Muhammad from Ahmad ibn al-Hassan ibn Ali from 'Amr ibn Sa'id from Musaddiq ibn Sadaqah from 'Ammar ibn Musa who has said the following:

"Abu 'Abd Allah, *'Alayhi al-Salam*, has said, 'Shroud can be made of Burd; if Burd is not available, then the whole shroud is of cotton. If a turban of cotton is not available, then Sabiriy fabric can be used for this purpose.'"

H 4346, Ch. 22, h 11

Ali ibn Muhammad has narrated from certain persons of his people from al-Washsha' from al-Husayn ibn al-Mukhtar who has said the following:

"Abu 'Abd Allah, *'Alayhi al-Salam*, has said, 'A deceased is not shrouded in black.'"

H 4347, Ch. 22, h 12

Muhammad ibn Yahya has narrated from Muhammad ibn Ahmad from Ahmad ibn Muhammad ibn 'Isa from al-Husayn ibn Rashid who has said the following:

"I once asked him (the Imam), *'Alayhi al-Salam*, about the fabrics made in al-Basrah in the form of Yemenite workmanship out of silk or cotton if it can be used to shroud a deceased? He (the Imam) said, 'If the amount of cotton in the fabric is more than the amount of silk, then it is permissible to use it for shrouding.'"

Chapter 23 - The Amount of Water Needed for Ghusl (bath) of a Deceased Person

H 4348, Ch. 23, h 1

A number of our people have narrated from Sahl ibn Ziyad from Ahmad ibn Muhammad from ibn abu Nasr from Fudayl Sukkarah who has said the following:

"I once asked abu 'Abd Allah, *'Alayhi al-Salam*, saying, 'I pray to Allah to keep my soul in service for your cause, how much water is needed for Ghusl (bath) of a deceased? He (the Imam) said, 'The Messenger of Allah said to Ali, *'Alayhi al-Salam*, "When I die, bring six pails of water from Ghars well (name of a well) and give me Ghusl (bath) with it. Thereafter shroud me and apply hunut on me. When you complete hunut (applying camphor), then make me sit up, then ask me whatever you want, by Allah, of whatever you ask I will give the right answer.""""

H 4349, Ch. 23, h 2

Ali ibn Ibrahim has narrated from his father from ibn abu 'Umayr from Hafs al-Bakhtariy who has said the following:

"Abu 'Abd Allah, *'Alayhi al-Salam*, has said that the Messenger of Allah said to Ali, *'Alayhi al-Salam*, "O Ali, when I die give me Ghusl (bath) with seven pails of water from Ghars well.""""

H 4350, Ch. 23, h 3

Muhammad ibn Yahya has said that Muhammad ibn al-Hassan who has narrated the following:

"I once wrote to abu Muhammad, *'Alayhi al-Salam*, 'How much water is needed for Ghusl (bath) of a deceased person?' The answer came with the signature of the Imam, 'The amount of water needed is to wash the dead body clean, by the will Allah.' He (the narrator) has said that he wrote again to him (the Imam) asking, 'Is it permissible to wash a deceased person where the water poured on him flows into the toilet or cesspool or if water with which one takes Wudu' flows in the toilet?' He (the Imam) wrote back to him with his signature, 'It does end up in the toilet.'"

H 4351, Ch. 23, h 4

Ali ibn Ibrahim has narrated from his father in a marfu' manner:

"The Sunnah about hunut (application of camphor) is thirteen dirham (in weight) and one third at most. He (the Imam) has said that Jibril came to the Messenger of Allah with hunut (camphor) that weighed forty dirhams. The Messenger of Allah divided it in three part: one for himself, one for Ali, and one for Fatimah, *'Alayhim al-Salam*.'"

H 4352, Ch. 23, h 5

A number of our people have narrated from Sahl ibn Ziyad ibn abu Najran from certain persons of his people who has said the following:

"Abu 'Abd Allah, *'Alayhi al-Salam*, has said, 'The minimum camphor for a deceased is one Mithqal (4.68 g).'"

In the narration of al-Kahiliy and Husayn ibn al-Mukhtar from abu 'Abd Allah, *'Alayhi al-Salam*, it is said that a balanced amount of camphor for this purpose is four Mithqal.

Chapter 24 - The Two Fresh Al-Jaridah (Twigs of Palm Tree)

H 4353, Ch. 24, h 1

Abu Ali al-Ash'ariy has narrated from Muhammad ibn 'Abd al-Jabbar and Muhammad ibn 'Isma'il from al-Fadl ibn Shadhan all from Safwan ibn Yahya from ibn Muskan from al-Hassan ibn Ziyad al-Sayqal who has said the following:

"Abu 'Abd Allah, *'Alayhi al-Salam*, has said, 'Two pieces of twig are placed with a deceased, one on the right and the other on the left.' He (the narrator) has said, that he (the Imam) said, 'Al-Jaridah (twig of palm tree) benefits both, believers and non-believers.'"

H 4354, Ch. 24, h 2

Muhammad ibn Yahya has narrated from Ahmad ibn Muhammad from Muhammad ibn 'Isma'il ibn Bazi' from Hanan ibn Sadir from Yahya ibn 'Ubadah al-Makkiy who has said the following:

"I heard Sufyan al-Thawriy asking him (the Imam) about greening. He (the Imam) said that once a man from al-Ansar died and the Messenger of Allah was asked to attend his funeral. He (the Messenger of Allah) asked one of the relatives of the deceased to green up their fellow man; greening people are very few.' They asked, 'What is greening?' He (the Messenger of Allah) replied, 'It is a fresh twig which is placed near the hands up to the collar bones.'"

H 4355, Ch. 24, h 3

Ali ibn Ibrahim has narrated from his father from 'Abd Allah ibn al-Mughirah, from a man from Yahya ibn 'Ubadah who has said the following:

"Abu 'Abd Allah, *'Alayhi al-Salam*, has said, 'Two pieces of fresh twigs one yard in length are placed with a deceased' - pointing with his hand – 'one end from collar bones to the hands wrapped with cloth.' He (the narrator) has said that the man then said, 'I met abu 'Abd Allah, *'Alayhi al-Salam*, afterwards and asked him (the Imam) about it. He (the Imam) said, 'Yes I spoke about it to Yahya ibn 'Ubadah.'"

H 4356, Ch. 24, h 4

Ali ibn Ibrahim has narrated from his father from Hammad ibn 'Isa from Hariz from Zurarah who has said the following:

"I once asked abu Ja'far, *'Alayhi al-Salam*, what happens if two fresh al-Jaridah (twig of palm tree) are not placed with a deceased? He (the Imam) said, 'Torture and accounting is kept away from him as long as the al-Jaridah (twig of palm tree) are fresh. All tortures take place in one day in one hour for a duration within which people return and leave the gravesite. The two al-Jaridah (twig of palm tree) (branches) are placed for this reason, and after they dry there will be no torture and accounting by the will of Allah.'"

H 4357, Ch. 24, h 5

Ali ibn Ibrahim has narrated from his father from ibn abu 'Umayr from Jamil ibn Darraj who has said the following:

"He (the Imam) has said, 'Al-Jaridah (twigs of palm tree) are of the size of one Shibr (ten inches) of which one is placed with one end near the collarbones downward as far as it reaches next to the skin, and the other on the left side near the collarbones downward as far as it reaches over the shirt.'"

H 4358, Ch. 24, h 6

A number of our people have narrated from Sahl ibn Ziyad from Ahmad ibn Muhammad from ibn abu Nasr from Muhammad ibn Sama'ah from al-Fudayl ibn Yasar who has said the following:

"Abu 'Abd Allah, *'Alayhi al-Salam*, has said that two pieces of al-Jaridah (twig of palm tree) are placed with a deceased: one on the right and the other on the left side.'"

H 4359, Ch. 24, h 7

Ali ibn Ibrahim has narrated from his father from 'Abd Allah ibn al-Mughirah from Hariz and Fudayl and 'Abd al-Rahman ibn abu 'Abd Allah who has said the following:

"Abu 'Abd Allah, *'Alayhi al-Salam*, was asked, 'Why a twig is placed with a deceased? He (the Imam) replied, 'Torture is kept away from him as long as it (twig) is fresh.'"

H 4360, Ch. 24, h 8

A number of our people have narrated from Sahl ibn Ziyad in a marfu' manner who has said the following:

"It was said to him (the Imam), 'I pray to Allah to keep my soul in service for your cause, because of the presence of fear I may not be able to place al-Jaridah (twig of palm tree) as you have told us.' He (the Imam) said, 'Place them just as it is possible for you to do.'"

H 4361, Ch. 24, h 9

Humayd ibn Ziyad has narrated from al-Hassan ibn Muhammad al-Kindiy from more than one person from Aban ibn 'Uthman from 'Abd al-Rahman ibn abu 'Abd Allah who has said the following:

"I once asked abu 'Abd Allah, *'Alayhi al-Salam*, about the twig which is placed in the grave. He (the Imam) said, 'It is not harmful.'"

H 4362, Ch. 24, h 10

A number of our people have narrated from Sahl ibn Ziyad from more than one person of our people who have said the following:

"We said to him (the Imam), *'Alayhi al-Salam*, 'We pray to Allah to keep our souls in service for your cause. What should we do if we cannot find al-Jaridah (twig of palm tree)? He (the Imam) said, 'Twig of berry tree is also good.' It then was asked, 'What should be done if twig of berry tree is also not found? He (the Imam) said, 'Then it is twig of al-Khilaf (certain tree).'"

H 4363, Ch. 24, h 11

Ali ibn Ibrahim has narrated from Ali ibn m h al-Qasaniy from Muhammad ibn Muhammad from Ali ibn Bilal who has said the following:

"I wrote to him (the Imam) asking about al-Jaridah (palm tree twig) if it is not available, can any other branch be used if palm tree is not available? He (the Imam) wrote, 'It is permissible if al-Jaridah (palm tree twig) is not available, but al-Jaridah (palm tree twig) is better; there is Hadith about it.'"

H 4364, Ch. 24, h 12

Ali ibn Ibrahim has narrated in another Hadith that the branch of pomegranate is placed in place of al-Jaridah (palm tree twig).

H 4365, Ch. 24, 13

Ali ibn Ibrahim has narrated from his father from ibn abu 'Umayr from Jamil who has said the following:

"I once asked him (the Imam) about al-Jaridah (palm tree twig) if they are to be placed under the cloth or over the cloths. He (the Imam) said, 'It is over the shirt and below al-Khasirah (waist).' I then asked on which side it should be placed. He (the Imam) said, 'It is placed on the right side.'"

Chapter 25 - Persons Dead Without Shower Due to Carnal Relations Hayd or Child Birth Reasons

H 4366, Ch. 25, h 1

Ali ibn Ibrahim has narrated from his father from Hammad ibn 'Isa from Hariz from Zurarah, in a Muzmar manner, who has said the following:

"I once said to him (the Imam), *'Alayhi al-Salam*, that there is one who has died after sexual relation but before Ghusl (bath). How is Ghusl (bath) prescribed for him and how much water is needed? He (the Imam) said, 'Only one Ghusl (bath) is sufficient for both reasons, each of which is inviolable requiring one inviolable act (Ghusl (bath)).'"

H 4367, Ch. 25, h 2
Muhammad ibn Yahya has narrated from Muhammad ibn Ahmad from Ahmad ibn al-Hassan ibn Ali from 'Amr ibn Sa'id from Musaddiq ibn Sadaqah from 'Ammar ibn Musa who has said the following:
"I once asked abu 'Abd Allah, *'Alayhi al-Salam*, about the case of a woman who dies during her child-birth, how Ghusl (bath) to be given for her? He (the Imam) said, 'It is just like cleansing Ghusl (bath) after blood discharge is over and so also is the case with a woman during her Hayd (menses) and after sexual relation: only one Ghusl (bath) is sufficient.'"

H 4368, Ch. 25, h 3
Sahl ibn Ziyad has narrated from ibn Mahbub and Ahmad ibn Muhammad in a Muzmar manner who has said the following:
"Abu 'Abd Allah, *'Alayhi al-Salam*, has said, 'A woman, who dies during her child-birth with a great deal of blood discharge, is placed in a clean bag of treated skin up to her bellybutton; then she is shrouded.'"

Chapter 26- Dead Woman with a Baby Moving Inside Her

H 4369, Ch. 26, h 1
Humayd ibn Ziyad has narrated from al-Hassan ibn Muhammad from Sama'ah from Muhammad ibn abu Hamzah from Ali ibn Yaqtin who has said the following:
"I once asked the virtuous servant of Allah about the case of a woman who dies with her child in her womb. He (the Imam), *'Alayhi al-Salam*, said, 'Her belly is opened to remove her child.'"

H 4370, Ch. 26, h 2
Sahl ibn Ziyad has narrated from 'Isma'il ibn Mahziyar from Ali ibn abu Hamzah who has said the following:
"I once asked abu 'Abd Allah, *'Alayhi al-Salam*, about the case of a woman who dies and the baby moves inside her belly; is it prescribed to cut open to take the baby out. He (the Imam) said, 'Yes, it must be cut open.' In the narration of ibn abu 'Umayr it is added that after taking out the baby the cut is stitched to close her belly."

H 4371, Ch. 26, h 3
A number of our people have narrated from Ahmad ibn Muhammad ibn Khalid from his father from ibn Wahab who has said the following:
"Abu 'Abd Allah, *'Alayhi al-Salam*, has said that 'Amir al-Mu'minin, *'Alayhi al-Salam*, has said, 'If a woman dies and in her belly is a child that moves, her belly is cut open to take the baby out.' He (the Imam), about the case of a woman in whose belly the baby dies and there is fear for her life, has said, 'A man can use his hand to take out the dead baby (if needed) cut in pieces.'"

Chapter 27 - Cutting of Nails and Hairs of Dead Person Undesirable

H 4372, Ch. 27, h 1

Ali ibn Ibrahim has narrated from his father from ibn abu 'Umayr from certain persons of his people who has said the following:

"Abu 'Abd Allah, *'Alayhi al-Salam,* has said, 'Nothing of the hairs or nails of a deceased is touched and if any of such things fall off, you must place them in his shroud.'"

H 4373, Ch. 27, h 2

It is a narration from him (narrator of previous Hadith) by his father from 'Abd Allah ibn al-Mughirah from Ghiyath who has said the following:

"Abu 'Abd Allah, *'Alayhi al-Salam,* has stated this Hadith. "Amir al-Mu'minin, *'Alayhi al-Salam,* has said that it is detestable to shave a dead persons' pubic hair, when giving Ghusl (bath), cut his nails or trim his hairs.'"

H 4374, Ch. 27, h 3

A number of our people have narrated from Sahl ibn Ziyad from ibn Mahbub from 'Abd al-Rahman ibn Mahziyar from Talhah ibn Zayd who has said the following:

"Abu 'Abd Allah, *'Alayhi al-Salam,* has said, 'Cutting the fingernails of a dead person, trimming hairs or shaving pubic hairs or softening body joints are detested matters.'"

H 4375, Ch. 27, h 4

Humayd ibn Ziyad has narrated from al-Hassan ibn Muhammad al-Kindiy from Ahmad ibn al-Hassan al-Mithamiy from Aban ibn 'Uthman from 'Abd al-Rahman ibn abu 'Abd Allah who has said the following:

"I once asked abu 'Abd Allah, *'Alayhi al-Salam,* about the case of a dead person whose body has hairs if it is required to shave or trim them. He (the Imam) said, 'Nothing as such must be touched. Just give him Ghusl (bath) and bury.'"

Chapter 28 - Things Coming Out of a Dead Body after Ghusl (bath)

H 4376, Ch. 28, h 1

A number of our people have narrated from Sahl ibn Ziyad from Ahmad ibn Muhammad from ibn abu Nasr from 'Abd Allah ibn Yahya al-Kahiliy who has said the following:

"Abu 'Abd Allah, *'Alayhi al-Salam,* has said, 'If anything comes out of the nostrils of a deceased, like blood and so on, after Ghusl (bath) and such things come in contact with turban or shroud, such parts (of shroud) must be cut off and disposed.'"

H 4377, Ch. 28, h 2

It is a narration from him (narrator of previous Hadith) by certain persons of his people in a marfu' manner who has said the following:

"He (the Imam), *'Alayhi al-Salam,* has said, 'After Ghusl (bath), if something happens, only that part is washed and repeating Ghusl (bath) is not required.'"

H 4378, Ch. 28, h 3

Ali ibn Ibrahim has narrated from his father from ibn abu 'Umayr from certain persons of his people who has said the following:

"Abu 'Abd Allah, *'Alayhi al-Salam*, has said, 'If after shrouding a certain part of it (cloth) becomes unclean, it must be cut off and disposed.'"

Chapter 29 - Washing of Persons of opposite Gender

H 4379, Ch. 29, h 1

Ali ibn Ibrahim has narrated from his father from ibn abu 'Umayr from Hammad ibn 'Isa from al-Halabiy who has said the following:

"Abu 'Abd Allah, *'Alayhi al-Salam*, was asked about a man who dies and there is no one to give him Ghusl (bath) except women. He (the Imam) said that his wife or a relative woman could give him Ghusl (bath). Women just pour water on him. In the case of a woman, her husband gives her Ghusl (bath) by reaching with his hand under her shirt.'"

H 4380, Ch. 29, h 2

Muhammad ibn Yahya has narrated from Ahmad ibn Muhammad from al-Husayn ibn Sa'id from Fadalah ibn Ayyub from 'Abd Allah ibn Sinan who has said the following:

"I once asked abu 'Abd Allah, *'Alayhi al-Salam*, about a man if he can look at his wife when she is dying or give her Ghusl (bath) if there is no one for her Ghusl (bath) and if a woman can look at her husband in such a condition. He (the Imam) said, 'It is not harmful. Only relatives of the woman may not like her husband to look as such that they dislike.'"

H 4381, Ch. 29, h 3

Muhammad ibn Yahya has narrated from Muhammad ibn al-Husayn from Safwan from al-'Ala' from Muhammad ibn Muslim who has said the following:

"I once asked him (the Imam), *'Alayhi al-Salam*, about a man if he can give Ghusl (bath) to his dead wife from behind a cloth. He (the Imam) said, 'Yes, he can do so from behind a cloth.'"

H 4382, Ch. 29, h 4

Humayd ibn Ziyad has narrated from al-Hassan ibn Muhammad al-kindiy from more than one person from Aban ibn 'Uthman from 'Abd al-Rahman ibn abu 'Abd Allah who has said the following:

"I once asked abu 'Abd Allah, *'Alayhi al-Salam*, about a man who dies and there is no one to give him Ghusl (bath) except women. He (the Imam) said, 'His wife can give him Ghusl (bath) or a woman of his relatives and other woman can just pour water from behind the cloth.'"

H 4383, Ch. 29, h 5

Muhammad ibn Yahya has narrated from Ahmad ibn Muhammad from Ali ibn al-Nu'man from Dawud ibn Farqad who has said the following:

"I once heard a friend of ours ask abu 'Abd Allah, *'Alayhi al-Salam*, about a woman who dies among men and none of them is of her relatives in that case can they give her Ghusl (bath) with her clothes on her. He (the Imam) said, 'Thereby that feeling is apt to get in them, instead they must only wash her both palms (hands).'"

H 4384, Ch. 29, h 6

Muhammad ibn Yahya has narrated from Ahmad ibn Muhammad from Ali ibn al-Hakam from al-Husayn ibn 'Uthman from Sama'ah who has said the following:

"I once asked him (the Imam), *'Alayhi al-Salam*, about the case of a woman who dies. He (the Imam) said, 'Her husband can reach out with his hand under her shirt up to the elbows.'"

H 4385, Ch. 29, h 7

A number of our people have narrated from Sahl ibn Ziyad from Ahmad ibn Muhammad from ibn abu Nasr from Dawud ibn Sarhan who has said the following:

"About a man who dies on a journey or a strage land and there is no one other than women with him, abu 'Abd Allah, *'Alayhi al-Salam*, has said, 'He is buried without Ghusl (bath).' He (the Imam) said that the same rule applies to woman in such condition unless her husband is among them, in which case he gives her Ghusl (bath) from behind the shield and pours water in a large amount on her body. A wife can give him Ghusl (bath) if he (her husband) dies. Women are different from men. Women are in a worse condition when they die.'"

H 4386, Ch. 29, h 8

Abu Ali al-Ash'ariy has narrated from Muhammad ibn 'Abd al-Jabbar and Muhammad ibn `Isma'il has narrated from al-Fadl ibn Shadhan from all from Safwan ibn Yahya from Mansur ibn Hazim who has said the following:

"I once asked abu 'Abd Allah, *'Alayhi al-Salam*, about a man who goes on a journey with his wife (and she dies), can he give her Ghusl (bath)? He (the Imam) said, 'Yes, he can do so and so also is the case of his mother and sister. Such person's private parts are covered with a piece of cloth.'"

H 4387, Ch. 29, h 9

A number of our people have narrated from Sahl ibn Ziyad from Ali ibn al-Hakam from Sayf ibn 'Amirah from Dawud ibn Farqad who has said the following:

"I once heard a friend of us ask abu 'Abd Allah, *'Alayhi al-Salam*, about a woman who dies among men and none of them is of her relatives if they can give her Ghusl (bath) with her clothes on her. He (the Imam) said, 'Thereby that feeling is apt to get in them, instead they must only wash her both palms (hands).'"

H 4388, Ch. 29, h 10

Sahl ibn Ziyad has narrated from ibn Mahbub from ibn Ri'ab from al-Halabiy who has said the following:

"About the case of a woman who dies and there is no other woman to give her Ghusl (bath), abu 'Abd Allah, *'Alayhi al-Salam*, has said, 'Her husband can reach out with his hand up to his elbow under her shirt to give her Ghusl (bath).'"

H 4389, Ch. 29, h 11

Ali ibn Ibrahim has narrated from his father from Hammad ibn 'Isa from Hariz from Muhammad ibn Muslim who has said the following:

"I once asked him (the Imam), *'Alayhi al-Salam*, about the case of a woman who dies, if her husband can give her Ghusl (bath). He (the Imam) said, 'Yes, but her relatives may hinder due to intolerance.'"

H 4390, Ch. 29, h 12

Muhammad ibn Yahya has narrated from Ahmad ibn Muhammad from Ahmad ibn al-Hassan from 'Amr ibn Sa'id from Musaddiq ibn Sadaqah from 'Ammar ibn Musa who has said the following:

"Abu 'Abd Allah, *'Alayhi al-Salam*, was asked about a Muslim man who dies on a journey and there is no other Muslim man with him but there are Christian men with him and his paternal and maternal aunts who are Muslimah how to be given Ghusl (bath) is give to him. He (the Imam) said, 'His aunts must give him Ghusl (bath) from behind his shirt and Christians must not come close to him.' It then was asked about a woman who dies on a journey and there are no other Muslim women except Christian women and her paternal and maternal uncles. He (the Imam) said, 'The uncles may give her Ghusl (bath). Christian women must not come close to her. Only the uncles give her Ghusl (bath) from behind a shield and water is poured from above the shield.' I then asked about a Muslim man who dies on a journey and there is no other Muslim man or women from his relatives but there are Christian men and none relative Muslim women. He (the Imam) said, 'Christian men themselves first take Ghusl (bath) to give him (the deceased) Ghusl (bath) because of the need.' He (the Imam) was asked about the case of a Muslim woman who dies and there are no other Muslim women with her or men of her relatives; but there is a Christian woman and non-relative Muslim men. He (the Imam) said, 'The Christian woman first herself must take Ghusl (bath) then she gives her (the deceased) Ghusl (bath).' He (the Imam) was asked about a case where on a journey a Christian man dies among the Muslims. He (the Imam) said, 'A Muslim cannot give him Ghusl (bath): it is not an honor (befitting) he cannot bury him and cannot stand on his grave.'"

H 4391, Ch. 29, h 13

Muhammad ibn Yahya has narrated from Ahmad ibn Muhammad ibn 'Isa from 'Abd al-Rahman ibn Salim from Mufaddal ibn 'Umar who has said the following:

"I once asked abu 'Abd Allah, *'Alayhi al-Salam*, 'Who gave Ghusl (bath) to Fatimah, *'Alayha al-Salam*? He (the Imam) said, 'That was `Amir al-Mu'minin, *'Alayhi al-Salam*. It seems as if you find it astonishing to hear such words.' He (the Imam) said to me, 'It seems you are strained because of what I told you.' I said, 'I pray to Allah to keep my soul in service for your cause, that is true.' He (the Imam) said to me, 'You must not be stressed out; she was a truthful one and no one other than a truthful one could give her Ghusl (bath). Consider the case of Maryam (Mary) who was given Ghusl (bath) by no one other than Jesus, *'Alayhi al-Salam*.' I then said, 'I pray to Allah to keep my soul in service for your cause, what do you say about the case of a woman who dies during a journey in the company of men among whom there is no one of her relatives or other woman. What they must do?' He (the Imam) said, 'Only those parts of her body are washed which Allah has made obligatory to be used for Tayammum. She is not touched and neither anything of her beauty which Allah, most Majestic, most Glorious, has covered must be exposed.' I then asked, 'What they must do?' He (the Imam) said, 'Only her palms, face and the backs of her hands are washed.'"

Chapter 30 - The Age of Children during Which Women Can Wash Their Bodies

H 4392, Ch. 30, h 1

Abu Ali al-Ash'ariy has narrated from Muhammad ibn 'Abd al-Jabbar from ibn Faddal from Yunus ibn Ya'qub from ibn Numayr, Mawla' al-Harith ibn al-Mughirah who has said the following:

"I once asked abu 'Abd Allah, *'Alayhi al-Salam*, up to what age a child can be given Ghusl (bath) by women? He (the Imam) replied, 'It is up to three years of age.'"

Chapter 31 - The Ghusl (bath) Necessary for Touching a Dead Body and Washing or Touching When the Body Is Still Warm or Has Become Cold

H 4393, Ch. 31, h 1

Ali ibn Ibrahim has narrated from his father from Hammad ibn 'Isa from Hariz who has said the following:

"Abu 'Abd Allah, *'Alayhi al-Salam*, has said, 'One who gives Ghusl (bath) to a dead person must himself also take a Ghusl (bath). I then asked, 'What is one required to do after touching a dead body when it is still warm? He (the Imam) said, 'Ghusl (bath) is not obligatory for him in such a case. One must take Ghusl (bath) after touching a dead body when it has become cold.' I then asked, 'What is the rule for one who places a dead body in the grave?' He (the Imam) said, 'Ghusl (bath) is not obligatory on him; he touches the cloth only.'"

H 4394, Ch. 31, h 2

Abu Ali al-Ash'ariy has narrated from Muhammad ibn 'Abd al-Jabbar from Safwan ibn Yahya from al-'Ala' ibn Razin from Muhammad ibn Muslim who has said the following:

"I once asked one of the two Imam, (abu Ja'far or abu 'Abd Allah), *'Alayhim al-Salam*, about a man who closes the eyes of a deceased if he must take Ghusl (bath) because of touching a dead body. He (the Imam) said, 'If he does it when the dead body's natural temperature is not lost, Ghusl (bath) is not obligatory on him; if he touches it after body temperature is lost, then he must take Ghusl (bath).' I then asked if one who gives Ghusl (bath) to the deceased is required to take Ghusl (bath). He (the Imam) said, 'Yes, he is required to take Ghusl (bath).' I then asked if he is required to take it before shrouding the deceased. He (the Imam) said, 'He gives Ghusl (bath) to the deceased first, then washes his own hands clean of any objects and shrouds the deceased before himself taking Ghusl (bath).' I then asked if those who carry the deceased are required to take Ghusl (bath). He (the Imam) said, 'No, they are not required to take Ghusl (bath).' I then asked if those who place the deceased in the grave are required to take Wudu'. He (the Imam) said, 'No, they are not required to take Wudu'; however, they can take Wudu' (Tayammum) with the soil of the grave if they so wanted.'"

H 4395, Ch. 31, h 3

A number of our people have narrated from Sahl ibn Ziyad from Ahmad ibn Muhammad from ibn abu Nasr from 'Abd Allah ibn Sinan who has said the following:

"Abu 'Abd Allah, *'Alayhi al-Salam*, has said, 'Those who give Ghusl (bath) to a deceased, themselves must take Ghusl (bath). If one kisses a deceased when the dead body is still warm, one is not required to take Ghusl (bath); but if he touches the dead body or kisses it when it has become cold, must take Ghusl (bath) and it is not harmful to touch or kiss after the dead body is given Ghusl (bath).'"

H 4396, Ch. 31, h 4

Ali ibn Ibrahim has narrated from his father from ibn abu 'Umayr from Hammad from al-Halabiy who has said the following:

"I once asked abu 'Abd Allah, *'Alayhi al-Salam*, about a man who touches a dead body: if it is proper for him to take Ghusl (bath) for it. He (the Imam) said, 'No, it is only necessary if it is the dead body of a human being.' I then asked about a man whose clothes become polluted because of contact with a dead body. He (the Imam) said, 'He must wash the polluted area.'"

H 4397, Ch. 31, h 5

Abu Ali al-Ash'ariy has narrated from Muhammad ibn 'Abd al-Jabbar from al-Hajjal from Tha'labah from Mu'ammar ibn Yahya who has said the following:

"I once heard abu 'Abd Allah, *'Alayhi al-Salam*, prohibit taking Ghusl (bath) because of entering the grave."

H 4398, Ch. 31, h 6

Muhammad ibn Yahya has narrated from Ahmad ibn Muhammad from al-Husayn ibn Sa'id from Fadalah ibn Ayyub from 'Isma'il ibn abu Ziyad who has said the following:

"Abu 'Abd Allah, *'Alayhi al-Salam*, has said that the Messenger of Allah kissed 'Uthman ibn Maz'un after his death."

H 4399, Ch. 31, h 7

A number of our people have narrated from Sahl ibn Ziyad from al-Hassan ibn Mahbub from ibn Ri'ab from Ibrahim who has said the following:

"Abu 'Abd Allah, *'Alayhi al-Salam*, has said that if a man's clothes come in contact with a dead body after the deceased is given Ghusl (bath), he is not required to wash them. If they become polluted because of such contact before the dead body is given Ghusl (bath) he must wash them.'"

H 4400, Ch. 31, h 8

Sahl ibn Ziyad has narrated from ibn abu Najran from 'Abd Allah ibn Sinan who has said the following:

"I once asked abu 'Abd Allah, *'Alayhi al-Salam*, if one who gives Ghusl (bath) to a dead person is required to take Ghusl (bath). He (the Imam) said, 'Yes, he is required to take Ghusl (bath).' I then asked if one who places the deceased in the grave is required to take Ghusl (bath). He (the Imam) said, 'No, he is not required to take Ghusl (bath) because he only touches the cloth.'"

Chapter 32 - Reason behind Washing a Dead Body for Burial and After Sexual Activities

H 4401, Ch. 32, h 1

Ali ibn Muhammad ibn 'Abd Allah has narrated from Ibrahim ibn 'Ishaq from Muhammad ibn Sulayman al-Daylamiy from his father who has said the following:

"Abu 'Abd Allah, *'Alayhi al-Salam*, has said that once 'Abd Allah ibn Qays al-Masir visited abu Ja'far, *'Alayhi al-Salam*, and said, 'Tell me why a dead body is given Ghusl (bath) because of carnal activities?' Abu Ja'far, *'Alayhi al-Salam*, said, 'I do not want to tell you.' He then left and thereafter found someone of the followers of the Imam. He said to him, 'It is very strange of you Shi'ah people. You consider this man as Divine guardian, obey him even if he asks you to worship him. I asked him a question but he had no answer for it.' A few days later he visited the Imam again, asked the same question and he (the Imam) said, 'I do not want to tell you.' 'Abd Allah ibn Qays then asked one of his people, 'Join the Shi'ah and pretend among them to be one of those who love the Imam. Condemn and denounce me. When it is time to perform Hajj come to me so I pay for your expenses; and then ask them to help you visit him (their Imam) Muhammad ibn Ali. When you are there, then ask him about why a dead person is given Ghusl (bath) because of carnal reasons.' The man joined the Shi'ah people until it was time to perform Hajj. During this time, he had observed the religious conditions of these people and had already accepted their belief, but did not tell ibn al-Qays about it for fear of being deprived of performing Hajj. When it was time for Hajj, he went to ibn al-Qays who provided him the expenses for Hajj. When he arrived in al-Madinah, his friends told him to stay behind until they informed the Imam about him and asked him for permission for a meeting. When they went to see abu Ja'far, *'Alayhi al-Salam*, he asked them, 'Where is your companion? You have not treated him with fairness.' They said, 'We did not know if you agreed to see him or not.' He then sent someone to bring him for a meeting. Abu Ja'far, *'Alayhi al-Salam*, welcomed him. He (the Imam) asked, 'How do you feel comparing what you have found with what you had before?' He replied, 'O child of the Messenger of Allah, I did not have anything.' He said, 'You have spoken the truth. Your worships in those days were easier than what they are today; truth is heavy and Satan is assigned to work hard against our Shi'ah but other people themselves work for him. I, however, will tell you about the question of al-Qays al-Masir before even you ask me about it and will leave it for you to decide whether to explain it to him or not. Allah, Most High, has created creative agents. When He decides to create a creature, He commands them (agents) to get something from the soil, which He has mentioned in His book. "From it (soil) We created you and to that soil We return you and take you out of that at another time." (20:57) Seed is then mixed with that soil from which they are created later after settling in the womb for forty nights. When four months are complete they (agents) ask, "Lord, what do you want to create out of it?" He then commands them to do what He wants to be done as regards the gender of the fetus being white or black. When the spirit comes out from the body, the seed comes out from that person just as it was, regardless of being young or grown up, male or female. For this reason the dead body is washed (just as) it is washed for carnal activities. He said, 'O child of the Messenger of Allah, I will never tell it to al-Qays al-Masir.' He said, 'It is up to you.'"

H 4402, Ch. 32, h 2

Ali ibn Ibrahim has narrated from his father from al-Nawfaliy, from al-Sakuniy who has said the following:

"Once, a person asked abu 'Abd Allah, *'Alayhi al-Salam*, 'Why does a dying person discharge (semen)?' He said, 'It is the seed from which he is created that he throws out.'"

H 4403, Ch. 32, h 3

Certain persons of our people have narrated from Ali ibn al-Hassan al-Mithamiy from Harun ibn Hamzah from certain persons of our people who has said the following:

"Ali ibn al-Husayn, *'Alayhi al-Salam*, has said that a creature does not die until the seed from which it is created comes out through his mouth or his eye."

Chapter 33 - The Reward for Washing a Believer for Burial

H 4404, Ch. 33, h 1

A number of our people have narrated from Sahl ibn Ziyad from al-Hassan ibn Mahbub from 'Abd Allah ibn Ghalib from Sa'd al-Iskaf who has said the following:

"This is a Hadith of abu Ja'far, *'Alayhi al-Salam*. He (the Imam) has said, 'If any believer, when washing the dead body of a believer says, "O Allah, this is the body of Your believing servant from which its spirit has come out and is just separated, please grant him forgiveness, and please grant him forgiveness."' Allah then forgives his one year's sins except the major ones."

H 4405, Ch. 33, h 2

Ali ibn Ibrahim has narrated from his father from ibn abu 'Umayr from Sa'd ibn Tarif who has said the following:

"Abu Ja'far, *'Alayhi al-Salam*, has said, 'If one washes a dead body and keeps the trust, Allah grants him forgiveness.' He was asked, 'What is the trust?' The Imam replied, 'Does not make public whatever he sees.'"

H 4406, Ch. 33, h 3

Ali ibn Ibrahim has narrated from his father from Hammad ibn 'Isa from Ibrahim ibn 'Umar who has said the following:

"Abu 'Abd Allah, *'Alayhi al-Salam*, has said, 'Any believing person who when washing the dead body of a believing person says, "O Allah grant him forgiveness," Allah then grants forgiveness to him also.'"

H 4407, Ch. 33, h 4

Muhammad ibn Yahya has narrated from Ahmad ibn Muhammad from ibn Sinan from abu al-Jarud who has said the following:

"Abu Ja'far, *'Alayhi al-Salam*, has said, 'One of the matters that Moses spoke about before Allah was this, "O Allah, what is the reward for one who washes a dead body?" The answer was, "I wash his sins as if his mother has just given him birth."'"

Chapter 34 - The Reward for Shrouding the Body of a Believing Person

H 4408, Ch. 34, h 1

Ali ibn Ibrahim has narrated from his father from ibn abu 'Umayr from Sayf ibn 'Amirah from Sa'd ibn Tarif who has said the following:

"Abu Ja'far, *'Alayhi al-Salam*, has said, 'One who provides shrouding (materials) for a believing person is like one whose dressing (needs) is guaranteed up to the Day of Judgment.'"

Chapter 35 - The Reward for One who Prepares the Grave for a Believing Person

H 4409, Ch. 35, h 1

Ali has narrated from his father from ibn abu 'Umayr from Sayf ibn 'Amira from Sa'd ibn Tarif who has said the following:

"Abu Ja'far, *'Alayhi al-Salam*, has said, 'One who prepares the grave for a believing person is like one who provides him a desirable dwelling up to the Day of Judgment.'"

Chapter 36a - The Required Depth of a Grave, the form of the Grave and Prepared Lahad for the Messenger of Allah

H 4410, Ch. 36a, h 1

Sahl ibn Ziyad has said that according to the narration of our people the depth of the grave is up to one's collarbones. Certain ones have said that it is up to one's chest and still others say that it is up to the whole height of a man, so one can pull the sheet over the head of those in the grave. The depth of Lahad is as high as one can sit straight inside. He (the narrator) has said that when Ali ibn al-Husayn, *'Alayhi al-Salam*, was about to die, he fainted for a while and then he removed the cloth and said, 'All praise belongs to Allah who has made us heirs of paradise. We can live wherever we like and this is good reward for those who do good deeds.' He (the Imam) then said, 'Dig for me (a grave) and sprinkle water properly.' He (the narrator) has said that he (the Imam), *'Alayhi al-Salam*, then pulled the sheet over his face and passed away.'" (Shahid al-Thani has said that fainting of the Imam in this Hadith is not in a literal sense; as long as an Imam is alive he is responsible and in a fainting condition one is not responsible).

(Lahad is a prepared room horizontally at the bottom of the grave as opposed to a vertical ditch in the center of the grave)

H 4411, Ch. 36a, h 2

Sahl has narrated from certain persons of his people from abu Hammam 'Isma'il ibn Hammad who has said the following:

"Abu Ja'far, *'Alayhi al-Salam*, when about to leave this world said, 'When I die dig a grave for me as a straight cut in the ground, as opposed to digging straight and then digging horizontally a passage to accommodate the body which is called Lahad. If people say that the Messenger of Allah was place in Lahad, accept it as true.'"

H 4412, Ch. 36a, h 3

Ali ibn Ibrahim has narrated from his father from ibn abu 'Umayr from Hammad ibn 'Uthman from al-Halabiy who has said the following:

"Abu 'Abd Allah, *'Alayhi al-Salam,* has said, 'Abu Talhah al-Ansariy prepared Lahad for the Messenger of Allah.'"

H 4413, Ch. 36a, h 4

Ali has narrated from his father from al-Nawfaliy from al-Sakuniy who has said the following:

"Abu 'Abd Allah, *'Alayhi al-Salam,* has said that the Holy prophet, prohibited digging the grave deeper than three hands (yards)."

Chapter 36b - Informing People to Attend a Funeral Service

H 4414, Ch. 36b, h 1

A number of our people have narrated from Sahl ibn Ziyad and Ali ibn Ibrahim from his father all from al-Hassan ibn Mahbub from abu Wallad and 'Abd Allah ibn Sinan all who has said the following:

"Abu 'Abd Allah, *'Alayhi al-Salam,* has said, 'The guardians of a deceased should inform the brothers (in belief) of the deceased about his death so they may attend his funeral services, perform prayer and appeal on his behalf for forgiveness (from Allah). Thus, a reward for them is written down as well as forgiveness. Also the person informing others about the funeral services earns a reward in addition to forgiveness for the deceased person.'"

H 4415, Ch. 36b, h 2

Abu Ali al-Ash'ariy has narrated from Muhammad ibn 'Abd al-Jabbar from Safwan ibn Yahya from Dharih al-Muharibiy who has said the following:

"I once asked abu 'Abd Allah, *'Alayhi al-Salam,* 'Should people be informed to attend the funeral of a deceased person?' He (the Imam) replied, 'Yes, people should be informed.'"

H 4416, Ch. 36b, h 3

Muhammad ibn Yahya has narrated from Ahmad ibn Muhammad from al-Husayn ibn Sa'id from al-Qasim ibn Muhammad from certain persons of his people who has said the following:

"Abu 'Abd Allah, *'Alayhi al-Salam,* has said that people should be informed to attend the funeral of a deceased person."

Chapter 37 - Expressions to Pronounce on Seeing a Dead Person

H 4417, Ch. 37, h 1

I do not know about him more of his name – from abu Hamzah who has said the following:

"Ali ibn al-Husayn, *'Alayhi al-Salam,* on seeing a dead body brought near, would say, 'All praise belongs to Allah who has not brought my life to an end.'"

H 4418, Ch. 37, h 2

Muhammad ibn Yahya has narrated from Musa ibn al-Hassan from abu al-Hassan al-Nahdi in a marfu‘ manner who has said the following:

"Abu Ja‘far, *'Alayhi al-Salam*, when seeing a dead person would say, 'All praise belongs to Allah who has not placed me among the masses whose lives have already ended.'"

H 4419, Ch. 37, h 3

Humayd has narrated from ibn Sama‘ah from 'Abd Allah ibn Jabalah from Muhammad ibn Mas'ud al-Ta'i from 'Anbasah ibn Mus'ab who has said the following:

"Abu 'Abd Allah, *'Alayhi al-Salam*, has said that the Messenger of Allah has said, 'If one finds a dead body brought from the opposite direction or just sees one and says, "Allah is great. This is what Allah and His Messenger have told us will happen to us and Allah and His Messenger have indeed spoken the truth. O Lord, increase our belief and submission. All praise belongs to Allah who is Most Majestic due to His power and who has subdued people by death," no angel is left in the heavens but will weep out of sympathy for the tone of his voice.'""

Chapter 38 - The Sunnah to Carry a Dead Body

H 4420, Ch. 38, h 1

Ali ibn Ibrahim has narrated from his father from more than one person from Yunus from Ali ibn Yaqtin from abu al-Hassan, *'Alayhi al-Salam*, who has said the following:

"Once, I heard the Imam saying, 'It is of the Sunnah (noble tradition) to lift up the front corner of the coffin on one's right shoulder. Thereafter one should move back to lift up the second corner of the coffin, then move to the other side of the coffin from the back side to lift up the third corner and lastly move (forward) to lift up the fourth corner on one's left shoulder.'"

H 4421, Ch. 38, h 2

Abu Ali al-Ash'ariy has narrated from Muhammad ibn 'Abd al-Jabbar from Ali ibn al-Hadid from Sayf ibn 'Amirah from 'Amr ibn Shimr from Jabir who has said the following:

"Abu Ja‘far, *'Alayhi al-Salam*, has said, 'It is of the Sunnah (noble tradition) to lift up all the four corners of the coffin (in a manner mentioned in the Hadith above). Other than this is extra and voluntary.'"

H 4422, Ch. 38, h 3

Ali ibn Ibrahim has narrated from his father from certain persons of his people from al-Fadl ibn Yunus who has said the following:

"I asked abu Ibrahim, *'Alayhi al-Salam*, about lifting up all four corners of a coffin. The Imam said, 'If you are in a place where you need to observe Taqiyah (in fearful condition), you should lift up the corner of the coffin where the right hand is, then lift up the corner where the right leg is. Thereafter you should return to the right side of the dead body and do not go around by the backside of the coffin. Thereafter lift up the corner where the left hand is and then lift up the corner where the left leg is, then go back to your place but do not go around by the backside of the coffin. When you are at the front, then do the same thing you did before. If you are not in the condition of Taqiyah, then the procedure of lifting up all four corners of the coffin, which is of the Sunnah, is to lift up the corner where the right hand (of the dead person) is. Thereafter one should lift up the corner where the right leg is, then the left leg and finally lift up the corner where the left hand is until the circle is complete.'"

H 4423, Ch. 38, h 4

Ali ibn Ibrahim has narrated from his father from ibn Faddal from Ali ibn 'Uqbah from Musa ibn 'Ukayl from al-'Ala' ibn Sayabah who has said the following:

"Abu 'Abd Allah, *'Alayhi al-Salam*, has said, 'Begin to lift up the coffin from the right side, then go around by the backside of the coffin to the other side then turn to the front like grinding stone (counterclockwise).'"

Chapter 39 - Walking Along with Procession for the Dead Body

H 4424, Ch. 39, h 1

Muhammad ibn Yahya has narrated from Ahmad ibn Muhammad from Muhammad ibn Isma'il from Muhammad ibn 'Adhafir from Ishaq ibn 'Ammar, who has said the following:

"Abu 'Abd Allah, *'Alayhi al-Salam*, has said, 'Walking behind the coffin of the deceased is more virtuous than walking in front of it.'"

H 4425, Ch. 39, h 2

A number of our people have narrated from Sahl ibn Ziyad from Muhammad ibn 'Uramah from Muhammad ibn 'Amr from Husayn ibn Ahmad al-Minqariy from Yunus ibn Zabyan who has said the following:

"Abu 'Abd Allah, *'Alayhi al-Salam*, has said, 'Walk in front of the coffin of a knowledgeable Muslim but do not walk in front of the coffin of a rejecter (of belief). In front of the coffin of a Muslim, angels who hasten to paradise walk, but in front of the coffin of an unbeliever, angels walk who hasten with him (the unbeliever) to hell.'"

H 4426, Ch. 39, h 3

A number of our people have narrated from Ahmad ibn abu 'Abd Allah from 'Amr ibn 'Uthman from Mufaddal ibn Salih from Jabir who has said the following:

"Abu Ja'far, *'Alayhi al-Salam*, has said, 'The Holy Prophet once was walking behind the coffin of a deceased person and he was asked, "O Messenger of Allah, why do you walk behind the coffin?" He replied, "I see angels walk in front of the coffin and we just follow them."'"

H 4427, Ch. 39, h 4

Abu Ali al-Ash'ariy has narrated from Muhammad ibn 'Abd al-Jabbar from Safwan ibn Yahya from al-'Ala' ibn Razin from Muhammad ibn Muslim who has said the following:

"I asked him [one of the two Imam] (abu Ja'far or abu 'Abd Allah, *'Alayhim al-Salam*, about walking in the funeral procession. He said, 'Walk in front or on the right or left side or behind it.'"

H 4428, Ch. 39, h 5

Humayd ibn Ziyad has narrated from al-Hassan ibn Muhammad al-Kindiy from more than one person from Aban ibn 'Uthman from Muhammad ibn Muslim who has said the following:

"Abu Ja'far, *'Alayhi al-Salam*, has said, '(In a funeral procession) walk in front or behind (the coffin).'"

H 4429, Ch. 39, h 6

Abu Ali al-Ash'ariy has narrated from Muhammad ibn 'Abd al-Jabbar from al-Hajjal from Ali ibn Shajarah from abu al-Wafa' al-Muradiy from Sadir who has said the following:

"Abu Ja'far, *'Alayhi al-Salam*, has said, 'If one wants to walk (in a funeral procession) like the honorable angels, then walk on either side of the coffin.'"

H 4430, Ch. 39, h 7

Ali ibn Ibrahim has narrated from his father from al-Nawfaliy from al-Sakuniy who has said the following:

"Someone asked abu 'Abd Allah, *'Alayhi al-Salam*, 'How should I walk in a funeral procession?' The Imam replied, 'Walk in front, or behind or on the right or left side of the coffin.' He (the Imam) then said, 'Do not walk in front if he is someone opposed to our belief; the angels of torment will come his way with all kinds of torment.'"

Chapter 40 - It Is Not Desirable to Ride in Funeral Procession

H 4431, Ch. 40, h 1

Ali ibn Ibrahim has narrated from his father from ibn abu 'Umayr from certain person of our people who has said the following:

"Abu 'Abd Allah, *'Alayhi al-Salam*, has said that the Messenger of Allah once saw a group of people riding behind the coffin in a funeral procession. He said, 'Why do these people not feel ashamed of following their companion while they have abandoned him in such condition?'"

H 4432, Ch. 40, h 2

Ali has narrated from his father from Hammad ibn 'Isa from Hariz from 'Abd al-Rahman ibn 'Abd Allah who has said the following :) who has said the following:

"Abu 'Abd Allah, *'Alayhi al-Salam*, has said, 'A man from Ansar (new Muslims of al-Madinah) of the companions of the Messenger of Allah died. The Messenger of Allah came out and joined the funeral procession walking. Someone from his companions said, "Why do you not ride, O Messenger of Allah?" He replied, "I do not like to ride when angels are walking." He refused to ride.'"

Chapter 41 - One Who Joins a Funeral Procession and then Returns

H 4433, Ch. 41, h 1

A number of our people have narrated from Sahl ibn Ziyad from al-Hassan ibn Mahbub from Ali ibn Ri'ab from Zurarah who has said the following:

"Once I was in the presence of abu Ja'far, *'Alayhi al-Salam*, in a funeral procession of one of his relatives. When he completed the prayer for a deceased, the guardian of the deceased said to abu Ja'far, *'Alayhi al-Salam*, 'Please return home. May Allah grant you the reward. Please do not become tired. You are not strong enough to walk.' I then said to abu Ja'far, *'Alayhi al-Salam*, 'He has given you permission to return. I am in need of something and I want to ask you about it.' Abu Ja'far, *'Alayhi al-Salam*, then said to me, 'It is a matter of virtue and reward which is proportionate to one's walking in the funeral procession. (You mentioned) his permission. We did not come with his permission and we will not return by his permission.'"

H 4434, Ch. 41, h 2

A number of our people have narrated from Ahmad ibn Muhammad ibn abu 'Abd Allah in a marfu' manner who has said the following:

"Abu 'Abd Allah, *'Alayhi al-Salam*, has said that the Messenger of Allah has said, 'Two kinds of commanders have no command. One is he who joins a funeral procession. He has no command to return home before the burial is complete, or he is given permission to return. The other is a man who performs Hajj along with a woman. He has no command to leave her alone before she completes all activities of her Hajj.'"

H 4435, Ch. 41, h 3

Ali ibn Ibrahim has narrated from his father from ibn Mahbub from Ali ibn Ri'ab from Zurarah who has said the following:

"Once abu Ja'far, *'Alayhi al-Salam*, joined a funeral procession for a man from Quraysh while I was with him. 'Ata' (ibn Rabah) was also there. A woman began to cry loudly. 'Ata' said, 'You should calm down or I must leave.' She did not calm down and 'Ata' returned. I then said to abu Ja'far, *'Alayhi al-Salam*, that 'Ata' has returned.' He asked, 'Why did he do so?' I said, 'A woman began to cry loudly. 'Ata' asked her, "Calm down or I return." She did not calm down thus he returned.' He (the Imam) said, 'Allow us to continue. If we saw falsehood alongside the truth and for that reason returned, we would not be yielding to the rights of a Muslim.' The narrator has said, 'When prayer for the deceased was performed, the guardian of the deceased came to abu Ja'far, *'Alayhi al-Salam*, and said, "Please return home. May Allah grant you good rewards and favors for your efforts. You are not strong enough to walk."' The Imam refused to return. I then said, 'He has given you permission to return. I need something and I want to ask you about it.' He said, 'Allow us to continue. We did not join the funeral procession by his permission, nor will we return by his permission. It is a matter of virtue and reward we seek, and such reward is proportionate to the amount of walking in the procession.'"

Chapter 42 - The Reward for Walking in a Funeral Procession

H 4436, Ch. 42, h 1

Ali ibn Ibrahim has narrated from his father from ibn abu 'Umayr from Sayf ibn 'Amirah from Jabir who has said the following:

"Abu Ja'far, *'Alayhi al-Salam*, has said, 'When a believing person is placed in the grave, it is announced then: "Paradise is the first gift for you and forgiveness for those who have escorted you."'"

H 4437, Ch. 42, h 2

Ali has narrated from his father and a number of our people have narrated from Sahl ibn Ziyad all from ibn Mahbub from Dawud al-Riqqiy, from a man of his people who has said the following:

"Abu 'Abd Allah, *'Alayhi al-Salam,* has stated this Hadith. 'Allah, the Most Majestic, the Most Glorious, for one's escorting the dead body of a believing person until it (the dead body) is buried, assigns seventy thousand angels of the escorting ones to escort him (escorting person) and ask forgiveness for him from the time he is taken out of his grave to the station (for Judgment).'"

H 4438, Ch. 42, h 3

Sahl ibn Ziyad has narrated from al-Hassan ibn Ali from Muhammad ibn al-Fudayl from Ishaq ibn 'Ammar who has said the following:

"Abu 'Abd Allah, *'Alayhi al-Salam,* has said that the first gift for a deceased believing person is forgiveness for those who escort him to his grave."

H 4439, Ch. 42, h 4

Muhammad ibn Yahya has narrated from Ahmad ibn Muhammad from Ali ibn al-Hakam from Sayf ibn 'Amirah from 'Amr ibn Shimr from Jabir who has said the following:

"Abu Ja'far, *'Alayhi al-Salam,* has said, 'If one escorts a deceased until the Salat (prayer) for a deceased is performed, his reward is one qirat and one who escorts the deceased up to the grave and until burial is complete, his reward is two qirat; and one qirat is of the size of the mountain of 'Uhud."

H 4440, Ch. 42, h 5

A number of our people have narrated from Sahl ibn Ziyad from ibn abu Najran from 'Asem ibn Hamid from abu Basir who has said the following:

"I heard abu Ja'far, *'Alayhi al-Salam,* say, 'If one walks in the procession for the burial of a deceased until Salat (prayer) for a deceased is complete and then returns back, his reward is one qirat. If one walks until burial is complete, his reward is two qirat and one qirat is of the size of the mountain of 'Uhud.'"

H 4441, Ch. 42, h 6

Abu Ali al-Ash'ariy has narrated from Muhammad ibn 'Abd al-Jabbar from ibn Faddal from Ali ibn 'Uqbah from Muyassir who has said the following:

"I heard abu Ja'far, *'Alayhi al-Salam,* say, 'If one escorts the dead body of a Muslim, on the Day of Judgment, he will be given four kinds of intercession opportunities. Whatever he says (in response), the angel says, "Likewise is for you also."'"

H 4442, Ch. 42, h 7

Muhammad ibn Yahya has narrated from Ahmad ibn Muhammad ibn 'Isa from al-Husayn ibn Sa'id from al-Husayn ibn 'Ulwan from Sa'd ibn Tarif from al-Asbagh ibn Nubatah who has said the following:

"'Amir al-Mu'minin, *'Alayhi al-Salam,* has said, 'If one escorts the body of a deceased, his reward is four qirat, one for escorting, one for Salat (prayer) for a deceased, one for waiting until burial is complete and one for offering condolences.'"

H 4443, Ch. 42, h 8

Muhammad ibn Yahya has narrated from Ahmad ibn Muhammad from ibn Sinan from abu al-Jarud who has said the following:

"Abu Ja'far, *'Alayhi al-Salam,* has said, 'One of the private conversations that Moses had with his Lord was this: "O Lord, what is the reward for one who escorts a deceased person?" The Lord said, "I assign angels of My angels who carry banners when escorting them from their graves to the station for Judgment.'"

Chapter 43 - The Reward for Lifting up the Coffin of a Dead Body

H 4444, Ch. 43, h 1

Ali ibn Ibrahim has narrated from his father from ibn abu 'Umayr from Sayf ibn 'Amirah, from Jabir who has said the following:

"Abu Ja'far, *'Alayhi al-Salam*, has said, 'If one lifts up (the coffin of) a deceased person from all of its four corners (at different times), Allah forgives his forty major sins."

H 4445, Ch. 43, h 2

Al-Husayn ibn Muhammad has narrated from Ishaq from Sa'dan ibn Muslim from Sulayman ibn Khalid from a man who has said the following:

"Abu 'Abd Allah, *'Alayhi al-Salam*, has said that if one holds the corner of the coffin, Allah forgives his twenty-five major sins; and if he lifts up all four corners (at different times) he comes out of all sins."

H 4446, Ch. 43, h 3

Abu Ali al-Ash'ariy has narrated from Muhammad ibn 'Abd al-Jabbar from al-Hajjal from Ali ibn Shajarah from 'Isa ibn Rashid from a man of his people who has said the following:

"I once heard abu 'Abd Allah, *'Alayhi al-Salam*, say, 'If one lifts up all four corners of the coffin Allah forgives his forty major sins.'"

(For such Ahadith about an act or issue of the five categories of deeds of the quality of Wujub, (Obligatory), Hurmat (Prohibited), Istihbab (Preference), Kirahat (Detestability) or Ibahah (Permissibility) one must consult fatwas of one's Mujtahid. The following chapters are best explained through fatwa, please consult fatwas.)

Chapter 44 - The Dead Bodies of Men, Women, Children and Slaves

H 4447, Ch. 44, h 1

A number of our people have narrated from Sahl ibn Ziyad Ahmad ibn Muhammad from ibn abu Nasr from al-'Ala' ibn Razin from Muhammad ibn Muslim who has said the following:

"I once asked him (the Imam), *'Alayhi al-Salam*, about performing Salat (prayer) for the dead bodies of men and women. He (the Imam) said, 'The dead bodies of men are placed near men and those of women behind the (dead) men.'"

H 4448, Ch. 44, h 2

Muhammad ibn Yahya has narrated from Muhammad ibn Ahmad from Ahmad ibn al-Husayn from Ali ibn 'Amr ibn Sa'id from Musaddiq ibn Sadaqah from 'Ammar al-Sabatiy who has said the following:

"I once asked abu 'Abd Allah, *'Alayhi al-Salam*, about the case of one who performs Salat (prayer) for one or two or three dead bodies, how is he to perform them. He (the Imam) said, 'If there are three or two or ten or less or more, he performs one Salat (prayer) with five Takbir (Allah is great beyond description) just as it is done for one deceased, and in so doing one has performed Salat (prayer) for all of them. The body of one deceased man is placed on the ground, the other is placed parallel to the hips of the first one and the head of the third is placed parallel to the hips of the second one similar to a ladder, until all of them are in place. When this is done, he then stands up in the middle and says five Takbir (Allah is great beyond description) doing what is done for one deceased person.' It then was asked, 'How Salat (prayer) is performed if there are the dead bodies of both men and women. He (the Imam) said, 'First, the bodies of men are arranged by placing the head of the second dead body parallel to the hips of the first one. When all the bodies of men are arranged in this way, then the head of the dead body of the first woman is placed parallel to the hips of the dead body of the last man, then the head of the other woman parallel to the hips of the first woman until all of them are arranged in this way. Then he stands in the middle, the middle of men, says Takbir (Allah is great beyond description) and performs Salat (prayer) for them just as performing Salat (prayer) for one deceased person.' He (the Imam) was asked about the case of a dead body that was found after Salat (prayer) with his head in place of his leg. He (the Imam) said, 'It is corrected and Salat (prayer) is performed again, even if the body is carried away but is not buried yet. Once the body is buried, time of Salat (prayer) is passed, and Salat (prayer) is not performed after burial.'"

H 4449, Ch. 44, h 3

A number of our people have narrated from Sahl ibn Ziyad from Muhammad ibn Sinan from Talhah ibn Zayd who has said the following:

"When abu 'Abd Allah, *'Alayhi al-Salam*, performed Salat (prayer) for a deceased man and a deceased woman, he (the Imam) would set forward woman, then the man. In the case of a slave and a free person, he (the Imam) would set forward the slave, then the free: and in the case of grown up and a minor, he set forward the minor then the grown up."

H 4450, Ch. 44, h 4

Abu Ali al-Ash'ariy has narrated from Muhammad ibn 'Abd al-Jabbar from Safwan ibn Yahya from al-'Ala' from Muhammad ibn Muslim who has said the following:

"I once asked one of the two Imam, (abu Ja'far or abu 'Abd Allah), *'Alayhim al-Salam*, about the case of deceased men and women as to how Salat (prayer) is performed for them. He (the Imam) said, 'Men are placed before women from the side of the Imam in a queue one after the other.'"

H 4451, Ch. 44, h 5

Muhammad ibn Yahya has narrated from Ahmad ibn Muhammad ibn 'Isa from ibn Faddal from ibn Bukayr from certain persons of his people who has said the following:

"About the case of the dead bodies of men, children and women, abu 'Abd Allah, *'Alayhi al-Salam*, has said, 'Women are placed first from the direction of al-Qiblah (al-Ka'bah). Then the children, and then men are placed, and the Imam stands next to the dead bodied of men.'"

H 4452, Ch. 44, h 6

Humayd ibn Ziyad has narrated from al-Hassan ibn Muhammad ibn Sama'ah from more than one person from Aban ibn 'Uthman from 'Abd al-Rahman ibn abu 'Abd Allah who has said the following:

"I once asked abu 'Abd Allah, *'Alayhi al-Salam*, about the case of the dead bodies of men and women collected together. He (the Imam) said, 'The dead bodied of men are placed first, according to the book of Ali, *'Alayhi al-Salam*.'"

Chapter 45 - Rare Ahadith

H 4453, Ch. 45, h 1

Ali ibn Ibrahim has narrated from his father from Yahya ibn Zakariya from his father Zakariya ibn Musa from al-Yasa' ibn 'Abd Allah al-Qummiy who has said the following:

"I once asked abu 'Abd Allah, *'Alayhi al-Salam*, about a man who performs Salat (prayer) for a dead body alone. He (the Imam) said, 'Yes, he can do so.' I then asked, 'Can two people perform Salat (prayer) for a dead body? He (the Imam) said, 'Yes, but one of them stands behind the other and not on his side.'"

H 4454, Ch. 45, h 2

A number of our people have narrated from Sahl ibn Ziyad from 'Isma'il ibn Mehran form Sayf ibn 'Amirah who has said the following:

"Abu 'Abd Allah, *'Alayhi al-Salam*, has said, 'Salat (prayer) for dead bodies are not performed wearing shoes, but it is not harmful to wear al-Khuff (slippers, socks).'"

H 4455, Ch. 45, h 3

Ali ibn Ibrahim has narrated from his father from al-Nawfaliy from al-Sakuniy who has said the following:

"Abu 'Abd Allah, *'Alayhi al-Salam*, has said, that the Messenger of Allah has said, 'The best row in Salat (prayer) is the first row but the best row in Salat (prayer) for dead bodies is the last one.' It was asked, 'Why is it so, O Messenger of Allah?' He (the Messenger of Allah) said, 'It is a curtain for women.'"

Chapter 46 - The Place Where the Person Performing Salat (Prayer) for a Dead Body Stands

H 4456, Ch. 46, h 1

Ali ibn Ibrahim has narrated from his father from 'Abd Allah ibn al-Mughirah from certain persons of our people who has said the following:

"Abu 'Abd Allah, *'Alayhi al-Salam*, has said that 'Amir al-Mu'minin) *'Alayhi al-Salam*, has said, 'When performing Salat (prayer) for a deceased woman one does not stand next to her midsection. Instead; one stands next to her chest, but when performing Salat (prayer) for a deceased man, one stands next to his midsection.'"

H 4457, Ch. 46, h 2

A number of our people have narrated from Sahl ibn Ziyad from Ahmad ibn Muhammad ibn abu Nasr from Musa ibn Bakr who has said the following:

"Abu al-Hassan *'Alayhi al-Salam*, has said, 'When performing Salat (prayer) for a deceased woman you must stand up next to her head and for a man stand up next to his midsection.'"

Chapter 47 - The Most Preferred Person to Perform Salat (Prayer) for a Dead Person

H 4458, Ch. 47, h 1

Ali ibn Ibrahim has narrated from his father from ibn abu 'Umayr from certain persons of his people who has said the following:

"Abu 'Abd Allah, *'Alayhi al-Salam*, has said, 'The nearest relative performs Salat (prayer) for a deceased or one whom such relative likes to perform Salat (prayer).'"

H 4459, Ch. 47, h 2

Muhammad ibn Yahya has narrated from Ahmad ibn Muhammad ibn 'Isa from al-Husayn ibn Sa'id from al-Qasim ibn Muhammad from Ali ibn abu Hamzah from abu Basir from who has said the following:

"I once said to abu 'Abd Allah, *'Alayhi al-Salam*, who is the most deserving to perform Salat (prayer) for a deceased woman? He (the Imam) said, 'It is her husband.' I then asked, 'Is her husband more deserving or her father, son or brother? He (the Imam) said, 'Yes, her husband is more deserving.'"

H 4460, Ch. 47, h 3

Ali ibn Ibrahim has narrated from his father from 'Isma'il ibn Marrar from Yunus from abu Basir from who has said the following:

"I once asked abu 'Abd Allah, *'Alayhi al-Salam*, about a deceased woman as to who is most deserving to perform Salat (prayer) for her. He (the Imam) said, 'Her husband deserves the most to perform Salat (prayer) for her.' I then asked, 'Is he more deserving than her father, brother or son? He (the Imam) said, 'Yes, he is more deserving.'"

H 4461, Ch. 47, h 4

Ali ibn Ibrahim has narrated from his father from Muhammad ibn Yahya from Talhah ibn Zayd who has said the following:

"Abu 'Abd Allah, *'Alayhi al-Salam*, has said, 'If the Imam is present, he is the most deserving of all people to perform Salat (prayer) for a deceased person.'"

H 4462, Ch. 47, h 5

A number of our people have narrated from Sahl ibn Ziyad Ahmad ibn Muhammad from ibn abu Nasr from certain persons of our people who has said the following:

"Abu 'Abd Allah, *'Alayhi al-Salam*, has said, 'The nearest relative performs Salat (prayer) for a deceased or one whom such relative likes to perform Salat (prayer).'"

Chapter 48 - Performing Salat (Prayer) for a Dead Person without Wudu'

H 4463, Ch. 48, h 1

Muhammad ibn Yahya has narrated from Ahmad ibn Muhammad ibn 'Isa from ibn Faddal from Yunus ibn Ya'qub who has said the following:

"I once asked abu 'Abd Allah, *'Alayhi al-Salam*, about performing Salat (prayer) for a deceased without Wudu'. He (the Imam) said, 'It is permissible; it is only Takbir (Allah is great beyond description), Tahlil (no one deserves worship except Allah), Tahmid (it is Allah only who deserves all praise), Tasbih (Allah is free of all defects) and Takbir (Allah is great beyond description).'"

H 4464, Ch. 48, h 2

Ali ibn Ibrahim has narrated from his father from ibn abu 'Umayr from Hammad ibn 'Isa from al-Halabiy who has said the following:

"Abu 'Abd Allah, *'Alayhi al-Salam*, was asked about a man who attends Salat (prayer) for a deceased without Wudu' and if he goes for Wudu' he misses Salat (prayer). He (the Imam) said, 'He can take Tayammum, then perform Salat (prayer).'"

H 4465, Ch. 48, h 3

Muhammad ibn 'Isma'il has narrated from al-Fadl ibn Shadhan and abu Ali al-Ash'ariy from Muhammad ibn 'Abd al-Jabbar all from Safwan ibn Yahya from 'Abd al-Hamid ibn Sa'id who has said the following:

"I once asked abu al-Hassan, *'Alayhi al-Salam*, about Salat (prayer) for a deceased when I do not have Wudu', and because of going for Wudu' I miss Salat (prayer) if I can perform it without Wudu'. He (the Imam) your being with Wudu' is more beloved to me.'"

H 4466, Ch. 48, h 4

Abu Ali al-Ash'ariy has narrated from Muhammad ibn 'Abd al-Jabbar from Safwan from al-'Ala' from Muhammad ibn Muslim who has said the following:

"I once asked one of the two Imam, (abu Ja'far or abu 'Abd Allah), *'Alayhim al-Salam*, about a man who suddenly comes across Salat (prayer) for a deceased without Wudu'. He (the Imam) said, 'He can say Takbir (Allah is great beyond description) along with them.'"

H 4467, Ch. 48, h 5

Muhammad ibn Yahya has narrated from Ahmad ibn Muhammad ibn 'Isa from al-Husayn ibn Sa'id from his brother al-Hassan from Zur'ah from Sama'ah who has said the following:

"I once asked him (the Imam), *'Alayhi al-Salam*, about a man who comes across a deceased without Wudu' and about what he should do. He (the Imam) said, 'He can thump his palms against the wall of bricks to have Tayammum.'"

Chapter 49 - Women's Performing Salat (Prayer) for a Dead Person

H 4468, Ch. 49, h 1

A number of our people have narrated from Sahl ibn Ziyad from al-Hassan ibn Ali ibn Faddal from Ali ibn 'Uqbah from woman of al-Hassan al-Sayqal from al-Hassan al-Sayqal who has said the following:

"I once asked abu 'Abd Allah, *'Alayhi al-Salam*, about women's performing Salat (prayer) for deceased people if there is no man present among them. He (the Imam) said, 'They all line up and no one of them stands up in front of others.'"

H 4469, Ch. 49, h 2

Abu Ali al-Ash'ariy has narrated from Muhammad ibn Salim from Ahmad ibn abu Nadr from 'Amr ibn Shimr from Jabir who has said the following:

"Abu Ja'far, *'Alayhi al-Salam*, has said, 'If no man is present, a woman leads (standing) in the middle with other women on her right and left, she in the middle says Takbir (Allah is great beyond description) until Salat (prayer) is complete.'"

H 4470, Ch. 49, h 3

Humayd ibn Ziyad has narrated from al-Hassan ibn Muhammad al-Kindiy from al-Mithamiy from Aban ibn 'Uthman from 'Abd al-Rahman ibn abu 'Abd Allah who has said the following:

"I once asked abu 'Abd Allah, *'Alayhi al-Salam*, about the case of a woman experiencing Hayd (menses), if she can perform Salat (prayer) for a deceased. He (the Imam) said, 'Yes, but she must not stand in the line; instead stand alone.'"

H 4471, Ch. 49, h 4

Ali ibn Ibrahim has narrated from his father from Hammad ibn 'Isa from Hariz from Muhammad ibn Muslim who has said the following:

"I once asked abu 'Abd Allah, *'Alayhi al-Salam*, about the case of a woman who experiences Hayd (menses) if she can perform Salat (prayer) for a deceased. He (the Imam) said, 'Yes, but she must not stand in the line of the others.'"

H 4472, Ch. 49, h 5

Hammad has narrated from Hariz from those whom he has mentioned who has said the following:

"Abu 'Abd Allah, *'Alayhi al-Salam*, has said, 'Woman experiencing Hayd (menses) can also perform Salat (prayer) for a deceased; there is no Ruku', and Sajdah. One experiencing sexual relation can take Tayammum and performs Salat (prayer) for a deceased.'"

Chapter 50 - The Time of Performing Salat (Prayer) for a Dead Person

H 4473, Ch. 50, h 1

Humayd ibn Ziyad has narrated from al-Hassan ibn Muhammad ibn Sama'ah from more than one person from Aban from Muhammad ibn Muslim who has said the following:

"I once asked abu 'Abd Allah, *'Alayhi al-Salam*, 'Is there any hour during which performing Salat (prayer) for a deceased is prohibited? He (the Imam) said, 'No, there is no such time.'"

H 4474, Ch. 50, h 2
Abu Ali al-Ash'ariy has narrated from Muhammad ibn 'Abd al-Jabbar from Safwan ibn Yahya from al-'Ala' ibn Razin from Muhammad ibn Muslim who has said the following:
"Abu Ja'far, *'Alayhi al-Salam*, has said, 'You can perform Salat (prayer) for a deceased anytime; it is not a Salat (prayer) with Ruku' (bowing down on one's knees) and Sujud (prostrations). Only on sunset and sunrise performing Salat (prayer) in which there is humbleness, Ruku' (bowing down on one's knees) and Sujud (prostrations) it is not desirable, because it sets and rises between the two Qarn (horns) of Satan.'" (Another meaning of the word 'Qarn' is a century)

Chapter 51 - Reason for Five Takbir in Salat (Prayer) for a Dead Person

H 4475, Ch. 51, h 1
Ali ibn Ibrahim has narrated from his father from in a mafu' manner the following:
"I asked abu 'Abd Allah, *'Alayhi al-Salam*, 'Why are there five Takbir in Salat (prayer) for a dead person?' He (the Imam) replied, 'From every Salat (prayer) of a day's Salat (prayer), one Takbir has come.'"

H 4476, Ch. 51, h 2
Ali ibn Ibrahim has narrated from his father from ibn abu 'Umayr from Hammad ibn 'Uthman and Hisham ibn Salim who has said the following:
"Abu 'Abd Allah, *'Alayhi al-Salam*, has said that the Messenger of Allah would say five Takbir for certain people, and four Takbir for other groups of people. When he (the Messenger of Allah) would say four Takbir in the Salat (prayer) for a dead man, he (the deceased) was suspected of hypocrisy."

H 4477, Ch. 51, h 3
Ali ibn Ibrahim has narrated from his father from ibn abu 'Umayr from Muhammad ibn Muhajir from his mother "Umm Salamah who has said the following:
"I once heard abu 'Abd Allah, *'Alayhi al-Salam*, say, 'When performing Salat (prayer) for a deceased, the Messenger of Allah would say Takbir (Allah is great beyond description), then say the two testimonies (I testify that only Allah deserves worship, He is one and has no partners and I testify that Muhammad is His servant and Messenger). He would then say Takbir then say, " O Allah, grant compensation to Muhammad and his family worthy of their services to Your cause" and pray for the prophets. Then say Takbir (Allah is great beyond description) and pray for the believing people, then say the fourth Takbir and pray for the deceased, then say Takbir and end the Salat (prayer). When Allah, most Majestic, most Glorious, prohibited praying for the hypocrites, he (the Messenger of Allah) would say Takbir, say the two testimonies, pray for the prophets, then say Takbir and pray for the believing people then say the fourth Takbir, end the Salat (prayer) and would not pray for the deceased.'"

H 4478, Ch. 51, h 4

Muhammad ibn Yahya has narrated from Ahmad ibn Muhammad from certain persons of his people from Sulayman ibn Ja'far al-Ja'fariy from his father who has said the following:

"Abu 'Abd Allah, *'Alayhi al-Salam,* has said that the Messenger of Allah has said, 'Allah, most Blessed, most High, made five Salat (prayer) obligatory, and from every Salat (prayer) there is one Takbir (Allah is great beyond description) in Salat (prayer) for a deceased.'"

H 4479, Ch. 51, h 5

A number of our people have narrated from Ahmad ibn Muhammad from Ali ibn al-Hakam from 'Uthman ibn 'Abd al-Malik al-Hadramiy from abu Bakr al-Hadramiy who has said the following:

"Abu Ja'far, *'Alayhi al-Salam,* once asked, 'O abu Bakr, do you know how much is Salat (prayer) for a deceased?' I replied, 'No, I do not know.' He (the Imam) said, 'It is five Takbir (Allah is great beyond description). Do you know from where are they taken?' I replied, 'No, I do not know.' He (the Imam) said, 'Five Takbir (Allah is great beyond description) are taken from five Salat (prayer), one Takbir from every Salat (prayer).'"

Chapter 52 - Salat (Prayer) for a Person in a Masjid

H 4480, Ch. 52, h 1

Muhammad ibn Yahya has narrated from Muhammad ibn al-Husayn from Musa ibn Talhah from abu Bakr ibn 'Isa ibn Ahmad al-'Alaviy who has said the following:

"Once I was in the Masjid when a dead body was brought in and I wanted to perform Salat (prayer) for the deceased. Abu al-Hassan, al-Awwal, *'Alayhi al-Salam,* came to me, placed his elbow against my chest and pushed me back all the way out of the Masjid and then said, 'O abu Bakr, Salat (prayer) for deceased people is not performed in Masjid.'"

Chapter 53 - Salat (Prayer) for a Believer's Dead Body, Takbir and Du'a

H 4481, Ch. 53, h 1

A number of our people have narrated from Sahl ibn Ziyad from Muhammad ibn 'Uramah from Zur'ah, from Muhammad ibn Sama'ah in a Muzmar manner has said the following:

"I once asked him (the Imam), *'Alayhi al-Salam,* about Salat (prayer) for a deceased. He (the Imam) said, 'You must say five Takbir (Allah is great beyond description) in this Salat (prayer). After first Takbir (Allah is great beyond description) say, "I testify that only Allah deserves worship, He is one and has no partners and I testify that Muhammad is His servant and Messenger. O Allah, grant compensation to Muhammad and his family worthy of their services to Your cause and to `A'immah who provide right guidance and forgive us, our brothers who were believers before us and do not allow jealousy against the believers to enter our hearts. O Lord, You are compassionate and merciful. O Lord grant forgiveness to our living people, to those who have died of the male, female believing people, place kindness in our hearts, those of the virtuous ones among us and grant us guidance in the disputed matters of the issues of truth by Your permission; You guide, whomever You will, to the right path." If the second Takbir is said (before you complete the above sayings), it is not harmful. You then say, "O Lord, this is Your servant, son of Your male and female servants. You know better than I about him do. He needs to receive mercy from You and You do not need him. O Lord forgive his sins, increase his good deeds, forgive him, have mercy upon him, lightup his grave, dictate to him his good argument, join him with his Holy prophet, do not deprive us of receiving rewards because of him and do not put us to trials after him." Say this until you complete all five Takbir.'"

(According to this Hadith there are five Takbir and after every Takbir there are the above recitations, which consist of the two testimonies, Salawat (O Allah, grant compensation to Muhammad and his family worthy of their services to Your cause), prayer for the believers and prayer for the deceased).

H 4482, Ch. 53, h 2

Ali ibn Ibrahim has narrated from his father from ibn abu 'Umayr from Hammad from al-Halabiy from Zurarah who has said the following:

"Abu 'Abd Allah, *'Alayhi al-Salam*, has said, 'In Salat (prayer) for a deceased say Takbir (Allah is great beyond description), then say, "O Allah, grant compensation to Muhammad and his family worthy of their services to Your cause," then say, "O Lord, this is Your servant the son of Your male and a female servant. I do not know about him except good but You know more about him than I know. O Lord if he is a person of good deeds, increase his good deeds, but if he is a person of bad deeds, forgive his sins, grant him mercy, make his grave spacious and make him of the friends of Muhammad, O Allah grant compensation to Muhammad and his family worthy of their services to Your cause." Then say the second Takbir (Allah is great beyond description). Then say, "O Lord, if he is a person of purity, purify him but if he is a sinner forgive him." Then say the third Takbir (Allah is great beyond description) and say, "O Lord, do not deprive us of receiving rewards because of him and do not put us to trial after him." Then say the fourth Takbir (Allah is great beyond description). Then say, "O Lord, write him (his name) with You among those of high status and replace him in his children whom he has left behind and make him of the friends of Muhammad, O Allah grant compensation to Muhammad and his family worthy of their services to Your cause." Then say the fifth Takbir (Allah is great beyond description) and end the Salat (prayer).'"

H 4483, Ch. 53, h 3

Ali ibn Ibrahim has narrated from his father from a number of our people have narrated from Sahl ibn Ziyad all from ibn Mahbub from abu Wallad who has said the following:

"I once asked abu 'Abd Allah, *'Alayhi al-Salam*, about Takbir over a deceased person. He (the Imam) said, 'There are five Takbir. In the first one say, "I testify that only Allah deserves worship, He is one and has no partners and I testify that Muhammad is His servant and Messenger. O Allah, I pray to You to grant compensation to Muhammad and his family worthy of their services to Your cause." Then say, "O Lord, this person, shrouded in front of us, is your servant and the son of Your servant whose soul You have taken to Yourself, and he is in need for your mercy and You do not need his being punished. O Lord, if he is a person of good deeds, increase his good deeds; if he is a person of bad deeds, forgive his sins." Then say the second Takbir and do the same after every Takbir.'"

H 4484, Ch. 53, h 4

Ali ibn Ibrahim has narrated from his father from ibn abu 'Umayr from Hammad from al-Halabiy who has said the following:

Abu 'Abd Allah, *'Alayhi al-Salam*, has said, 'In Salat (prayer) for a deceased say Takbir (Allah is great beyond description) and the testimony and say, "We are from Allah and to Allah we return. All praise belongs to Allah, Lord of the worlds, Lord of death and life. O Allah, I pray to You to grant compensation to Muhammad and his family worthy of their services to Your cause. O Allah I pray to You to grant Muhammad the best of rewards for his favors to his followers and for his preaching the message of his Lord." Then say, "O Lord, this is Your servant, the son of Your male and a female servant. His forehead is in Your control. He has left this world, he is in need of Your mercy, and You do not need his being punished. O Lord, we do not know about him anything except good; but You know more about him than we know. O Lord, if he is a person of good deeds, increase his good deeds. If he is a person of bad deeds, forgive his sins, grant him mercy, forgive him through your mercy, join him with your Holy prophet, and keep him on the unchangeable word in the worldly life and in the hereafter. O Lord, make us to walk on the path of guidance and guide him and us to the right path. O Lord, grant (us) forgiveness, O Lord grant (us) forgiveness." Then say the second Takbir. Repeat what you have said after every Takbir (Allah is great beyond description) until you say all five Takbir (Allah is great beyond description).'"

H 4485, Ch. 53, h 5

A number of our people have narrated from Sahl ibn Ziyad from Muhammad ibn 'Isa from Yunus who has said the following:

"I once asked al-Rida', *'Alayhi al-Salam*, saying, 'I pray to Allah to keep my soul in service for your cause. People raise their hands during the first Takbir (Allah is great beyond description) in Salat (prayer) for a deceased but not in the rest of Takbir and if should I raise my hand in the first Takbir only or in all Takbir. He (the Imam) said, 'Raise your hand in all Takbir.'"

H 4486, Ch. 53, h 6

Ali ibn Muhammad has narrated from Ali ibn al-Hassan from Ahmad ibn 'Abd al-Rahim abu al-Sakhr from 'Isma'il ibn 'Abd al-Khaliq ibn 'Abd Rabbihi who has said the following:

"Abu 'Abd Allah, *'Alayhi al-Salam*, has said, 'In Salat (prayer) for a deceased say, 'O Lord, You have created this soul and You have caused it to die. You know all of its secret and public matters. We have come to You to mediate before You in his favor, so accept our intercession. O Lord, entrust it with those whom it took as supreme power and raise it with those whom it loved.'"

Chapter 54 - There is No Particular Du'a or Salam in Salat (Prayer) for a Dead Body

H 4487, Ch. 54, h 1

Ali ibn Ibrahim has narrated from his father from ibn abu 'Umayr from ibn 'Udhaynah from Muhammad ibn Muslim and Zurarah from and Mu'ammar ibn Yahya and 'Isma'il al-Ju'fiy who has said the following:

"Abu Ja'far, *'Alayhi al-Salam*, has said, 'There is no particularly prescribed prayer to say in Salat (prayer) for a deceased. You can pray whatever prayer you like; and the most deserving is the believing person who has just died and that such prayer begins with prayer for the Messenger of Allah by saying, 'O Allah, grant compensation to Muhammad and his family worthy of their services to Your cause.'"

H 4488, Ch. 54, h 2

A number of our people have narrated from Sahl ibn Ziyad from Muhammad ibn Sinan from 'Abd Allah ibn Muskan from al-Halabiy who has said the following:

"Abu 'Abd Allah, *'Alayhi al-Salam*, has said, 'There is no Salam (the phrase of offering greeting of peace) to end Salat (prayer) for a deceased.'"

H 4489, Ch. 54, h 3

Ali ibn Ibrahim has narrated from his father from ibn abu 'Umayr from Hammad ibn 'Uthaman from al-Halabiy from Zurarah who has said the following:

"Abu Ja'far, and abu 'Abd Allah, *'Alayhi al-Salam*, have said, 'There is no Salam (the phrase of offering greeting of peace) to end Salat (prayer) for a deceased.'"

Chapter 55 - Saying More Than Five Takbir in Salat (Prayer) for a Dead Person

H 4490, Ch. 55, h 1

A number of our people have narrated from Sahl ibn Ziyad from Ahmad ibn Muhammad from ibn abu Nasr from al-Muthanna' ibn al-Walid from Zurarah from who has said the following:

"Abu Ja'far, *'Alayhi al-Salam*, has said, 'The Messenger of Allah said seventy Salat (prayers) for Hamzah.'"

H 4491, Ch. 55, h 2

Ali ibn Ibrahim has narrated from his father from ibn abu 'Umayr from Hammad from al-Halabiy who has said the following:

"Abu 'Abd Allah, *'Alayhi al-Salam*, has said, ''Amir al-Mu'minin, *'Alayhi al-Salam*, in Salat (prayer) for Sahl ibn Hunayf who was a Badriy, (participant in the battle of Badr) said five Takbir. He (the Imam then walked for a while, then placed him on the ground and said another five Takbir and so on until he had said twenty-five Takbir.'"

H 4492, Ch. 55, h 3

Muhammad ibn Yahya has narrated from Ahmad ibn Muhammad from al-Husayn ibn Sa'id from al-Qasim ibn Muhammad from Ali ibn abu Hamzah from abu Basir from who has said the following:

"Abu Ja'far, *'Alayhi al-Salam,* has said, 'The Messenger of Allah in Salat (prayer) for Hamzah said seventy Takbir and `Amir al-Mu'minin) Ali said twenty five Takbir in Salat (prayer) for Sahl ibn Hunayf. He (the Imam) said, 'Each time `Amir al-Mu'minin said five Takbir as new people arrived saying that we did not have a chance to attend Salat (prayer) for him so `Amir al-Mu'minin would ask to place him on the ground and he (the Imam) say five Takbir until he arrived to his grave.'"

Chapter 56 - Salat (Prayer) For a Person of Weak Understanding of Faith and One Who Does Not Know the Truth

H 4493, Ch. 56, h 1

Ali ibn Ibrahim has narrated from his father from Hammad ibn 'Isa from Hariz from Muhammad ibn Muslim who has said the following:

"One of the two Imam, *'Alayhim al-Salam,* has stated this Hadith: 'There are people of weak understanding who do not understand prayer for the Holy prophet, and for the believing people - male and female. In Salat (prayer) for such people you should say, "Our Lord, forgive those who repent and follow your path and save them from the fire of hell. . ." Read to the end of verse 8 of Chapter 40 of the Holy Quran.'"

H 4494, Ch. 56, h 2

Ali ibn Ibrahim has narrated from his father from ibn abu 'Umayr from 'Umar ibn `Udhaynah from Fudayl ibn Yasar who has said the following:

"Abu Ja'far, *'Alayhi al-Salam,* has said, 'When you perform Salat (prayer) for a believing person, pray for him and strive in your appeal in favor of the deceased person. If he is of those who keep matters on hold (of waqifiy belief) or of weak understanding say, 'Takbir (Allah is great beyond description) and, O Lord, forgive those who have repented, followed your path and protect them against the suffering of the hell fire.'"

H 4495, Ch. 56, h 3

Ali ibn Ibrahim has narrated from his father from ibn abu 'Umayr from Hammad ibn 'Uthaman from al-Halabiy who has said the following:

"Abu 'Abd Allah, *'Alayhi al-Salam,* has said, 'If the deceased is a person of weak understanding, say, "O Lord, forgive those who have repented and followed Your path and protect them against suffering of the hell fire." If you do not know the condition of the deceased, then say, "O Lord, if this deceased is of those who love good and people of goodness, then forgive him, have mercy on him and ignore his shortcomings." If the deceased is a person of weak understanding, ask forgiveness for him in the form of intercession, not because of his right upon you as believing in Divine Authority of `A'immah, *'Alayhim al-Salam.*'"

H 4496, Ch. 56, h 4

Ali ibn Ibrahim has narrated from his father from ibn Faddal from certain persons of his people who has said the following:

"Abu 'Abd Allah, *'Alayhi al-Salam*, has said, 'Expressing kindness and compassion has two aspects: The aspect of al-Walayah (guardianship) and that of intercession.'"

H 4497, Ch. 56, h 5
Ali ibn Ibrahim has narrated from his father from 'Abd Allah ibn al-Mughirah from a man from Sulayman ibn Khalid who has said the following:
"Abu 'Abd Allah, *'Alayhi al-Salam*, has said to say this, '(I testify that only Allah deserves worship, He is one and has no partners and I testify that Muhammad is His servant and Messenger). O Allah, I pray to You to grant compensation to Muhammad and his family worthy of their services to Your cause. O Lord, accept his intercession, brighten his face and increase the number of his followers. O Lord, forgive me, grant me mercy and accept my repentance. O Lord, forgive those who repent, follow your path and save them from the fire of hell. . . .' (40:7) If the deceased is a believing person, he goes to paradise; if he is not a believer, he goes out of it.'"

H 4498, Ch. 56, h 6
A number of our people have narrated from Sahl ibn Ziyad from al-Hassan ibn Mahbub from 'Abd Allah ibn Ghalib from Thabit abu al-Miqdam who has said the following:
"Once I was with abu Ja'far, *'Alayhi al-Salam*, when a deceased from the people who believe in predestination was brought; and I was near him (the Imam) and heard him (the Imam) say, 'O Lord, it is You who have created these souls and You cause them to die and give them life. You know their secrets and their public affairs better than we know. You know the permanent and temporary ones among them. O Lord, this is Your servant. I do not know anything evil about him and You know better about him. We have come to intercede in his favor after his death. If he deserves, accept our intercession in his favor and raise him with those whom he loves.'"

Chapter 57 - Salat (Prayer) for a Dead Person Hostile to `A'immah

H 4499, Ch. 57, h 1
Ali ibn Ibrahim has narrated from his father from ibn abu 'Umayr from Hammad ibn 'Isa from al-Halabiy who has said the following:
"Abu 'Abd Allah, *'Alayhi al-Salam*, has said, 'When 'Abd Allah ibn 'Ubay ibn Salul died, the Holy prophet attended his funeral. 'Umar said to the Messenger of Allah, "O Messenger of Allah, has Allah not forbidden you from standing on his grave?" He (the Messenger of Allah) remained silent. He ('Umar) said, "O Messenger of Allah, has Allah not forbidden you from standing on his grave?" He (the Messenger of Allah) said, 'Fie upon you, how you could tell what I say? I said, "O Lord, fill his belly with fire, fill his grave with fire and make him feel the heat of fire."' Abu 'Abd Allah, *'Alayhi al-Salam*, then said, 'He made the Messenger of Allah to expose what he disliked.'"

H 4500, Ch. 57, h 2

A number of our people have narrated from Sahl ibn Ziyad and Ali ibn Ibrahim has narrated from his father all from ibn Mahbub from Ziyad ibn 'Isa from 'Amir ibn al-Simt who has said the following:

"Abu 'Abd Allah, *'Alayhi al-Salam*, has said that a man of the hypocrites died. Al-Husayn ibn Ali, *'Alayhi al-Salam*, attended his funeral; at this time one of his followers met him and asked, 'O so and so, where do you want to go?' He (the follower) said, 'I am running away from the dead body of this hypocrite and from having to perform Salat (prayer) for him.' Al-Husayn ibn Ali, *'Alayhi al-Salam*, said, 'Just stay on my right side and say what I say.' When the guardian of the deceased said Takbir, al-Husayn ibn Ali, *'Alayhi al-Salam*, said, 'O Lord, condemn so and so a thousand times together and without difference. O Lord, make this one of Your servant to suffer in Your land and make him suffer the heat of fire, make him suffer the most severe of Your punishment; he loved Your enemies, he was hostile to Your friends and he hated the family of Your Holy prophet.'"

H 4501, Ch. 57, h 3

Sahl ibn Ziyad has narrated from ibn abu Najran from Safwan al-Jammal who has said the following:

"Abu 'Abd Allah, *'Alayhi al-Salam*, has said that a man of the hypocrites died and al-Husayn, *'Alayhi al-Salam*, came out walking. One of his followers came and he (the Imam) asked, 'Where are you going?' He replied, 'I am running away from the dead body of this hypocrite to avoid performing Salat (prayer) for him.' Al-Husayn, *'Alayhi al-Salam*, said, 'Stand next to me and say what you will hear I will say.' He (the Imam) then raised his hands and said, 'O Lord, humiliate a servant who is one of Your servants in Your land. O Lord, make him feel the heat of Your fire. O Lord, make him suffer the most severe of suffering from Your creation because he loved Your enemies, he was an enemy of Your friends and hated the family of Your Holy prophet.'"

H 4502, Ch. 57, h 4

Ali ibn Ibrahim has narrated from his father from ibn abu 'Umayr from Hammad from al-Halabiy who has said the following:

"Abu 'Abd Allah, *'Alayhi al-Salam*, has said, 'When you pray against the enemy of Allah say, "O Lord, we do not know of so and so except that he is Your enemy and the enemy of Your messenger. O Lord, fill up his grave with fire as well as his belly and hasten him to the fire, because he loved Your enemies, he was an enemy of Your friends and hated the family of Your Holy prophet. O Lord, constrict down his grave.' When his body is picked up, then say, 'O Lord, do not raise him and do not purify him.'"

H 4503, Ch. 57, h 5

Ali ibn Ibrahim has narrated from his father from Hammad ibn 'Isa from Hariz from Muhammad ibn Muslim who has said the following:

"One of the two Imam, (abu Ja'far or abu 'Abd Allah), *'Alayhim al-Salam*, has said, 'If the dead person is one who refuses the truth say, 'O Lord, fill up his belly with fire as well as his grave. Make snakes and scorpions dominate him.' This is what abu Ja'far, *'Alayhi al-Salam*, said about an evil woman of banu

'Umayyah against whom my father prayed and said this expression, "Make Satan her companion." Muhammad ibn Muslim has said that he then asked him (the Imam), 'For what reason snakes and scorpions are placed in her grave?' He (the Imam) said, 'It is because snakes bite her and scorpions sting her and Satans give her company.' I then asked, 'Will she feel the pain?' He (the Imam) said, 'Yes, very severely.'"

H 4504, Ch. 57, h 6

A number of our people have narrated from Sahl ibn Ziyad from Ahmad ibn Muhammad from ibn abu Nasr who has said the following:

"He (the Imam), *'Alayhi al-Salam*, has said, say, 'O Lord, humiliate a servant who is one of Your servants in Your land. O Lord, make him feel the heat of Your fire. O Lord, make him suffer the most severe of suffering from Your creation because, he was an enemy of Your friends, he loved Your enemies and hated the family of Your Holy prophet.'"

H 4505, Ch. 57, h 7

Muhammad ibn Yahya has narrated from Ahmad ibn Muhammad from 'Abd Allah al-Hajjal from Hammad ibn 'Uthaman from abu' Abd Allah or from those whom he has mentioned who has said the following:

"Abu 'Abd Allah, *'Alayhi al-Salam,* has said, 'Once a woman of banu 'Umayyah died and I was present in her funeral. When they performed Salat (prayer) and picked her body when on the hands of men he (the Imam) said, 'O Lord, put her down and do not raise her and do not cleanse her.' He (the Imam) said, 'She was an enemy of Allah –I think he said- and our (enemy).'"

Chapter 58 - Arrival of Another Dead Body During Salat (Prayer) for One Already There

H 4506, Ch. 58, h 1

Muhammad ibn Yahya has narrated from al-'Amrakiy from Ali ibn Ja'far from his brother Musa ibn Ja'far, *'Alayhi al-Salam*, who has said the following:

"I once asked him (the Imam), *'Alayhi al-Salam*, about the case of a people who just have said Takbir (Allah is great beyond description) for Salat (prayer) of a deceased that another dead body is placed on the ground. What are they to do? He (the Imam) said, 'They can leave the first one until they complete all Takbir for the second one. They can complete all Takbir for the first one and do the remaining for the last one, either way is not harmful.'"

Chapter 59 - Placing the Dead Body in front of the Grave

H 4507, Ch. 59, h 1

A number of our people have narrated from Sahl ibn Ziyad from Muhammad ibn Sinan from Muhammad ibn 'Ajlan who has said the following:

"Abu 'Abd Allah, *'Alayhi al-Salam*, has said, 'You must not make it heavy for your deceased by placing him in the grave. Place him two or three yards away from the grave on the ground so that he can get ready.'"

H 4508, Ch. 59, h 2

Ali ibn Muhammad has narrated from Muhammad ibn Ahmad al-Khurasaniy from his father from Yunus who has said the following:

"I heard a Hadith from abu al-Hassan, Musa, *'Alayhi al-Salam*, that whenever I remember it in a house I feel as if it is tightening upon me. He (the Imam) said, 'When a deceased is placed in front of his grave, give him a chance for a while; he readies himself for interrogation.'"

Chapter 60 - Rare Ahadith

H 4509, Ch. 60, h 1

Muhammad ibn Yahya has narrated from Ahmad ibn Muhammad from al-Husayn ibn Sa'id from al-Nadr ibn al-Suwayd from Yahya ibn 'Imran al-Halabiy from 'Abd Allah ibn Muskan from Zurarah who has said the following:

"Once I was with of abu Ja'far, *'Alayhi al-Salam*, when a man from Ansar was also there. A funeral procession passed by and the Ansariy man stood up; but abu Ja'far, *'Alayhi al-Salam*, did not do so, and I remained sitting with him. The Ansariy remained standing until the procession passed by and then he sat down. The Imam asked, 'What made you stand up?' He replied, 'I saw al-Husayn ibn Ali do as I did.' Abu Ja'far, *'Alayhi al-Salam*, said, 'By Allah, al-Husayn did not do so and no one from us (Ahl al-Bayt) has ever done so.' The Ansariy then said, 'What you just said has placed me in doubt. I thought I had seen him (al-Husayn) doing so.'"

H 4510, Ch. 60, h 2

A number of our people have narrated from Sahl ibn Ziyad from ibn abu Najran from Muthanna al-Hannat who has said the following:

"Abu 'Abd Allah, *'Alayhi al-Salam*, has said that Ali ibn Al-Husayn, *'Alayhi al-Salam*, was sitting when (people with) the dead body passed by. People stood up when the dead body appeared. Ali ibn Al-Husayn, *'Alayhi al-Salam*, said, 'Once, (people with) the dead body of a Jewish person passed by; the Messenger of Allah was sitting on (the side of) way. He did not like the dead body of Jewish person higher over his head and to avoid this he stood up."

Chapter 61 - Entering and Coming out of the Grave

H 4511, Ch. 61, h 1

A number of our people have narrated from Sahl ibn Ziyad from ibn Mahbub from 'Abd al-'Aziz al-'Abdiy from ibn abu Ya'fur who has said the following:

"Abu 'Abd Allah, *'Alayhi al-Salam*, has said that no one should enter a grave with shoes, slippers, turbans, gowns or hats."

H 4512, Ch. 61, h 2

Ali ibn Ibrahim has narrated from his father from ibn abu 'Umayr from Ali ibn Yaqtin who has said the following:

"I heard abu al-Hassan, *'Alayhi al-Salam*, say, 'You must not enter a grave wearing a turban, a hat, shoes, or a shawl. You should open up your buttons, thus is the tradition of the Messenger of Allah. You should ask protection from Allah against Satan, the one condemned to be stoned. You should read Fatihah al-Kitab, Chapters 113, 114, 112 and Ayat al-Kursiy. If possible, one should make the side of his face touch the earth, keep saying the testimonies of faith and speak of Allah as much as one knows until he is in the presence of his guardian (Imam al-Mahdi).'"

H 4513, Ch. 61, h 3

Muhammad ibn Yahya has narrated from Muhammad ibn Ahmad from Muhammad ibn 'Abd Allah al-Misma'iy from Isma'il ibn Yasar al-Wasitiy from Sayf ibn 'Amirah from abu Bakr al-Hadramiy who has said the following:

"Abu 'Abd Allah, *'Alayhi al-Salam*, has said that you must not enter a grave wearing a turban, a shawl, a gown, or shoes. You should open your buttons.' I then asked, 'Can one wear al-Khuff (slippers or socks)?' He replied, 'There is no offense in wearing al-Khuff if needed or because of fear.'"

H 4514, Ch. 61, h 4

Ali ibn Muhammad has narrated from his father from al-Nawfaliy from al-Sakuniy who has said the following:

"Abu 'Abd Allah, *'Alayhi al-Salam*, has said that whoever enters a grave should come out only from the side where the feet are placed."

H 4515, Ch. 61, h 5

A number of our people have narrated from Sahl ibn Ziyad in a marfu' manner the following:

"He (the Imam), *'Alayhi al-Salam*, has said, 'One may enter a grave from whatever direction he likes, but should come out from the side where the feet are placed.'"

"In another Hadith it is said, 'The Messenger of Allah has said, "Every house has a door. The door of a grave is from the side where feet are placed."'"

Chapter 62 - People Who Should and Those Who Should Not Enter a Grave

H 4516, Ch. 62, h 1

Ali ibn Ibrahim has narrated from his father from Salih al-Sindiy from Ja'far ibn Bashir from 'Abd Allah ibn Rashid who has said the following:

"Abu 'Abd Allah, *'Alayhi al-Salam*, has said that a man may enter the grave of his father, but a father should not enter the grave of his sons."

H 4517, Ch. 62, h 2

Ali ibn Ibrahim has narrated from his father from ibn abu 'Umayr from Hafs ibn al-Bakhtariy and others who has said the following:

"Abu 'Abd Allah, *'Alayhi al-Salam*, has said that it is undesirable for a man to enter the grave of his sons."

H 4518, Ch. 62, h 3

Ali has narrated from his father from ibn abu 'Umayr from Muhammad ibn abu Hamzah from a man who has said the following:

"When Isma'il, son of abu 'Abd Allah, passed away, abu 'Abd Allah, *'Alayhi al-Salam*, went to the grave site, allowed his body to reach the ground, and said,

'I pray to Allah to grant you mercy and favors.' He did not enter the grave; and he said, 'This is how the Holy Prophet did when Ibrahim died.'"

H 4519, Ch. 62, h 4

Abu Ali al-Ash'ariy has narrated from Muhammad ibn 'Abd al-Jabbar from 'Abd Allah al-Hajjal from Tha'labah ibn Maymun from Zurarah who has said the following:

"I asked abu 'Abd Allah, *'Alayhi al-Salam*, 'How many should enter a grave?' He replied, 'It is up to the guardian of the deceased. He may ask an odd or even number of people.'"

H 4520, Ch. 62, h 5

A number of our people have narrated from Sahl ibn Ziyad and Ali ibn Ibrahim has narrated from his father all from al-Nawfaliy from al-Sakuniy from 'Abd Allah, *'Alayhi al-Salam*, who has said the following:

"Amir al-Mu'minin, *'Alayhi al-Salam*, has said, 'It is of the Sunnah (tradition) of the Messenger of Allah that no one should enter the grave of a woman except those who could see her in her lifetime.'"

H 4521, Ch. 62, h 6

Sahl ibn Ziyad has narrated from Muhammad ibn 'Uramah from Ali ibn Maysarah from Ishaq ibn 'Ammar who has said the following:

"Abu 'Abd Allah, *'Alayhi al-Salam*, has said that a husband is more rightful to place his wife in the grave."

H 4522, Ch. 62, h 7

Humayd ibn Ziyad has narrated from al-Hassan ibn Muhammad al-Kindiy from Ahmad ibn al-Hassan al-Mithamiy from Aban from 'Abd Allah ibn Rashid who has said the following:

"I was with abu 'Abd Allah, *'Alayhi al-Salam*, when Isma'il, his son passed away. The dead body was brought down in the grave. Thereafter he (the Imam) allowed his body to reach the ground on the side of the grave facing the direction of Qiblah. Then he said, 'This is how the Messenger of Allah did on the death of Ibrahim.' He then said, 'A man may enter the grave of his father but a father, should not enter the grave of his sons.'"

H 4523, Ch. 62, h 8

A number of our people have narrated from Sahl ibn Ziyad from Muhammad ibn al-Walid from Yahya ibn 'Amr from 'Abd Allah ibn Rashid from 'Abd Allah al-'Anbariy who has said the following:

"Once I asked abu 'Abd Allah, *'Alayhi al-Salam*, 'Can a man bury his son?' He replied, 'He does not bury him in the soil.' I (the narrator) then asked, 'Can a son bury his father?' He replied, 'Yes, there is no offense in it.'"

Chapter 63 - Preparation for Placing a Deceased in the Grave

H 4524, Ch. 63, h 1

Ali ibn Ibrahim has narrated from his father from ibn abu 'Umayr from Hammad from al-Halabiy who has said the following:

"Abu 'Abd Allah, *'Alayhi al-Salam*, has said that you should place a deceased, after his arrival near the grave, in it from the side where you intend to place his feet. When the deceased is placed in the grave, read Ayatu al-Kursiy and say, '(I begin) in the name of Allah, in the way of Allah and on the path of the Messenger of Allah. O Allah, make his grave comfortably spacious and join him with his prophet, who with his family are *'Alayhim al-Salam.'* Then say what you have just said in Salat (prayer) for the deceased only once nearby, 'O Allah, if he is a person of good deed, increase his good deeds and if he is a person of bad deeds, please forgive him, have mercy on him and ignore his sins.' You should ask forgiveness for him as much as possible. The Imam said, 'Ali ibn al-Husayn, *'Alayhi al-Salam*, at the time of placing a deceased in the grave would say, "O Allah make his place spacious on both sides, accept his good deeds and grant him happiness from Your side.""'

H 4525, Ch. 63, h 2

Muhammad ibn Yahya has narrated from Ahmad ibn Muhammad ibn 'Isa from al-Husayn ibn Sa'id and Muhammad ibn Khalid, all from al-Nadr ibn al-Suwayd from Yahya ibn 'Imran from Harun ibn Kharijah from abu Basir who has said the following:

"Abu 'Abd Allah, *'Alayhi al-Salam*, has said to say this, when you place a deceased in the grave, '(I begin) in the name of Allah, with Allah and on the path of the Messenger of Allah. O Allah, take him to Your mercy and not to Your punishment.' Say, when the deceased is placed in the grave, with your hand on his ear, 'Allah is your Lord, al-Islam is your religion, Muhammad is your prophet, Quran is your book and Ali is your Imam.'"

H 4526, Ch. 63, h 3

A number of our people have narrated from Sahl ibn Ziyad from al-Hassan ibn Mahbub from al-'Ala' ibn Razin from Muhammad ibn Muslim who has said the following:

"I asked one of the two Imam, *'Alayhim al-Salam*, about a deceased. He said, 'Place him in the grave from the side of the feet. Keep the grave above the ground by four open fingers and make it four cornered.'"

H 4527, Ch. 63, h 4

Sahl ibn Ziyad has narrated from Muhammad ibn Sinan from Muhammad ibn 'Ajlan who has said the following:

"Abu 'Abd Allah, *'Alayhi al-Salam*, has said to place a deceased gently in the grave. The person from the side of his head, when he is placed in the grave, should speak of the names of Allah. He should also say 'Allahumma Salli 'Ala Muhammad wa 'Ali Muhammad (O Allah grant Muhammad and his family a compensation worthy of their serving Your cause).' He should ask protection with Allah against Satan; read al-Fatihah al-Kitab, chapters 113, 114, 112 of the Holy Quran and Ayatu al-Kursiy. If possible, one should place the side of his face on the soil without covering, say the testimonies, and speak of Allah whatever he knows until he is in the presence of his guardian (Imam al-Mahdi)."

H 4528, Ch. 63, h 5

Muhammad ibn Yahya has narrated from Muhammad ibn Isma'il from Ali ibn al-Hakam from Muhammad ibn Sinan from Mahfuz al-Iskaf who has said the following:

"Abu 'Abd Allah, *'Alayhi al-Salam*, has said that the person nearest in kinship to the deceased should enter the grave for burial near his head, remove the shroud from the right side of his face, place it on earth, with his mouth near the ear of the deceased, say three times, 'Listen and understand.' Allah is your Lord,

Muhammad is your prophet, al-Islam is your religion, so and so is your Imam. Listen and understand. He should repeat this dictation three times.'"

H 4529, Ch. 63, h 6

Ali ibn Ibrahim has narrated from his father from Hammad ibn 'Isa from Hariz from Muhammad ibn Muslim from one of the two Imam the following:

"The Imam, *'Alayhi al-Salam*, said, 'When a deceased is placed in the grave you should say, "(I begin) in the name of Allah, in the way of Allah and according to the traditions of the Messenger of Allah. (O Allah), this, Your servant, son of Your servant has become Your guest and You are the best host. O Allah, make his grave spacious and join him with his prophet. O Allah, all we know of him is good but You are more knowledgeable about him than we are." When you place the slab, (to cover his grave) say, "O Allah, find connections for his loneliness and comfort for his dread. Settle with him from Your mercy a mercy that will suffice him of the mercy of those other than Yourself." When coming out of the grave say, "We are for Allah and to Him we return. All praise belongs to Allah, Lord of the worlds. O Allah, raise his position in the highest of high places, make a successor among those whom he has left behind, who suffer grief, O Lord of the worlds."'"

H 4530, Ch. 63, h 7

It is a narration from him (narrator of previous Hadith) by his father from Hammad from Hariz from Zurarah who has said the following:

"He (the Imam), *'Alayhi al-Salam*, has said, that when you place a deceased in his grave, read Ayatu al-Kursiy and hold his right shoulder with your hand, then say, 'O so and so say, "I accept Allah as the Lord, al-Islam as the religion, Muhammad as the prophet and Ali as the Imam." Then mention the Imam of his time.'"

H 4531, Ch. 63, h 8

A number of our people have narrated from Sahl ibn Ziyad and Muhammad ibn Yahya from Ahmad ibn Muhammad all from ibn Mahbub from abu Ayyub from Sama'ah who has said the following:

"I asked abu 'Abd Allah, *'Alayhi al-Salam*, 'What should we say when placing a deceased from us in the grave?' He said to say, 'O Allah, this is Your servant so and so son of Your servant who has become Your guest and You are the best host. He is in need of Your mercy. O Allah, all we know from him is good. You know his secrets. We are only witnesses about his appearances. O Allah, make the earth spacious on his both sides. Dictate to him the statement of authority (that he needs) and make this day the best of days that he has ever lived. Make this grave the best house where he has ever lived. Place him in the best of what he has ever experienced. Make his entrance spacious, comfort his dread, forgive his sins and do not deprive us of the reward (because of him) and do not make us to go astray thereafter.'"

H 4532, Ch. 63, h 9

Ali ibn Ibrahim has narrated from his father from ibn abu 'Umayr from more than one person of our people who has said the following:

"Abu 'Abd Allah, *'Alayhi al-Salam*, has said that a shroud should be cut open from where the head of the deceased is when he is placed in the grave."

H 4533, Ch. 63, h 10

Humayd ibn Ziyad has narrated from al-Hassan ibn Muhammad ibn Sama'ah from certain individuals of his people from Aban from 'Abd al-Rahman ibn Sayabah from abu 'Abd Allah, who has said the following:

"Abu 'Abd Allah, *'Alayhi al-Salam*, has said, 'You should place the deceased in the grave gently.'"

H 4534, Ch. 63, h 11

A number of our people have narrated from Ahmad ibn Muhammad from 'Uthman ibn 'Isa from Sama'ah who has said the following:

"Abu 'Abd Allah, *'Alayhi al-Salam*, has said that when you place a deceased in the grave say, 'O Allah [this is] Your servant son of a male servant and a female servant who has become Your guest and You are the best host.' When you send the body upward from where the feet are to be placed to the place for the head say, '(I begin) in the name of Allah, with Allah and according to the tradition of the Messenger of Allah. O Allah, (send him) to Your mercy but not to Your punishment. O Allah, make his grave spacious, dictate him the statement of his authority, make him steadfast upon the solid words, protect him and us against the torment of fire.' When earth is leveled upon him say, 'O Allah, make the earth spacious on his both sides. Raise his spirit toward the spirits of the believing people in the high places and join him with righteous ones.'"

(Chapter 64 is best explained by fatwa.)

Chapter 64 - Preparing Lahad and the Materials Needed

H 4535, Ch. 64, h 1

Ali ibn Ibrahim has narrated from his father from Ali ibn Muhammad al-Qasaniy who has said the following:

"Once Ali ibn Bilal wrote to abu al-Hassan, *'Alayhi al-Salam*, about the condition of a grave asking, 'Someone may die in our area but the ground of the grave is wet.' We pave it (the floor) with teak (wooden board) or cover it in this way, is this permissible? He (the Imam) wrote the answer, 'It is permissible.'"

H 4536, Ch. 64, h 2

Ali ibn Ibrahim has narrated from his father from Salih ibn Sindiy from Ja'far ibn Bashir from Yahya ibn abu al-'Ala' who has said the following:

"Abu 'Abd Allah, *'Alayhi al-Salam*, has said, 'Shuqran, Mawla' of the Messenger of Allah spread a sheet (blanket) in his grave.'"

H 4537, Ch. 64, h 3

Muhammad ibn Yahya has narrated from Ahmad ibn Muhammad from Ali ibn al-Hakam from Husayn ibn 'Uthman from ibn Muskan from Aban ibn Taghlib who has said the following:

"I once heard abu 'Abd Allah, *'Alayhi al-Salam*, say, 'Ali, *'Alayhi al-Salam*, placed bricks on the grave of the Holy prophet.' I then asked, 'If one places tiles on the grave is it harmful to the deceased?' He (the Imam) said, 'No, it is not harmful.'"

Chapter 65 - Who Should Fill Soil in the Grave and How

H 4538, Ch. 65, h 1

Ali ibn Ibrahim has narrated from his father from ibn abu 'Umayr from Dawud ibn al-Nu'man who has said the following:

"I heard abu al-Hassan, *'Alayhi al-Salam*, say, 'It is what Allah wills, not what people will.' When he approached the grave, he kept to a side and sat down. When the deceased was placed in the grave, he stood up and filled three handfuls of soil in the grave, one at a time."

H 4539, Ch. 65, h 2

Ali ibn Ibrahim has narrated from his father, from al-Nawfaliy from al-Sakuniy who has said the following:

"Abu 'Abd Allah, *'Alayhi al-Salam*, has said that when you fill soil in the grave of a deceased say, '(It is) out of faith in You (O Allah) and an acknowledgement of Your resurrection. This is what Allah and His Messenger have promised us.' He (the Imam) said that Amir al-Mu'minin, *'Alayhi al-Salam*, has said, 'I heard the Messenger of Allah say, "Whoever fills soil in the grave of a deceased saying this expression, Allah grants him the reward of one good deed for each particle."'"

H 4540, Ch. 65, h 3

Ali ibn Ibrahim has narrated from his father from certain individuals of his people from 'Ala' ibn Razin from Muhammad ibn Muslim who has said the following:

"I was with abu Ja'far, *'Alayhi al-Salam*, in a funeral procession for one of our companions. When they buried him, he (the Imam) stood up next to his grave, then filled soil toward his head, three handfuls. He then extended his palm over the grave, and then said, 'O Allah make earth spacious on his both sides, raise his spirit to Yourself and grant him happiness from Your side and settle his grave with Your mercy so much so that it suffices him of the mercy of all things other than Your mercy,' then he (the Imam) left."

H 4541, Ch. 65, h 4

Ali ibn Ibrahim has narrated from his father from ibn abu 'Umayr from Jamil ibn Darraj from 'Umar ibn 'Udhaynah who has said the following:

"I saw abu 'Abd Allah, *'Alayhi al-Salam*, fill soil in the grave of a deceased. He held it (soil) in his hand for a while then tossed it in the grave and did not do more than three handfuls. I asked him about it and he replied, 'O 'Umar I was saying, "It is out of faith in You (O Allah), and an acknowledgement of Your resurrecting (people). This is what Allah and His Messenger have promised us. Allah and His Messenger are truthful. This has only increased our faith and acceptance." This is how the Messenger of Allah would do and thus it has become a tradition.'"

H 4542, Ch. 65, h 5

Ali ibn Ibrahim has narrated from Ya'qub ibn Yazid from Ali ibn Asbat from 'Ubayd ibn Zurarah who has said the following:

"A son of one of the companions of abu 'Abd Allah, *'Alayhi al-Salam*, died. Abu 'Abd Allah attended the funeral. When the deceased was placed in the grave, his father went forward to toss soil into his grave. Abu 'Abd Allah held his hand and said, 'You must not toss soil on him. No one of his relatives should do so. The Messenger of Allah has prohibited a father and relatives to do so.' We asked him (the Imam), 'O son of the Messenger of Allah, do you prohibit in this case only?' He replied, 'I prohibit from tossing soil in the grave of your relatives; it causes hardheartedness and those suffering from hardheartedness are away from their Lord.'"

Chapter 66 - Preparing Four Corners of the Grave and Sprinkling Water on It

H 4543, Ch. 66, h 1

Muhammad ibn Yahya has narrated from Ahmad ibn Muhammad from al-Hassan ibn Ali from ibn Bukayr from Qudamah ibn Za'idah who has said the following:

"I heard abu Ja'far, *'Alayhi al-Salam*, say, 'The Messenger of Allah placed his son Ibrahim in a basket-shaped place in the grave and made the surface into a square shape.'"

H 4544, Ch. 66, h 2

A number of our people have narrated from Ahmad ibn Muhammad ibn Khalid from 'Uthman ibn 'Isa from Sama'ah who has said the following:

"Abu 'Abd Allah, *'Alayhi al-Salam*, has said, 'It is preferable to place two fresh twigs of palm tree with the deceased in the grave, raise the surface of the grave above ground by four inches, sprinkle water on it and then leave it alone.'"

H 4545, Ch. 66, h 3

Humayd ibn Ziyad has narrated from al-Hassan ibn Muhammad ibn Sama'ah from more than one person from Aban from 'Abd al-Rahman ibn abu 'Abd Allah who has said the following:

"I once asked him (the Imam), *'Alayhi al-Salam*, about one's placing his hand over the grave, its significance and why it is done. He (the Imam) said, 'The Messenger of Allah had done so over the grave of his son after sprinkling water.' He (the narrator) has said that I then asked, 'How should I place my hand over the graves of the Muslims?' He (the Imam) pointed with his hand, placed it on the ground, then raised it while he was facing al-Qiblah (al-Ka'bah).'"

H 4546, Ch. 66, h 4

Ali ibn Ibrahim has narrated from his father from ibn abu 'Umayr from ibn 'Udhaynah from Zurarah from who has said the following:

"Abu Ja'far, *'Alayhi al-Salam*, has said, 'The Messenger of Allah would do something over the grave of the people from the tribe of banu Hashim and he would not do on other Muslims' graves. After performing Salat (prayer) for a deceased from banu Hashim, sprinkling water over his grave, he would place his hand over the grave while his fingers pressed in the clay. Strangers or travelers who came in the town and saw a new grave with marks of the fingers of the Messenger of Allah on it could tell that someone from banu Hashim has died. They would ask, 'Who from the family of Muhammad, O Allah grant compensation to Muhammad and his family worthy of their services to Your cause, has died?'"

H 4547, Ch. 66, h 5

Ali ibn Ibrahim has narrated from his father from ibn abu 'Umayr from Hammad ibn 'Isa who has said the following:

"Abu 'Abd Allah, *'Alayhi al-Salam*, has said, 'One day my father during his illness said to me, 'Son, call certain people from Quraysh and people of al-Madinah, so I can appoint them as witness.' I then called a number of people. He said, 'O Ja'far, when I die, give Ghusl (bath) to me, place me in the shroud, raise the surface of my grave by four fingers above the ground and sprinkle water on it.' When they left I asked, 'Father, had you commanded me, I would have done all these things. Why did you decide to call these people to be witnesses?' He said, 'My son I did it so no one will raise any disputes against you.'"

H 4548, Ch. 66, h 6

Ali ibn Ibrahim has narrated from his father from ibn abu 'Umayr from certain persons of his people who has said the following:

"About spraying water on the grave abu 'Abd Allah, *'Alayhi al-Salam*, has said, 'Suffering is withdrawn from it as long as the moisture exists.'"

H 4549, Ch. 66, h 7

A number of our people have narrated from Sahl ibn Ziyad from Muhammad ibn Sinan from Talhah ibn Zayd who has said the following:

"Abu 'Abd Allah, *'Alayhi al-Salam*, has said that sprinkling water over a new grave was during the time of the Messenger of Allah."

H 4550, Ch. 66, h 8

Ali ibn Ibrahim has narrated from his father from Hammad ibn 'Isa from Hariz from Zurarah from who has said the following:

"Abu 'Abd Allah, *'Alayhi al-Salam*, has said, 'When you complete the grave sprinkle water on it, then place your hand near the head of the deceased and depress your hand on it after sprinkling water.'"

H 4551, Ch. 66, h 9

Humayd ibn Ziyad has narrated from al-Hassan ibn Muhammad from more than one person from Aban from 'Abd Allah ibn 'Ajalan who has said the following:

"Abu Ja'far, *'Alayhi al-Salam*, stood on the grave of one of his followers and said, 'O Lord, grant company in his loneliness, comfort his fear and settle down with him of your mercy that much which will make him free from want from others except yourself.'"

H 4552, Ch. 66, h 10

Aban has narrated from Muhammad ibn Muslim who has said the following:

"Abu Ja'far, *'Alayhi al-Salam*, has said, 'Prayers are said when a deceased is placed in his grave and the surface of the grave is raised above the ground by four fingers.'"

H 4553, Ch. 66, h 11

Muhammad ibn Yahya has narrated from certain persons of our people from Ahmad ibn Muhammad ibn abu Nasr from `Isma'il who has that narrated to me abu al-Hassan al-Dallal from Yahya ibn 'Abd Allah who has said the following:

"I once heard abu 'Abd Allah, *'Alayhi al-Salam*, say, 'It does not harm the family of a deceased among you to prevent his fear of meeting al-Munkar and al-Nakir (interrogating angels).' I (the narrator) then asked, 'How can they do so?' He (the Imam) said, 'When the deceased is left alone, the nearest relative is left behind near the deceased who places his mouth near the head of the deceased and calls loudly, 'O so and so, son of so and so, or daughter of so and so, are you still true to the covenant (belief) with which you departed us. The testimony that states, 'I testify that only Allah deserves worship, He is one and has no partners and I testify that Muhammad is His servant and Messenger, master of the prophets. I testify that Ali is `Amir al-Mu'minin (master of the believers) and master of the executors (of the wills of the prophets). I testify that whatever Muhammad, *'Alayhi al-Salam*, has brought from Allah is all true, that death is a truth, resurrection is a truth and that Allah will raise everyone from the grave.' He (the Imam) said, 'Al-Munkar then says to Nakir, 'Allow us to turn away from him; his argument (authoritative statements of his belief) are dictated to him.'"

Chapter 67 - Using Clay or Lime over the Grave

H 4554, Ch. 67, h 1

Ali ibn Ibrahim has narrated from his father from al-Nawfaliy from al-Sakuniy who has said the following:

"Abu 'Abd Allah, *'Alayhi al-Salam*, has said, 'You must not apply clay to the grave which is not of the clay of that grave.'"

H 4555, Ch. 67, h 2

Humayd ibn Ziyad has narrated from al-Hassan ibn Muhammad from more than one person from certain persons of his people who has said the following:

"Abu 'Abd Allah, *'Alayhi al-Salam*, has said, 'The grave of the Messenger of Allah is covered with red color pebbles."

H 4556, Ch. 67 h 3

A number of our people have narrated from Sahl ibn Ziyad ibn Mahbub from Yunus ibn Ya'qub who has said the following:

"When abu al-Hassan, *'Alayhi al-Salam*, returned from Baghdad to al-Madinah, one of his daughters died in Fayd. He (the Imam) buried her and commanded certain people of his followers to build her grave with lime, write her name on the tombstone and place it on the grave."

H 4557, Ch. 67, h 4

Ali ibn Ibrahim has narrated from his father from al-Nawfaliy from al-Sakuniy who has said the following:

"Abu 'Abd Allah, *'Alayhi al-Salam*, has said, 'The Holy prophet prohibited adding of such soil into the grave which has not come from that grave.'"

Chapter 68 - The Soil Where a Person Is Buried

H 4558, Ch. 68, h 1

A number of our people have narrated from Ahmad ibn Muhammad ibn 'Isa from ibn Muskan from Muhammad ibn Muslim who has said the following:

"One of the two Imam, *'Alayhim al-Salam*, has said, 'From whatever soil one is created in that soil one is buried also.'"

H 4559, Ch. 68, h 2

A number of our people have narrated from Sahl ibn Ziyad from al-Hajjal from ibn Bukayr from abu Minhal from al-Harith ibn al-Mughirah who has said the following:

"I once heard abu 'Abd Allah, *'Alayhi al-Salam*, say, 'When al-Nutfah (seed, sperm) falls in the womb Allah, most Majestic, most Glorious, sends an angel who takes from the soil in which he is to be buried and dissolves it into the al-Nutfah. His heart continues yearning for that place until he is buried therein.'"

Chapter 69 - Condolences and the Obligations of the People of the Deceased

H 4560, Ch. 69, h 1

A number of our people have narrated from Sahl ibn Ziyad from Muhammad ibn Isma'il from Muhammad ibn 'Adhafir from Ishaq ibn 'Ammar who has said the following:

"Abu 'Abd Allah, *'Alayhi al-Salam*, has said that condolence is offered only near the grave. Thereafter people should disperse so that if something should happen to the deceased no one can hear the voice."

H 4561, Ch. 69, h 2

Ali ibn Ibrahim has narrated from his father from ibn abu 'Umayr from certain persons of his people who has said the following:

"Abu 'Abd Allah, *'Alayhi al-Salam*, has said that condolences should be offered to the people of the deceased after burial takes place."

H 4562, Ch. 69, h 3

Abu Ali al-Ash'ariy has narrated from Muhammad ibn 'Abd al-Jabbar from al-Hajjal from Ishaq ibn 'Ammar (in a maqtu' manner) who has said the following:

"He (the Imam), *'Alayhi al-Salam*, has said that condolences should be offered only near the grave. Thereafter people should return so that they cannot hear the voice if anything happens to the deceased."

H 4563, Ch. 69, h 4

A number of our people have narrated from Ahmad ibn Muhammad ibn Khalid from his father from certain persons of his people who has said the following:

"Abu 'Abd Allah, *'Alayhi al-Salam*, has said that the necessary condolence should be offered after burial takes place."

H 4564, Ch. 69, h 5

Ali ibn Ibrahim has narrated from his father from ibn abu 'Umayr from al-Qasim ibn Muhammad from al-Husayn ibn 'Uthman who has said the following:

"When Ismai'l ibn abu 'Abd Allah, *'Alayhi al-Salam*, died, abu 'Abd Allah walked to the coffin (stretcher) barefoot and without a gown."

H 4565, Ch. 65, h 6

Ali ibn Ibrahim has narrated from ibn abu 'Umayr from certain persons of his people who has said the following:

"Abu 'Abd Allah, *'Alayhi al-Salam,* has said that people of the deceased should remove their gowns. This can serve as a sign to show that they are of the people of the deceased."

H 4566, Ch. 69, h 7

Muhammad ibn Yahya has narrated from Ahmad ibn Muhammad from Ali ibn al-Hakam, from Rifa'ah al-Nakhkhas from a man who has said the following:

"Once abu 'Abd Allah, *'Alayhi al-Salam,* offered condolences to a man because of the death of his son, saying, 'Allah is better for your son than you are, and the reward from Allah is better for you than your son.' When he (Imam) heard him crying loudly, he returned to him saying, 'The Messenger of Allah died. Is this not enough lesson for you?' He said, 'He (my son) was drunk.' The Imam said, 'There are three things before him: The testimony, "No one deserves to be worshipped except Allah, the mercy and kindness of Allah and the intercession of the Messenger of Allah." Either one of these will save him, if Allah so will.'"

H 4567, Ch. 69, h 8

Al-Husayn ibn Muhammad has narrated from Ahmad ibn Ishaq from Sa'dan ibn Muslim from abu Basir who has said the following:

"Abu 'Abd Allah, *'Alayhi al-Salam,* has said that people of the deceased should not wear their gowns. They should wear only shirts so people can recognize them."

H 4568, Ch. 69, h 9

Ali ibn Ibrahim has narrated from his father and Muhammad ibn Isma'il from al-Fadl ibn Shadhan all from ibn abu 'Umayr from Hisham ibn al-Hakam who has said the following:

"I observed (Imam) Musa, *'Alayhi al-Salam,* offer condolences before and after burial."

H 4569, Ch. 65, h 10

A number of our people have narrated from Sahl ibn Ziyad from ibn Mehran who has said the following:

"Abu Ja'far, the second, *'Alayhi al-Salam,* wrote to a man, 'I was informed of your suffering from the death of your son, Ali. I was also informed that he was the most beloved among your sons to you. It so happens that Allah, the Most Majestic, the Most Glorious, takes away from a father or other people the most beloved to his people so as to increase their reward for their suffering. May Allah increase your reward, grant you patience and strengthen your heart; He is Most powerful. May Allah very soon grant you one to replace him and I hope that Allah has already made it happen.'"

Chapter 70 - The Reward for One Who Offers Condolences to a Saddened Person

H 4570, Ch. 70, h 1
Ali ibn Ibrahim has narrated from his father from Al-Nawfaliy from al-Sakuniy who has said the following:
"Abu 'Abd Allah, *'Alayhi al-Salam*, has narrated from his ancestors who have said that the Messenger of Allah has said, 'If one offers condolences to a saddened person, he will be given a well beautified dress on the station for Judgment ."

H 4571, Ch. 70, h 2
A number of our people have narrated from Ahmad ibn Muhammad ibn Khalid from his father from Wahab who has said the following:
"Abu 'Abd Allah, *'Alayhi al-Salam*, has said that the Messenger of Allah has said, 'If one offers condolences to a depressed person, one will have a reward equal to his (depressed person's) reward without any reduction in the reward for the latter, the sorrowful party.'"

(The following chapters are best explained by fatwa, please consult fatwa.)

Chapter 71 - A Woman Dies with Baby Moving Inside

H 4572, Ch. 71, h 1
Ali ibn Ibrahim has narrated from his father from ibn abu 'Umayr from certain persons of his people who has said the following:
"Abu 'Abd Allah, *'Alayhi al-Salam*, was asked, 'If a woman dies with a child moving in her womb, is her belly to be opened to take the child out?' He (the Imam) said, 'Yes, and her belly is stitched to close.'"

H 4573, Ch. 71, h 2
A number of our people have narrated from Ahmad ibn Muhammad ibn Khalid from Wahab ibn Wahab who has said the following:
"Abu 'Abd Allah, *'Alayhi al-Salam*, has said that `Amir al-Mu'minin, *'Alayhi al-Salam*, has said, 'If a woman dies with the child moving in her womb whose life is in danger, her belly is opened and the child is taken out.'

"About a woman whose child dies in her womb and her life is in danger, he (the Imam) said, 'It is permissible for a man to enter his hand inside, cut it (the dead body) to take it out if there is no woman around."

Chapter 72 - Ghusl (bath) for Children and Salat (Prayer) for Them

H 4574, Ch. 72, h 1
A number of our people have narrated from Sahl ibn Ziyad from Ahmad ibn Muhammad from al-Husayn ibn Musa from Zurarah from who has said the following:
"Abu 'Abd Allah, *'Alayhi al-Salam*, has said, 'A miscarried child (fetus) after four months is given Ghusl (bath).'"

H 4575, Ch. 72, h 2

Ali ibn Ibrahim has narrated from his father from ibn abu 'Umayr from Hammad ibn 'Isa from al-Halabiy and Zurarah who has said the following:

"Abu 'Abd Allah, *'Alayhi al-Salam*, was asked about Salat (prayer) of a child. He (the Imam) said, 'There is Salat (prayer) for him when he is able to understand it (Salat (prayer)).' I (the narrator) then asked, 'When it becomes obligatory for him? He (the Imam) said, 'It is when he is six years old and there is fasting on him when he is able to fast.'"

H 4576, Ch. 72, h 3

Ali ibn Ibrahim has narrated from his father from ibn abu 'Umayr from 'Umar ibn `Udhaynah from Zurarah from who has said the following:

"I saw a son of abu 'Abd Allah, *'Alayhi al-Salam*, during the life time of abu Ja'far, *'Alayhi al-Salam*, called 'Abd Allah Fatim moved in. I asked him about their Mawla' next to him, 'Who is he next to you?' He replied, 'He is my Mawla' (servant or follower).' The Mawla', joking with him said, 'I am not your Mawla'.' He said, 'That is worse for you.' That boy was hurt and he died. (They carried) his body to al-Baqi' cemetery in a basket. Abu Ja'far, *'Alayhi al-Salam*, came out to join the funeral wearing a jubbah which was yellow, a yellow turban and a yellow shawl of khazz (a certain kind of fur). He (the Imam) walked to al-Baqi' while leaning on me for support. People offered condolences for his grandchild. In al-Baqi' abu Ja'far, *'Alayhi al-Salam*, moved forward and performed Salat (prayer) for the deceased boy with four Takbir. He then commanded to bury him. He (the Imam) then holding my hand moved away and then said, 'Salat (prayer) was not performed for deceased children. `Amir al-Mu'minin, *'Alayhi al-Salam*, would command to bury them (children) without performing Salat (prayer). I performed Salat (prayer) only because of people of al-Madinah. I do not like their saying, 'They do not perform Salat (prayer) for their children.'"

H 4577, Ch. 72, 4

Muhammad ibn Yahya has narrated from Ahmad ibn Muhammad ibn 'Isa from Muhammad ibn Khalid and al-Husayn ibn Sa'id from al-Nadr ibn Suwayd from Yahya ibn 'Imran from ibn Muskan from Zurarah from who has said the following:

"One of the sons of Abu Ja'far, *'Alayhi al-Salam*, died. He (the Imam) was informed of his death and he commanded for Ghusl (bath) and shroud. He (the Imam) walked in his funeral and performed Salat (prayer). A prayer mat was spread and he (the Imam) stood on it, then he (the Imam) stood on his grave until he was free, then moved away and I (the narrator) also moved away. I walked along with him (the Imam). He (the Imam) said that Salat (prayer) was not performed in such cases, but people did things and we also do like them. I (the narrator) then asked, 'When Salat (prayer) is obligatory?' He (the Imam) said, 'It is necessary when he understands Salat (prayer) and he is six years old. I (the narrator) asked, 'What do you say about children?' He (the Imam) said, 'The Messenger of Allah was asked about them and he said that Allah knows best about what they have done.'"

H 4578, Ch. 72, h 5

Muhammad ibn Yahya has narrated from Ahmad ibn Muhammad from Ali ibn 'Isma'il from 'Uthman ibn 'Isa from Zur'ah from Sama'ah who has said the following:

"I once asked abu al-Hassan, al-Awwal, *'Alayhi al-Salam,* about a miscarried child whose body is complete if Ghusl (bath) is necessary as well as al-Lahad (a horizontal or vertical) ditch in the grave). He (the Imam) said, 'All of such things are necessary.'"

H 4579, Ch. 72, h 6

A number of our people have narrated from Sahl ibn Ziyad from Ali ibn Mehran from Muhammad ibn al-Fudayl who has said the following:

"I once wrote to abu Ja'far, *'Alayhi al-Salam,* asking about what is done for a miscarried child. He (the Imam) wrote to me, 'A miscarried child is buried with his blood in his place (right away).'"

H 4580, Ch. 72, h 7

Ali ibn Ibrahim has narrated from his father from 'Amr ibn Sa'id from Ali ibn 'Abd Allah who has said the following:

"I heard abu al-Hassan Musa, *'Alayhi al-Salam,* say, 'When Ibrahim son of the Messenger of Allah passed away, three traditions were established. One tradition is that on that day a sun eclipse took place and people said that it is because of the death of the son of the Messenger of Allah. The Messenger of Allah went on the pulpit, praised Allah and glorified Him; then said, "O people the sun and the moon are two signs of the signs of Allah which move because of His command and in obedience to Him. Their eclipse is not because of the death or life of anyone. If one or both of them eclipse perform Salat (prayer) for eclipse." He climbed down the pulpit and performed Salat (prayer) because of eclipse with the people. When he completed his Salat (prayer) by saying the last phrase, the greeting, he (the Messenger of Allah) said, "O Ali, you must prepare my son for burial." Ali, *'Alayhi al-Salam,* gave Ghusl (bath) to Ibrahim, hunut and shroud. He brought the deceased out and the Messenger of Allah joined the funeral until they arrived near his grave. People said, "The Messenger of Allah has forgotten Salat (prayer) for Ibrahim due to shock because of his death." He (the Messenger of Allah) stood up straight and said, "O people, Jibril just informed me of what you have thought about my forgetting Salat (prayer) for my son, Ibrahim, because of shock due to his death. You must know that it is not as you think it is. In fact the Most Kind and Most Aware one has made five Salat (prayer) obligatory on you and for your dead people. He has made five Takbir necessary, one Takbir from each Salat (prayer). He has commanded me to perform Salat (prayer) only for those who have performed Salat (prayer)." He (the Messenger of Allah) then said, "O Ali, climb down and place my son in al-Lahad." He (Ali) climbed down and placed Ibrahim in Lahad. People said, "It is not proper for people to climb down in the grave of their sons because the Messenger of Allah has not done so." The Messenger of Allah said to them, "O people, it is not unlawful for you to climb down in the grave of your sons, but I do not find it safe for you to do so because on opening the shroud of your sons Satan may play with you to cause a shock and you lose your reward." He (the Messenger of Allah) thereafter, moved away and left the graveyard.'"

H 4581, Ch. 72, h 8

Ali has narrated from Ali ibn Shirah from Muhammad ibn Sulayman from Husayn al-Harshush from Hisham ibn Salim who has said the following:

"I once said to abu 'Abd Allah, *'Alayhi al-Salam*, that people speak against us and do not accept our words, 'there is no Salat (prayer) for a deceased child'; he has not performed any Salat (prayer). They say, 'You say that there is no Salat (prayer) for those who have not performed any Salat (prayer).' We say, 'Yes that is true.' They say, 'Consider if a Christian or a Jew becomes a Muslim, then he dies within the same hour, then what is the answer?' He (the Imam) said, 'Ask them to consider the case of this man, new Muslim, if he within the same hour falsely accuses a human being. What is his obligation because of his committing such sin? They will say that he is subject to punishment according to law. When they say this, then it is said to them, 'If a child who has not performed any Salat (prayer) accuses a human being falsely, is he subjected to punishment according to law? They will say that he is not subject to any punishment. It then is said to them that you are right. Salat (prayer) is necessary for one who has performed Salat (prayer) and those who are subject to punishment according to law. Salat (prayer) is not necessary for one on whom Salat (prayer) is not obligatory or enduring punishment according to law.'"

Chapter 73 - People Drowned or Struck Dead

H 4582, Ch. 73, h 1

Ali ibn Ibrahim has narrated from his father from ibn abu 'Umayr from Hisham ibn al-Hakam who has said the following:

"About people found dead because of a sudden shock or drowned, abu al-Hassan, *'Alayhi al-Salam*, has said to wait three days unless a change in their condition takes place earlier.'"

H 4583, Ch. 73, h 2

Muhammad ibn Yahya has narrated from Ahmad ibn Muhammad ibn 'Isa from Ali ibn al-Hakam from Sayf ibn 'Amirah from Ishaq ibn 'Ammar who has said the following:

"I once asked him (the Imam), *'Alayhi al-Salam*, if there is Ghusl (bath) for one who has died because of drowning. He (the Imam) said, 'Yes, there is Ghusl (bath) and he is freed (of doubtful condition).' I then asked, 'How is he freed?' He (the Imam) said, 'He is left for three days before burial and so also is the case of one found dead because of a sudden shock. People think he is dead, perhaps he is not dead.'"

H 4584, Ch. 73, h 3

Ali ibn Ibrahim has narrated from his father from al-Nawfaliy from al-Sakuniy who has said the following:

"Abu 'Abd Allah, *'Alayhi al-Salam*, has said that `Amir al-Mu'minin, *'Alayhi al-Salam*, has said, 'Ghusl (bath) of one who has died because of drowning is necessary.'"

H 4585, Ch. 73, h 4

Muhammad ibn Yahya has narrated from Muhammad ibn Ahmad ibn al-Hassan from 'Amr ibn Sa'id from Musaddiq ibn Sadaqah from 'Ammar who has said the following:

"Abu 'Abd Allah, *'Alayhi al-Salam*, has said, 'One who has died because of drowning is kept until there is a change and his death becomes certain; then his Ghusl (bath) and shroud are done.' He (the narrator) has said that he (the Imam) was asked about one who has died because of a sudden shock. He (the Imam) said, 'If it (death) is because of sudden shock, he is kept for two days, then his Ghusl (bath) and shroud are done.'"

H 4586, Ch. 73, h 5
Ali ibn Ibrahim has narrated from Muhammad ibn 'Isa from Yunus from `Isma'il ibn 'Abd Allah al-Khaliq, brother of Shihab ibn 'Abd Rabbihi who has said the following:
"Abu 'Abd Allah, *'Alayhi al-Salam*, has said, 'Burial is delayed, unless there is a change, because of five kinds of reasons for death: Death because of drowning, sudden shock, internal (illness pain), crushed and smoke (fumigation).'"

H 4587, Ch. 73, h 6
Ahmad ibn Mehran has narrated from Muhammad ibn Ali from Ali ibn abu Hamzah who has said the following:
"In one of the years many people in Makkah died because of a great deal of lightning and thunder. I visited abu Ibrahim, *'Alayhi al-Salam*, and he, without asking, initiated stating, 'It is proper to delay for three days the burial of one who has died because of drowning and sudden shock unless the spread of smell proves his death.' I then said, 'I pray to Allah to keep my soul in service for your cause, are you telling me that many people are buried alive? He (the Imam) said, 'Yes, O Ali, many people were buried alive and they did not die but in their graves.'"

Chapter 74 - People Killed

H 4588, Ch. 74, h 1
Muhammad ibn Yahya has narrated from Muhammad ibn Ahmad from Ali ibn al-Hakam from al-Husayn ibn 'Uthman from ibn Muskan from Aban ibn Taghlib who has said the following:
"I once asked abu 'Abd Allah, *'Alayhi al-Salam*, about those who are killed in the way of Allah, are Ghusl (bath), shroud and hunut done for them? He (the Imam) said, 'They are buried as they are found in their clothes, unless found alive, then die in which case Ghusl (bath), shroud, hunut and Salat (prayer) are done for them. The Messenger of Allah performed Salat (prayer) for Hamzah and his body was placed in the shroud because his clothes were looted.'"

H 4589, Ch. 74, h 2
Ali ibn Ibrahim has narrated from his father from Hammad from Hariz from `Isma'il ibn Jabir and Zurarah from who has said the following:
"I once asked abu Ja'far, *'Alayhi al-Salam*, about the martyr who is buried with his blood (not washed clean). He (the Imam) said, 'Yes, he is buried in his clothes, with his blood, without, hunut and Ghusl (bath) and is buried as he is found.' He (the Imam) then said, 'The Messenger of Allah buried his uncle Hamzah in his clothes, with his blood, in which he was hurt and the Holy prophet used his own gown for him, but it came short from the side of his legs. He (the Messenger of Allah) asked for 'Idhkhir (a certain plant) as cover and he

then covered him, performed Salat (prayer) - seventy Salat (prayer) and seventy Takbir.'"

H 4590, Ch. 74, h 3

Humayd ibn Ziyad has narrated from al-Hassan ibn Muhammad from more than one person from Aban from abu Maryam who has said the following:

"I once heard abu 'Abd Allah, *'Alayhi al-Salam*, say, 'A martyr if found alive is given Ghusl (bath), shroud, hunut and Salat (prayer) is performed for him. If he is found dead he is buried in his clothes.'"

H 4591, Ch. 74, h 4

A number of our people have narrated from Ahmad ibn Muhammad ibn Khalid from his father from abu al-Jawza' from al-Husayn ibn 'Ulwan from 'Amr ibn Khalid from Zayd ibn Ali from his ancestors, *'Alayhi al-Salam*, who has said the following:

"'Amir al-Mu'minin, *'Alayhi al-Salam*, has said, 'Skull-cap, shoes, turban, loincloth and trousers are removed from a martyr unless they have become bloody in which case, they are left with, him and everything tied down with him is turned loose and open.'"

H 4592, Ch. 74, h 5

Ali ibn Ibrahim has narrated from his father from ibn Mahbub ibn Sinan from Aban ibn Taghlib who has said the following:

"I once heard abu 'Abd Allah, *'Alayhi al-Salam*, say, 'Those who are killed in the way of Allah are buried with their clothes without Ghusl (bath) unless Muslims find him alive and then he dies afterward, in which case Ghusl (bath), shroud and hunut are done for him. The Messenger of Allah buried Hamzah with his clothes without Ghusl (bath) but he (the Messenger of Allah) performed Salat (prayer) for him.'"

Chapter 75a - People Consumed By Beasts, Birds, Pieces of Bodies of Those Killed or Burnt

H 4593, Ch. 75a, h 1

Muhammad ibn Yahya has narrated from al-'Amrakiy from Ali ibn Ja'far from his brother, who has said the following:

"I once asked abu al-Hassan, *'Alayhi al-Salam*, about one who is consumed by beasts and birds, and only his bones without flesh are left. He (the Imam) said, 'Ghusl (bath), shroud and Salat (prayer) are done and then it is buried. If the deceased is found into two halves, Salat (prayer) is performed for the part which has the heart with it.'"

H 4594, Ch. 75a, h 2

Ali ibn Ibrahim has narrated from his father from Ahmad ibn Muhammad ibn abu Nasr from Jamil ibn Darraj from Muhammad ibn Muslim who has said the following:

"Abu Ja'far, *'Alayhi al-Salam*, has said, 'If one is killed and only flesh without bones are found, Salat (prayer) is not obligatory for it. If bones without flesh are found, there is Salat (prayer) for it.'"

"He (the narrator) has said, 'It is narrated that Salat (prayer) is not obligatory for a head found without the body.'"

H 4595, Ch. 75a, h 3

A number of our people have narrated from Ahmad ibn Muhammad ibn Khalid from his father from certain persons of his people who has said the following:

"Abu 'Abd Allah, *'Alayhi al-Salam*, has said, 'A man who is found being killed, if there is a complete part of the body, it is buried after Salat (prayer) for it. If a complete part is not found it is buried without Salat (prayer).'"

H 4596, Ch. 75a, h 4

A number of our people have narrated from Sahl ibn Ziyad from Ayyub ibn Nuh in a marfu' manner who has said the following:

"Abu 'Abd Allah, *'Alayhi al-Salam*, has said, 'If a piece is cut from a man, it is dead. In case of one's touching, whatever piece has bone in it Ghusl (bath) becomes obligatory, if bone is not found in it, Ghusl (bath) is not obligatory.'"

H 4597, Ch. 75a, h 5

Sahl ibn Ziyad has narrated from 'Abd Allah ibn al-Husayn from certain persons of his people who has said the following:

"Abu 'Abd Allah, *'Alayhi al-Salam*, has said, 'If a man is cut in two pieces, Salat (prayer) is performed on the part in which the heart exists.'"

H 4598, Ch. 75a h 6

A number of our people have narrated from Ahmad ibn Muhammad from ibn Khalid from abu al-Jawza' from al-Husayn ibn 'Ulwan from 'Amr ibn Khalid from Zayd ibn Ali from his ancestors who has said the following:

"'Amir al-Mu'minin, *'Alayhi al-Salam*, was asked about a man who was burnt. He (the Imam) instructed them to pour water on him well, then perform Salat (prayer) for the deceased.'"

H 4599, Ch. 75a, h 7

Ali ibn Ibrahim has narrated from his father from Ali ibn Ma'bad from al-Dihqan from Drust from abu Khalid who has said the following:

"He (the Imam), *'Alayhi al-Salam*, has said, 'You must give Ghusl (bath) to every dead person because of drowning, being killed by beasts and by all other causes except those who are killed between two lines of fighters, who only if found alive, are given Ghusl (bath), otherwise, Ghusl (bath) is not required.'"

Chapter 75b - People Who Die in Ships and Cannot Be Brought Ashore or Are Naked

H 4600, Ch. 75b, h 1

Abu Ali al-Ash'ariy has narrated from Muhammad ibn 'Abd al-Jabbar and Muhammad ibn 'Isma'il from al-Fadl ibn Shadhan all from Safwan ibn Yahya from ibn Muskan from Ayyub al-Hurr who has said the following:

"Abu 'Abd Allah, *'Alayhi al-Salam*, was asked about one who dies in a ship in the ocean. He (the Imam) said, 'The deceased is placed in a vat and with its opening sealed is thrown into the water.'"

H 4601, Ch. 75b, h 2

Humayd ibn Ziyad has narrated from al-Hassan ibn Muhammad from more than one person from Aban from a man who has said the following:

"Abu 'Abd Allah, *'Alayhi al-Salam*, was asked about one who dies in the company of people in the ocean. He (the Imam) said, 'Ghusl (bath), shroud and Salat (prayer) are done for him and with some weight tied to him is thrown in the ocean.'"

H 4602, Ch. 75b, h 3

A number of our people have narrated from Sahl ibn Ziyad in a marfu' manner has said the following:

"Abu 'Abd Allah, *'Alayhi al-Salam*, has said, 'If one dies in a ship and it is not possible to bring him to the shore, shroud and hunut are done for him, after wrapping in a piece of cloth, is thrown into the water.'"

H 4603, Ch. 75b, h 4

A number of our people have narrated from Ahmad ibn Muhammad ibn abu Nasr from Marwan ibn Muslim from 'Ammar ibn Musa who has said the following:

"I once asked abu 'Abd Allah, *'Alayhi al-Salam*, 'What do you say about a people who walk during a journey on the sea shore; they find a dead man who is naked, thrown out by the ocean and they also are naked except for a loin cloth on them; how do they perform Salat (prayer) for him when he is naked? They do not have extra clothes with them to use as shroud for him. He (the Imam) said, 'A grave is dug and he is placed in it and with a piece of brick placed on his private parts, Salat (prayer) is performed for him and then he is buried.' I (the narrator) asked. 'Can Salat (prayer) be made after he is buried? He (the Imam) said, 'Once a deceased is buried Salat (prayer) is not performed, nor when he is naked and before his private parts are covered.'"

Chapter 76 - Salat (Prayer) for Persons Crucified, Stoned or Dead for Capital Punishment

H 4604, Ch. 76, h 1

A number of our people have narrated from Sahl ibn Ziyad from Muhammad ibn al-Hassan ibn Shammun from 'Abd Allah ibn 'Abd al-Rahman from Misma' Kirdin who has said the following:

"Abu 'Abd Allah, *'Alayhi al-Salam*, has said, 'Ghusl (bath), hunut, and shroud are done for people stoned to death, male or female, prior to executing stoning, then Salat (prayer) is performed. Ghusl (bath), hunut, shrouding and Salat (prayer) for one executed because of retaliation are also done before the execution.'"

H 4605, Ch. 76, h 2

Ali ibn Ibrahim has narrated from his father from abu Hashim al-Ja'fariy who has said the following:

"I once asked abu al-Hassan al-Rida, *'Alayhi al-Salam*, about one who is crucified. He (the Imam) said, 'Do you not know that my grandfather performed Salat (prayer) for his uncle?' I said, 'I know it but I do not understand it clearly.' He (the Imam) said, 'I explain it for you. If the face of the person crucified is toward al-Qiblah (al-Ka'bah), stand near his right shoulder. If his back is toward al-Qiblah (al-Ka'bah), then stand near his left shoulder but if it is between the east and west and his left shoulder toward al-Qiblah (al-Ka'bah), then stand near his right shoulder. If his right shoulder is toward al-Qiblah (al-Ka'bah), then stand near his left shoulder. To whichever direction he is, do not keep away from his shoulders and keep your face toward east or west, and do not stand face to face with him. You must not turn your back to him.' Abu Hashim has said that I then said, 'I certainly understood, by the will of Allah, I understood it by Allah.'"

H 4606, Ch. 76, h 3
Muhammad ibn Yahya has narrated from Ahmad ibn Muhammad from al-'Abbas ibn Ma'ruf from Ya'qubiy from Musa ibn 'Isa from Muhammad ibn Muyassir from Harun ibn al-Jahm from al-Sakuniy who has said the following:
"Abu 'Abd Allah, *'Alayhi al-Salam*, has said that the Messenger of Allah has said, 'You must not keep a crucified person on (the woods) for more than three days, after which the deceased must be brought down and buried.'"

Chapter 77 - The Obligations of the Neighbors toward the People of the Deceased and Mourning Ceremonies

H 4607, Ch. 77, h 1
Ali ibn Ibrahim has narrated from his father from ibn abu 'Umayr from Hafs ibn al-Bakhtariy (and from) Hisham ibn Salim who has said the following:
"Abu 'Abd Allah, *'Alayhi al-Salam*, has said that when Ja'far ibn abu Talib was martyred, the Messenger of Allah instructed Fatimah, *'Alayha al-Salam*, to prepare food for Asma' bint 'Umays for three days and visit her with a group of her women everyday for three days. This formed the tradition to prepare food for the people of the deceased for three days."

H 4608, Ch. 77, h 2
Ali ibn Ibrahim has narrated from his father from Hammad from Hariz from Zurarah who has said the following:
"Abu Ja'far, *'Alayhi al-Salam*, has said, 'Mourning ceremony is organized for a deceased for three days, beginning from the day of his death.'"

H 4609, Ch. 77, h 3
Al-Husayn ibn Muhammad has narrated from Ahmad ibn Ishaq from Sa'dan from abu Basir who has said the following:
"Abu 'Abd Allah, *'Alayhi al-Salam*, has said that neighbors of the people of a deceased should prepare food for them (people of the deceased) for three days."

H 4610, Ch. 77, h 4
Ali ibn Ibrahim has narrated from his father from Hammad ibn 'Isa from Hariz or others who has said the following:
"Abu Ja'far, *'Alayhi al-Salam*, said in his will that eight hundred dirhams should be spent to organize a memorial service for his death. He considered it as part of the tradition; the Messenger of Allah had said, 'Prepare food for the family of Ja'far; they are preoccupied (with the death of Ja'far).'"

H 4611, Ch. 77, h 5

Muhammad ibn Yahya has narrated from Ahmad ibn Muhammad from Ali ibn al-Hakam from 'Abd Allah al-Kahiliy who has said the following:

"Once I said to abu al-Hassan, *'Alayhi al-Salam*, 'My wife and the wife of ibn Marid went to join a memorial service, and I tried to stop them but my wife said, "If it is unlawful then stop us so we desist, but if it is not unlawful then why should you stop us? If one of us will die no one will come to us."' Abu al-Hassan, *'Alayhi al-Salam*, then said, 'You are asking about rights. My father would send my mother and mother of Farwah to meet the terms of the rights of the people of al-Madinah.'"

H 4612, Ch. 77, h 6

Ahmad ibn Muhammad al-Kufiy has narrated from ibn Jumhur from his father from Muhammad ibn Sinan from al-Mufaddal ibn 'Umar who has said the following:

"He has also said that al-Asamm has narrated to us from Hariz from Muhammad ibn Muslim from abu 'Abd Allah, *'Alayhi al-Salam*, who has said the following:

''Amir al-Mu'minin, *'Alayhi al-Salam*, has said, "Instruct your families to speak good words when someone among you dies. When father of Fatimah, *'Alayha al-Salam*, died, daughters of children of Hashim supported her and she said to them, 'Ignore eulogies but you must pray (to Allah).'""'"

Chapter 78 - Suffering Due to the Death of a Son

H 4613, Ch. 78, h 1

A number of our people have narrated from Ahmad ibn Muhammad from Muhammad ibn Isma'il from ibn Bazi' from abu Isma'il al-Sarraj who has said the following:

"Abu 'Abd Allah, *'Alayhi al-Salam*, has said that a son whom one sends (to the next life) is better than seventy sons who survive after one's death, who have mounted their horses and are ready to march for the cause of Allah."

H 4614, Ch. 78, h 2

Abu Ali al-Ash'ariy has narrated from Muhammad ibn Salim from Ahmad ibn al-Nadhr from 'Amr ibn Shimr from Jabir who has said the following:

"Abu Ja'far, *'Alayhi al-Salam*, has said, 'The Messenger of Allah went to see Khadijah when al-Qasim, her son, had just passed away and she was weeping. He then asked her, "Why do you weep?" She said, "My milk flows out thus I weep." He then said, "O Khadijah, will you not be happy when on the Day of Judgment you proceed to the door of paradise and he will come to you, hold your hand and lead you to the best of the dwellings therein and such (reward) is for every believing person? Allah, the Most Majestic, the Most Glorious, is best honorable judge. He would never take away the fruit of the hearts of believing people, and make him suffer thereafter in any way or form."'"

H 4615, Ch. 78, h 3

Muhammad ibn Yahya has narrated from Ahmad ibn Muhammad ibn 'Isa and a number of our people from Sahl ibn Ziyad all from ibn Mehran who has said the following:

"A man once wrote to abu Ja'far, the second, *'Alayhi al-Salam*, complaining due to his suffering from the death of his sons and the intensity of his grief. The

Imam wrote to him, 'Do you know that Allah, the Most Majestic, the Most Glorious, chooses from the property and sons of the believing people the most valuable items so He will reward him in the same way (with most valuable reward)?'"

H 4616, Ch. 78, h 4

Ali ibn Ibrahim has narrated from his father, from al-Nawfaliy from al-Sakuniy who has said the following:

"Abu 'Abd Allah, *'Alayhi al-Salam,* has said that the Messenger of Allah has said, 'When a son of a believing person dies - Allah knows what the servant (of Allah) may say - Allah, the Most Holy, the Most High, says to His angels, "Have you taken the soul of the son of My servant out of his body?" They reply, "Yes, O Lord, we have done so." He then asks, "What did My servant say?" They say, "He praised You and said, 'We are for Allah and to Him we return.'" Allah, the Most Holy, the Most High, then says, "So you took away the fruit of his heart and the delight of his eyes but he praised Me and spoke of his return to Me. (For his reward) build a house for him in paradise and call it the house of al-Hamd (praising Allah)."'"

H 4617, Ch. 78, h 5

A number of our people have narrated from Ahmad ibn Muhammad ibn Khalid from Isma'il ibn Mehran from Sayf ibn 'Amirah who has said that abu 'Abd al-Rahman from abu Basir who has said the following:

"I heard abu 'Abd Allah, *'Alayhi al-Salam,* say, 'When Allah, the Most Majestic, the Most Glorious, loves a servant, He takes away the soul of his most beloved son to Himself.'"

H 4618, Ch. 78, h 6

It is narrated from him (narrator of above Hadith) Isma'il ibn Mehran from Sayf ibn 'Amirah from 'Amr ibn Shimr from Jabir who has said the following:

"Abu 'Abd Allah, *'Alayhi al-Salam,* has said that if two sons of any Muslim die and he considers it a decision of Allah, the Most Majestic, the Most Glorious, as such and obediently agrees, they (his sons) will protect him against fire by the permission of Allah, most High."

H 4619, Ch. 78, h 7

It is narrated from him (narrator of above Hadith) from Isma'il ibn Mehran from 'Amr ibn Shimr from Jabir who has said the following:

"Abu Ja'far, *'Alayhi al-Salam,* has said, 'When Tahir son of the Messenger of Allah passed away, the Messenger of Allah forbade Khadijah from weeping. She said, 'Yes, O Messenger of Allah, I agree, but I noticed that my milk flowed out; thus I wept.' He then said, 'Would you not agree if you find him standing near the door of paradise and on seeing you, hold your hand and lead you into paradise to the most clean and fine ones therein?' She then said, 'Is that how it is?' He said, 'Allah is Most Majestic and Honorable. He does not take away the fruits of the heart of (His own) servant who exercises patience, praises Him and agrees with His decision. Allah due to His Glory and Honor does not cause him any suffering.'"

H 4620, Ch. 78, h 8
Ali ibn Ibrahim has narrated from his father and Muhammad ibn Isma'il has narrated from al-Fadl ibn Shadhan all from ibn abu 'Umayr from ibn Bukayr who has said the following:
"Abu 'Abd Allah, *'Alayhi al-Salam*, has said that the reward for a believing person for the death of his sons is paradise, whether he exercise patience or not."

H 4621, Ch. 78, h 9
Ibn abu 'Umayr has narrated from 'Abd al-Rahman ibn Hajjaj who has said the following:
"Abu 'Abd Allah or abu al-Hassan, *'Alayhi al-Salam*, has said, 'Allah, the Most Majestic, the Most Glorious, likes a servant whose son dies but he praises Allah. Allah says, "My angels, look to My servant. I took away his soul but he praises and thanks Me."'"

H 4622, Ch. 78, h 10
Muhammad ibn Yahya has narrated from Salmah ibn al-Khattab from Ali Sayf ibn 'Amirah from his father from 'Amr ibn Shimr from Jabir who has said the following:
"Abu Ja'far, *'Alayhi al-Salam*, has said, 'Whoever considers the death of his sons as his savings with Allah, the Most Majestic, the Most Glorious, they will protect him against fire by the permission of Allah, the Most Majestic, the Most Glorious."

Chapter 79 - Offering Condolences and Solace

H 4623, Ch. 79, h 1
A number of our people have narrated from Sahl ibn Ziyad from Ali ibn al-Hakam from Sulayman ibn 'Amr al-Nakha'iy who has said the following:
"Abu 'Abd Allah, *'Alayhi al-Salam*, has said that if one experiences grief and sorrow due to someone's death, he should compare this with that which one has experienced due to the death of the Holy Prophet."

H 4624, Ch. 79, h 2
Muhammad ibn Yahya has narrated from Ahmad ibn Muhammad ibn 'Isa from Muhammad ibn Sinan from 'Ammar ibn Marwan from Zayd al-Shahham from 'Amr ibn Sa'id al-Thaqafiy who has said the following:
"Abu Ja'far, *'Alayhi al-Salam*, has said, 'If you suffer sorrow and grief about yourself, your property or children, then remind yourself of the sorrow and grief you have suffered due to the death of the Messenger of Allah; creatures have never suffered any grief as this (death of the Messenger of Allah).'"

H 4625, Ch. 79, h 3
A number of our people have narrated from Ahmad ibn Muhammad ibn Khalid from Isma'il ibn Mehran from Sayf ibn 'Amirah from 'Amr ibn Shimr from 'Abd Allah ibn al-Walid al-Ju'fiy from a man from his father who has said the following:
"When `Amir al-Mu'minin, Ali passed away, al-Hassan informed Al-Husayn, *'Alayhim al-Salam*, about it. He was in al-Mada'in (a place near Baghdad) at that time. When he read the letter, he said, 'How intense and great is this sorrow! Even though the Messenger of Allah has said that if you experience grief and sorrow, remind yourself of your sorrow and grief about me. It is very true that no sorrow and grief is more intense and greater than the sorrow and grief for him, he has certainly spoken the truth.'"

H 4626, Ch. 79, h 4

Ali ibn Ibrahim has narrated from his father from ibn abu 'Umayr from Hisham ibn Salim who has said the following:

"Abu 'Abd Allah, *'Alayhi al-Salam*, has said that when the Messenger of Allah passed away they (people) heard a voice, but did not see anyone in person, saying, 'Every soul is to experience the taste of death. You will certainly receive your reward on the Day of Judgment. Whoever is saved from the fire and is admitted in paradise, has become successful indeed.' It also said, 'In (the mercy of) Allah are good consequences for everyone who dies, solace for all forms of sorrow and compensation for every loss. In Allah, you must trust and in Him only place your hope. Deprived person, in reality, is one who is deprived of the rewards from Allah.'"

H 4627, Ch. 79, h 5

Muhammad ibn Yahya has narrated from Salmah ibn al-Khattab from Sulayman ibn Sama'ah from Al-Husayn ibn al-Mukhtar who has said the following:

"Abu 'Abd Allah, *'Alayhi al-Salam*, has said that when the Messenger of Allah passed away, Jibril (the archangel) came to them when the Holy Prophet was covered with a sheet of cloth, and in the house there were Ali, Fatimah, al-Hassan and Al-Husayn, *'Alayhim al-Salam*. He said, 'Assalamu 'Alaykum' (you are *'Alayhim al-Salam*), O family of the house of mercy. Every soul must experience the taste of death. You will receive your reward (from Allah) on the Day of Judgment only. Those who are saved from fire and are admitted into paradise are indeed successful. The worldly life is only a deceitful means. In Allah, the Most Majestic, the Most Glorious, alone is solace for all kinds of sorrow, good consequences for everyone who dies and proper compensation for all kinds of losses. In Allah, you must trust and in Him alone you must place your hopes. A truly deprived person is one who is deprived of rewards from Allah. This is the last time for my coming to this world.' They said, 'We heard his voice but did not see his person.'"

H 4628, Ch. 79, h 6

It is narrated from him (narrator of above Hadith) from Salmah from Ali ibn Sayf from his father from abu 'Usamah Zayd al-Shahham who has said the following:

"Abu 'Abd Allah, *'Alayhi al-Salam*, has said that when the Messenger of Allah passed away condolences were offered. Someone came to them and they felt his presence but did not see his person. He said, 'Assalamu 'Alaykum' (you are *'Alayhim al-Salam*), O people of the house and may Allah grant you favors and blessings. Every soul must experience the taste of death. You will receive your reward (from Allah) on the Day of Judgment only. Those who are saved from fire and are admitted into paradise are indeed successful. The worldly life is only a means of deceit. In Allah, the Most Majestic, the Most Glorious, alone is solace for all kinds of sorrow, good consequences for everyone who dies and proper compensation for all kinds of losses. In Allah, you must trust and in Him alone, you must place your hopes. A truly deprived person is one who is deprived of rewards from Allah. 'al-Salamu 'Alaykum' (you are *'Alayhim al-Salam*), [O people of the house and may Allah grant you favors and blessings].'"

H 4629, Ch. 79, h 7

It is narrated from him (narrator of above Hadith) from Ali ibn Sayf from his father from abu al-Jarud who has said the following:

"He (the narrator) has narrated a similar Hadith from abu Ja'far, *'Alayhi al-Salam*, with this addition. 'I asked, who were in the house?' He replied, 'They were Ali, Fatimah, al-Hassan and Al-Husayn, *'Alayhim al-Salam*.'"

H 4630, Ch. 79, h 8

It is narrated from him (narrator of above Hadith) from Salmah from Muhammad ibn 'Isa al-Armaniy from Al-Husayn ibn 'Ulwan from 'Abd Allah ibn al-Walid who has said the following:

"Abu Ja'far, *'Alayhi al-Salam*, has said, when the Holy Prophet passed away, someone came to them and stood at door of the house. He offered them greeting of peace and then said, 'O family of Muhammad, every soul must experience the taste of death. You will receive your reward (from Allah) on the Day of Judgment only. Those who are saved from fire and are admitted into paradise are indeed successful. The worldly life is only a means of deceit. In Allah, the Most Majestic, the Most Glorious, alone is solace for all kinds of sorrow, good consequences for everyone who dies and proper compensation for all kinds of losses. In Allah, you must trust and assign Him alone to be the person in charge of your affairs; and with His support for you alone, you must in grief and sorrow, agree. A truly affected person is one who is deprived of the rewards from Allah. Assalamu 'Alaykum (you are *'Alayhim al-Salam*) and may Allah grant you favors and blessings.' No one saw him. Someone in the family said, 'This is an angel from heaven. Allah, the Most Majestic, the Most Glorious, has sent him to you to offer you condolences.' Someone else said, 'He was al-Khadhiru who came to offer you condolences on the death of your Prophet.'"

Chapter 80 - Patience, Impatience and to Acknowledge (the Reality of) Death

H 4631, Ch. 80, h 1

A number of our people have narrated from Sahl ibn Ziyad from Ahmad ibn Muhammad ibn abu Nasr and al-Hassan ibn Ali all from abu Jamilah from Jabir from abu Ja'far, who has said the following:

"Once I asked abu Ja'far, *'Alayhi al-Salam*, 'What is impatience and outcry?' He replied, 'An intense form of impatience is to cry aloud expressing certain words as al-Wayl or howling or beating of the face or chest or pulling out of hairs from the forehead. Whoever organizes a lamentation ceremony has abandoned patience. If one exercises patience and acknowledges the reality of death saying, "To Allah we belong and to Him we return," praises and thanks Allah, the Most Majestic, the Most Glorious, he has agreed with the decision of Allah. His reward becomes due with Allah, otherwise, Allah's system of the working of things prevails, but he is condemned and Allah turns his efforts void and fruitless.'"

H 4632, Ch. 80, h 2

Ali ibn Ibrahim has narrated from his father from 'Amr ibn 'Uthman from abu Jamilah, from Jabir from abu Ja'far, *'Alayhi al-Salam*, a similar Hadith

H 4633, Ch. 80, h 3

Al-Husayn ibn Muhammad has narrated from 'Abd Allah ibn 'Amir from Ali ibn Mahziyar from Ali ibn Isma'il al-Mithamiy from Rib'iy ibn 'Abd Allah who has said the following:

"Abu 'Abd Allah, *'Alayhi al-Salam*, has said that patience and misfortune race toward a believing person but misfortune finds him exercising patience. Outcry and impatience race toward an unbeliever person and misfortune finds him in outcry and impatience."

H 4634, Ch. 80, h 4

Ali ibn Ibrahim has narrated from his father, from al-Nawfaliy from al-Sakuniy who has said the following:

"Abu 'Abd Allah, *'Alayhi al-Salam*, has said that the Messenger of Allah has said, 'If a Muslim strikes his hand against his thigh due to suffering and sorrow, it causes his deeds to become void and fruitless.'"

H 4635, Ch. 80, h 5

Ali ibn Ibrahim has narrated from his father from ibn abu 'Umayr from 'Abd Allah ibn Sinan from Ma'ruf ibn Kharrabuz who has said the following:

"Abu Ja'far, *'Alayhi al-Salam*, has said, 'Whoever of the servants (of Allah) after suffering a misfortune, upon recalling any of his suffering and sorrow, acknowledges it and exercises patience, if it befalls him suddenly, Allah forgives his past sins. Whenever thereafter upon recalling any of his suffering sorrow acknowledges it (saying 'to Allah we belong and to Him we return'), Allah forgives his sins that may have taken place in between (the two occasions of recalling).'"

H 4636, Ch. 80, h 6

Ali has narrated from his father from ibn abu 'Umayr from Dawud ibn Razin who has said the following:

"Abu 'Abd Allah, *'Alayhi al-Salam*, has said that if one recalls his suffering a misfortune even after a long time and says, 'To Allah we belong and to Him we return, all praise belongs to Allah Lord of the worlds; O Lord, grant me favors for my suffering a misfortune and replace my losses with something better,' his reward for this is equal to that he deserved upon suffering it the first time."

H 4637, Ch. 80, h 7

A number of our people have narrated from Sahl ibn Ziyad and Muhammad ibn Yahya from Ahmad ibn Muhammad from ibn Mahbub from Ishaq ibn 'Ammar who has said the following:

"Abu 'Abd Allah, *'Alayhi al-Salam*, has said that, O Ishaq, do not count a misfortune in which you were granted patience, thus you deserved reward from Allah, the Most Majestic, the Most Glorious. A misfortune is that in which due to acting impatiently, one is deprived of rewards for that suffering."

H 4638, Ch. 80, h 8

A number of our people have narrated from Sahl ibn Ziyad from al-Hassan ibn Ali from Ali ibn 'Uqbah from the woman of al-Hassan al-Sayqal who has said the following:

"Abu 'Abd Allah, *'Alayhi al-Salam*, has said that it is not advisable to cry loudly for a deceased or teardown one's clothes."

H 4639, Ch. 80, h 9

Sahl has narrated from Ali ibn Hassa'n from Musa ibn Bakr who has said the following:

"Abu al-Hassan the 1st, *'Alayhi al-Salam*, has said, 'A man's striking his hand on his thigh, when suffering a misfortune, causes suspension of his rewards for his suffering.'"

H 4640, Ch. 80, h 10

Sahl has narrated from al-Hassan ibn Ali from al-Fudayl ibn Muyassir who has said the following:

"We were in the presence of abu 'Abd Allah, *'Alayhi al-Salam*, when a man came and complained before him about a misfortune that he had suffered. Abu 'Abd Allah, *'Alayhi al-Salam*, said, 'If you exercise patience, you will be rewarded and if you do not exercise patience, Allah's system of working of things will apply to you without change and you will be counted a sinner.'"

H 4641, Ch. 80, h 11

Al-Husayn ibn Muhammad has narrated from 'Abd Allah ibn 'Amir from Ali ibn Mahziyar from al-Hassan ibn Muhammad ibn Mahziyar from al-Qutaybah al-A'sha' who has said the following:

"Once I visited abu 'Abd Allah, *'Alayhi al-Salam*, to also visit his son who was ill. I met him at the door and he was sorrowful and depressed. I asked, 'May Allah keep my soul in service of your cause, how is your child?' He replied, 'By Allah, he is about to die.' He then went inside the house and after a while came back to us, he looked bright and without any sign of depression. I had a longing that this can be a sign of the recovery of the child and I asked, 'May Allah keep my soul in service of your cause, how is the child?' He replied, 'He just passed away.' I then asked, 'May Allah keep my soul in service of your cause, I found you, when the child was still alive, so much depressed and sad but now, when the child is dead, I see you have changed so much with brightness. How is all this happened?' He replied, 'We, the family of the Holy Prophet, cry (to Allah) for help before the fall of misfortune but once the command of Allah is issued, we accept it and submit ourselves to His command.'"

H 4642, Ch. 80, h 12

Muhammad ibn Yahya has narrated from Ahmad ibn Muhammad ibn 'Isa from Al-Husayn ibn Sa'id from al-Nadr ibn Suwayd from al-Qasim ibn Sulayman from Jarrah al-Mada'iniy who has said the following:

"Abu 'Abd Allah, *'Alayhi al-Salam*, has said that howling for a deceased is not proper, and it should not happen but people do not know. Exercising patience is better."

H 4643, Ch. 80, h 13

Ali ibn Ibrahim has narrated from his father from Hammad ibn 'Isa from Al-Husayn ibn al-Mukhtar from 'Ala' ibn Kamil who has said the following:

"Once, I was sitting with abu 'Abd Allah, *'Alayhi al-Salam*, when someone inside the house began to cry loudly. Abu 'Abd Allah, *'Alayhi al-Salam*, stood up and then sat down saying, 'To Allah we belong and to Him we return,' and continued his Hadith until he finished and then said, 'We love to enjoy the wellbeing of our own selves, our children and our properties. If the systems of the working of things bring something upon us, then we have no right to love anything other than what Allah loves to happen to us.'"

H 4644, Ch. 80, h 14

Abu Ali al-Ash'ariy has narrated from Muhammad ibn 'Abd al-Jabbar from ibn Faddal from Yunus ibn Ya'qub from certain persons of our people who have said the following:

"Once a group of people came to visit abu Ja'far, *'Alayhi al-Salam,* to find out how one of his children suffering from illness was doing. They found him deeply concerned, grieved and restless. The narrator has said that they said, 'By Allah, if something happens to him (the child), we are afraid we will see something from him (the Imam) that we will not like to see.' The narrator has said that within a short time they began to hear weeping and crying for him. On the other hand, the Imam came to them, relaxed, free of concerns and totally changed from his previous conditions. They said, 'May Allah keep our souls in the service of your cause, from seeing your condition we were afraid that if something happens, we may see things that will cause us a great deal of sorrow.' The Imam then said to them, 'We love to enjoy the wellbeing of whatever we love, but when the command of Allah comes we submit ourselves to what He loves.'"

Chapter 81 - The Reward for offering Condolences

H 4645, Ch. 81, h 1

Muhammad ibn Yahya has narrated from Ahmad ibn Muhammad from ibn Sinan from abu al-Jarud who has said the following:

"Abu Ja'far, *'Alayhi al-Salam,* has said, 'One of the matters that Moses privately said to his Lord was this, "O Lord, what is the reward for one who offers condolences to one who has suffered from the death of one's son?" The Lord replied, "I will extend My shadow (protection) on him on the (extremely hot) day when there will be no shadows except My shadow."'"

H 4646, Ch. 81, h 2

Abu Ali al-Ash'ariy has narrated from Muhammad ibn 'Abd al-Jabbar from Muhammad ibn Hassa'n from al-Hassan ibn Al-Husayn from Ali ibn 'Abd Allah from Ali ibn Mansur from Isma'il al-Jawziy who has said the following:

"Abu 'Abd Allah, *'Alayhi al-Salam,* has said that the Messenger of Allah has said, 'Whoever offers condolences to a sorrowful person will, on the Station for clearance of accounts, receive a dress that will be presented to him.'"

H 4647, Ch. 81, h 3

It is narrated from him (narrator of above Hadith) from Muhammad ibn Ali from 'Isa ibn 'Abd Allah al-'Amriy from his father from his grandfather from his father, *'Alayhi al-Salam,* who has said the following:

"Amir al-Mu'minin, *'Alayhi al-Salam,* has said, 'Whoever offers condolences to a sorrowful person due to the death of his son, Allah will provide him shadow (protection) from His throne on the Day when there will be no shadow except His shadow.'"

H 4648, Ch. 81, h 4

A number of our people have narrated from Ahmad ibn Muhammad ibn Khalid from his father from Wahab who has said the following:

"Abu 'Abd Allah, *'Alayhi al-Salam*, has said that the Messenger of Allah has said, 'Whoever offers condolences to a person who is suffering sorrow and grief due to the death of his son, will receive a reward equal to that for the affected party without any reduction in the reward for the later mentioned.'"

Chapter 82 - About offering Solace

H 4649, Ch. 82, h 1

A number of our people have narrated from Ahmad ibn Muhammad from 'Uthman ibn 'Isa from Mehran ibn Muhammad who has said the following:

"I heard abu 'Abd Allah, *'Alayhi al-Salam*, say, 'When a person dies, Allah sends an angel to the most distressed person of his family. The angel wipes the heart of that person to forget the pain of his sorrow and grief. Were this not to happen, the world would cease to develop or gain anything.'"

H 4650, Ch. 82, h 2

Ali ibn Ibrahim has narrated from his father from ibn abu 'Umayr from Hisham ibn Salim who has said the following:

"Abu 'Abd Allah, *'Alayhi al-Salam*, has said that Allah, the Most Blessed, the Most High, has granted people three favors: He has made dead bodies to give out foul smell; otherwise, no friend would ever bury a friend. He has made solace to take effect; otherwise, reproduction would halt. He has assigned a creature over this grain (to destroy it); otherwise, the kings would store (hoard) them as gold and silver are treasured (in hiding)."

H 4651, Ch. 82, h 3

Muhammad ibn Yahya has narrated from Muhammad ibn Al-Husayn from 'Uthman ibn 'Isa from Mehran ibn Muhammad who has said the following:

"I once heard abu 'Abd Allah, *'Alayhi al-Salam*, say, 'When a person dies, Allah sends an angel to the most distressed person of his family. The angel wipes the heart of that person to forget the pain of his sorrow and grief. Were this not to happen, the world would cease to develop or gain anything.'"

Chapter 83 - Visiting of the Graves

H 4652, Ch. 83, h 1

Ali ibn Ibrahim has narrated from his father from ibn abu 'Umayr from Hafs ibn al-Bakhtariy and Jamil ibn Darraj who has said the following:

"Abu 'Abd Allah, *'Alayhi al-Salam*, has said that they (people of the cemetery) take comfort in you. When you disappear from them they become afraid."

H 4653, Ch. 83, h 2

A number of our people have narrated from Ahmad ibn Muhammad from 'Uthman ibn 'Isa from Sama'ah who has said the following:

"I asked (the Imam), *'Alayhi al-Salam*, about visiting graves and building Masjids there. He said, 'There is no offense in visiting graves, but Masjid must not be built there.'"

H 4654, Ch. 83, h 3

Ali ibn Ibrahim has narrated from his father from ibn abu 'Umayr from Hisham ibn Salim who has said the following:

"I heard the Imam, *'Alayhi al-Salam*, say, 'Fatimah, *'Alayha al-Salam*, lived for seventy-five days after her father but she was never seen smiling or laughing. Every week she would visit the graves of the martyrs twice on Mondays and Thursdays and would say, "There was the Prophet and there were the pagans."'"

H 4655, Ch. 83, h 4

A number of our people have narrated from Sahl ibn Ziyad from Muhammad ibn Sinan from Ishaq ibn 'Ammar from abu al-Hassan, *'Alayhi al-Salam*, who has said the following:

"I asked the Imam, *'Alayhi al-Salam*, 'Does a believing deceased notice who has visited his grave?' He replied, 'Yes, and he continues to take comfort in his visitor as long as he is near his grave. When the visitor stands up and leaves the gravesite he (the deceased) becomes afraid and lonely.'"

H 4656, Ch. 83, h 5

Ali ibn Ibrahim has narrated from his father from 'Abd Allah ibn al-Mughirah from 'Abd Allah ibn Sinan who has said the following:

"I asked abu 'Abd Allah, *'Alayhi al-Salam*, 'How should one offer greeting of peace to the people of the graves?' He said, 'Yes, (it has an answer). Say, "(May Allah grant) peace to the dwellings of the Muslims and believing people. You have departed us and we, by the will of Allah, will join you."'"

H 4657, Ch. 83, h 6

A number of our people have narrated from Sahl ibn Ziyad and Muhammad ibn Yahya from Ahmad ibn Muhammad all from ibn Mahbub from ''Amr ibn abu al-Miqdam who has said the following:

"Once abu Ja'far, *'Alayhi al-Salam*, and I passed by al-Baqi' cemetery. We then passed by the grave of a person from al-Kufah who was a Shi'ah Muslim. The narrator has said that the Imam stood on his grave and said, 'O Lord, grant him mercy and kindness in his loneliness, provide him company in his solitude, comfort him in his distress and give him such serenity, through Your mercy, that can suffice him in place of the kindness and mercy of everyone beside You. Join him with those whom he loved (accepted as his guardians).'"

H 4658, Ch. 83, h 7

Abu Ali al-Ash'ariy has narrated from Muhammad ibn 'Abd al-Jabbar and Muhammad ibn Isma'il from al-Fadl ibn Shadhan all from Safwan ibn Yahya from Mansur ibn Hazim in a Muzmar manner who has said the following:

"He (the Imam) has said, 'As a greeting of peace to the people of the graves say, "May Allah grant you peace which was wished for you by the town of a believing people, and we by the will of Allah are about to join you."'"

H 4659, Ch. 83, h 8

Muhammad ibn Yahya has narrated from Ahmad ibn Muhammad ibn 'Isa from Al-Husayn ibn Sa'id from al-Nadr ibn Suwayd from al-Qasim ibn Sulayman from Jarrah al-Mada'iniy who has said the following:

"I asked abu 'Abd Allah, *'Alayhi al-Salam*, 'How should one offer greeting of peace to the people of the graves?' He replied, say, 'May Allah grant peace to the Muslims and believing ones of this dwelling place. May Allah grant mercy upon those of us who have preceded us (to the next life) and those who will follow and we, by the will of Allah, are about to join you.'"

H 4660, Ch. 83, h 9

Muhammad ibn Yahya has narrated from Muhammad ibn Ahmad who has said the following:

"I was in Fayd (a place near Makkah). Ali ibn Bilal and I went to visit the grave of Muhammad ibn Isma'il ibn Bazi' and Ali ibn Bilal said, 'The dweller of this grave narrated to me from al-Rida', *'Alayhi al-Salam*, the following:

"If one visits the grave of his brother (in belief), places his hand over the grave and reads Chapter 97 of the Holy Quran seven times he, on the distressful Day (of Judgment) will be granted full protection and peace.""'"

H 4661, Ch. 83, h 10

Ahmad ibn Muhammad al-Kufiy has narrated from ibn Jumhur from his father from Muhammad ibn Sinan from Mufaddal ibn 'Umar and from 'Abd Allah ibn 'Abd al-Rahman al-Asamm from Hariz from Muhammad ibn Muslim who has said the following:

"Abu 'Abd Allah, *'Alayhi al-Salam*, has said that 'Amir al-Mu'minin, *'Alayhi al-Salam*, has said, 'Visit your dead people; they become happy due to your visit. One of you should ask for his wishes near the grave of his father and near the grave of his mother through the prayers that one may say for them.'"

Chapter 84 - Dead People Visit Their Families

H 4662, Ch. 84, h 1

Ali ibn Ibrahim has narrated from his father from ibn abu 'Umayr from Hafs ibn al-Bakhtariy who has said the following:

"Abu 'Abd Allah, *'Alayhi al-Salam*, has said that a believing deceased person visits his family. He observes such matters that he loves and what he dislikes is kept hidden from him. A deceased unbeliever person also visits his family but observes what he dislikes and things that he loves are kept hidden from him. Certain ones of these people visit his family every Friday and others visit proportionate to their deeds."

H 4663, Ch. 84, h 2

Muhammad ibn Yahya has narrated from Ahmad ibn Muhammad from Ali ibn al-Hakam from Ali ibn abu Hamzah from abu Basir who has said the following:

"Abu 'Abd Allah, *'Alayhi al-Salam*, has said that every believing and unbeliever person visits his family everyday just after midday. If he finds his family performing good deeds, he praises and thanks Allah for this. When an unbeliever finds his family in good deeds, he laments and regrets (for his lost opportunities)."

H 4664, Ch. 84, h 3

A number of our people have narrated from Sahl ibn Ziyad from ibn Mahbub from Ishaq ibn 'Ammar who has said the following:

"I (the narrator) asked abu al-Hassan al-Awwal, *'Alayhi al-Salam*, about a deceased person's visiting his family. He replied, 'Yes, (this is a fact).' I then asked, 'How often do such visits take place?' He replied, 'In a Friday (week), in a month and in a year, depending upon his status.' I then asked, 'In what form does he visit his family?' He replied, 'He visits them in the form of a fine bird. He drops on their walls and oversees them. If he finds them in good deeds, he becomes happy, and if he finds them in evil deeds or in need, he becomes depressed and sorrowful.'"

H 4665, Ch. 84, h 4

It is narrated from him (narrator of above Hadith) from Isma'il ibn Mehran from Durust ibn abu Mansur al-Wasitiy from Ishaq ibn 'Ammar from 'Abd al-Rahim al-Qasir who has said the following:

"I asked the Imam, *'Alayhi al-Salam*, 'Does a deceased believing person visit his family?' He replied, 'Yes, he asks his Lord for permission; then by His permission with two angels he comes to his family in the form of some kind of a bird. He turns arround his house and observes his family and hears whatever they say.'"

H 4666, Ch. 84, h 5

It is narrated from him (narrator of above Hadith) from Muhammad ibn Sinan from Ishaq ibn 'Ammar who has said the following:

"I asked abu al-Hassan al-Awwal, *'Alayhi al-Salam*, 'Does a believing deceased person visit his family?' He replied, 'Yes, he does.' I then asked, 'How often does he visit them?' He replied, 'It depends upon their merits. Certain ones among them visit every day, others visit every other day, and still others among them visit after every three days.' I then found in the course of his conversation indications that said, 'The least among them in merits visit their family once every Friday.' I then asked, 'What time of the day do such visits take place?' He replied, 'It takes place very soon after midday or so.' I then asked, 'In what form does he come?' He replied, 'He comes in the form of a sparrow or smaller than a sparrow. Allah sends with him an angel who shows what he likes and hides from him what he dislikes. He then observes what makes him happy and returns very much delighted.'"

Chapter 85 - A Dying Person Observes His Properties, Children and Deeds Just Before His Death

H 4667, Ch. 85, h 1

Ali ibn Ibrahim has narrated from his father from 'Amr ibn 'Uthman and a number of our people, from Sahl ibn Ziyad from Ahmad ibn Muhammad ibn abu Nasr and al-Hassan ibn Ali all from abu Jamilah Mufaddal ibn Salih from Jabir from 'Abd al-'A'la' and Ali ibn Ibrahim from Muhammad ibn 'Isa from Yunus from Ibrahim from 'Abd al-'A'la' from Suwayd ibn Ghafalah who has said the following:

"Amir al-Mu'minin, *'Alayhi al-Salam*, has said, 'When a child of Adam finds himself in the first day of his next life and the last day of his worldly life, his property, children and deeds are pictured before him. He then turns to his property and says, "By Allah, I was very greedy and stingy about you. In what ways can you help me?" It will say, "All you can do is to take your shroud from me." He then turns to his children saying, "I loved you, protected you all the time. In what ways can you help me?" They will say, "We can take you to your grave and bury you therein." He then turns to his deeds and asks, "By Allah, I had very little inclination to perform you and felt burdened because of you. In what ways can you help me now?" His deed will say, "I am your companion in your grave up to the day you will be resurrected, until we both will be brought before your Lord."' The Imam then said, 'If he is a friend of Allah, a person, the best of people with fragrance, the best in beauty, and in the best of dresses comes to him and says, "I have brought you the happiness and fragrance of paradise of blessings and you are most welcome." He will then ask, "Who are you?" The person says, "I am your good deeds. You now move from the worldly life to paradise." He knows those who wash his body for burial and begs those who carry his coffin to hurry up. When he is placed in his grave, two angels will come with their hairs dragging on the ground and tearing the earth with their feet, with thunderous sounds and their eyes like swift lightening. They will ask, "Who is your Lord? What is your religion and who is your prophet?" He will reply, "Allah is my Lord, Islam is my religion and Muhammad, O Allah grant compensation to Muhammad and his family worthy of their services to Your cause, is my prophet." The two angels will then say, "May Allah keep you steadfast in what you love and are happy therewith." This is a reference to the words of Allah, most Majestic, most Glorious, "Allah keeps the believers steadfast in the unchanging words, in this world and in the next life" (14:26). The two angels then open up his grave as far as his eyes can see, and a door to paradise and then say to him, "Rest delightfully like a blessed young person," because Allah, the Most Majestic, the Most Glorious, has said, "People of paradise, on that day will have the best station and resting place" (25:26). The Imam then said, 'If he is an enemy of his Lord, Allah's ugliest creatures with the ugliest dress, appearance and smell will come to him and say, "Your place is boiling water and to suffer heat." He knows people who wash his body for burial and begs those who carry his body to his grave to hold him back. When he is placed in his grave, the two examiners will come to him, remove his shroud away and ask him, "Who is your Lord? What is your religion and who is your prophet?" He will say, "I do not know." They will say, "You did not know and you never had any guidance." They will strike him at the front part of his head with a crashing hammer that they carry. The sound of this strike will frighten all creatures of Allah, the Most Majestic, the Most Glorious, except man and Jinn. They then open a door to hell for him and say to him, "Lie down here in worst condition, due to lack of space, as if squeezed like the iron spike into the tip of spears." It will force his brain to squirt out of his toe and fingernails through the tissues of his flesh. Allah then gives his control to the snakes, scorpions and the creatures of earth that keep biting him until Allah will resurrect him from his grave. He will wish for the coming of the Day of Judgment because of suffering in his wicked condition."'

"Jabir has said that abu Ja'far has said that the Holy Prophet has said, 'When watching the camels and sheep graze, before being commissioned as a prophet - there is no prophet who did not shepherd sheep - I could see them, while in safe and protected place and nothing around them, suddenly become excited and jump around frightened. I would say, "What is this strange phenomenon?" Once, Jibril (Gabriel) told me that when an unbeliever in his grave is struck on his head by the interrogating angels, all creatures of Allah, except man and Jinn, hear the sound of that (horrifying) strike and become frightened. I then said, "This is because of only one strike on the head of a disbeliever. I seek refuge with Allah against the (rest of the) torments in the grave.""'

H 4668, Ch. 85, h 2

Sahl ibn Ziyad has narrated from al-Hassan ibn Ali from Bashir al-Dahhan from abu 'Abd Allah, *'Alayhi al-Salam*, and Ali ibn Ibrahim has narrated from Muhammad ibn 'Isa, from Yunus from abu Jamilah from Jabir, abu Ja'far from Jabir ibn 'Abd Allah who has said the following:

"The Messenger of Allah has said that when an enemy of Allah is taken to his grave, he keeps saying to those who carry his coffin, 'Why do you not listen to me, O my brethren, I complain before you about what has happened to me, one of your wicked brethren. The enemy of Allah (Satan) deceived me. He placed me in trouble but did not help me to escape. He swore before me that he was my good advisor but betrayed me. I complain before you against the worldly attractions that made me a conceited person, so much so that I felt satisfied with them; they destroyed me. I complain before you against friends of worldly desires who promised me great favors, but then denounced and betrayed me. I complain before you against my children whom I protected and gave preference over my own self, who consumed my properties but abandoned me. I complain before you against the properties from which I did not pay Allah's dues and the responsibility for which was left upon me, but its profits went to the others. I complain before you against the house on which I spent all of my earnings, but it became a dwelling of the others. I complain before you against my long stay in my grave from which I hear, "I am a dwelling full of worms, a dwelling which is very dark, frightening and very congested." O brethren, hold me back as long as you can and avoid facing what I have faced. I have been given the news of my suffering, the heat of fire that burns me, the humiliation and lowliness, and the anger of the Most Majestic, the Almighty Lord. How great is the loss of being careless and unconcerned about Allah and His chosen people! How lengthy is the time of crying and moaning! I have no one whose intercession for me is accepted. I have no friend who may feel pity about me. I wish I had a chance to become one of the believing people.'"

H 4669, Ch. 85, h 3

Muhammad ibn Yahya has narrated from Muhammad ibn al-Husayn from 'Amr ibn 'Uthman from Jabir from abu Ja'far *'Alayhi al-Salam*, a similar Hadith with the following addition:

"He continues pleading (and crying) until he is placed in his grave. When he is placed in his grave, his spirit is then returned to his body and the two angels come to his grave and examine him." "The narrator has that abu Ja'far, *'Alayhi al-Salam*, would weep whenever this Hadith was mentioned."

H 4670, Ch. 85, h 4

Ali ibn Ibrahim has narrated from Muhammad ibn 'Isa from Yunus from 'Amr ibn Shimr from Jabir who has said the following:

"Ali ibn al-Husayn, *'Alayhi al-Salam*, has said, 'We do not know how to deal with people. If we tell them that we have heard (such and such Hadith) from the Messenger of Allah, they laugh, and to remain silent (to neglect our mission) is not possible for us.' The narrator has said that Damrah ibn Ma'bad then said, 'You then should narrate to us (of such) Ahadith.' The Imam, *'Alayhi al-Salam*, then said, 'Do you know what an enemy of Allah says when his body is placed on the stretcher?' We replied, 'No, we do not know.' The Imam then said, 'He says to those who carry his coffin, "Why is it that you do not listen to my complaints against Allah's enemy who deceived me in taking me to wickedness and then did not help me to escape there-from? I complain before you against those with whom I established brotherly relations but they all betrayed me. I complain before you against the children whom I protected all the time but they also abandoned me. I complain before you against the house upon which I spent all my earnings but other people began to dwell therein. Please be kind and gentle to me and do not rush me up to my grave."' Damrah then said, 'O abu al-Hassan, if this man can say such things, he then may almost stand up on the shoulders of those who carry him.' The narrator has said that Ali ibn al-Husayn, *'Alayhi al-Salam*, then said, 'O Allah, if Damrah has made fun of Hadith of the Messenger of Allah, then hold him like an angry person does.' The narrator has said that after forty days he died. He had a servant who after his burial came to Ali ibn al-Husayn, *'Alayhi al-Salam*. He sat next to the Imam who asked, 'Wherefrom are you coming O so and so?' He replied, 'I have come from the burial of Damrah. I placed my face over him (his grave) when he was buried and I heard his voice which I recognized. It was just as I knew it was in his lifetime. I heard him saying, "Woe is upon you, O Damrah ibn Ma'bad. Today all friends have abandoned you and your destination has become hell, wherein is your dwelling, a place of rest at night and in the morning." The narrator has said that Ali ibn al-Husayn, *'Alayhi al-Salam*, then said, 'I plead before Allah for safety. Such is the recompense for those who make fun of the Ahadith of the Messenger of Allah.'"

Chapter 86 - Interrogations in the Grave - Who Is Interrogated and Who Is Not

H 4671, Ch. 86, h 1

Abu Ali al-Ash'ariy has narrated from Muhammad ibn 'Abd Al-Jabbar from al-Hajjal from Tha'labah from abu Bakr al-Hadramiy who has said the following:

"Abu 'Abd Allah, *'Alayhi al-Salam*, has said, 'No one is interrogated in the grave except those whose faith and belief is pure or those whose disbelief is total, others, besides these, are left alone.'"

H 4672, Ch. 86, h 2

A number of our people have narrated from Sahl ibn Ziyad from 'Abd al-Rahman ibn abu Najran from 'Abd Allah ibn Sinan who has said the following:

"Abu 'Abd Allah, *'Alayhi al-Salam*, has said that the only people who are interrogated in the grave are those whose belief or disbelief is absolute and total, and people other than these are left alone."

H 4673, Ch. 86, h 3

Abu Ali al-Ash'ariy has narrated from Muhammad ibn 'Abd al-Jabbar from Muhammad ibn Isma'il from Mansur ibn Yunus from ibn Bukayr who has said the following:

"Abu Ja'far, *'Alayhi al-Salam*, has said, the only ones interrogated in the grave are those whose belief or disbelief is absolute and total, and people other than such ones are left alone."

H 4674, Ch. 86, h 4

Muhammad ibn Yahya has narrated from Ahmad ibn Muhammad ibn 'Isa from al-Husayn ibn Sa'id from al-Nadr ibn al-Suwayd from Yahya al-Halabiy from Burayd ibn Mu'awiyah from Muhammad ibn Muslim who has said the following:

"Abu 'Abd Allah, *'Alayhi al-Salam*, has said, 'The only ones interrogated in the grave are those whose belief or disbelief is absolute and total.'"

H 4675, Ch. 86, h 5

It is narrated from him (narrator of above Hadith) from Ahmad ibn Muhammad from Al-Husayn from al-Nadr ibn al-Suwayd from Yahya al-Halabiy from Harun ibn Kharijah from abu Basir who has said the following:

"Abu 'Abd Allah, *'Alayhi al-Salam*, has said that a person is interrogated in the grave while he is pressed hard from all sides."

H 4676, Ch. 86, h 6

A number of our people have narrated from Ahmad ibn Muhammad ibn Khalid from 'Uthman ibn 'Isa from Ali ibn abu Hamzah from abu Basir who has said the following:

"I asked abu 'Abd Allah, *'Alayhi al-Salam*, 'Can anyone remain safe from the pressure of the grave?' The Imam said, 'I seek protection against it from Allah. How few are those who remain safe from the pressure in the grave! When Ruqiyyah was murdered..., the Messenger of Allah stood on her grave and raised his head toward the sky, his eyes flooded with tears, and said to people, "I thought of her and her condition in the grave moved me to a weeping state. I pleaded before Allah to give her safety from the pressure of the grave as a gift for me."' He (the Imam) has said that the Messenger of Allah then said, "O Lord, save Ruqiyyah from the pressure of the grave as gift to me." Allah then granted him that gift. The Messenger of Allah took part in the funeral of Sa'd in which seventy thousand angels had also taken part. The Messenger of Allah raised his head to the sky and said, 'Even (a person like) Sa'd undergoes the pressure of the grave.' I then said to the Imam, 'It is said that he (Sa'd) would not pay much attention to the uncleanness from his urine.' He replied, 'May Allah grant protection, it was due to his harsh manners toward his family (wife).' The Imam then said that mother of Sa'd said, 'How fortunate are you, O Sa'd!' the Messenger of Allah then said, 'O mother of Sa'd, please do not consider it (granting an opportune) an obligation upon Allah.'"

H 4677, Ch. 86, h 7

Muhammad ibn Yahya has narrated from Ahmad ibn Muhammad ibn 'Isa from al-Hassan ibn Ali from Ghalib ibn 'Uthman from Bashir al-Dahhan who has said the following:

"Abu 'Abd Allah, *'Alayhi al-Salam*, has said that the two interrogating angels (Munkar and Nakir) will come to the person who is just buried. Their voice sounds like thunder, their eyes like swift lightening, tearing the earth with their incisors, they strike the earth with their hairs and ask the deceased, 'Who is your Lord and what your religion is?' The Imam then said, 'If the deceased is a believer he will say, "Allah is my Lord and Islam is my religion." They will then ask the deceased, "What do you say about this man who appeared among you?" The deceased will ask, "Are you asking me about Muhammad, the Messenger of Allah?" They then ask, "Do you testify that he is the Messenger of Allah?" He will say, "Yes, I do testify that he is the Messenger of Allah." They then will say, "Rest to sleep without dreams." They will open his grave by nine yards and a door to paradise where he can observe his seat.

'If the deceased is an unbeliever, the two angels will come to him and present before him will also be Satan with his eyes made of brass. The angels will ask him, "Who is your Lord, what is your religion and what do you say about this man who appeared among you?" The deceased will say, "I do not know." The angels then leave him with Satan who then will expose him to ninety-nine such serpents that even if one of them would blow in earth, no plant thereafter can grow therein. The angels open to him a door to hell wherein he can observe his seat.'"

H 4678, Ch. 86, h 8

A number of our people have narrated from Sahl ibn Ziyad from Muhammad ibn al-Hassan ibn Shammun from 'Abd Allah ibn 'Abd al-Rahman from 'Abd Allah ibn al-Qasim from abu Bakr al-Hadramiy who has said the following:

"I asked abu Ja'far, *'Alayhi al-Salam*, 'May Allah grant you well being, who are interrogated in the grave?' The Imam replied, 'The only ones interrogated in the grave are those whose belief or disbelief is absolute and total.' The narrator has said that I then asked, 'What about the rest of these creatures?' The Imam replied, 'They, by Allah, will be left alone.' The narrator has said that I then asked about the phrase: 'What will they be asked about?' The Imam replied, 'They will be questioned about Divine authority established among you. The believers will be asked, "What do you say about so and so son of so and so?" The believer will say, "He is my Imam." They then will say, "Rest to sleep; may Allah grant rest to your eyes."' They will open to him a door to paradise whereby he keeps receiving gifts up to the Day of Judgment. They ask an unbeliever, "What do you say about so and so son of so and so?" He will say, "I have heard about him but I do not know who he is." The angels will say, "May you never know!"' The Imam then said, 'The two angels will open a door of fire to him from which he will suffer up to the Day of Judgment.'"

H 4679, Ch. 86, h 9

Muhammad ibn Yahya from Ahmad ibn Muhammad ibn 'Isa from Ali ibn Hadid from Jamil from 'Amr ibn al-Ash'ath who has said the following:

"I heard abu 'Abd Allah, *'Alayhi al-Salam*, say that a man is interrogated in his grave. If he remains steadfast (in his belief), his grave is then made spacious by nine yards, a door to paradise is then opened for him and it is said to him, 'Rest to sleep like a newly wedded person with delightful heart.'"

H 4680, Ch. 86, h 10

A number of our people have narrated from Sahl ibn Ziyad from 'Abd al-Rahman ibn abu Najran from 'Asem ibn Humayd from abu Basir who has said the following:

"I heard abu 'Abd Allah, *'Alayhi al-Salam*, say, 'When a person is placed in his grave, two angels come to him, one from the right, the other from the left, and Satan whose eyes are made of brass stands before his eyes. The two angels will ask, "What do you say about the man who lived among you?"' The Imam then said, 'This causes him a terrifying alarm. If a believing person, he says, "Are you asking about Muhammad, the Messenger of Allah?" The two angels will then say to him, "Rest to sleep without dreams therein." They will make his grave spacious by nine yards. He then observes his seat in paradise.' This is what Allah, the Most Majestic, the Most Glorious, has mentioned (in His Book), 'Allah keeps the believers steadfast upon the firmly established word both in this and in the next life.' (14:26) If he is an unbeliever, the two angels will ask, "Who is the man who appeared among you?" He will say, "I do not know." The two angels will then leave him with Satan.'"

H 4681, Ch. 86, h 11

Muhammad ibn Yahya has narrated from Ahmad ibn Muhammad from al-Husayn ibn Sa'id from Ibrahim ibn abu al-Balad from certain persons of his people who has said the following:

"Abu al-Hassan Musa, *'Alayhi al-Salam*, has said, that a believing person in his grave will be asked, 'Who is your Lord?' He will reply, 'Allah is my Lord.' He is then asked, 'What is your religion?' He will reply, 'Islam is my religion.' He is then asked, 'Who is your prophet?' He will reply, 'Muhammad is my prophet.' He is then asked, 'Who is your Imam?' He will reply, 'So and so is my Imam.' He is asked, 'How did you come to know that he is your Imam?' He will reply, 'It is a matter to which Allah guided me and kept me steadfast therewith.' It then will be said to him, 'Rest to sleep without dreams like the sleep of newly wedded person.' A door to paradise is then opened to him through which fragrance and happiness of paradise continue to come to him. He will then say, 'Lord, allow the Day of judgment to come quicker so I can return to my family and property.' An unbeliever is asked, 'Who is your Lord?' He replies, 'Allah is my Lord.' He is then asked, 'Who is your prophet?' He replies, 'Muhammad is my prophet.' He is then asked, 'What is your religion?' He replies, 'Islam is my religion.' He is then asked, 'How did you come to know it?' He replies, 'People said so and so did I.' The two angels will then strike him with a war-club on his head such that even all man and Jinn together cannot bear (its pain). The Imam then said, 'He will melt like lead. Then they will return his soul to his body and place his heart between two boards of fire and he will plead, "O Lord, please delay the coming of the Day of Judgment."'"

H 4682, Ch. 86, h 12

Muhammad ibn Yahya has narrated from Ahmad ibn Muhammad ibn 'Isa from al-Husayn ibn Sa'id from al-Qasim ibn Muhammad from Ali ibn abu Hamzah from abu Basir who has said the following:

"Abu 'Abd Allah, *'Alayhi al-Salam*, has said that when a believing person is taken out of his home, the angels escort him to his grave in a crowded manner until they arrive on his grave. The earth then says to him, 'You are most welcome. By Allah, I loved that people like you walk on me. You will see what I will do for you.' His grave will be opened up for him as far as his eyes can see, and then the two angels of grave, the dweller therein, Munkar and Nakir, enter into his grave, send his soul in him up to his loin, make him rise to sit upright and ask him, 'Who is your Lord?' He then replies, 'Allah is my Lord.' They then ask, 'What is your religion?' He replies, 'Islam is my religion.' They then ask, 'Who is your prophet?' He then replies, 'Muhammad is my prophet.' They then ask, 'Who is your Imam?' He then replies, 'So and so is my Imam.' Then someone calls from the heaven, 'My servant has told the truth. Furnish his grave from the furnishing of paradise and open for his grave a door to paradise, dress him from the dresses of paradise until he will come to Us; what is with Us for him is better.' Then it is said to him, 'Rest to sleep like a newly wedded person, rest sleeping without dreams.' The Imam then said, 'If he is an unbeliever, the angels escort him to his grave while they all condemn him until they arrive on his grave; and the earth says, "You are not welcome at all. By Allah, I hated that people like you walk on me. However, you will see what I will do to you today." The grave then presses him with a huge force until his sides join each other. The Imam then said, 'Then the angels of the grave, the dwellers of the grave, Munkar and Nakir, enter his grave.'

"Abu Basir then asked, 'May Allah keep my soul in your service, do they (the angels) come to the believer and the unbeliever with the same shape and form?' The Imam replied, 'No, they do not do so.' The Imam then said, 'They then make him sit upright and send his soul in him up to his loin and ask him, "Who is your Lord?" He will hesitate and say, "I heard people say (so and so)." They will say, "May you never know." They then will ask, "What is your religion?" He will hesitate. They will say, "May you never know." They will ask, "Who is your prophet?" He will say, "I heard people say (so and so)." They will say, "May you never know." They then will ask him about the Imam of his time.' The Imam then said, 'Someone from the heaven then calls saying, "My servant has lied. Furnish his grave with the furnishing of fire, dress him with the dress of fire, open for him a door to fire until he comes before Us and what is with Us for him is much worse." They then strike him with a war-club three times and each strike sets his grave on fire. The force of each strike can turn the mountains of Makkah into ashes.'

"The Imam then said, 'Allah then allows serpents to bite him repeatedly and Satan to make him suffer sadness.' The Imam also said, 'All creatures of Allah except man and Jinn hear his punishment. He can hear the sound of their shoes walking and the sound of their fingers being cracked and this is what Allah has mentioned in His book, "Allah keeps the believers steadfast upon the firmly established word in this world and in the next life and Allah causes to mislead the unjust and He does as He wills."''" (14:26)

H 4683, Ch. 86, h 13

Ali ibn Ibrahim has narrated from his father from ibn Mahbub from 'Abd Allah ibn Kulum from abu Sa'id who has said the following:

"Abu 'Abd Allah, *'Alayhi al-Salam*, has said that when a believing person is placed in his grave, his prayer appears on his right side, Zakat (his paying charity) on his left side, his good manners above him and his patience stands on one side. When the angels, who interrogate him, enter his grave, his patience will say to his prayer and Zakat, 'Help your friend. If you fail, then I will defend him.'"

H 4684, Ch. 86, h 14

Ali ibn Muhammad has narrated from Muhammad ibn Ahmad al-Khurasaniy from his father who has said the following:

"Abu 'Abd Allah, *'Alayhi al-Salam*, has said, 'When a deceased person is placed in his grave, someone appears before him and says, "O so and so, there were three of us. One was your means of sustenance that is no more because of the coming of the time of your death. The other one was your family who left you and has returned home. I was your deeds and I have remained with you but I was the least important of the three before you."'"

H 4685, Ch. 86, h 15

It is narrated from him (narrator of the above Hadith) from his father in a marfu' manner who has said the following:

"Abu 'Abd Allah, *'Alayhi al-Salam*, has said that a deceased is asked in his grave about five issues. He is asked about his prayer, Zakat (paying charity), his Hajj, his fasting and about our, Ahl al-Bayt's wilayah (guardianship) over him. Wilayah then from one side of the grave says to the others, 'If you face any deficiency in your task (of protecting him), leave it for me to suffice.'"

H 4686, Ch. 86, h 16

Ali ibn Ibrahim has narrated from Muhammad ibn 'Isa from Yunus who has said the following:

"I asked him (the Imam), *'Alayhi al-Salam*, about one who dies because of being hanged, 'Is such a person punished in the form of the pressure of the grave?' He replied, 'Yes, Allah, the Most Majestic, the Most Glorious, sends the air to place huge pressures on him.'"

H 4687, Ch. 86, h 17

The following is narrated in another Hadith:

"Someone asked abu 'Abd Allah, 'Does a person who dies because of being hanged to death, suffer the severe pressure of the grave?' The Imam said, 'The Lord of the earth is also the Lord of the air. Allah, the Most Majestic, the Most Glorious, inspires the air and it applies a pressure on the deceased which is greater than the pressure in the grave.'"

H 4688, Ch. 86, h 18

Humayd ibn Ziyad has narrated from al-Hassan ibn Muhammad ibn Sama'ah from more than one person from Aban from abu Basir from one of the two Imam who has said the following:

"When Ruqiyyah, daughter of the Messenger of Allah passed away, the Messenger of Allah said, 'You now join the people of good deeds of our predecessors like 'Uthman ibn Maz'un and his friends.' The Imam said, 'Fatimah, *'Alayha al-Salam*, stood on the edge of the grave with her tears falling into the grave, and the Messenger of Allah allowed his tears to fall in his clothes. While standing he (the Messenger of Allah) prayed saying, "I am aware of her weakness and pray to Allah, the Most Majestic, the Most Glorious, to grant her protection against the pressure of the grave."'"

Chapter 87 - The Statements that Graves Make Every Day

H 4689, Ch. 87, h 1

Muhammad ibn Yahya has narrated from Muhammad ibn al-Husayn from 'Abd al-Rahman ibn abu Hashim from Salim who has said the following:

"Abu 'Abd Allah, *'Alayhi al-Salam,* has said that every gravesite speaks three times every day, 'I am the house of soil, I am the house of misfortune and I am the house of worms.' The Imam then said, 'When a believing person enters the grave it says, "You are most welcome. By Allah I loved you when you walked on me. Why then should I not love you when you are inside of me? You will see what I can do for you." His grave opens for him as far as he can see and a door for him opens to paradise where he can see his seat. There-from a man comes out, the like of whom in beauty he had never seen before, and he asks, "Who are you, O servant of Allah? I have never seen before anyone more beautiful than you." He will reply, "I am your good opinion that you possessed and your good deeds that you performed."' The Imam then said, 'Then his spirit or soul is taken to be placed in paradise where he had seen his dwelling and it is said to him, "Rest here to the delight of your eyes." Then he continues feeling the joy and fragrance of the breeze from paradise with his body until he is resurrected.' The Imam then said, 'When an unbeliever enters the grave, it says, "You are not welcome at all. By Allah, I hated you when you walked on me and it is more so now that you are inside of me, and you will see how much I hate you."' The Imam then said, 'The grave then applies a huge pressure upon him and turns him into ashes. Then he turns back into his form as before. Then it opens a door for him to the fire where he observes his seat therein.' The Imam then said, 'Thereafter a man comes out to him, the like of whom in ugliness he had never seen before.' The Imam also said that he then asks, 'Who are you, O servant of Allah? I have never seen anyone uglier than you.' He replies, 'I am your evil deeds that you performed and your filthy opinion.' The Imam then said, 'His soul is then taken to be placed where he had observed his seat in the fire. Thereafter blows of fire continue striking his body that feels the pain and heat thereof until the Day of Resurrection. Allah will allow ninety-nine very poisonous serpents to bite him. If any of them may blow to the earth, nothing can grow therein.'"

H 4690, Ch. 87, h 2

A number of our people have narrated from Sahl ibn Ziyad from al-Hassan ibn Ali from Ghalib ibn 'Uthman from Bashir al-Dahhan who has said the following:

"Abu 'Abd Allah, *'Alayhi al-Salam,* has said that the grave has a statement every day. It says, 'I am the house of loneliness. I am the terrifying house and I am the house of worms. I am the grave. I can be a garden of the gardens of paradise or a pit of the pits of hell.'"

H 4691, Ch. 87, h 3

Muhammad ibn Yahya has narrated from Ahmad ibn Muhammad ibn 'Isa from Ahmad ibn Muhammad from 'Abd al-Rahman ibn Hammad from 'Amr ibn Yazid who has said the following:

"I said to abu 'Abd Allah, *'Alayhi al-Salam,* 'I have heard you say, "All of our Shi'ah will be in paradise just as they are."' He said, 'I have told you the truth.

All of them, by Allah, will be in paradise.' The narrator has said that I then said, 'May Allah keep my soul in your service, the sins are many and the major ones.' He said, 'On the Day of Judgment, all of you will be in paradise through the intercession of the Holy Prophet, which is obeyed or through the intercession of an executor of the will of the Holy Prophet. However I am afraid for you in Barzakh.' I then asked, 'What is Barzakh?' He replied, 'It is the grave from his death to the Day of Judgment.'"

Chapter 88 - About the Spirits (Souls) of the Believers

H 4692, Ch. 88, h 1

Ali ibn Muhammad has narrated from Ali ibn al-Hassan from al-Husayn ibn Rashid, from al-Murtajil ibn Mu'ammar from Dharih al-Muharibiy, from 'Ubadah al-Asadiy from Habbah al-'Uraniy who has said the following:

"Once I went out along with `Amir al-Mu'minin toward the backside of the city of Kufah. He stood on Wadiy al-Salam (valley of peace). He seemed like speaking to certain people. I stood as he was until I became tired. I then sat down until I became bored. I then stood up until I began to feel as it happened before. I then sat down until I became bored again. I then stood up and pulled my gown together and said, 'O `Amir al-Mu'minin, I have become concerned about your standing for so long. You should rest for a while.' I then spread my gown so he could sit on it. He then said to me, 'O Habbah, it was only a conversation with Mu'min (believer) or feeling comfortable with.' I then asked, 'Are they such, O `Amir al-Mu'minin?' He replied, 'Yes, were it to be revealed to you, you could have seen them in groups and circles in Ihtiba' position, speaking to each other.' I then asked, 'Are they in the form of spirits or do they have bodily shapes?' He replied, 'They are in the form of spirits. Whenever and wherever any believing person dies his spirit is told to leave for Wadi al-Salam. It is a piece of paradise of Eden.'" (Ihtiba' is when one sits with his thighs against his belly and forms a ring with a piece of cloth for support around his trunk and knees or holds them against his belly with his hands).

H 4693, Ch. 88, h 2

A number of our people have narrated from Sahl ibn Ziyad from al-Hassan ibn Ali from Ahmad ibn 'Umar in marfu' manner from abu 'Abd Allah, the following:

"I said to abu 'Abd Allah, *'Alayhi al-Salam*, 'My brother is in Baghdad and I am afraid that he may die there.' He said, 'Why should you worry about wherever he dies? Indeed, Allah sends to Wadi al-Salam the soul of every believing person who dies in the east or west of the earth.' I then asked, 'Where is Wadi al-Salam?' 'It is behind the city of Kufah,' He (the Imam) replied. 'It is as if I see them in circles and circles, sitting and talking to each other,' the Imam explained.'"

Chapter 89 - Another Chapter about the Souls of the Believing People

H 4694, Ch. 92, h 1

Ali ibn Ibrahim has narrated from his father from al-Hassan ibn Mahbub from abu Wallad al-Hannat who has said the following:

"I asked abu 'Abd Allah, *'Alayhi al-Salam*, 'May Allah keep my soul in service for your cause, they narrate that the souls of the believing people are kept in the craw of green birds that live around the Throne.' The Imam replied, 'Believing people are very much respectable before Allah. He does not keep them in the craw of birds. In fact, He keeps them in bodies like their bodies.'"

H 4695, Ch. 92, h 2

A number of our people have narrated from Sahl ibn Ziyad from 'Abd al-Rahman ibn abu Najran from Muthanna al-Hannat from abu Basir who has said the following:

"Abu 'Abd Allah, *'Alayhi al-Salam*, has said, 'The souls of the believing people are in a tree of paradise. They eat and drink of fruits and water thereof, and say, "O Lord, make the Day of Judgment to come for us, make what You had promised to come true and allow the last of us to join our first."'"

H 4696, Ch. 92, h 3

Sahl ibn Ziyad has narrated from 'Isma'il ibn Mehran from Durust ibn abu Mansur from ibn Muskan from abu Basir who has said the following:

"Abu 'Abd Allah, *'Alayhi al-Salam*, has said that the souls (spirits) with the quality of body are in a tree in paradise where they get to know each other and ask questions. Whenever a new coming soul (spirit) joins them, they say, 'Leave him alone. He has just experienced a huge terrifying experience.' Then they ask him, 'What is so and so and so and so doing?' If he says, 'I left him in his lifetime,' they wish the best for him; but if he says, 'He died', they say, 'He then has fallen into the deep (hell).'"

H 4697, Ch. 92, h 4

Ali ibn Ibrahim has narrated from his father from ibn abu 'Umayr from Muhammad ibn 'Uthman from abu Basir who has said the following:

"I once asked abu 'Abd Allah, *'Alayhi al-Salam*, about the souls (spirits) of believing people. He said, 'They are in chambers in paradise, they eat and drink thereof and say, "O Lord, make it the Day of Judgment, allow what You had promised us to come true and join the last of us with those who were first."'"

H 4698, Ch. 92, h 5

Ali has narrated from his father from Muhsin ibn Ahmad from Muhammad ibn Hammad from Yunus ibn Ya'qub who has said the following:

"Abu 'Abd Allah, *'Alayhi al-Salam*, has said that when a dying person dies, other spirits gather around him and ask, 'Who is still alive and who is dead?' If someone is dead and has not joined them they say, 'He then has fallen into the deep.' Others among them say, 'Leave him alone so he can gain comfort from what he has experienced from death.'"

H 4699, Ch. 89, h 6

Muhammad ibn Yahya has narrated from Ahmad ibn Muhammad ibn 'Isa from Muhammad ibn Khalid from al-Qasim ibn Muhammad from al-Husayn ibn Ahmad from Yunus ibn Zabyan who has said the following:

'Once I was with abu 'Abd Allah, *'Alayhi al-Salam*, and he asked, 'What do people say about the spirits of the believers?' I then replied, 'They say that they live in the craws of green birds in chandlers in paradise under the Throne.' Abu 'Abd Allah, *'Alayhi al-Salam*, then said, 'Allah is free of all defects. A believer is highly respected in the sight of Allah. He does not place them (the spirits of believers) in the craws of birds. O Yunus, when that (death) comes Muhammad, Ali, Fatimah, al-Hassan and al-Husayn, *'Alayhim al-Salam*, and the angels of high ranks before Allah come. When Allah, the Most Majestic, the Most Glorious, causes him to die, the spirit is transferred to a form like his form in the world. They (spirits) eat and drink. When a new coming soul (spirit) joins them, they recognize him through his form which he had in the world.'"

H 4700, Ch. 89, h 7

Muhammad ibn Ahmad has narrated from al-Husayn ibn Sa'id from his brother al-Hassan from Zur'ah from abu Basir who has said the following:

"Once, I said to abu 'Abd Allah, *'Alayhi al-Salam*, 'We speak about the spirits of the believing people that they live in the craws of green birds that graze in paradise and seek shelter in chandlers under the Throne.' He said, 'No, they certainly are not in the craws of birds.' I then asked, 'Where are they then?' He replied, 'They are in a garden in the shape of bodies in paradise.'"

Chapter 90 - About the Souls (spirits) of the Unbelievers

H 4701, Ch. 90, h 1

Ali ibn Ibrahim has narrated from his father from ibn abu 'Umayr from Muhammad ibn 'Uthman from abu Basir who has said the following:

"I once asked abu 'Abd Allah, *'Alayhi al-Salam*, about the souls (spirits) of the pagans. He replied, 'They are in the fire where they are punished. They say, "O Lord, do not make it the Day of Judgment for us. Do not allow what You have promised us to come true and do not join the last of us with our first."'"

H 4702, Ch. 90, h 2

A number of our people have narrated from Sahl ibn Ziyad from 'Abd al-Rahman ibn abu Najran from Muthanna from abu Basir who has said the following:

"Abu 'Abd Allah, *'Alayhi al-Salam*, has said that the souls (spirits) of the unbelievers are exposed to hellfire. They say, 'O Lord, do not make any Day of Judgment for us. Do not allow what You have promised us to come true and do not join the last of us with our first ones.'"

H 4703, Ch. 93, h 3

Muhammad ibn Yahya has narrated from Muhammad ibn Ahmad through the chain of his narrators has said the following:

"'Amir al-Mu'minin, *'Alayhi al-Salam*, has said, 'The worst well in the fire is the well of Barahut in which the souls (spirits) of unbelievers live.'"

H 4704, Ch. 93, h 4

A number of our people have narrated from Sahl ibn Ziyad and Ali ibn Ibrahim has narrated from his father all from Ja'far ibn Muhammad al-Ash'ariy from al-Qaddah who has narrated the following:

"Abu 'Abd Allah from his ancestors, *'Alayhi al-Salam*, has narrated that `Amir al-Mu'minin, *'Alayhi al-Salam*, has said, 'The worst water on earth is the water of Barahut which is in Hadramawt where the souls (spirits) of unbelievers camp.'"

H 4705, Ch. 93, h 5

Ali ibn Ibrahim has narrated from his father from al-Nawfaliy from al-Sakuniy who has said the following:

"Abu 'Abd Allah, *'Alayhi al-Salam*, has said that the Messenger of Allah has said, 'The worst ones among Jews are the Jews of Baysan, the worst ones among Christians are the Christians of Najran. The best water on earth is the water of Zamzam and the worst water on earth is the water of Barahut and it is in the valley of Hadramawt where the souls and spirits of unbelievers camp.'"

Chapter 91 - Worldly Garden

H 4706, Ch. 91, h 1

A number of our people have narrated from Ahmad ibn Muhammad as well as Sahl ibn Ziyad and Ali ibn Ibrahim has narrated from his father, all from ibn Mahbub from Ali ibn Ri'ab from Durays al-Kunasiy who has said the following:

"I said to abu Ja'far, *'Alayhi al-Salam*, 'People say that our Euphrates gushes forth from the Garden (paradise). How can that be the case? It flows from the west and many springs and waters of valleys fall into it.' The narrator has that abu Ja'far, *'Alayhi al-Salam*, then said while I was listening, 'Allah has a garden. Allah has created it in the west. The waters of your Euphrates come from there and to this (garden) the souls (spirits) of believing people travel from their graves every evening. They descend upon its fruits, eat thereof, enjoy, meet others and get to know them. At dawn they move from the garden and remain in the air between earth and the sky, fly back and forth; at sunrise they visit their graves, meet in the air and get to know each other.' The Imam then said, 'Allah has a fire in the east. He has created it for the souls (spirits) of the unbelievers. They eat from Zaqqum (the fruit of the infernal tree) and drink from its boiling water all night; at dawn they move to a valley in Yemen called 'Barahut', which is hotter than the fire of the world, where they meet and get to know each other. In the evening they return to the fire. They remain in this condition until the Day of Judgment.' The narrator has said that I then asked, 'May Allah keep you well, in what condition do the people remain who believe in one Creator, and who seek nearness (to Allah) through the prophet-hood of Muhammad, O Allah grant compensation to Muhammad and his family worthy of their services to Your cause? They are of the Muslims who have sinned and they die. They have no Imam and do not acknowledge your Divine Authority.' He said, 'They remain in their pit (graves) and do not come out from there. For those of them who have done good deeds and who have not expressed animosity (toward us), a line is drawn for them to the garden, which Allah has created in the west. Through this the garden happiness comes to their grave until the Day of Judgment when they come before Allah. He then shows them the account of their good and bad deeds and thereafter they are sent to paradise or to the fire. Their case depends on Allah's Judgment.' The Imam then said, 'In the same way He deals with the feeble-minded, the dimwitted ones, children and the children of Muslims who die before maturity. However, for those of the people of Qiblah (people who face Ka'bah during their prayers) who express animosity (toward Ahl al-Bayt) a line is drawn to the fire, which Allah has created in the east, wherefrom heat and flame and smoke and jets of hot water reach them until the Day of Judgment. Thereafter their destination will be to hot water, then to the fire, which will attack them. Then it will be said to them, "To whom, other than Allah, would you invite people? Where is your Imam whom you had chosen other than the Imam whom Allah had made for people?""'

H 4707, Ch. 91, h 2
Ali ibn Ibrahim has narrated from his father from Ahmad ibn Muhammad ibn abu Nasr from al-Husayn ibn Muyassir who has said the following:
"I asked abu 'Abd Allah, *'Alayhi al-Salam*, about the garden of Adam, *'Alayhi al-Salam*. He said, 'It was a garden of the gardens of the world on which the sun and moon rise. Had it been of the gardens of the hereafter, he would have never been expelled there from.'"

Chapter 92 - The Children

H 4708, Ch. 92, h 1
Ali ibn Ibrahim has narrated from his father from Hammad, from Hariz from Zurarah who has narrated the following:
"I asked abu Ja'far, *'Alayhi al-Salam*, 'Had the Messenger of Allah been asked about children?' He said, 'Indeed he was asked and he said, "Allah knows better about their deeds."' The Imam then said, 'O Zurarah, do you know His words, "Allah knows better of what they had been doing?"' I replied, 'I do not know.' The Imam said, 'Allah has a wish in the matter. On the Day of Judgment Allah, the Most Majestic, the Most Glorious, will bring the children together as well as the people who have died between the intervals (the time between the passing away of one prophet and the coming of the other). He will bring the elderly who lived in the time of the Holy Prophet but had lost understanding, were the deaf, and the dumb who do not understand, the insane ones and the dimwitted who do not understand. Every one of such people will argue before Allah, the Most Majestic, the Most Glorious. Allah sends an angel from among His angels who lights up a fire and then Allah sends another angel who says to them, 'Your Lord commands you to jump in it (fire). Whoever of them jumps, for him it will turn cool and peaceful and he is admitted to paradise and those who disobey go to the fire.'"

H 4709, Ch. 92, h 2
A number of our people have narrated from Sahl ibn Ziyad for more than one person who, in a marfu' manner, have said the following:
"He (the Holy Prophet) was asked about the children and he replied, 'On the Day of Judgment Allah will bring all of them together, light up for them a fire

and command them to throw themselves in it. Those of them who are fortunate in the knowledge of Allah, the Most Majestic, the Most Glorious, throw themselves in the fire and it turns cool and peaceful to them. Those of them who are not fortunate in the knowledge of Allah, they refuse to throw themselves in the fire and Allah then orders them to the fire and they will say, "O Lord, You commanded us to the fire and the pen has not moved against us." The Almighty will say, "I just commanded you face to face but you did not obey Me: how would you obey Me through sending you my messengers in an unseen condition?'"

"In another Hadith it is said that the children of the believing people are joined with their parents and the children of the pagans are joined with their parents as this is stated in the words of Allah, the Most Majestic, the Most Glorious, 'The offspring of the believers will also follow them to paradise. Therefore, We shall join their offspring to them because of their faith. We shall not reduce anything from their deeds. Everyone will be responsible for his own actions.'" (52:21)

H 4710, Ch. 92, h 3

Muhammad ibn Yahya has narrated from Ahmad ibn Muhammad from al-Husayn ibn Sa'id from al-Nadr ibn al-Suwayd from Yahya al-Halabiy from ibn Muskan from Zurarah who has said the following:

"I asked abu Ja'far, *'Alayhi al-Salam*, about the children, and he said, 'The Messenger of Allah was asked about the children and infants, and he replied, "Allah knows best about what they had been doing."'"

H 4711, Ch. 92, h 4

Ali ibn Ibrahim has narrated from his father from ibn abu 'Umayr from 'Umar ibn 'Udhaynah from Zurarah who has said the following:

"I asked abu 'Abd Allah, *'Alayhi al-Salam*, about children who die before maturity and he replied, 'The Messenger of Allah was asked about them and he said, "Allah knows best about what they may do."' Then he turned to me and said, 'O Zurarah, do you know what the Messenger of Allah meant thereby?' I said, 'No, I do not know.' He said, 'He meant to say, "You must not say anything about them but leave their affairs to Allah (to deal with)."'"

H 4712, Ch. 92, h 5

A number of our people have narrated from Sahl ibn Ziyad from Ali ibn al-Hakam from Sayf ibn 'Amirah from ibn Bukayr who has said the following:

"This is about the words of Allah, the Most Majestic, the Most Glorious, that read,'. . . (The bountiful paradise is for the pious ones) and for the believers and their offspring who have followed them (parents) in belief, whom We shall join with their parents therein. . . . (52:21).' Abu 'Abd Allah, *'Alayhi al-Salam*, has said, 'The children even though may have had shortcomings in their deeds, they will be joined with their parents to grant delightfulness to the eyes of the parents.'"

H 4713, Ch. 92, h 6

Ali ibn Ibrahim has narrated from his father from ibn abu 'Umayr from Hisham who has said the following:

"Abu 'Abd Allah, *'Alayhi al-Salam*, has said that the Messenger of Allah was asked about those who die in the interval (between the passing away of one prophet and coming of the other), those who have not committed sins, and people with severe mental conditions. He replied, 'Allah argues against them by lighting up a fire and telling them to walk in it. Those who go in the fire it becomes cool and peaceful for them and to those who refuse Allah will say, "Consider, I just commanded you but you disobeyed Me."'"

H 4714, Ch. 92, h 7

Through the same chain of narrators it is said:

"Abu 'Abd Allah, *'Alayhi al-Salam*, has said, 'An argument will be made against three kinds of people: dumb people, children, and those who have died in the interval between the passing away and coming of a prophet. A fire will be brought before them and they will be commanded to go in it. Those who go in the fire, it will turn cool and peaceful for them. Those who refuse to go in the fire, Allah, the most Blessed, the most High, will say, "Consider, I just commanded you but you disobeyed Me."'"

Chapter 93 - The Rare Ahadith

H 4715, Ch. 93 h 1

Ali ibn Ibrahim has narrated from his father from Nuh ibn Shu'ayb from Shihab ibn 'Abd Rabbihi who has narrated the following:

"I once asked abu 'Abd Allah, *'Alayhi al-Salam*, about the case of a man who is involved in sexual relations and he gives Ghusl (bath) to a dead person or one who has given Ghusl (bath) to a dead person, then performs sexual relation with his wife. He (the Imam) said, 'It is the same and it is not harmful. If he is involved in sexual relation, he washes his hand, then gives Ghusl (bath) to a dead person, then takes Wudu', can go to his wife for sexual relation, only one Ghusl (bath) is sufficient for both reasons.'"

H 4716, Ch. 93 h 2

Ali has narrated from his father from 'Abd Allah ibn al-Mughirah from al-Sakuniy who has said the following:

"Abu 'Abd Allah, *'Alayhi al-Salam*, has said that when a person is about to die, the angel of death ties him down; otherwise, he will not calm down."

H 4717, Ch. 93, h 3

Abu Ali al-Ash'ariy has narrated from Muhammad ibn 'Abd Jabbar from abu Muhammad al-Hudhaliy from Ibrahim ibn Khalid al-Qattan from Muhammad ibn Mansur al-Sayqal from his father who has said the following:

"I complained before abu 'Abd Allah, *'Alayhi al-Salam*, about feeling extremely sad for the death of my son and I feared for my sanity. He said, 'When something like this happens, allow your tears to flow; it gives you relief.'"

H 4718, Ch. 93, h 4

Ali ibn Ibrahim has narrated in a marfu' manner the following:

"When Dharr, son of abu Dharr passed away, abu Dharr wiped his grave with his hand and said, 'May Allah grant you mercy, O Dharr, by Allah, you were kind to me and I am satisfied with you. By Allah, I am not disappointed due to your death and I do not need anyone beside Allah. Had it not been for fear from the next life I would have been happy to be in your place. My sadness for you (my concern about your condition in the next life) has kept me from sadness due to your death. By Allah, I do not weep because of your death but I weep for you because of what you may face in the next life. I do not know what I have said about you and what is said about you.' Then he said, 'O Lord, I have waived in his favor my rights that You had set on him. Please waive in his favor Your rights on him; You are more generous than I.'"

H 4719, Ch. 93, h 5

A number of our people have narrated from Sahl ibn Ziyad from 'Uthman ibn 'Isa from a number of our people has narrated the following:

"When abu Ja'far passed away abu 'Abd Allah, *'Alayhi al-Salam*, commanded (his people) to light a lamp in the house where he lived until abu 'Abd Allah passed away. Thereafter abu al-Hassan did a similar thing in the house where abu 'Abd Allah lived until he was taken to Iraq and thereafter I do not know what happened."

H 4720, Ch. 93, h 6

Ali ibn Ibrahim has narrated from his father from ibn abu 'Umayr from Hammad from al-Halabiy who has said the following:

"I asked abu 'Abd Allah, *'Alayhi al-Salam*, 'Who was the initiator of coffins for deceased people?' He replied, 'Fatimah, *'Alayha al-Salam*, was the one.'"

H 4721, Ch. 93, h 7

Muhammad ibn Yahya has narrated from Muhammad ibn Ahmad from Ahmad ibn al-Hassan from 'Amr ibn Sa'id from Musaddiq ibn Sadaqah from 'Ammar ibn Musa who has said the following:

"Abu 'Abd Allah, *'Alayhi al-Salam*, was asked, 'Does the body of a dead person decay?' He replied, 'Yes, nothing of the flesh and bones will be left except the clay from which he is created. This does not decay and it remains in the grave with a round shape until he is created from it just as before.'"

H 4722, Ch. 93, h 8

Ali ibn Ibrahim has narrated from his father and Ahmad ibn Muhammad al-Kufiy from certain persons of his people from Safwan ibn Yahya from Yazid ibn Khalifah al-Khawlaniy who is Yazid ibn Khalifah al-Harithiy who has said the following:

...(Fatwah best explains this hadith)

H 4723, Ch. 93, h 9

Ali ibn Ibrahim has narrated from his father from al-Nawfaliy from al-Sakuniy who has said the following:

"Abu 'Abd Allah, *'Alayhi al-Salam*, has said that if a man keeps his shroud ready, because of looking at it, he is entitled to a reward each time he looks at it."

H 4724, Ch. 93, h 10

It is narrated through the same chain of narrator, as the above Hadith, the following:

"Amir al-Mu'minin, *'Alayhi al-Salam*, was suffering from a severe eye illness and the Holy Prophet visited him for this reason. He groaned loudly because of severe pain. The Holy Prophet said, 'Is it impatience or severe pain?' He replied, 'O Messenger of Allah, I have never experienced such a severe pain.' He said, 'O Ali, when the angel of death goes to remove the soul of an unbeliever from his body, he takes with him a number of roasting bars of fire with which he removes his (unbeliever's) soul from his body, and then hell roars.' Ali, *'Alayhi al-Salam*, then sat upright saying, 'O Messenger of Allah, please repeat what you just said; it made me forget the severe pain altogether.' He then asked, 'Will anyone from your followers face such a condition?' The Messenger of Allah replied, 'Yes, an unjust ruler, those who unjustly consume the property of orphans and those who present a false testimony.'"

H 4725, Ch. 93, h 11

Through the same chain of narrators, as the above Hadith, it is narrated who has said the following:

"Abu 'Abd Allah, *'Alayhi al-Salam*, has said that the Holy Prophet has said, 'There is relieved and relieving. The relieved is the believing person who because of death is freed. He is relieved from worldly suffering and hard works like worshipping and so forth, after which he enjoys the bounties and comforts of the next life. The relieving or relieved from, is a criminal because of whose death the two keeper angels are relieved, his servants, his family and the land on which he had been walking.'"

H 4726, Ch. 93, h 12

A number of our people have narrated from Sahl ibn Ziyad from al-Nawfaliy from al-Sakuniy who has said the following:

"Abu 'Abd Allah, *'Alayhi al-Salam*, has said that if a person keeps his shroud ready, for each time he looks on it he is entitled to one reward."

H 4727, Ch. 93, h 13

Sahl ibn Ziyad has narrated from Ali ibn Ibrahim has narrated from his father all from ibn Mahbub from Ali ibn Ri'ab who has said the following:

"I heard abu al-Hassan, the first, saying, 'When a believing person dies, angels, the pieces of land on which he had performed his worship, and the doors of the heavens through which his deeds were raised all weep for him. Because of his death, an irreparable crack appears in Islam; the believing people serve as a fortress for Islam like the fortress of the protective walls around a city.'"

H 4728, Ch. 93, h 14

Sahl ibn Ziyad has narrated from Muhammad ibn Ali from Isma'il ibn Yasar from 'Amr ibn Yazid who has said the following:

"Abu 'Abd Allah, *'Alayhi al-Salam*, has said that if forty people take part in the funeral of a person and say the following: 'O Allah, we do not know anything about him. All we know is good deeds,' Allah, the Most Majestic, the Most Glorious, will say, 'I accept your testimony and forgive him for things that he did but you had no knowledge of.'"

H 4729, Ch. 93, h 15

Sahl has narrated from Ahmad ibn Muhammad ibn abu Nasr from Hammad ibn 'Uthaman from 'Amir ibn 'Abd Allah who has said the following:

"I heard abu 'Abd Allah, *'Alayhi al-Salam*, say, 'On the gravesite of Ibrahim, son of the Messenger of Allah, there was a palm tree that provided shadow and it would turn as the sun moved to provide shadow for the site but when it dried up, the gravesite became old and indistinguishable.'"

H 4730, Ch. 93, h 16

Al-Husayn ibn Muhammad has narrated from 'Abd Allah ibn 'Amir from Ali ibn Mahziyar from Hammad ibn 'Isa from Mu'awiyah ibn 'Ammar who has said the following:

"Al-Bara' ibn Ma'rur al-Tamimiy al-Ansariy was in al-Madinah and the Messenger of Allah was in Makkah. He died when the Messenger of Allah and Muslims would face Jerusalem during prayer. He said in his will that when he died, the Messenger of Allah should place him facing Qiblah in the grave. This became a Sunnah (tradition). He also said in his will that one-third of his properties should be given to the needy. A verse in the Holy Quran was revealed about one-third of the properties of a deceased and it became an established Sunnah (tradition)."

H 4731, Ch. 93, h 17

Ali ibn Ibrahim has narrated from his father from ibn abu 'Umayr from Hisham ibn Salim who has said the following:

"Abu 'Abd Allah, *'Alayhi al-Salam*, has said that Jibril (Gabriel) came to the Holy Prophet and said, 'O Muhammad, live as you wish, but you will certainly die; love whoever you wish, but you will certainly depart him, and act as you wish but one day you will face your deeds.'"

H 4732, Ch. 93, h 18

Ibn abu 'Umayr has narrated from Ayyub from abu 'Ubaydah who has said the following:

"Once I said to abu Ja'far, *'Alayhi al-Salam*, 'Please speak to me about things whereby I can benefit.' He said, 'O abu 'Ubaydah, speak of death very often. Whoever speaks of death very often restrains from the worldly matters (sins).'"

H 4733, Ch. 93, h 19

Ibn abu 'Umayr has narrated from al-Hakam ibn Ayman from Dawud al-Abzariy who has said the following:

"Abu Ja'far, *'Alayhi al-Salam*, has said, 'A caller announces the following every day: 'Children of Adam, give birth for death, accumulate wealth for annihilation and build for destruction.'"

H 4734, Ch. 93, h 20

Ibn abu 'Umayr has narrated from Ali ibn abu Hamzah from abu Basir who has said the following:

"Once I complained before abu 'Abd Allah, *'Alayhi al-Salam*, about the disturbance of temptation in my mind. He (the Imam) said, 'O abu Muhammad, speak (think) of your joints coming apart in your grave, and of your relatives abandoning you after your burial, worms coming out from your nose and other worms consuming your flesh; this will help you to overcome temptations.' Abu Basir has said, 'By Allah, whenever I did as he had told me to do I felt free from temptations.'"

H 4735, Ch. 93, h 21

Abu Ali al-Ash'ariy has narrated from Muhammad ibn 'Abd al-Jabbar from ibn Faddal from Ali ibn 'Uqbah from 'Asbat ibn Salim Mawla Aban who has said the following:

"I said to abu 'Abd Allah, *'Alayhi al-Salam*, 'May Allah keep my soul in service for your cause, does the angel of death know whose soul he has to remove from his body?' He said, 'No, he does not know. It is the ascribes who come down from the heavens and say, "Remove the soul of so and so, son of so and so."'"

H 4736, Ch. 93, h 22

Ali ibn Ibrahim has narrated from his father from ibn abu 'Umayr from Hisham ibn Salim who has said the following:

"Abu 'Abd Allah, *'Alayhi al-Salam*, has said that the angel of death examines five times every day the faces of every member of all families regardless of their living in homes built of hairs or fur."

H 4737, Ch. 93, h 23

Muhammad ibn Yahya has narrated from Ahmad ibn Muhammad from Muhammad ibn Sinan from those who narrated to him who has said the following:

"Abu 'Abd Allah, *'Alayhi al-Salam*, has said that whoever keeps his shroud ready at his home is not considered a neglectful person. He is rewarded whenever he looks at it."

H 4738, Ch. 93, h 24

Ali ibn Ibrahim has narrated from his father from 'Amr ibn 'Uthaman from al-Mufaddal ibn Salih from Zayd al-Shahham who has said the following:

"Abu 'Abd Allah, *'Alayhi al-Salam*, was asked about the angel of death saying, 'Is it true, as it is said that he observes the whole earth like a bowl on his palm and stretches his hand to it as he likes?' He replied, 'Yes, that is true.'"

H 4739, Ch. 93, h 25

Muhammad ibn Yahya has narrated from Ahmad ibn Muhammad ibn 'Isa from al-Husayn ibn Sa'id from Fadalah ibn Ayyub from abu al-Maghra' who has said that Ya'qub al-Ahmar narrated to me saying the following:

"Once we visited abu 'Abd Allah, *'Alayhi al-Salam*, to offer condolences because of the death of Isma'il. He expressed sympathy toward him and said, 'Allah, the Most Majestic, the Most Glorious, offered condolences to the Holy Prophet for his own death saying, "You die and they all die (39:32)," and "Every soul tests the agony of death (3:182)."' He further added saying, 'All inhabitants of earth will die until no one will be left, then all inhabitants of the heavens will die until no one will be left except the angel of death, the carriers of the Throne, Jibril and Mikhail.' He then said, 'The angel of death then will come in the presence of Allah, the Most Majestic, the Most Glorious, and it will be said - even though He knows - to him, "Who is left?" He will say, "Lord, no one is left except the angel of death, the carriers of the Throne, Jibril and Mikhail." It will be said to him, "Tell Jibril and Mikhail to die." The angels will say, "O Lord, they are Your trusted messengers." He then will say, "I have decided that all living things must die." Then the angel of death will come until he stands up in the presence of Allah, the Most Majestic, the Most Glorious, and he will be asked – even though He knows-, "Who is left?" He will say, "O Lord, no one is left except the angel of death and the carriers of the Throne." He will say, "Tell the carriers of the throne to die."' The Imam then said, 'He will then come forward, sad, depressed and unable to look up. It then will be asked, "Who is left?" He will reply, "O Lord, no one is left except the angel of death." It then will be said to him, "Die, O angel of death." He will die. He then will hold the earth in His right hand, the heavens in His left hand and will say, "Where are those who were considered as My partners and where are those who were taken as Lords besides Me?""'"

H 4740, Ch. 93, h 26

Ali ibn Ibrahim has narrated from his father from 'Amr ibn 'Uthman from Mufaddal ibn Salih from Jabir who has said the following:

"Abu Ja'far, *'Alayhi al-Salam*, has said, 'The Messenger of Allah has said, 'Jibril (Gabriel) has informed me that an angel of the angels of Allah had a great position before Allah, the Most Majestic, the Most Glorious, but then this angel was to be disciplined. He was made to descend down to earth. He went to prophet Idris and requested him saying, "You have a great position before Allah, please intercede for me before your Lord." He prayed for three nights without lapse, fasted three days without break and then pleaded before Allah, the Most High in an early morning about the angel and the angel said, "You have been granted your request and my wing is freed. I would like to compensate you for this favor. You may ask me for help if you need." He said, "If you can show me the angel of death, you may do so, so that I try to get comfortable with him because, on remembering him nothing seems enjoyable to me." The angel spread his wing and said, "Climb on" and he ascended up in search for the angel of death in heaven above the world. He was told to ascend higher. They met him between the fourth and the fifth heavens, and the angel asked, "Why is it that I see you, O angel of death, frowning?" He replied, "It is strange. I, while under the shadow of the Throne, am commanded to remove the soul of a man between the fourth and the fifth heavens." Idris heard it, he found it very difficult and fell off the wing of the angel. His soul was removed from his body at the spot. About this Allah, the Most Majestic, the Most Glorious, has said, "We raised him to a high (exalted) place (19:65).""'"

H 4741, Ch. 93, h 27

Muhammad ibn Yahya has narrated from Ahmad ibn Muhammad from Ali ibn al-Nu'man from ibn Muskan from Dawud ibn Farqad (abu Yazid) from ibn abu Shaybah al-Zuhriy who has said the following:

"Abu Ja'far, *'Alayhi al-Salam*, has said, 'The Messenger of Allah has said, "(I remind you about) death, (I remind you about) death! Indeed death is inevitable. Death comes along with certain things. It comes with happiness, comfort and the blessed turn to lofty paradise, prepared for the people of eternity, for which they had worked assiduously, with great interest. Death comes along with certain things. It comes with misfortune, regret, with a turn to loss and extremely hot fire, which is prepared for the dwellers of deceitful abode which they had been seeking with great interest." The Messenger of Allah then said, "To those who deserve guardianship and protection of Allah and salvation, death seems as if it is before their eyes. The worldly ambitions are kept backward, but if one is under the guardianship of Satan, in his case misfortune and worldly ambitions come before his eyes, and the reality of death is kept backward.' The Imam then said, 'The Messenger of Allah was asked, "Who is the most intelligent believer?" He replied, "Those who think about death very often and are very serious to prepare themselves for death."'""

H 4742, Ch. 93, h 28

Ali ibn Ibrahim has narrated from his father from ibn abu 'Umayr from Hisham ibn Salim from abu Hamzah who has said the following:

"I heard Ali ibn al-Husayn, *'Alayhi al-Salam*, say, 'The case of one who denies death is very odd indeed, while he sees people die every day and night. So also is the case of one who denies the next life while he observers the present life.'"

H 4743, Ch. 93, h 29

Muhammad ibn Yahya has narrated from al-Husayn ibn Ishaq from Ali ibn Mahziyar from Fadalah ibn Ayyub from Sa'dan from 'Ajlan abu Salih who has said the following:

"Abu 'Abd Allah, *'Alayhi al-Salam*, said to me, 'O abu Salih, when you help lift up someone's coffin, consider it to be yourself being carried, as if you asked your Lord to give you a chance for returning back to the worldly life and your plea is granted. Think of how to live the new life.' The narrator has said that the Imam then said, 'It is very odd indeed about the people whose predecessors are held back from returning to the present life and their successors are told to leave, but they are playfully unconcerned.'"

H 4744, Ch. 93, h 30

It is narrated from the same narrator as the previous Hadith from Fadalah from Isma'il ibn abu Ziyad who has said the following:

"Abu 'Abd Allah, *'Alayhi al-Salam,* has said that `Amir al-Mu'minin, *'Alayhi al-Salam*, has said, 'One who counts tomorrow as part of his life, he has not paid proper attention to death.' The Imam then said that `Amir al-Mu'minin has said, 'Any servant of Allah who cherishes long-term worldly expectations, he becomes involved in bad deeds.' `Amir al-Mu'minin would say, 'A servant of Allah who sees his death fast approaching, he dislikes the deeds for the sake of the worldly life.'"

H 4745, Ch. 93, h 31

Muhammad has narrated from Ahmad ibn Muhammad from al-Husayn ibn Sa'id from al-Husayn ibn 'Ulwan from 'Amr ibn Shimr from Jabir who has said the following:

"I asked abu Ja'far, *'Alayhi al-Salam*, about the moment of the angel of death. The Imam said, 'Have you not seen people sitting and suddenly face a heart attack? No one of them in such condition is able to speak. That is the moment of the angel of death who examines them.'"

H 4746, Ch. 90, h 32

Ali ibn Ibrahim has narrated from his father from 'Amr ibn 'Uthman from al-Mufaddal ibn Salih from Jabir who has said the following:

"I asked abu Ja'far, *'Alayhi al-Salam*, about the words of Allah, the Most Holy, the Most High, 'And it is said, "Who is able to provide curing charm?"' (75:28-30) The Imam said, 'That is a son of Adam who on facing death says, "Is there a physician?" "And he finds it to be the departing," means that he becomes certain about departing his loved ones.' The Imam then read, 'When one leg turns around the other,' means when the present life turns into the life hereafter, "then it is the time to be driven to your Lord" means to the Lord of the worlds is the destination.'"

H 4747, Ch. 93, h 33

Muhammad ibn Yahya has narrated from al-Husayn ibn Ishaq from Ali ibn Mahziyar from Ali ibn Isma'il al-Maythamiy from 'Abd al-'A'la Mawla 'Ala Sam who has said the following:

"I asked abu 'Abd Allah, *'Alayhi al-Salam*, about the words of Allah, most Majestic, most Glorious, 'We count for them a strict account' (19:78). The Imam asked, 'What do you know about it?' I replied, 'It means counting of days.' The Imam said, 'No, because parents do such counting. It means counting of exhaling and inhaling of one's breath.'"

H 4748, Ch. 93, h 34

It is narrated from the narrator of the previous Hadith from Fadalah from Musa ibn Bakr from Zurarah who has said the following:

"Abu Ja'far, *'Alayhi al-Salam*, has said, 'Life and death are two creatures of the creatures of Allah. When death comes then it enters in man. In whatever things death enters, life goes out of that place.'"

H 4749, Ch. 93, h 35

A number of our people have narrated from Sahl ibn Ziyad from certain persons of his people from Muhammad ibn Sukayn who has said the following:

"I asked abu 'Abd Allah, *'Alayhi al-Salam*, about an expression about the death of a person, 'Allah has given preference to so and so.' The Imam said, 'It is not desirable.' Someone then asked about the expression, 'So and so is ready to give away his soul generously.' The Imam said, 'There is no offense in such expression. Is it not a fact that a dying person opens his mouth once, twice or three times? Giving away of one's soul generously happens when one observes his rewards with Allah, the Most Majestic, the Most Glorious, when before, one was so tightfisted about it.'"

H 4750, Ch. 93, h 36

Ali ibn Ibrahim has narrated from his father from ibn abu 'Umayr from Hisham ibn Salim who has said the following:

"Abu 'Abd Allah, *'Alayhi al-Salam*, has said that a people in the past had asked their prophet, 'Pray to your Lord to stop death from ending our lives.' He prayed and death was stopped from ending their lives. Their number multiplied and it caused congestion to their dwellings and birth rate increased so much so that a man needed to feed his father, grandfather, mother, grandfather of his grandfather, take care of their hygiene and look after them. It stopped them from working to make a living. They then asked their prophet to appeal to his Lord to return them to their previous conditions. Their prophet asked his Lord. He then returned them to their previous conditions.'"

H 4751, Ch. 93, h 37

Ali ibn Muhammad has narrated from certain persons of our people from Ali ibn al-Hakam from Rabi' ibn Muhammad from 'Abd Allah ibn Sulaym al-'Amiriy who has said the following:

"Jesus, son of Mary, went to the gravesite of John, son of Zachariah, and he had asked the Lord to bring him back to life for him. He called him and he replied, came out of his grave and asked, 'What do you want from me?' He replied, 'I want you to comfort me as you did before your death.' He said, 'O Jesus, the heat of death which took me still has not calmed down and you want me to return to the worldly life; thus the heat of death returns to me again.' He (Jesus) left him alone and he (John) returned to his grave.'"

H 4752, Ch. 93, h 38

Ali ibn Ibrahim has narrated from his father from ibn Mahbub from abu Ayyub from Yazid al-Kunasiy who has said the following:

"Abu Ja'far, *'Alayhi al-Salam*, has said, 'Certain youth from the children of Israelite kings were devoted worshippers. Worshipping was a practice among the children of the Israelite kings. These youth decided to travel around in the land. They passed by a gravesite above the road. Winds had almost wiped out its marks. They said to each other, "We should pray to Allah to bring out our fellow from his grave so that we can ask him about his experience of dying." They prayed to Allah and their prayer was as follows: "You are our Lord. O Lord, no one other than You is our Lord. You are the eternal inventor, never unaware, the ever living who never dies. Every day You work. You know all things without being taught. Please bring this deceased out of his grave by Your power."' The Imam said that a man with hairs of his head and beard all gray came out of the grave shaking dust off his head, terrified and gazing to the sky and asked them, "What has made you stand on my grave?" They replied, "We called you so we can ask about your experience of facing death." He replied, "I have remained in my grave for ninety-nine years, but the pain and hardship of experiencing death have not gone away, and its bitterness is still in my throat." They asked, "Were your hairs of head and beard all gray on the day you died?" He replied, "No, but when I heard the cry, 'come out,' the ashes of my bones came together with my soul (spirit) and I took a breath in it and then came out, terrified and gazing to the sky following the voice that called me and that made my hairs to turn all gray.""'"

H 4753, Ch. 93, h 39

Ali has narrated from his father from al-Nawfaliy from al-Sakuniy who has said the following:

"Abu 'Abd Allah, *'Alayhi al-Salam*, has said that the Holy prophet has said, 'One of the signs of the coming of the Day of Judgment is the spread of paralysis and sudden death.'"

H 4754, Ch. 93, h 40

Ali ibn Muhammad has narrated from Salih ibn abu Hammad in a marfu' manner has said the following:

"'Amir al-Mu'minin, *'Alayhi al-Salam*, once visited Ash'ath ibn Qays to offer condolences for the death of his brother, called, 'Abd al-Rahman. 'Amir al-Mu'minin told him, 'If you express grief, you have observed the right of relatives; but if you exercise patience you have observed the right of Allah. If you exercise patience, you cannot escape destiny but you will be praised, and if you express grief, still you cannot escape destiny but you will be blamed.' Ash'ath then said to him, 'We are for Allah and to Him we return.' `Amir al-Mu'minin then asked, 'Do you know what its explanation is?' Ash'ath replied, 'No, you are the end and limit of knowledge.' The Imam said, 'Your saying, "we are for Allah," is your professing that you are owned (by Allah) and your saying, "to Him we return", is your professing to die.'"

H 4755, Ch. 93, h 41

Muhammad ibn Yahya in a marfu' manner has narrated the following:

"`Amir al-Mu'minin, *'Alayhi al-Salam*, has said, 'A prophet of the prophets prayed against his followers. It was said to him, "I will make their enemy to dominate them." He said, "No, I do not want this." It was told to him that hunger would dominate them. He said, "No." He then was asked, "What do you want?" He replied, "I want for them a pressing death to seize the heart with grief and reduce the number." Plague was then sent upon them.'"

H 4756, Ch. 93, h 42

A number of our people have narrated from Sahl ibn Ziyad from Ali ibn Asbat who in a marfu' manner has said the following:

"During an unfortunate occasion abu 'Abd Allah, *'Alayhi al-Salam*, would say, 'I praise Allah who has not caused any suffering in my religion. I praise Allah who could have made my misfortune greater than this if He so wished. I praise Allah for the fact which if He wanted to come into existence, it would come into being.'"

H 4757, Ch. 93, h 43

Ali ibn Ibrahim has narrated from his father from al-Nadr ibn al-Suwayd, from al-Qasim ibn Sulayman from 'Abd al-Hamid ibn abu Ja'far al-Farra' who has said the following:

"Once, one of the teeth of abu Ja'far, *'Alayhi al-Salam*, came off. He placed it on his palm and then said, 'All praise belongs to Allah.' Then he said, 'O Ja'far, when I die and you bury me, bury this also with me.' After a while another tooth came off. He placed it on his palm and said, 'All praise belongs to Allah. O Ja'far, when I die, then bury this with me.'"

H 4758, Ch. 93, h 44

Ali ibn Ibrahim has narrated from his father from Bakr ibn Muhammad al-Azdiy who has said the following:

"This is about the words of Allah, 'Death from which you run away will take your life and then you will be returned to the One who knows the unseen and seen. He, then will inform you of what you have done.' (62:6) Abu 'Abd Allah, *'Alayhi al-Salam*, has said that you count years, then the months, then days, then hours and then each breath. When their time comes it will do so without allowing them to live one hour thereafter or die one hour before.'" (7:33)

H 4759, Ch. 93, h 45

A number of our people have narrated from Sahl ibn Ziyad from Ja'far ibn Muhammad from ibn al-Qaddah who has said the following:

"Abu 'Abd Allah, *'Alayhi al-Salam*, has said that the Holy Prophet once heard a woman who on the death of 'Uthman ibn Maz'un said, 'Good for you enjoying paradise, O abu al-Sa'ib!' The Holy Prophet then said, 'How would you know it to be so? It is enough for you to say, "He loved Allah, most Majestic, most Glorious, and His Messenger."' When Ibrahim, son of the Messenger of Allah died, the eyes of the Messenger of Allah flooded with tears and the Holy Prophet said, 'Eyes shed tears, hearts become sad; but we do not say anything that angers the Lord. O Ibrahim, we are sad for you.' The Holy Prophet then saw some kind of gap in the grave and fixed it with his hand saying, "When anyone of you does something, he should do it properly." He then said, "Join, (O Ibrahim) your predecessors, people of good deeds like 'Uthman ibn Maz'un."'

H 4760, Ch. 93, h 46

A number of our people have narrated from Sahl ibn Ziyad from Ali ibn Mahziyar who has said the following:

"Once a man wrote to abu Ja'far, *'Alayhi al-Salam*, and complained before him about his suffering the death of his son. He then has said that the Imam wrote back to him saying, 'You should be aware of the fact that Allah, the Most Majestic, the Most Glorious, chooses from the property and children of the believers the best ones, so He may reward him for it.'"

This is the end of the Book about dying people - of the book, al-Kafi compiled by abu Ja'far (Muhammad ibn Ya'qub) al-Kulayniy (rh). May Allah grant him blessings. All praise belongs to Allah alone. May Allah grant blessings upon Muhammad and his family as a whole. Following is the book of Prayer.

In the Name of Allah, the Beneficient, the Merciful

Part Four: The Book of Prayer

Chapter 1 - The Excellence of Prayer

H 4761, Ch. 1, h 1

The compiler of this book, Muhammad ibn Ya'qub al-Kulayniy, has said that Muhammad ibn Yahya has narrated from Ahmad ibn Muhammad ibn 'Isa from al-Hassan ibn Mahbub from Mu'awiyah ibn Wahab who has said the following:

"I asked abu 'Abd Allah, *'Alayhi al-Salam*, 'What is the best thing through which a servant of Allah may become closer to his Lord that is also most beloved to Allah, the Most Majestic, the Most Glorious?' The Imam replied, 'I do not know anything after knowing (knowing Allah and His religion) more excellent than this prayer. Consider what the pious servant of Allah, Jesus son of Mary has said, "He (the Lord) has advised me to pray and pay Zakat as long as I live."'"

H 4762, Ch. 1, h 2

Ali ibn Ibrahim has narrated from Muhammad ibn 'Isa from Yunus from Harun ibn Kharijah from Zayd al-Shahham who has said the following:

"I heard abu 'Abd Allah, *'Alayhi al-Salam*, say, 'The most beloved deed in the sight of Allah, the Most Majestic, the Most Glorious, is Salat (prayer). Prayer is the last item in the wills of the prophets. How nice it is of a man who takes a shower or Wudu' properly and then moves away where no one can notice his presence when he is in Ruku' or Sajdah! When a servant of Allah is in Sajdah which he prolongs, Iblis (Satan) will say crying, "Woe is on me, he (this servant of Allah) obeys Him but I disobeyed, he is doing Sajdah but I refused to do so."'"

H 4763, Ch. 1, h 3

Ali ibn Muhammad has narrated from Sahl ibn Ziyad from al-Washsha' who has said the following:

"I heard al-Rida', *'Alayhi al-Salam*, say, 'The condition wherein a servant of Allah, the Most Majestic, the Most Glorious, is nearest and closest to Him is in Sajdah. It is because of the words of Allah, the Most Majestic, the Most Glorious, "Prostrate (do Sajdah) and become close."'"

H 4764, Ch. 1, h 4

Ali ibn Ibrahim has narrated from Muhammad ibn 'Isa from Yunus from Yazid ibn Khalifah who has said the following:

"I heard abu 'Abd Allah, *'Alayhi al-Salam*, say, 'When a person praying stands up for Salat (prayer), mercy from the horizons of the sky descends upon him as well as from the horizons of earth, angels surround him and one angel says, "Had this person praying known what Salat (prayer) is he would not stop performing Salat (prayer)."'"

H 4765, Ch. 1, h 5

Muhammad ibn al-Hassan has narrated from Sahl ibn Ziyad from ibn Mahbub from abu Hamzah who has said the following:

"Abu Ja'far, *'Alayhi al-Salam*, has said, 'The Messenger of Allah has said, 'When a believing servant of Allah stands up for Salat (prayer), Allah looks upon him - or he said that Allah turns toward him - as long as he is in his Salat (prayer). At such time, mercy covers him up to the horizons of the sky and angels surround him up to the horizons of the sky. Allah appoints an angel who stands up over his head and says, "O praying person, had you known who is looking at you, to who you are speaking and whispering, you would never turn away or leave this place."'''"

H 4766, Ch. 1, h 6

Abu Dawud has narrated from al-Husayn ibn Sa'id from Muhammad ibn al-Fudayl who has said the following:

"Abu al-Hassan al-Rida, *'Alayhi al-Salam*, has said, 'Salat (prayer) is a means for every pious person to getting nearer to Allah.'"

H 4767, Ch. 1, h 7

It is a narration from him (narrator of previous Hadith) by al-Husayn ibn Sa'id from Safwan ibn Yahya from ibn Muskan from Isma'il ibn 'Ammar from abu Basir who has said the following:

"Abu 'Abd Allah, *'Alayhi al-Salam*, has said, 'Performing an obligatory Salat (prayer) is more virtuous than performing one Hajj. Performing one Hajj is more virtuous than giving in charity one whole house full of gold.'"

H 4768, Ch. 1, h 8

A group of our people has narrated from Ahmad ibn Muhammad ibn 'Isa from al-Husayn ibn Sa'id from Fadalah from 'Abd Allah ibn Sinan who has said the following:

"Abu 'Abd Allah, *'Alayhi al-Salam*, has said that once a man passed by the Holy Prophet while he was doing some work around one of his rooms. He asked, 'O Messenger of Allah, can I help you?' He (the Holy Prophet) replied, 'If you like, you may do so.' When the work finished the Messenger of Allah asked, 'Can I do anything for you?' 'Paradise,' the man pleaded. The Messenger of Allah looked into the sky then said, 'Yes, (paradise is your reward).' When he was leaving the Messenger of Allah said, 'O servant of Allah, you must assist us by prolonging your Sajdah.'"

H 4769, Ch. 1, h 9

Ahmad ibn Idris has narrated from Muhammad ibn 'Abd al-Jabbar from Safwan from Hamzah ibn Humran from 'Ubayd ibn Zurarah from abu 'Abd Allah, who has said the following:

"The Messenger of Allah has said, 'Salat (prayer) is like the poles of a tent. If the poles are established then the ropes, pegs and the covering work, but if the poles break, none of the ropes, pegs and covering work.'"

H 4770, Ch. 1, h 10

Muhammad ibn Isma'il has narrated from al-Fadl ibn Shadhan from Hammad ibn 'Isa from Ibrahim ibn 'Umar al-Yamaniy from those who narrated to him the following:

"Abu 'Abd Allah, *'Alayhi al-Salam*, about the words of Allah, the Most Majestic, the Most Glorious, 'Good deeds eliminate bad deeds' (11:116) has said, 'It is a reference to the Salat (prayer) of a believing person during the night that eliminate his bad deeds he has done during the day.'"

H 4771, Ch. 1, h 11

Ali ibn Ibrahim has narrated from his father from ibn abu 'Umayr from Hafs ibn al-Bakhtariy who has said the following:

"Abu 'Abd Allah, *'Alayhi al-Salam,* has said that whoever's one Salat (prayer) Allah accepts He does not punish him and whoever's one good deed He accepts He does not punish him."

H 4772, Ch. 1, h 12

Muhammad ibn Yahya has narrated from Salmah ibn al-Khattab from al-Husayn ibn Sayf from his father who has said the following:

"Narrated to me the one who had heard abu 'Abd Allah, *'Alayhi al-Salam,* say, 'Whoever performs a Salat (prayer) of two Rak'at in which he is aware of what he says, when he finishes them no sin remains upon him before Allah.'"

H 4773, Ch. 1, h 13

Muhammad ibn Yahya has narrated from 'Abd Allah ibn Muhammad ibn 'Isa from his father from 'Abd Allah ibn al-Mughirah formal-Sakuniy who has said the following:

"The Messenger of Allah has said, 'Salat (prayer) is a balance. Whoever maintains it balanced receives his part properly balanced.'"

Chapter 2 - Those Who Preserve Salat (prayer) and Those Who Lose

H 4774, Ch. 2, h 1

Ali ibn Ibrahim has narrated from Muhammad ibn 'Isa from Yunus ibn 'Abd al-Rahman from 'Abd al-Rahman ibn al-Hajjaj from Aban ibn Taghlib who has said the following:

"Once I performed Salat (prayer) with abu 'Abd Allah, *'Alayhi al-Salam,* in Muzdalifah (a place in Makkah). When he completed Salat (prayer) he turned to me and said, 'O Aban, the five times Salat (prayer) every day is obligatory. Those who properly observe the rules about these prayers and perform them in their designated times they, on the Day of Judgment, will come in the presence of Allah with their established covenant before Him, because of which they will be admitted in paradise. Those who ignore the rules about Salat (prayer) and ignore the times designated for them, they will come in the presence of Allah without having any established covenant with Him. He then will decide about them. He may punish or forgive them as He will wish.'"

H 4775, Ch. 2, h 2

Al-Husayn ibn Muhammad al-Ash'ariy has narrated from 'Abd Allah ibn 'Amir from Ali ibn Mahziyar ibn abu 'Umayr from 'Abd al-Rahman ibn al-Hajjaj from Aban ibn Taghlib who has said the following:

"Once I performed Maghrib (evening) Salat (prayer) with abu 'Abd Allah, *'Alayhi al-Salam,* in Muzdalifah. When he completed, he called for Salat (prayer) and performed al-'Isha' (late evening) prayer without any delay between the two prayers (evening and late evening). One year later I performed Salat (prayer) with him. He prayed Maghrib then he stood up for Nafl (optional)

Salat (prayer). He performed four Rak'at, then he said Iqamah (called for Salat (prayer) and prayed al-'Isha prayer (late evening)) and then he turned to me saying, 'O Aban, these five times Salat (prayers) are obligatory. Those who perform them and do not ignore their designated times, they will come in the presence of Allah, on the Day of Judgment, with an established covenant before Him, because of which they will be admitted in paradise. Those who do not perform them in their designated times and ignore the rules about them, then it will be up to Him. He may forgive them or punish them as He will wish.'"

H 4776, Ch. 2, h 3

Ali ibn Ibrahim has narrated from Muhammad ibn 'Isa from Yunus ibn 'Abd al-Rahman from Yunus ibn 'Ammar who has said the following:

"Someone asked abu 'Abd Allah, *'Alayhi al-Salam*, while I was present, 'What is the rule about a man who is in Salat (prayer) free of negative feelings but then he feels self-importance?' Imam replied, 'If in the beginning his intention was only for his Lord, then such feeling does not affect his prayer negatively, he should continue his Salat (prayer) and Satan is humiliated.'"

H 4777, Ch. 2, h 4

A group of our people has narrated from Ahmad ibn Muhammad ibn 'Isa from al-Husayn ibn Sa'id from Fadalah from Husayn ibn 'Uthman from Sama'ah from abu Basir who has said the following:

"I heard abu Ja'far, *'Alayhi al-Salam*, say, 'Every mistake in Salat (prayer) is dropped thereby except that Allah, the Most High, completes it with optional prayers. The first item of deeds with which one is judged is Salat (prayer). If Salat (prayer) is accepted, other deeds are also accepted. If Salat (prayer) is raised in the beginning of its designated time, it comes to the person who prayed it all white and radiant, saying, "You preserved me, may Allah protect you." If Salat (prayer) is raised in other times without observance of the rules about it Salat (prayer) returns back to the person who has performed it, all black and dark, saying, "You wasted me away, may Allah lay you waste."'"

H 4778, Ch. 2, h 5

Muhammad ibn Yahya has narrated from Ahmad ibn Muhammad from al-Husayn from Muhammad ibn al-Fudayl who has said the following:

"I asked the pious servant of Allah about the words of Allah, the Most Majestic, the Most Glorious, 'Those who make mistakes in their prayer.' Imam replied, 'It means loss of prayer.'"

H 4779, Ch. 2, h 6

Ali ibn Ibrahim has narrated from his father from ibn abu 'Umayr from 'Umar ibn 'Udhaynah from Zurarah who has said the following:

"A man entered the Masjid when the Messenger of Allah was present. He began to perform Salat (prayer) without properly doing Ruku' and Sajdah. He (the Messenger of Allah) said, 'He acted like a crow picking up grain from the ground. If he dies with his Salat (prayer) of such condition he dies in a religion other than my religion.'"

H 4780, Ch. 2, h 7

It is a narration from him (narrator of previous Hadith) by his father from Hammad from Hariz from Zurarah who has said the following:

"Abu Ja'far, *'Alayhi al-Salam*, has said, 'You must not consider your Salat (prayer) insignificant; the Holy Prophet said when he was about to pass away, "Those who consider their Salat (prayer) insignificant are not of my people, as well as those who drink intoxicating liquor. They will not be able to come to me at the pond of al-Kawthar, no by Allah (they will not be able to do so).""'"

H 4781, Ch. 2, h 8

Ali ibn Muhammad has narrated from Sahl ibn Ziyad from al-Nawfaliy from al-Sakuniy who has said the following:

"Abu 'Abd Allah, *'Alayhi al-Salam*, has said that the Messenger of Allah has said, 'Satan continues to be afraid of a believing person as long as he protects his five times daily Salat (prayers), but when he loses them, Satan becomes daring, then he takes him into great sins.'"

H 4782, Ch. 2, h 9

Muhammad ibn Yahya has narrated from Ahmad ibn Muhammad ibn 'Isa from al-Husayn ibn Sa'id from Safwan ibn Yahya from al-'is ibn al-Qasim who has said the following:

"Abu 'Abd Allah, *'Alayhi al-Salam*, has said, 'A man may become fifty years old, but Allah has accepted not even one Salat (prayer) from him. What can be more serious than this? By Allah, you may also find someone in your neighborhood who performs Salat (prayer) with you, but is not accepted from him due to his considering it insignificant. Allah, the Most Majestic, the Most Glorious, does not accept anything other than what is good. How then He will accept what he considers insignificant?'"

H 4783, Ch. 2, h 10

Muhammad ibn Yahya has narrated from Ahmad ibn Muhammad from Ali ibn al-Hakam from Hisham ibn Salim who has said the following:

"Abu 'Abd Allah, *'Alayhi al-Salam*, has said that when a man stands up for Salat (prayer) but considers it insignificant, Allah, the Most Holy, the Most High, says to His angels, 'Look at this servant of Mine. It seems as if he thinks someone other than Me is a person in charge of fulfilling his needs. Does he not know that I am the One who fulfills all of his needs by My own hand?'"

H 4784, Ch. 2, h 11

Ali ibn Ibrahim has narrated from his father from Hammad and Muhammad ibn Yahya from Ahmad ibn Muhammad from Hammad ibn 'Isa from Hariz from Zurarah who has said the following:

"Abu Ja'far, *'Alayhi al-Salam*, has said, 'When a man completes one Salat (prayer) properly, all of his other prayers are accepted; even though they may not be complete. If he loses them, altogether, none of his Salat (prayer) is accepted, and not even his optional or obligatory prayers are counted. Optional Salat (prayer) are accepted only after obligatory prayers are accepted. If one does not perform obligatory prayers, optional prayers are not accepted; they are to complete therewith the shortcomings of the obligatory ones."

H 4785, Ch. 2, h 12

It narrated through the same chain of narrators from Hariz from al-Fudayl who has said the following:

"I asked abu Ja'far, *'Alayhi al-Salam*, about the words of Allah, the Most Majestic, the Most Glorious, 'Those who are protective of their Salat (prayers)" (23:9). The Imam said, 'It means obligatory prayer.' I then asked about, 'Those who are ever observing their prayer' (70:23). The Imam said, 'It means optional prayers.'"

H 4786, Ch. 2, h 13

Muhammad ibn Yahya has narrated from Ahmad ibn Muhammad from al-Husayn ibn Sa'id from Fadalah ibn Ayyub from Dawud ibn Farqad who has said the following:

"I asked abu 'Abd Allah, *'Alayhi al-Salam*, about the words of Allah, 'Salat (prayer) was made obligatory in designated times' (4:105). The Imam replied, 'It is an established obligation. If you performed earlier or delayed a little, it is not harmful as long as you did not lose them altogether. Allah, the Most Majestic, the Most Glorious, says about a people, "They lost Salat (prayer) and followed their lustful desires so they face deviation" (19:60).'"

H 4787, Ch. 2, h 14

Ali ibn Ibrahim has narrated from his father from ibn Mahbub from Jamil ibn Darraj from certain persons of his people who has said the following:

"Abu Ja'far, *'Alayhi al-Salam*, has said, 'Whoever of the believers preserves his obligatory Salat (prayers) and performs them in time, he is not of the neglectful people.'"

H 4788, Ch. 2, h 15

Muhammad ibn Yahya has narrated from Ahmad ibn Muhammad from Muhammad ibn 'Isma'il from abu 'Isma'il al-Sarraj from ibn Muskan from abu Basir who has said the following:

"Abu al-Hassan the first, *'Alayhi al-Salam*, has said, 'When my father was about to pass away he said, "My son, those who consider Salat (prayers) insignificant will not be able to benefit from our intercession."'"

H 4789, Ch. 2, h 16

Muhammad has narrated from Sahl ibn Ziyad from al-Nawfaliy from al-Sakuniy from Ja'far from his father who has said the following:

"The Messenger of Allah has said, 'Everything has a face. The face of your religion is Salat (prayer), no one of you, therefore, must deface his religion. Everything has a nose. The nose of Salat (prayer) is al-Takbir (saying, "Allah is greater than can be described").'"

(Chapters 3-15, practical rules about prayer are best expressed in the form of fatwa.)

Chapter 3 - Salat (Prayer) Is Made Obligatory

H 4790, Ch. 3, h 1

Ali ibn Ibrahim has narrated from his father from Hammad ibn 'Isa and Muhammad ibn Yahya has narrated from Ahmad ibn Muhammad ibn 'Isa and Muhammad ibn 'Isma'il from al-Fadl ibn Shadhan all Hammad ibn 'Isa from Hariz from Zurarah who has said the following:

"I once asked abu Ja'far, *'Alayhi al-Salam*, about how much of Salat (prayer) Allah, most Majestic, most Glorious, has made obligatory. He (the Imam) said, 'During one day and night five Salat (prayer) are made obligatory.' I then asked, 'Has He named and explained them in His book?' He (the Imam) said, 'Yes, Allah, most High has said to His Holy Prophet, "Perform Salat (prayer) after the sun declines to the west, on midday until the darkness of the night." (17:78).The sun declines on midday. There are four Salat (prayer) between midday and the darkness of the night. Allah has named, explained and timed them. Darkness of night is in midnight. He, most Blessed, most High has then said, ". . . and the recitation (performing Salat (prayer)) at dawn and recitation at dawn was witnessed (attended by the angels of the day and those of the nights)." These are five Salat (prayers). Allah, most High about this issue has said, "Perform Salat (prayer) on both ends of the day, [which is sunset and morning], and in a part of the night." (11:116) This is al-'Isha' Salat (prayer) He, most High has said, "Preserve Salat (prayer) especially the middle Salat (prayer)." (2:239) Middle Salat (prayer) is al-Zuhr Salat (prayer) which is the first Salat (prayer) the Messenger of Allah performed. It is in the middle of two Salat (prayer) during the day, the morning and al-'Asr Salat (prayer). In some of the recitations it is said, "Preserve Salawat (prayers) and the middle Salat (prayer)." Middle Salat (prayer) is al-'Asr Salat (prayer).' About the words of Allah, "Stand up praying before Allah," he (the Imam) said, 'This verse was revealed on Friday when the Messenger of Allah was on a journey. The Messenger of Allah prayed before Allah on Friday and left it in that condition during a journey or when at home. For those at home he added two Rak'ats. He reduced two Rak'at which the Holy Prophet, had added on Friday for people when at home, because of the two sermons which a prayer leader delivers. Those who perform Friday prayer without congregation, they perform it four Rak'at like al-Zuhr Salat (prayer) in other days.'"

H 4791, Ch. 3, h 2

Through the chain of his narrators Hammad has narrated from Hariz from Zurarah who has said the following:

"Abu Ja'far, *'Alayhi al-Salam*, has said, 'Of Salat (prayer) Allah has made ten Rak'at obligatory on His servants. In such Salat (prayer) there are the recitations; thus, conjectures, mistakes in such Salat (prayer) are not acceptable. The Messenger of Allah added seven Rak'ats in which conjectures, mistakes are dealt with according to certain rules, but there are no recitations in them.'"

H 4792, Ch. 3, h 3

Through the chain of his narrators Hammad has narrated from Hariz from Zurarah who has said the following:

"'Abu Ja'far, *'Alayhi al-Salam*, has said, 'Allah has made Salat (prayer) obligatory. The Messenger of Allah has established ten kinds of traditions in Salat (prayer): Salat (prayer) at home and during a journey. Salat (prayer) due to fear is of three kinds. There is Salat (prayer) because of sun eclipse and moon eclipse. There is Salat (prayer) of the two 'Id. There is Salat (prayer) for rain and (lastly) Salat (prayer) for a deceased.'"

H 4793, Ch. 3, h 4

Hammad has narrated from Hariz from Zurarah from who has said the following:

"About the words of Allah, most Majestic, most Glorious, 'Salat (prayer) in Mawqut (with certain timing) form was written on believers' abu Ja'far, *'Alayhi al-Salam*, has said, 'it means obligatory.'"

H 4794, Ch. 3, h 5

Hammad has narrated from Hariz from Zurarah from who has said the following:

"I once asked abu Ja'far, *'Alayhi al-Salam*, about what is obligatory in Salat (prayer). He (the Imam) said, 'Time, al-Tahur (cleansing), facing al-Qiblah (al-Ka'bah), paying attention, al-Ruku', al-Sujud and praying. The rest are optional in an obligatory duty.'"

H 4795, Ch. 3, h 6

Ali ibn Ibrahim has narrated from his father from Hammad ibn 'Isa who has said the following:

"Abu 'Abd Allah, *'Alayhi al-Salam*, has said, 'Salat (prayer) has four thousand limits (rules).'"

"In another Hadith it is said that in Salat (prayer) there are four thousand doors (chapters)."

H 4796, Ch. 3, h 7

Ali ibn Ibrahim has narrated from his father from ibn abu 'Umayr from 'Umar ibn 'Udhaynah from Zurarah who has said the following:

"Abu Ja'far, *'Alayhi al-Salam*, has said, 'There are ten Rak'at in Salat (prayer). There are two for al-Zuhr, two for al-'Asr, two Rak'at of Morning, two Rak'at of al-Maghrib and two Rak'at of al-'Isha' al-Akhirah. In these many of Salat (prayer) conjectures (mistakes) are not acceptable. If one faces conjectures in such Salat (prayer), he performs it again. They are Salat (prayer) which Allah, most Majestic, most Glorious, made obligatory on believers in al-Quran. He (Allah) delegated Muhammad, *'Alayhi al-Salam*, and he (the Holy prophet) increased seven Rak'at. They are of Sunnah and have no recitations. They have Tasbih (Allah is free of all defects), Tahlil, (no one deserves worship except Allah) Takbir (Allah is great beyond description), and prayer. Conjectures in these Rak'at are (dealt with according to certain rules). The Messenger of Allah increased two Rak'at for those at home in al-Zuhr, al-'Asr, al-'Isha', al-Akhirah and one Rak'at to al-Maghrib for those at home as well as for those on a journey.'"

H 4797, Ch. 3, h 8

Ali ibn Ibrahim has narrated from his father from ibn abu 'Umayr from Hammad from al-Halabiy who has said the following:

"Abu 'Abd Allah, *'Alayhi al-Salam*, has said, 'Acts of Salat (prayer) fall in three categories; They are Tahur (cleansing), Ruku' (bowing down on one's knees), and Sujud (prostration).'"

Chapter 4 - The Timing of Salat (Prayer), the Beginning, the End and the Outstanding Phases

H 4798, Ch. 4, h 1

Ali ibn Ibrahim has narrated from his father from ibn abu 'Umayr from 'Umar ibn `Udhaynah from Zurarah from who has said the following:

"I once was sitting in the presence of abu 'Abd Allah, *'Alayhi al-Salam,* and Humran ibn `A'yan was also present. Humran asked him (the Imam), 'What do you say about the words of Zurarah with which I do not agree?' Abu 'Abd Allah, *'Alayhi al-Salam,* asked, 'What are they?' Humran said, 'Zurarah says that the time for Salat (prayer) was delegated to the Messenger of Allah. He was the one who determined them.' Abu 'Abd Allah, *'Alayhi al-Salam,* asked, 'What do you (Humran) say about it?' I (Humran) said, 'Jibril came to him (the Holy prophet) on the first day with the first time and on the last day with the last time. Jibril then said, 'In between there are times for Salat (prayer).' Abu 'Abd Allah, *'Alayhi al-Salam,* then said, 'O Humran, Zurarah says that Jibril came to the Messenger of Allah only to give him an indication. Zurarah is right. Allah left it to Muhammad, O Allah grant compensation to Muhammad and his family worthy of their services to Your cause, who made the determination. Jibril provided him with an indication about it.'"

H 4799, Ch. 4, h 2

A number of our people have narrated from Ahmad ibn Muhammad ibn 'Isa from Muhammad ibn al-Hassan ibn 'Allan from Hammad ibn 'Isa and from Safwan ibn Yahya from Rib'iy ibn 'Abd Allah from al-Fudayl ibn Yasar who has said the following:

"Abu Ja'far, *'Alayhi al-Salam,* has said, 'Of the things certain ones are of a longer timing and others are of shorter timing. Salat (prayer) is of longer timing. It can be performed earlier and later. Friday Salat (prayer) is of a short timing. On Friday its time is a Sa'ah which then vanish. The time for al-'Asr Salat (prayer) on Friday is the time for al-Zuhr on other days.'"

H 4800, Ch. 4, h 3

Ali ibn Ibrahim has narrated from Muhammad ibn 'Isa from Yunus ibn 'Abd al-Rahman from 'Abd Allah ibn Sinan who has said the following:

"I once heard abu 'Abd Allah, *'Alayhi al-Salam,* say, 'For every Salat (prayer) there are two kinds of timings; the beginning of time is the outstanding one, and no one has the right to call the end of two kinds of timings as a time, without good reason, and for no reason.'"

H 4801, Ch. 4, h 4

Muhammad ibn Yahya has narrated from Ahmad ibn Muhammad from al-Husayn ibn Sa'id from Fadalah ibn Ayyub Mu'awiyah ibn 'Ammar or ibn Wahab who has said the following:

"Abu 'Abd Allah, *'Alayhi al-Salam,* has said, 'For every Salat (prayer) there are two kinds of timings and the outstanding one is the beginning of time.'"

H 4802, Ch. 4, h 5

Ali ibn Ibrahim has narrated from his father from ibn abu 'Umayr from 'Umar ibn `Udhaynah from Zurarah who has said the following:

"I once said to abu Ja'far, *'Alayhi al-Salam*, 'I pray to Allah to keep you well, of the timing for Salat (prayer), what portion is better? Is it the beginning, the middle or the end of time?' He (the Imam) said, 'It is the beginning of it; the Messenger of Allah has said, "Allah, most Majestic, most Glorious, loves of good things the most that which is done earlier."'"

H 4803, Ch. 4, h 6

Muhammad ibn Yahya has narrated from Salmah ibn al-Khattab from Ali ibn Sayf ibn 'Amirah from his father from Qutaybah al-'A'sha' who has said the following:

"Abu 'Abd Allah, *'Alayhi al-Salam*, has said, 'The outstanding quality of the beginning of the time for Salat (prayer) is like the outstanding quality of the next life compared to the worldly life.'"

H 4804, Ch. 4, h 7

Al-Husayn ibn Muhammad has narrated from Muhammad ibn Ahmad ibn Ishaq from Bakr ibn Muhammad al-Azdiy who has said the following:

"Abu 'Abd Allah, *'Alayhi al-Salam*, has said, 'The outstanding quality of the beginning of time for Salat (prayer) compared with the end of time for Salat (prayer) is better for a man than his children and belongings.'"

H 4805, Ch. 4, h 8

Muhammad ibn Yahya has narrated from Ahmad ibn Muhammad from Hammad from Hariz from Zurarah who has said the following:

"Abu Ja'far, *'Alayhi al-Salam*, has said, 'You must note that the beginning of time always is better, so act faster for the good as much as you can. The most beloved of deeds in the sight of Allah, most Majestic, most Glorious, is that which a servant continues even if it is very little.'"

H 4806, Ch. 4, h 9

Ahmad ibn Idris and others have narrated from Muhammad ibn Ahmad from Muhammad ibn al-Husayn from his father from Mansur ibn Hazim or others who has said the following:

"Abu 'Abd Allah, *'Alayhi al-Salam*, has said that Ali ibn al-Husayn, *'Alayhi al-Salam*, has said, 'Those who pay proper attention to the timing for Salat (prayer) do not seek to complete worldly pleasures.'"

Chapter 5 - The Time of Noon and Afternoon Salat (Prayer)

H 4807, Ch. 5, h 1

Ali ibn Ibrahim has narrated from Muhammad ibn 'Isa from Yunus from Yazid ibn Khalifah who has said the following:

"I once said to abu 'Abd Allah, *'Alayhi al-Salam*, that 'Umar ibn Hanzalah has reported to us from you about timing (for Salat (prayer)). Abu 'Abd Allah, *'Alayhi al-Salam*, then said, 'If so, he does not fabricate things to call them to be from us.' I (the narrator) then said that he quotes your statement. It says, 'The first Salat (prayer) that Allah made obligatory on His Holy prophet was al-Zuhr Salat (prayer). Allah, most Majestic, most Glorious, has said, "Perform Salat (prayer) from the time of declining of the sun toward the west at noontime" (17:78), so when the sun declines toward the west at noontime, there is no other obstacle except your Nafl (optional Salat (prayer)). This time continues until the shadow of an object becomes equal to its length and that is the end of this time. When the shadow of an object becomes equal to its length, it is the time for al-'Asr Salat (prayer) which continues until the shadow of an object becomes double its length and that is evening.' He (the Imam) said, 'He has spoken the truth.'"

H 4808, Ch. 5, h 2

Muhammad ibn Yahya has narrated from Salmah ibn al-Khattab from Ali ibn Sayf ibn 'Amirah from his father form 'Umar ibn Hanzalah who has said the following:

"Abu 'Abd Allah, *'Alayhi al-Salam*, has said, 'When the sun declines toward the west at noontime, it is time for al-Zuhr Salat (prayer) except that there is Nafl (optional Salat (prayer) before al-Zuhr Salat (prayer). It is up to you to spend a longer time for it or a short one.'"

H 4809, Ch. 5, h 3

Ali ibn Ibrahim has narrated from his father from ibn abu 'Umayr from Dharih al-Muharibiy who has narrated the following:

"I once asked abu 'Abd Allah, *'Alayhi al-Salam*, 'When can I perform al-Zuhr Salat (prayer)?' He (the Imam) said, 'Perform the eight Rak'at (the optional Salat (prayer) when the sun declines (toward the west at noontime), then perform al-Zuhr. Thereafter perform your optional Salat (prayer) for a longer or short time, then perform al-'Asr Salat (prayer).'"

H 4810, Ch. 5, h 4

Al-Husayn ibn Muhammad al-Ash'ariy has narrated from 'Abd Allah ibn 'Amir from Ali ibn Mahziyar from Fadalah ibn Ayyub from al-Husayn ibn 'Uthman from ibn Muskan formal-Harith ibn al-Mughirah and 'Umar ibn Hanzalah and Mansur ibn Hazim who have said the following:

"We would measure the sun in al-Madinah by the yards. Abu 'Abd Allah, *'Alayhi al-Salam*, said, 'Allow me to show you a way clearer than this. When the sun declines toward the west at noontime, it is the time for al-Zuhr Salat (prayer), except for the optional Salat (prayer) before it, which is up to you to make it longer or shorter.'"

"Sa'id has narrated from Musa al-Hassan from al-Hassan ibn al-Husayn al-Lu'lu'iy from Safwan ibn Yahya from al-Harith ibn al-Mughirah al-Nadriy and 'Umar ibn Hanzalah:

"In a similar Hadith it is said, 'It is up to you to make the optional one light thereafter, or make it longer, thereafter is the time (for al-Zuhr).'"

H 4811, Ch. 5, h 5

A number of our people have narrated from Ahmad ibn Muhammad from al-Husayn ibn Sa'id from al-Qasim ibn 'Urwah from 'Ubayd ibn Zurarah from who has said the following:

"Abu 'Abd Allah, *'Alayhi al-Salam*, has said that when the sun declines (toward the west at noontime), it is the time for two Salat (prayer) except that this is before that."

"Also Sa'd has narrated from al-Husayn ibn Sa'id and Muhammad ibn Khalid al-Barqiy and al-'Abbas ibn Ma'ruf all from al-Qasim and Ahmad ibn Muhammad ibn 'Isa from al-Barqiy from al-Qasim:

"In a similar Hadith it is said, 'Time for al-Zuhr and al-'Asr together has come' and in addition, it is said that you are in the time for both of them (al-Zuhr and al-'Asr Salat (prayer)) until it is sunset."

H 4812, Ch. 5, h 6

Muhammad ibn Yahya has narrated from Muhammad ibn al-Husayn from 'Abd al-Rahman ibn abu Hashim al-Bajaliy from Salim abu Khadijah who has said the following:

"Once, when I also was present, a human being asked abu 'Abd Allah, *'Alayhi al-Salam*, 'I may enter a Masjid when certain persons of our people perform al-'Asr and others perform al-Zuhr Salat (prayer).' He (the Imam) said, 'I have commanded them to do so; were they to perform at one time they would have been recognized and caught by their necks.'"

H 4813, Ch. 5, h 7

Ali ibn Ibrahim has narrated from his father from Salih ibn Sa'id from Yunus from certain persons of his people who has said the following:

"I once asked abu 'Abd Allah, *'Alayhi al-Salam*, about the meaning of Hadith that says, 'Perform al-Zuhr Salat (prayer) when the sun is equal to one length or two, one yard or two or one step or two steps from this and from there. When is it and how is it? At certain times is half of one step.' He (the Imam) said that in the Hadith is it said, 'An object's shadow' and not the shadow of an object' is because the shadow of an object may appear in different sizes, sometimes longer and sometimes shorter, but an object is an object all the time and it does not change. Hadith has said that it is one yard or two yards, one step or two steps." Thus one yard or two yards have become explanation of one length or two lengths during the time when an object's shadow is of the size of one yard and two object's shadows of the size of two yards. Therefore one object's or two objects' shadows and one yard or two yards are in agreement with each other in times as understood one, explaining the other and supported thereby. At a given time, for example at one O'clock, when an object's shadow is of the size of one yard the time (for Salat (prayer)) is one yard of an object's shadow and the object is a yard of the shadow. When an object's shadow is less or more, the time is measured in yards or two yards. This is the explanation of one length and a yard or two yards.'" (The theme of Hadith is obvious; it only may need a little thinking to grasp it fully.)

H 4814, Ch. 5, h 8

Ali ibn Muhammad has narrated from Sahl ibn Ziyad from Muhammad ibn al-Hassan from 'Abd Allah ibn 'Abd al-Rahman from Misma' ibn 'Abd Malik who has said the following:

"He (the Imam), *'Alayhi al-Salam*, has said, 'When you complete al-Zuhr Salat (prayer), it is time for al-'Asr Salat (prayer) except that before it there is Nafl (optional Salat (prayer) and it is up to you to make it lengthy or a short one.'"

Chapter 6 - The Times of Maghrib and 'Isha' Salat (Prayer)

H 4815, Ch. 6, h 1

Muhammad ibn Yahya has narrated from Ahmad ibn Muhammad from Ali ibn Ahmad ibn 'Ushaym from certain persons of our people who has said the following:

"I once heard abu 'Abd Allah, *'Alayhi al-Salam*, say, 'It is time for al-Maghrib Salat (prayer) when the redness disappears in the east. Do you know how it happens?' I replied, 'No, I do not know.' He (the Imam) said that it is because the east is under-hanged in relation to the west like this.' He (the Imam) raised his right hand over his left hand. 'When it is sunset here, the redness disappears there.'"

H 4816, Ch. 6, h 2

Muhammad ibn Yahya has narrated from Ahmad ibn Muhammad ibn Khalid and al-Husayn ibn Sa'id from al-Qasim ibn al-'Urwah from Burayd ibn Mu'awiyah who has said the following:

"Abu Ja'far, *'Alayhi al-Salam*, 'When the redness disappears from this side, that is, from the east, it is proof that it is sunset in the east and west.'"

H 4817, Ch. 6, h 3

Ali ibn Muhammad and Muhammad ibn al-Hassan from Sahl ibn Ziyad from ibn Mahbub from abu Wallad Who has said the following:

"Abu 'Abd Allah, *'Alayhi al-Salam*, has said, 'Allah has created a barrier of darkness from near the east and has appointed for it an angel. When it is sunset, that angel fills up his hand with it, then faces toward the west, following the brightness and it moves out of his two hands little by little. He passes by until he comes to the west at the time of the disappearance of brightness; then he leaves darkness into darkness, then he returns to the east and, when it is dawn, he spreads his wings and drives the darkness from the east toward the west until he comes in the west at sunrise.'"

H 4818, Ch. 6, h 4

Ali ibn Muhammad has narrated from Sahl Ziyad from Muhammad ibn Isa from ibn abu 'Umayr from those whom he has mentioned who has said the following:

"Abu 'Abd Allah has said, 'The disappearance of the disk (the sun), the necessary time to discontinue fasting is when facing its direction and the disappearance of the redness that rise from the east upon its reaching overhead toward the west at such time fasting is discontinued; the (disappearance of the disk (sunset) has taken place.'"

H 4819, Ch. 6, h 5

Ali ibn Ibrahim has narrated from his father from Hammad ibn Isa from Hariz from Zurarah who has said the following:

"Abu Ja'far, *'Alayhi al-Salam*, has said, 'It is time of al-Maghrib when the disc disappears, (sunset takes place). If you see the disc latter when you have already performed Salat (prayer), you must perform Salat (prayer) again, continue fasting, avoid eating if you have taken anything of food.'"

H 4820, Ch. 6, h 6

Ali ibn Ibrahim has narrated from Muhammad ibn Isa from Yunus from Yazid ibn Khalifah who has the following

"I once said to abu 'Abd Allah, *'Alayhi al-Salam*, that 'Umar ibn Hanzalah has reported something from you about the timing. Abu 'Abd Allah, *'Alayhi al-Salam*, said, 'Rest assured, he does not forge untrue reports from us.' I said that he has said, 'It is the time of sunset when the disk disappears (sunset takes place) except that the Messenger of Allah when tired on a journey delayed al-Maghrib and performed both of them together with al-'Isha' He (the Imam) said, 'He has spoken the truth.' He (the Imam) said that the time of al-'Isha' is from when brightness disappears, up to one-third of the night and the time for dawn Salat (prayer) is from when it is clear up till the rays come out.'"

H 4821, Ch. 6, h 7

A number of our people have narrated from Ahmad ibn Muhammad from al-Husayn ibn Sa'id from al-Nadr ibn Suwayd from 'Abd Allah ibn Sinan who has said the following:

"I once heard abu 'Abd Allah, *'Alayhi al-Salam*, say, 'It is time for al-Maghrib Salat (prayer) when it is sunset and its (sun's) disc disappears.'"

H 4822, Ch. 6, h 8

Al-Husayn ibn Muhammad al-Ash'ariy has narrated from 'Abd Allah ibn 'Amir from Ali ibn Mahziyar from Hammad ibn 'Isa from Hariz from Zayd al-Shahham who has said the following:

"I once asked abu 'Abd Allah, *'Alayhi al-Salam*, about the time of al-Maghrib. He (the Imam) said that Jibril brought to the Holy prophet, two timings for every Salat (prayer) except al-Maghrib Salat (prayer). The time for al-Maghrib is when it becomes obligatory.'"

H 4823, Ch. 6, h 9

He has narrated it from Zurarah and al-Fudayl who have said the following:

"Abu Ja'far, *'Alayhi al-Salam*, has said, 'For every Salat (prayer) there are two timings except al-Maghrib; its timing is one and it is the time when it becomes obligatory. It ends with the disappearance of al-Shafaq (redness in the west).'"

"It is also narrated that there are two timings for al-Maghrib and it ends with the disappearance of al-Shafaq (redness). It does not disagree with the previous Hadith that says it has one time; because al-Shafaq is the redness. The time between sunset and disappearance of al-Shafaq is not very long. The sign of sunset is when redness reaches past one's overhead when facing the direction of sunset, and it is a short time. The time between the reaching of the redness in the western horizon and its disappearance is not more than a time that takes one to complete al-Maghrib Salat (prayer) and its Nawafil (optional) Salat (prayer), if they are performed comfortably. I have examined it many times and for this reason the timing for al-Maghrib is narrow."

H 4824, Ch. 6, h 10

Muhammad ibn Yahya has narrated from Ahmad ibn Muhammad ibn 'Isa from ibn Faddal who has said the following:

"Ali ibn Asbat once asked abu al-Hassan, *'Alayhi al-Salam*, when we were listening, about the brightness if it is redness or whiteness. He (the Imam) said,

'It is the redness; in the case of the condition of whiteness, it (virtuous time for al-Maghrib) remains up to one third of the night.'"

H 4825, Ch. 6, h 11

Muhammad ibn Yahya has narrated from Ahmad ibn Muhammad from 'Abd Allah ibn Muhammad al-Hajjal from Tha'labah ibn Maymun from 'Imran ibn Ali al-Halabiy who has said the following:

"I once asked abu 'Abd Allah, *'Alayhi al-Salam*, about when al-'Atmah (al-'Isha') becomes obligatory? He (the Imam) said, 'When al-Shafaq (redness) disappears. Al-Shafaq is the redness.' 'Ubayd Allah then said, 'I pray to Allah to keep you well, after the disappearance of redness there remains a strong light visible.' Abu 'Abd Allah, *'Alayhi al-Salam*, said, 'Brightness (al-Shafaq) is the redness and light (or rays) are not from al-Shafaq.'"

H 4826, Ch. 6, h 12

A number of our people have narrated from Ahmad ibn Muhammad from ibn al-Husayn ibn Sa'id from al-Qasim ibn 'Urwah from 'Ubayd ibn Zurarah who has said the following:

"Abu 'Abd Allah, *'Alayhi al-Salam*, has said, 'When it is sunset, it is time for two Salat (prayer) except that this is before that.'"

H 4827, Ch. 6, h 13

Al-Husayn ibn Muhammad has narrated from Mu'alla' ibn Muhammad from al-Washsha' from Aban from abu Basir from who has said the following:

"Abu Ja'far, *'Alayhi al-Salam*, has said that the Messenger of Allah has said, 'If it was not because of al-Shafaq (bright redness), I would have delayed al-'Isha' Salat (prayer) up till passing of one-third of night.'" It is also narrated, "up till midnight.'"

H 4828, Ch. 6, h 14

Muhammad ibn Yahya has narrated from Salmah ibn al-Khattab from Muhammad ibn al-Walid from Aban ibn 'Uthman from 'Umar ibn Yazid who has said the following:

"Abu 'Abd Allah, *'Alayhi al-Salam*, has said, 'The time for al-Maghrib Salat (prayer) on a journey remains until passing of one-fourth of the night.'"

H 4829, Ch. 6, h 15

Ali ibn Muhammad has narrated from Sahl ibn Ziyad from Ali ibn al-Rayyan who has said the following:

"I once wrote to the man (the Imam) *'Alayhi al-Salam*, and asked about a man who is within the house. The walls do not allow him to see the redness in the west to find about al-Shafaq (redness) and the time for al-'Isha' al-Akhirah. When must he perform Salat (prayer) and what should he do? He (the Imam), *'Alayhi al-Salam*, signed the answer that said, 'He performs it (al-'Isha') when on this side, stars appear and al-Maghrib when just few stars appear. The clarity of sunset is from the appearance of few stars until their clearly becoming visible.'"

H 4830, Ch. 6, h 16

Ali ibn Muhammad and Muhammad ibn al-Hassan have narrated from Sahl ibn Ziyad from 'Isma'il ibn Mehran who has said the following:

"I once, wrote to al-Rida', *'Alayhi al-Salam*, to ask a question. 'Our people have said that when the sun declines toward the west at noontime, it is the time of al-

Zuhr and al-'Asr Salat (prayers). When it is sunset it is time of al-Maghrib and al-'Isha' al-Akhirah Salat (prayers) except that this is before this. It is the same for one at home or on a journey and the time of al-Maghrib remains until passing of one-fourth of night.' He (the Imam) wrote to me, 'That is how the timing is, except that the time of al-Maghrib is short and its end is when redness disappears, turning to whiteness in the western horizon.'"

Chapter 7 - The Time of Morning Salat (Prayer)

H 4831, Ch. 7, h 1

Ali ibn Muhammad has narrated from Sahl ibn Ziyad from Ali ibn Mahziyar from who has said the following:

"Abu al-Hassan ibn al-Husayn once wrote to Abu Ja'far, al-Thaniy, *'Alayhi al-Salam*, 'With me, I pray to Allah to keep my soul in service for your cause, people of your followers disagree on timing of dawn Salat (prayer). Certain ones of them perform when it is the first dawn in which a rectangular line appears in the sky, and others among them perform the morning Salat (prayer) when it (brightness) is at the bottom of the horizon and it has just appeared. I do not know which one is better, so I perform my Salat (prayer) in that time. If you consider it proper, instruct me about the time, which is better. Define it for me and how I should deal with the moon and the dawn with which it is not distinguishable, until it becomes red and it is dawn; and how should I deal with clouds and what are the limits for it during a journey or when one is at home. I will follow your instructions.' He (the Imam) wrote back with his own handwriting and I read it:

"Dawn, Allah has granted you kindness, is when the white line appears sideways; and it is not vertical, during which time you do not perform Salat (prayer) on a journey or when at home until it is obvious. Allah, most Blessed, most High, does not leave His creatures in confusion in this matter so He has said, 'Eat and drink until a white line appears from a darkness line at dawn.' (2:187) The white line is that which is sideways and after the appearance of which eating and drinking become unlawful because of fasting, and so also Salat (prayer) becomes obligatory at such time.'"

H 4832, Ch. 7, h 2

Ali ibn Muhammad has narrated from Sahl ibn Ziyad from Ahmad ibn Muhammad from ibn abu Nasr from 'Abd al-Rahman ibn Salim from Ishaq ibn 'Ammar who has said the following:

"I once asked abu 'Abd Allah, *'Alayhi al-Salam*, to teach me about the most excellent time for the morning Salat (prayer). He (the Imam), *'Alayhi al-Salam*, said, 'About the coming of dawn, Allah, most Majestic, most Glorious, says, "You must perform Salat (prayer)) and the recitation at dawn. The recitation at dawn certainly was witnessed." (17:78) It is a reference to the morning Salat (prayer) which is witnessed (attended) by the angels of the night and the angels of the day. When a servant of Allah performs Salat (prayer) at dawn, it is written in his favor twice: once by the angels of the night and once by the angels of the day.'"

H 4833, Ch. 7, h 3

Ali ibn Ibrahim has narrated from his father from ibn abu 'Umayr from Ali ibn 'Atiyyah who has said the following:

"Abu 'Abd Allah, *'Alayhi al-Salam*, has said, 'Dawn is when you find a white line like the whiteness of Sur' (a certain section of Euphrates river in Iraq)'"

H 4834, Ch. 7, h 4

Ali ibn Muhammad ibn 'Isa has narrated from Yunus from Yazid ibn Khalifah who has said the following:

"Abu 'Abd Allah, *'Alayhi al-Salam*, has said, 'The time for morning Salat (prayer) is when it (the white line) appears until the coming out of rays (of the sun).'"

H 4835, Ch. 7, h 5

Ali has narrated from his father ibn abu 'Umayr from Hammad al-Halabiy who has said the following:

"Abu 'Abd Allah, *'Alayhi al-Salam*, has said, 'The time for morning Salat (prayer) begins when dawn opens, until morning (with rays) brightens the sky. It is not proper to delay purposely; however, there is time for those who are preoccupied, forget or are sleeping.'"

H 4836, Ch. 7, h 6

Ali ibn Ibrahim has narrated from Ali ibn Muhammad al-Qasaniy from Sulayman ibn Hafs al-Marwaziy who has said the following:

"Abu al-Hassan, al-'Askariy, *'Alayhi al-Salam*, has said, 'At midnight a white spot appears in the middle of the sky like a pillar of iron, because of which it gives light in the world. This is there for an hour, then it goes out and it becomes dark. When there is one-third of the night left, whiteness appears in the east, which gives light to the world and it after an hour goes out. That is the time for Salat (prayer) of night. It then becomes dark before dawn: then the true dawn appears from the east.' He (the Imam) said, 'Those who like to perform Salat (prayer) of night at midnight that is for them.'"

Chapter 8 - The Time of Salat (Prayer) In a Cloudy Day, Windy and One Who Has Performed Salat (Prayer) Without Facing the Direction of Qiblah

H 4837, Ch. 8, h 1

Muhammad ibn Yahya has narrated from Muhammad ibn al-Husayn from 'Uthman ibn 'Isa from Sama'ah, who has said the following:

"I once asked him (the Imam), *'Alayhi al-Salam*, about performing Salat (prayer) during the night and during the day when the sun, the moon and stars cannot be seen. He (the Imam) said, 'Strive to come up with your best opinion about al-Qiblah (al-Ka'bah).'"

H 4838, Ch. 8, h 2

Ali ibn Ibrahim has narrated from his father from ibn abu 'Umayr from abu 'Abd Allah, al-Farra' who has said the following:

"A man from our people once said to abu 'Abd Allah, *'Alayhi al-Salam*, 'In a cloudy day sometimes the identifying the exact time becomes confusing.' He (the Imam) said, 'Are you aware of the existence of these birds, in Iraq, called al-Dikah (rooster)?' He (the man) replied, 'Yes, I am aware.' He (the Imam) said, 'When they raise their voices and others respond, it is the time when the sun declines toward the west at noontime, or that he (the Imam) said, 'You must perform Salat (prayer).'"

H 4839, Ch. 8, h 3

Al-Husayn ibn Muhammad has narrated from 'Abd Allah ibn 'Amir, from Ali ibn Mahziyar from Fadalah ibn Ayyub, from 'Abd al-Rahman ibn abu 'Abd Allah who has said the following:

"Abu 'Abd Allah, *'Alayhi al-Salam*, has said, 'You may perform a Salat (prayer) without facing al-Qiblah (al-Ka'bah). You must perform it again, only if you realize it in time. If the time is gone, it is not obligatory for you to perform it again.'"

H 4840, Ch. 8, h 4

Through the same chain of narrators as that of the previous Hadith it is narrated from Fadalah from Aban from Zurarah who has said the following:

"Abu Ja'far, *'Alayhi al-Salam*, about a man who performs the morning Salat (prayer) during the night mistakenly because of moon light and then goes to sleep until sunrise and he then is informed of having performed his morning Salat (prayer) during the night, has said, 'He must perform it again.'"

H 4841, Ch. 8, h 5

Ali ibn Muhammad has narrated from Sahl ibn Ziyad from Muhammad ibn Ibrahim al-Nawfaliy from al-Husayn ibn al-Mukhtar from a man who has said the following:

"I once said to abu 'Abd Allah, *'Alayhi al-Salam*, 'I am a Mu'adhdhin (caller for Salat (prayer)). On a cloudy day I cannot find when time for a Salat (prayer) begins.' He (the Imam) said, 'When the rooster crows three times consecutively, it is time when the sun has declined toward the west at noontime, thus it is time for Salat (prayer).'"

H 4842, Ch. 8, h 6

Muhammad ibn Yahya has narrated from Salmah ibn al-Khattab, from Yahya ibn Ibrahim ibn abu al-Bilad from his father from abu Basir from who has said the following:

"Abu 'Abd Allah, *'Alayhi al-Salam*, has said, 'One who performs a Salat (prayer) when it is not its time; his Salat (prayer) is not valid.'"

H 4843, Ch. 8, h 7

Muhammad ibn Yahya has narrated from Ahmad ibn Muhammad from Hammad from Hariz from Zurarah who has said the following:

"Abu Ja'far, *'Alayhi al-Salam*, has said, 'Al-Taharriy (investigation) is always sufficient in the issue of finding al-Qiblah (al-Ka'bah).'"

H 4844, Ch. 8, h 8

Ahmad ibn Idris and Muhammad ibn Yahya have narrated from Muhammad ibn Ahmad from Ahmad ibn al-Hassan ibn Ali from 'Amr ibn Sa'id from Musaddiq ibn Sadaqah from 'Ammar al-Sabatiy who has said the following:

"Abu 'Abd Allah, *'Alayhi al-Salam*, has said that a man may perform a Salat (prayer) without facing proper al-Qiblah (al-Ka'bah). He may realize it before completing the Salat (prayer). If his face is within one hundred eighty degrees of the al-Qiblah (al-Ka'bah) he must turn to al-Qiblah (al-Ka'bah) as soon as he realizes. If his back is toward al-Qiblah (al-Ka'bah), he must discontinue the Salat (prayer), then turn to al-Qiblah (al-Ka'bah) and begin the Salat (prayer) again.'"

H 4845, Ch. 8, h 9

Muhammad ibn Yahya has narrated from Ahmad ibn Muhammad from ibn abu 'Umayr from Hisham ibn Salim from Sulayman ibn Khalid who has said the following:

"I once asked abu 'Abd Allah, *'Alayhi al-Salam*, about a man who is in unpopulated land on a cloudy day and performs Salat (prayer) facing a wrong direction. Clouds then clear and he finds out about his Salat (prayer) having been performed facing a wrong direction. What he must do? He (the Imam) said, 'If there is still time, he must do his Salat (prayer) again but if the time is passed, then whatever investigation he has done is sufficient.'"

H 4846, Ch. 8, h 10

It is a narration from him (narrator of previous Hadith) by Ahmad ibn Muhammad from al-Husayn ibn Sa'id from ibn abu 'Umayr from certain persons of our people from Zurarah who has said the following:

"I once asked abu Ja'far, *'Alayhi al-Salam*, about al-Qiblah (al-Ka'bah) for one who is confused. He (the Imam) said, 'He performs as he wishes.' It is also narrated that he performs Salat (prayer) facing four directions."

H 4847, Ch. 8, h 11

Muhammad ibn Yahya has narrated from Ahmad ibn Muhammad from al-Husayn ibn Sa'id from ibn abu 'Umayr from 'Isma'il ibn Rabah who has said the following:

"Abu 'Abd Allah, *'Alayhi al-Salam*, has said, 'If you perform Salat (prayer) and you think it is time, when in fact is not time yet, but the time comes when you are still performing that Salat (prayer) it is sufficient.'"

H 4848, Ch. 8, h 12

Ali ibn Ibrahim has narrated from his father from ibn abu 'Umayr from Hammad from al-Halabiy who has said the following:

"I once asked abu 'Abd Allah, *'Alayhi al-Salam*, 'Did the Messenger of Allah perform Salat (prayer) facing Bayt al-Maqdis?' He (the Imam) replied, 'Yes, he did so.' I then asked, 'Would he turn his back toward al-Ka'bah?' He (the Imam) replied, 'When in Makkah he did not do so; but when he migrated to al-Madinah, he did so until he turned to al-Ka'bah.'"

Chapter 9 - Performing Two Salat (Prayer) Soon After the Other

H 4849, Ch. 9, h 1

Muhammad ibn Yahya has narrated from Ahmad ibn Muhammad from Ali ibn al-Hakam from 'Abd Allah ibn Bukayr from Zurarah who has said the following:

"Abu 'Abd Allah, *'Alayhi al-Salam*, has said, 'The Messenger of Allah performed al-Zuhr and al-'Asr Salat (prayers) when the sun declined (toward the west at noontime) in congregation without any reason. He also performed al-Maghrib and al-'Isha' Salat (prayer) in congregation before disappearing of al-Shafaq (redness) without any reason to do so. The Messenger of Allah did so to make it easier for his followers.'"

H 4850, Ch. 9, h 2

Ali ibn Muhammad has narrated from Sahl ibn Ziyad from Ahmad ibn Muhammad from ibn abu Nasr from 'Abd Allah ibn Sinan who has said the following:

"I once was present in Masjid of the Messenger of Allah, during the time of al-Maghrib Salat (prayer) in a rainy evening. When it was near al-Shafaq (redness), they called and performed Salat (prayer) of al-Maghrib. People were given time to perform two Rak'at Salat (prayer), then the caller stood in his place in Masjid, called for Salat (prayer) and they performed al-'Isha' Salat (prayer). People then left for their homes. I asked abu 'Abd Allah, *'Alayhi al-Salam*, about it. He (the Imam) said, 'Yes, the Messenger of Allah had certainly done so.'"

H 4851, Ch. 9, h 3

Muhammad ibn Yahya has narrated from Salmah ibn al-Khattab from al-Husayn ibn Sayf from Hammad ibn 'Uthman from Muhammad ibn Hakim who has said the following:

"I once heard abu al-Hassan, *'Alayhi al-Salam*, say, 'If you perform two Salat (prayer), one after the other, do not perform optional Salat (prayer) between them.'"

H 4852, Ch. 9, h 4

Ali ibn Muhammad has narrated from Muhammad ibn Musa from Muhammad ibn 'Isa from ibn Faddal from Hammad ibn 'Uthman who has said the following:

"Muhammad ibn Hakim narrated to me that he had heard abu al-Hassan, *'Alayhi al-Salam*, say, 'Performing two Salat (prayer) soon one after the other is when no optional Salat (prayer) is performed between them. When optional Salat (prayer) is performed between them, they are not performed soon one after the other.'"

H 4853, Ch. 9, h 5

Ali ibn Muhammad has narrated from al-Fadl ibn Muhammad ibn Yahya ibn Zakariya from Aban from Safwan al-Jammal who has said the following:

"Abu 'Abd Allah, *'Alayhi al-Salam*, performed with us al-Zuhr and al-'Asr Salat (prayer) after the sun declined (toward the west at noontime), with one Adhan and two 'Iqamah, and said, 'I need to do something, so you can perform optional Salat (prayer).'"

H 4854, Ch. 9, h 6

Muhammad ibn Yahya has narrated from Muhammad ibn Ahmad from 'Abbas al-Naqid who has said the following:

"My belongings and associates were scattered and I complained about it before abu Muhammad, *'Alayhi al-Salam*. He (the Imam) said, 'Perform al-Zuhr and al-'Asr Salat (prayer) soon after the other; you will see whatever you love.'"

Chapter 10 - The Salat (Prayer) Any Time

H 4855, Ch 10, h 1

Ali ibn Ibrahim has narrated from Muhammad ibn 'Isa from Yunus ibn Hashim ibn Sa'id al-Mukariy from abu Basir from who has said the following:

"Abu 'Abd Allah, *'Alayhi al-Salam*, has said, 'There are five Salat (prayer) which you can perform anytime you want. Such Salat (prayer) are because of eclipse, for a deceased, for 'Ihram, for making up a missed one, for Tawaf from dawn to sunrise and after al-'Asr until night.'"

H 4856, Ch. 10, h 2

Muhammad ibn 'Isma'il has narrated from al-Fadl ibn Shadhan and Ahmad ibn Idris from Muhammad ibn 'Abd al-Jabbar all from Safwan ibn Yahya Mu'awiyah ibn 'Ammar who has said the following:

"Abu 'Abd Allah, *'Alayhi al-Salam*, has said, 'Five Salat (prayer) are not neglected in any condition. Such Salat (prayer) are after performing Tawaf, when you are about to have Ihram, for eclipse, to make up when remembering one forgotten and Salat (prayer) for a deceased.'"

H 4857, Ch. 10, h 3

Ali ibn Ibrahim has narrated from his father from Hammad from Hariz from Zurarah who has said the following:

"Abu Ja'far, *'Alayhi al-Salam*, has said, 'There are four kinds of Salat (prayer) which a man can perform anytime. Such are Salat (prayer) after remembering a forgotten one, two Rak'at after obligatory Tawaf, because of eclipse and Salat (prayer) for a deceased. You can perform these kinds of Salat (prayer) at any hour.'"

Chapter 11 - Performing Optional Salat (Prayer) at the Time of Obligatory Salat (Prayer) and the Times Not to Perform Salat (Prayer)

H 4858, Ch. 11, h 1

Al-Husayn ibn Muhammad al-Ash'ariy has narrated from 'Abd Allah ibn 'Amir from Ali ibn Mahziyar from Fadalah ibn Ayyub from al-Husayn ibn 'Uthman from ibn Muskan from Zurarah who has said the following:

"He (the Imam), *'Alayhi al-Salam*, once said to me, 'Do you know why one and two yards are set?' I (the narrator) said, 'Why are they set?' He (the Imam) said, 'It is because of obligatory Salat (prayer). You can perform optional Salat (prayer) soon after the sun declines (to the west at noontime) until it become one yard, but if you begin the obligatory one, you do not perform optional Salat (prayer).'"

H 4859, Ch. 11, h 2

Muhammad ibn Yahya has narrated from Ahmad ibn Muhammad from ibn Faddal Yunus ibn Ya'qub from Minhal who has said the following:

"I once asked abu 'Abd Allah, *'Alayhi al-Salam*, about the time when I should not perform any optional Salat (prayer) after the sun declines toward the west at noontime. He (the Imam) replied, 'When it is one yard until it is like it (twice as much).'"

H 4860, Ch. 11, h 3

Muhammad ibn Yahya has narrated from Muhammad ibn al-Husayn from 'Uthman ibn 'Isa from Sama'ah who has said the following:

"I once asked him (the Imam), *'Alayhi al-Salam*, about a man who comes to Masjid when people there have completed their Salat (prayer). Should he begin the obligatory or optional before the obligatory? He (the Imam) said, 'If it is a good time it is not harmful to perform optional Salat (prayer) before obligatory. If he fears that time may end, he must begin the obligatory, which is the right of Allah, most Majestic, most Glorious, then perform optional Salat (prayer) whatever he wants. The time for optional Salat (prayer) is longer. One can perform in the beginning of the time for obligatory optional ones, unless one is afraid of passing of the time of obligatory one. It is better when one performs alone to begin with obligatory, if it is time for it, so that it is performed during the excellent time which is in the beginning of time. It is not prohibited to perform optional Salat (prayer) at the beginning of time up to near the end of the time.'"

H 4861, Ch. 11, h 4

Muhammad ibn Yahya has narrated from Ahmad ibn Muhammad from al-Husayn ibn Sa'id from 'Uthman ibn 'Isa from Ishaq ibn 'Ammar who has said the following:

"I once asked him (the Imam), *'Alayhi al-Salam*, 'Can I perform optional Salat (prayer) in the time for obligatory one?' He (the Imam) replied, 'Yes, you can do so in the beginning of time if you are with the Imam who leads you in Salat (prayer). If you are alone, then perform the obligatory first.'"

H 4862, Ch. 11, h 5

Ali ibn Ibrahim has narrated from his father from ibn abu 'Umayr from abu Ayyub from Muhammad ibn Muslim who has said the following:

"I once said to abu 'Abd Allah, *'Alayhi al-Salam*, 'When the time for obligatory Salat (prayer) comes, should I perform optional Salat (prayer) or begin the obligatory one?' He (the Imam) said, 'It is better to begin with obligatory. Al-Zuhr is delayed to one yard from Zawal (declining of the sun toward the west at noontime) by one yard for Salat (prayer) of repentant people.'"

H 4863, Ch. 11, h 6

Ali ibn Ibrahim has narrated from his father from ibn abu 'Umayr from abu Ayyub from Muhammad ibn Muslim who has said the following:

"I once asked abu 'Abd Allah, *'Alayhi al-Salam*, 'When the time for obligatory Salat (prayer) comes, can I perform optional Salat (prayer) or begin with obligatory Salat (prayer)?' He (the Imam) replied, 'It is better to begin with the obligatory Salat (prayer).'"

H 4864, Ch. 11, h 7

Ali ibn Ibrahim has narrated from his father from ibn abu 'Umayr from 'Umar ibn 'Udhaynah from a number of our people who has said the following:

"They had heard abu Ja'far, *'Alayhi al-Salam,* say, "Amir al-Mu'minin, *'Alayhi al-Salam,* would not perform Salat (prayer) during the day until Zawal (declining of the sun toward the west at noontime). During the night he would not perform any Salat (prayer) after al-'Isha' up until midnight. It means that it is not time for obligatory or optional Salat (prayer); the Messenger of Allah has defined all times. However, to perform a make-up for obligatory or performing optional Salat (prayer) before or after is not harmful.'"

H 4865, Ch. 11, h 8

Ali ibn Ibrahim has narrated from his father from in a marfu' manner the following;

"Once a man mentioned before abu 'Abd Allah, *'Alayhi al-Salam,* the Hadith which is narrated from abu Ja'far, *'Alayhi al-Salam,* that says, 'The sun emerges from between the two horns of Satan.' He (the Imam) said, 'Yes, Iblis has found a throne between the sky and earth. When the sun rises and people prostrate at that time, Iblis then says to his other Satans, 'Children of Adam perform Salat (prayer) for me.'"

H 4866, Ch. 11, h 9

Ali ibn Muhammad has narrated from Sahl ibn Ziyad from al-Husayn ibn Rashid from al-Husayn ibn Aslama who has said the following:

"I once said to abu al-Hassan al-Thaniy, *'Alayhi al-Salam,* 'In the market place I come to know that it is time but it becomes difficult (to perform Salat (prayer)) after I enter the market place (for business).' He (the Imam) said, 'Satan nears the sun during three conditions, at sunrise, Zawal (declining of the sun toward the west at noontime) and at sunset. You must perform Salat (prayer) after Zawal (declining of the sun toward the west at noontime); Satan wants to mislead you from the right path.'"

Chapter 12 - One Who Goes to Sleep Before Performing Salat (Prayer) or Forgets

H 4867, Ch. 12, h 1

Ali ibn Ibrahim has narrated from his father from and Muhammad ibn 'Isma'il from al-Fadl ibn Shadhan all from Hammad ibn 'Isa from Hariz from Zurarah who has said the following:

"Abu Ja'far, *'Alayhi al-Salam,* has said, 'If you forget to perform Salat (prayer) or perform it without Wudu' and miss Salat (prayers) which you must perform, begin with what is first. Say Adhan and 'Iqamah, then perform it, thereafter perform what is after this with just 'Iqamah for every Salat (prayer).' Abu Ja'far, *'Alayhi al-Salam,* has said, 'If you have already performed al-Zuhr, then remembered that you have missed the morning Salat (prayer), perform the morning Salat (prayer) in whatever hour you remember even if it is after al-'Asr. Whenever you remember a Salat (prayer) that you have missed, perform it.' Abu Ja'far, *'Alayhi al-Salam,* has said, 'If you forget to perform al-Zuhr until you perform al-'Asr, then remember in the middle of Salat (prayer) or after you complete a Salat (prayer) consider it the first one (al-Zuhr which is missed). Then perform al-'Asr; it is a four Rak'at in place of another four Rak'at. If you remember that you have not performed the first one and you are in the middle of al-'Asr from which you have performed only two Rak'at consider it the first (al-

Zuhr), then perform the two remaining Rak'at. Then stand up and perform al-'Asr. If you remember that you have not performed al-'Asr until it is time of al-Maghrib and you are not afraid of running short of its time, perform al-'Asr, thereafter perform al-Maghrib. If you have performed al-Maghrib, stand up to perform al-'Asr. If you have performed two Rak'at of al-Maghrib, then you remember that you have missed al-'Asr; consider it al-'Asr then complete it with another two Rak'at, say Salam and thereafter perform al-Maghrib. If you have performed al-'Isha' al-Akhirah, but you have forgotten al-Maghrib, stand up to perform al-Maghrib. If you remember when you have performed two Rak'at of al-'Isha' al-Akhirah or you just have stood up for the third Rak'at, consider it al-Maghrib then say Salam and thereafter perform al-'Isha' al-Akhirah. If you forget al-'Isha' al-Akhirah until you perform the morning Salat (prayer), perform al-'Isha' al-Akhirah thereafter. If you remember in the first Rak'at or in the second Rak'at of the morning Salat (prayer), consider it al-'Isha', thereafter perform the morning Salat (prayer), say Adhan and 'Iqamah. If both al-Maghrib and al-'Isha' al-Akhirah are missed, begin with these ones first before the morning Salat (prayer), first al-Maghrib and then al-'Isha' al-Akhirah. If you are afraid of the running short of the time of the morning Salat (prayer) if you perform the two first, begin with al-Maghrib, then morning Salat (prayer), then al-'Isha'. If you are afraid of running short of the time of the morning Salat (prayer), if you begin with al-Maghrib, begin with the morning Salat (prayer) then al-Maghrib and al-'Isha'. Begin with the first one because it is a Qada' (make-up for). Start whichever you want. You must not perform except after the rising of sun rays.' I (the narrator) then asked, 'Why is that?' He (the Imam) said, 'Because you are not afraid of missing them.'"

H 4868, Ch. 12, h 2

Ali ibn Muhammad has narrated from Sahl ibn Ziyad from Muhammad ibn Sinan from ibn Muskan from abu Basir from who has said the following:

"I once asked him (the Imam), *'Alayhi al-Salam*, about a man who forgets al-Zuhr until it is time of al-'Asr. He (the Imam) said, 'He begins with al-Zuhr and so also one begins with Salat (prayer) which is forgotten, unless one is afraid of the running short of the time of Salat (prayer), in which case one begins with that for which there is still time, thereafter performs what one has forgotten.'"

H 4869, Ch. 12, h 3

Ali ibn Ibrahim has narrated from his father from ibn abu 'Umayr from ibn 'Udhaynah from Zurarah who has said the following:

"Abu Ja'far, *'Alayhi al-Salam*, was once asked about a man who performs Salat (prayer) without Tahur (cleansing) or forgets it (Salat (prayer)) or goes to sleep. He (the Imam) said, 'He performs its Qada' (compensatory prayer) in whatever hour he remembers during the night or day. If the time for a Salat (prayer) comes and he has not yet completed what he was to perform as Qada' (compensatory prayer) he completes what he is to do unless is afraid of running short of the time of Salat (prayer) of present time. Such Salat (prayer) is of greater priority in matters of its time thus, he performs it and when this is complete, he performs that which was missed in the past, and he does not perform any optional Salat (prayer) even one Rak'at, until completion of all obligatory ones.'"

H 4870, Ch. 12, h 4

Muhammad ibn Yahya has narrated from Ahmad ibn Muhammad from al-Husayn ibn Sa'id and Muhammad ibn Khalid all from al-Qasim ibn 'Urwah from 'Ubayd ibn Zurarah from his father who has said the following:

"Abu Ja'far, *'Alayhi al-Salam,* has sad, 'You may miss a Salat (prayer) and remember it in another time. If you think you can perform Qada' (compensatory prayer) for the one missed when there is still enough time left to perform the present Salat (prayer), begin to do so. Allah, most Majestic, most Glorious, says, "Perform Salat (prayer) to remember (speak of) Me" but if you know that with performing Qada' (compensatory prayer) for what you have missed, the time for the present one will end, then begin with the present Salat (prayer). Thereafter perform Qada' (compensatory prayer) for the one missed in the past.'"

H 4871, Ch. 12, h 5

Al-Husayn ibn Muhammad has narrated from Muhammad al-Ash'ariy from Mu'alla' ibn Muhammad from al-Washsha' from Aban ibn 'Uthman from 'Abd al-Rahman ibn abu 'Abd Allah who has said the following:

"I once asked abu 'Abd Allah, *'Alayhi al-Salam,* about a man who has forgotten a Salat (prayer) until the time for next Salat (prayer). He (the Imam) said, 'If one misses a Salat (prayer) because of forgetting or sleep, he must perform it as soon as he remembers. If he remembers it during performing another Salat (prayer), he begins with that which is forgotten. If he remembers while performing Salat (prayer) of al-Maghrib behind an Imam, he completes it with an additional Rak'at, thereafter performs al-Maghrib and then al-'Atmah, (al-'Isha' al-Akhirah) thereafter. If he is performing al-'Atmah alone and two Rak'at of it are complete when he remembers that he has forgotten al-Maghrib, he completes it with one more Rak'at to finish its three Rak'at for al-Maghrib, then performs al-'Atmah thereafter.'"

H 4872, Ch. 12, h 6

Muhammad ibn 'Isma'il has narrated from al-Fadl ibn Shadhan from Safwan ibn Yahya who has said the following:

"I once asked abu al-Hassan, *'Alayhi al-Salam,* about a man who forgets al-Zuhr until it is sunset and has performed al-'Asr. He (the Imam) said, 'Abu Ja'far, *'Alayhi al-Salam,* or my father would say, "If he can perform Qada' (compensatory prayer) for it before the time for al-Maghrib ends, he must do so, otherwise, he performs al-Maghrib then Qada' (compensatory prayer) for that which is missed.'"

H 4873, Ch. 12, h 7

Ali ibn Ibrahim has narrated from his father from ibn abu 'Umayr from Hammad from al-Halabiy who has said the following:

"I once asked abu 'Abd Allah, *'Alayhi al-Salam,* about a man who leads people for al-'Asr, then he remembers during Salat (prayer) that he has not performed the one before. He (the Imam) said, 'He considers it (Salat (prayer) he is performing) as the one before which is missed and thereafter perform al-'Asr again and the people proceed with their Salat (prayer).'"

H 4874, Ch. 12, h 8

Muhammad ibn Yahya has narrated from Ahmad ibn Muhammad from 'Uthman ibn 'Isa from Sama'ah ibn Mehran who has said the following:

"I once asked him (the Imam), *'Alayhi al-Salam*, about a man who forgets to perform the morning Salat (prayer) until it is sunrise. He (the Imam) said, 'He performs it whenever he remembers. The Messenger of Allah remained sleeping during the time for the morning Salat (prayer) until sunrise, then he performed it Qada' (compensatory prayer) when he woke up but moved away from his place, then performed Salat (prayer).'"

H 4875, Ch. 12, h 9

Muhammad ibn Yahya has narrated from Ahmad ibn Muhammad from Ali ibn al-Nu'man from Sa'id al-'Araj who has said the following:

"I once heard abu 'Abd Allah, *'Alayhi al-Salam*, say, 'The Messenger of Allah remained sleeping during the time of the morning Salat (prayer) and Allah, most Majestic, most Glorious, made him to remain sleeping until sunrise and this was a blessing from Him for the people. Consider, when one remains sleeping until sunrise, people reproach him saying, "You do not avoid sins in matters of Salat (prayer)." This became a Sunnah, tradition and guideline. If one man says to another man, "You remained sleeping during the time of Salat (prayer), he can respond saying, 'the Messenger of Allah also remained sleeping.'" Thus, it became a Sunnah and guideline and a blessing, which Allah, most Glorious, granted this nation.'"

H 4876, Ch. 12, h 10

Ali ibn Ibrahim has narrated from his father from ibn abu 'Umayr from Hammad from Hariz from Zurarah and Fudayl who has said the following:

"This is about the words of Allah. most Blessed is whose name, 'Salat (prayer) was written as obligatory upon people.' (4:103) Abu Ja'far, *'Alayhi al-Salam*, has said, 'It means that it was obligatory, not that it is obligatory for a limited time so that if it is performed after the limited time, it does not fulfill the obligation. Had it been so Sulayman son of Dawud would have been destroyed when he performed his Salat (prayer) in a time, which was other than the time of that Salat (prayer). However, he performed when he remembered.' He (the Imam) then said, 'If you are certain or have doubts in its time that you did not perform, you must perform it again. If you face a doubt after its time has ended, there has an obstacle come into existence, so a repeat is not required from you because of doubt, unless you are certain. If you become certain you must perform in whatever condition you are.'"

H 4877, Ch. 12, h 11

Ali ibn Ibrahim has narrated from his father from 'Abd Allah ibn al-Mughirah from those who m he has mentioned who has said the following:

"I once asked abu 'Abd Allah, *'Alayhi al-Salam*, about a man who remains sleeping during the time of al-'Atmah and does not wake up until after midnight.

He (the Imam) said, 'He performs that Salat (prayer) and remains fasting until the morning.'"

Chapter 13 - Construction of the Masjid of the Holy Prophet

H 4878, Ch. 13, h 1

Ali ibn Muhammad and Muhammad ibn al-Hassan have narrated from Sahl ibn Ziyad from Ahmad ibn Muhammad from ibn abu Nasr and Ali ibn Ibrahim has narrated from his father from 'Abd Allah ibn al-Mughirah from 'Abd Allah ibn Sinan who has said the following:

"I heard abu 'Abd Allah, *'Alayhi al-Salam*, say, 'The Messenger of Allah built his Masjid with an arrangement of one brick. The number of Muslims increased and they asked, "O Messenger of Allah, issue a command to expand the Masjid." He responded positively and commanded to expand it and it was expanded. It was built with an arrangement of one and a half bricks. Then Muslims became greater in number and they asked the Messenger of Allah to expand the Masjid again. He agreed and commanded to increase the size of the Masjid and this time, the walls were built with an arrangement of bricks. (The arrangements of bricks, as mentioned, apply more clearly to the width of the wall). When during the warm season it became hot, they asked the Messenger of Allah to provide shadow. He agreed and commanded them to do so, they placed beams of palm tree trunks over which branches and bushes were placed. They remained until it rained and water leaked down upon them. They asked, "O Messenger of Allah, we wish you command to cover the roof of the Masjid with clay." The Messenger of Allah said to them, "There must be no trellises like the trellis of Moses." It remained in that form until the Holy prophet passed away. The height of the walls before placing the roof was of the size of the height of a man. When the length of its shadow would become of the size of one yard, which is of the size of a goat, they would perform Salat (prayer) soon after noontime. When its length doubled, they would perform 'Al-'Asr Salat (prayer).'"

H 4879, Ch. 13, h 2

Ali ibn Ibrahim has narrated from his father from ibn abu 'Umayr from Hammad ibn 'Isa from al-Halabiy who has said the following:

"I asked abu 'Abd Allah, *'Alayhi al-Salam*, about the Masjid which was built for a pious purpose. He (the Imam) replied, 'It is Masjid al-Quba''"

H 4880, Ch. 13, h 3

Ahmad ibn Idris and other people have narrated from Ahmad ibn Muhammad from Ali ibn 'Isma'il from Muhammad ibn 'Amr ibn Sa'id who has said that Musa ibn 'Ukayl narrated from 'Abd al-'A'la' from Mawla Ala Sam who has said the following:

"I asked abu 'Abd Allah, *'Alayhi al-Salam*, 'What was the size of Masjid of the Messenger of Allah?' He (the Imam) replied, 'It was three thousand and six hundred square yards.'"

Chapter 14 - Forming a Barrier between One Performing Salat (Prayer) and Those Passing in Front of Him

H 4881, Ch. 14, h 1

Muhammad ibn Yahya has narrated from Ahmad ibn Muhammad from al-Hassan ibn Mahbub from Mu'awiyah ibn Wahab who has said the following:

"Abu 'Abd Allah, *'Alayhi al-Salam*, has said, 'The Messenger of Allah would place his staff in front of the place where he performed Salat (prayer).'"

H 4882, Ch. 14, h 2

A number of our people have narrated from Ahmad ibn Muhammad from al-Husayn ibn Sa'id from ibn Sinan from ibn Muskan from abu Basir from who has said the following:

"Abu 'Abd Allah, *'Alayhi al-Salam*, has said, 'The length of the staff of the Messenger of Allah was one yard and he would place it in his front for a barrier between himself and people passing by.'"

H 4883, Ch. 14, h 3

Muhammad ibn Yahya has narrated from Ahmad ibn Muhammad from 'Uthman ibn 'Isa from ibn Muskan from ibn abu Ya'fur who has said the following:

"I once asked abu 'Abd Allah, *'Alayhi al-Salam*, about a man whose Salat (prayer) is discontinued because of something moving in front of him. He (the Imam) said, 'Things do not discontinue Salat (prayer) of the believer, but guard it as much as you can.'"

"In the narration of ibn Muskan from abu Basir from abu 'Abd Allah, *'Alayhi al-Salam*, it is said that things do not discontinue Salat (prayer), not a dog, donkey and woman, but place a barrier in front of yourselves, of the size of one yard high above ground; it is enough of a barrier.'"

Al-Kulayniy has said that it is better to establish a barrier with something, which you can place in front of yourselves and those passing-by. If you did not do so, it is not harmful because the one for whom one performs Salat (prayer) is closer than passing-by one, but it is a matter of the discipline of Salat (prayer) and its respect.

H 4884, Ch. 14, h 4

Ali ibn Ibrahim has narrated from his father in a marfu' manner from Muhammad ibn Muslim who has said the following:

"Once, abu Hanifah went to see abu 'Abd Allah, *'Alayhi al-Salam*. On his arrival he said, 'I saw your son Musa perform Salat (prayer) while people passed by in front of him; but he did not stop them and it is questionable.' Abu 'Abd Allah, *'Alayhi al-Salam*, asked to call Musa. He was called and he asked, 'Son, abu Hanifah says that you were performing Salat (prayer) and people passed by in front of you, but you did not stop them.' He replied, 'Yes, O father, the One for whom I was performing Salat (prayer) was closer to me than people passing by in front of me. Allah, most Majestic, most Glorious, says, "We are closer to him than the jugular vein."' (50:16) The narrator has said that he (the Imam) then embraced him and then said, 'I pray to Allah to keep me and my mother in service for your cause, O reservoir of secrets.' (Imam's response is to show the significance of Salat (prayer) not to compromising any excellence.)"

(The following chapter (15) is best explained by fatwa.)

Chapter 15 - Women Performing Salat (Prayer) in Front of Men or Men Performing Salat (Prayer) With Women in Front

H 4885, Ch. 15, h 1

Ali ibn Ibrahim has narrated from his father from Hammad from Hariz who has said the following:

"I once asked abu 'Abd Allah, *'Alayhi al-Salam,* about the case of a woman who performs Salat (prayer) on the side of the man nearby. He (the Imam) said, 'If there is a distance of one Rahl (yard), it is not harmful.

H 4886, Ch. 15, h 2

Al-Husayn ibn Muhammad has narrated from Mu'alla' ibn Muhammad from al-Washsha' from Aban ibn 'Uthman from 'Abd al-Rahman ibn abu 'Abd Allah who has said the following:

"I once asked abu 'Abd Allah, *'Alayhi al-Salam,* about a man who performs Salat (prayer) when a woman is parallel with him on the right or left. He (the Imam) said, 'It is not harmful if she is not performing Salat (prayer)'"

H 4887, Ch. 15, h 3

Ali ibn Muhammad has narrated from Sahl ibn Ziyad from ibn Sinan from ibn Muskan from abu Basir from who has said the following:

"I once asked abu 'Abd Allah, *'Alayhi al-Salam,* about a man and a woman performing Salat (prayer) at the same time and the woman is on his right parallel. He (the Imam) said, 'No, unless there is a distance of one shibr or one yard between the two of them.'"

H 4888, Ch 15, h 4

Ali ibn Muhammad has narrated from Sahl ibn Ziyad from Ahmad ibn Muhammad from ibn abu Nasr from al-'Ala' from Muhammad ibn Muslim who has said the following:

"I once asked one of the two Imam, *'Alayhim al-Salam,* about a man who performs Salat (prayer) in one corner of the room and his wife or daughter parallel with him in another corner of the room. He (the Imam) said, 'He should not do so. If there is a distance of one shibr between them it is enough for him.' I asked him (the Imam) about a man and woman share ride in a carriage and perform Salat (prayer) at the same time. He (the Imam) said, 'No, man performs Salat (prayer) first, then the woman.'"

H 4889, Ch. 15, h 5

Muhammad ibn Yahya has narrated from Muhammad ibn al-Hassan from Ja'far ibn Bashir from Hammad ibn 'Uthman from Idris ibn 'Abd Allah al-Qummiy who has said the following:

"I once asked abu 'Abd Allah, *'Alayhi al-Salam,* about a man who performs Salat (prayer) and a woman is in his view, standing on furnishing on his side. He (the Imam) said, 'If she is sitting, it is not harmful, but if she is performing Salat (prayer), then it is not acceptable.'"

H 4890, Ch. 15, h 6

Muhammad ibn Yahya has narrated from Ahmad ibn Muhammad from ibn Faddal from Ali ibn al-Hassan ibn Ribat from certain persons of our people who has said the following:

"Abu 'Abd Allah, *'Alayhi al-Salam,* has said, 'The Messenger of Allah would perform Salat (prayer) while 'A'ishah slept sideways in front of him, while she did not perform Salat (prayer).'"

H 4891, Ch. 15, h 7

Muhammad ibn Yahya has narrated from Ahmad ibn Muhammad from ibn Faddal from ibn Bukayr from those who he has mentioned who has said the following:

"I once asked abu 'Abd Allah, *'Alayhi al-Salam,* about a woman who performs Salat (prayer) on the side or parallel with a man. He (the Imam) said, 'If her Sujud (prostration) is with his Ruku' (bowing down on one's knees), it is not harmful.'"

(Ahadith 1-7 of this Chapter are best explained by fatwa.)

Chapter 16 - Humility during Salat (prayer) and the Contemptibility of Playfulness during Prayer

H 4892, Ch. 16, h 1

Ali ibn Ibrahim has narrated from his father and Muhammad ibn 'Isma'il from Fadl ibn Shadhan all from Hammad ibn 'Isa from Hariz from Zurarah who has said the following:

"Abu Ja'far, *'Alayhi al-Salam,* has said, 'When you stand up for Salat (prayer) you should be prepared (attentive) for prayer; what will be counted in your favor of prayer will be only that in which you were attentive. You should not play during Salat (prayer) with your hands, head and beard, and do not speak in your soul. You should not yawn, stretch or fold your hands one over the other; this is what the Zoroastrians would do. You should not mask your face, feel urged (for urination), keep your feet far apart from each other like camels do, should not sit on your heels, place your arms flat on the ground, crack your fingers; anyone of such things causes a defect in Salat (prayer). You should not stand for Salat (prayer) in a lazy mode, slumbering or feeling burdened; each one of such things is of behaviors of hypocrites. Allah, the Most Glorious, has forbidden the believers to stand up for prayer in a lazy mode, that is, feeling sleepy. He has said about the hypocrites, "When they stand up for Salat (prayer) they do so in a lazy mode and just to show off to people and they do not speak of (remember) Allah but very little" (4:141).'"

H 4893, Ch. 16, h 2

Ali ibn Ibrahim has narrated from his father from al-Hassan ibn abu al-Hassan al-Farisiy from those who narrated to him who has said the following:

"Abu 'Abd Allah, *'Alayhi al-Salam,* has said that the Messenger of Allah has said, 'Allah has made twenty-four things contemptible for you to do and has forbidden you to do them. Allah dislikes that you act as playful during Salat (prayer).'"

H 4894, Ch. 16, h 3

Ali ibn Ibrahim has narrated from his father from ibn abu 'Umayr from Hammad from al-Halabiy who has said the following:

"Abu 'Abd Allah, *'Alayhi al-Salam*, has said that when you are in your Salat (prayer), you must be humble and attentive in it; Allah, the Most Majestic, the Most Glorious, has said, 'Those who are humble during their Salat (prayer) (are of the true believers)' (23:3)."

H 4895, Ch. 16, h 4

A number of our people have narrated from Ahmad ibn Muhammad and abu Dawud all from al-Husayn ibn Sa'id from Ali ibn abu Jahmah from Jahm ibn Hamid who has said the following:

"Abu 'Abd Allah, *'Alayhi al-Salam*, has said that his (Imam's) father has said that when Ali ibn al-Husayn, *'Alayhi al-Salam*, would stand up for Salat (prayer), he seemed like the trunk of a tree. Not anything of his body would move except what the wind would move.'"

H 4896, Ch. 16, h 5

Muhammad ibn Isma'il has narrated from al-Fadl ibn Shadhan from Hammad ibn Isa from Rib'iy ibn 'Abd Allah from al-Fudayl ibn Yasar who has said the following:

"Abu 'Abd Allah, *'Alayhi al-Salam*, has said that when Ali ibn al-Husayn, *'Alayhi al-Salam*, would stand up for Salat (prayer), the color of his face change and in sajdah he remained so long until (his face) became drenched with perspiration (and tears)."

H 4897, Ch. 16, h 6

Ali ibn Ibrahim has narrated from his father from Hammad from Hariz from Zurarah who has narrated the following:

"Abu Ja'far, *'Alayhi al-Salam*, has said that when you face the direction of al-Qiblah (al-Ka'bah) you must not turn your face away from it; it destroys your Salat (prayer). Allah, most Majestic, most Glorious, has said to His Holy prophet, O Allah grant compensation to Muhammad and his family worthy of their services to Your cause, about the obligatory Salat (prayer). 'You must turn your face to the Masjid al-Haram (the Sacred Masjid). Wherever you are you must turn your faces toward it.' (2:144) Your eyes must be cast down instead of being raised to the sky and your eye must remain before your face on the place for your Sujud (prostrations).'"

H 4898, Ch. 16, h 7

Al-Husayn ibn Muhammad has narrated from Mu'alla' ibn Muhammad from al-Hassan ibn Ali al-Washsha' from Aban ibn 'Uthman from al-Fudayl ibn Yasar from one of the two Imam, *'Alayhim al-Salam*, who has said the following:

"About a man's yawning and stretching during Salat (prayer) the Imam, *'Alayhi al-Salam*, has said, 'It comes from Satan over which he has no control (but one should control things that cause it to happen).'"

H 4899, Ch. 16, h 8

Muhammad ibn Yahya has narrated from Ahmad ibn Muhammad ibn 'Isa from Ahmad ibn Muhammad ibn abu Nasr from abu al-Walid who has said the following:

"I was sitting in the presence of abu 'Abd Allah, *'Alayhi al-Salam*, when Najiyyah abu Habib asked the Imam saying, 'May Allah keep my soul in service for your cause, I have a flour-mill. During the night I wake up (for Salat (prayer)) and notice from the mill that the servant is gone to sleep. (Can) I then knock at the wall to wake him up?' The Imam replied, 'Yes, you are in the condition of obeying Allah, the Most Majestic, the Most Glorious, when you are seeking to make a living.'"

(Please consult a fatwa also.)

H 4900, Ch. 16, h 9
Muhammad ibn Yahya has narrated from Ahmad ibn Muhammad ibn 'Isa in a marfu' manner who has said the following:
"Abu 'Abd Allah, *'Alayhi al-Salam*, has said that when you stand up for Salat (prayer), you must not play with your beard, your head or with pebbles while you pray, except when you prepare (pebbles) as you are about to do sajdah in which case it is not an offense."

Chapter 17 - Weeping and Appealing for One's Needs in Salat (prayer)

H 4901, Ch. 17, h 1
Muhammad ibn Yahya has narrated from Ahmad ibn Muhammad from 'Uthman ibn 'Isa from Sama'ah who has said the following:
"Abu 'Abd Allah, *'Alayhi al-Salam*, has said, 'One, when reading from the Holy Quran, should, upon coming across a verse that speaks of prayer or warning, ask Allah for what is good that one hopes for and for safety from fire and torment.'"

H 4902, Ch. 17, h 2
Al-Husayn ibn Muhammad has narrated from Mu'alla' ibn Muhammad from al-Washsha' from Hammad ibn 'Uthman from Sa'id al-Bayya' al-Sabiriy who has said the following:
"I asked abu 'Abd Allah, *'Alayhi al-Salam*, 'Can a person weep during Salat (prayer)?' The Imam replied, 'It is a matter of great congratulations even if it (tears) is of the size of the head of a fly.'"

H 4903, Ch. 17, h 3
Ali ibn Ibrahim has narrated from his father from ibn abu 'Umayr from Hammad from al-Halabiy who has said the following:
"I asked abu 'Abd Allah, *'Alayhi al-Salam*, 'What should a man who performs Salat (prayer) with an Imam do if they come across a verse that speaks of paradise or fire?' The Imam said, 'In such case (during prayer) he may ask Allah for protection against fire or for admission in paradise.'"

H 4904, Ch. 17, h 4
Muhammad ibn Yahya has narrated from Ahmad ibn Muhammad from ibn Faddal from ibn Bukayr from 'Ubayd ibn Zurarah who has said the following:
"I once asked abu 'Abd Allah, *'Alayhi al-Salam*, about reading a chapter of the book in the form of an appeal for help in Salat (prayer) like Chapter 112. He (the Imam) said, 'If you read it in the form of appeal for help it is not harmful.'"

H 4905, Ch. 17, h 5

Ali ibn Ibrahim has narrated from his father from Hammad ibn 'Isa from certain persons of his people who has said the following:

"Abu 'Abd Allah, *'Alayhi al-Salam*, has said, 'Whatever (words) with which you speak to Allah in Salat (prayer) is not harmful.'"

(Ahadith 4-5 of this Chapter are best explained by fatwas.)

Chapter 18 - Commencement of Adhan, Iqamah, and the Excellence of Reading them

H 4906, Ch. 18, h 1

Ali ibn Ibrahim has narrated from his father from ibn abu 'Umayr from 'Umar ibn `Udhaynah from Zurarah from and al-Fadl who has said the following:

"Abu Ja'far, *'Alayhi al-Salam*, has said, 'When the Messenger of Allah was taken to the heaven upon his arrival in Bayt al-Ma'mur at the time of Salat (prayer), Jibril (Gabriel) said Adhan and Iqamah. The Messenger of Allah went ahead to lead and the angels and prophets lined up behind Prophet Muhammad for prayer.'"

H 4907, Ch. 18, h 2

Ali ibn Ibrahim has narrated from his father from ibn abu 'Umayr from Hammad from Mansur ibn Hazim who has said the following:

"Abu 'Abd Allah, *'Alayhi al-Salam*, has said that when Jibril (Gabriel) descended with Adhan to the Messenger of Allah, he was resting and his head was on Amir al-Mu'minin Ali's lap. Jibril then read Adhan and Iqamah. When the Messenger of Allah woke up he asked, 'O Ali, did you hear it?' He replied, 'Yes, I did.' He (the Messenger of Allah) asked, 'Do you remember it?' He (Ali) replied, 'Yes, I remember.' He (the Messenger of Allah) then said, 'Call Bilal and teach him.' Ali then called Bilal and taught him Adhan and Iqamah.'"

H 4908, Ch. 18, h 3

Ali ibn Ibrahim has narrated from Muhammad ibn 'Isa ibn 'Ubayd from Yunus from Aban ibn 'Uthman from `Isma'il al-Ju'fiy who has said the following:

"I once heard abu Ja'far, *'Alayhi al-Salam*, say, 'Adhan and 'Iqamah consist of thirty-five letters.' He (the Imam) counted them by his hand one by one; Adhan eighteen letters and 'Iqamah seventeen letters."

H 4909, Ch. 18, h 4

Ahmad ibn Idris has narrated from Ahmad ibn Muhammad from al-Husayn ibn Sa'id from ibn abu Najran from Safwan al-Jammal who has said the following:

"I once heard abu 'Abd Allah, *'Alayhi al-Salam*, say, 'Adhan is twice and twice and 'Iqamah is twice and twice.'"

H 4910, Ch. 18, h 5

Muhammad ibn `Isma'il has narrated from al-Fadl ibn Shadhan from Hammad ibn 'Isa from Hariz from Zurarah who has said the following:

"Abu Ja'far, *'Alayhi al-Salam*, once said, 'O Zurarah, begin Adhan with four Takbir (Allah is great beyond description) and end it with two Takbir (Allah is great beyond description) and two Tahlil, (no one deserves worship except Allah).'"

H 4911, Ch. 18, h 6

Ali ibn Ibrahim has narrated from Muhammad ibn 'Isa from Yunus from Mu'awiyah ibn Wahab who has said the following:

"I once asked abu 'Abd Allah, *'Alayhi al-Salam*, about tathwib (yawning) in Adhan and 'Iqamah. He (the Imam) said, 'We do not know it (experience it).'"

H 4912, Ch 18, h 7

Ali ibn Ibrahim has narrated from his father from Hammad ibn 'Isa from Hariz from Zurarah who has said the following:

"Abu Ja'far, *'Alayhi al-Salam*, has said, 'When you say Adhan say Alif and al-Ha' (two letters of Arabic alphabet) clearly and say O Allah, grant compensation to Muhammad and his family worthy of their services to Your cause whenever you mention his name or someone else mentions his name in Adhan or in other expressions.'"

H 4913, Ch. 18, h 8

Ali ibn Ibrahim has narrated from his father from ibn abu 'Umayr from Hammad from al-Halabiy who has said the following:

"Abu 'Abd Allah, *'Alayhi al-Salam*, has said that if you recite both Adhan and Iqamah, two rows of angels perform Salat (prayer) behind you. If you recite just Iqamah, only one row of angels performs Salat (prayer) behind you."

(Ahadith 3- 8 are best express in the form of fatwa.)

H 4914, Ch. 18, h 9

Muhammad ibn Yahya has narrated from Ahmad ibn Muhammad from al-Husayn ibn Sa'id from al-Qasim ibn Muhammad from Ali ibn abu Hamzah from abu Basir from who has said the following:

"I once asked one of the two Imam, *'Alayhi al-Salam*, 'Is one Adhan sufficient? He (the Imam) said, 'If you perform Salat (prayer) in congregation, there is one Adhan and one 'Iqamah. If you are alone and you are in a hurry so you do not lose something, then one 'Iqamah is sufficient, except the morning Salat (prayer) and al-Maghrib in which case, it is proper to say Adhan for them as well as 'Iqamah; they are not shortened as other Salat (prayers) are done.'"

H 4915, Ch. 18, h 10

Abu Dawud has narrated from al-Husayn ibn Sa'id from Fadalah from al-Husayn ibn 'Uthman from 'Amr ibn abu Nasr who has said the following:

"I once asked abu 'Abd Allah, *'Alayhi al-Salam*, "Can a man speak during Adhan?' He (the Imam) said, 'It is not harmful.' I then asked, about 'Iqamah. He (the Imam) said, 'No, it is not acceptable.'"

H 4916, Ch. 18, h 11

Ali ibn Ibrahim has narrated from his father from ibn abu 'Umayr from Hammad from al-Halabiy who has said the following:

"He (the Imam), *'Alayhi al-Salam*, has said, 'It is not harmful if a man says Adhan without Wudu' but he does not say 'Iqamah without it.'"

H 4917, Ch. 18, h 12

Ali ibn Ibrahim has narrated from his father from Salih ibn Sa'id from Yunus from ibn Muskan from abu Basir from who has said the following:

"I once asked him (the Imam), *'Alayhi al-Salam*, about a man who joins an Imam when he is saying Salam. He (the Imam) said, 'He is not required to repeat Adhan. He can join them with their Adhan, however if he finds them leaving, he then repeats Adhan.'"

H 4918, Ch. 18, h 13

Muhammad ibn Yahya has narrated from Ahmad ibn Muhammad from ibn al-Hassan ibn Ali from 'Amr ibn Sa'id from Musaddiq ibn Sadaqah from 'Ammar al-Sabatiy who has said the following:

"Once abu 'Abd Allah, *'Alayhi al-Salam*, was asked about Adhan if one who is not well versed can say Adhan. He (the Imam) said, 'Adhan does not come right and it is not permissible to say Adhan unless one is a Muslim man and knowledgeable. If he knows Adhan he says it, if he is not well versed it is not permissible for him to say it or 'Iqamah. One is not permitted to assign him to lead in Salat (prayer).' He (the Imam) was asked about a man who says Adhan and 'Iqamah so he can perform Salat (prayer) alone, and then another man comes and says, 'Allow us to perform Salat (prayer) in congregation.' Is it permissible that they perform Salat (prayer) with that Adhan and 'Iqamah?' He (the Imam) said, 'No, but he says Adhan and 'Iqamah.'"

H 4919, Ch. 18, h 14

Muhammad ibn 'Isma'il has narrated from al-Fadl ibn Shadhan from Safwan from al-'Ala' ibn Razin from Muhammad ibn Muslim who has said the following:

"Abu 'Abd Allah, *'Alayhi al-Salam*, has said, 'If a man forgets Adhan and 'Iqamah until he is in Salat (prayer), if he remembers before recitation he says O Allah, grant compensation to Muhammad and his family worthy of their services to Your cause and says 'Iqamah but if he has done the recitation he completes Salat (prayer)."

H 4920, Ch. 18, h 15

Muhammad ibn Yahya has narrated from Ahmad ibn Muhammad from Hammad from Hariz from Zurarah who has said the following:

"Abu 'Abd Allah, *'Alayhi al-Salam*, has said, 'If one by mistake, mixes up Adhan he repeats to correct the mix up all the way to the end.'"

H 4921, Ch. 18, h 16

Ali ibn Muhammad has narrated from Sahl ibn Ziyad from Ahmad ibn Muhammad from ibn abu Nasr who has said the following:

"Abu al-Hassan, *'Alayhi al-Salam*, has said, 'A man says Adhan when sitting but does not say 'Iqamah unless he is standing. You can say Adhan when riding but do not say 'Iqamah unless you are on the ground.'"

H 4922, Ch. 18, h 17

Ali ibn Ibrahim has narrated from his father from ibn abu 'Umayr from Hammad from al-Halabiy who has said the following:

"I once asked abu 'Abd Allah, *'Alayhi al-Salam*, 'Can a man say Adhan without facing al-Qiblah (al-Ka'bah)?' He (the Imam) said, 'If during saying the testimonies he faces al-Qiblah (al-Ka'bah), then it is not harmful.'"

H 4923, Ch. 18, h 18

Muhammad ibn 'Isma'il has narrated from al-Fadl ibn Shadhan from ibn abu 'Umayr from Jamil ibn Darraj who has said the following:

"I once asked abu 'Abd Allah, *'Alayhi al-Salam*, if a woman is required to say Adhan and 'Iqamah. He (the Imam) said, 'No, she is not required.'"

H 4924, Ch. 18, h 19

Ahmad ibn Idris has narrated from Ahmad ibn Muhammad from al-Husayn ibn Sa'id from Fadalah ibn Ayyub from Aban ibn 'Uthman from abu Maryam al-Ansariy who has said the following:

"I once heard abu 'Abd Allah, *'Alayhi al-Salam*, say, 'Women for 'Iqamah only say Takbir (Allah is great beyond description) and the two testimonies; (I testify that only Allah deserves worship, He is one and has no partners and I testify that Muhammad is His servant and Messenger).'"

H 4925, Ch. 18, h 20

Muhammad ibn Yahya has narrated from Muhammad ibn al-Husayn from Muhammad ibn 'Isma'il from Salih ibn 'Uqbah from abu Harun al-Makfuf who has said the following:

"Abu 'Abd Allah, *'Alayhi al-Salam*, has said, 'O abu Harun, 'Iqamah is part of Salat (prayer). When you say it do not speak or point with your hands.'"

H 4926, Ch. 18, h 21

Through the same chain of narrators as that of the previous Hadith the following is narrated from Salih ibn 'Uqbah from Sulayman ibn Salih who has said the following:

"Abu 'Abd Allah, *'Alayhi al-Salam*, has said, 'No one among you says 'Iqamah for Salat (prayer) when walking, riding or resting unless one is ill. One remains well placed during 'Iqamah like in Salat (prayer). In 'Iqamah one is in Salat (prayer).'"

H 4927, Ch. 18, h 22

Al-Husayn ibn Muhammad al-Ash'ariy has narrated from 'Abd Allah ibn 'Amir from Ali ibn Mahziyar from ibn abu 'Umayr from abu Ayyub from Mu'adh ibn Kathir who has said the following:

"Abu 'Abd Allah, *'Alayhi al-Salam*, has said, 'A man may enter a Masjid and is not following his companion in Salat (prayer). He finds the Imam has only one verse to recite or two verses. He is afraid of not being able to join the Imam in Ruku' (bowing down on one's knees) if he says Adhan or 'Iqamah. He can say, 'Salat (prayer) has began, Salat (prayer) has began, Allah is great beyond description, Allah is great beyond description. No one deserves worship except Allah,' he then can begin al-Salat (prayer).'"

H 4928, Ch. 18, h 23

Muhammad ibn Yahya has narrated from Ahmad ibn Muhammad ibn 'Isa from al-Husayn ibn Sa'id from al-Nadr ibn Suwayd from Yahya ibn 'Imran ibn Ali al-Halabiy who has said the following:

"I once asked abu 'Abd Allah, *'Alayhi al-Salam*, about Adhan before dawn. He (the Imam) said, 'If it is for congregation, it is not acceptable, but if one is alone, then it is not harmful.'"

H 4929, Ch. 18, h 24

Muhammad ibn al-Husayn has narrated from Sahl ibn Ziyad from Ahmad ibn Muhammad from ibn abu Nasr who has said the following:

"Abu al-Hassan, *'Alayhi al-Salam*, has said, 'There is sitting between Adhan and 'Iqamah for all Salat (prayer) if before 'Iqamah, other Salat (prayer) is not performed.'"

H 4930, Ch. 18, h 25

Ali ibn Ibrahim has narrated from his father from Ali ibn Mahziyar from certain persons of our people from 'Isma'il ibn Jabir who has said the following:

"Abu 'Abd Allah, *'Alayhi al-Salam,* would say Adhan and someone else would say 'Iqamah.' He (the narrator) has said that Abu 'Abd Allah, *'Alayhi al-Salam,* would say 'Iqamah and someone else would say Adhan.'"

H 4931, Ch. 18, h 26

A group of our people has narrated from Ahmad ibn Muhammad ibn 'Isa from Muhammad ibn Sinan from al-Hassan ibn al-Sariy who has said the following:

"Abu 'Abd Allah, *'Alayhi al-Salam*, has said, 'Adhan is said with Tartil (articulation slowly) and 'Iqamah is said quickly.'"

H 4932, Ch. 18, h 27

Muhammad ibn Yahya has narrated from Ahmad ibn Muhammad from ibn abu Najran in a marfu' manner who has said the following:

"Three things on the Day of Judgment are on sands of musk. One of them is one who says Adhan just for the sake of Allah."

H 4933, Ch. 18, h 28

Muhammad has narrated from Ahmad from al-Husayn ibn Sa'id from al-Nadr ibn Suwayd from Yahya ibn 'Imran al-Halabiy from Muhammad ibn Marwan who has said the following:

"I heard abu 'Abd Allah, *'Alayhi al-Salam*, say, 'One who recites Adhan receives forgiveness for the sins as big as the space his voice fills and everything hearing him bears witness to this fact.'"

(Ahadith 9-28 are best expressed in the form of fatwa.)

H 4934, Ch. 18, h 29

Muhammad ibn 'Isma'il has narrated from al-Fadl ibn Shadhan from Hammad ibn 'Isa from Rib'iy ibn 'Abd Allah from Muhammad ibn Muslim who has said the following:

"Abu Ja'far, *'Alayhi al-Salam*, has said, 'When someone recited Adhan, the Messenger of Allah on hearing him would say everything the person reciting Adhan would say."

H 4935, Ch. 18, h 30

Ali ibn Muhammad has narrated from Sahl ibn Ziyad from ibn Mahbub from Jamil ibn Salih from al-Harith ibn al-Mughirah al-Nadriy who has said the following:

"Abu 'Abd Allah, *'Alayhi al-Salam*, has said that one may hear someone recite Adhan and say, 'I testify that no one deserves to be worshipped except Allah and I testify that Muhammad is the Messenger of Allah and I affirm and acknowledge.' If he also says, 'I testify that no one deserves to be worshipped except Allah and that Muhammad is the Messenger of Allah and I consider them both sufficient for me against all who deny and reject these (the two testimonies). I seek assistance from those who affirm and testify to the two testimonies.' His reward is equal to the number of those who have denied and rejected them and those who have affirmed and testified to these testimonies."

H 4936, Ch. 18, h 31

Ali ibn Muhammad has narrated from Sahl ibn Ziyad from ibn Mahbub from 'Abd Allah ibn Sinan who has said the following:

"Abu 'Abd Allah, *'Alayhi al-Salam*, has said that the height of the wall of the Masjid of the Messenger of Allah was equal to the height of a man. He, the Messenger of Allah would say to Bilal, 'When time comes, O Bilal, climb on the wall and raise your voice with Adhan. Allah has assigned a wind to raise Adhan to the heaven and that the angels upon hearing Adhan from the people of earth say, "This is the voice of the followers of Prophet Muhammad about oneness of Allah, the Most Majestic, the Most Glorious." They ask forgiveness for the followers of Muhammad, O Allah grant compensation to Muhammad and his family worthy of their services to Your cause, until they complete that prayer.'"

H 4937, Ch. 18, h 32

Al-Husayn ibn Muhammad has narrated from 'Abd Allah ibn 'Amir from Ali ibn Mahziyar from al-Husayn ibn Asad from Ja'far ibn Muhammad ibn Yaqzan in a marfu' manner from the Imam who has said the following:

"He (the Imam), *'Alayhi al-Salam*, has said, 'When one completes reciting Adhan and sits down he should say, "O Lord, make my heart virtuous, my livelihood constant, my sustenance to come continuously and assign for me a place near the grave of your prophet to rest and dwell."'"

H 4938, Ch. 18, h 33

Ali ibn Mahziyar has narrated from Muhammad ibn Rashid who has said that narrated to me Hisham ibn Ibrahim who has said the following:

"I complained before abu al-Hassan al-Rida, *'Alayhi al-Salam*, against an illness and that I do not have any child. He commanded me, 'Recite Adhan in your home loudly.' I followed his instruction. The illness was gone and my children became numerous." Muhammad ibn Rashid has said, 'I was always ill, myself, a group of my servants and my family. When I heard the above Hadith from Hisham I practiced it. Allah removed the illness from me and my family altogether.'"

H 4939, Ch. 18, h 34

Muhammad ibn Yahya has narrated from Ahmad ibn Muhammad from ibn Mahbub from Ali ibn abu Hamzah from abu Basir from who has said the following:

"Abu 'Abd Allah, *'Alayhi al-Salam*, has said, 'If when saying Adhan one repeats the phrases of the 'testimonies' or 'come to Salat (prayer)' or 'to salvation' three times or more with the intention of calling people to come together, it is not harmful.'"

H 4940, Ch. 18, h 35

A group has narrated from Ahmad ibn Muhammad ibn 'Isa from al-Husayn ibn Sa'id from Sulayman al-Ja'fariy who has said the following:

"I once heard him (the Imam), *'Alayhi al-Salam*, say, 'Say Adhan in your house; it repels Satan and it is a beloved thing to do for the sake of children.'"

(Hadith 34 and 35 are best be explained by fatwa.)

Chapter 19 - Words to Say When Entering and Leaving a Masjid

H 4941, Ch. 19, h 1

Ali ibn Ibrahim has narrated from his father from Salih ibn Sa'id al-Rashidiy from Yunus who has said the following:

"'A'immah, *'Alayhim al-Salam*, have said, 'When entering a Masjid, it is better to step in with the right foot and to step out with left foot when leaving a Masjid."

H 4942, Ch. 19, h 2

Ali has narrated from his father from 'Abd Allah ibn al-Mughirah from 'Abd Allah ibn Sinan who has said the following:

"Abu 'Abd Allah, *'Alayhi al-Salam*, has said that when entering and leaving a Masjid say, 'Allahumma Salli 'Ala Muhammad wa 'Ali Muhammad (O Allah grant Muhammad and his family a compensation worthy of their serving Your cause).'"

H 4943, Ch. 19, h 3

It is a narration from him (narrator of previous Hadith) by his father from al-Husayn ibn Sa'id from Fadalah from Aban and Mu'awiyah ibn Wahab who have said the following:

"Abu 'Abd Allah, *'Alayhi al-Salam*, has said that when you stand up for Salat (prayer), say this: 'O Allah, I consider Muhammad, O Allah grant compensation to Muhammad and his family worthy of their services to Your cause, to be in front of me in Your presence along with my wishes and needs and I turn to You through him. For the sake of his position before You, grant me honor in this and the next world and include me among those near You. Make my Salat (prayer) accepted through him, my sins forgiven and my prayer and wishes granted. You are forgiving and merciful.'""

H 4944, Ch. 19, h 4

Al-Husayn ibn Muhammad has narrated from 'Abd Allah ibn 'Amir from Ali ibn Mahziyar from Ja'far ibn Muhammad al-Hashimiy from abu Hafs al-'Attar –Shaykh of the people of Madinah who has said the following:

"I heard abu 'Abd Allah, *'Alayhi al-Salam*, say. 'The Messenger of Allah has said, "When any one of you after completing an obligatory Salat (prayer), wants to leave a Masjid he should stand at the door and say, 'O Lord You called me and I answered Your call. I performed my obligatory Salat (prayer). I want to move in Your land as You have commanded me. Now I ask You to help me to act in Your obedience, avoid making You angry with me and suffice me in matters of my sustenance through Your mercy.'"'"

Chapter 20 - The Opening Readings When Commencing Salat (prayer)

H 4945, Ch. 20, h 1

Ali ibn Ibrahim has narrated from his father from ibn abu 'Umayr from Jamil ibn Darraj from Zurarah who has said the following:

"One of the two Imam, *'Alayhim al-Salam*, has said, 'Raise your hands when commencing Salat (prayer) on the sides of your face and do not raise them all the way farther.'"

H 4946, Ch. 20, h 2

It is a narration from him (narrator of previous Hadith) by his father from Hammad from Hariz from Zurarah who has said the following:

"Abu Ja'far, *'Alayhi al-Salam*, has said, 'When you stand up for Salat (prayer) say Takbir (Allah is great beyond description) and raise your hands. Do not allow your palms (hands) to rise higher than your ears. Keep them on the sides of your face.'"

H 4947, Ch. 20, h 3

It is a narration from him (narrator of previous Hadith) by his father Hammad ibn 'Isa from Hariz from Zurarah who has said the following:

"He (the Imam), *'Alayhi al-Salam*, has said, 'The least for Takbir (Allah is great beyond description) facing (al-Qiblah (al-Ka'bah)) is to say it once. Three times is good and seven times is better.'"

H 4948, Ch. 20, h 4

Muhammad ibn 'Isma'il has narrated from al-Fadl ibn Shadhan from Hammad ibn 'Isa from Mu'awiyah ibn 'Ammar who has said the following:

"Abu 'Abd Allah, *'Alayhi al-Salam*, has said, 'If you are leading others in Salat (prayer) one Takbir (Allah is great beyond description) is sufficient; with you there can be people who need to go after their needs, weak people and the old ones.'"

H 4949, Ch. 20, h 5

Ali ibn Ibrahim has narrated from his father from ibn abu 'Umayr from Mu'awiyah ibn 'Ammar who has said the following:

"Abu 'Abd Allah, *'Alayhi al-Salam*, has said, 'The number of Takbir (Allah is great beyond description) in all five obligatory Salat (prayer) is ninety-five of which are Takbir (Allah is great beyond description) during five Qunut.'"

H 4950, Ch. 20, h 6

He (Ali ibn Ibrahim) has narrated it also from his father from 'Abd Allah ibn al-Mughirah.

In explaining he has said that in al-Zuhr there are twenty-one, in al-'Asr twenty-one, in al-Maghrib sixteen, in al-'Isha' al-Akhirah twenty-one and in the morning Salat (prayer) there are eleven and in the five Qunut there are five Takbir (Allah is great beyond description).

H 4951, Ch. 20, h 7

Ali ibn Ibrahim ibn Hashim has narrated from his father from ibn abu 'Umayr from Hammad ibn 'Uthman from al-Halabiy who has said the following:

"Abu 'Abd Allah, *'Alayhi al-Salam*, has said that as introduction for prayer raise your hands and open them, then say three times, 'Allah is great and then say, 'O Lord, You are the true owner. No one other than You deserves to be worshipped. You are free of all defects. I have wronged myself so forgive my sins; no one other than You is able to forgive sins.' Then say two times, 'Allah is great.' Then say, '(O Lord), here I am to obey Your command and asking help from You (to accomplish my duty); all good is in Your hands and evil has no way toward You. Guided are those whom You have granted guidance. There is no place of refuge from You (Your anger) except in Your presence. You are free of all defects and compassionate, the most Blessed, the most High. You are free of all defects and You are the Lord of the House.' Then say two times, 'Allah is great.' Then say. 'I have turned my face toward the One who has created the skies and the earth. He has knowledge of the unseen and seen. I am humble before and submitted to the will of Allah and I am not one of the pagans. My Salat (prayer), my practices, my life and my death are all for the sake of Allah, Cherisher of the worlds. He has no partner. I am commanded to speak as such and I am the first Muslim.' Then seek refuge with Allah against Satan, who is subject to stoning and then read al-Fatihah."

H 4952, Ch. 20, h 8

Ali ibn Ibrahim has narrated from his father from Hammad ibn 'Isa who has said the following:

"Abu 'Abd Allah, *'Alayhi al-Salam*, one day asked me, 'Do you know how to perform Salat (prayer) properly?' I said, 'I keep the book of Hariz with me in Salat (prayer).' The Imam said, 'Nevermind, O Hammad. Stand up and perform Salat (prayer).' The narrator has said, 'I then stood up in his presence, facing the direction of Qiblah (Makkah). I began performing Salat (prayer), with Ruku' and Sajdah.' He then said, "O Hammad, you do not know how to perform Salat (prayer) properly. It is a shame for a man of your people who at the age of sixty or seventy cannot even perform one Salat (prayer) according to its complete rules and manners.' Hammad has said, 'I belittled myself very much at this point. I then asked him saying, "I pray to Allah to keep my soul in service for your cause teach me how to perform Salat (prayer) properly."' Abu 'Abd Allah, *'Alayhi al-Salam*, stood up straight facing the direction of Qiblah. He allowed his hands to rest on his thighs, with his fingers close side by side, kept his feet near each other, only leaving between them a distance of three fingers opened up, with his toes facing the direction of Qiblah without allowing them to deviate from this direction and with humbleness said, 'Allah is great.' He then recited al-Hamd (the first Chapter of the Holy Quran) with clarity and fluency and Chapter 112 of the Holy Quran. He then paused for a breath while still standing and raised his hands up to the sides of his face and said, 'Allah is great,' while still standing. He then bent down for Ruku' (kneeling). He then placed his palms over his knees allowing them to be filled up with his knees that were separate from each other, and pressed them backward until his back became so straightly level that even if there had been a drop of water or oil it would not flow to any side. He stretched his neck forward, lowered his eyes and then said with clarity and fluency three times, 'I praise my Lord, the Great, Who is free of all defects.' He then stood up straight. While standing straight he said, 'Allah hears all those who praise Him.' He then while standing raised his hands up to the sides of his face and said, 'Allah is great.' Then he bowed down for sajdah. He opened his palms with his fingers close side by side, placed them near his knees on the sides next to his face and said, 'I praise my Lord, the most High who is free of all defects,' three times. He did not place any other part of his body on any other part thereof. He performed sajdah on eight parts of his bones: his palms, knees, big toes of his feet, his forehead and his nose. He (the Imam) said, 'Placing seven parts of these bones on the ground is obligatory during sajdah but one of them (the nose) is not obligatory. This is what Allah has spoken of in the Quran, "The parts of the body to be placed on the ground during sajdah belong to Allah, you then must not worship anyone other than Allah." (72:17) Such parts are forehead, palms, knees and big toes of feet. Placing one's nose on the ground is optional.' He then raised his head from sajdah. When he sat up straight, he then said, 'Allah is great.' He then sat on his left thigh placing the back of his right foot over the sole of his left foot and then said, 'I seek forgiveness from Allah, my Lord and turn to Him in repentance.' He then said, 'Allah is great.' Then he bowed down for second sajdah, saying therein what he said in the first sajdah. He did not place any other part of his body on any other part during Ruku' or sajdah. He spread his elbows and did not place his arms on the ground. In this way, he performed two Rak'ats of Salat (prayer). He (the Imam) kept the fingers of his hands close side by side when saying the two testimonies in a sitting position. When he finished saying the testimonies, he then read Salam and said, 'O Hammad, you must perform Salat (prayer) like this.'"

(Ahadith 2-7 are best explained by fatwa.)

Chapter 21/22 - Recitations in Salat (prayer)

H 4953, Ch. 21/22, h 1

Ali ibn Ibrahim has narrated from Muhammad ibn 'Isa from Yunus from Mu'awiyah ibn 'Ammar who has said the following:

"I once asked abu 'Abd Allah, *'Alayhi al-Salam*, 'When I stand up for Salat (prayer) can I read, "In the name of Allah, most Beneficent, most Merciful" in the beginning of the recitation?' He (the Imam) said, 'Yes, you can do so.' I then asked, 'When I complete reading al-Fatihah can I read "In the name of Allah, most Beneficent, most Merciful" in the beginning of the chapter?' He (the Imam) said, 'Yes, you can do so.'"

H 4954, Ch. 21/22, h 2

Muhammad ibn Yahya has narrated from Ahmad ibn Muhammad from Ali ibn Mahziyar from Yahya ibn abu 'Imran al-Hamdaniy who has said the following:

"I once wrote to abu Ja'far, *'Alayhi al-Salam*, and asked. 'I pray to Allah to keep my soul in service for your cause, what do you say about a man who says "In the name of Allah, most Beneficent, most Merciful" in the beginning of 'Umm al-Kitab, when performing Salat (prayer) alone. After completing 'Umm al-Kitab he does not say it before the chapter (surah) and al-'Abbasiy says that it is not harmful?' He (the Imam) wrote with his own handwriting, 'He reads it again, he reads it again twice to emphasise against al-'Abbasiy.'"

(Ahadith 1-2 are best explained in the form of fatwa.)

H 4955, Ch. 21/22, h 3

Muhammad ibn Yahya has narrated from Ali ibn al-Hassan ibn Ali from ‘Abbad ibn Ya‘qub from ‘Amr ibn Mus’ab from Furat ibn Ahnaf who has said the following:

“I heard abu Ja‘far, *‘Alayhi al-Salam,* say, ‘Every book that has come from the heavens begins with “In the name of Allah, the Beneficent, the Merciful.”’ When you read, ‘In the name of Allah, the Beneficent, the Merciful’ it is then not an offense not to read: ‘I seek refuge with Allah against Satan, the condemned one.’ When you read, ‘In the name of Allah, the Beneficent, the Merciful’, it protects you from things between the sky and earth.”

H 4956, Ch. 21/22, h 4

Ali ibn Ibrahim has narrated from Muhammad ibn ‘Isa from Yunus ibn ‘Abd al-Rahman from abu Ayyub al-Khazzaz from Muhammad ibn Muslim who has said the following:

“I once asked abu ‘Abd Allah, *‘Alayhi al-Salam,* ‘Is there any temporary recitation in Salat (prayer)? He (the Imam) replied, ‘No, except Friday in which you recite al-Jumu‘ah, and al-Munafiqun, (Chapters 62 and 63).’”

H 4957, Ch. 21/22, h 5

Ali has narrated from his father from ‘Abd Allah ibn al-Mughirah from Jamil who has said the following:

“Abu ‘Abd Allah, *‘Alayhi al-Salam,* has said, ‘If you are behind an Imam when he completes reading al-Hamd you say, ‘all praise belongs to Allah, Cherisher of the worlds,’ and do not say ‘Amen.’”

(Ahadith 4-5 are best explained in the form of fatwa.)

H 4958, Ch. 21/22, h 6

Ali ibn Ibrahim has narrated from his father from ibn abu ‘Umayr from ‘Umar ibn ‘Udhaynah and ibn Bukayr from Zurarah who has said the following:

“Abu Ja’far, *‘Alayhi al-Salam,* has said, ‘Of recitations and prayers, only such recitations and prayers are counted which one has made his own self to hear.’”

H 4959, Ch. 21/22, h 7

Abu Dawud has narrated from al-Husayn ibn Sa‘id from Muhammad ibn Sinan from ibn Muskan from Hassan al-Sayqal who has said the following:

“I once asked abu ‘Abd Allah, *‘Alayhi al-Salam,* ‘Is it sufficient for me to read just al-Fatihah in an obligatory Salat (prayer) if I am in a hurry or something causes me to move quickly?’ He (the Imam) replied, ‘It is not harmful.’”

H 4960, Ch. 21/22, h 8

Muhammad ibn Yahya has narrated from al-Husayn ibn abu Najran from Safwan al-Jammal who has said the following:

“Abu ‘Abd Allah, *‘Alayhi al-Salam,* once led us in al-Maghrib Salat (prayer) and recited al-Ma‘udhatayn in two Rak‘at.”

H 4961, Ch. 21/22, h 9

Ali ibn Ibrahim has narrated from Muhammad ibn ‘Isa from Yunus from ‘Abd Allah ibn Sinan who has said the following:

"Abu 'Abd Allah, *'Alayhi al-Salam*, has said, 'It is permissible for one suffering from illness to recite just al-Fatihah in an obligatory Salat (prayer) as well as for one in good health in Qada' (compensatory prayer) of optional Salat (prayer) missed during the day or night.'"

H 4962, Ch. 21/22, h 10

Muhammad ibn Yahya has narrated from Muhammad ibn al-Husayn from Safwan from ibn Bukayr from Zurarah who has said the following:

"Abu Ja'far, *'Alayhi al-Salam*, has said, 'It is undesirable to recite two Surah (chapters) together in an obligatory Salat (prayer) but in an optional one it is not harmful.'"

(Ahadith 7-11 are best explained in the form of fatwa.)

H 4963, Ch. 21/22, h 11

Muhammad ibn Yahya through the chain of his narrators has narrated who has said the following:

"Abu 'Abd Allah, *'Alayhi al-Salam*, has said that it is not desirable to recite all of Chapter 112 in one breath."

H 4964, Ch. 21/22, h 12

Ahmad ibn Idris has narrated from Muhammad ibn Ahmad from Muhammad ibn 'Abd al-Hamid from Sayf ibn 'Amirah from Mansur ibn Hazim who has said the following:

"Abu 'Abd Allah, *'Alayhi al-Salam*, has said, 'You must not read less than a Surah (Chapter) in an obligatory Salat (prayer) or more.'"

H 4965, Ch. 21/22, h 13

Abu Dawud has narrated from Ali ibn Mahziyar from through chain of his narrators from Safwan al-Jammal who has said the following:

"I once heard abu 'Abd Allah, *'Alayhi al-Salam*, say, 'Salat (prayer) of repenting people with all fifty of them there is Chapter 112.'"

H 4966, Ch. 21/22, h 14

Muhammad ibn Yahya has narrated from Muhammad ibn al-Husayn from Muhammad ibn 'Isma'il from Salih ibn 'Uqbah from abu Harun al-Makfuf who has said the following:

"A man once asked abu 'Abd Allah, *'Alayhi al-Salam*, when I was present, 'How much one recites when it is Zawal (declining of the sun toward the west at noontime)?' He (the Imam) said, 'One recites eighty verses.' The man then left. He (the Imam) said, 'O abu Harun, have you ever seen an old man more strange than this man who asked me about something which I answered but did not ask me about its explanation? This is a man about whom people of Iraq think, is the wisest among them. O abu Harun, al-Hamd has seven verses and 112 has three verses all together become ten verses. At noontime there are eight Rak'at and this makes it eighty verses.'" (According to 'A'immah Chapter 112 may consist of three verses).

H 4967, Ch. 21/22, h 15

It is a narration from him (narrator of previous Hadith) by Muhammad ibn al-Husayn from ibn Mahbub from ibn Ri'ab from al-Halabiy who has said the following:

"I once asked abu 'Abd Allah, *'Alayhi al-Salam*, 'Can one recite in Salat (prayer) with his clothes on his mouth? He (the Imam) said, 'It is not harmful if his ears can hear his humming.'"

H 4968, Ch. 21/22, h 16

Ahmad ibn Idris has narrated from Muhammad ibn Ahmad from Ya'qub ibn Yazid from Muhammad ibn abu Hamzah from those whom he has mentioned who has said the following:

"Abu 'Abd Allah, *'Alayhi al-Salam*, has said, 'When performing Salat (prayer) with them (other people) it is sufficient to recite like speaking to one's soul.'"

H 4969, Ch. 21/22, h 17

Ali ibn Ibrahim has narrated from his father from al-Nawfaliy from al-Sakuniy who has said the following:

"Abu 'Abd Allah, *'Alayhi al-Salam*, has said, 'The recitation of a speechless person in Talbiyah, Tashahhud and readings from al-Quran in Salat (prayer) is by moving his tongue and pointing with his finger.'"

H 4970, Ch. 21/22, h 18

It is a narration from him (narrator of previous Hadith) by Muhammad ibn Ahmad from Ahmad ibn al-Hassan ibn Ali ibn Faddal from 'Amr ibn Sa'id al-Mada'iniy from Musaddiq ibn Sadaqah from 'Ammar ibn Musa who has said the following:

"I once asked abu 'Abd Allah, *'Alayhi al-Salam*, about a man who forgets a letter of the recitation and remembers it in Ruku' (bowing down on one's knees); is it permissible for him to recite in Ruku'? He (the Imam) said, 'No, it is not permissible but he recites in Sujud (prostration).'"

H 4971, Ch. 21/22, h 19

Ali ibn Muhammad has narrated from Sahl ibn Ziyad from Ahmad ibn 'Ubdus from Muhammad ibn Zawiyah from abu Ali ibn Rashid who has said the following:

"I said to abu al-Hassan, *'Alayhi al-Salam*, 'May Allah keep my soul in service for your cause, you have written to Muhammad ibn al-Faraj telling him that the most excellent recitation in obligatory Salat (prayer) are chapters 97 and 112 of the Holy Quran. I feel uneasy reciting them in morning Salat (prayer).' The Imam said, 'You should not feel uneasy to recite them, by Allah, excellence is in reciting these two chapters.'"

(Ahadith 12-19 are best explained in the form of fatwa.)

H 4972, Ch. 21/22, h 20

Muhammad ibn Yahya has narrated from Ahmad ibn Muhammad from al-Husayn ibn Sa'id from al-Qasim ibn Muhammad from Safwan al-Jammal who has said the following:

"I performed Salat (prayer) for many days in congregation led by abu 'Abd Allah, *'Alayhi al-Salam*, and in Salat (prayer) which is not recited loudly, he would read Bismillah, (in the name of Allah, most Beneficent, most Merciful) aloud in both Surah (chapters)."

H 4973, Ch. 21/22, h 21

It is a narration from him (narrator of previous Hadith) by Ahmad ibn Muhammad from 'Uthman ibn 'Isa from Sama'ah who has said the following:

"I once asked him (the Imam), *'Alayhi al-Salam*, about the words of Allah, most Majestic, most Glorious, 'Do not be loud in your Salat (prayer) nor very quiet.' (17:110) He (the Imam) said, 'Quiet is when you do not hear it, and loud is when you raise your voice very loud.'"

H 4974, Ch. 21/22, h 22

Ali ibn Ibrahim has narrated from his father from 'Abd Allah ibn al-Mughirah who has said that narrated to him Mu'adh ibn Muslim who has said the following:

"Abu 'Abd Allah, *'Alayhi al-Salam*, has said, 'You must not miss reading Surah (chapter) 112 and 109 in seven instances. Read them in the two Rak'at before dawn, in the two Rak'at at noontime, in the two Rak'at after al-Maghrib, in the first two Rak'at of the night Salat (prayer), the two Rak'at for Ihram. Read them in the two Rak'at of the morning if you begin the morning with them and the two Rak'at for Tawaf.'" "In another Hadith it is said that in all of these Surah (Chapter) 112 is read first and in the second Rak'at is Surah (Chapter) 109 except for the two Rak'at before the morning in which Surah (Chapter) 109 is read first and in the second Rak'at Surah (chapter) 112 is read."

H 4975, Ch. 21/22, h 23

Muhammad ibn Yahya has narrated from Ahmad ibn Muhammad from Ali ibn al-Hakam from al-'Ala' ibn Razin from Muhammad ibn Muslim who has said the following:

"Abu 'Abd Allah, *'Alayhi al-Salam*, was asked about a man who leads people in Salat (prayer) and makes a mistake. He (the Imam) said, 'Those behind him open it up for him (help to correct him).'"

H 4976, Ch. 21/22, h 24

Ali ibn Ibrahim has narrated from his father from al-Nawfaliy from al-Sakuniy who has said the following:

"Abu 'Abd Allah, *'Alayhi al-Salam*, has said that a man may stand up in a certain place to perform Salat (prayer). He then wants to move forward. He in such case stops reading when he is walking forward, until he reaches the place that he wants, then reads.'"

H 4977, Ch. 21/22, h 25

Al-Husayn ibn Muhammad has narrated from as ibn 'Amir from Ali ibn Mahziyar from Fadalah ibn Ayyub from al-Husayn ibn 'Uthman from 'Amr ibn abu Nasr who has said the following:

"I once said to abu 'Abd Allah, *'Alayhi al-Salam*, that a man stands up for Salat (prayer), wants to read a Surah (chapter) and he reads Surah (chapter) 112 and Surah (chapter) 109. He (the Imam) said, 'He can discontinue reading any Surah (chapter) except Surah (chapter) 112 and Surah (chapter) 109.'"

H 4978, Ch. 21/22, h 26

Muhammad ibn Yahya has narrated from Ahmad ibn Muhammad from Ali ibn al-Hakam from Sayf ibn 'Amirah from Dawud ibn Farqad from Sabir Mawla' Bassam who has said the following:

"Once, abu 'Abd Allah, *'Alayhi al-Salam*, led us in al-Maghrib Salat (prayer). He read al-M'udhatayn (chapters 113, 114) and said that they are of al-Quran.'"

H 4979, Ch. 21/22, h 27

Ali ibn Ibrahim has narrated from Muhammad ibn 'Isa from Yunus ibn 'Abd al-Rahman from 'Abd Allah ibn Sinan who has said the following:

"I once said to abu 'Abd Allah, *'Alayhi al-Salam,* 'Is it necessary for an Imam to read so that people behind him can hear his reading even if they are many?' He (the Imam) said, 'He reads moderately; Allah, most Blessed, most High, has said, "Do not be very loud in your Salat (prayer) nor very quiet."''" (17:110)

H 4980, Ch. 21/22, h 28
Ali ibn Muhammad has narrated from 'Isa from Yunus from al-'Ala' from Muhammad ibn Muslim who has said the following:
"I once asked him (the Imam), *'Alayhi al-Salam,* about one who does not read al-Fatihah in his Salat (prayer). He (the Imam) said, 'His Salat (prayer) is not valid. He must begin with it (al-Fatihah) that which is read aloud or quietly.' I then asked, 'Which one is more beloved to you: if one is afraid or in a hurry, is it reading a Surah (chapter) or al-Fatihah of al-Kitab?' He (the Imam) said, 'al-Fatihah of al-Kitab is more beloved.'"

(Ahadith 20-28 are best explained in the form of fatwa.)

Chapter 23 - Reading Chapters of the Holy Quran Which Involve Obligatory Sajdah

H 4981, Ch. 23, h 1
A group has narrated from Ahmad ibn Muhammad ibn 'Isa from al-Husayn ibn Sa'id from al-Nadr ibn Suwayd 'Abd Allah ibn Sinan who has said the following:
"Abu 'Abd Allah, *'Alayhi al-Salam,* has said, 'If you read of al-'Aza''im something for which there is Sajdah (prostration), do not say Takbir (Allah is great beyond description) before Sajdah (prostration) but say it when raising your head from Sajdah (prostration). Al-'Aza''im are four: Ha mim al-Sajdah, Tanzil, al-Najm and 'Iqra' bisme rabbik.'" (Chapters 32, 41, 53 and 96)

H 4982, Ch. 23, h 2
Muhammad ibn Yahya has narrated from Ahmad ibn Muhammad from al-Husayn ibn Sa'id from al-Qasim ibn Muhammad from Ali ibn abu Hamzah from abu Basir from who has said the following:
"He (the Imam), *'Alayhi al-Salam,* has said, 'If anything of the four al-'Aza''im is read and you hear them, perform Sajdah (prostration), even if you are not with a valid Wudu', or have experienced sexual relation, even if a woman does not perform Salat (prayer) (due to Hayd (menses)). In the case of the rest of al-Quran, you can perform Sajdah (prostration) or do not perform, it is your choice.'"

H 4983, Ch. 23, h 3
Ali ibn Ibrahim has narrated from Muhammad ibn 'Isa from 'Ubayd ibn Yunus ibn 'Abd al-Rahman from 'Abd Allah ibn Sinan who has said the following:
"I once asked abu 'Abd Allah, *'Alayhi al-Salam,* about a man who has heard Sajdah (prostration) is read. He (the Imam) said, 'He is not required to perform Sajdah (prostration) unless he is quiet and listening to the reading or performs Salat (prayer) with his Salat (prayer) (he reader of the Chapter with Sajdah (prostration) being the Imam). If one reads Sajdah (prostration) when

performing Salat (prayer) in one side and you are performing Salat (prayer) in another side, you do not do Sajdah (prostration) even on hearing such reading.'"

H 4984, Ch. 23, h 4

Ahmad ibn Idris from Ahmad ibn Muhammad from al-Husayn ibn Sa'id from Fadalah ibn Ayyub from al-Husayn ibn 'Uthman from Sama'ah from abu Basir from who has said the following:

"Abu 'Abd Allah, *'Alayhi al-Salam*, has said that if you perform Salat (prayer) with a people and the Imam reads bisme rabbik (Chapter 96) or something of al-'Aza'im, completes his reading and does not do Sajdah (prostration), you just make a gesture for it. A woman experiencing Hayd (menses) must perform Sajdah (prostration) when listening to such reading.'"

H 4985, Ch. 23, h 5

Ali ibn Ibrahim has narrated from his father from ibn abu 'Umayr from Hammad from al-Halabiy who has said the following:

"Abu 'Abd Allah, *'Alayhi al-Salam*, was asked about a man who reads (verses) Sajdah (prostration) in the last Surah (chapter). He (the Imam) said, 'He must perform Sajdah (prostration), then stand up, read al-Fatihah al-Kitab, then perform Ruku' (bowing down on one's knees) and Sajdah (prostration).'"

H 4986, Ch. 23, h 6

Muhammad ibn Yahya has narrated from Ahmad ibn Muhammad from al-Husayn ibn Sa'id from al-al-Qasim ibn 'Urwah from ibn Bukayr from Zurarah who has said the following:

"One of the two Imam, *'Alayhim al-Salam*, has said, 'You must not read anything of al-'Aza''im in any of obligatory Salat (prayer); Sajdah (prostration) becomes an addition in an obligatory Salat (prayer).'"

Chapter 24 - Reading in the Last Two Rak'at and Tasbih Therein

H 4987, Ch. 24, h 1

Al-Husayn ibn Muhammad has narrated from 'Abd Allah ibn 'Amir from Ali ibn Mahziyar from al-Nadr ibn Suwayd from Muhammad ibn abu Hamzah from Mu'awiyah ibn 'Ammar who has said the following:

"I once asked abu 'Abd Allah, *'Alayhi al-Salam*, about reading in the case of one who performs behind an Imam in last two Rak'at. He (the Imam) said, 'He reads al-Fatihah al-Kitab and everyone behind him reads Tasbih. When performing Salat (prayer) alone, read (al-Fatihah) in the two last Rak'at or say Tasbih if you like.'"

H 4988, Ch. 24, h 2

Muhammad ibn 'Isma'il has narrated from al-Fadl ibn Shadhan from Hammad ibn 'Isa from Hariz from Zurarah who has said the following:

"I once asked abu Ja'far, *'Alayhi al-Salam*, about what is a sufficient reading in the last two Rak'at. He (the Imam) said, 'Say Tasbih (Allah is free of all defects), Tahmid (it is Allah only who deserves all praise), Tahlil (no one deserves worship except Allah), and Takbir (Allah is great beyond description). Say Takbir (Allah is great beyond description), then assume Ruku' (bowing down on one's knees) position.'"

Chapter 25 - Ruku‘ (Kneeling) and Readings therein and When Standing up Straight Thereafter

H 4989, Ch. 25, h 1

Muhammad ibn Yahya has narrated from Ahmad ibn Muhammad ibn ‘Isa from Hammad ibn ‘Isa from Hariz from Zurarah and Ali ibn Ibrahim has narrated from his father from Hammad from Hariz from Zurarah who has said the following:

“Abu Ja’far, *‘Alayhi al-Salam*, has said, ‘When you want to kneel for Ruku‘ say, ‘Allah is great’ before it, then assume Ruku‘ position and say, ‘O Lord, I have knelt down for You, I am submitted to You, I believe in You, and I plead before You to be my attorney. You are my Lord. My heart, my ears, my eyes, my hairs, my skin, my flesh, my blood, my bone marrow, my bones, my nerves and all that my legs support of me are humble before You without reservations, arrogance or tiredness.’ Say three times, ‘My Lord, the great, is free of all defects and I praise Him,’ with clarity and fluency. In Ruku‘ position you should level up your feet with a distance of one shibr (eight inches) between them, place your palms over your knees, first your right palm on the right knee, and then the left palm over your left knee. Open your fingers and make them to hold the sides of your knees, keep your back straight, stretch your neck forward and keep your eyes to look between your feet. Then, while standing straight, say, ‘Allah hears all who praise Him. All praise belongs to Allah, Lord of the worlds, the owner of might and majesty. Greatness belongs to Allah, Lord of the worlds,’ raise your voice when saying this, then raise your hands for saying ‘Allah is great’ and then bow down for sajdah.”

H 4990, Ch. 25, h 2

Muhammad ibn `Isma‘il has narrated from al-Fadl ibn Shadhan from ibn abu ‘Umayr from Jamil ibn Darraj who has said the following:

“I once asked abu ‘Abd Allah, *‘Alayhi al-Salam*, about what one says when performing behind an Imam when he says, ‘Allah hears all those who praise him.’ He (the Imam) said that he must say, ‘All praise belong to Allah, Cherisher of the worlds’ and lowers his voice.’”

H 4991, Ch. 25, h 3

Ali ibn Ibrahim has narrated from his father from Hammad ibn ‘Isa from Hariz from Zurarah who has said the following:

“Abu Ja‘far, *‘Alayhi al-Salam*, has said, ‘When you decide to assume Ruku‘ (bowing down on one’s knees) and Sajdah (prostration) position, raise your hands, say Takbir (Allah is great beyond description), then assume Ruku‘ (bowing down on one’s knees) and Sajdah (prostration) position.’”

H 4992, Ch. 25, h 4

Muhammad ibn Yahya has narrated from Ahmad ibn Muhammad from al-Husayn ibn Sa‘id from Fadalah ibn Ayyub from abu al-Mighra’ from abu Basir who has said the following:

“Abu ‘Abd Allah, *‘Alayhi al-Salam*, has said that `Amir al-Mu’minin has said, ‘One who does not straighten his back during Salat (prayer), his Salat (prayer) is not valid.’”

H 4993, Ch. 25, h 5

Al-Husayn ibn Muhammad has narrated from 'Abd Allah ibn 'Amir from Ali ibn Mahziyar from Muhammad ibn 'Isma'il ibn Bazi' who has said the following:

"I saw abu al-Hassan, *'Alayhi al-Salam*, perform Ruku' (bowing down on one's knees) and make it lower than all of those whom I have seen performing Ruku'. He spread, in the position of Ruku' his arms like wings.'"

H 4994, Ch. 25, h 6

Ahmad ibn Idris has narrated from Ahmad ibn Muhammad from al-Husayn ibn Sa'id from al-Qasim ibn Muhammad from a man from abu Basir from who has said the following:

"Abu 'Abd Allah, *'Alayhi al-Salam*, has said, 'When you stand up straight after Ruku' (bowing down on one's knees), make your back (bones) stand straight (vertically), otherwise, one's Salat (prayer) is not considered Salat (prayer).'"

H 4995, Ch. 25, h 7

Muhammad ibn Yahya has narrated from Ahmad ibn Muhammad from al-Sindiy ibn al-Rabi' from Sa'id ibn Janah who has said the following:

"I once was in the presence of abu Ja'far, *'Alayhi al-Salam*, in his home in al-Madinah. He initiating a conversation saying, 'One who completes his Ruku' (bowing down on one's knees) does not face any dread in the grave.'"

H 4996, Ch. 25, h 8

Muhammad ibn Yahya has narrated from Muhammad ibn al-Husayn from Ja'far ibn Bashir form Hammad from Hisham who has said the following:

"I once asked abu 'Abd Allah, *'Alayhi al-Salam*, 'Is it sufficient for me to say Tahlil, (no one deserves worship except Allah) and Takbir (Allah is great beyond description) in Ruku' (bowing down on one's knees) instead of Tasbih (Allah is free of all defects). He (the Imam) said, 'Yes, it is sufficient.'"

H 4997, Ch. 25, h 9

Ahmad ibn Idris has narrated from Muhammad ibn Ahmad from Ya'qub ibn Yazid from ibn abu 'Umayr from Ali ibn 'Uqbah who has said the following:

"Once abu al-Hassan, *'Alayhi al-Salam*, saw me, in al-Madinah when I performed Salat (prayer). I bent down my head and stretched in my Ruku' (bowing down on one's knees). He (the Imam) sent me a message that said, 'You must not do so (when you are in Ruku').'"

(Ahadith 2-9 are best explained in the form of fatwa.)

Chapter 26 - Sajdah, Readings and Recitations therein in Obligatory Salat (prayer) and Optional Salat (prayer) and Readings between the Two Sajdah

H 4998, Ch. 26, h 1

Ali ibn Ibrahim has narrated from his father from ibn abu 'Umayr from Hammad ibn 'Uthman from al-Halabiy who has said the following:

"Abu 'Abd Allah, *'Alayhi al-Salam*, has said that when you bow down for sajdah say, 'Allah is great,' then say, 'O Lord, I have bowed down to prostrate before You, I believe in You, submitted myself to You, have appealed to You to be my attorney and You are my Lord. My face has prostrated before the One who has created it, who has cut out for it a hearing means and a seeing means (ears and eyes). All praise belongs to Allah, the Lord of the worlds. Allah is most Blessed and the best Creator.' Then say, 'My Lord, the most High, is free of all defects,' three times. While sitting straight between the two prostrations, say, 'O Lord, forgive me, grant me mercy, grant me protection, and defend me against my enemies. I am in great need of the good that You have sent to me. Blessed is Allah, Lord of the worlds.'"

H 4999, Ch. 26, h 2

A group of people has narrated from Ahmad ibn Muhammad from al-Husayn ibn Sa'id from Fadalah ibn Ayyub from 'Abd Allah ibn Sinan from Hafs al-'A'war who has said the following:

"Abu 'Abd Allah, *'Alayhi al-Salam,* has said that Imam Ali, *'Alayhi al-Salam,* when prostrating would place his chest also on the ground like a skinny being."

H 5000, Ch. 26, h 3

Al-Husayn ibn Muhammad has narrated from 'Abd Allah ibn 'Amir from Ali ibn Mahziyar from Muhammad ibn Isma'il who has said the following:

"I saw abu al-Hassan, *'Alayhi al-Salam,* when prostrating, move three of his fingers one after the other slightly as if counting rosary and then raise his head from prostration."

H 5001, Ch. 26, h 4

Muhammad ibn Yahya has narrated from Ahmad ibn Muhammad and Muhammad ibn al-Husayn from al-Hassan ibn Mahbub from, abu Ja'far al-Ahwal from abu 'Ubaydah al-Hadhdha' who has said the following:

"I heard abu Ja'far, *'Alayhi al-Salam,* say when prostrating, '(O Lord,) I plead before You through the right of Muhammad, Your beloved one, to change my bad deeds to good ones and hold my accountability very little.' In the second prostration said, '(O Lord,) I plead before You through the right of Muhammad, Your beloved one, to suffice me in (my) needs in this world and all frightening matters up to paradise.' In the third sajdah said, '(O Lord,) I plead before You through the right of Muhammad, Your beloved one, to forgive my sins, be it a great deal or a smaller amount and accept my very few (good deeds).' In the fourth sajdah he said, '(O Lord,) I plead before You through the right of Muhammad, Your beloved one, to admit me in paradise, make me of its dwellers, save me from the effect of fire through Your mercy, and, O Allah, grant Muhammad and his family a compensation worthy of their serving Your cause.'"

H 5002, Ch. 26, h 5

A group has narrated from Ahmad ibn Muhammad from al-Husayn ibn Sa'id from al-Nadr ibn Suwayd from 'Abd Allah ibn Sinan from 'Abd Allah ibn Sulayman who has said the following:

"I asked abu 'Abd Allah, *'Alayhi al-Salam,* about a man who whenever mentioning the Holy Prophet during his Ruku' or sajdah in obligatory Salat (prayer), would say, 'O Allah grant Muhammad and his family a compensation worthy of their serving Your cause.' The Imam said, 'Yes, saying such words, after the mention the name of the Holy Prophet is like saying, "Allah is great,"

"Allah is free of all defects." There is a reward for ten good deeds for it and eighteen angels rush forward to take it up to deliver to him.""'

H 5003, Ch. 26, h 6

Ahmad ibn Muhammad from has narrated from al-Husayn ibn Sa'id from Fadalah from Aban from 'Abd al-Rahman ibn Sayabah who has said the following:

"I once asked abu 'Abd Allah, *'Alayhi al-Salam*, 'Can I plead (before Allah) in Sajdah (prostration)?' He (the Imam) said, 'Yes, you can do so. Plead for the worldly and the hereafter; He is the Lord of the world and the Lord of the life to come.'" (Hadith 6 is best explained by fatwa.)

H 5004, Ch. 26, h 7

Muhammad ibn 'Isma'il has narrated from Fadl ibn Shadan from ibn abu 'Umayr from Jamil ibn Darraj who has said the following:

"Abu 'Abd Allah, *'Alayhi al-Salam*, once said that a position nearest to Allah during one's prayer is the position of prostration. 'What do you say during your prostration?' I said, 'May Allah keep my soul in service for your cause; teach me what I should say.' The Imam told me to say, 'O Lord of lords, O King of kings, O Master of masters, O Mightier than mighty ones, and O Lord of those who are worshipped, O Allah grant Muhammad and his family a compensation worthy of their serving Your cause, please grant my such and such wishes.' Then say, 'I am your servant and my forehead is in your control'; then ask for your wishes that you like; He is generous and nothing seems great before him.'"

H 5005, Ch. 26, h 8

Muhammad ibn Yahya has narrated from Ahmad ibn Muhammad from ibn abu 'Umayr from Hisham ibn Salim from Muhammad ibn Muslim who has said the following:

"Abu Basir once on the way to Makkah performed Salat (prayer) with us as the leader and while in Sajdah (prostration) said, 'O Lord, - a camel of their camel man was lost-, return to so and so his camel.' Muhammad has said that I then went to visit abu 'Abd Allah, *'Alayhi al-Salam*, and informed him (about what abu Basir had said in Sajdah (prostration)). He (the Imam) asked, 'Did he do so? I replied, 'Yes, he did.' He (the Imam) remained quiet. I then asked, 'Must I perform Salat (prayer) again?' He (the Imam) replied, 'No, (it is not necessary).'"

(Hadith 8 is best explained in the form of fatwa.)

H 5006, Ch. 26, h 9

Ahmad ibn Idris has narrated from Ahmad ibn Muhammad from ibn Mahbub from Ishaq ibn 'Ammar who has said the following:

"Abu 'Abd Allah, *'Alayhi al-Salam*, has said, 'I would prepare the bed for my father and wait for his coming until he would go to sleep; then I would leave to go to bed. One night he delayed and I went to the Masjid to search him. This was the time when people had already left and it was quite calm out there. I found him in the Masjid prostrating and there was no one in the Masjid except him. I heard his affectionate plea saying, "(O Lord,) You are free of all defects, You are my Lord, in all truth, there is no doubt. I have prostrated before You, my Lord as (Your) slave and a sole servant. O Lord, my deeds are weak, so please increase them for me. O Lord, save me from Your punishment on the Day when Your servants are resurrected and turn to me to accept my repentance. You accept repentance and grant mercy.''''

H 5007, Ch. 26, h 10

Ahmad has narrated from ibn Mahbub from abu Jarir al-Rawasiy who has said the following:

"I heard abu al-Hassan Musa, *'Alayhi al-Salam*, say, 'O Lord, I pray to You to grant me comfort at the time of death and forgiveness at the time of issuing judgments repeatedly."

H 5008, Ch. 26, h 11

Muhammad ibn Yahya has narrated from Ahmad ibn Muhammad from al-Hajjal from 'Abd Allah ibn Muhammad from Tha'labah ibn Maymun from 'Abd Allah ibn Hilal who has said the following:

"I once complained before abu 'Abd Allah, *'Alayhi al-Salam*, about the difficulties we faced and deprivation from our belongings. He (the Imam) said, 'You must plead (before Allah) when you are in Sajdah (prostration) position; the nearest position to Allah for a servant of Allah is one's position in Sajdah (prostration).' I then asked, 'Can I plead (before Allah) in obligatory Salat (prayer) and mention my needs?' He (the Imam) replied, 'Yes, you can do so; the Messenger of Allah had done so. He pleaded (before Allah) against a people and mentioned their names and the names of their fathers. After him Ali, *'Alayhi al-Salam*, also had done so.'"

(Hadith 11 is best explained in the form of fatwa.)

H 5009, Ch. 26, h 12

A group of our people has narrated from Ahmad ibn Muhammad ibn 'Isa from al-Husayn ibn Sa'id from al-Qasim ibn Muhammad from Ali ibn abu Hamzah from abu Basir who has said the following:

"Abu Ja'far, *'Alayhi al-Salam*, has said, 'Once, the Holy Prophet, when he was with 'A'ishah, during the night decided to perform optional Salat (prayer). 'A'ishah woke up and searched around for him with her hand but did not find him. She thought he might have gone to her slave girl. She got up searching around and stepped on his neck when he was prostrating, weeping and saying, '(O Lord,) my person and my imagination have prostrated before You and my heart believes in You. I come to You with bounties and confess my great sin. I have done a bad deed. I have done injustice to myself so forgive me; no one forgives a great sin except You. I seek refuge with Your pardon from Your punishment, I seek refuge with Your pleasure from Your anger, I seek refuge with Your mercy from Your punishment and I seek refuge with You from You. I can never praise or admire You sufficiently. You are as You have praised Yourself. I ask forgiveness from You and turn to You in repentance.' When he came back he asked, ''A'ishah, why did you hurt my neck? Were you afraid that I might go to your slave girl?'''

H 5010, Ch. 26, h 13

Muhammad ibn Yahya has narrated from Ahmad ibn Muhammad from his father from the one whom he has mentioned from Muhammad ibn abu Hamzah from his father who has said the following:

"If one says during his Ruku', sajdah or standing position, 'Allahumma Salli 'Ala Muhammad wa 'Ali Muhammad (O Allah grant Muhammad and his family a compensation worthy of their serving Your cause),' Allah writes for him the reward for a sajdah, Ruku' or standing for worship."

H 5011, Ch. 26, h 14

Ali ibn Ibrahim has narrated from his father from ibn abu 'Umayr from Ja'far ibn Ali who has said the following:

"I saw abu al-Hassan, *'Alayhi al-Salam*, doing sajdah for after Salat (prayer), his arms spread on the ground and his chest and belly placed on the ground when praying."

H 5012, Ch. 26, h 15

Ali ibn Ibrahim has narrated from Yahya ibn 'Abd al-Rahman ibn Khaqan who has said the following:

"I saw abu al-Hassan, the third doing sajdah for Shukr (thanksgiving), his arms spread on the ground and his chest and belly placed on the ground. I asked him about it and he said, 'This is what we like.'"

H 5013, Ch. 26, h 16

Ali ibn Muhammad has narrated from Sahl from Ahmad ibn 'Abd al-'Aziz who has said that narrated to him certain persons of our people saying:

"When abu al-Hassan the first, *'Alayhi al-Salam*, raised his head from last sajdah of witr prayer he said, 'This is a position of one whose good deeds are due to Your bounties and whose thanksgiving is weak, but his sin is great. He does not have anything other than Your defending him and granting him mercy. You have said in Your book revealed to Your Holy Prophet and Messenger, "They sleep at night very little and in the morning ask forgiveness for their sins" (51: 18-19). My sleep has been very long and my standing for Salat (prayer) very little. This is morning. I ask You to forgive me my sin, like the one who is unable to harm himself, or benefit, control his death, life or resurrection.' Then he, *'Alayhi al-Salam*, would bow down to prostrate."

H 5014, Ch. 26, h 17

Ali ibn Ibrahim has narrated from his father from 'Abd Allah ibn Jundab who has said the following:

"I asked abu al-Hassan, *'Alayhi al-Salam*, about what to say in prostration for thanksgiving because our people are not of the same idea about it. He told me to say the following in a prostrating position: 'O Lord, I beg You to bear witness, I beg Your angels, Your prophets, messengers and all of Your creatures to bear witness (to my testimony) that You are Allah. You are my Lord. Islam is my religion and Muhammad is my prophet. Ali and all of my `A'immah so and so' - mentioning one by one – 'al-Hassan, al-Husayn, Ali ibn al-Husayn, Muhammad ibn Ali, Ja'far ibn Muhammad, Musa ibn Ja'far, Ali ibn Musa, Muhammad ibn Ali, Ali ibn Muhammad, al-Hassan ibn Ali and al-Mahdi are my `A'immah, *'Alayhim al-Salam*. I have acknowledged their divine authority and as my guardians, I love them and I denounce their enemies. O Lord, I plead before You through the blood of the one who suffered injustice,' - three times - 'O Lord I plead before You through Your firm undertaking of granting victory to Your friends – those whom You have entrusted with Your Authority- over Your enemy as well as their enemy. O Allah, I appeal before You to grant Muhammad and those members of his family who have safeguarded their trust compensation. Grant them a compensation worthy of their services to Your cause. O Lord, I request You to grant me comfort after suffering' – three times. Then place the right side of your face on the ground. Say, 'O my protector at times when all means become useless and the whole wide world seems to have become narrow, O my creator due to His mercy not because of being in need of such creation, O Allah, grant proper compensation to Muhammad and those members of his family who have safeguarded their trust.' Then place the left side of your face on the ground and say, 'O subjugator of tyrants and bestowing honor to the oppressed ones. I swear by Your majesty that my efforts are exhausted' – three times. Then say, 'O the affectionate one, the One who grants favors, O the One who removes great hardships' – three times. Then bow down for prostration and say one hundred times, 'Shukran' (I thank You, O Lord); then ask from Allah what you need by the will of Allah, the most High.'"

H 5015, Ch. 26, h 18

Ali ibn Ibrahim has narrated from Ali ibn Muhammad al-Qasaniy from Sulayman ibn Hafs al-Marwaziy who has said the following:

"I wrote to abu al-Hassan Musa ibn Ja'far, *'Alayhi al-Salam*, about prostration for thanksgiving. He wrote back to me. 'It is one hundred times 'Shukran' (O Lord, I thank You), or if you like, say ''Afwan' (O Lord, I beg forgiveness from You) one hundred times.'"

H 5016, Ch. 26, h 19

A number of our people have narrated from Ahmad ibn Muhammad ibn 'Isa from Ali ibn al-Hakam from Muhammad ibn Sulayman from his father who has said the following:

"Once I accompanied abu al-Hassan, Musa ibn Ja'far, *'Alayhim al-Salam*, to see some of his properties. He readied himself for noontime Salat (prayer). When he finished he bowed down to prostrate before Allah. I heard him saying with a sad voice and tears causing an unevenness of sound in his throat, 'O Lord, I have disobeyed You with my tongue. Had You wanted, I swear by Your majesty, You could have made it dumb. I have disobeyed You with my eyes. Had You wanted, I swear by Your majesty, You could have made them blind. I have disobeyed You with my ears. Had You wanted, I swear by Your majesty, You could have made them deaf. I have disobeyed You with my hands. Had You wanted, I swear by Your majesty, You could have crippled them. I have disobeyed You with my legs. Had You wanted, I swear by Your majesty, You could have paralyzed them. I have disobeyed You with my genital organ. Had You wanted, I swear by Your majesty, You could have made it barren. I have disobeyed You with all parts of my body which You have gifted me with and this is not the way I should have returned Your favors.' The narrator has said that I counted his saying 'al-'Afw' one thousand times. He then made the right side of his face touch the ground and I heard him saying in a sad voice, 'I have come to You with sin and bad deeds, I have done injustice to myself so forgive me; no one is able to forgive sins except You, O my Lord'- three times. Then he made the left side of his face touch the ground and I heard him say, '(O Lord,) forgive the one who has bad deeds and has accumulated sins but is humble and has confessed his sins'- three times. Then he raised his head."

H 5017, Ch. 26, h 20

Muhammad ibn Yahya has narrated from Ahmad ibn Muhammad from Ali ibn al-Hakam from Malik ibn 'Atiyyah from Yunus ibn 'Ammar who has said the following:

"Once I said to abu 'Abd Allah, *'Alayhi al-Salam*, may Allah keep my soul in service for your cause, about this thing that has appeared on my face, people say that Allah, the Most Majestic, the Most Holy, does not allow it to cause suffering to one who means anything to Him.' The Imam said, 'No, that is not so. The fingers of the believing person among the people of Pharaoh were such that bones were visible and he would speak to people extending his hand forward: "O people, follow the messengers"' (36:20). The Imam then said, 'When it is the beginning of the last third of the night, make Wudu' and stand up for prayer that you (usually) perform. In the last Sajdah (prostration) of the first two Rak'at say, "O the Most High, O the Most Great, O the Beneficent, O the Merciful, O the Hearer of the pleas for help. You are the conferrer of the good, grant al-Salat (favors) upon Muhammad and his family. Facilitate for me of the good things of this and of the good things of the next world that much which You deem proper. Divert away from me the evil of this and the next world that much that You deem proper and relieve me from this pain;' - mention it by its name – 'it has caused me anguish and sadness,' and be persistent in your pleading and prayer.'"

"The narrator has said that before his reaching al-Kufa Allah had totally relieved him from that illness.'"

H 5018, Ch. 26, h 21

A number of our people have narrated from Ahmad ibn Muhammad al-Barqiy from Muhammad ibn Ali from Sa'dan from a man who has said the following:

"Abu 'Abd Allah, *'Alayhi al-Salam*, in prostration would say the following: '(O Lord), my aging face has prostrated before Your ever remaining, eternal and great face. My submissive face has prostrated before Your majestic face. My poor face has prostrated before the self-sufficient, gracious, most High and great face of my Lord. My Lord, I beg You to forgive me for what has happened and what will happen. My Lord, do not allow my afflictions to intensify. Do not allow my enemy to rejoice at my misfortunes. My Lord, do not make my destiny to end up in a bad form. O Lord, there is no one except You to defend me against or prevent evil matters to afflict me. O Allah, grant Muhammad and his family compensation worthy of their serving Your cause, grant them the best form of compensation, grant them the best of Your blessings. O Lord, I seek Your protection against Your strength. O Lord, I seek Your protection against all forms of Your anger and displeasure. You are free of all defects. No one deserves to be worshipped except You, Cherisher of the worlds.'"

" He (the Imam) said that `Amir al-Mu'minin Ali, *'Alayhi al-Salam*, would say the following in prostrating position: 'O Lord, grant mercy to my submissive condition before You and my pleading to You, and to my feeling afraid among people and comfortable with You, O gracious One.' He would also say, 'O Lord, You gave me good advice but I failed to learn a lesson. You warned me about committing what You have prohibited but I failed to observe Your prohibitions. You granted me bounties as long as I have lived but I failed to give You thanks. O Lord, I beg You to forgive me, O Lord, I beg You to forgive me, O gracious One, I beg You to grant me comfort at the time of dying. I beg You to forgive me at the time of issuing judgment.'"

"Abu Ja'far, *'Alayhi al-Salam*, in prostration condition would say the following: 'No one deserves worship except You. You deserve worship in all truth and without doubts. I have prostrated before You, my Lord as (Your) slave and a sole servant. O Most great, my (good) deeds are weak, so please increase them for me, O gracious Lord. O compassionate Lord, forgive my sins and crimes and accept my deeds, O gracious Lord. O most powerful Lord, I seek protection with You against failure or tolerating injustice. O Lord, from You come bounties and You grant the ability to appreciate such bounties. With You are the reward due to your generosity and benevolence and Your graciously caring.'"

H 5019, Ch. 26, h 22

Ali ibn Muhammad has narrated from Sahl ibn Ziyad from Ya'qub ibn Yazid from Ziyad ibn Marwan who has said the following:

"Abu al-Hassan, *'Alayhi al-Salam*, in prostration position would say, 'O Lord, I seek Your protection against the fire of incessant heat. I seek Your protection against the fire which remains ever-new, I seek Your protection against the fire in which no one's thirst is quenched; I seek Your protection against the fire in which the naked is never dressed up.'"

H 5020, Ch. 26, h 23

Muhammad ibn Yahya has narrated from Ahmad ibn Muhammad from ibn Mahbub from ibn Ri'ab from abu 'Ubaydah al-Hadhdha' who has said the following:

"Abu 'Abd Allah, *'Alayhi al-Salam*, has said, 'When anyone of you may recite the chapters of the Holy Quran wherein is the verse calling for prostration, in the prostration for such recitation you should say, "O Lord, I have prostrated before You as a servant and in submission before You. I do not assume arrogance in worshipping You, refrain or consider myself by far exalted than performing acts of worship. The fact is that I am a weak servant, afraid and seeking (Your) protection."'"

H 5021, Ch. 26, h 24

Ali ibn Muhammad has narrated from Sahl ibn Ziyad from Ali ibn al-Rayyan from certain individuals of our people who has said the following:

"I complained before abu 'Abd Allah, *'Alayhi al-Salam*, about an illness in a mother of my child. He told me to tell her to say the following in prostration after completing an obligatory Salat (prayer), 'O my Lord, O my master, O Allah, grant Muhammad and his family a compensation worthy of their serving Your cause, grant me a cure from such and such illness.' It was because of this that Ja'far ibn Sulayman was saved from the fire, the Imam explained. The narrator has said that I mentioned this Hadith to certain individuals of our people; he said, 'I know the following to be as part of this Hadith, "O Lord, O compassionate, O merciful, O my Lord, O my master, grant me my such and such needs.""'

H 5022, Ch. 26, h 25

Ali ibn Muhammad has narrated from certain individuals of our people from ibn abu 'Umayr from Ziyad al-Qandiy who has said the following:

"I wrote to abu al-Hassan the first, *'Alayhi al-Salam*, to teach me a supplication. I am suffering from a situation - he was imprisoned in Baghdad. They had accused him in matters of their properties. The Imam wrote to him instructing him to say it in Salat (prayer), in a prolonged prostration. 'O the One who does not need anyone ' - for one breathe, then say, 'O the One to whom pleading does not do anything but to increase His generosity and grace.' Say it for one breath, then say, 'O Lord of lords, You are the One, You are the One and You are the One in whom there is hope while from all others all hope is cut off, O most High, most Great.' Ziyad has said, 'I practiced the above supplication and my hardships were removed and I was set free.'"

(The following chapters are best explained by fatwa.)

Chapter 27 - Minimum and Maximum Tasbih in Ruku' and Sajdah

H 5023, Ch. 27, h 1

Muhammad ibn Yahya has narrated from Ahmad ibn Muhammad from Ali ibn al-Hakam from 'Uthman ibn 'Abd al-Malik from abu Bakr al-Hadramiy who has said the following:

"Abu Ja'far, *'Alayhi al-Salam*, once asked me, 'Do you know what the limits of Ruku' (bowing down on one's knees) and Sujud (prostration) are?' I replied, 'No, I do not know them.' He (the Imam) said, 'Say Tasbih (my Lord, (Allah) most Great, is free of all defects and I praise Him) in Ruku' three times. In Sujud position say, 'My Lord, (Allah) most High, is free of all defects and I praise Him. One who reduces one of these Tasbih has reduced one-third of his Salat (prayer). One who has reduced two of them has reduced two-thirds of his Salat (prayer) and one who does not say Tasbih has lost his Salat (prayer).'"

H 5024, Ch. 27, h 2

Al-Husayn ibn Muhammad has narrated from 'Abd Allah ibn 'Amir from Ali ibn Mahziyar from ibn Faddal from Ahmad ibn 'Umar al-Halabiy from his father from Aban ibn Taghlib who has said the following:

"I once went to visit abu 'Abd Allah, *'Alayhi al-Salam*, when he performed Salat (prayer). I counted his Tasbih in Ruku' (bowing down on one's knees) and Sujud (prostration) which were sixty Tasbih.'"

H 5025, Ch. 27, h 3

Muhammad ibn Yahya has narrated from Ahmad ibn Muhammad from ibn Faddal from ibn Bukayr from Hamzah ibn Humran and al-Hassan ibn Ziyad who have said the following:

"Once we went to visit abu 'Abd Allah, *'Alayhi al-Salam*, when there a group of people was with him. He (the Imam) performed al-'Asr Salat (prayer) with them and we had already performed our Salat (prayer). We counted the number of

Tasbih (my Lord, (Allah) most Great, is free of all defects) thirty-three or thirty-four times. One of them (narrators) in his Hadith has said that the number of his Tasbih (my Lord, (Allah) most Great, is free of all defects and I praise Him) in both Ruku‘ and Sujud (prostration) were of the same number. This is because he (the Imam) knew they were ready for lengthy Ruku‘ and Sujud (prostration). This also is because of a Hadith that it is better for an Imam to make it light and perform Salat (prayer) according to the condition of the weakest of the people (performing Salat (prayer) with him).’”

H 5026, Ch. 27, h 4

Ali ibn Ibrahim has narrated from Muhammad ibn ‘Isa from Yunus ibn ‘Abd al-Rahman from Mu‘awiyah ibn ‘Ammar who has said the following:

“I once asked abu ‘Abd Allah, *‘Alayhi al-Salam*, ‘How many Tasbih is sufficient in Ruku‘ (bowing down on one’s knees) and in Sujud (prostration) in the case of one suffering from illness?’ He (the Imam) said, ‘One Tasbih is sufficient.’”

H 5027, Ch. 27, h 5

Ali has narrated from his father from ‘Abd Allah ibn al-Mughirah from Hisham ibn al-Hakam who has said the following:

“Abu ‘Abd Allah, *‘Alayhi al-Salam*, has said, ‘No word is lighter, easier and more eloquent for the tongue than Subhana Allah (Allah is free of all defects).’ I (the narrator) then asked, ‘Can I say Tahlil (no one deserves worship except Allah), Tahmid (it is Allah only who deserves all praise) and Takbir (Allah is great beyond description), instead of Tasbih (Allah is free of all defects)?’ He (the Imam) said, ‘Yes, all of them are speaking of Allah.’ I (the narrator) said, ‘We know the meaning of Tahmid (it is Allah only who deserves all praise) and Tahlil (no one deserves worship except Allah). What is the explanation of Tasbih (Allah is free of all defects)?’ He (the Imam) said, ‘It is to speak of the glory of Allah, consider when a man is marveled because of something says, ‘Subhana Allah (Allah is free of all defects).’’”

H 5028, Ch. 27, h 6

Ali ibn Muhammad has narrated from certain persons of our people from Marwak ibn ‘Ubayd from certain persons of his people who has said the following:

“I once said to abu Ja‘far, *‘Alayhi al-Salam*, ‘I am an Imam of the village. During Salat (prayer) I hear the sound of their shoes walking when I am in Ruku‘ (bowing down on one’s knees).’ He (the Imam) said, ‘Wait in your Ruku‘ for the length of your Ruku‘ until the sound stops, otherwise, you can rise to stand up straight.’”

Chapter 28 - Objects on Which Sajdah Is Permissible and What Is Undesirable

H 5029, Ch. 28, h 1

Muhammad ibn Yahya has narrated from Ahmad ibn Muhammad ibn ‘Isa from Muhammad ibn Khalid and al-Husayn ibn Sa‘id from al-Qasim ibn ‘Urwah from abu al-‘Abbas al-Fadl ibn ‘‘Abd al-Malik who has said the following:

"Abu 'Abd Allah, *'Alayhi al-Salam*, has said, 'You must not perform Sujud (prostration) on anything except earth or on what grows from earth except cotton and linen.'"

H 5030, Ch. 28, h 2

Ali ibn Ibrahim has narrated from his father from and Muhammad ibn 'Isma'il from al-Fadl ibn Shadhan all from Hammad ibn 'Isa from Zurarah who has said the following:

"I once asked abu Ja'far, *'Alayhi al-Salam*, 'Can I perform Sajdah (prostration) on asphalt? He (the Imam) said, 'No, also not on cotton, wool, anything from animals, food, fruits of earth and not on anything of clothing.'"

H 5031, Ch. 28, h 3

Muhammad ibn Yahya has narrated from Ahmad ibn Muhammad from al-Hassan ibn Mahbub who has said the following:

"I once asked abu al-Hassan, *'Alayhi al-Salam*, about lime which is fired with feces (dung) and bones of dead animals, then is used in the construction of Masjid. Is performing Sajdah (prostration) permissible on it?' He (the Imam) wrote with his own hand writing, 'Water and fire have cleansed it.'"

H 5032, Ch. 28, h 4

Muhammad ibn Yahya has narrated from Ahmad ibn Muhammad from Muhammad ibn Sinan from ibn Muskan from al-Halabiy who has said the following:

"Abu 'Abd Allah, *'Alayhi al-Salam*, has said, 'Once my father asked for a prayer mat but I was not fast enough, so he took a handful of pebbles, placed them on the furnishing and performed Sajdah (prostration) on them.'"

H 5033, Ch. 28, h 5

Ali ibn Ibrahim has narrated from his father from ibn abu 'Umayr from 'Umar ibn 'Udhaynah from Fudayl ibn Yasar and Burayd ibn Mu'awiyah who has said the following:

"One of the two Imam, *'Alayhim al-Salam*, has said, 'It is not harmful to stand on a prayer mat made of hairs and wool if one performs Sajdah (prostration) on earth, but if it is of the plants of earth, it is not harmful to stand on it and perform Sajdah (prostration) on it.'"

H 5034, Ch. 28, h 6

Ahmad ibn Idris and others have narrated Ahmad ibn Muhammad from Ali ibn 'Isma'il from Muhammad ibn 'Umar ibn Sa'id who has said the following:

"Abu al-Hassan, *'Alayhi al-Salam*, has said, 'You must not perform Sajdah (prostration) on graves and on a mix of lime and construction compound.'"

H 5035, Ch. 28, h 7

Ali ibn Muhammad and others have narrated from Sahl ibn Ziyad from Ali ibn Rayyan who has said the following:

"Certain ones of our people once wrote to him (the Imam) through Ibrahim ibn 'Uqbah, asking abu Ja'far, *'Alayhi al-Salam*, about performing Salat (prayer) on prayer mats made in al-Madinah. He (the Imam) wrote in answer, 'You can perform Salat (prayer) on what is made with threads but not on that which is made with leather stripes.' Our people were not clear about the meaning of 'thread' and 'stripe', so I presented a line of poem by Taabbata Sharran (name of a person) that said, 'As if they are threads of Mariy which are twisted and attached.' Mariy was a weaving man who worked with ropes and twines.

H 5036, Ch. 28, h 8

Muhammad ibn Yahya has narrated through the chain of narrators has said the following:

"Abu 'Abd Allah, *'Alayhi al-Salam*, has said, 'Performing Sujud (prostration) on earth is obligatory and on a prayer mat is a tradition."

H 5037, Ch. 28, h 9

Ahmad ibn Muhammad from Sahl ibn Ziyad from Muhammad ibn al-Walid from Yunus from Ya'qub who has said the following:

"Abu 'Abd Allah, *'Alayhi al-Salam*, has said, 'You must not perform Sajdah (prostration) on gold or on silver.'"

H 5038, Ch. 28, h 10

Ali ibn Ibrahim has narrated from his father from Muhammad ibn Yahya from Ghiyath ibn Ibrahim who has said the following:

"Ja'far, *'Alayhi al-Salam*, has narrated from his father from Ali, *'Alayhi al-Salam*, who have said, 'One must not perform Sajdah (prostration) on an item on which none of the parts of his body rests.'" (According to Arabic footnote this Hadith is because of Taqiyah)

H 5039, Ch. 28, h 11

Ahmad ibn Muhammad has narrated from al-Husayn ibn Sa'id from Fadalah from Aban from 'Abd al-Rahman ibn abu 'Abd Allah from Humran from who has said the following:

"One of the two Imam, (abu Ja'far or abu 'Abd Allah), *'Alayhim al-Salam*, has said, 'My father would perform Sajdah (prostration) on a prayer mat. He would place it on Tanfash (carpet) and perform Sajdah (prostration) on it. If there was no prayer mat, he placed pebbles on Tanfash and performed Sajdah (prostration) on it.'"

H 5040, Ch. 28, h 12

Muhammad ibn Yahya has narrated from Ahmad ibn Muhammad from al-Husayn ibn Sa'id from Fadalah from Jamil ibn Darraj who has said the following:

"Abu 'Abd Allah, *'Alayhi al-Salam*, disliked performing Sajdah (prostration) on a piece of paper with writing on it.'"

H 5041, Ch. 28, h 13

Muhammad ibn Yahya has narrated from al-'Amrakiy al-Naysaburiy from Ali ibn Ja'far from his brother Musa ibn Ja'far, *'Alayhim al-Salam*, has said the following:

"I once asked him (the Imam), *'Alayhi al-Salam*, about a man who performs Sajdah (prostration) on wet growing items. He (the Imam) said, 'If your forehead touches the ground it is not harmful.' I asked about stationary grass on the ground and dry leaves while he touches the ground. He (the Imam) said, 'It is not harmful.'"

H 5042, Ch. 28, h 14

Muhammad ibn Yahya has narrated from Muhammad ibn al-Husayn who has said the following:

"Certain ones of our people wrote to abu al-Hassan, the previous one, *'Alayhi al-Salam*, asking about Salat (prayer) on glass. He has said that when my letter finished I thought and said to myself that it is something that grows from earth, so I do not need to write and ask him (the Imam). He (the Imam) wrote to me, 'You must not perform Salat (prayer) on glass even though your soul has spoken to you that it is of what earth grows. However, it is from salt and sand and they both are metamorphosed.'"

Chapter 29 - Placing the Forehead on the Ground

H 5043, Ch. 29, h 1

Ali ibn Ibrahim has narrated from his father from Hammad ibn 'Isa from Hariz from Zurarah who has said the following:

"Abu Ja'far, *'Alayhi al-Salam*, has said, 'The entire forehead, from the hairline to the eyebrows is for Sajdah (prostration). Whatever of this area falls on the ground of the size of a dirham or of the size of a finger's tip is sufficient.'"

H 5044, Ch. 29, h 2

It is a narration from him (narrator of previous Hadith) by his father from 'Abd Allah ibn al-Mughirah who has said the following:

"Reported to me the one who had heard, abu 'Abd Allah, *'Alayhi al-Salam*, say, 'Salat (prayer) does not come into being until one's nose touches what his forehead has touched.'"

H 5045, Ch. 29, h 3

Muhammad ibn `Isma'il has narrated from al-Fadl ibn Shadhan from Safwan ibn Yahya from Mu'awiyah ibn 'Ammar who has said the following:

"Abu 'Abd Allah, *'Alayhi al-Salam*, has said, 'If you place your forehead on an uneven place, do not raise it to place on a proper place: instead drag it on the ground.'"

H 5046, Ch. 29, h 4

Ali ibn Ibrahim has narrated from his father from ibn abu 'Umayr from 'Abd Allah ibn Sinan who has said the following:

"I once asked abu 'Abd Allah, *'Alayhi al-Salam*, about the place of Sujud (prostration) if it can be higher than the place where one stands. He (the Imam) said, 'No, it must be level.' In another Hadith about the place of Sujud (prostration) which is higher than the place on which one stands, it is said that if it is of the height of a brick it is not harmful.'"

H 5047, Ch. 29, h 5

Muhammad ibn Yahya has narrated from Ahmad ibn Muhammad from al-Husayn ibn Sa'id from Safwan ibn Yahya from Ishaq ibn 'Ammar from certain persons of his people from Musadif who has said the following:

"On my forehead there was a dimple so I would perform Sajdah (prostration) on one side. Abu 'Abd Allah, *'Alayhi al-Salam*, noticed it and asked, 'What is this?' I replied, 'I cannot perform Sajdah (prostration) because of the pimple so I perform Sajdah (prostration) on one side.' He (the Imam) said, 'You must not do so, instead make a dent, then place the dimple in the dent area so your forehead touches the ground.'"

H 5048, Ch. 29, h 6

Ahmad ibn Muhammad from through the chain of his narrators has said the following:

"Abu 'Abd Allah, *'Alayhi al-Salam,* was asked about the case of one on whose forehead there is something because of which he is not able to perform Sajdah (prostration) on it. He (the Imam) said, 'He places his chin on the ground; Allah, most Majestic, most Glorious, has said, "They fall down on their chins prostrating."'" (17:107)

H 5049, Ch. 29, h 7

Muhammad ibn 'Isma'il has narrated from al-Fadl ibn Shadhan, from Safwan ibn Yahya Ishaq ibn 'Ammar from ''Abd al-Malik ibn 'Amr who has said the following:

"I saw abu 'Abd Allah, *'Alayhi al-Salam,* leveled the pebbles when he wanted to perform Sujud (prostration)."

H 5050, Ch. 29, h 8

Muhammad has narrated from al-Fadl from Hammad ibn 'Isa from Hariz from Muhammad ibn Muslim who has said the following:

"I once asked abu 'Abd Allah, *'Alayhi al-Salam,* 'Can one blow at the place where he places his forehead for prostration?' He (the Imam) replied, 'No, he cannot do so.'"

H 5051, Ch. 29, h 9

Muhammad ibn Yahya has narrated from Ahmad ibn Muhammad from al-Husayn ibn Sa'id from Fadalah from Aban from 'Abd al-Rahman ibn abu 'Abd Allah who has said the following:

"I once asked abu 'Abd Allah, *'Alayhi al-Salam,* about a man who performs Sajdah (prostration) wearing a turban which prevents his face from falling on the earth. He (the Imam) said, 'No, it is not sufficient until his forehead touches the earth.'"

Chapter 30 - Manners of Standing and Sitting Positions in Salat (prayer)

H 5052, Ch. 30, h 1

Ali has narrated from his father from Hammad ibn 'Isa and Muhammad ibn Isma'il from al-Fadl ibn Shadhan from Hammad ibn 'Isa and Muhammad ibn Yahya from Ahmad ibn Muhammad from Hammad ibn 'Isa from Hariz from Zurarah who has said the following:

"Abu Ja'far, *'Alayhi al-Salam,* has said, 'When you stand up for Salat (prayer) do not allow one foot to touch the other, leave between them a distance of one finger at the least and one Shibr (about 8 inches) at most. Allow your shoulders to relax and leave your hands alone. Do not crisscross your fingers. Instead they should be kept on your thighs on its front side and your eyes should look at the place for prostration. During Ruku' position line up your feet with a distance of one shibr in between them, allow your fingers to hold on to your knees. Place your right palm on your right knee before placing the left palm on your left knee. Allow your fingers to reach to the sides of your knees and stretch your fingers when placed on your knees. If during Ruku' the tips of your fingers reach your knees it is sufficient but I like that your palm should rest on your knees so you can allow your finger to hold to your knees while they (knees) are kept apart. Your back should be straight, your neck stretched forward and your looks should be kept between your feet.

“When you are ready for prostration, raise your hands for saying “Allah is great”, then bow down for prostration. First your hands should be placed on the ground, before your knees, together but do not place your forearms on the ground as beasts do. You must not place your forearms on your knees or thighs but open them up as wings with your elbows. You must not touch your knees with your palms and do not place them very close to your face. Place them in between level with your shoulders. You must not place them in front of your knees. Place them a little out, extend them on the ground and keep them a little toward you. If there is some cloth underneath, it does not matter, and if you allow them to be placed on the ground it is better. You must not keep your fingers apart from each other during your sajdah but keep them close side by side.’ The Imam said, ‘When you sit up straight for reading the testimonies, keep your knees touching the ground and a little apart from each other. The back of your left foot should be on the ground, the back of you right foot should be placed on the bottom of your left foot and both hips should be placed on the ground as well as the tip of the big toe of your right foot. You should never sit on both your feet; it may hurt you. You should not sit on the ground; in this way some parts of you are sitting on the others and you cannot bear sitting this way for reading the testimonies and supplications.’”

H 5053, Ch. 30, h 2

Through the same chain of narrators as that of the previous Hadith, it is narrated Hammad ibn ‘Isa from Hariz from Zurarah who has said the following:

“He (the Imam), *‘Alayhi al-Salam*, has said, ‘When a woman stands up for Salat (prayer) she should place her feet close to each other and should not keep them apart from each other. She should keep her hands over her chest over her breast. In Ruku‘ position she should place her hands above her knees on her thighs so as not to bend down very much to lift up her rear end. When sitting she should sit on her posteriors unlike a man. When bowing down for prostration she should first bring down her knees before her hands, then place herself on the ground. When sitting she should keep her thighs together and raise her knees from the ground. When moving to stand up a woman should rise upward without allowing her rear end to be seen being lifted up first.”

H 5054, Ch. 30, h 3

A group has narrated from Ahmad ibn Muhammad ibn ‘Isa from al-Husayn ibn Sa‘id from Fadalah ibn Ayyub from al-Husayn ibn ‘Uthman from Sama‘ah from abu Basir who has said the following:

“Abu ‘Abd Allah, *‘Alayhi al-Salam*, has said, ‘You must not sit, between the two sajdah, placing your hips on your heels.’”

H 5055, Ch. 30, h 4

Ahmad ibn Muhammad has narrated from al-Husayn ibn Sa‘id from ‘Uthman ibn ‘Isa from ibn Muskan from ibn abu Ya‘fur who has said the following:

“Abu ‘Abd Allah, *‘Alayhi al-Salam*, has said, ‘When a woman performs Sajdah (prostration) she must stretch her arms.’”

H 5056, Ch. 30, h 5

Ahmad ibn Muhammad has narrated from al-Husayn ibn Sa'id from Fadalah ibn Ayyub from Mu'alla' abu 'Uthman from Mu'alla' ibn Khunayth who has said the following:

"I once heard abu 'Abd Allah, *'Alayhi al-Salam*, say, 'Ali ibn al-Husayn, *'Alayhi al-Salam*, while bowing down for Sajdah (prostration) would say Takbir (Allah is great beyond description).'"

(Ahadith 4-5 are best be explained by fatwa.)

H 5057, Ch. 30, h 6

Ali ibn Ibrahim has narrated from his father from ibn abu 'Umayr from Hammad ibn 'Uthman from al-Halabiy who has said the following:

"Abu 'Abd Allah, *'Alayhi al-Salam*, has said, 'When one is in prostration position and wants to stand up, he should not make his hand into a fist placed on the ground, instead he should open his palms without placing his posteriors on the ground.'"

H 5058, Ch. 30, h 7

Ali ibn Ibrahim has narrated from his father from al-Husayn ibn Sa'id from Fadalah from Aban from 'Abd al-Rahman ibn abu 'Abd Allah who has said the following:

"I once asked abu 'Abd Allah, *'Alayhi al-Salam*, about woman when sitting during Salat (prayer). He (the Imam) said, 'She keeps her thighs together.'"

H 5059, Ch. 30, h 9

Muhammad ibn Yahya has narrated from Ahmad ibn Muhammad from ibn Faddal from ibn Bukayr from certain persons of our people who has narrated the following:

"He (the Imam), *'Alayhi al-Salam*, has said that woman when performing Sajdah (prostration) should not spread herself and man should spread himself on the ground.'"

H 5060, Ch. 30, h 10

It is a narration from him (narrator of previous Hadith) by Ahmad ibn Muhammad from Hammad from Hariz from a man who has said the following:

"I once asked abu Ja'far, *'Alayhi al-Salam*, about the words of Allah, 'Perform Salat (prayer) for the sake of your Lord and offer sacrifice. . . .'(108:2) He (the Imam) said, 'Offering sacrifice' is a reference to standing in a level posture by keeping one's back and neck level.' He (the Imam) said, 'You must not place your hand on your other hand; Majus (Zoroastrians) people would do so. You must not cover your mouth, do not hold your limbs tightly together and do not squat (sit on one's heels) and do not place your arms flat on the ground.'"

(Ahadith 7-9 above and the following chapters are best explained in the form of fatwa).

Chapter 31 - Tashahhud after the First Two Rak'at and After the Fourth Rak'at and Al-Taslim

H 5061, Ch. 31, h 1

Muhammad ibn Yahya has narrated from Ahmad ibn Muhammad ibn 'Isa from al-Husayn ibn Sa'id from 'Uthman ibn 'Isa from Mansur ibn Hazim from Bakr ibn Habib who has said the following:

"I once asked abu Ja'far, *'Alayhi al-Salam*, about Tashahhud (the testimony of belief). He (the Imam) said, 'Had it been as they say that it was obligatory people would have been destroyed. People only said what was easy of what they knew. If you praise Allah it is sufficient.'"

H 5062, Ch. 31, h 2

In another Hadith it is said that it is narrated from Safwan from Mansur from Bakr ibn Habib who has said the following:

"I once asked abu Ja'far, *'Alayhi al-Salam*, 'What should I say in Tashahhud (testimonies of belief) and Qunut (supplication after recitation in second Rak'at)?' He (the Imam) said, 'Say of the best you know; had it been something definite people would have been destroyed.'"

H 5063, Ch. 31, h 3

Muhammad ibn Yahya has narrated from Ahmad ibn Muhammad from al-Hajjal, from Tha'labah ibn Maymun from Yahya ibn Talhah from Sawrah ibn Kulayb who has said the following:

"I once asked abu Ja'far, *'Alayhi al-Salam*, about the minimum of what is sufficient for Tashahhud (testimonies of belief). He (the Imam) said, 'It is the two testimonies of belief."

H 5064, Ch. 31, h 4

Muhammad ibn Yahya has narrated from Ahmad ibn Muhammad from Ali ibn al-Nu'man form Dawud ibn Farqad from Ya'qub ibn Shu'ayb who has said the following:

"I once asked abu 'Abd Allah, *'Alayhi al-Salam*, 'Can I say in Tashahhud (testimonies of belief), 'Whatever is good is for Allah and whatever is evil is for those other than Allah?' He (the Imam) said, 'That is what Ali, *'Alayhi al-Salam*, would say.'"

H 5065, Ch. 31, h 5

Ali ibn Ibrahim has narrated from his father from ibn abu 'Umayr from Hafs ibn al-Bakhtariy who has said the following:

"Abu 'Abd Allah, *'Alayhi al-Salam*, has said, 'It is proper for the Imam to make people behind him hear Tashahhud (testimonies of belief) and they must not make him to hear anything from them.'"

H 5066, Ch. 31, h 6

Muhammad ibn Yahya has narrated from Ahmad ibn Muhammad from al-Husayn ibn Sa'id from Fadalah ibn Ayyub from Al-Husayn ibn 'Uthman from ibn Muskan from al-Halabiy who has said the following:

"Abu 'Abd Allah, *'Alayhi al-Salam*, once said to me, 'Whatever you say of Allah and the Holy prophet is of Salat (prayer). As soon as you say the phrase, 'I appeal before Allah to send peace on us and on the virtuous servants of Allah', you have ended Salat (prayer).'"

H 5067, Ch. 31, h 7

Through the same chain of narrators as that of the previous Hadith the following is narrated from ibn Muskan from abu Basir who has said the following:

"Abu 'Abd Allah, *'Alayhi al-Salam*, has said, 'When you are in the row (of people performing Salat (prayer)), say the phrase of offering greeting of peace, one to your right side and one to your left side, because from your left someone says the phrase of offering greeting of peace to you. If you are the Imam, then say Salam (the phrase of offering greeting of peace) facing al-Qiblah (al-Ka'bah).'"

H 5068, Ch. 31, h 8

Muhammad ibn Yahya has narrated from Ahmad ibn Muhammad from 'Uthman ibn 'Isa from Sama'ah who has said the following:

"Abu 'Abd Allah, *'Alayhi al-Salam,* has said, 'When you want to move away after completing Salat (prayer) move to your right side.'"

H 5069, Ch. 31, h 9

Muhammad ibn Yahya has narrated from Ahmad ibn Muhammad from al-Husayn ibn Sa'id from Fadalah ibn Ayyub from Al-Husayn ibn 'Uthman from ibn Muskan from 'Anbasah ibn Mus'ab who has said the following:

"I once asked abu 'Abd Allah, *'Alayhi al-Salam,* about a man who performs Salat (prayer) behind an Imam and there is no one on his left side; how he says the phrase of offering greeting of peace?' He (the Imam) said, 'He says the phrase of offering greeting of peace only once to his right side.'"

H 5070, Ch. 31, h 10

Through the same chain of narrators as that of the previous Hadith the following is narrated from Fadalah ibn Ayyub from Sayf ibn 'Amirah from abu Bakr al-Hadramiy who has said the following:

"Abu 'Abd Allah, *'Alayhi al-Salam,* has said, 'When you want to stand up after a Rak'at use your hands for support and say, 'By the means of Allah and His power I stand up and sit down. Ali, *'Alayhi al-Salam,* would do and say so.'"

H 5071, Ch. 31, h 11

Muhammad ibn Yahya has narrated from Ahmad ibn Muhammad from Hammad ibn 'Isa from Hariz from Muhammad ibn Muslim who has said the following:

"Abu 'Abd Allah, *'Alayhi al-Salam,* has said, 'When you sit up straight after the first two Rak'at, say Tashahhud (testimonies of belief), then when standing up say, "By the means of Allah and His power I stand up and sit down."'"

Chapter 32 - Al-Qunut in Obligatory and Optional Salat (prayer)

H 5072, Ch. 32, h 1

Muhammad ibn Yahya and others have narrated from Ahmad ibn Muhammad ibn 'Isa from al-Husayn ibn Sa'id from ibn abu 'Umayr and from Safwan ibn Yahya from ibn Bukayr from Muhammad ibn Muslim who has said the following:

"I once asked abu Ja'far, *'Alayhi al-Salam,* about Qunut (supplication after recitation in second Rak'at) in the five daily Salat (prayer). He (the Imam) said, 'Say Qunut in all of them.' I afterwards asked abu 'Abd Allah, *'Alayhi al-Salam,* about Qunut. He (the Imam) said, 'You must not have any doubt about (the need for Qunut) in whatever you say aloud.'"

H 5073, Ch. 32, h 2

Ahmad has narrated from al-Husayn from ibn abu Najran from Safwan al-Jammal who has said the following:

"Whenever I performed Salat (prayer) led by abu 'Abd Allah, *'Alayhi al-Salam*, I found him (the Imam) say Qunut (supplication after recitation in second Rak'at) in every Salat (prayer); those which are said aloud as well as those said silently."

H 5074, Ch. 32, h 3

Ali ibn Ibrahim has narrated from his father from ibn Faddal from ibn Bukayr from abu Basir who has said the following:

"I once asked abu 'Abd Allah, *'Alayhi al-Salam*, about Qunut (supplication after recitation in second Rak'at). He (the Imam) said, 'It is in Salat (prayer) in which recitation is loudly?' I (the narrator) then said to him (the Imam), 'I asked your father about it and he said that it is in all of the five daily Salat (prayer).' He (the Imam) then said, 'I pray to Allah to grant favors to my father, the companions of my father asked him and he informed them of the truth. Thereafter skeptics came to me and I made a presentation according to Taqiyah.'"

H 5075, Ch. 32, h 4

Ali ibn Muhammad ibn 'Isa has narrated from Yunus ibn 'Abd al-Rahman from Muhammad ibn Fudayl from al-Harith ibn al-Mughirah who has said the following:

"Abu 'Abd Allah, *'Alayhi al-Salam*, has said, 'Say Qunut (supplication after recitation in second Rak'at) before Ruku' (bowing down on one's knees) in every two Rak'at in obligatory Salat (prayer) or optional ones'"

H 5076, Ch. 32, h 5

Muhammad ibn 'Isma'il has narrated from al-Fadl ibn Shadhan, from ibn abu 'Umayr, from 'Abd al-Rahman ibn Hajjaj who has said the following:

"I once asked abu 'Abd Allah, *'Alayhi al-Salam*, about Qunut (supplication after recitation in second Rak'at). He (the Imam) said, 'It is in every Salat (prayer); obligatory or optional.'"

H 5077, Ch. 32, h 6

Through the same chain of narrators as that of the previous Hadith the following is narrated from Yunus from Wahab ibn ''Abd Rabbihi who has said the following:

"Abu 'Abd Allah, *'Alayhi al-Salam*, has said, 'Whoever omits Qunut (supplication after recitation in second Rak'at) in dislike his Salat (prayer) is not anything.'"

H 5078, Ch. 32, h 7

Ali ibn Ibrahim has narrated from his father from ibn abu 'Umayr from Zurarah who has said the following:

"Abu Ja'far, *'Alayhi al-Salam*, has said, 'There is Qunut (supplication after recitation in second Rak'at) in every Salat (prayer) in the second Rak'at before Ruku' (bowing down on one's knees).'"

H 5079, Ch. 32, h 8

Muhammad ibn Yahya has narrated from Ahmad ibn Muhammad from al-Husayn ibn Sa'id from Fadalah ibn Ayyub from Aban ibn 'Isma'il ibn al-Fadl who has said the following:

"I once asked abu 'Abd Allah, *'Alayhi al-Salam*, about Qunut (supplication after recitation in second Rak'at) and what is said in it. He (the Imam) said, 'Say whatever Allah makes to come out from your tongue. I do not know of anything definite for it.'"

H 5080, Ch. 32, h 9

Muhammad ibn Yahya has narrated from Ahmad ibn Muhammad from al-Husayn ibn Sa'id from Fadalah from Aban from 'Abd al-Rahman ibn abu 'Abd Allah, who has said the following:

"Abu 'Abd Allah, *'Alayhi al-Salam*, has said, 'Al-Qunut in obligatory Salat (prayer) is pleading (before Allah) and in Witr it is to ask forgiveness (from Allah).'"

(Ahadith 1-9 are best explained in the form of fatwa.)

H 5081, Ch. 32, h 10

Muhammad ibn Isma'il has narrated from al-Fadl ibn Shadhan from Hammad ibn 'Isa from Hariz from Zurarah who has said the following:

"I asked abu Ja'far, *'Alayhi al-Salam*, about a man who has forgotten al-Qunut then remembers somewhere on the way. The Imam said, 'He should turn toward Qiblah and say it.' He then said, 'I do not like a man's ignoring traditions of the Messenger of Allah or abandoning them altogether.'"

H 5082, Ch. 32, h 11

Muhammad ibn Yahya has narrated from Ahmad ibn Muhammad from al-Husayn ibn Sa'id from al-Qasim ibn Muhammad from Ali ibn abu Hamzah from abu Basir who has said the following:

"I asked abu 'Abd Allah, *'Alayhi al-Salam*, about the minimum form of al-Qunut. He said, 'It is five times saying, "Allah is free of all defects."'"

H 5083, Ch. 32, h 12

Ali ibn Ibrahim has narrated from his father from ibn abu 'Umayr from Sa'd ibn abu Khalaf who has said the following:

"Abu 'Abd Allah, *'Alayhi al-Salam*, has said, 'It is sufficient for al-Qunut to say, "O Lord, forgive us, grant us mercy, good health and pardon us in this world and in the next life; You have power over all things."'"

H 5084, Ch. 32, h 13

Muhammad ibn 'Isma'il has narrated from al-Fadl ibn Shadhan from ibn abu 'Umayr from Mu'awiyah ibn 'Ammar who has said the following:

"Abu 'Abd Allah, *'Alayhi al-Salam*, has said, 'I do not know of any Qunut (supplication after recitation in second Rak'at) except before Ruku' (bowing down on one's knees).'"

H 5085, Ch. 32, h 14

Muhammad ibn Yahya has narrated from Ahmad ibn Muhammad from al-Husayn ibn Sa'id who has said the following:

"Ya'qub ibn Yaqtin narrated to me saying, 'I once asked the virtuous servant of Allah about Qunut (supplication after recitation in second Rak'at) in al-Witr, the morning Salat (prayer) and Salat (prayer) which is said aloud before Ruku' (bowing down on one's knees) or after Ruku'. He (the Imam) said, 'It is before Ruku' when you complete your recitation.'"

H 5086, Ch. 32, h 15
Ali ibn Muhammad has narrated from Sahl ibn Ziyad Ya'qub ibn Yazid from Ziyad al-Qandiy from Durust from Muhammad ibn Muslim who has said the following:
"He (the Imam), *'Alayhi al-Salam*, has said, 'There is Qunut (supplication after recitation in second Rak'at) in every Salat (prayer); obligatory or optional.'"

(Ahadith 13-15 are best explained in the form of fatwa.)

Chapter 33 - Prayers after Salat (a special form of prayer)

H 5087, Ch. 33, h 1
Ali ibn Ibrahim has narrated from his father from ibn abu 'Umayr from Hammad from al-Halabiy who has said the following:
"Abu 'Abd Allah, *'Alayhi al-Salam*, has said, 'It is not proper for an Imam to move from his place after saying the phrase of offering greeting of peace before people behind him complete their Salat (prayer). He (the narrator) has said that I asked him (the Imam) about a man who leads others in Salat (prayer) if it is necessary for him to say follow up supplications, after the phrase of offering greeting of peace, along with those who have followed him in Salat (prayer). He (the Imam) said, 'He says Tasbih (Allah is free of all defects) and thereafter whoever wants leaves for their needs and a man does not say the follow up supplications because the Imam is doing so.'"

H 5088, Ch. 33, h 2
Ali has narrated from his father from Hammad from Hariz from abu Basir from who has said the following:
"Whoever leads a people in Salat (prayer) must sit down after the phrase of offering greeting of peace and must not leave that place until those behind him complete (their Salat (prayer)) which is completed after (the Salat (prayer) of the Imam). It is obligatory for every Imam if they know that there are people who have not completed their Salat (prayer). When he finds out that everyone has completed and no one is left he then can go wherever he wants.'"

(Ahadith 1 and 2 are best explained in the form of fatwa.)

H 5089, Ch. 33, h 3
Muhammad ibn Yahya has narrated from Ahmad ibn Muhammad from Ali ibn Hadid from Manur ibn Yunus from those whom he has mentioned who has said the following:
"Abu 'Abd Allah, *'Alayhi al-Salam*, has said, 'If after completing an obligatory Salat (prayer), one remains in his place for ta'qib (praying and speaking to Allah) up to the time of the next Salat (prayer), he is a guest of Allah and it is a right in his favor before Allah to honor His guest.'"

H 5090, Ch. 33, h 4
Al-Husayn ibn Muhammad has narrated from Mu'alla' ibn Muhammad from al-Washsha' from Aban ibn 'Uthman from al-Hassan ibn al-Mughirah who has said the following:
"I heard abu 'Abd Allah, *'Alayhi al-Salam*, say, 'The excellence of prayer, after an obligatory Salat (prayer), over prayers after non-obligatory Salat (prayer), is like the excellence of obligatory Salat (prayer) over non-obligatory Salat

(prayer).' The Imam then said, 'Pray to Allah and do not say that matters are settled. Prayer is worshipping. Allah, the Most Majestic, the Most Glorious, has said, "Those who belittle worshipping Me will go to hell in humiliation." He has also said, "Pray to Me. I answer your prayers." (40:60) The Imam then said, 'When you want to pray to Allah, you should speak of His glory. You should praise Him, speak of His Majesty, say that He is the only Lord who must be worshipped and speak of His praise. You should say, "Allahumma Salli 'Ala Muhammad wa 'Ali Muhammad (O Allah grant Muhammad and his family a compensation worthy of their serving Your cause)," then ask for your needs, you will receive what you need.'"

H 5091, Ch. 33, h 5

Ali ibn Ibrahim has narrated from his father from Hammad from Hariz from Zurarah who has said the following:

"Abu Ja'far, *'Alayhi al-Salam,* has said, 'Prayer after an obligatory Salat (prayer) is better than after non-obligatory Salat (prayer).'"

H 5092, Ch. 33, h 6

Al-Husayn ibn Muhammad al-Ash'ariy has narrated from 'Abd Allah ibn 'Amir from Ali ibn Mahziyar from Fadalah ibn Ayyub from 'Abd Allah ibn Sinan who has said the following:

"Abu 'Abd Allah, *'Alayhi al-Salam,* has said, 'One who reads Tasbih of Fatimah al-Zahra', *'Alayha al-Salam,* after an obligatory Salat (prayer) and before moving his legs away from his position Allah forgives him and he should begin with al-Takbir (Allahu Akbar).'"

H 5093, Ch. 33, h 7

A number of our people have narrated from Ahmad ibn Muhammad ibn Khalid from Yahya ibn Muhammad, from Ali ibn al-Nu'man from ibn abu Najran from a man who has said the following:

"Abu 'Abd Allah, *'Alayhi al-Salam,* has said, 'If one speaks of the glory of Allah after completing an obligatory Salat (prayer) in the form of Tasbih of Fatimah al-Zahra', *'Alayha al-Salam,* one hundred times and following this says, "No one deserves to be worshipped except Allah," Allah forgives him.'"

H 5094, Ch. 33, h 8

A number of our people have narrated from Ahmad ibn Muhammad from 'Amr ibn 'Uthman from Muhammad ibn 'Adhafir who has said the following:

"Once my father and I went to see abu 'Abd Allah, *'Alayhi al-Salam,* and my father asked him about Tasbih of Fatimah al-Zahra', *'Alayha al-Salam.* The Imam said, 'Allahu Akbar' thirty four times. Then he said, 'Al-Hamdu Li Allah' up to sixty-seven. He then said, 'Subhana Allah' up to one hundred. He was counting all of them with his hand in one successive order to one hundred."

H 5095, Ch. 33, h 9

Ali ibn Muhammad has narrated from Sahl ibn Ziyad from Muhammad ibn 'Abd al-Hamid from Safwan from ibn Muskan from abu Basir who has said the following:

"Abu 'Abd Allah, *'Alayhi al-Salam,* has said that one should begin Tasbih of Fatimah, *'Alayha al-Salam,* with Takbir (Allah is great) thirty-four times, Tahmid (all praise belongs to Allah) thirty-three times and Tasbih (Allah is free of all defects) thirty-three times."

H 5096, Ch. 33, h 10

Muhammad ibn Yahya has narrated from Muhammad ibn al-Husayn from Muhammad ibn Isma'il ibn Bazi' from al-Khaybariy from al-Husayn ibn Thuwayr and abu Salmah al-Sarraj who have said the following:

"We heard abu 'Abd Allah, *'Alayhi al-Salam*, express condemnations against four men and four women after every obligatory Salat (prayer) naming so and so and so on and Mu'awiyah, Hind and 'Umm al-Hakam, sister of Mu'awiyah."

H 5097, Ch. 33, h 11

Ahmad ibn Idris from Muhammad ibn Ahmad in a marfu' manner has said the following:

"Abu 'Abd Allah, *'Alayhi al-Salam*, has said, 'If you face uncertainty about Tasbih of Fatimah al-Zahra', *'Alayha al-Salam*, say it again.'"

H 5098, Ch. 33, h 12

It is narrated from the narrator of previous Hadith from Muhammad ibn Ahmad from Ya'qub ibn Yazid from Muhammad ibn Ja'far from those whom he has mentioned has said the following:

"Abu 'Abd Allah, *'Alayhi al-Salam*, would say Tasbih of Fatimah al-Zahra', *'Alayha al-Salam*, continuously without interruption."

H 5099, Ch. 33, h 13

Muhammad ibn Yahya has narrated from Muhammad ibn al-Husayn from Muhammad ibn Ismai'l ibn Bazi' from Salih ibn 'Uqbah from abu Harun al-Makfuf who has said the following:

"Once abu 'Abd Allah, *'Alayhi al-Salam*, said, 'O abu Harun, we command our children to read Tasbih of Fatimah al-Zahra', *'Alayha al-Salam*, just as we command them to say Salat (prayer). You must hold to it; whoever holds to it does not become unfortunate.'"

H 5100, Ch. 33, h 14

Through the same chain of narrators as the previous Hadith it is narrated from Salih ibn 'Uqbah from 'Uqbah who has said the following:

"Abu Ja'far, *'Alayhi al-Salam*, has said, 'In worshipping Allah in the form of praises no other thing is better than Tasbih of Fatimah al-Zahra', *'Alayha al-Salam*. If anything other than this could make a better gift the Messenger of Allah would have instead given to Fatimah al-Zahra', *'Alayha al-Salam*.'"

H 5101, Ch. 33, h 15

It is narrated from the same narrator as the previous Hadith from abu Khalid al-Qammat who has said the following:

"I heard abu 'Abd Allah, *'Alayhi al-Salam*, say, 'Tasbih of Fatimah al-Zahra', *'Alayha al-Salam*, every day after every Salat (prayer) is more beloved to me than one thousand Rak'at prayer every day.'"

H 5102, Ch. 33, h 16

Ali ibn Ibrahim has narrated from his father from Hammad from Hariz from Zurarah who has said the following:

"Abu Ja'far, *'Alayhi al-Salam*, has said, 'The least that you should say after an obligatory Salat (prayer) is to say, 'O Lord, I ask from You of all good which Your knowledge has encompassed, and seek refuge with You against every evil thing that Your knowledge has encompassed. O Lord, I ask from You good health in all of my affairs and I seek refuge with You against failures in this life and torment in the next life.'"

H 5103, Ch. 33, h 17

A number of our people have narrated from Ahmad ibn Muhammad ibn Khalid from his father from al-Qasim ibn 'Urwah from abu al-'Abbas al-Fadl ibn 'Abd al-Malik who has said the following:

"Abu 'Abd Allah, *'Alayhi al-Salam*, has said, 'Prayers are answered in four conditions and instances of time: One is the prayer during one's doing Salat (prayer) of Witr, after Salat (prayer) of Fajr (Morning Prayer), after Salat (prayer) at noon time and upon completion of Salat (prayer) of Maghrib (after sunset).'"

H 5104, Ch. 33, h 18

Muhammad ibn Yahya has narrated from 'Abd Allah ibn Muhammad ibn 'Isa from Ali ibn al-Hakam from Aban from Muhammad al-Wasitiy who has said the following:

"I heard abu 'Abd Allah, *'Alayhi al-Salam*, say, 'Do not go away before saying the following after every Salat (prayer): "I seek protection, for myself and whatever my Lord has given me, with Allah, the only One self-sufficient, who does not have any children. He Himself is not anyone's child. There is no one like Him (Chapter 112 of Holy Quran). I seek protection, for myself and for whatever my Lord has given me, with the Lord who has brought about the opening, against whatever evil He has created, against the evil of incoming darkness, the evil of those who perform magic and against the ill desires of envious ones (Chapter 113 of the Holy Quran). I seek protection, for myself and for whatever my Lord has given me, with the Cherisher of the people, the owner of the people, the Lord of the people against the evil temptation of al-Khannas, who incites the heart of people, in the form of Jinn and man (Chapter 114 of the Holy Quran).""'"

H 5105, Ch. 33, h 19

Ali ibn Ibrahim has narrated from his father from Hammad ibn 'Isa from Hariz from Zurarah, who has said the following:

"Abu Ja'far, *'Alayhi al-Salam*, has said, 'Do not forget' – or that he said 'you must not forget appealing before Allah after every obligatory Salat (prayer) about the two essential matters.' I then asked, 'What are the two essential matters?' The Imam replied, 'Appealing before Allah for paradise and seeking refuge with Allah against the fire.'"

H 5106, Ch. 33, h 20

Muhammad ibn Yahya and Ahmad ibn Idris have narrated from Muhammad ibn Ahmad from Ali ibn Muhammad al-Qasaniy from Muhammad ibn 'Isa from Sulayman ibn Hafs al-Marwaziy who has said the following:

"The man, *'Alayhi al-Salam*, wrote to me the following: 'During sajdah when expressing thanks to Allah say, "Shukran" one hundred times – or if you wanted – say "'Afwan 'Afwan.""'"

H 5107, Ch. 33, h 21

Muhammad ibn al-Hassan has narrated from Sahl ibn Ziyad through his chain of narrators from Sama'ah ibn Mehran who has said the following:

"Abu 'Abd Allah, *'Alayhi al-Salam*, has said, 'Whoever's fingers may move faster than his tongue it is counted in his favor (according to the movement of the former).'"

H 5108, Ch. 33, h 22

A number of our people have narrated from Ahmad ibn Muhammad from Ali ibn al-Hakam from Dawud al-'Ijliy Mawla' of abu al-Mighra' who has said the following:

"I heard abu 'Abd Allah, *'Alayhi al-Salam*, say, 'Three things are given the power to hear creatures. They are paradise, the fire and al-Hur al-'Ayn. When a servant of Allah completes his Salat (prayer) then pleads and says, "O Lord, set me free from the fire, admit me in paradise and join me as a pair with al-Hur al-'Ayn." The fire then says, "O Lord, Your servant has pleaded before You to set him free from me, so please set him free." Paradise will say, "O Lord, Your servant has prayed to You to make me his dwelling so please make his wish to come true." Al-Hur al-'Ayn will say, "O Lord, Your servant has prayed to be joined in pairs with us so please make his wish to come true." But if he goes away after completing his Salat (prayer) without praying to Allah for any of these things, al-Hur al-'Ayn will say, "This servant of Allah has abstained from being joined in pairs with us." Paradise will say, "This servant has abstained from praying to live in me." The fire will say, "This servant is ignorant about me."'"

H 5109, Ch. 33, h 23

Ahmad ibn Muhammad has narrated in a marfu' manner a prayer that can be said after every Salat (prayer):

"Abu 'Abd Allah, *'Alayhi al-Salam*, has said that if one has an illness or pain somewhere in his body he, after completing a Salat (prayer), should touch the place of his sajdah with his hand. He should say this prayer and wipe, seven times, on the painful or ailing part of his body. "(O Lord, it is You), O the One who has pressed the earth upon the water, held the air in the sky, chosen for Himself the most beautiful names. - Allahumma Salli 'Ala Muhammad wa 'Ali Muhammad, (O Allah grant Muhammad and his family a compensation worthy of their serving Your cause), - please make my such and such wishes to come true and grant me good health in such and such conditions."'"

H 5110, Ch. 33, h 24

Muhammad ibn Yahya has narrated from Ahmad ibn Muhammad ibn 'Isa from Muhammad ibn 'Isma'il from abu 'Isma'il al-Sarraj from Ali ibn Shajarah from Muhammad ibn Marwan who has said the following:

"Abu 'Abd Allah, *'Alayhi al-Salam*, has said, 'Wipe with your right hand your forehead after Maghrib Salat (prayer) after sunset and other Salawat (prayers) and say, "In the name of Allah besides whom no one deserves to be worshipped. He has the knowledge of the unseen and seen, the Beneficent, the Merciful. O Lord, I seek refuge with You against anxiety, sadness, illness, deficiencies, lowliness, humiliation and the apparent and concealed indecencies."'"

H 5111, Ch. 33, h 25

Ali ibn Ibrahim has narrated from his father from al-Husayn ibn Sa'id from Fadalah from al-'Ala' from Muhammad ibn Muslim who has said the following:

"I asked abu Ja'far, *'Alayhi al-Salam*, about Tasbih. The Imam replied, 'I do not know of any Tasbih in a prescribed manner except Tasbih of Fatimah al-Zahra', *'Alayha al-Salam*, and to say ten times after the morning, "No one deserves to be worshipped except Allah alone Who has no partner. To Him belongs the kingdom and He deserves all praise. He gives life and causes death, causes death and gives life. In His hand is all good and He has power over all things," but one may say as many Tasbih as one likes.'"

H 5112, Ch. 33, h 26

Muhammad ibn Yahya has narrated from Ahmad ibn Muhammad from Muhammad ibn Sinan from 'Abd al-Malik al-Qummiy from Idris his brother who has said the following:

"I heard abu 'Abd Allah, *'Alayhi al-Salam*, say, 'When you complete your Salat (prayer) say this. "O Lord, I follow Your religion in obedience to You under Your guardianship, the guardianship of Your messenger and the guardianship of `A'immah, the first to the last Imam. . ." You should mention the name of each Imam. Then say, "O Lord, I follow Your religion in obedience to You and under their guardianship. I am happy for the excellence that You have granted them without being arrogant or assuming arrogance against what You have revealed in Your book in the form of that which is reached to us as well as what is not reached us. I believe, affirm and submit to such facts. I am happy with that with which You are happy, O Lord. I seek thereby Your happiness and the eternal living in the next life. I am fearful and I desire to be (acceptable) before You. Give me life as long as You will with this (belief), cause me to die with it (belief) when You cause me to die and raise me when You raise me with it (belief). If I may have had shortcomings in the past, I repent before You and I desire to come before You for the bounties You own. I plead before You to protect me against disobedience to You and do not leave me to myself for a blinking of an eye as long as You keep me living, no less or more than such time. The soul motivates toward evil, except those whom You through Your mercy protect, O Most Merciful, Most Beneficent. I plead before You to protect me with (my) obedience to You until I die with it (belief in and obedience to You) when You are happy with me and make my life end up with salvation. Please do not ever turn me away from it (salvation); there is no power without You.""""

H 5113, Ch. 33, h 27

Al-Husayn ibn Muhammad has narrated from Mu'alla' ibn Muhammad from al-Washsha' from Aban from Muhammad al-Wasitiy who has said the following:

"I heard abu 'Abd Allah, *'Alayhi al-Salam*, saying, 'Do not go away before saying the following after every Salat (prayer). "I seek protection for myself and whatever my Lord has given me from Allah, the only One self-sufficient, who does not have any children, nor Himself is anyone's child and there is no one like Him." (Chapter 112 of Holy Quran) "I seek protection for myself and for whatever my Lord has given me from the Lord who has brought about the opening, against whatever evil He has created, against the evil of incoming darkness, the evil of those who perform magic and against the ill desires of envious ones." (Chapter 113 of the Holy Quran). "I seek protection for myself and for whatever my Lord has given me with the Lord of the people, the owner of the people, the Lord of the people against the evil temptation of al-Khannas, who incites the heart of people, in the form of Jinn and man.'" (Chapter 114 of the Holy Quran).

H 5114, Ch. 33, h 28

Ali ibn Muhammad has narrated from Sahl ibn Ziyad from Ali ibn Mahziyar who has said the following:

"Muhammad ibn Ibrahim wrote to abu al-Hassan, *'Alayhi al-Salam*, 'My master, if you deem it proper, teach me a prayer that I can read after every Salat (prayer) so Allah will grant me good, both in this and the next life.' The Imam wrote to him, 'Say, O Lord, I seek refuge with Your gracious presence, Your unassailable majesty and Your unstoppable power, against the evil of this world as well as those in the next life and against the misfortune of all illnesses.'"

(The following chapters are best explained by fatwa.)

Chapter 34 - The Case of One Whose Wudu' Is Invalidated Before Al-Taslim

H 5115, Ch. 34, h 1

Muhammad ibn Yahya has narrated from Ahmad ibn Muhammad ibn 'Isa from al-Husayn ibn Sa'id from Fadalah ibn Ayyub from ibn Bukayr from 'Ubayd ibn Zurarah who has said the following:

"I once asked abu 'Abd Allah, *'Alayhi al-Salam*, about a man who performs obligatory Salat (prayer) but when he raises his head from the second Sajdah (prostration) of the fourth Rak'at his Wudu' becomes invalid. He (the Imam) said, 'His Salat (prayer) is ended; what remains is Tashahhud (testimonies of belief). Tashahhud (testimonies of belief) is Sunnah (a tradition) in Salat (prayer). He takes wudu,' returns to his place or a clean place to say Tashahhud (testimonies of belief).'"

H 5116, Ch. 34, h 2

Ali ibn Ibrahim has narrated from his father from ibn abu 'Umayr from 'Umar ibn 'Udhaynah from Zurarah who has said the following:

"Wudu' of a man may become invalid after he raises his head from the last Sajdah (prostration) before Tashahhud (testimonies of belief). Abu Ja'far, *'Alayhi al-Salam*, has said, 'He moves to take Wudu' and if he wants to return to Masjid or if he wants in his house, sits down to say Tashahhud (testimonies of belief) and the phrase of offering greeting of peace. If his Wudu' becomes invalid after Tashahhud (testimonies of belief), his Salat (prayer) is passed.'"

Chapter 35 - Mistake in Opening of Salat (Prayer)

H 5117, Ch. 35, h 1

Ali ibn Ibrahim ibn Hashim has narrated from his father from ibn abu 'Umayr from Jamil and Muhammad ibn 'Isma'il from al-Fadl ibn Shadhan from ibn abu 'Umayr from Jamil ibn Darraj from Zurarah who has said the following:

"I once asked abu Ja'far, *'Alayhi al-Salam*, about one who forgets the opening Takbir (Allah is great beyond description). He (the Imam) said, 'He says it again.'"

H 5118, Ch. 35, h 2

Al-Husayn ibn Muhammad al-Ash'ariy has narrated from 'Abd Allah ibn 'Amir from Ali ibn Mahziyar from Fadalah from Aban from al-Fadl ibn 'Abd al-Malik or ibn abu Ya'fur who has said the following:

"About a man who performs Salat (prayer) but forgets to say the opening Takbir (Allah is great beyond description) if Takbir (Allah is great beyond description) for Ruku' (bowing down on one's knees) is sufficient. Abu 'Abd Allah, *'Alayhi al-Salam*, has said, 'It is not sufficient. He performs Salat (prayer) again when he finds out that he has not said the Takbir (Allah is great beyond description).'"

H 5119, Ch. 35, h 3

Muhammad ibn Yahya in a marfu' manner has narrated from the following:

"Al-Rida, *'Alayhi al-Salam*, has said, 'An Imam carries and sustains the conjectures of those who are behind him except the opening Takbir (Allah is great beyond description).'"

Chapter 36 - Mistake in Recitation

H 5120, Ch. 36 h 1

Muhammad ibn 'Isma'il has narrated from al-Fadl ibn Shadhan from Hammad ibn 'Isa from Rib'iy ibn 'Abd Allah from Muhammad ibn Muslim who has said the following:

"One of the two Imam, *'Alayhim al-Salam*, has said, 'Allah has made Ruku' (bowing down on one's knees) and Sujud (prostrations) obligatory. Recitation is Sunnah. Whoever omits recitation willfully performs Salat (prayer) again. Whoever forgets recitation his Salat (prayer) is complete and he is not obligated for anything in this matter.'"

H 5121, Ch. 36, h 2

Muhammad ibn Yahya has narrated from Ahmad ibn Muhammad from al-Husayn ibn Sa'id from al-Qasim ibn Muhammad, from Ali ibn abu Hamzah from abu Basir, from who has said the following:

"I once asked abu 'Abd Allah, *'Alayhi al-Salam*, about a man who forgets 'Umm al-Quran (al-Fatihah). He (the Imam) said, 'If he has not yet reached Ruku' position, he recites it again.'"

H 5122, Ch. 36, h 3

Muhammad ibn Yahya has narrated from Ahmad ibn Muhammad from ibn Faddal from Yunus ibn Ya'qub from Mansur ibn Hazim who has said the following:

"I once said to abu 'Abd Allah, *'Alayhi al-Salam*, 'I performed the obligatory Salat (prayer) but forgot the recitation in all of my Salat (prayer). He (the Imam) asked, 'Did you complete Ruku' (bowing down on one's knees) and Sujud (prostrations)?' I replied, 'Yes, I did so.' He (the Imam) said, 'Your Salat (prayer) is complete if it was because of forgetfulness.'"

Chapter 37 - Mistake in Ruku'

H 5123, Ch. 37, h 1

Muhammad ibn Yahya has narrated from Ahmad ibn Muhammad from al-Husayn ibn Sa'id from Fadalah ibn Ayyub from al-Husayn ibn 'Uthman from ibn Muskan from abu Basir who has said the following:

"I once asked abu 'Abd Allah, *'Alayhi al-Salam*, about a man who in a standing position doubts and does not know if he has performed Ruku' (bowing down on one's knees) or not. He (the Imam) said, 'He performs Ruku' and Sajdah (prostration).'"

H 5124, Ch. 37, h 2

Ali ibn Ibrahim has narrated from his father from and Muhammad ibn 'Isma'il from al-Fadl ibn Shadhan all from ibn abu 'Umayr from Rifa'ah who has said the following:

"I once asked abu 'Abd Allah, *'Alayhi al-Salam*, about a man who forgets performing Ruku' (bowing down on one's knees) until he performs Sajdah (prostration) and stands up. He (the Imam) said, 'He performs Salat (prayer) again.'"

H 5125, Ch. 37, h 3

Ali ibn Ibrahim has narrated from his father from ibn abu 'Umayr from 'Umar ibn 'Udhaynah from Zurarah who has said the following:

"Abu Ja'far, *'Alayhi al-Salam*, has sad, 'If one is certain that he has increased one Rak'at in an obligatory Salat (prayer) he disregards it and performs that Salat (prayer) again if he has certainty.'"

Chapter 38 - Mistake in Sujud (prostrations)

H 5126, Ch. 38, h 1

Ali ibn Ibrahim has narrated from his father from ibn abu 'Umayr from Hammad from al-Halabiy who has said the following:

"Abu 'Abd Allah, *'Alayhi al-Salam*, was asked about a man who becomes confused and does not know if he has done one or two Sajdah (prostrations). He (the Imam) said, 'He performs another Sajdah (prostration) and after completion of Salat (prayer) two Sajdah (prostration) because of mistake is not necessary.'"

H 5127, Ch. 38, h 2

Muhammad ibn Yahya has narrated from Ahmad ibn Muhammad from al-Husayn ibn Sa'id from Muhammad ibn Sinan from ibn Muskan from abu Basir from who has said the following:

"I once asked abu 'Abd Allah, *'Alayhi al-Salam*, about a man who doubts and does not know if he has performed one or two Sajdah (prostrations). He (the Imam) said, 'He performs Sajdah (prostration) to ascertain that it is two Sajdah (prostrations).'"

H 5128, Ch. 38, h 3

It is a narration from him (narrator of previous Hadith) by Ahmad ibn Muhammad from Ahmad ibn Muhammad ibn abu Nasr and Ali ibn Muhammad from Sahl ibn Ziyad from Ahmad ibn Muhammad ibn abu Nasr who has said the following:

"I once asked abu al-Hassan, *'Alayhi al-Salam*, about a man who performs one Rak'at of Salat (prayer), then he remembers in the second Rak'at in Ruku' (bowing down on one's knees) position that he has omitted one Sajdah (prostration) of the first Rak'at. He said, 'Abu al-Hassan, *'Alayhi al-Salam*, would say that if you omit Sajdah (prostration) in the first Rak'at and do not know if it is one or two; perform Salat (prayer) again until it is correct to say that two Sajdah (prostrations) are performed.'"

H 5129, Ch. 38, h 4
Ali ibn Ibrahim has narrated from his father from ibn abu 'Umayr from 'Amr ibn 'Uthman al-Khazzaz from al-Mufaddal ibn Salih from Zayd al-Shahham who has said the following:
"About a man who doubts and does not know if he has performed one or two Sajdah (prostrations), abu 'Abd Allah, *'Alayhi al-Salam*, has said, 'He performs one more Sajdah (prostration).'"

Chapter 39 - Mistake in the First Two Rak'at

H 5130, Ch. 39, h 1
Muhammad ibn al-Hassan and others have narrated from Sahl ibn Ziyad from Muhammad ibn Sinan from ibn Muskan from 'Anbasah ibn Mus'ab who has said the following:
"Once, abu 'Abd Allah, *'Alayhi al-Salam*, said to me, 'If you doubt in the first two Rak'at, perform your Salat (prayer) again.'"

H 5131, Ch. 39, h 2
Al-Husayn ibn Muhammad has narrated from 'Abd Allah ibn 'Amir from Ali ibn Mahziyar from al-Husayn ibn Sa'id from Zur'ah ibn Muhammad from Sama'ah who has said the following:
"He (the Imam), *'Alayhi al-Salam*, has said, 'If one doubts in the first two Rak'at of al-Zuhr, al-'Asr and al-'Atmah and does not know he has performed one or two, he must perform his Salat (prayer) again.'"

H 5132, Ch. 39, h 3
Muhammad ibn 'Isma'il has narrated from al-Fadl ibn Shadhan and Ali ibn Ibrahim has narrated from his father from all from Hammad ibn 'Isa from Hariz from Zurarah who has said the following:
"I once said to one of the two Imam, *'Alayhi al-Salam*, 'There is a man who does not know if he has performed one or two. He (the Imam) said, 'He performs his Salat (prayer) again.' I then asked, 'There is a man who does not know if he has performed two or three. He (the Imam) said, 'If he doubts after entering the third Rak'at, he continues his Salat (prayer), then performs one more (Rak'at); and he is not obligated for anything in this matter and he says the phrase of offering greeting of peace.' I then asked, 'One does not know if it is the second or fourth (Rak'at).' He (the Imam) said, 'He says the phrase of offering greeting of peace and performs two Rak'at, says the phrase of offering greeting of peace and he is not obligated for anything in this matter.'"

H 5133, Ch. 39, h 4
Muhammad ibn Yahya has narrated from Ahmad ibn Muhammad from al-Hassan ibn Ali al-Washsha' and al-Husayn ibn Muhammad from Mu'alla' ibn Muhammad from al-Hassan ibn Ali al-Washsha' who has said the following:
"Abu al-Hassan, al-Rida, *'Alayhi al-Salam*, once said to me, 'In the first two Rak'at it is performing again and confusion in the second two Rak'at (has remedies).'"

Chapter 40 -Mistake in the Morning, al-Maghrib and Friday Salat (Prayer)

H 5134, Ch. 40, h 1

Ali ibn Ibrahim has narrated from his father from and Muhammad ibn `Isma'il from al-Fadl ibn Shadhan all from ibn abu 'Umayr from Hafs ibn al-Bakhtariy and others who has said the following:

"Abu 'Abd Allah, *'Alayhi al-Salam*, has said, 'If you doubt in al-Maghrib Salat (prayer) perform it again. If you doubt in the morning Salat (prayer) perform it again.'"

H 5135, Ch. 40, h 2

Ali ibn Ibrahim has narrated from his father from Hammad, from Hariz from Muhammad ibn Muslim who has said the following:

"I once asked abu 'Abd Allah, *'Alayhi al-Salam*, about a man who performs Salat (prayer) but does not know if he has performed one or two (Rak'at). He (the Imam) said, 'He performs it again to ascertain that he has completed it and so also is the case with Friday, al-Maghrib and Salat (prayer) on a journey.'"

H 5136, Ch. 40, h 3

Al-Husayn ibn Muhammad al-Ash'ariy has narrated from 'Abd Allah ibn 'Amir from Ali ibn Mahziyar from Fadalah ibn Ayyub from Sayf ibn 'Amirah from abu Bakr al-Hadramiy who has said the following:

"I once performed al-Maghrib Salat (prayer) with my people but after two Rak'at I said the phrase of offering greeting of peace and someone from them said, 'You performed only two Rak'at.' I performed it again. I then informed abu 'Abd Allah, *'Alayhi al-Salam*, about it and he said, 'Perhaps you performed it again.' I said, 'Yes, I did so.' He (the narrator) has said that he (the Imam) smiled and said, 'You only had to stand up and perform one Rak'at.'"

H 5137, Ch. 40, h 4

Ali ibn Ibrahim has narrated from Muhammad ibn 'Isa from Yunus from a man who has said the following:

"Abu 'Abd Allah, *'Alayhi al-Salam*, has said, 'There is no confusion (acceptable) in al-Maghrib and morning Salat (prayer).'"

Chapter 41 - Mistakes in Salat (Prayer) of Three or Four Rak'at

H 5138, Ch. 41, h 1

Muhammad ibn Yahya and others has narrated from Ahmad ibn Muhammad from al-Husayn ibn Sa'id from Fadalah from al-Husayn ibn 'Uthman from Sama'ah from abu Basir who has said the following:

"I once asked him (the Imam), *'Alayhi al-Salam*, about a man who performs Salat (prayer) but does not know if he is in the third or fourth Rak'at. He (the Imam) said, 'It depends on what his guessing indicates. If he according to his guess thinks it is the third or fourth he accepts it along with his soul, then performs two Rak'at in which he reads al-Fatihah al-Kitab only.'"

H 5139, Ch. 41, h 2

It is a narration from him (narrator of previous Hadith) by Ahmad ibn al-Husayn from Fadalah from al-Husayn ibn abu al-'Ala' who has said the following:

"Abu 'Abd Allah, *'Alayhi al-Salam*, has said, 'If one's guess settles on his performing three or four Rak'at, he says the phrase of offering greeting of peace, then performs two Rak'at and four Sujud (prostrations) with al-Fatihah al-Kitab in a sitting position and says Tashahhud (testimonies of belief).'"

H 5140, Ch. 41, h 3

Ali ibn Ibrahim has narrated from his father and Muhammad ibn 'Isma'il from al-Fadl ibn Shadhan all from Hammad ibn 'Isa from Hariz from Zurarah who has said the following:

"I once asked one of the two Imam, *'Alayhim al-Salam*, about a man who performs Salat (prayer) but does not know if he is in the second or fourth Rak'at but he knows that he has performed two Rak'at. He (the Imam) said, 'He performs two Rak'at and four Sujud (prostrations). He does it in a standing position with al-Fatihah al-Kitab and Tashahhud (testimonies of belief) and he is not obligated for anything in this matter. If he does not know he is in the third or fourth and if he has secured three Rak'at, he stands up to perform one more Rak'at and he is not obligated for anything in this matter. He does not destroy his certainty with doubt and doubt does not enter into certainty. No one of them mixes with the other but doubt is destroyed by certainty and he completes with certainty, based on certainty and does not depend on doubt in no condition whatsoever.'"

H 5141, Ch. 41, h 4

Ali ibn Ibrahim has narrated from Muhammad ibn 'Isma'il from Yunus from ibn Muskan from ibn abu Ya'fur who has said the following:

"I once asked abu 'Abd Allah, *'Alayhi al-Salam*, about a man who does not know if he has performed two Rak'at or four. He (the Imam) said, 'He says Tashahhud (testimonies of belief) and the phrase of offering greeting of peace, then stands up to perform two Rak'at and four Sujud (prostrations) in which he reads al-Fatihah al-Kitab, thereafter says Tashahhud (testimonies of belief) and the phrase of offering greeting of peace. If he has, in fact, performed four Rak'at, the two Rak'at are optional; but if they were two Rak'at, then these two Rak'at complete the four, and if he has spoken something other than what is part of Salat (prayer) he performs two Sajdah (prostrations) because of mistake.'"

H 5142, Ch. 41, h 5

Hammad has narrated from Hariz from Muhammad ibn Muslim who has said the following:

"He (the Imam), *'Alayhi al-Salam*, has said, 'The case of doubt whether it is three or four or if it is two or four is of the same position. If one doubts and does not know if he has performed three or four and his doubt about both sides are equal', he (the Imam) said, 'Such person stands up and completes (Salat (prayer)). He then sits down, says Tashahhud (testimonies of belief) and the phrase of offering greeting of peace then performs two Rak'at and four Sujud (prostrations) in a sitting position. If his doubt has a greater side toward four, he says Tashahhud (testimonies of belief) and the phrase of offering greeting of peace then reads al-Fatihah al-Kitab and performs Ruku' (bowing down on one's knees) and Sajdah (prostration) then reads and performs two Sajdah (prostration), says Tashahhud (testimonies of belief) and the phrase of offering greeting of peace. If the greater side of his doubt is toward two Rak'at, he stands up, performs two Rak'at, says Tashahhud (testimonies of belief) and the phrase of offering greeting of peace.'"

H 5143, Ch. 41, h 6

Ali ibn Ibrahim has narrated from his father from ibn abu 'Umayr from certain persons of his people who has said the following:

"Abu 'Abd Allah, *'Alayhi al-Salam*, about the case of one who performs Salat (prayer) and doubts if he has performed two or four Rak'at, has said, 'He stands up and performs two Rak'at in a standing position. He then says the phrase of offering greeting of peace, then performs two Rak'at in a sitting position, and says the phrase of offering greeting of peace. If, in fact, they were four Rak'at the two Rak'at become optional; otherwise, they complete the four Rak'at.'"

H 5144, Ch. 41, h 7

Muhammad ibn Yahya has narrated from Ahmad ibn Muhammad from al-Husayn ibn Sa'id from Fadalah ibn Ayyub from Aban from 'Abd al-Rahman ibn Sayabah and abu al-'Abbas who has said the following:

"Abu 'Abd Allah, *'Alayhi al-Salam*, has said, 'If you do not know whether you have performed three or four Rak'at and your thought settles on three, then consider it three. If your thought settles on four, say Salam (the phrase of offering greeting of peace) and end Salat (prayer). If your guess is equal; end Salat (prayer), then perform two Rak'at in a sitting position.'"

H 5145, Ch. 41, h 8

Ali ibn Ibrahim has narrated from his father from ibn abu 'Umayr from Hammad ibn 'Uthman from al-Halabiy who has said the following:

"Abu 'Abd Allah, *'Alayhi al-Salam*, has said, 'You may not know whether you have performed two or four Rak'at and your guess about one side is not greater than the other side. You must say Tashahhud (testimonies of belief) and Salam (the phrase of offering greeting of peace), then perform two Rak'at and four Sujud (prostrations). Read in them 'Umm al-Quran, then say Tashahhud (testimonies of belief) and Salam (the phrase of offering greeting of peace). If, in fact, you had performed two Rak'at these two complete the four and if, in fact, you had performed four, these two become optional. If you do not know whether you have performed three or four Rak'at and your guess about one side is not greater than the other; say Salam (the phrase of offering greeting of peace), then perform two Rak'at in a sitting position. Read in them al-Fatihah al-Kitab. If your guess about three is greater, then perform the fourth Rak'at. Do not perform two Sajdah (prostration) because of mistake. If your guess about four is greater; say Tashahhud (testimonies of belief) and Salam (the phrase of offering greeting of peace) then perform two Sajdah (prostration) because of mistake.'"

H 5146, Ch. 41, h 9

Muhammad ibn Yahya has narrated from Ahmad ibn Muhammad from Ali ibn Hadid from Jamil certain persons of our people who have said the following:

"Abu 'Abd Allah, *'Alayhi al-Salam*, has said, 'One may not know whether he has performed three or four and his guess about both sides is equal. (For such case) he (the narrator) has said that he (the Imam) said, 'If his guess is equal about three and four, he has the choice to perform one Rak'at standing or two Rak'at in a sitting position and four Sujud (prostrations) in a sitting position.' He (the Imam), *'Alayhi al-Salam*, about a man who does not know if he has performed two or four Rak'at and his guess about four is greater or about two Rak'at, he (the Imam) said that he performs two Rak'at and four Sujud (prostrations). He (the Imam) said, 'If your guess about two Rak'at and four is equal, then this and the case of doubt about whether it is three or four Rak'at is not the same.'"

Chapter 42 - Mistake about Four or Five Rak'at

H 5147, Ch. 42, h 1

Ali ibn Ibrahim has narrated from his father from ibn abu 'Umayr from ibn 'Udhaynah from Zurarah who has said the following:

"I once heard abu Ja'far, *'Alayhi al-Salam*, say, 'The Messenger of Allah has said, "If one of you doubts in his Salat (prayer) and does not know if he has increased or decreased, he performs two Sajdah (prostration) while sitting." The Messenger of Allah has called it humiliating (Satan).'"

H 5148, Ch. 42, h 2

Ali ibn Ibrahim has narrated from his father from ibn abu 'Umayr from ibn 'Udhaynah from Zurarah and ibn Bukayr ibn A'yan who has said the following:

"Abu Ja'far, *'Alayhi al-Salam*, has said, 'If one of you is certain that he has increased something in his obligatory Salat (prayer) he does not depend on it and performs his Salat (prayer) again if he is certain of such increase.'"

H 5149, Ch. 42, h 3

Ali ibn Ibrahim has narrated from Muhammad ibn 'Isa from Yunus ibn 'Abd al-Rahman from 'Abd Allah ibn Sinan who has said the following:

"Abu 'Abd Allah, *'Alayhi al-Salam*, has said, 'If you do not know whether you have performed four or five; then perform two Sujud (prostrations) because of mistake after Salam (the phrase of offering greeting of peace) and after the two Sujud (prostrations), say Salam.'"

H 5150, Ch. 42, h 4

Muhammad ibn Yahya has narrated from Ahmad ibn Muhammad ibn 'Isa from 'Uthman ibn 'Isa from Sama'ah who has said the following:

"He (the Imam), *'Alayhi al-Salam*, has said, 'If one knows the kind of mistake he has made and completes it then Sajdah (prostration) for mistake is not necessary for him. Sajdah (prostration) for mistake is upon one who does not know if he has increased or decreased something in Salat (prayer).'"

H 5151, Ch. 42, h 5

Al-Husayn ibn Muhammad has narrated from 'Abd Allah ibn 'Amir from Ali ibn Mahziyar from Fadalah ibn Ayyub from Aban ibn 'Uthman from abu Basir from who has said the following:

"Abu 'Abd Allah, *'Alayhi al-Salam*, has said, 'If one increases something in his Salat (prayer) he performs it again.'"

H 5152, Ch. 42, h 6
Muhammad ibn Yahya has narrated from Ahmad ibn Muhammad from Hammad ibn 'Isa from Shu'ayb from abu Basir who has said the following:
"Abu 'Abd Allah, *'Alayhi al-Salam*, has said, 'If you do not know whether you have performed five Rak'at or four, perform two Sajdah (prostration) because of mistake after Salam (the phrase of offering greeting of peace) in a sitting position and thereafter say Salam (the phrase of offering greeting of peace).'"

Chapter 43 - Speaking During Salat (Prayer), or Turning Away Before Completion

H 5153, Ch. 43, h 1
Muhammad ibn Yahya has narrated from Ahmad ibn Muhammad ibn 'Isa from 'Uthman ibn 'Isa from Sama'ah ibn Mehran who has said the following:
"Abu 'Abd Allah, *'Alayhi al-Salam*, has said, 'If one knows the kind of mistake he has made, he completes it, and Sajdah (prostration) for mistake is not necessary for him. The Messenger of Allah performed al-Zuhr Salat (prayer) with people as two Rak'at, then he mistakenly said Salam (the phrase of offering greeting of peace). Dhu al-Shamalayn asked him, "O Messenger of Allah, is anything revealed about Salat (prayer)?" The Messenger of Allah asked, "Why is that?" He said that it is because you performed two Rak'at. The Messenger of Allah then asked others, "Do you also say what he says?" They replied, "Yes, he is right." The Messenger of Allah stood up, completed Salat (prayer) with them and performed two Sajdah (prostration) with them because of mistake.' He (the narrator) has said that I then asked, 'What do you say about the case of one who performs two Rak'at and thinks that it is four, then says Salam (the phrase of offering greeting of peace) and moves away; then remembers after moving away that he has performed two Rak'at? He (the Imam) said, 'He performs it again from the beginning.' He (the narrator) has said that he then asked, 'Why did the Messenger of Allah not perform again? He only completed with them whatever remained of his Salat (prayer). He (the Imam) said, 'It is because the Messenger of Allah had not left his place. If one does not leave his place, he completes what is deficient of his Salat (prayer), provided, he has secured the first two Rak'at.'"

H 5154, Ch. 43, h 2
Ali ibn Ibrahim has narrated from his father from ibn abu 'Umayr from 'Umar from Fudayl ibn Yasar who has said the following:
"Abu Ja'far, *'Alayhi al-Salam*, about a man who performs two Rak'at obligatory, then forgets and stands up before sitting between them, has said, 'He sits down until he has not assumed Ruku' (bowing down on one's knees). His Salat (prayer) is complete. If he does not remember until he assumes Ruku', he then continues and after Salam (the phrase of offering greeting of peace) performs two Sajdah (prostration) because of mistake in a sitting position.'"

H 5155, Ch. 43, h 3

A number of our people have narrated from Ahmad ibn Muhammad al-Barqiy from Mansur ibn al-'Abbas from 'Amr ibn Sa'id from al-Hassan ibn Sadaqah who has said the following:

"I once asked abu al-Hassan al-Awwal, *'Alayhi al-Salam*, 'Did the Messenger of Allah say Salam (the phrase of offering greeting of peace) in the first two Rak'at while his status was as it was? He (the Imam) said, 'Yes; Allah, most Majestic, most Glorious, willed to give them (people) proper understanding.'"

H 5156, Ch. 43, h 4

Muhammad ibn Yahya has narrated from Muhammad ibn al-Husayn Ahmad ibn Muhammad from Muhammad ibn 'Isma'il from al-Fadl ibn Shadhan all from Safwan ibn Yahya from 'Abd al-Rahman ibn al-Hajjaj who has said the following:

"I once asked abu 'Abd Allah, *'Alayhi al-Salam*, about a man who speaks because of forgetfulness in Salat (prayer) saying, 'Straighten your rows.' He (the Imam) said, 'He completes his Salat (prayer), then performs two Sajdah (prostration).' I then asked, 'Are the two Sajdah (prostration) because of mistake after or before Salam (the phrase of offering greeting of peace)?' He (the Imam) said, 'It is afterward.'"

H 5157, Ch. 43, h 5

Ali ibn Ibrahim has narrated from his father from ibn abu 'Umayr from Hammad from al-Halabiy who has said the following:

"Abu 'Abd Allah, *'Alayhi al-Salam*, has said, 'In the two Sajdah (prostration) because of mistake say, 'In the name of Allah and with Allah, O Allah, grant compensation to Muhammad and his family worthy of their services to Your cause.' Al-Halabiy has said that I heard him (the Imam) in another time say, 'In the name of Allah and with Allah, O Holy prophet, Allah has granted you kindness and blessings.'"

H 5158, Ch. 43, h 6

Muhammad ibn Yahya has narrated from Ahmad ibn Muhammad ibn 'Isa from Ali ibn al-Nu'man from Sa'id al-'A'raj who has said the following:

"I heard abu 'Abd Allah, *'Alayhi al-Salam*, say, 'The Messenger of Allah once said Salam (the phrase of offering greeting of peace) in two Rak'at and those behind him asked, "O Messenger of Allah, has something happened to Salat (prayer)?" The Messenger of Allah asked, "Why is that?" They replied, "You performed only two Rak'at." The Messenger of Allah then asked, "Was it so, O Dhu al-Yadayn?" – he was also called Dhu al-Shamalayn - He replied, "Yes, it was so." The Messenger of Allah based his Salat (prayer) on that and completed it as four Rak'at.' He (the Imam) said, 'Allah made him to forget to grant and make it a mercy for the nation (his followers). Is it not true that if a man does so, he is reproached and is told that his Salat (prayer) is not accepted? If today someone experiences such condition he says that the Messenger of Allah has established a Sunnah (tradition) and it has become a guideline to follow. He (the Messenger of Allah) then performed two Sajdah (prostration) because of speaking.'"

H 5159, Ch. 43, h 7

Muhammad ibn Yahya has narrated from Ahmad ibn Muhammad from al-Husayn ibn Sa'id from al-Qasim ibn Muhammad from Ali ibn abu Hamzah who has said the following:

"Abu 'Abd Allah, *'Alayhi al-Salam*, has said, 'If you stand up in the first two Rak'at without saying Tashahhud (testimonies of belief), then remember before Ruku' (bowing down on one's knees), you must sit down. You must say Tashahhud (testimonies of belief). In case, if you do not remember until Ruku', then continue your Salat (prayer) as you are. When you end, perform two Sajdah (prostration) without Ruku', then say Tashahhud (testimonies of belief) which you had missed.'"

H 5160, Ch. 43, h 8

Ali ibn Ibrahim has narrated from his father from ibn abu 'Umayr from Hammad ibn 'Uthman from al-Halabiy who has said the following:

"Abu 'Abd Allah, *'Alayhi al-Salam* has stated this Hadith. He (the Imam) has said, 'You may stand up in the two Rak'at of al-Zuhr or others without saying Tashahhud (testimonies of belief) and remember it in the third Rak'at before Ruku' (bowing down on one's knees), you must sit down, then say Tashahhud (testimonies of belief), then stand up and complete your Salat (prayer). In case, if you do not remember until Ruku', then continue your Salat (prayer) until the end. When you complete it, then perform two Sajdah (prostration) because of mistake after Salam (the phrase of offering greeting of peace) and before speaking.'"

H 5161, Ch. 43, h 9

Ali ibn Ibrahim has narrated from Muhammad ibn 'Isa from Yunus from Mu'awiyah ibn 'Ammar who has said the following:

"I once asked him (the Imam), *'Alayhi al-Salam*, about a man who mistakenly stands up where he was to sit or sits down where he was to stand up. He (the Imam) said, 'He performs two Sajdah (prostration) after Salam (the phrase of offering greeting of peace) which are destroyers to destroy Satan.'"

Chapter 44 - Facing Doubts about Salat (Prayer) As a Whole, Not Knowing if It Is Increased or Decreased, One Facing Mistakes Very Often, Mistakes in Optional Salat (prayer) and Mistakes of an Imam and Those behind Him

H 5162, Ch. 44, h 1

Muhammad ibn Yahya has narrated from Ahmad ibn Muhammad ibn 'Isa from Muhammad ibn Khalid from Sa'd ibn Sa'd from Safwan who has said the following:

"Abu al-Hassan, *'Alayhi al-Salam*, has said, 'If you do not know how many Rak'at you have performed and your guess does not settle anywhere, perform your Salat (prayer) again.'"

H 5163, Ch. 44, h 2

Ali ibn Ibrahim has narrated from his father from Hammad ibn 'Isa and Muhammad ibn 'Isma'il from al-Fadl ibn Shadhan from Hammad ibn 'Isa from Hariz from Zurarah and abu Basir who have said the following:

"We once asked him (the Imam), *'Alayhi al-Salam*, about a man who doubts very often and does not know how many Rak'at he has performed and how many Rak'at remain. He (the Imam) said, 'He performs again.' We then asked, 'It becomes a great many on him, because every time he performs again he doubts.' He (the Imam) said, 'He continues with his doubts.' He (the Imam) then said, 'You must not allow the filth to mix with your souls by discontinuing your Salat (prayer) to feed him. Satan, the filthy gets used to whatever habit he is allowed. One of you may continue with his guess and do not discontinue Salat (prayer) very often. If one does so several times, doubt does not return to him.' Zurarah has said that he (the Imam) then said, 'The filthy wants to be obeyed. If he is disobeyed, he does not come back to anyone of you.'"

H 5164, Ch. 44, h 3

Hammad has narrated from ibn abu Ya'fur who has said the following:

"Abu 'Abd Allah, *'Alayhi al-Salam*, has said, 'If you doubt and do not know if you have performed three or two or one or four, perform Salat (prayer) again and do not continue with doubt.'"

H 5165, Ch. 44, h 4

Ali ibn Ibrahim has narrated from his father from al-Nawfaliy from al-Sakuniy who has said the following:

"Abu 'Abd Allah, *'Alayhi al-Salam*, has said, 'Once a man came to the Holy prophet, and said, "O Messenger of Allah, I complain before you against misgivings I face in my Salat (prayer) so much so that I do not know how much I have performed, increased or decreased. He (the Messenger of Allah) said, 'When you begin your Salat (prayer) hit your left thigh with your right forefinger and say, 'In the name of Allah, I choose Allah, the all-knowing and all-hearing as my attorney against Satan, condemned to be stoned, thus, you slaughter and repel him.'"

H 5166, Ch. 44, h 5

Ali ibn Ibrahim has narrated from Muhammad ibn 'Isa from Yunus from a man who has said the following:

"I once asked abu 'Abd Allah, *'Alayhi al-Salam*, about the case of an Imam who leads four or five people in Salat (prayer). Of these people two of them say Tasbih (Allah is free of all defects) indicating that it is three Rak'at and three of them say Tasbih (Allah is free of all defects) to indicate that it is four Rak'at. These ones say to stand up, these ones say to sit down, and the Imam is inclined toward one side or has equal guess about both sides. What is he to do? He (the Imam) said, 'Imam does not have mistakes if those behind him preserve (the order of Salat) with their certainty and those behind the Imam do not have mistakes if the Imam does not have mistakes. There is no mistake (applicable) in mistakes, (about the number of Rak'at) correctable in al-Maghrib, in the morning Salat (prayer), in the first two Rak'at of every Salat (prayer) and in optional Salat (prayer). If those behind the Imam differ with the Imam then it is upon him and upon them to observe caution by performing again for ascertainment.'"

H 5167, Ch. 44, h 6

Ali ibn Ibrahim has narrated from Muhammad ibn 'Isa from Yunus fro, al-'Ala' ibn Razin from Muhammad ibn Muslim who has said the following:

"I once asked one of the two Imam, *'Alayhim al-Salam*, about mistakes in optional Salat (prayer). He (the Imam) said, 'There is not anything upon him.'"

H 5168, Ch. 44, h 7

Ali ibn Ibrahim has narrated from his father from and Muhammad ibn 'Isma'il from al-Fadl ibn Shadhan all from ibn abu 'Umayr from Hafs ibn al-Bakhtariy who has said the following:

"Abu 'Abd Allah, *'Alayhi al-Salam*, has said, 'Mistake is not applicable in the case of an Imam, in the case of those behind an Imam, and it is not applicable about a mistake in a mistake or about repeat of the repeat.'"

H 5169, Ch. 44, h 8

Muhammad ibn Yahya has narrated from Muhammad ibn al-Husayn from Safwan from al-'Ala' from Muhammad ibn Muslim who has said the following:

"Abu Ja'far, *'Alayhi al-Salam*, has sad, 'If mistakes become many on you then continue in your Salat (prayer), eventually it may leave you alone; it is from Satan.'"

H 5170, Ch. 44, h 9

Muhammad ibn Yahya has narrated from Ahmad ibn Muhammad from ibn Faddal from ibn Bukayr from 'Ubayd Allah al-Halabiy who has said the following:

"I once asked abu 'Abd Allah, *'Alayhi al-Salam*, about mistakes which befall on me a great deal. He (the Imam) said, 'Incorporate your Salat (prayer) properly.' I then asked, 'What is incorporating?' He (the Imam) said, 'It is saying three Tasbih (Allah is free of all defects) in Ruku' (bowing down on one's knees) and in Sujud (prostrations).' "It is narrated that if one makes mistakes in optional Salat (prayer) he considers it to be of the lesser side."

(The following to the next chapter seems to be like fatwa of al-Kulayni (rh) that he has summarized)

"All the cases of mistakes are seventeen in number. In seven of them it is necessary to perform Salat (prayer) again. (1) One case is when one forgets the opening Takbir (Allah is great beyond description) which one does not remember until Ruku' (bowing down on one's knees) (2) The second case is when one forgets Ruku' (bowing down on one's knees) and Sujud (prostrations). (3) The third case is when one forgets and does not know if he has performed one or two Rak'at. (4) The fourth case is when one forgets something in al-Maghrib and in the morning Salat (prayer). (5) It is when one increases something in his Salat (prayer). (6) It is when one does not know if he has increased or decreased and his guess does not settle anywhere. (7) It is when one moves away from Salat (prayer) before completing.

"There are those conditions in which performing Salat (prayer) again is not necessary. Only two Sajdah (prostration) because of mistake is necessary. Of such cases is: (1) when one says Salam (the phrase of offering greeting of peace) in two Rak'at then speaks before moving away his face from al-Qiblah (al-

Ka'bah). He completes his Salat (prayer), then performs two Sajdah (prostration) because of mistake. (2) One who forgets Tashahhud (testimonies of belief) and does not sit down in two Rak'at and it is missed until Ruku' (bowing down on one's knees) in the third Rak'at. He performs two Sajdah (prostration) because of mistake and makes up for Tashahhud (testimonies of belief) which is missed. (3) One who does not know if he has performed four or five, has to perform two Sajdah (prostration) because of mistake. (4) One who by mistake speaks in his Salat (prayer) improperly, like commanding or prohibiting because of forgetfulness and not in a willful manner. He performs two Sajdah (prostration). Sajdah (prostration) is necessary in these four cases. Of such cases are where performing Salat (prayer) again is not necessary as well as Sajdah (prostration) because of mistake. (1) One is he who corrects his mistake before it is late like one who is to stand up but instead sits down or is to sit down but stands up then remembers it before entering in another condition, in such case he is to perform Qada' (perform a compensatory) for it. (2) Another is he who says Salam (the phrase of offering greeting of peace) in the first two Rak'at then remembers. He completes before he speaks in which case the rules for mistake is not applicable to his case. (3) The rule for mistake does apply to the case of one behind an Imam who remembers and (4) as well as to the case of an Imam if people behind him remember. (5) The rule for mistake does not apply to mistake in a mistake. (6) The rule for does not apply to a mistake in optional Salat (prayer) and the rule for mistake does not apply to a repeat in optional Salat (prayer). These are six cases where repeat is not necessary as well as two Sajdah (prostration) because of mistake.

"One who doubts about the opening Takbir (Allah is great beyond description) and does not know if he has said it or not, he is to say it when he remembers before Ruku', then does the recitation then Ruku'. If one doubts in Ruku' and does not know if he has said the opening Takbir (Allah is great beyond description) or not, he continues his Salat (prayer) and he is not obligated for anything in this matter. If he becomes certain of not saying the opening Takbir (Allah is great beyond description), he performs his Salat (prayer) again. If one doubts when he is standing and he does not know if he has performed Ruku' or not, he performs Ruku' to ascertain his performing Ruku'. If one performs Ruku', then remembers that he has already performed Ruku', he sends himself down to Sajdah (prostration) without raising his head from Ruku' in Ruku'. If he continues and raises his head from Ruku', then remembers that he has already performed Ruku', he performs his Salat (prayer) again; he has increased in his Salat (prayer) one Rak'at. One who performs Sajdah (prostration) and because of doubt does not know if one has performed Ruku' or not, one continues his Salat (prayer) and he is not obligated for anything in this matter, because of his doubt unless one becomes certain that one has not performed Ruku'. In this case one performs his Salat (prayer) again. If one performs Sajdah (prostration) and does not know if one has performed one or two Sajdah (prostration), one is to perform another Sajdah (prostration) to ascertain performing two Sajdah (prostration). If one performs Sajdah (prostration) and remembers that he has already performed two Sajdah (prostration), one is to perform his Salat (prayer) again, because of increase in his Salat (prayer) one Sajdah (prostration). If one doubts after standing and does not know if one has performed one or two Sajdah (prostration) one is to continue his Salat (prayer) and he is not obligated for anything in this matter. If one is certain that one has performed only one Sajdah (prostration), one is to perform another Sajdah (prostration) and he is not obligated for anything in this matter. If one reads Surah (chapter) then remembers that one has performed only one Sajdah (prostration), one is to perform another Sajdah (prostration), then stand up to complete the recitation and perform Ruku' and he is not obligated for anything in this matter. If one performs Ruku' and becomes certain that one has not performed any Sajdah (prostration) but only one Sajdah (prostration) or has not performed any Sajdah (prostration) at all, one is to perform Salat (prayer) again.'"

Mistakes in Tashahhud (testimonies of belief)

"If one by mistake stands up before Tashahhud (testimonies of belief) in two Rak'at, he is to sit down and say Tashahhud, if he has not reached in Ruku' (bowing down on one's knees), then stand up and continues his Salat (prayer) and he is not obligated for anything in this matter. If one has assumed Ruku' and learns that one has not said Tashahhud, continues one's Salat (prayer) and when one ends his Salat (prayer) performs two Sajdah (prostration) because of mistake and he is not obligated for anything in the condition of doubt as long one is not certain."

Mistakes about Two or Four Rak'at

"One who doubts and does not know if one has performed two or four Rak'at, if one's guess settles on four, one says Salam (the phrase of offering greeting of peace) and he is not obligated for anything in this matter. If one's guess settles on one's performing two Rak'at, one performs two more Rak'at and he is not obligated for anything in this matter if one's guess is equal, one says Salam (the phrase of offering greeting of peace), then performs two Rak'at in a standing position with al-Fatihah al-Kitab. If, in fact, one has performed two Rak'at these two Rak'at complete the four and if, in fact, one has performed four Rak'at these two become optional Salat (prayer).

Mistake about Two or Three Rak'at

"One who doubts and does not know if one has performed two or three Rak'at and his guess settles on the side of two Rak'at, one is to perform two more Rak'at and he is not obligated for anything in this matter. If one's guess settles on the side of three, one then is to perform one more Rak'at and he is not obligated for anything in this matter. If one's guess does not settle on either side and one is certain of performing two Rak'at, one is to perform one Rak'at in a standing position, then say Salam (the phrase of offering greeting of peace) and performs two Rak'at in a sitting position with al-Fatihah al-Kitab. If one, in fact, has performed two Rak'at, the two Rak'at performed in a standing position before Salam (the phrase of offering greeting of peace) complete the four Rak'at. The two Rak'at in a sitting position are in place of one Rak'at and his Salat (prayer) is complete. If one has performed three Rak'at the one Rak'at performed in a standing position completes the four Rak'at and the two Rak'at one has performed in a sitting position are counted as optional Salat (prayer).

Mistakes about Four or Three Rak'at

"One who doubts and does not know if one has performed three or four and his guess settles on the side of three Rak'at, one is to perform one Rak'at, then say Salam (the phrase of offering greeting of peace) and he is not obligated for anything in this matter. If one's guess settles on the side of four, one says Salam and he is not obligated for anything in this matter. If one's guess settles on three and four, one says Salam with his doubtful condition and performs two Rak'at in a sitting position with al-Fatihah al-Kitab. If one has performed three the two Rak'at are counted as one to complete the four, and if one has performed four Rak'at these two are counted as optional Salat (prayer) in one's favor.

Mistakes about Four or Five Rak'at

"One who doubts and does not know if one has performed four or five Rak'at, if one's guess settles on the side of four, one is to say Salam (the phrase of offering greeting of peace) and he is not obligated for anything in this matter. If one's guess settles on five one performs his Salat (prayer) again. If one's guess about both sides are equal one is to say Salam, then perform two Sajdah (prostration) because of mistake which are destroyers (of Satan).

Chapter 45 - Matters Accepted From Salat (Prayer) of a Forgetful Person

H 5171, Ch. 45, h 1

Muhammad ibn Yahya has narrated from Ahmad ibn Muhammad from al-Husayn ibn Sa'id from al-Nadr ibn Suwayd from Hisham ibn Salim from Muhammad ibn Muslim who has said the following:

"I once said to abu 'Abd Allah, *'Alayhi al-Salam*, ''Ammar al-Sabatiy has narrated from you a Hadith.' He (the Imam) asked, 'What Hadith is it?' I then said, 'He narrates that Sunnah is obligatory.' He (the Imam) said, 'Where does he go! Where does he go! I did not speak to him as such. I only said to him that when performing Salat (prayer) if one is attentive toward it, does not speak to one's soul in it and does not make mistakes in it, Allah comes forward eagerly to what is performed eagerly. Perhaps one half is raised, one fourth, one third or one fifth is raised. We command to perform Sunnah only to complete what is missed of obligatory ones.'"

H 5172, Ch. 45, h 2

Muhammad ibn Yahya has narrated from Ahmad ibn Muhammad from ibn abu 'Umayr Hisham ibn Salim from Muhammad ibn Muslim who has said the following:

"Abu Ja'far, *'Alayhi al-Salam*, has said, 'Of Salat (prayer) of a servant (of Allah) sometimes one-half, sometimes one-third, one-fourth or one-fifth is raised. Whatever is raised is only what one has performed with love from his heart. We only command to perform optional Salat (prayer) to complete what it is cut short of obligatory ones.'"

H 5173, Ch. 45, h 3

It is a narration from him (narrator of previous Hadith) by Ahmad ibn Muhammad from al-Husayn ibn Sa'id from al-Qasim ibn Muhammad from Ali ibn abu Hamzah from abu Basir from who has said the following:

"Once, when I was present, a man said to abu 'Abd Allah, *'Alayhi al-Salam*, 'I pray to Allah to keep my soul in service for your cause, I make a great number of mistakes in my Salat (prayer).' He (the Imam) said, 'Has anyone remained safe thereby?' I (the narrator) then said, 'I think no one makes as many mistakes as I do.' Abu 'Abd Allah, *'Alayhi al-Salam*, then said to him, 'O abu Muhammad, sometimes of Salat (prayer) of a servant (of Allah) one-third is raised, sometimes one-half or three-fourth or less or more depending upon the quantity of one's mistakes in that Salat (prayer). However, it is completed with his optional Salat (prayer).' Abu Basir then said to him (the Imam), 'I think, optional Salat (prayer) should not be omitted in any condition.' Abu 'Abd Allah, *'Alayhi al-Salam*, then said, 'Yes, it should not be omitted.'"

H 5174, Ch. 45, h 4

Ali ibn Ibrahim has narrated from his father and Muhammad ibn 'Isma'il from al-Fadl ibn Shadhan all from Hammad ibn 'Isa from Hariz from Fudayl ibn Yasar who has said the following:

"Abu Ja'far, and abu 'Abd Allah, *'Alayhim al-Salam*, have said, 'Of your Salat (prayer) only that much is for you which you have performed with love. If one instills delusion in Salat (prayer) or omits it altogether, then such Salat (prayer) is rolled up and is struck against the face of its owner.'"

H 5175, Ch. 45, h 5

Ali ibn Ibrahim has narrated from his father from 'Abd Allah ibn al-Mughirah who has said the following:

"It is in the book of Hariz who has said that once I forgot about my being in obligatory Salat (prayer) until Ruku' (bowing down on one's knees). Can I make my intention for it to be an optional Salat (prayer)? He (the Imam), *'Alayhi al-Salam*, said, 'It is what you had stood up for. If you stood up to perform an obligatory Salat (prayer) then doubts entered, you are still in obligatory Salat (prayer). If you stood up for optional Salat (prayer) then made your intention for obligatory Salat (prayer), you were still in optional Salat (prayer). If you stood up for obligatory then you remembered optional Salat (prayer) which was due, you were to complete it as obligatory.'"

Chapter 46 - Things That Invalidate Salat (Prayer) Like Laughing, Invalidating Wudu', Making a Gesture, Forgetting and So on

H 5176, Ch. 46, h 1

A group has narrated from Ahmad ibn Muhammad ibn 'Isa, from al-Husayn ibn Sa'id, from his brother al-Hassan, from Zur'ah, from Sama'ah who has said the following:

"I once asked him (the Imam), *'Alayhi al-Salam*, about laughing if it destroys Salat (prayer). He (the Imam) said, 'Smiling does not destroy Salat (prayer) but laughing loudly destroys it.'"

"It (the above Hadith) also is narrated from Ahmad ibn Muhammad from 'Uthman ibn 'Isa from Sama'ah."

H 5177, Ch. 46, h 2

Ali ibn Ibrahim has narrated from his father from ibn abu 'Umayr from Hammad from al-Halabiy who has said the following:

"I once asked abu 'Abd Allah, *'Alayhi al-Salam*, about a man who experiences nostril bleeding in Salat (prayer). He (the Imam) said, 'If it is possible for him to reach on his right, left or forward when still facing al-Qiblah (al-Ka'bah), he washes it clean, then completes the remaining of his Salat (prayer). If he cannot find water without turning away from al-Qiblah (al-Ka'bah), his Salat (prayer) is discontinued.'"

H 5178, Ch. 46, h 3

Muhammad ibn Yahya has narrated from Muhammad ibn al-Husayn from Safwan ibn Yahya from 'Abd al-Rahman ibn al-Hajjaj who has said the following:

"I once asked abu al-Hassan, *'Alayhi al-Salam*, about a man who feels something in his abdomen and he is able to bear it. Can he perform Salat (prayer) in that condition or not? He (the Imam) said, 'If he can remain patient without fear of hastening his Salat (prayer), he completes his Salat (prayer) and exercise patience.'"

H 5179, Ch. 46, h 4

Muhammad ibn Yahya has narrated from Ahmad ibn Muhammad and Muhammad ibn al-Husayn from Muhammad ibn 'Isma'il ibn Bazi' from Mansur ibn Yunus from abu Bakr al-Hadramiy who has said the following:

"Abu Ja'far, and abu 'Abd Allah, *'Alayhim al-Salam*, would say, 'Only four things discontinue Salat (prayer): defecation, urination, gas and sound.'"

H 5180, Ch. 46, h 5

Ali ibn Ibrahim has narrated from Muhammad ibn 'Isa from Yunus from al-'Ala' from Muhammad ibn Muslim who has said the following:

"About a man who during Salat (prayer) touches his nose and finds blood; one of the two Imam, abu Ja'far or abu 'Abd Allah, *'Alayhim al-Salam*, has said, 'If it is dry he throws it away and it is not harmful.'"

H 5181, Ch. 46, h 6

Ali ibn Ibrahim has narrated from his father from ibn abu 'Umayr from Jamil ibn Darraj from Zurarah who has said the following:

"Abu 'Abd Allah, *'Alayhi al-Salam*, has said, 'Laughing does not invalidate Wudu' but it invalidates Salat (prayer).'"

H 5182, Ch. 46, h 7

It is a narration from him (narrator of previous Hadith) by ibn abu 'Umayr from Hammad from al-Halabiy who has said the following:

"Once abu 'Abd Allah, *'Alayhi al-Salam*, was asked about one who, while in Salat (prayer), needs something. He (the Imam) said, 'He can make a gesture with his head and with his hand or say Tasbih (Allah is free of all defects), and a woman in such condition can clap her hand.'"

H 5183, Ch. 46, h 8

Ali ibn Muhammad has narrated from Sahl ibn Ziyad from Muhammad ibn al-Hassan al-Shammun from 'Abd Allah ibn 'Abd al-Rahman al-Asamm from Misma' abu Sayyar who has said the following:

"Abu 'Abd Allah, *'Alayhi al-Salam*, has said, 'The Holy prophet once heard behind him a click like one's cracking his finger in his Salat (prayer). After ending his Salat (prayer) the Holy prophet, said, 'That is his share from his Salat (prayer).'"

H 5184, Ch. 46, h 9

Al-Husayn ibn Muhammad has narrated from 'Abd Allah ibn 'Amir from Ali ibn Mahziyar from Fadalah from al-'Ala' from Muhammad ibn Muslim who has said the following:

"I once asked abu Ja'far, *'Alayhi al-Salam*, about a man who experiences nose bleeding and vomiting while in Salat (prayer). What is he to do? He (the Imam) said, 'He turns to wash his nose and comes back to his Salat (prayer). If he has spoken, he must perform his Salat (prayer) again, but he does not need Wudu'.'"

H 5185, Ch. 46, h 10

Ali ibn Ibrahim has narrated from his father from ibn abu 'Umayr from Hammad from al-Halabiy who has said the following:

"I once asked abu 'Abd Allah, *'Alayhi al-Salam*, about a man whose Salat (prayer) is discontinued because of something passing in front of him. He (the Imam) said, 'Salat (prayer) of a Muslim does not become discontinued by anything; however, protect as much as you can.' He (the narrator) has said, 'I then asked him (the Imam) about a man who experiences nose bleeding which does not stop until the time of Salat (prayer). He (the Imam) said, 'He fills his nose up with something, then performs Salat (prayer), but does not take a long time if he fears bleeding.' He (the narrator) has said that he (the Imam) said, 'If he experiences nose bleeding in obligatory Salat (prayer) without break he performs his Salat (prayer) again if he has turned away from al-Qiblah (al-Ka'bah) before completing. If he has said Tashahhud (testimonies of belief), then he is not required to perform again.'"

H 5186, Ch. 46, h 11

Al-Husayn ibn Muhammad al-Ash'ariy has narrated from 'Abd Allah ibn 'Amir from Ali ibn Mahziyar from Fadalah from Aban from Salmah ibn abu Hafs who has said the following:

"Abu 'Abd Allah, *'Alayhi al-Salam*, has said, 'Ali, *'Alayhi al-Salam*, would say, 'Nose bleeding does not discontinue Salat (prayer) nor vomiting, or blood. If one feels a pinch he can hold another man's hand of the people in the rows to come forward, if he is an Imam, to lead.'"

H 5187, Ch. 46, h 12

Muhammad ibn Yahya has narrated from Muhammad ibn al-Husayn from Safwan from al-'Ala' from Muhammad ibn Muslim who has said the following:

"I once asked abu Ja'far, *'Alayhi al-Salam*, if a man in Salat (prayer) can turn around. He (the Imam) said, 'No, and he must not crack his fingers also.'"

Chapter 47 - Offering greeting of peace to a Person Performing Salat (Prayer) and Sneezing in Salat (prayer)

H 5188, Ch. 47, h 1

Muhammad ibn Yahya has narrated from Ahmad ibn Muhammad from 'Uthman ibn 'Isa from Sama'ah who has said the following:

"I once asked abu 'Abd Allah, *'Alayhi al-Salam*, about a man who is offered Salam (the phrase of offering greeting of peace) while he performs Salat (prayer). He (the Imam) said, 'He responds saying, "Salamun 'Alaykum," but he does not say, "'Alaykum al-Salam." The Messenger of Allah once was standing in Salat (prayer) when 'Ammar ibn Yasir passed by and offered Salam (the phrase of offering greeting of peace). The Holy prophet responded in this way.'"

H 5189, Ch. 47, h 2

Ali ibn Ibrahim has narrated from his father from ibn abu 'Umayr from Hammad from al-Halabiy who has said the following:

"Abu 'Abd Allah, *'Alayhi al-Salam*, has said, 'In case of sneezing in Salat (prayer) one should say, 'Tahmid, (all praise belongs to Allah).'"

H 5190, Ch. 47, h 3

Muhammad ibn Yahya has narrated from Ahmad ibn Muhammad from ibn Faddal from Mu'alla' abu 'Uthman from abu Basir who has said the following:

"I once asked abu 'Abd Allah, *'Alayhi al-Salam*, 'In Salat (prayer) I hear sneezing, can I then praise Allah and say, "O Allah, grant compensation to Muhammad and his family worthy of their services to Your cause?"' He (the Imam) said, 'Yes, when your brother (in belief) sneezes while you are in Salat (prayer) say, "All praise belongs to Allah. O Allah, grant compensation to Muhammad and his family worthy of their services to Your cause; even if there is an ocean between you and your friend, say, 'O Allah, grant compensation to Muhammad and his family worthy of their services to Your cause.'"'"

Chapter 48 - Killing Insects, and So on during Salat (Prayer)

H 5191, Ch. 48, h 1

Muhammad ibn Yahya has narrated from Ahmad ibn Muhammad, from Hammad from Hariz from Muhammad ibn Muslim who has said the following:

"I once asked abu 'Abd Allah, *'Alayhi al-Salam*, about a man who in Salat (prayer) sees a snake or scorpion; can he kill it if it is hurting? He (the Imam) said, 'Yes, he can do so.'"

H 5192, Ch. 48, h 2

Ali ibn Ibrahim has narrated from his father from ibn abu 'Umayr from Hammad ibn 'Uthman from al-Halabiy who has said the following:

"I once asked abu 'Abd Allah, *'Alayhi al-Salam*, about a man who kills, a bug, flea, lice or a fly while in Salat (prayer), does it invalidate his Salat (prayer) and Wudu'? He (the Imam) said, 'No, it does not do so.'"

H 5193, Ch. 48, h 3
Muhammad ibn Yahya has narrated from Ahmad ibn Muhammad from and Muhammad ibn al-Husayn from 'Uthman ibn 'Isa from Sama'ah who has said the following:
"I once asked him (the Imam), *'Alayhi al-Salam*, about a man who is standing in obligatory Salat (prayer) when he remembers his bag or property and he is afraid of loss or destruction of such items. He (the Imam) said, 'He can discontinue his Salat (prayer) to secure such items then perform his Salat (prayer) again.' I then asked him (the Imam), 'What happens if he is in obligatory Salat (prayer) when a stumper (animal) or his stumper escapes and he is afraid of its getting lost or causing him difficulties?' He (the Imam) said, 'It is not harmful if he discontinues his Salat (prayer).'"

H 5194, Ch. 48, h 4
Al-Husayn ibn Muhammad has narrated from 'Abd Allah ibn 'Amir, from Ali ibn Mahziyar from Fadalah ibn Ayyub, from Aban from Muhammad who has said the following:
"When Abu Ja'far, *'Alayhi al-Salam*, would see lice in Masjid he would cover it with sand."

H 5195, Ch. 48, h 5
Muhammad ibn 'Isma'il has narrated from al-Fadl ibn Shadhan from Hammad ibn 'Isa from Hariz from those who narrated to him who has said the following:
"Abu 'Abd Allah, *'Alayhi al-Salam*, has said, 'When you are in obligatory Salat (prayer) and see your slave escaping or your debtor who owes you a certain amount of property, or a snake because of which you are afraid for your life, you can discontinue your Salat (prayer) follow the slave or debtor or kill the snake.'"

H 5196, Ch. 48, h 6
Ali ibn Ibrahim has narrated from Muhammad ibn 'Isa from Yunus from 'Abd Allah ibn Sinan who has said the following:
"Abu 'Abd Allah, *'Alayhi al-Salam*, has said, 'If you see lice in the Masjid when you are in Salat (prayer) cover it in the sand."

Chapter 49 - Building a Masjid, Items Taken from It, Invalidating Wudu' and Sleeping in Masjid and So On

H 5197, Ch. 49, h 1
Ali ibn Ibrahim has narrated from his father from ibn abu 'Umayr from Hisham ibn al-Hakam from au 'Ubaydah al-Hadhddha' who has said the following:
"I heard abu 'Abd Allah, *'Alayhi al-Salam*, say, 'If one builds a Masjid, Allah builds for him a house in paradise.' Abu 'Ubaydah has said, 'Abu 'Abd Allah, *'Alayhi al-Salam*, once passed by on the way to Makkah and I had built a Masjid with stones and asked him, "I pray to Allah to keep my souls in the service of your cause , I hope this will be of those (houses in paradise)." He (the Imam) said, "Yes, it will be so.""""

H 5198, Ch. 49, h 2
Ali ibn Muhammad has narrated from Sahl ibn Ziyad from Ahmad ibn Muhammad from ibn abu Nasr from Aban 'Uthman from abu al-Jarud who has said the following:

"I once asked abu Ja'far, *'Alayhi al-Salam,* about the case of a Masjid which is in a house and the people of the house want to expand it to a certain extent or relocate it in another place. He (the Imam) said, 'It is not harmful.' He (the narrator) has said that he then asked him (the Imam) about a place which is filthy, then it is cleansed and is made a Masjid. He (the Imam) said, 'Soil is poured on it until it is covered; it is cleaner.'"

H 5199, Ch. 49, h 3

Muhammad ibn 'Isma'il has narrated from al-Fadl ibn Shadhan from Safwan from al-'Is who has said the following:

"I once asked abu 'Abd Allah, *'Alayhi al-Salam,* about al-Biya' and churches if they can be changed into Masjid. He (the Imam) said, 'Yes, it is possible.'"

H 5200, Ch. 49, h 4

Ali ibn Ibrahim has narrated from his father from ibn abu 'Umayr from Hammad ibn 'Isa from al-Halabiy who has said the following:

"Abu 'Abd Allah, *'Alayhi al-Salam,* once was asked about Masjid, which is made to also provide shadow, if performing Salat (prayer) therein is undesirable. He (the Imam) said, 'Yes, it is as such but today it is not harmful for you. Had there been justice you would see how it is dealt with.' He (the narrator) has said that he then asked, 'Can arms be hanged in Masjid? He (the Imam) said, 'Yes, it is permissible; however, it is not permissible in the greater Masjid; my grandfather prohibited a man trimming an arrow in the Masjid.'"

H 5201, Ch. 49, h 5

Muhammad ibn Yahya has narrated from Ahmad ibn Muhammad from ibn Mahbub from 'Abd al-Rahman ibn al-Hajjaj from Ja'far ibn Ibrahim who has said the following:

"Ali ibn al-Husayn, *'Alayhi al-Salam,* has said that the Messenger of Allah has said, 'If you hear someone reciting poems in Masjid say to him, "May Allah tear your mouth, Masjid is built only for al-Quran (to read)."'"

H 5202, Ch. 49, h 6

Al-Husayn ibn Ali al-'Alaviy has narrated from al-Hassan ibn al-Husayn al-'Uraniy from 'Amr ibn Jumay' who has said the following:

"I once asked abu Ja'far, *'Alayhi al-Salam,* if it is permissible to perform Salat (prayer) in a Masjid with pictures. He (the Imam) said, 'I dislike it, however, today it is not harmful to you. Had justice been established you would see how it is dealt with.'"

H 5203, Ch. 49, h 7

Ali ibn Muhammad has narrated from Sahl ibn Ziyad from Muhammad ibn al-Husayn ibn Shammun from 'Abd Allah ibn 'Abd al-Rahman from Misma' abu Sayyar who has said the following:

"Abu 'Abd Allah, *'Alayhi al-Salam,* has said, "The Messenger of Allah has prohibited speaking jargon language in Masjid (expressions understood by two people or a group only)."'

H 5204, Ch. 49, h 8

Ali ibn Ibrahim has narrated from Muhammad ibn 'Isa from Yunus from al-'Ala' from Muhammad ibn Muslim who has said the following:

"One of the two Imam, *'Alayhim al-Salam*, has said, 'The Messenger of Allah prohibited unsheathing of swords and trimming arrows in the Masjid saying, "Masjid is built for something other than such things."'"

H 5205, Ch. 49, h 9

Muhammad ibn Yahya has narrated from Ahmad ibn Muhammad from al-Husayn ibn Sa'id from Fadalah ibn Ayyub from Rifa'ah ibn Musa who has said the following:

"I once asked abu 'Abd Allah, *'Alayhi al-Salam*, about taking Wudu' in Masjid and he disliked it because of defecation and urination."

H 5206, Ch. 49, h 10

Ali ibn Ibrahim has narrated from Muhammad ibn 'Isa from Yunus from Mu'awiyah ibn Wahab who has said the following:

"I once asked abu 'Abd Allah, *'Alayhi al-Salam*, about sleeping in Masjid al-Haram and Masjid of the Holy prophet. He (the Imam) said, 'Yes, they can do so, where else can people sleep?'"

H 5207, Ch. 49, h 11

It is a narration from him (narrator of previous Hadith) by his father from Hammad from Hariz from Zurarah who has said the following:

"I once asked abu Ja'far, *'Alayhi al-Salam*, about sleeping in Masjid. He (the Imam) said, 'It is not an offense, except two Masjids: Masjid of the Holy prophet and Masjid al-Haram.' He (the narrator) has said that he (the Imam) would in certain parts of the night hold my hand and move to one side where he would sit and speak in Masjid al-Haram and perhaps sleep and I also sleep. I then spoke to him about it and he (the Imam) said that it is undesirable to sleep in Masjid al-Haram that was in the time of the Messenger of Allah but sleeping in this area is not an offense.'"

H 5208, Ch. 49, h 12

A group has narrated from Ahmad ibn Muhammad from al-Husayn ibn Sa'id from Muhammad ibn Mehran al-Karkhiy from 'Abd Allah ibn Sinan who has said the following:

"I once asked abu 'Abd Allah, *'Alayhi al-Salam*, about a man who is in Masjid in Salat (prayer) and wants to spit away. He (the Imam) said, 'He can do it toward his left and if he is not in Salat (prayer); he must not do so in front of al-Qiblah (al-Ka'bah) but do so toward his left or right sides.'"

H 5209, Ch. 49, h 13

Al-Husayn ibn Muhammad has narrated from 'Abd Allah ibn 'Amir from Ali ibn Mahziyar from who has said the following:

"I once saw abu Ja'far, al-Thaniy, *'Alayhi al-Salam*, emit saliva in Masjid al-Haram between al-Yemaniy corner and the Blackstone and did not bury it.'"

H 5210, Ch. 49, h 14

Al-Husayn ibn Muhammad has narrated from in a marfu' manner from ibn abu 'Umayr from certain persons of his people who has said the following:

"I once said to abu 'Abd Allah, *'Alayhi al-Salam*, 'I dislike performing Salat (prayer) in their Masjid.' He (the Imam) said, 'You must not dislike it; every Masjid is built on the grave of a prophet or the executor of the will of a prophet who was murdered and that site received a sprinkle of his blood and Allah loved to be spoken of therein. So you can perform obligatory Salat (prayer) therein as well as optional Salat (prayer) and what you need to perform as Qada' (compensatory prayer).'"

H 5211, Ch. 49, h 15

Muhammad ibn Yahya has narrated from Ahmad ibn Muhammad from Hammad ibn 'Isa from al-Husayn ibn al-Mukhtar from abu Usamah Zayd al-Shahham who has said the following:

"I once asked abu 'Abd Allah, *'Alayhi al-Salam*, about the words of Allah, most Majestic, most Glorious, 'You must not go near Salat (prayer) while you are drunk.' (4:46) He (the Imam) said, 'It is a reference to sleep.'"

H 5212, Ch. 49, h 16

A group of our people has narrated from Ahmad ibn Muhammad from al-Husayn ibn Sa'id from Fadalah ibn Ayyub from ibn Sinan from 'Umar ibn Yazid who has said the following:

"Abu 'Abd Allah, *'Alayhi al-Salam*, has said, 'Nothing of sleep is permissible in Salat (prayer).'"

(Ahadith 2-16 are best explained in the form of fatwa.)

Chapter 50 - Excellence of Salat (prayer) in Congregation

H 5213, Ch. 50, h 1

Ali ibn Ibrahim has narrated from his father from ibn abu 'Umayr from 'Umar ibn 'Udhaynah from Zurarah who has said the following:

"I asked abu 'Abd Allah, *'Alayhi al-Salam*, 'People say that performing Salat (prayer) in congregation is more virtuous than twenty-five Salat (prayer) performed alone. Is this true?' The Imam replied, 'What they say is right.' I then asked, 'Can two people be considered a congregation?' He, *'Alayhi al-Salam*, said, 'Yes, but one should stand on the right side of the prayer leader.'"

H 5214, Ch. 50, h 2

A group has narrated from Ahmad ibn Muhammad from al-Husayn ibn Sa'id from Hammad ibn 'Isa from Muhammad ibn Yusuf from his father who has said the following:

"I heard abu Ja'far, *'Alayhi al-Salam*, say, 'Al-Juhaniy came to the Holy Prophet and asked, "O Messenger of Allah, I live in open land (unpopulated) with my family, children, and slaves. I say Adhan and 'Iqamah and lead them in Salat (prayer). Are we considered a congregation?" The Messenger of Allah replied, "Yes, you are a congregation." He then asked, "O Messenger of Allah, sometimes the slaves follow the drops from the cloud, then my family, children and I remain home. I say Adhan and Iqamah and lead them in Salat (prayer). Are we considered a congregation?" The Messenger of Allah replied, "Yes, you are a congregation." He then asked, "O Messenger of Allah, sometimes my children go out after the cattle, only then my family and I remain home. I then say Adhan and Iqamah and lead them in Salat (prayer). Am I a congregation?" The Messenger of Allah replied, "Yes, you are a congregation." He then asked, "O Messenger of Allah, the female (his wife) goes for her things to do and I then remain by myself. I then say Adhan and Iqamah and perform Salat (prayer). Am I a congregation?" The Messenger of Allah replied, "Yes, the believer, by himself is a congregation."'"

H 5215, Ch. 50, h 3

Ali ibn Ibrahim has narrated from his father from al-Nawfaliy, from al-Sakuniy who has said the following:

"Abu 'Abd Allah, *'Alayhi al-Salam*, has said, 'The Messenger of Allah has said, "If one performs the five Salat (prayer) in congregation you should think good about him."'"

H 5216, Ch. 50, h 4

A group has narrated from Ahmad ibn Muhammad from al-Husayn ibn Sa'id from Muhammad ibn Sinan from Ishaq ibn 'Ammar who has said the following:

"Abu 'Abd Allah, *'Alayhi al-Salam*, has said, 'Should a man among you who may sell his slave girl to someone, not feel embarrassed, if she says that her previous owner would not attend Salat (prayer) in congregation?'"

H 5217, Ch. 50, h 5

Ali ibn Ibrahim has narrated from his father and Muhammad ibn `Isma'il from al-Fadl ibn Shadhan all Hammad ibn 'Isa from Hariz from Zurarah who has said the following:

"I once was sitting in the presence of abu Ja'far, *'Alayhi al-Salam*, when a man came to him and said, 'I pray to Allah to keep my soul in service for your cause, I am a man in the neighborhood of the Masjid of my people. If I do not perform Salat (prayer) with them, they turn against me and say that I am so and so. He (the Imam) said, 'When you say this, notice that `Amir al-Mu'minin, *'Alayhi al-Salam*, has said, "Whoever hears the call and does not respond without good reason, his Salat (prayer) is nothing of value."' The man then left and he (the Imam) said to him, 'You must not ignore performing Salat (prayer) with them and behind every Imam.' When he left I said to him (the Imam), 'I pray to Allah to keep my soul in service for your cause, your words to this man seem very big to me when he asked your fatwa especially if he is not of the believing people. He (the Imam) laughed, then said, 'From now on I want to see you nowhere else but here, O Zurarah. What other greater proof you need than the fact that he does not perform Salat (prayer) behind him?' He (the Imam) then said, 'Have you not seen (found, understood) me saying, "Perform Salat (prayer) in your Masjid. Perform Salat (prayer) behind your `A'immah (plural of Imam).'"

H 5218, Ch. 50, h 6

Hammad has narrated from Hariz from Zurarah and al-Fudayl who have said the following:

"We once asked him (the Imam), 'Is Salat (prayer) in congregation obligatory?' He (the Imam) said, 'Salat (prayer) is obligatory but congregating for it in general is not obligatory; however, it is of the Sunnah. Whoever omits it in disregard and in disregard of the group of believers without good reason, his Salat (prayer) is nothing of value.'"

H 5219, Ch. 50, h 7

Al-Husayn ibn Muhammad al-Ash'ariy from Mu'alla' ibn Muhammad from al-Washsha' from al-Mufaddal ibn Salih from Jabir who has said the following:

"Abu Ja'far, *'Alayhi al-Salam*, has sad, 'Those of you who are just behind the Imam are people of forbearance and wisdom, so that if Imam forgets or becomes tired they can help. The excellent row is the first row and excellent in the first row is the place nearest to the Imam. The height of the excellence of Salat (prayer) in congregation over Salat (prayer) of a man alone is twenty-five degrees in paradise.'"

H 5220, Ch. 49, h 8

Ali ibn Muhammad has narrated from Sahl ibn Ziyad through the same chain of his narrators has said following:

"He (the Imam) has said, 'The excellence of performing Salat (prayer) in the center of the rows over that in the left is like the excellence of performing Salat (prayer) in congregation over performing Salat (prayer) alone individually.'"

H 5221, Ch. 49, h 9

Muhammad ibn 'Isma'il has narrated from al-Fadl ibn Shadhan from ibn abu 'Umayr from Hafs ibn al-Bakhtariy who has said the following:

"Abu 'Abd Allah, *'Alayhi al-Salam*, has said, 'It is counted in your favor if you join them even if you do not follow them, just like it is counted in your favor when you are with those whom you follow.'"

(Ahadith 5-9 are best explained in the form of fatwa.)

Chapter 51 - Performing Salat (prayer) behind one Who Is not Qualified to Lead Others

H 5222, Ch. 51, h 1

Muhammad ibn Yahya al-'Attar has narrated from Ahmad ibn Muhammad from al-Hassan ibn Ali ibn Faddal from ibn Bukayr from Zurarah who has said the following:

"I once asked abu 'Abd Allah, *'Alayhi al-Salam*, 'In Salat (prayer) with an Imam I complete the recitation before he does.' He (the Imam) said, 'Leave one verse, speak of the glory of Allah and praise Him and when he (the Imam) completes, read that verse, then perform Ruku' (bowing down on one's knees).'"

H 5223, Ch. 51, h 2

It is a narration from him (narrator of previous Hadith) by Ahmad from 'Abd Allah ibn Muhammad al-Hajjal from Tha'labah from Zurarah who has said the following:

"I once asked abu Ja'far, *'Alayhi al-Salam*, about performing Salat (prayer) behind those who oppose our belief. He (the Imam) said, 'To me they are but walls (scarecrows).'"

H 5224, Ch. 51, h 3

Muhammad ibn 'Isma'il has narrated from Ishaq ibn 'Ammar from the one who has asked abu 'Abd Allah, *'Alayhi al-Salam*, has said the following:

I once asked abu 'Abd Allah, *'Alayhi al-Salam*, 'Can I perform Salat (prayer) behind one whom I do not follow and complete recitation when he has not yet completed?' He (the Imam) said, 'Say Tasbih (Allah is free of all defects) until he completes.'"

H 5225, Ch. 51, h 4

Ali ibn Ibrahim has narrated from his father from ibn abu 'Umayr from Hammad ibn 'Uthaman from al-Halabiy who has said the following:

"Abu 'Abd Allah, *'Alayhi al-Salam*, has said, 'When you perform Salat (prayer) behind an Imam who is not qualified, read behind him the recitation, regardless, you hear him or not.'"

H 5226, Ch. 51, h 5

Ali ibn Muhammad has narrated from Sahl ibn Ziyad from Ali ibn Mahziyar from Ali ibn Rashid who has said the following:

"I said to abu Ja'far, *'Alayhi al-Salam*, 'You have different friends, thus, I perform Salat (prayer) behind every one of them.' The Imam said, 'Do not perform Salat (prayer) behind anyone whom you cannot trust in matters of his religion.' He then said, 'I have many friends.' I said, 'You have many companions.' He then immediately, before I could mention their names, said, 'No, (do not mention their names). Ali ibn Hadid requires you to do this. Is this what Ali ibn Hadid commands you to do?' I replied, 'Yes, that is correct.'"

H 5227, Ch. 51, h 6

Ali ibn Ibrahim has narrated from his father from Hammad from Hariz from Zurarah who has said the following:

"I once asked abu Ja'far, *'Alayhi al-Salam*, 'Certain people have narrated that `Amir al-Mu'minin performed four Rak'at after Friday without any interval of saying Salam (the phrase of offering greeting of peace) in between. He (the Imam) said, 'O Zurarah, `Amir al-Mu'minin performed Salat (prayer) behind a sinful one. When he said Salam (the phrase of offering greeting of peace) and moved away `Amir al-Mu'minin stood up, performed four Rak'at without interval in between by means of saying Salam (the phrase of offering greeting of peace). A man from his side then said, 'O abu al-Hassan you performed four Rak'at without interval in between.' He (`Amir al-Mu'minin)) said, 'They were four similar Rak'at' and remained quiet. By Allah, he did not understand what he said.'"

H 5228, Ch. 51, h 7

Muhammad ibn Yahya has narrated from Ahmad ibn Muhammad from Ali ibn Hadid from Jamil ibn Darraj from Humran ibn `A'yan who has said the following:

"I once said to Abu Ja'far, *'Alayhi al-Salam*, 'I pray to Allah to keep my soul in service for your cause, we perform Salat (prayer) with these people on Friday and they perform in a certain time. What must we do? He (the Imam) said, 'Perform Salat (prayer) with them.' Humran then went to Zurarah and said to him, 'We are commanded to perform Salat (prayer) with them with their Salat (prayer).' Zurarah said, 'This cannot be accepted without interpretation.' Humran said to him, 'Come and hear it from him (the Imam).' He (the narrator) has said that both went to him (the Imam) and Zurarah said, 'I pray to Allah to keep my soul in service for your cause, Humran thinks you have commanded us to perform Salat (prayer) with them and I did not accept it.' He (the Imam) said to us, 'Ali ibn al-Husayn, *'Alayhi al-Salam*, would say two Rak'at with them and when they would complete he stand up to perform two more Rak'at.'"

(Ahadith 1-7 are best explained by fatwa.)

Chapter 52 - Who Is an Undesirable Leader in Salat (prayer)? Can a Slave Lead Salat (prayer)? Who Is Most Rightful to Lead Salat (prayer)

H 5229, Ch. 52, h 1

A group has narrated from Ahmad ibn Muhammad from al-Husayn ibn Sa'id from Fadalah ibn Ayyub from al-Husayn ibn 'Uthman from ibn Muskan from abu Basir from who has said the following:

"Abu 'Abd Allah, *'Alayhi al-Salam*, has said, 'Five kinds of people are not to lead other people in Salat (prayer) in all circumstances: People suffering from leprosy, insanity, one born out of wedlock and al-A'ra`biy Arab of the desert.'"

H 5230, Ch. 52, h 2

Ali ibn Ibrahim has narrated from his father from al-Nawfaliy from al-Sakuniy who has said the following:

"Abu 'Abd Allah, *'Alayhi al-Salam*, has said that `Amir al-Mu'minin said, 'One bonded cannot lead in Salat (prayer) those who are free, one paralyzed cannot lead those in good health, one with Tayammum cannot lead those with Wudu', a blind cannot lead others in the wilderness unless directed to al-Qiblah (al-Ka'bah).'"

H 5231, Ch. 52, h 3

Through the chain of narrators as that of the previous Hadith is the following narration:

"If two people disagree and one says, 'I was your Imam' and the other says, 'I was your Imam' he (the Imam) said, 'Both persons' Salat (prayer) is complete.' I (the narrator) then asked, 'What happens if each one says, 'I followed you.' He (the Imam) said, 'Both persons' Salat (prayer) is invalid. They must perform it again.'"

H 5232, Ch. 52, h 4

Ali ibn Ibrahim has narrated from his father from Hammad from Hariz from Zurarah who has said the following:

"I once asked abu Ja'far, *'Alayhi al-Salam*, about performing Salat (prayer) behind a slave. He (the Imam) said, 'It is not an offense if he has good understanding of fiqh (Islamic laws) and there is no one excelling him in fiqh (Islamic laws). He (the narrator) has said that he then asked, 'Can I perform Salat (prayer) behind a blind man?' He (the Imam) said, 'Yes, if there is someone who shows him the direction and he is more excellent than others present.' He (the Imam) then said, '`Amir al-Mu'minin, *'Alayhi al-Salam*, has said, "No one of you must perform Salat (prayer) behind one suffering from leprosy, an insane man, one punished by law, one born of wedlock, behind a desert dwelling Arab and the immigrant (drifting) must not lead Salat (prayer)"'"

H 5233, Ch. 52, h 5

Ali ibn Muhammad and others have narrated from Sahl ibn Ziyad from ibn Mahbub from ibn Ri'ab from abu 'Ubaydah who has said the following:

"I once asked abu 'Abd Allah, *'Alayhi al-Salam*, about a people of our companions who come together then Salat (prayer) time comes. Certain ones among them say to the others, 'O so and so lead.' He (the Imam) said, 'The Messenger of Allah has said that the most learned in al-Quran is to lead. If all of them are equally learned in al-Quran, the first to migrate among them, if all are equal in migration, then the oldest among them, if all are equal in age, then the most learned among them in the Sunnah and most learned in religion is to lead. No one of you must lead one in his house or the one with authority in his dominion.'"

H 5234, Ch. 52, h 6

Ali ibn Ibrahim has narrated from his father from 'Abd Allah ibn al-Mughirah from Ghiyath ibn Ibrahim who has said the following:

"Abu 'Abd Allah, *'Alayhi al-Salam*, has said, 'It is not an offense if a young boy, who has not become an adult, leads a people and says Adhan.'"

(Ahadith 1-6 and the following chapters are best explained in the form of fatwa.)

Chapter 53 - Men Lead Salat (Prayer) for Women and Women Lead Salat (Prayer) for Women

H 5235, Ch. 53, h 1

Muhammad ibn Yahya has narrated from Ahmad ibn Muhammad from Muhammad ibn Sinan from ibn Muskan from abu al-'Abbas who has said the following:

"I once asked abu 'Abd Allah, *'Alayhi al-Salam*, about a man who leads the woman in his house in Salat (prayer). He (the Imam) said, 'Yes, he can do so and she stands behind him.'"

H 5236, Ch. 53, h 2

A group has narrated from Ahmad ibn Muhammad from al-Husayn ibn Sa'id from Fadalah from ibn Sinan from Sulayman ibn Khalid who has said the following:

"I once asked abu 'Abd Allah, *'Alayhi al-Salam*, about a woman's leading other women in Salat (prayer). He (the Imam) said, 'She can do so if they all follow her in optional Salat (prayer), but not in obligatory Salat (prayer), and she is not to lead them, instead she stands up in their middle.'"

H 5237, Ch. 53, h 3

Ahmad ibn al-Husayn has narrated from Fadalah from Hammad ibn 'Uthaman from Ibrahim ibn Maymun who has said the following:

"I once asked abu 'Abd Allah, *'Alayhi al-Salam*, about a man who leads women in obligatory Salat (prayer) where there are no other men. He (the Imam) said, 'Yes, he can do so and if there is a child he stands up on his side.'"

Chapter 54 - Performing Salat (Prayer) Behind a Qualified Person, Recitation behind Him and His Responsibilities

H 5238, Ch. 54, h 1

Muhammad ibn Yahya has narrated from Muhammad ibn al-Husayn from Muhammad ibn 'Isma'il from al-Fadl ibn Shadhan all from Safwan ibn Yahya from 'Abd al-Rahman ibn al-Hajjaj who has said the following:

"I once asked abu 'Abd Allah, *'Alayhi al-Salam,* about performing Salat (prayer) behind an Imam if I must do the recitation. He (the Imam) said, 'Salat (prayer) in which recitation is not aloud, it is assigned to him. So you do not recite behind him, and for Salat (prayer) in which recitation is done aloud, he is commanded to recite aloud so people behind him remain silent; thus, if you hear him, remain silent, and if you do not hear him, then you are to recite.'"

H 5239, Ch. 54, h 2

Ali ibn Ibrahim has narrated from his father from ibn abu 'Umayr from Hammad ibn 'Uthaman from al-Halabiy who has said the following:

"Abu 'Abd Allah, *'Alayhi al-Salam,* has said, 'If you perform Salat (prayer) behind one whom you follow, do not do the recitation behind him, regardless if you hear his recitation or not, except, when it is a Salat (prayer) in which recitation is done aloud and you do not hear then you are to recite.'"

H 5240, Ch. 54, h 3

Ali has narrated from his father from Hammad from Hariz from Zurarah who has said the following:

"One of the two Imam, *'Alayhi al-Salam,* has said, 'If you perform Salat (prayer) behind an Imam whom you follow then remain silent and say Tasbih (Allah is free of all defects) to yourself only.'"

H 5241, Ch. 54, h 4

It is a narration from him (narrator of previous Hadith) by his father from 'Abd Allah ibn al-Mughirah from Qutaybah who has said the following:

"Abu 'Abd Allah, *'Alayhim al-Salam,* has said, 'When you perform Salat (prayer) behind an Imam and are happy with him in Salat (prayer) of which recitation is to be read aloud and you do not hear his recitation, then recite to yourself, but if you hear a humming sound, do not recite.'"

H 5242, Ch. 54, h 5

Muhammad ibn Yahya has narrated from Ahmad ibn Muhammad from Ali ibn Hadid from Jamil ibn Darraj from Zurarah who has said the following:

"I once asked one of the two Imam, *'Alayhim al-Salam,* if the Imam is responsible for Salat (prayer) of the people. He (the Imam) said, 'No, he is not responsible.'"

H 5243, Ch. 54, h 6

Muhammad ibn Ahmad has narrated from Muhammad from Hammad ibn 'Isa from Hariz from Zurarah from Muhammad ibn Muslim who has said the following:

"Abu Ja'far, *'Alayhi al-Salam,* has said that 'Amir al-Mu'minin would say, 'One who recites when performing Salat (prayer) behind an Imam whom he follows and dies, he has died in a religion other than Fitrah (Islam).'"

Chapter 55 - A Prayer Leader Whose Wudu' Is Invalid or Is without al-Qiblah (al-Ka'bah)

H 5244, Ch. 55, h 1

Ali ibn Ibrahim ibn Hashim has narrated from his father and Muhammad ibn 'Isma'il from al-Fadl ibn Shadhan all from Hammad ibn 'Isa from Hariz Muhammad ibn Muslim who has said the following:

"I once asked abu 'Abd Allah, *'Alayhi al-Salam*, about a man who leads a people in Salat (prayer) but does not have a valid Wudu' and informs them after Salat (prayer). He (the Imam) said, 'Only he, but not they, must perform again.'"

H 5245, Ch. 55, h 2

Ali has narrated from his father from ibn abu 'Umayr from Hammad from al-Halabiy who has said the following:

"I once asked abu 'Abd Allah, *'Alayhi al-Salam*, about a blind man who leads a people in Salat (prayer) and is not facing al-Qiblah (al-Ka'bah). He (the Imam) said, 'Only he, but not they, performs again; they had made the effort (about al-Qiblah (al-Ka'bah)).'"

H 5246, Ch. 55, h 3

Muhammad ibn Yahya has narrated from Ahmad ibn Muhammad from Ali ibn Hadid from Jamil from Zurarah who has said the following:

"I once asked one of the two Imam, *'Alayhim al-Salam*, about a man who leads a people in Salat (prayer) of two Rak'at and then informs them that he does not have a valid Wudu'. He (the Imam) said, 'People must complete their Salat (prayer); there is no responsibility on Imam.'"

H 5247, Ch. 55, h 4

Ali ibn Ibrahim has narrated from his father from ibn abu 'Umayr from certain persons of his people who has said the following:

"About the case of a people who traveled from certain mountainous area of Khurasan and a man would lead them in Salat (prayer), when in al-Kufah they found out that he was a Jew, Abu 'Abd Allah, *'Alayhi al-Salam*, has said, 'They are not required to perform their Salat (prayer) again.'"

Chapter 56 - One Who Has Performed Salat (Prayer) but Wants to Join a Congregation or Has Led a People and Wants to Perform Again

H 5248, Ch. 56, h 1

Muhammad ibn 'Isma'il has narrated from al-Fadl ibn Shadhan and Ali ibn Ibrahim has narrated from his father from all from ibn abu 'Umayr from Hafs ibn al-Bakhtariy who has said the following:

"I once asked abu 'Abd Allah, *'Alayhi al-Salam*, about a man who performs Salat (prayer) alone then finds a congregation. He (the Imam) said, 'He can perform Salat (prayer) with them and make it to be an obligatory one.'"

H 5249, Ch. 56, h 2

Ali ibn Muhammad has narrated from Sahl ibn Ziyad from Muhammad ibn al-Walid from Yunus ibn Ya'qub from abu Basir from who has said the following:

"I once said to abu 'Abd Allah, *'Alayhi al-Salam*, 'I enter Masjid and Salat (prayer) begins while I have already performed Salat (prayer). He (the Imam) said, 'You can perform Salat (prayer) with them; Allah chooses the lovelier one of the two.'"

H 5250, Ch. 56, h 3

Muhammad ibn Yahya has narrated from Ahmad ibn Muhammad from ibn abu 'Umayr from Hisham ibn Salim from Sulayman ibn Khalid who has said the following:

"I once asked abu 'Abd Allah, *'Alayhi al-Salam*, about a man who enters Masjid and begins Salat (prayer). While he is standing up in Salat (prayer) Adhan is said and Salat (prayer) begins. He (the Imam) said, 'He can perform it as a two Rak'at, then commence Salat (prayer) with the Imam and the two Rak'at has to be optional Salat (prayer)'"

H 5251, Ch. 56, h 4

A group has narrated from Ahmad ibn Muhammad from al-Husayn ibn Sa'id from Ya'qub ibn Yaqtin who has said the following:

"I once said to abu al-Hassan, *'Alayhi al-Salam*, 'I pray to Allah to keep my soul in service for your cause, it is time for al-Zuhr and we are not able to come down for Salat (prayer) in time until they come down. We come down with them and perform Salat (prayer). They quickly leave and we stand up to perform al-'Asr and show them as if we perform Ruku' (bowing down on one's knees). They then come down for al-'Asr and lead us. Can we perform Salat (prayer) with them? He (the Imam) said, 'Perform Salat (prayer) with them. May Allah never grant them any Salat (prayer).'"

H 5252, Ch. 56, h 5

Muhammad ibn Yahya has narrated from Ahmad ibn Muhammad from Muhammad ibn 'Isma'il who has said the following:

"I once wrote to abu al-Hassan, *'Alayhi al-Salam*, 'I go to Masjid with my neighbors and others and they ask me to lead Salat (prayer) with them, when I have already performed Salat (prayer) before coming to them. Perhaps certain ones have followed me in Salat (prayer) that I have already performed and they are people of weak understanding and the ignorant ones. I dislike leading. I have performed in such condition that I have mentioned. Command me so I obey and follow your command by the will of Allah. He (the Imam) wrote to me, 'You must lead them in Salat (prayer).'"

H 5253, Ch. 56, h 6

Ali ibn Ibrahim has narrated from his father from ibn abu 'Umayr from Hammad from al-Halabiy who has said the following:

"Abu 'Abd Allah, *'Alayhi al-Salam*, has said, 'Whoever performs Salat (prayer) with them in the first row it is as if he has performed Salat (prayer) with the Messenger of Allah.'"

H 5254, Ch. 56, h 7

Muhammad ibn Yahya has narrated from Ahmad ibn Muhammad from 'Uthman ibn 'Isa from Sama'ah who has said the following:

"I once asked him (the Imam), *'Alayhi al-Salam*, about a man who performs Salat (prayer) and has completed only one Rak'at of an obligatory Salat (prayer) that the Imam arrives. He (the Imam) said, 'If he is an Imam who possesses the quality of justice, he performs one more Rak'at, completes and makes it an optional Salat (prayer). He joins the Imam in his Salat (prayer) as is. If he (the Imam) does not have the quality of justice, he (the man) continues with his Salat (prayer) as is. He performs one more Rak'at with him (the Imam) and sits down for a time within which one can say: I testify that only Allah deserves worship, He is one and has no partners and I testify that Muhammad is His servant and Messenger. He then completes his Salat (prayer) with him as possibly he can; Taqiyah (fear) provides great chances and there is nothing performed in Taqiyah for which one is not rewarded by the will of Allah.'"

H 5255, Ch. 56, h 8

A group has narrated from has narrated from Ahmad ibn Muhammad from form al-Husayn ibn Sa'id from al-Haytham ibn Waqid from al-Husayn ibn 'Abd Allah al-Arjaniy who has said the following:

"Abu 'Abd Allah, *'Alayhi al-Salam*, has said, 'If one performs Salat (prayer) in his house then comes to one of their Masjid and performs Salat (prayer) with them, he leaves with all of their good deeds.'"

Chapter 57 - One Performing Salat (Prayer) Partially behind an Imam Who then Asks Him to Lead because of Losing his Wudu'

H 5256, Ch. 57, h 1

Muhammad ibn Yahya has narrated from Muhammad ibn al-Husayn from Safwan from 'Abd al-Rahman ibn al-Hajjaj who has said the following:

"I once asked abu 'Abd Allah, *'Alayhi al-Salam*, about a man who joins the congregation in the second Rak'at which is the first for him. What is he to do when the Imam sits down? He (the Imam) said, 'He displays readiness to stand up (by raising his knees from the ground and placing his palms on the ground), does not allow himself to sit down. When it is the third Rak'at for the Imam and the second for him, he waits a little while to say Tashahhud (testimonies of belief), then joins the Imam.' He (the narrator) has said that he then asked him (the Imam) about one who joins a congregation in the two last Rak'at of Salat (prayer) and what is one to do about recitation. He (the Imam) said, 'Recite in them; they are the first two Rak'at for you and do not make the beginning of your Salat (prayer) its end.'"

H 5257, Ch. 57, h 2

Muhammad ibn 'Isma'il has narrated from al-Fadl ibn Shadhan from ibn abu 'Umayr from Jamil ibn Darraj from Muhammad ibn Muslim who has said the following:

"Abu 'Abd Allah, *'Alayhi al-Salam*, has said, 'If you cannot join in Takbir (Allah is great beyond description) for Ruku' (bowing down on one's knees) do not enter (congregational Salat (prayer)) in that Rak'at.'"

H 5258, Ch. 57, h 3

Ali ibn Muhammad and Muhammad ibn al-Hassan have narrated from Sahl ibn Ziyad from Ahmad ibn Muhammad from ibn abu Nasr from al-Mithamiy from Ishaq ibn Yazid who has said the following:

"I once said to abu 'Abd Allah, *'Alayhi al-Salam*, I pray to Allah to keep my soul in service for your cause, the Imam is one Rak'at ahead of me which is the first for me and the second for him. Do I say Tashahhud (testimonies of belief) when I sit down? He (the Imam) said, 'Yes, Tashahhud (testimonies of belief) is but a blessing.'"

H 5259, Ch. 57, h 4

Muhammad ibn Yahya has narrated from 'Abd Allah ibn Muhammad ibn 'Isa from Ali ibn al-Hakam from Aban ibn 'Uthman from 'Abd al-Rahman ibn abu 'Abd Allah who has said the following:

"Abu 'Abd Allah, *'Alayhi al-Salam*, has said, 'If the Imam is one Rak'at ahead and you join in the last recitation, recite in the third Rak'at for him which is the second for you. You must do so even if you cannot join him for more than one Rak'at in which you recited as well as in the one that follows. If he is one Rak'at ahead of you, sit down in the second Rak'at for you and the third for him until the row stand up in line.' He (the narrator) has said that he (the Imam) said, 'If you find the Imam in Sajdah (prostration) remain where you are until he raises his head, and if he is sitting, you also sit down, and if he is standing, stand up.'"

H 5260, Ch. 57, h 5

Ali ibn Ibrahim has narrated from his father from ibn abu 'Umayr from Hammad ibn 'Uthaman from al-Halabiy who has said the following:

"Abu 'Abd Allah, *'Alayhi al-Salam*, has said, 'If you join the Imam for one Rak'at, say Takbir (Allah is great beyond description). You must perform Ruku' (bowing down on one's knees) before he raises his head (from Ruku'). You have joined for one Rak'at but if he raises his head before you are in Ruku', you have missed one Rak'at.'"

H 5261, Ch. 57, h 6

Muhammad ibn Yahya has narrated from Ahmad ibn Muhammad from Ali ibn al-Nu'man from ibn Muskan from Sulayman ibn Khalid who has said the following:

"Abu 'Abd Allah, *'Alayhi al-Salam*, has said, 'If a man finds the Imam in Ruku' (bowing down on one's knees), says Takbir (Allah is great beyond description) while his back is straight and performs Ruku' before the Imam raises his head, has joined for one Rak'at.'"

H 5262, Ch. 57, h 7

Muhammad ibn `Isma'il has narrated from al-Fadl ibn Shadhan from ibn abu 'Umayr from Mu'awiyah ibn 'Ammar who has said the following:

"I once asked abu 'Abd Allah, *'Alayhi al-Salam*, about a man who comes to Masjid when they are in Salat (prayer) and the Imam is one Rak'at ahead or more. The Imam faces a problem and holds his hand when he is the closest to him and makes him to lead. He (the Imam) said, 'He completes Salat (prayer) of the people, then sits down until they complete Tashahhud (testimonies of belief), he makes a gesture to his right and lifts and it (gesture) is considered saying

Salam (the phrase of offering greeting of peace) and completion of their Salat (prayer) and he completes whatever he is yet to complete.'"

H 5263, Ch. 57, h 8

It is a narration from him (narrator of previous Hadith) by al-Fadl and Ali ibn Ibrahim has narrated from his father all from Hammad ibn 'Isa from Hariz from Zurarah who has said the following:

"I once asked abu Ja'far, *'Alayhi al-Salam*, about a man who comes to a people during their Salat (prayer) and he is not intending it to be Salat (prayer). Their Imam faces invalidation of his Wudu' and holds the hand of this man and makes him to lead. He performs Salat (prayer) with them. Is his Salat (prayer) sufficient to complete their Salat (prayer) while he has not intended it to be Salat (prayer)? He (the Imam) said, 'It is not proper for a man to come to a people in their Salat (prayer) and not intend it to be Salat (prayer). It is proper for him to intend it to be Salat (prayer). If he has already performed Salat (prayer) he has another Salat (prayer). Otherwise, he must not come to them; their Salat (prayer) is sufficient for them even if he did not intend it to be Salat (prayer).'"

H 5264, Ch. 57, h 9

Ali ibn Ibrahim has narrated from his father from ibn abu 'Umayr from Hammad from al-Halabiy who has said the following:

"I once asked abu 'Abd Allah, *'Alayhi al-Salam*, about a man who leads Salat (prayer) with a people and performs one Rak'at; then he dies. He (the Imam) said, 'They make another man to lead and count it as one Rak'at, leave the dead body behind them and then take Ghusl (bath) for touching a dead body.'"

H 5265, Ch. 57, h 10

Muhammad ibn Yahya has narrated from Ahmad ibn Muhammad from Marwak ibn 'Ubayd from Ahmad ibn al-Nadr from a man who has said the following:

"Abu Ja'far, *'Alayhi al-Salam*, once asked, 'What do they say about a man who has missed two Rak'at of the Imam's Salat (prayer)?' I replied, 'They say that he is to recite al-Hamd and Surah (chapter) in them.' He (the Imam) said, 'He turns his Salat (prayer) backward by making its first the last.' I then asked, 'How is he to do it?' He (the Imam) said, 'He recites al-Fatihah al-Kitab in every Rak'at.'"

H 5266, Ch. 57, h 11

Muhammad ibn Yahya has narrated from Ahmad ibn Muhammad from Ali al-Nu'man from al-Husayn ibn abu al-'Ala' who has said the following:

"I once asked abu 'Abd Allah, *'Alayhi al-Salam*, 'I come to the Imam when he is one Rak'at ahead of me in the morning Salat (prayer). When he says Salam (the phrase of offering greeting of peace) I, thinking to have completed, remain speaking of Allah until sunrise. At sunrise I stood up and remembered that the Imam was one Rak'at ahead of me.' He (the Imam) said, 'If you are still in your place, complete it with one Rak'at but if you have moved away, perform your Salat (prayer) again.'"

H 5267, Ch. 57, h 12

A group of our people has narrated from Ahmad ibn Muhammad from al-Husayn ibn Sa'id from Fadalah ibn Ayyub from al-Husayn ibn 'Uthman from Sama'ah from abu Basir from who has said the following:

"I once asked him (the Imam), *'Alayhi al-Salam*, about a man who performs Salat (prayer) with a people and he thinks it is the first (al-Zuhr) but it is al-'Asr. He (the Imam) said, 'He considers it the first and perform al-'Asr.'"

"In another Hadith it is said, 'If he knows that it is al-'Asr and has not performed the one before, he is not to join them.'"

H 5268, Ch. 57, h 13

Muhammad ibn Yahya has narrated from Ahmad ibn Muhammad from Ali ibn Hadid from Jamil from who has said the following:

"I once asked one of the two Imam, *'Alayhim al-Salam*, about the case of an Imam who leads a people and remembers that his Wudu' is not valid. He moves away and holds the hand of another man to make him lead and he does not know how much is performed. He (the Imam) said, 'He performs Salat (prayer) with them and if he makes a mistake, the people remind him by saying Tasbih (Allah is free of all defects) to complete Salat (prayer) as it was before him.'"

H 5269, Ch. 57, h 14

Ali ibn Ibrahim has narrated from his father from 'Abd Allah ibn al-Mughirah from Ghiyath ibn Ibrahim who has said the following:

"Abu 'Abd Allah, *'Alayhi al-Salam*, was asked about one who raises his head before the Imam. Is he to return to Ruku' (bowing down on one's knees) if the Imam delays, or raise his head?' He (the Imam) said, 'No, he must not raise his head.'"

Chapter 58 - One Joining a Row, Alone in One Row or Away From the Prayer Leader More Than One Step

H 5270, Ch. 58, h 1

A group has narrated from Ahmad ibn Muhammad from al-Husayn ibn Sa'id from Hammad ibn 'Isa from Mu'awiyah ibn Wahab who has said the following:

"I once saw abu 'Abd Allah, *'Alayhi al-Salam*, entering Masjid al-Haram during al-'Asr Salat (prayer), when he was near the rows, they performed Ruku' (bowing down on one's knees). He (the Imam) performed Ruku' (bowing down on one's knees) alone and two Sajdah (prostration). He (the Imam) then stood up and walked until he joined the rows.'"

H 5271, Ch. 58, h 2

Muhammad ibn 'Isma'il has narrated from al-Fadl ibn Shadhan from Hammad ibn 'Isa from Rib'i from Muhammad ibn Muslim who has said the following:

"I once asked him (the Imam), *'Alayhi al-Salam*, 'Can a man move backward in Salat (prayer)?' He (the Imam) said, 'No, he cannot do so.' I then asked, 'Can he move forward?' He (the Imam) said, 'Yes, as much as he wants to al-Qiblah (al-Ka'bah).'"

H 5272, Ch. 58, h 3

Muhammad ibn Yahya has narrated from Ahmad ibn Muhammad from 'Uthman ibn 'Isa from Sa'id al-A'raj who has said the following:

"I once asked abu 'Abd Allah, *'Alayhi al-Salam*, about a man who comes to Salat (prayer) and does not find a place in the rows. Can he stand up alone until Salat (prayer) is complete? He (the Imam) said, 'Yes, it is not an offense to stand parallel to the Imam.'"

H 5273, Ch. 58, h 4

Ali ibn Ibrahim has narrated from his father from Hammad ibn 'Isa from Hariz from Zurarah who has said the following:

"Abu Ja'far, *'Alayhi al-Salam*, has said, 'If a people perform Salat (prayer) and there is a space between them and the Imam, which cannot be covered by one step, that Imam is not their Imam. Any row which performs Salat (prayer) following an Imam and the space between this and the row in front is more than can be covered by one step it is not of that (row). If there is a barrier or wall in between, it is not a Salat (prayer) for them unless one is in front of a door.' He (the narrator) has said that he (the Imam) said, 'These arches did not exist in the time of anyone. The tyrants have invented them. Salat (prayer) of those who perform behind them, following those who perform inside is not valid Salat (prayer).' Abu Ja'far, *'Alayhi al-Salam*, has said, 'The rows must be complete, connected with each other and there must be a space of one step between two rows. The space must be of the length of human body that falls (when in Sajdah (prostration)).'"

H 5274, Ch. 58, h 5

Muhammad ibn Yahya has narrated from 'Abd Allah ibn Muhammad ibn 'Isa from Ali ibn al-Hakam from Aban from 'Abd al-Rahman ibn abu 'Abd Allah who has said the following:

"Abu 'Abd Allah, *'Alayhi al-Salam*, has said, 'When you enter a Masjid and the Imam is in Ruku' (bowing down on one's knees) and you think that if you walked all the way to join, he raises his head before you join. Say Takbir (Allah is great beyond description) perform Ruku', and if he raised his head, perform Sajdah (prostration) where you are, and if he stood up, join the row, and if he sits down sit down in your place, and when he stands up, join the row.'"

H 5275, Ch. 58, h 6

Ali ibn Ibrahim has narrated from his father from ibn abu 'Umayr from Hammad from al-Halabiy who has said the following:

"Abu 'Abd Allah, *'Alayhi al-Salam*, has said, 'I do not see any problem in the rows between the pillars.'"

H 5276, Ch. 58, h 7

Ahmad ibn Idris and others have narrated from Muhammad ibn Ahmad from Ahmad ibn al-Hassan ibn Ali from 'Amr ibn Sa'id from Musaddiq ibn Sadaqah from 'Ammar al-Sabatiy who has said the following:

"I once asked abu 'Abd Allah, *'Alayhi al-Salam*, about a man who finds the Imam in sitting position saying Tashahhud (testimonies of belief) and there is no one behind him except one man on his right side. He (the Imam) said, 'He does not go ahead of the Imam or behind the man, but sits down behind the Imam;

and when the Imam says Salam (the phrase of offering greeting of peace), the man stands up and completes his Salat (prayer).'"

H 5277, Ch. 58, h 8

Muhammad ibn Yahya has narrated from Ali ibn Ibrahim ibn Hashim in a marfu' manner who has said the following:

"I once saw abu 'Abd Allah, *'Alayhi al-Salam*, performing Salat (prayer) while standing in a corner of his house near the wall, all others on his right side and no one on his left."

H 5278, Ch. 58, h 9

Ahmad ibn Idris and others have narrated from Muhammad ibn Ahmad from Ahmad ibn al-Hassan from Ali from 'Amr ibn Sa'id from Musaddiq ibn Sadaqah from 'Ammar al-Sabatiy who has said the following:

"I once asked him (the Imam), *'Alayhi al-Salam*, about a man who performs Salat (prayer) with a people who are in a place lower than his place in which he performs Salat (prayer). He (the Imam) said, 'If the Imam is in a place which is higher than their place like a raised place, a platform, their Salat (prayer) is not permissible. He (the Imam) said, 'It is not harmful if he is higher by one shibr (8 inches). Or it is more or less in a gully if the land is stretched, or there is a raised place, the Imam stands on a higher place, those behind him in a lower place and the land is extended, except that they are on a sloping place.' He (the narrator) has said that he (the Imam) was asked, 'What happens if the Imam stands below the place where people behind him stand?' He (the Imam) said, 'It is not harmful.' He (the Imam) said, 'If a man is on the roof or so and the Imam is on a place below, it is permissible for one to perform Salat (prayer) behind him to follow his Salat (prayer) even if it is very high.'"

H 5279, Ch. 58, h 10

Muhammad ibn Yahya has narrated from Ahmad ibn Muhammad who has the following:

Al-Husayn has mentioned that he (the Imam),'Alayhi al-Salam, commanded a man, who was asking him (the Imam) about a man who was performing Salat (prayer) on the side of a man standing on his left. He did not know (that he is to stand on the right side of the Imam) and then he learned in his Salat (prayer) how he is to do. He (the Imam) commanded to turn him to his right.'"

Chapter 59 - Performing Salat (Prayer) Inside Ka'bah, on its Top, al-Biya', Churches and Places where Performing Salat (prayer) Is Undesirable

H 5280, Ch. 59, h 1

Ali ibn Ibrahim has narrated from his father from Muhammad ibn 'Isa from Yunus from 'Abd Allah ibn Sinan who has said the following:

"I once asked abu 'Abd Allah, *'Alayhi al-Salam*, about performing Salat (prayer) in al-Biya' and churches. He (the Imam) said, 'Sprinkle, then perform Salat (prayer).' He (the narrator) has said that he then asked him (the Imam) about the houses of Zoroastrians. He (the Imam) said, 'Sprinkle and perform Salat (prayer).'"

H 5281, Ch. 59, h 2

Muhammad ibn Yahya has narrated from Ahmad ibn Muhammad from Hammad ibn 'Isa from Hariz from Muhammad ibn Muslim who has said the following:

"I once asked abu 'Abd Allah, *'Alayhi al-Salam*, about performing Salat (prayer) in camel's barn. He (the Imam) said, 'If you are afraid for your effects, sweep it and wash it. It is not harmful to perform Salat (prayer) in sheep barns.'"

H 5282, Ch. 59, h 3

It is a narration from him (narrator of previous Hadith) by Ahmad ibn Muhammad and Muhammad ibn al-Husayn from 'Uthman ibn 'Isa from Sama'ah who has said the following:

"He (the Imam), *'Alayhi al-Salam*, said, 'You must not perform Salat (prayer) in places where horses, mules and donkeys are kept.'"

H 5283, Ch. 59, h 4

Ali ibn Muhammad has narrated from Sahl ibn Ziyad from Ahmad ibn Muhammad ibn abu Nasr from someone who had asked abu 'Abd Allah, *'Alayhi al-Salam*, has the following:

"I once asked abu 'Abd Allah, *'Alayhi al-Salam*, about the al-Qiblah (al-Ka'bah) side of the wall of a Masjid from which sewage, in which people urinate, leaks. He (the Imam) said, 'If the leakage is from the sewage, do not perform Salat (prayer) there; but if the leakage is from something else, it is not an offense to perform Salat (prayer) there.'"

H 5284, Ch. 59, h 5

Ali ibn Ibrahim has narrated from his father from ibn abu 'Umayr from Hammad from al-Halabiy who has said the following:

"I once asked abu 'Abd Allah, *'Alayhi al-Salam*, about the barn of sheep. He (the Imam) said, 'You can perform Salat (prayer) there but do not perform Salat (prayer) in the place where camels are kept, unless you are afraid for loss of your property, in which case, you can sweep and sprinkle water on it, then perform Salat (prayer) there.' I then asked abu 'Abd Allah, *'Alayhi al-Salam*, about performing Salat (prayer) on a roadside. He (the Imam) said, 'It is not an offense to perform Salat (prayer) in such place but not in the middle of a road.' He (the Imam) said, 'It is undesirable to perform Salat (prayer) on salt grounds unless there is a soft area on which the forehead can rest in a level manner.' He (the narrator) has said that he then asked him (the Imam) about performing Salat (prayer) in al-Bi'ah (Church). He (the Imam) said, 'If you can face al-Qiblah (al-Ka'bah), then it is not an offense to perform Salat (prayer) there.' He (the narrator) has said that I saw him (the Imam) in rest areas on the road to Makkah sometimes sprinkle water on the place for his forehead during Sajdah (prostration), and perform Sajdah (prostration) when still wet, as he (the Imam) sometimes would not sprinkle water if it was fine (already wet).

"He (the narrator) has said that he asked him (the Imam) about a man who sails in water and time for Salat (prayer) arrives. He (the Imam) said, 'If he is in a war only making gestures for Salat (prayer) is sufficient but if he is a merchant, he is not to sail before performing Salat (prayer).'"

H 5285, Ch. 59, h 6

Muhammad ibn Yahya has narrated from Ahmad ibn Muhammad from 'Abd al-Majid from abu Jamilah from abu 'Usamah who has said the following:

"Abu 'Abd Allah, *'Alayhi al-Salam*, has said, 'Do not perform Salat (prayer) in a house in which there is a Zoroastrian, but it is not a offense if there is a Jew or a Christian.'"

H 5286, Ch. 59, h 7

Muhammad ibn Yahya has narrated from Ahmad ibn Muhammad from Ahmad ibn Muhammad from ibn abu Nasr who has said the following:

"I once said to abu al-Hassan, *'Alayhi al-Salam*, 'We were in al-Bayda' (name of a place) toward the end of the night. I took Wudu', brushed my teeth and I intended to perform Salat (prayer), then it occurred to me. Is it permissible to perform Salat (prayer), in al-Bayda' in the carriage? He (the Imam) said, 'Do not perform Salat (prayer) in al-Bayda'.' I then asked, 'What are the limits of al-Bayda'?' He (the Imam) said, 'Abu Ja'far, *'Alayhi al-Salam*, would on reaching Dhat al-Jaysh travel faster. He (the Imam) would not perform Salat (prayer) until reaching Mu'arras of the Holy prophet.' I then asked, 'Where is Dhat al-Jaysh?' He (the Imam) said, 'It is three miles before al-Hafirah.'"

H 5287, Ch. 59, h 8

It is a narration from him (narrator of previous Hadith) by Ahmad ibn Muhammad from Muhammad ibn al-Fadl who has said the following:

"Al-Rida', *'Alayhi al-Salam*, has said, 'Do not perform Salat (prayer) on any road which is used, regardless, it has a main path or not. It is not proper to perform Salat (prayer) on it.' I then asked, 'Where then one can perform Salat (prayer)?' He (the Imam) said, 'On its right or left sides.'"

H 5288, Ch. 59, h 9

Muhammad ibn Yahya and others has narrated from Muhammad ibn Ahmad from Ayyub ibn Nuh who has said the following:

"I once asked abu al-Hassan, the last, *'Alayhi al-Salam*, 'It becomes the time for Salat (prayer) and one is in al-Bayda' (name of a place). What is he to do?' He (the Imam) said, 'One moves away from the center toward the right or left, then performs Salat (prayer).'"

H 5289, Ch. 59, h 10

Al-Husayn ibn Muhammad has narrated from 'Abd 'Abd Allah ibn 'Amir from Ali ibn Mahziyar from Fadalah ibn Ayyub from Mu'awiyah ibn 'Ammar who has said the following:

"Abu 'Abd Allah, *'Alayhi al-Salam*, has said, 'It is undesirable to perform Salat (prayer) in three locations of roads. They are al-Bayda' which is Dhat al-Jaysh, Dhat al-Salasil, and Dajnan (names of places).' He (the narrator) has said that he (the Imam) then said, 'It is not an offense to perform Salat (prayer) above the main road but it is undesirable to perform Salat (prayer) on the main road.'"

H 5290, Ch. 59, h 11

Muhammad ibn Yahya has narrated from Ahmad ibn Muhammad from ibn Faddal from certain persons of our people who have said the following:

"Abu 'Abd Allah, *'Alayhi al-Salam*, has said, 'Salat (prayer) is not performed in al-Shuqrah valley.'"

H 5291, Ch. 59, h 12

Ali ibn Muhammad ibn 'Abd Allah has narrated from ibn al-Barqiy from his father from 'Abd Allah ibn al-Fadl from those who narrated to him has said the following:

"Abu 'Abd Allah, *'Alayhi al-Salam*, has said, 'Salat (prayer) is not performed in ten places, such as in clay, water, bath houses, on graves, on main roads, ant's colonies, camel's barns, water beds, salt grounds and on snow.'"

H 5292, Ch. 59, h 13

Muhammad ibn Yahya has narrated from Ahmad ibn Muhammad from Ahmad ibn al-Hassan ibn Ali from 'Amr ibn Sa'id from Musaddiq ibn Sadaqah from 'Ammar al-Sabatiy who has said the following:

"I once asked abu 'Abd Allah, *'Alayhi al-Salam*, about what is clay on which Sajdah (prostration) cannot be performed. He (the Imam) said, 'Clay is that on which one's forehead sinks lower and lower without remaining in one place on earth.' I asked about a man who performs Salat (prayer) on graves. He (the Imam) said, 'It is not permissible unless he places something between himself and the graves when performing Salat (prayer), like a distance of ten yards from his front side and from his back side, ten yards from the right and ten yards from the left; then he can perform Salat (prayer) if he wanted.'"

H 5293, Ch. 59, h 14

Muhammad ibn Yahya has narrated from Ahmad ibn Muhammad from Dawud al-Sarmiy who has said the following:

"I once said to abu al-Hassan, *'Alayhi al-Salam*, 'I may go in this direction and may not find a place to perform Salat (prayer) because of snow. He (the Imam) said, 'If possible, do not perform Sajdah (prostration) on snow and if not, then level it and perform Sajdah (prostration) on it.'"

"In another Hadith it is said, 'Perform Sajdah (prostration) on your clothes.'"

H 5294, Ch. 59, h 15

Muhammad ibn Yahya has narrated from 'Imran ibn Musa and Muhammad ibn Ahmad from Ahmad ibn al-Hassan ibn Ali from 'Amr ibn Sa'id from Musaddiq ibn Sadaqah from 'Ammar al-Sabatiy who has said the following:

"I once asked abu 'Abd Allah, *'Alayhi al-Salam*, about a man who performs Salat (prayer) and in front of him there is an open copy of Quran. He (the Imam) said, 'No, it is not permissible.' I then asked, 'What happens if it is in a cover?' He (the Imam) said, 'Yes, it is permissible.' He (the Imam) said, 'One is not to perform Salat (prayer) with a fire in front of him, or iron.' He (the Imam) was asked about a man who performs Salat (prayer) with a chandelier hanging in his front with fire in it except that it is his view. He (the Imam) said, 'When it is higher it is evil. One is not to perform Salat (prayer) with it in one's view.'"

H 5295, Ch. 59, h 16

Muhammad has narrated from al-'Amrakiy from Ali ibn Ja'far who has said the following:

"I once asked abu al-Hassan, *'Alayhi al-Salam*, about a man who performs Salat (prayer) with a lamp placed in his front in the direction of al-Qiblah (al-Ka'bah). He (the Imam) said, 'It is not proper for him to face fire.' It is also narrated that it is not an offense because the One for whom Salat (prayer) is performed is closer to one (person performing Salat (prayer)).'"

H 5296, Ch. 59, h 17

Muhammad ibn al-Hassan and Ali ibn Muhammad have narrated from Sahl ibn Ziyad from ibn Mahbub, from Ali ibn Ri'ab from Jamil ibn Salih, from Fudayl ibn Yasar who has said the following:

"I once said to abu 'Abd Allah, *'Alayhi al-Salam*, 'I stand up for Salat (prayer) and see feces in the direction of al-Qiblah (al-Ka'bah). He (the Imam) said, 'Keep away from it as much as you can and do not perform Salat (prayer) on a main road.'"

H 5297, Ch. 59, h 18

A group has narrated from Ahmad ibn Muhammad from al-Husayn ibn Sa'id from Fadalah ibn Ayyub from al-'Ala' from Muhammad ibn Muslim who has said the following:

"One of the two Imam, *'Alayhim al-Salam*, has said, 'Do not perform obligatory Salat (prayer) in al-Ka'bah.'"

"In another Hadith it is narrated that Salat (prayer) is performed toward four directions if one has no choice but to do so."

H 5298, Ch. 59, h 19

A group has narrated from Ahmad ibn Muhammad from Muhammad from al-Husayn ibn Sa'id from Fadalah from al-Husayn ibn 'Uthman from ibn Muskan from Khalid abu 'Isma'il who has said the following:

"I once asked abu 'Abd Allah, *'Alayhi al-Salam*, 'Can one perform Salat (prayer) on abu Qubays (name of the hill) facing the direction of al-Qiblah (al-Ka'bah)? He (the Imam) said, 'There is no offense in it.'"

H 5299, Ch. 59, h 20

A group has narrated from Ahmad ibn Muhammad from al-Husayn ibn Sa'id from Safwan ibn Yahya from al-'Ala' from Muhammad ibn Muslim who has said the following:

"I once asked one of the two Imam, *'Alayhim al-Salam*, about pictures in the house. He (the Imam) said, 'There is no offense in it if it is on your right, left, behind you or under your feet. If it is in the direction of al-Qiblah (al-Ka'bah), then cover it with a piece of cloth.'"

H 5300, Ch. 59, h 21

Ali ibn Muhammad has narrated from Ishaq ibn Muhammad from 'Abd al-Salam ibn Salih who has said the following:

"I once asked al-Rida', *'Alayhi al-Salam*, about the case of one who at the time of Salat (prayer) is on the top of al-Ka'bah. He (the Imam) said, 'If he stands up there is no al-Qiblah (al-Ka'bah) for him; however, he lies down on his back and opens his eyes to the sky and keeps in his heart al-Qiblah which is in the heaven, al-Bayt al-Ma'mur, does the recitation and for Ruku' (bowing down on one's knees) closes his eyes. When intending to raise his head from Ruku' opens his eyes and for Sujud (prostrations) he does the same.'"

H 5301, Ch. 59, h 22

Ali ibn Ibrahim has narrated from his father from ibn abu 'Umayr from certain persons of his people who has said the following:

"Abu 'Abd Allah, *'Alayhi al-Salam*, about pictures on furnishings which come in one's view has said, 'If there is one eye for it, it is not harmful but if it has two eyes then it is not permissible.'"

H 5302, Ch. 59, h 23

Muhammad ibn Yahya has narrated from Ahmad ibn Muhammad, from Hammad from Hariz from Zurarah and Ali ibn Hadid who have said the following:

"We once asked abu 'Abd Allah, *'Alayhi al-Salam*, about a roof on which there is urine. Can one perform Salat (prayer) there? He (the Imam) said, 'If sun rays and wind can reach it and it is dry, there is no offense in it unless it is used as a urinating place.'"

H 5303, Ch. 59, h 24

Muhammad ibn Yahya has narrated from Ahmad ibn Muhammad from Ahmad ibn al-Hassan ibn Ali from 'Amr ibn Sa'id from Musaddiq ibn Sadaqah from 'Ammar al-Sabatiy who has said the following:

"Abu 'Abd Allah, *'Alayhi al-Salam*, has said, 'Salat (prayer) is not performed in a house where wine and intoxicating items exist.'"

H 5304, Ch. 59, h 25

Ali ibn Ibrahim has narrated from Muhammad ibn 'Isa from Yunus from Hammad from 'Amir ibn Nu'aym who has said the following:

"I once asked abu 'Abd Allah, *'Alayhi al-Salam*, about the case of these houses where people lodge, in which there is urine of animals and dung, where Jews and Christians enter. How is one to perform Salat (prayer)? He (the Imam) said, 'Perform Salat (prayer) on your clothes.'"

H 5305, Ch. 59, h 26

Al-Husayn ibn Muhammad has narrated from Mu'alla' ibn Muhammad from al-Hassan ibn Ali al-Washsha' from Aban from 'Amr ibn Khalid who has said the following:

"Abu Ja'far, *'Alayhi al-Salam*, has said, 'Jibril said, "O Messenger of Allah, we do not enter a house in which there are pictures of a human being, or a house used for urinating or a house where a dog exists."'"

H 5306, Ch. 59, h 27

Abu Ali al-Ash'ariy has narrated from Muhammad ibn 'Abd al-Jabbar from Safwan from ibn Muskan from Muhammad Marwan who has said the following:

"Abu 'Abd Allah, *'Alayhi al-Salam*, has said that the Messenger of Allah has said, 'Jibril came to me and said, "We the community of angels do not enter a house in which a dog exists, or there is a statue of a body or there is a pot with urine in it."''

Chapter 60 - Performing Salat (Prayer) In One Piece of Cloth, How Much clothing a woman Needs, Salat (prayer) of Naked People and Putting One's Clothes in a Certain Manner, Garb with a Sash

H 5307, Ch. 60, h 1

Ali ibn Ibrahim has narrated from his father and Muhammad ibn `Isma'il from al-Fadl ibn Shadhan all from Hammad ibn 'Isa from Hariz from Muhammad ibn Muslim who has said the following:

"I once asked one of the two Imam, *'Alayhim al-Salam*, about a man who performs Salat (prayer) in one shirt or a gown of a single layer or stuffed (of several layers), one without a loincloth. He (the Imam) said, 'If one is wearing a shirt which is of a densely woven fabric or a gown which does not have a long opening (on its sides), then it is not an offense to use them in Salat (prayer). Or if it is one piece of fabric which is placed on the right shoulder and then one end sent under the left arm and turned back over the shoulder and so on or a pant (pajama) in which case one is to secure it with something like even a piece of rope to one's shoulders.'"

H 5308, Ch. 60, h 2

Muhammad ibn Yahya has narrated from Ahmad ibn Muhammad from Ali ibn al-Hakam from fro al-'Ala' ibn Razin from Muhammad ibn Muslim who has said the following:

"I once saw abu Ja'far, *'Alayhi al-Salam*, perform Salat (prayer) wearing a loincloth, not very large, secured to his neck by a knot. I then asked him (the Imam) about a man who performs Salat (prayer) in one shirt. He (the Imam) said, 'It is not an offense if it is woven densely, and a woman performs Salat (prayer) in a loose outer garment and veil, if the outer garment is densely woven, that is, provides covering.' I then asked saying, 'Allah has granted you blessings, is a slave-girl to cover her head in Salat (prayer)? He (the Imam) said, 'A slave girl is not required to have a veil.'"

H 5309, Ch. 60, h 3

Al-Husayn ibn Muhammad has narrated from 'Abd Allah ibn 'Amir Ali ibn Mahziyar from al-Nadr ibn Suwayd from Hisham ibn Salim from Sulayman ibn Khalid who has said the following:

I once asked abu 'Abd Allah, *'Alayhi al-Salam*, about a man who leads a people in Salat (prayer) wearing a shirt without a gown. He (the Imam) said, 'It is not proper for him to perform Salat (prayer) without a gown or turban to dress up with.'"

H 5310, Ch. 60, h 4

Ali ibn Ibrahim has narrated from his father from Hammad ibn 'Isa from Hariz from Zurarah who has said the following:

"Abu Ja'far, *'Alayhi al-Salam*, has said, 'Never use Iltihaf al-Samma'. I then asked, 'What is Iltihaf al-Samma'?' He (the Imam) said, 'It is to insert clothes under your arms and secure them on one shoulder (as if placing yourself in a bag).'"

H 5311, Ch. 60, h 5

Ali ibn Muhammad in a marfu' manner has narrated the following:

"About a man who performs Salat (prayer) wearing a pant (pajama) with no other clothes, abu 'Abd Allah, *'Alayhi al-Salam,* has said, 'He is to secure it with a drawstring to his shoulder.'"

H 5312, Ch. 60, h 6

Muhammad ibn Yahya has narrated from Ali ibn Hadid from Jamil who has said the following:

"Murazim once asked abu 'Abd Allah, *'Alayhi al-Salam,* when I was present, about a man who performs Salat (prayer) when at home, wearing a loincloth. He (the Imam) said, 'He is to secure it with a handkerchief or turban to his neck when wearing.'"

H 5313, Ch. 60, h 7

Muhammad ibn Yahya has narrated from Ahmad ibn Muhammad from Ali ibn al-Hakam from Hisham ibn Salim from abu Basir from who has said the following:

"Abu 'Abd Allah, *'Alayhi al-Salam,* has said, 'It is not proper to throw a loincloth over a shirt when performing Salat (prayer) or use a loincloth on a shirt when performing Salat (prayer); it is of the manner of dressing in the pre-Islamic age of darkness.'"

H 5314, Ch. 60, h 8

Muhammad ibn Yahya has narrated from Ahmad ibn Muhammad, from ibn Mahbub from ibn Ri'ab from Ziyad ibn Suqah who has said the following:

"Abu Ja'far, *'Alayhi al-Salam,* has said, 'It is not an offense if one of you perform Salat (prayer) in one piece of cloth and his loincloth is not secured; religion of Muhammad, O Allah grant compensation to Muhammad and his family worthy of their services to Your cause, is upright.'"

H 5315, Ch. 60, h 9

Ahmad ibn Idris has narrated from Muhammad ibn 'Abd al-Jabbar from Safwan ibn Yahya from Rifa'ah who has said the following:

"The person who had heard abu 'Abd Allah, *'Alayhi al-Salam,* narrated to me about a man who performs Salat (prayer) in one piece of cloth using it as a loincloth. He (the Imam) said, 'There is no offense in it if he raises it up to his chest.'"

H 5316, Ch. 60, h 10

It is a narration from him (narrator of previous Hadith) by Ahmad ibn Muhammad from Ahmad ibn al-Hassan ibn Ali from 'Amr ibn Sa'id from Musaddiq ibn Sadaqah 'Ammar al-Sabatiy who has said the following:

"I once asked abu 'Abd Allah, *'Alayhi al-Salam,* about a man who when performing Salat (prayer) enters his hands under his clothes. He (the Imam) said, 'It is not an offense if he has other clothes on him, like a loincloth or pant (pajama); otherwise, it is not permissible, however, entering one hand is not harmful.'"

H 5317, Ch. 60, h 11

Muhammad ibn Yahya has narrated from Ahmad ibn Muhammad from al-Husayn ibn Sa'id from 'Uthman ibn 'Isa from ibn Muskan from ibn abu Ya'fur who has said the following:

"Abu 'Abd Allah, *'Alayhi al-Salam,* has said, 'Women perform Salat (prayer) in three pieces of clothes: Loincloth, an outer garment with sleeves, and a yashmak. It is not harmful if she uses the Yashmak as a veil and if she does not find, she can use two pieces of clothes using one as loincloth and the other as a veil.' I (the narrator) then asked, 'Can she use an outer garment and a sheet without a head scarf?' He (the Imam) said, 'It is not an offense if she uses the sheet as a head scarf and if it is not enough, she can wear it lengthwise.'"

H 5318, Ch. 60, h 12

Al-Husayn ibn Muhammad has narrated from 'Abd Allah ibn 'Amir from Ali ibn Mahziyar from Hammad ibn 'Isa from Shu'ayb from abu Basir who has said the following:

"Abu 'Abd Allah, *'Alayhi al-Salam*, has said, 'It is not an offense if a man performs Salat (prayer) with his clothes on his back and shoulder to allow them to hang downward to the ground and he does not use it as a bed-sheet, as I am told it is done so.'"

H 5319, Ch. 60, h 13

Muhammad ibn Yahya has narrated from Muhammad ibn al-Husayn from 'Uthman ibn 'Isa from Sama'ah who has said the following:

"I once asked him (the Imam), *'Alayhi al-Salam*, about a man who wraps himself up in one piece of cloth. He (the Imam) said, 'He does not wrap himself up in one piece of cloth, but if he uses it as an outer garment that covers his shoulders, it is not harmful.'"

H 5320, Ch. 60, h 14

Ali ibn Ibrahim has narrated from his father from ibn abu 'Umayr from Hammad from al-Halabiy who has said the following:

"Abu 'Abd Allah, *'Alayhi al-Salam*, has said, 'It is not proper for a Muslim woman to wear of the veils and outer garment the kind that does not provide any covering.'"

H 5321, Ch. 60, h 15

A group has narrated from Ahmad ibn Muhammad from al-Husayn ibn Sa'id from his brother Zur'ah from Sama'ah who has said the following:

"I once asked him (the Imam), *'Alayhi al-Salam*, about a man who is in wilderness and has no other clothes except one piece and has experienced sexual relation in it. He does not have water. What must he do? He (the Imam) said, 'He takes Tayammum and performs Salat (prayer) in a sitting position and makes gestures.'"

H 5322, Ch. 60, h 16

Ali ibn Ibrahim has narrated from his father from Hammad from Hariz from Zurarah who has said the following:

"I once asked abu Ja'far, *'Alayhi al-Salam*, about a man who sails in a boat while naked or his clothes are looted and does not find anything to perform Salat (prayer) with. He (the Imam) said, 'He performs Salat (prayer) by making gestures and a woman in such condition places her hand over her vagina, and if a man, he places his hand over his private part. They sit and make gestures and do not perform Sajdah (prostration) or Ruku' (bowing down on one's knees) so their back is exposed. Their Salat (prayer) is by gestures by their heads.' He (the Imam) said, 'If they are in water or sea with waves they do not perform Sajdah (prostration) and they are exempt from facing (the direction of al-Qiblah (al-Ka'bah)). They make gestures: their rising and lowering is gestures.'"

Chapter 61 - Kinds of Clothes in Which It Is Undesirable to Perform Salat (Prayer) As Well As Otherwise

H 5323, Ch. 61, h 1

Ali ibn Ibrahim has narrated from his father from ibn abu 'Umayr from ibn Bukayr who has said the following:

"Zurarah once asked abu 'Abd Allah, *'Alayhi al-Salam*, about foxes, fennec and squirrel and so on of hair. He (the Imam) then took out a book that he (the Imam) thought was of the dictations of the Messenger of Allah and it said, 'Salat (prayer) performed with hair of everything of inedible flesh is unlawful. Thus, Salat (prayer) performed with the fur, hair, skin, urine, dung, milk and with everything from such animals is invalid and unacceptable until one performs with something else which Allah has made of edible flesh.' He (the Imam) then said, 'O Zurarah, this is from the Messenger of Allah; preserve it. O Zurarah, if it is from edible animal, performing Salat (prayer) with its fur, urine, hair, dung, milk and everything from it is permissible, if you know that proper slaughtering has taken place, which makes it clean. If it is from something which is not made lawful for you to consume as food but is made unlawful, performing Salat (prayer) with it is invalid, regardless if slaughtered properly or not.'"

H 5324, Ch. 61, h 2

Ali ibn Muhammad ibn 'Abd Allah has narrated from Ishaq al-'Alaviy from al-Hassan ibn Ali from Muhammad ibn Sulayman al-Daylamiy from 'Aytham ibn Aslam al-Najashiy from abu Basir who has said the following:

"I once asked abu 'Abd Allah, *'Alayhi al-Salam*, about Salat (prayer) with furs. He (the Imam) said, 'Ali ibn al-Husayn was sensitive to cold and fur from Hijaz was not sufficient for him because tanning is by the pod of a species of a tree. He would send for fur from Iraq and he (the Imam) used it, but during Salat (prayer) removed it as well as the shirt underneath the fur. When asked about it he (the Imam) answered, 'People of Iraq consider using of skins of dead animals as lawful. They think tanning makes them clean.'"

H 5325, Ch. 61, h 3

Through the same chain of narrators as that of the previous Hadith the following is narrated from Muhammad ibn Sulayman from Ali ibn abu Hamzah who has said the following:

"I once asked abu 'Abd Allah, and abu al-Hassan, *'Alayhi al-Salam*, about clothes of fur in Salat (prayer). He (the Imam) said, 'Do not perform Salat (prayer) with it unless it is made clean, by properly slaughtering.' I then asked, 'Is proper slaughtering done with iron? He (the Imam) said, 'Yes, if it is of edible flesh.' I then asked about that which is of edible flesh other than sheep. He (the Imam) said, 'It is not an offense to use fur of squirrel; it is an animal that does not eat flesh and it is not of that which the Messenger of Allah prohibited; the Messenger of Allah prohibited everything that has dogtooth and claw.'"

H 5326, Ch. 61, h 4

Ali ibn Ibrahim has narrated from his father from ibn abu 'Umayr from Hammad from al-Halabiy who has said the following:

"Abu 'Abd Allah, *'Alayhi al-Salam*, has said, 'It is undesirable to perform Salat (prayer) in fur except those made in al-Hijaz or that you know is properly slaughtered.'"

H 5327, Ch. 61, h 5

Ali ibn Muhammad has narrated from 'Abd Allah ibn Ishaq al-'Alaviy from al-Hassan ibn Ali from Muhammad ibn 'Abd Allah ibn Hilal from 'Abd al-Rahman ibn al-Hajjaj who has said the following:

"I once said to abu 'Abd Allah, *'Alayhi al-Salam*, 'I enter al-Suq (market place) of Muslims, meaning thereby these people who are called Muslims and buy from them fur for business purposes. I ask the owner, 'Is it of properly slaughtered animals?' He says, 'Yes, it is of properly slaughtered animals.' Can I sell it as that from properly slaughtered animals? He (the Imam) said, 'No, you cannot do so; however, it is not an offense to sell it and say that the one from whom you purchased has said that it is from properly slaughtered animals.' I then asked, 'What has destroyed it?' He (the Imam) said, 'It is because people of Iraq consider dead animals as clean, thinking that tanning makes it lawful and it is its properly slaughtering and then they do not remain satisfied without saying that it is from the Messenger of Allah.'"

H 5328, Ch. 61, h 6

Muhammad ibn Yahya and others has narrated from Ahmad ibn Muhammad from ibn Mahbub from 'Asem ibn Humayd from Ali ibn al-Mighra' who has said the following:

"I once asked abu 'Abd Allah, *'Alayhi al-Salam*, about the case of dead animals if any benefit thereby is permissible. He (the Imam) said, 'No, there is no lawful benefit in it.' I then said, 'We are told that the Messenger of Allah once passed by the dead body of a goat and said, 'What has happened to the owners of this goat? If they could not benefit from its flesh they could benefit from its skin.' He (the Imam) said, 'That goat belonged to Sawdah, daughter of Zam'ah, wife of the Holy prophet. It was an emaciated ewe and its flesh was not useable, so they left until it died. Thus, the Holy prophet, said, 'If the owners could not benefit from its flesh why did they not benefit from its skin after slaughtering it properly.'"

H 5329, Ch. 61, h 7

Ali ibn Muhammad has narrated from Sahl ibn Ziyad from Ali ibn Mahziyar from Muhammad ibn al-Hassan al-Ash'ariy who has said the following:

"Certain individuals of our people once wrote to abu Ja'far, *'Alayhi al-Salam*, asking, 'What do you say about fur purchased from al-Suq (marketplace)? He (the Imam) replied, 'If it is (lawfully) guaranteed, then it is not an offense to buy it.'"

H 5330, Ch. 61, h 8

Ahmad ibn Idris has narrated from Muhammad ibn 'Abd al-Jabbar from Ali ibn Mahziyar from a man who had has said the following:

"He had asked him (the Imam) about performing Salat (prayer) with foxes (things from it) and he (the Imam) prohibited him to perform Salat (prayer) in such things and with the clothes which is the next layer. He (the man) did not know which layer was meant; the one touching the furs or the one touching one's skin. He (the Imam) wrote with his handwriting that said, 'It is the one that touches the skin. He (the narrator) has said that he then asked abu al-Hassan that he had asked him (the Imam) about this issue and he (the Imam) had said, 'Do not perform Salat (prayer) with the clothes which are on its top as well as that which is beneath.'"

H 5331, Ch. 61, h 9

Ali ibn Mahziyar from has said the following:

"Ibrahim ibn 'Uqbah once wrote to him (the Imam), *'Alayhi al-Salam*, asking, 'People here make socks and waistbands from the fur of foxes. Is it permissible to perform Salat (prayer) with it without Taqiyah (fear) or necessity? He (the Imam) wrote with his hand writing, 'It is not permissible to perform Salat (prayer) with it.'"

H 5332, Ch. 61, h 10

Ahmad ibn Idris has narrated from Muhammad ibn 'Abd al-Jabbar who has said the following:

"I once wrote to abu Muhammad, *'Alayhi al-Salam*, asking if it is permissible to perform Salat (prayer) with a cap of pure silk or silk brocade. He (the Imam) wrote, 'It is not lawful to perform Salat (prayer) with pure silk.'"

H 5333, Ch. 61, h 11

Ali ibn Muhammad has narrated from 'Abd Allah ibn Ishaq al-'Alaviy from al-Hassan ibn Ali from Muhammad ibn Sulayman al-Daylamiy from Furayt from ibn abu Ya'fur who has said the following:

"Once I was in the presence of abu 'Abd Allah, *'Alayhi al-Salam*, when a man of al-Khazzazin came and said, 'I pray to Allah to keep my soul in service for your cause, 'What do you say about performing Salat (prayer) with al-Khazz? He (the Imam) said, 'It is not an offense to perform Salat (prayer) with it.' A man then said to him (the Imam), 'I pray to Allah to keep my soul in service for your cause, it is dead and it is manufactured and I know it. Abu 'Abd Allah, *'Alayhi al-Salam*, said, 'I know it more than you do.' The man said, 'It is manufactured and no one knows more than I know.' Abu 'Abd Allah, *'Alayhi al-Salam*, then smiled and asked, 'Do you say that it is an animal that comes from water? Or you say that it is caught from water and is brought out and when it is away from water it dies?' The man said, 'You spoke the truth, I pray to Allah to keep my soul in service for your cause, that is how it is.' Abu 'Abd Allah, *'Alayhi al-Salam*, said to him, 'So you say that it is an animal that walks on four feet and it is not like whales in the case of which its properly being slaughtered is its coming out of the water.' The man said, 'Yes, by Allah that is what I say how it is.' Abu 'Abd Allah, *'Alayhi al-Salam*, said, 'Allah, most High has made it lawful and its proper slaughtering is its dying like whales for which proper slaughtering is its dying.'"

H 5334, Ch. 61, h 12

Muhammad ibn Yahya has narrated from Ahmad ibn Muhammad from Muhammad ibn Khalid from `Isma'il ibn Sa'd al-Ahwas who has said the following:

"I once asked abu al-Hassan al-Rida', *'Alayhi al-Salam*, about performing Salat (prayer) with the skin of beasts. He (the Imam) said, 'Do not perform Salat (prayer) with it.' He (the narrator) has said that he then asked him (the Imam) about performing Salat (prayer) with Abrisam (silk). He (the Imam) said, 'No, it is not permissible.'"

H 5335, Ch. 61, h 13

Muhammad ibn Yahya has narrated from certain persons of our people from Ali ibn 'Uqbah from Musa ibn 'Ukayl al-Numayriy who has said the following:

"I once asked abu 'Abd Allah, *'Alayhi al-Salam*, about a man who on a journey has a knife in his slipper without which he cannot do anything or it is in his pant, and a key which he is afraid of losing it, or that around his midsection is a belt in which there is iron. He (the Imam) said, 'It is not an offense to have a knife, or a belt for a traveler in case he needs them as well as a key for which one is afraid about forgetting it. It is not an offense to have a sword or weapons during a war and in other times. It is not permissible to perform Salat (prayer) with iron; it is Najis (unclean) and metamorphosed.'"

H 5336, Ch. 61, h 14

Ali ibn Muhammad and Muhammad ibn al-Hassan has narrated from Sahl ibn Ziyad from Ali ibn Mahziyar from abu Ali ibn Rashid who has said the following:

"I once asked abu Ja'far al-Thaniy, *'Alayhi al-Salam*, about furs if performing Salat (prayer) with it is permissible. He (the Imam) asked, 'Which kind of fur is it?' I replied, 'Fennec, squirrel and sable. He (the Imam) said, 'You can perform Salat (prayer) with fennec and squirrel. Do not perform Salat (prayer) with the fur of sable.' I then asked about foxes. He (the Imam) said, 'No, you cannot perform Salat (prayer) with it but you can wear it after Salat (prayer). I then asked, 'Can I perform Salat (prayer) with the layer of clothes next to it?' He (the Imam) said, 'No, you cannot do so.'"

H 5337, Ch. 61, h 15

Ali ibn Ibrahim has narrated from Ahmad ibn 'Abddeyl from ibn Sinan from 'Abd Allah ibn Jundab from Sufyan ibn al-Simt who has said the following:

"Abu 'Abd Allah, *'Alayhi al-Salam*, has said, 'If a man covers himself with a loincloth up to his two breast he can perform Salat (prayer) with it. He (the narrator) has said that he read in the letter of Muhammad ibn Ibrahim to abu al-Hassan, *'Alayhi al-Salam*, in which he had asked about fennec if it is permissible to perform Salat (prayer) with it. He (the Imam) had written, 'It is not an offense to perform Salat (prayer) with it.' He had written asking about the skins of foxes and he (the Imam) had written, 'It is undesirable.' He had written asking about lining of silk (not the one from silkworm) if performing Salat (prayer) with it is permissible. He (the Imam) had written, 'It is permissible.'"

H 5338, Ch. 61, h 16

Ali ibn Muhammad has narrated from 'Abd Allah ibn Ishaq from those whom he has mentioned from Muqatil ibn Muqatil who has said the following:

"I once asked abu al-Hassan, *'Alayhi al-Salam*, about performing Salat (prayer) with sable, squirrel and fox. He (the Imam) said, 'There is nothing good with all of it except squirrel which is an animal that does not eat meat.'"

H 5339, Ch. 61, h 17

Ali ibn Ibrahim has narrated from Muhammad ibn 'Isa from Yunus from 'Abd Allah ibn Sinan who has said the following:

"Abu 'Abd Allah, *'Alayhi al-Salam*, disliked to perform Salat (prayer) with clothes that had portraits on them.'"

H 5340, Ch. 61, h 18

Muhammad ibn Yahya has narrated from Ahmad ibn Muhammad and Muhammad ibn al-Husayn from 'Uthman ibn 'Isa from Sama'ah from abu Basir who has said the following:

"I once asked abu Ja'far, *'Alayhi al-Salam*, about the shawl made by Zoroastrians if I can perform Salat (prayer) with it. He (the Imam) asked, 'Can it be washed with water?' I replied, 'Yes, it can be washed.' He (the Imam) said, 'It is not an offense to perform Salat (prayer) with it.' I then asked about cloths made by the weavers if I can perform Salat (prayer) with it. He (the Imam) said, 'Yes, you can do so.'"

H 5341, Ch. 61, h 19

Muhammad ibn 'Isma'il has narrated from al-Fadl ibn Shadhan from Safwan ibn Yahya from al-'Is ibn al-Qasim who has said the following:

"I once asked abu 'Abd Allah, *'Alayhi al-Salam*, about a man who performs Salat (prayer) with clothes of woman, with her loincloth and uses her veil as a turban. He (the Imam) said, 'It is acceptable if she is trusted.'"

H 5342, Ch. 61, h 20

Al-Husayn ibn Muhammad has narrated from 'Abd Allah ibn 'Amir from Ali ibn Mahziyar from Fadalah ibn Ayyub from Hammad ibn 'Uthman who has said the following:

"I once asked abu 'Abd Allah, *'Alayhi al-Salam*, about a man who performs Salat (prayer) with black dirhams which have portraits on them. He (the Imam) said, 'It is not an offense if they are hidden.'"

H 5343, Ch. 61, 21

In the narration of 'Abd al-Rahman ibn al-Hajjaj narrated from him (the Imam) who has said the following:

"He (the Imam), *'Alayhi al-Salam*, has said, ' People must protect their properties. When performing Salat (prayer) with their belongings around, such things are kept behind them but are not placed between them and al-Qiblah (al-Ka'bah)."

H 5344, Ch. 61, h 22

Muhammad ibn Yahya has narrated from Ahmad ibn Muhammad from ibn Faddal from Hammad ibn 'Uthaman who has said the following:

"Abu 'Abd Allah, *'Alayhi al-Salam*, has said, 'It is undesirable to perform Salat (prayer) in clothes dyed with sharply saturated colors.'"

H 5345, Ch. 61, h 23

Muhammad ibn Yahya in a marfu' manner has said the following:

"Abu 'Abd Allah, *'Alayhi al-Salam*, has said, 'Perform Salat (prayer) with your own handkerchief but not with others' handkerchief.'"

H 5346, Ch. 61, h 24

Muhammad ibn Yahya in a marfu' manner has said the following:

"Abu 'Abd Allah, *'Alayhi al-Salam*, has said, 'You must not perform Salat (prayer) in cloths that are shaffa or suffa, that is, that which is painted.'"

"In another Hadith it is said, 'Do not perform Salat (prayer) in black clothes; however, black slipper, cloak or turban is not harmful.'"

H 5347, Ch. 61, h 25

Ahmad ibn Idris has narrated from Muhammad ibn Ahmad al-Sayyariy from abu Yazid al-Qasmiy, Qasmah is a village in Yeman in Basra, who has said the following:

"I once asked abu al-Hassan al-Rida', *'Alayhi al-Salam*, about al-Darish skin from which slippers are made. He (the Imam) said, 'Do not perform Salat (prayer) with them because it is tanned with the leftover of dogs.'"

H 5348, Ch. 61, h 26

A number of our people have narrated from Ahmad ibn Muhammad who, in a marfu' manner has said the following:

"Abu 'Abd Allah, *'Alayhi al-Salam*, about pure al-Khazz has said, 'It is not an offense to perform Salat (prayer) with it, but do not perform Salat (prayer) with that which is mixed with fur of foxes or other things.'"

H 5349, Ch. 61, h 27

A number of our people have narrated from Ahmad ibn Muhammad, from al-Barqiy from his father from al-Nadr ibn Suwayd from al-Qasim ibn Sulayman from Jarrah al-Mad'iniy who has said the following:

"Abu 'Abd Allah, *'Alayhi al-Salam*, has said that he disliked wearing a shirt which has brocaded hems, cloths of silk embroideries and red saddlecloth; it is a saddlecloth of Satan.'":

H 5350, Ch. 61, h 28

Muhammad ibn 'Isma'il has narrated from al-Fadl ibn Shadhan from Safwan ibn Yahya from ibn Muskan from al-Halabiy who has said the following:

"I once asked abu 'Abd Allah, *'Alayhi al-Salam*, about the slippers that we buy from the market if we can perform Salat (prayer) with them. He (the Imam) said, 'Perform Salat (prayer) with them until you are told that it exactly is from dead animals.'"

H 5351, Ch. 61, h 29

A number of our people have narrated from Ahmad ibn Muhammad from who, in a marfu' manner has said the following:

"Abu 'Abd Allah, *'Alayhi al-Salam*, has said, 'Performing Salat (prayer) is undesirable except in three items: slippers, turban, and cloak.'"

H 5352, Ch. 61, h 30

Ali ibn Muhammad has narrated from Sahl ibn Ziyad from Muhsin ibn Ahmad from those whom he has mentioned who has said the following:

"I once asked abu 'Abd Allah, *'Alayhi al-Salam*, if I can perform Salat (prayer) with a black cap. He (the Imam) said, 'Do not perform Salat (prayer) with it; it is of the clothes of people of the fire.'"

H 5353, Ch. 61, h 31

Ali has narrated from Sahl ibn Ziyad from certain persons of his people from al-Hassan ibn al-Jahm who has said the following:

"I once said to abu al-Hassan, *'Alayhi al-Salam*, that I visit the market and buy a slipper but I do not know if it is from properly slaughtered animal or not. He (the Imam) said, 'Perform Salat (prayer) with it.' I then asked, 'Can I use such shoes?' He (the Imam) said, 'It is the same as slippers.' I then said, 'I am not comfortable with it.' He (the Imam) asked, 'Do you dislike what abu al-Hassan, *'Alayhi al-Salam*, would do?'"

H 5354, Ch. 61, h 32

Muhammad ibn Yahya has narrated from Ahmad ibn Muhammad from Ibrahim ibn Mahziyar who has said the following:

"I once asked him (the Imam), *'Alayhi al-Salam*, about a Jurmuq (a larger slipper worn over another one) if it is permissible to perform Salat (prayer) with it and I showed it to him (the Imam) and he (the Imam) said, 'It is permissible to perform Salat (prayer) with it.'"

H 5355, Ch. 61, h 33

Muhammad ibn Yahya has narrated from al-'Amrakiy from Ali ibn Ja'far who has said the following:

"I once asked abu al-Hassan, *'Alayhi al-Salam*, about a man who performed Salat (prayer) with a bird in his sleeve. He (the Imam) said, 'If he is afraid about it then it is not harmful.' He (the narrator) has said that he then asked him (the Imam) about anklets if women and children could use them during Salat (prayer). He (the Imam) said, 'It is not an offense if they are silent, but if they make noise then it is not permissible.'"

H 5356, Ch. 61, h 34

Ali ibn Ibrahim has narrated from his father from Ahmad ibn Muhammad from ibn abu al-Fadl al-Mada'iniy from those who narrated to him who has said the following:

"Abu 'Abd Allah, *'Alayhi al-Salam*, has said, 'A man does not perform Salat (prayer) with a waistband which has an iron key.'"

H 5357, Ch. 61, h 35

Ali has narrated from his father from al-Nawfaliy from al-Sakuniy who has said the following:

"Abu 'Abd Allah, *'Alayhi al-Salam*, has said that the Messenger of Allah has said, 'A man does not perform Salat (prayer) wearing an iron ring.'"

"It is narrated that if a key is inside cover then it is not an offense."

(Ahadith 1-35 of this chapter are best explained by fatwa.)

Chapter 62 - Rules about Performing Salat (Prayer) in an Unclean Cloth Regardless One Knows it or Not

H 5358, Ch. 62, h 1

Al-Husayn ibn Muhammad has narrated from 'Abd Allah ibn 'Amir Ali ibn Mahziyar from Safwan from al-'Is ibn al-Qasim who has said the following:

"I once asked abu 'Abd Allah, *'Alayhi al-Salam*, about a man who performs Salat (prayer) wearing another man's clothes for many days, then the owner of clothes inform him that he does not wear them for Salat (prayer). He (the Imam) said, 'He does not need to perform any of his Salat (prayer) again.'"

H 5359, Ch. 62, h 2

Through the same chain of narrators as that of the previous Hadith it is narrated from Ali ibn Mahziyar from Fadalah ibn Ayyub from 'Abd Allah ibn Sinan who has said the following:

"I once asked abu 'Abd Allah, *'Alayhi al-Salam*, about a man who performs Salat (prayer) and there is feces of human being, cat or dog in his clothes, 'Must he perform his Salat (prayer) again?' He (the Imam) said, 'He is not required to perform his Salat (prayer) again, if he did not know about it.'"

H 5360, Ch. 62, h 3

Ahmad ibn Idris has narrated from Ahmad ibn Muhammad ibn 'Isa from al-Nadr ibn Suwayd from abu Sa'id al-Mukariy from abu Basir who has said the following:

"Abu Ja'far, or abu 'Abd Allah, *'Alayhi al-Salam*, has said, 'You are not required to perform your Salat (prayer) again, because of blood that you did not see except that which is from Hayd (menses), a small amount or otherwise, you see it or not are all the same.'"

H 5361, Ch. 62, h 4

Ali ibn Ibrahim has narrated from Muhammad ibn 'Isa from Yunus from certain persons of who narrated to him who has said the following:

"Abu 'Abd Allah, *'Alayhi al-Salam*, has said, 'If your clothes come in contact with wine or intoxicating al-Nabidh (a kind of wine), you must wash it, if you know the area but if you do not know the area then wash all of that cloth and if you have performed Salat (prayer) with it perform it again.'"

H 5362, Ch. 62, h 5

Ali ibn Muhammad has narrated from Sahl ibn Ziyad from Khayran al-Khadim who has said the following:

"I once wrote to the man, *'Alayhi al-Salam*, asking him about clothes which come in contact with wine and flesh of pig, if I can perform Salat (prayer) wearing such cloth or not. Our people have differences on the issue. Certain ones say, 'You can perform Salat (prayer) with it because only drinking is unlawful.' Certain others say, 'You must not perform Salat (prayer) wearing them.' He (the Imam) wrote, 'You must not perform Salat (prayer) wearing them: it is rijs (filthy).' I then asked abu 'Abd Allah, *'Alayhi al-Salam*, about someone who borrows clothes from one whom he knows consumes al-Jirry (scale-less fish) or drinks wine. He then returns what he has borrowed. Can he perform Salat (prayer) wearing them before washing? He (the Imam) said, 'He does not perform Salat (prayer) wearing them before washing.'"

H 5363, Ch. 62, h 6

Ali ibn Ibrahim has narrated from Muhammad ibn 'Isa from Yunus ibn 'Abd al-Rahman from ibn Muskan from abu Basir who has said the following:

"I once asked abu 'Abd Allah, *'Alayhi al-Salam*, about a man who performs two Rak'at Salat (prayer) wearing clothes in which one has experienced sexual relation, then he comes to know it. He (the Imam) said, 'He is required to perform it from the beginning.' He (the narrator) has said that he then asked him (the Imam) about one who performs Salat (prayer) wearing clothes in which sexual relation is experienced or there is blood in it. He completes his Salat (prayer) then he comes to know it. He (the Imam) said, 'His Salat (prayer) is passed. He is not required to perform it again.'"

H 5364, Ch. 62, h 7

Muhammad ibn Yahya has narrated from al-Hassan ibn Ali ibn 'Abd Allah from 'Abd Allah ibn Jabalah from Sayf from Mansur al-Sayqal who has said the following:

"I once asked abu 'Abd Allah, *'Alayhi al-Salam*, about a man who experiences sexual relation during the night and takes Ghusl (bath). In the morning finds semen in his clothes. He (the Imam) said, 'All praise belongs to Allah who has not left anything without a limit. If he gets up in the morning and looks but does not find anything, he is not required to perform his Salat (prayer) again, but if he gets up and does not look, he is required to perform his Salat (prayer) again.'"

H 5365, Ch. 62, h 8

Muhammad ibn Yahya has narrated from Ahmad ibn Muhammad from Ali ibn al-Hakam from al-'Ala' from Muhammad ibn Muslim who has said the following:

I once asked one of the two Imam, *'Alayhim al-Salam*, about a man who finds blood in clothes of his brother while he is performing Salat (prayer). He (the Imam) said, 'He is not required to inform him until he completes his Salat (prayer) again.'"

H 5366, Ch. 62, h 9

Ali ibn Ibrahim has narrated from his father from 'Abd Allah ibn al-Mughirah from 'Abd Allah ibn Sinan who has said the following:

"I once asked abu 'Abd Allah, *'Alayhi al-Salam*, about a man who finds semen or blood in his clothes. He (the Imam) said, 'If he learns before performing Salat (prayer) that there is semen in his clothes, then performs Salat (prayer) in it without washing; he is required to perform his Salat (prayer) again, but if he did not know, he is not required to perform his Salat (prayer) again. If he thinks that something has happened then investigates but does not see anything it is sufficient to pour water on it.'"

H 5367, Ch. 62, h 10

Muhammad ibn Yahya has narrated from Ahmad ibn Muhammad from Muhammad ibn Sinan from ibn Muskan who has said the following:

"I once sent a question to abu 'Abd Allah, *'Alayhi al-Salam*, through Ibrahim ibn Maymun and told him to ask him (the Imam) about the case of a drop of urine found on one's thigh but one performs Salat (prayer) and then remembers that he has not washed it. He (the Imam) said, 'He is required to perform his Salat (prayer) again.'"

H 5368, Ch. 62, h 11

Al-Husayn ibn Muhammad has narrated from 'Abd Allah ibn 'Amir from Ali ibn Mahziyar from Fadalah from Aban from 'Abd al-Rahman ibn abu 'Abd Allah who has said the following:

"I once asked abu 'Abd Allah, *'Alayhi al-Salam*, about a man who performs Salat (prayer) with clothes in which there is feces of human beings or cat or dog, if he is required to perform his Salat (prayer) again. He (the Imam) said, 'If he did not know he is not required to perform his Salat (prayer) again.'"

H 5369, Ch. 62, h 12

Ali ibn Muhammad has narrated from 'Abd Allah ibn Sinan who has said the following:

"Abu 'Abd Allah, *'Alayhi al-Salam*, has said, 'Wash your clothes clean because of urine of all inedible animals.'"

H 5370, Ch. 62, h 13

Ahmad ibn Idris has narrated from Muhammad ibn Ahmad from Ahmad ibn al-Hassan ibn Ali from 'Amr ibn Sa'id from Musaddiq ibn Sadaqah from 'Ammar who has said the following:

"I once asked abu 'Abd Allah, *'Alayhi al-Salam*, about a man who vomits in his clothes, if he can perform Salat (prayer) in them without washing. He (the Imam) said, 'It is not an offense to do so.'"

H 5371, Ch. 62, h 14

Al-Husayn ibn Muhammad has narrated from 'Abd Allah ibn 'Amir from Ali ibn Mahziyar from and Muhammad ibn Yahya from Ahmad ibn Muhammad from Ali and Ali ibn Muhammad from Sahl ibn Ziyad from Ali ibn Mahziyar who has said the following:

"I read in the letter of 'Abd Allah ibn Muhammad to abu al-Hassan, *'Alayhi al-Salam*, in which he has said, 'I pray to Allah to keep my soul in service for your cause. Zurarah has narrated for abu Ja'far, and abu 'Abd Allah, *'Alayhim al-Salam*, about wine which pollutes one's clothes that the two Imam had said, "It is not an offense to perform Salat (prayer) with such clothes. Only drinking wine is unlawful." People other than Zurarah have narrated from abu 'Abd Allah, *'Alayhi al-Salam*. He (the Imam) has said, "If wine or al-Nabidh (a kind of wine) or any intoxicating thing pollutes your clothes, wash if you know the area of contact. If you do not know the area of contact, then wash all of such clothes. If you have performed Salat (prayer) with it perform such Salat (prayer) again." Please instruct me which one I must follow. He (the Imam) wrote with his signature, "You must follow the words of abu 'Abd Allah, *'Alayhi al-Salam*."'"

H 5372, Ch. 62, h 15

Muhammad ibn Yahya has narrated from certain persons of our people from abu Jamil al-Basriy who have said the following:

"Yunus and I were in Baghdad. I walked with him in the market. An owner of beer opened the container of his beer and drops from it came in contact with clothes of Yunus and I saw him depressed until it became Zawal (declining of the sun toward the west at noontime). I asked him, 'O abu Muhammad, do you want to perform Salat (prayer)?' He said, 'I do not want to perform Salat (prayer) until I return home and wash this wine from my clothes.' I then said, 'Is this your opinion or it is something you narrate.' He said, 'Hisham ibn al-Hakam has narrated that he asked abu 'Abd Allah, *'Alayhi al-Salam*, about beer. He (the

Imam) said, 'Do not drink it; it is unknown wine. If it pollutes your clothes, wash them clean.'"

H 5373, Ch. 62, h 16

Al-Husayn ibn Muhammad has narrated from Mu'alla' ibn Muhammad, from Muhammad ibn 'Abd Allah al-Wasitiy, from al-Qasim al-Sayqal who has said the following:

"I once wrote to al-Rida', *'Alayhi al-Salam*, saying, 'I make sword sheathing of leather from dead donkeys. My clothes come in contact with it and I perform Salat (prayer) with them. He (the Imam), *'Alayhi al-Salam*, wrote to me, 'Find other clothes for your Salat (prayer).' I then wrote to abu Ja'far, the second, *'Alayhi al-Salam*, saying, 'I would write to your father, *'Alayhi al-Salam*, about such and such issues. It became difficult for me and I then began to make them from leather of wild donkeys, properly slaughtered.' He (the Imam) wrote to me, 'All good deeds require patience, I pray to Allah to grant you blessings. If what you do is from wild ones and properly slaughtered, then it is not harmful.'"

Chapter 63 - Rules about Performing Salat (Prayer) With a Mask on One's Face, with Dyes, Does not Take out One's Hands from Under One's Clothes during Salat (prayer)

H 5374, Ch. 63, h 1

Muhammad ibn 'Isma'il has narrated from al-Fadl ibn Shadhan, from Hammad ibn 'Isa from Rib'iy, from Muhammad ibn Muslim who has said the following:

"I once asked abu Ja'far, *'Alayhi al-Salam*, about a man's performing Salat (prayer) with his face veiled. He (the Imam) said, 'It is not permissible while on the ground; however, while riding on a stumper is not an offense.'"

H 5375, Ch. 63, h 2

Muhammad ibn Yahya has narrated from Ahmad ibn Muhammad from al-Husayn ibn Sa'id from Fadalah ibn Ayyub from al-Husayn ibn 'Uthman from ibn Muskan from abu Bakr al-Hadramiy who has said the following:

"I once asked abu 'Abd Allah, *'Alayhi al-Salam*, about a man who performs Salat (prayer) with dyes (paint) on him. He (the Imam) said, 'He must not perform Salat (prayer) while it is on him. He must remove it when he wants to perform Salat (prayer).' I (the narrator) then asked, 'Is it acceptable if it is inside a piece of fabric which is clean?' He (the Imam) said, 'He must not perform Salat (prayer) while it is on him and a woman also must not perform Salat (prayer) while it is on her.'"

H 5376, Ch. 63, h 3

Ali ibn Ibrahim has narrated from his father from ibn abu 'Umayr from 'Abd al-Rahman ibn al-Hajjaj who has said the following:

"I once was with abu 'Abd Allah, *'Alayhi al-Salam*, when 'Abd al-Malik al-Qummiy came and asked saying, 'I pray to Allah to keep you well, I perform Sajdah (prostration) and my hands are inside my clothes. He (the Imam) said, 'If you want, you can do so.' He (the narrator) has said that he (the Imam) then said, 'I, by Allah, am not afraid for you because of this and things similar to it.'"

H 5377, Ch. 63, h 4

Muhammad ibn Yahya has narrated from Ahmad ibn Muhammad from Ali ibn al-Nu'man from those who he has mentioned who has said the following:

"Abu 'Abd Allah, *'Alayhi al-Salam*, about a man who performs Sajdah (prostration) on the saddle while on horseback, has said, 'He must clear the place for his Sajdah (prostration).'"

H 5378, Ch. 63, h 5

Muhammad ibn Yahya has narrated from Ahmad ibn Muhammad from ibn Mahbub from Musadif who has said the following:

"Abu 'Abd Allah, *'Alayhi al-Salam*, about a man who bundles up his hairs on the top of his head, has said, 'He is required to perform his Salat (prayer) again.'" (Fatwa best explains this Hadith.)

Chapter 64 - Salat (Prayer) of Children and When Should They Begin Salat (Prayer)

H 5379, Ch. 64, h 1

Ali ibn Ibrahim has narrated from his father from ibn abu 'Umayr from Hammad from al-Halabiy who has said the following:

"Abu 'Abd Allah, *'Alayhi al-Salam*, has said, 'We instruct our children to perform Salat (prayer) when they are five years old. Instruct your children to perform Salat (prayer) when they are seven years old. We instruct our children to fast when they are seven years old if they can endure fasting even up to midday, or more than this or less. When thirst bothers them and hunger they discontinue the fast. This is to familiarize them with fasting to build their endurance to fast. So instruct your children to fast when they are nine years old and for as much of the day they can fast. When thirst bothers them, then you should allow them to discontinue their fast.'"

H 5380, Ch. 64, h 2

Muhammad ibn 'Isma'il has narrated from al-Fadl ibn Shadhan from Hammad ibn 'Isa from Rib'iy ibn 'Abd Allah from Fudayl ibn Yasar who has said the following:

"Ali ibn al-Husayn, *'Alayhi al-Salam*, would instruct children to perform Salat (prayer) of al-Maghrib and al-'Isha' soon, one after the other, saying that it is better for them than falling asleep."

H 5381, Ch. 64, h 3

Al-Husayn ibn Muhammad has narrated from Mu'alla' ibn Muhammad from al-Washsha' from al-Mufaddal ibn Salih from Jabir who has said the following:

"I once asked abu Ja'far, *'Alayhi al-Salam*, about children when they line up for obligatory Salat (prayer). He (the Imam) said, 'Do not push them back from obligatory but separate them from each other (boys from girls).'"

Chapter 65 - Rules about the Very Old or One with an Illness

H 5382, Ch. 65, h 1

Ali ibn Ibrahim has narrated from his father from Hanan ibn Sadir from his father who has said the following:

"I once asked abu Ja'far, *'Alayhi al-Salam*, 'Do you perform optional Salat (prayer) in a sitting position? He (the Imam) replied, 'I perform them in a sitting position only from the time I have gained this much weight and reached this age.'"

H 5383, Ch. 65, h 2

Muhammad ibn Yahya has narrated from Ahmad ibn Muhammad from al-Husayn ibn Sa'id from al-Qasim ibn Muhammad from Ali ibn abu Hamzah from abu Basir who has said the following:

"I once said to abu Ja'far, *'Alayhi al-Salam*, that we speak and say that whoever performs Salat (prayer) in a sitting position without good reason, his two Rak'at are counted as one Rak'at and his two Sajdah (prostration) are counted as one Sajdah (prostration). He (the Imam) said, 'It is not that way. It is complete for you.'"

H 5384, Ch. 65, h 3

Ali ibn Ibrahim has narrated from his father from ibn abu 'Umayr from Jamil ibn Darraj who has said the following:

"I once asked abu 'Abd Allah, *'Alayhi al-Salam*, about a man who suffers from an illness. In what condition he is allowed to perform Salat (prayer) in a sitting position? He (the Imam) said, 'A man is unwell and experiences anguish; however, he knows better about himself. When he is able he must stand up.'"

H 5385, Ch. 65, h 4

Muhammad ibn Yahya has narrated from Ahmad ibn Muhammad from Hammad ibn 'Isa from Hariz from Muhammad ibn Muslim who has said the following:

"I once asked abu 'Abd Allah, *'Alayhi al-Salam*, about a man and a woman who lose their eyesight. Physicians say that they can treat them within a month or forty nights while they remain lying down on their back. Can they perform Salat (prayer) in this condition? He (the Imam) gave permission saying, '(Permission is granted to) those who are compelled and they are not rebels and transgressors. It is not a sin on them. (2:168)'"

H 5386, Ch. 65, h 5

Ali ibn Ibrahim has narrated from his father from ibn abu 'Umayr from Hammad from al-Halabiy who has said the following:

"I once asked abu 'Abd Allah, *'Alayhi al-Salam*, about a man who suffers from an illness and is not able to stand up and perform Sujud (prostrations). He (the Imam) said, 'He is required to perform his Salat (prayer) by making gestures with his head, and placing his forehead on the ground is lovelier to me.'"

H 5387, Ch. 65, h 6

Al-Husayn ibn Muhammad has narrated from 'Abd Allah ibn 'Amir in a marfu' manner from Jamil ibn Darraj from Zurarah who has said the following:

"Abu Ja'far, *'Alayhi al-Salam*, has said, 'People suffering from illness can make gestures in their Salat (prayer).'"

H 5388, Ch. 65, h 7

Ali ibn Muhammad has narrated from Sahl ibn Ziyad ibn abu Nasr from ibn Bukayr from Muhammad ibn Muslim who has said the following:

"I once asked abu Ja'far, *'Alayhi al-Salam*, about the case of one who suffers from an internal illness because of which is not able to control anal discharge. He (the Imam) said, 'He continues his Salat (prayer) wherever in Salat (prayer) he is.'"

H 5389, Ch. 65, h 8

Al-Husayn ibn Muhammad has narrated from 'Abd Allah ibn 'Amir from Ali ibn Mahziyar from Fadalah from Aban from Zurarah who has said the following:

"I once asked abu Ja'far, *'Alayhi al-Salam*, about a man who performs Salat (prayer) in a sitting position. He recites Surah (chapter). When he wants to complete it he stands up then performs Ruku' (bowing down on one's knees). He (the Imam) said, 'His Salat (prayer) is like that of the one who performs it in a standing position.'"

H 5390, Ch. 65, h 9

Ali ibn Ibrahim has narrated from his father from 'Abd Allah ibn al-Mughirah from Mu'awiyah ibn Maysarah who has said the following:

"Sinan once asked abu 'Abd Allah, *'Alayhi al-Salam*, about a man who during Salat (prayer) stretches one of his legs in his front while he is sitting. He (the Imam) said, 'It is not harmful.' I do not think except that he (the Imam) said it about one with health problems or illness.

"In another Hadith it is said that he can perform Salat (prayer) folding his legs in a square shape or stretch them, all of it is permissible."

H 5391, Ch. 65, h 10

Ali ibn Ibrahim has narrated from his father from 'Abd Allah ibn al-Mughirah from Sama'ah who has said the following:

"He (the Imam), *'Alayhi al-Salam*, was asked about the captive of the pagans. It becomes time for Salat (prayer) and the captor does not allow him to perform Salat (prayer). He (the Imam) said, 'He performs Salat (prayer) by making gestures.'"

H 5392, Ch. 65, h 11

Ali has narrated from his father from ibn Mahbub from abu Hamzah who has said the following:

"About the words of Allah, most Majestic, most Glorious, '. . . those who speak of Allah, standing, sitting and while lying on their sides. . .' (32:15) abu Ja'far, *'Alayhi al-Salam*, has said, 'A healthy person performs Salat (prayer) standing. One suffering from an illness performs Salat (prayer) sitting, and 'on their sides' is for one who is weaker than a patient who performs Salat (prayer) in a sitting position.'"

H 5393, Ch. 65, h 12

Ali has narrated from his father from those who narrated to him who has said the following:

"Abu 'Abd Allah, *'Alayhi al-Salam*, has said, 'One suffering from an illness performs Salat (prayer) in a sitting position; if one cannot do this also, one does so while lying on one's back, says Takbir (Allah is great beyond description) then recites. For Ruku' (bowing down on one's knees) closes his eyes, then says Tasbih (Allah is free of all defects), then opens his eyes. Opening one's eyes is considered standing up from Ruku‘ (bowing down on one’s knees). For Sajdah (prostration) one closes one’s eyes, then says Tasbih (Allah is free of all defects) and then opens one’s eyes which is considered raising one’s head from Sajdah (prostration). Then one says Tashahhud (testimonies of belief) and ends Salat (prayer).’”

H 5394, Ch. 65, h 13

Ahmad ibn Idris has narrated from Muhammad ibn Ahmad from Ahmad ibn al-Hassan from ‘Amr ibn Sa‘id from Musaddiq ibn Sadaqah who has said the following:

“I once asked abu ‘Abd Allah, *‘Alayhi al-Salam*, about a man who suffers from an illness: if it is permissible to stand up on his floor furnishing and perform Sajdah (prostration) on earth. He (the Imam) said, ‘If the furnishing is thick of the size of a brick or less, he can stand up on it and perform Sajdah (prostration) on earth, but if it is more than that, then it is not permissible.’”

Chapter 66 - Rules about Salat (Prayer) of Fainted or Ill Persons

H 5395, Ch. 66, h 1

Muhammad ibn Yahya has narrated from Ahmad ibn Muhammad from Ali ibn Hadid from Murazim who has said the following:

“I once asked abu ‘Abd Allah, *‘Alayhi al-Salam*, about the case of one who is ill and is not able to perform Salat (prayer). He (the Imam) said, ‘One whom Allah has over powered, then Allah is the first to pardon.’”

H 5396, Ch. 66, h 2

Muhammad ibn Yahya has narrated from Ahmad ibn Muhammad from al-Hajjal from Tha’labah ibn Maymun from Ma‘mar ibn ‘Umar who has said the following:

“I once asked abu Ja‘far, *‘Alayhi al-Salam*, about one suffering from illness if one is required to perform one’s Salat (prayer) again which is missed during the time of fainting condition. He (the Imam) said, ‘No, one is not required to perform such Salat (prayer) again.’”

H 5397, Ch. 66, h 3

Ali ibn Ibrahim has narrated from Muhammad ibn ‘Isa from Yunus from Ibrahim al-Khazzaz abu Ayyub who has said the following:

“I once asked abu ‘Abd Allah, *‘Alayhi al-Salam*, about a man who remains fainted for several days, unable to perform any Salat (prayer), who then gains consciousness; if he is required, what is missed, to perform his Salat (prayer) again. He (the Imam) said, ‘He is not obligated to perform it again.’”

H 5398, Ch. 66, h 4

Ali ibn Muhammad and Muhammad ibn al-Hassan has narrated from Sahl ibn Ziyad from ibn Mahbub from ibn Ri’ab from abu Basir who has said the following:

“I once asked one of the two Imam, *‘Alayhim al-Salam*, about a patient who faints and then gains consciousness, if he is required to perform his Salat (prayer) again. He (the Imam) said, ‘He is required to perform only those Salat (prayer) again for which there was still time after his gaining consciousness.’”

H 5399, Ch. 66, h 5

Ali ibn Ibrahim has narrated from his father from Hammad, from Hariz from Muhammad ibn Muslim who has said the following:

"I once said to him (the Imam), *'Alayhi al-Salam*, 'There is a man who has become ill and has omitted optional Salat (prayer).' He (the Imam) said, 'O Muhammad, it is not obligatory Salat (prayer). If he performs, it is a good deed that he does. If he did not do, he is not required to perform it.'"

H 5400, Ch. 66, h 6

A group has narrated from Ahmad ibn Muhammad from al-Husayn ibn Sa'id from Safwan from al-'Is ibn al-Qasim who has said the following:

"I once asked abu 'Abd Allah, *'Alayhi al-Salam*, about a man upon whom Salat (prayer) for one year has accumulated because of illness. He (the Imam) said, 'He is not required to perform such Salat (prayer).'"

H 5401, Ch. 66, h 7

Ali ibn Ibrahim has narrated from his father from and Muhammad ibn `Isma'il from al-Fadl ibn Shadhan all from ibn abu 'Umayr from Hafs ibn al-Bakhtariy who has said the following:

"I once heard abu 'Abd Allah, *'Alayhi al-Salam*, say about one fainted because of illness, 'Whomever Allah overpowers, Allah is the first to pardon.'"

Chapter 67 - The Excellence of Friday and its Night

H 5402, Ch. 67, h 1

Muhammad ibn Yahya has narrated from Ahmad ibn Muhammad from Hammad ibn 'Isa from al-Husayn ibn al-Mukhtar from abu Basir who has said the following:

"I heard abu Ja'far, *'Alayhi al-Salam*, saying, 'The sun does not shine on anything (other days) more excellent than Friday.'"

H 5403, Ch. 67, h 2

It is a narration from him (narrator of previous Hadith) by Ahmad ibn Muhammad from al-Husayn ibn Sa'id from al-Nadr ibn al-Suwayd from 'Abd Allah ibn Sinan from Hafs al-Bakhtariy from Muhammad ibn Muslim who has said the following:

"Abu Ja'far, *'Alayhi al-Salam*, has said, 'On Fridays, prominent angels come down with paper of silver and pens of gold and sit on the doors of Masjids on chairs of light and write people according to their grades such as first, second . . . until the Imam (prayer leader) comes out. When he comes out they (angels) roll up their pages and do not descend again until next Friday.'"

H 5404, Ch. 67, h 3

Ahmad has narrated from al-Husayn from al-Nadr ibn al-Suwayd from 'Abd Allah ibn Sinan who has said the following:

"Abu 'Abd Allah, *'Alayhi al-Salam*, has said, 'The Messenger of Allah loved it, when traveling or coming home in winter, to be on Friday nights.' Abu 'Abd Allah, *'Alayhi al-Salam*, has also said, 'Allah has chosen something from everything. From days He has chosen Friday.'"

H 5405, Ch. 67, h 4

The narrator of previous Hadith has also narrated from al-Nadr from 'Abd Allah ibn Sinan who has said the following:

"Abu 'Abd Allah, *'Alayhi al-Salam*, has said, 'The hour of Friday wherein prayers are answered is the time when the prayer leader completes the sermons, until people get ready in rows for Salat (prayer). The other hour is the time at the end of the day to sunset.'"

H 5406, Ch. 67, h 5

Ali ibn Muhammad has narrated from Sahl ibn Ziyad from ibn abu Nasr who has said the following:

"Abu al-Hassan al-Rida, *'Alayhi al-Salam*, has said, that the Messenger of Allah has said, 'Friday is the master of days. On this day Allah increases good deeds and obliterates bad deeds, raises the degrees, answers prayers, removes hardships and makes great wishes come true. It is the day wherein Allah increases the number of those He emancipates and sets free from fire. Whoever prays in this day to Allah with full knowledge of His rights and respect, it then becomes necessary for Allah, the Most Majestic, the Most Glorious, to emancipate and free him from the fire. If he dies on this day or night, he has died a martyr and will be resurrected with full protection. Whoever neglects to respect Him and fails to observe His right, it then becomes a right upon Allah, the Most Majestic, the Most Glorious, to make him feel the heat of hell unless he repents.'"

H 5407, Ch. 67, h 6

Muhammad ibn Yahya has narrated from 'Abd Allah ibn Muhammad from Ali ibn al-Hakam from Aban who has said the following:

"Abu 'Abd Allah, *'Alayhi al-Salam*, has said, 'For Friday there are rights and respect, you must not fail to observe them or have shortcomings in worshipping Allah or in striving to become nearer to Him through good deeds and through refraining from all prohibited matters. Allah on this day increases good deeds, obliterates bad deeds and raises degrees of excellence.' The narrator has said that the Imam then said, 'Friday night is like its day. If you can, stay awake all night in Salat (prayer) and supplication; your Lord in the beginning of Friday night (commands an angel who) descends to the first heaven, (he) increases good deeds, obliterates bad deeds and Allah's kindness is vast and graceful.'"

H 5408, Ch. 67, h 7

Muhammad ibn Yahya has narrated from Muhammad ibn Musa from al-'Abbas ibn The Ma'ruf from ibn abu Najran from 'Abd Allah ibn Sinan from ibn abu Ya'fur from abu Hamzah who has said the following:

"Abu Ja'far, *'Alayhi al-Salam*, has said, in answer to a question, 'How was Friday called Friday?' The Imam said, 'Allah, the Most Majestic, the Most Glorious, brought His creatures under the Divine Authority of Muhammad, *'Alayhi al-Salam*, and the Executor of his will during "the divine Covenant session", and that session was called "al-Jumu'ah" (the assembly) because of His calling His creatures together.'"

H 5409, Ch. 67, h 8

Muhammad ibn Yahya has narrated from Muhammad ibn al-Husayn from Ali ibn al-Nu'man from 'Umar ibn Yazid from Jabir who has said the following:

"Someone asked abu Ja'far, *'Alayhi al-Salam*, about Friday and its night. The Imam replied, 'Friday night is the finest; its day is brilliant. There is no other day in which sunset takes place with as many rescued from the fire as is on Friday. If one dies on Friday while fully acknowledging the rights of Ahl al-Bayt (people of this house), Allah writes for him the certificate of freedom from the fire and punishment. If one dies on a Friday night, he is set free from the fire.'"

H 5410, Ch. 67, h 9

Muhammad ibn Yahya has narrated from Ahmad ibn Muhammad from Muhammad ibn Khalid from al-Nadr ibn al-Suwayd from 'Abd Allah ibn Sinan who has said the following:

"Abu 'Abd Allah, *'Alayhi al-Salam*, has said, 'Allah has given excellence to Friday over other days. On Friday, decoration and beautification takes place in paradise for those who attend it (Friday). You race to paradise proportionate to the degree of your attending Friday. On Friday the doors of heavens open for the deeds of servants (of Allah).'"

H 5411, Ch. 67, h 10

Ali ibn Muhammad and Muhammad ibn al-Hassan have narrated from Sahl ibn Ziyad from Ahmad ibn Muhammad from al-Mufaddal ibn Salih from Jabir ibn Yazid who has said the following:

"I asked abu Ja'far, *'Alayhi al-Salam*, about the words of Allah, the Most Majestic, the Most Glorious, 'Hasten to remember Allah. . . .' (62:9). He replied, 'It means do good deeds and do it promptly; it is a busy day for the Muslims. The reward for the deeds of the Muslims is proportionate to the degree of its business. Both good and bad deeds double on this day.' The narrator has said that abu Ja'far, *'Alayhi al-Salam*, has said, 'By Allah, I have received reports that the companions of the Holy Prophet would prepare themselves on Thursday for Friday; it is a busy day for the Muslims.'"

H 5412, Ch. 67, h 11

Muhammad ibn Yahya has narrated from Ahmad ibn Muhammad from al-Husayn ibn Sa'id from Ibrahim ibn abu al-Balad from certain individuals of his people who have said the following:

"Abu Ja'far or abu 'Abd Allah, *'Alayhi al-Salam*, has said, 'There is no other day on which sun shines more excellent than Friday. The words of birds, on meeting each other, on this day are, "Peace, peace. It is a good day."'"

H 5413, Ch. 67, h 12

Muhammad ibn Yahya has narrated from Ahmad ibn Muhammad from ibn abu Nasr from Mu'awiyah ibn 'Ammar who has said the following:

"I asked abu 'Abd Allah, *'Alayhi al-Salam*, about the hour on Friday in which prayer of a believing person is answered. He replied, 'Yes, it is the time when the Imam comes out.' I then said, 'Imam may come early or late.' He said, 'It is when the sun declines toward the west at midday.'"

H 5414, Ch. 67, h 13

Ali ibn Muhammad has narrated from Sahl ibn Ziyad from 'Amr ibn 'Uthman from Muhammad ibn 'Adhafir from 'Umar ibn Yazid who has said the following:

"Abu 'Abd Allah, *'Alayhi al-Salam*, said to me, 'O 'Umar, on Friday nights angels by the number of atoms come to earth with pens of gold and papers of silver in their hands. They write no other thing until Saturday except about Allahumma Salli 'Ala Muhammad wa 'Ali Muhammad (O Allah grant

Muhammad and his family a compensation worthy of their serving Your cause). I pray to Allah to grant them such rewards. You should say, "Allahumma Salli 'Ala Muhammad wa 'Ali Muhammad (O Allah grant Muhammad and his family a compensation worthy of their serving Your cause) a great deal." The Imam also said, 'O 'Umar, it is of the Sunnah (tradition the Holy Prophet) to say, "Allahumma Salli 'Ala Muhammad wa 'Ali Muhammad (O Allah grant Muhammad and his family a compensation worthy of their serving Your cause)" every Friday one thousand times and one hundred times on other days.'"

H 5415, Ch. 67, h 14

Ali ibn Ibrahim has narrated from his brother, Ishaq ibn Ibrahim, from Muhammad ibn `Isma'il ibn Bazi' who has said the following:

"I once asked al-Rida', *'Alayhi al-Salam*, 'Is it true, as I have heard that Friday is the shortest day?' He replied, 'That is true.' I then said, 'I pray to Allah to keep my soul in service for your cause, how can it be so?' He replied, 'Allah, the most Blessed, the most High, brings together the spirits of the pagans under the eye of the sun. When the sun stalls, Allah causes the pagans to be punished with sun's stalling for an hour. On Friday, however, the sun does not stall, so Allah exempts them from being punished due to the excellence of Friday, thus, there is no stalling for the sun on that day.'" (This is a mutashabih Hadith, thus, the Imam can best explain it).

Chapter 68 - Sprucing up on Fridays

H 5416, Ch. 68, h 1

Ali ibn Ibrahim has narrated from Muhammad ibn 'Isa from Yunus ibn 'Abd al-Rahman from Hisham ibn al-Hakam who has said the following:

"Abu 'Abd Allah, *'Alayhi al-Salam*, has said, 'Everyone of you should take a shower, apply fragrance, comb your beard, dress up in your best dress and prepare himself for Friday. On that day, he should be serene and dignified. He should make his worshipping his Lord to be the best and do as much good as he can; Allah watches over the people of earth to double their good deeds.'"

H 5417, Ch. 68, h 2

Muhammad ibn Yahya has narrated from Ahmad ibn Muhammad from al-Husayn ibn Sa'id from Muhammad ibn al-Husayn from 'Umar al-Jurjaniy from Muhammad ibn al-'Ala' who has said the following:

"I heard abu 'Abd Allah, *'Alayhi al-Salam*, say, 'One may, on Friday trim his mustache and fingernails. In so doing if one says, "(I do this) in the name of Allah and because of the Sunnah (traditions) of the Holy Prophet, Muhammad, and his family," Allah writes for him for every hair and piece of fingernail a reward equal to freeing a slave. He will not become ill to a harmful degree except the illness that causes his death.'"

H 5418, Ch. 68, h 3

Muhammad ibn Yahya has narrated from Muhammad ibn al-Husayn from Safwan ibn Yahya from Mansur ibn Hazim who has said the following:

"Abu 'Abd Allah, *'Alayhi al-Salam*, has said, 'Both men and women should take a shower on Friday when at home. On the journey men should take a shower on Friday.'"

H 5419, Ch. 68, h 4

Ali ibn Ibrahim has narrated from his father from Hammad ibn 'Isa from Hariz from Zurarah who has narrated the following:

"Abu Ja'far, *'Alayhi al-Salam*, has said, 'You must not ignore Ghusl (bath) on Friday; it is a sunnah. You should use perfumes, dress up in you proper dress and you should complete your Ghusl (bath) before noontime. At Zawal (declining of the sun toward the west at noontime) rise up with calmness and dignity for prayer.' He (the Imam) said, 'Ghusl (bath) on Friday is obligatory.'"

H 5420, Ch. 68, h 5

Ali has narrated from his brother from 'Isma'il ibn 'Abd al-Khaliq from Muhammad ibn Talhah who has said the following:

"Abu 'Abd Allah, *'Alayhi al-Salam*, has said, 'Trimming one's mustache, fingernails and applying al-Khatmi (officinal or marshmallow) to one's head on Friday removes one's poverty and increases one's sustenance.'"

H 5421, Ch. 68, h 6

Muhammad ibn Yahya has narrated from Muhammad ibn al-Husayn from Musa ibn Sa'dan from 'Abd Allah ibn Sinan who has said the following:

"Abu 'Abd Allah, *'Alayhi al-Salam*, has said, 'One who trims his mustache and fingernails and washes his head with marshmallow on Friday, he is like one who sets free a human being.'"

H 5422, Ch. 68, h 7

Muhammad ibn 'Isma'il has narrated from al-Fadl ibn Shadhan from ibn abu 'Umayr from Hafs ibn al-Bakhtariy who has said the following:

"Abu 'Abd Allah, *'Alayhi al-Salam*, has said, 'Trimming one's mustache, and fingernails every Friday is protection against leprosy.'"

H 5423, Ch. 68, h 8

Ali ibn Ibrahim has narrated from his father from and Muhammad ibn 'Isma'il fom from al-Fadl ibn Shadhan all from Hammad ibn 'Isa from Hariz from Zurarah and al-Fudayl who has narrated the following:

" We once asked him (the Imam), *'Alayhi al-Salam*, if taking Ghusl (bath) after dawn on Friday is sufficient. He (the Imam) replied, 'Yes it is sufficient.'"

H 5424, Ch. 68, h 9

Hammad has narrated from Hariz from certain persons of our people who has narrated the following:

Abu Ja'far, *'Alayhi al-Salam*, has said, 'Taking Ghusl (bath) on Friday is necessary, regardless of whether one is at home or on a journey. If one forgets, one must take Ghusl (bath) the next day. In the case of a person suffering from an illness it is permissible not to take a Ghusl (bath).'"

(Ahadith 8-9 are best explained in the form of fatwa.)

H 5425, Ch. 68, h 10

A number of our people have narrated from Ahmad ibn Muhammad from ibn Faddal from ibn Bukayr who has said the following:

"Abu 'Abd Allah, *'Alayhi al-Salam*, has said, 'Washing one's head with marshmallow every Friday is protection against leprosy and insanity.'"

(The following chapters are best explained by fatwa.)

Chapter 69 - Obligation of Friday Salat (prayer)

H 5426, Ch. 69, h 1

Muhammad ibn Yahya has narrated from Ahmad ibn Muhammad from al-Husayn ibn Sa'id from al-Nadr ibn Suwayd from 'Asem ibn Humayd from abu Basir and Muhammad ibn Muslim who have said the following:

"Abu 'Abd Allah, *'Alayhi al-Salam*, has said, 'In every seven days Allah, most Majestic, most Glorious, has made thirty-five Salat (prayer) obligatory upon every Muslim to attend except five kinds of people: Those suffering from illness, slaves, travelers, women and children.'"

H 5427, Ch. 69, h 2

Ali ibn Ibrahim has narrated from his father from ibn abu 'Umayr from Jamil ibn Darraj from Muhammad ibn Muslim and Zurarah who have said the following:

"Abu Ja'far, *'Alayhi al-Salam*, has said, 'Friday Salat (prayer) is not obligatory upon those who are two farsakh (about six miles) away (from the location of the congregation).'"

H 5428, Ch. 69, h 3

Ali has narrated from his father from Hammad from Hariz from ibn Muslim who has said the following:

"I once asked abu 'Abd Allah, *'Alayhi al-Salam*, about Friday. He (the Imam) said, 'It (Friday Salat (prayer)) is obligatory up on those who live within two farsakh. If the distance is more than this then it is not obligatory on him.'"

H 5429, Ch. 69, h 4

Ali has narrated from his father from ibn abu 'Umayr from ibn 'Udhaynah from Zurarah who has said the following:

"Abu Ja'far, *'Alayhi al-Salam*, has said, 'The sermons and Friday Salat (prayer) are not valid without the presence of five people, the fifth of whom is the Imam.'"

H 5430, Ch. 69, h 5

Al-Husayn ibn Muhammad has narrated from 'Abd Allah ibn 'Amir from Ali ibn Mahziyar from Fadalah from Aban ibn 'Uthman from abu al-'Abbas who has said the following:

"Abu 'Abd Allah, *'Alayhi al-Salam*, has said, 'Minimum number of attending people for Friday Salat (prayer) is seven or at least five people.'"

H 5431, Ch. 69, h 6

Muhammad ibn 'Isma'il has narrated from al-Fadl ibn Shadhan and Ali ibn Ibrahim has narrated from his father from all from Hammad ibn 'Isa from Hariz from Zurarah who has said the following:

"Abu Ja'far, *'Alayhi al-Salam,* has said, 'From one Friday to the next Friday Allah has made thirty-five Salat (prayer) obligatory. Of these one is made obligatory to be performed in congregation and that is Friday Salat (prayer). He has exempted nine kinds of people: Of such people are children, the elderly, the insane, the travelers, the slaves, the women, people suffering from illness, the blind and those who live beyond two farsakh.'"

H 5432, Ch. 69, h 7

Ali ibn Ibrahim has narrated from his father from 'Abd Allah ibn al-Mughirah from Jamil from Muhammad ibn Muslim who has said the following:

"Abu Ja'far, *'Alayhi al-Salam,* has said, 'There must be a distance of three miles between two congregations for Friday Salat (prayer). Friday Salat (prayer) without sermon is not valid. If there is a distance of three miles between two congregation for Friday Salat (prayer), then each congregation can come together (for Friday Salat (prayer)).'"

Chapter 70 - The Time for Friday and 'Asr Salat (prayer)

H 5433, Ch. 70, h 1

Muhammad ibn `Isma'il has narrated from al-Fadl ibn Shadhan from Hammad ibn 'Isa from Rib'iy and Muhammad ibn Yahya from Muhammad ibn al-Husayn from 'Uthman ibn 'Isa from Sama'ah all who has said the following:

"Abu 'Abd Allah, *'Alayhi al-Salam,* has said that Abu 'Abd Allah, *'Alayhi al-Salam,* has said, 'The time of al-Zuhr on Friday begins at Zawal (declining of the sun toward the west at noontime)."

H 5434, Ch. 70, h 2

Ali ibn Ibrahim has narrated from Muhammad ibn 'Isa from Yunus ibn 'Abd al-Rahman from 'Abd Allah ibn Sinan who has said the following:

"Abu 'Abd Allah, *'Alayhi al-Salam,* has said, 'On Friday when it is Zawal (declining of the sun to ward the west at noontime), then you can begin the obligatory Salat (prayer).'"

H 5435, Ch. 70, h 3

Muhammad ibn Yahya has narrated from Ahmad ibn Muhammad from al-Husayn ibn Sa'id from al-Nadr ibn Suwayd from Muhammad ibn abu Hamzah from Sufyan ibn al-Simt who has said the following:

"I once asked abu 'Abd Allah, *'Alayhi al-Salam,* about the time of al-'Asr Salat (prayer) on Friday. He (the Imam) said, 'It is at the time of al-Zuhr Salat (prayer) during the days other than Fridays.'"

H 5436, Ch. 70, h 4

Muhammad ibn Yahya has narrated from Ahmad ibn Muhammad from Muhammad ibn Khalid from al-al-Qasim ibn 'Urwah from Muhammad ibn abu 'Umayr who has said the following:

"I once asked abu 'Abd Allah, *'Alayhi al-Salam,* about Salat (prayer) of Friday. He (the Imam) said, 'Jibril brought it with a short period of time. When it is Zawal (declining of the sun toward the west at noontime) then perform it.' I (the narrator) then asked, 'When it is Zawal, must I perform two Rak'at, then Friday Salat (prayer)?' Abu 'Abd Allah, *'Alayhi al-Salam,* said, 'I, however, when it is

Zawal, do not begin anything before obligatory Salat (prayer).' Al-Qasim has said that ibn Bukayr would perform two Rak'at when he had doubts about the commencement of Zawal. When he became certain of the commencement of Zawal he commenced the obligatory Salat (prayer) on Friday.'"

(The following chapter is best explained in the form of fatwa.)

Chapter 71 - Friday Prayer Leader's Getting ready for Friday Prayer, His Sermon and Quietly Listening

H 5437, Ch. 71, h 1

Muhammad ibn Yahya has narrated from Muhammad ibn al-Husayn and Ahmad ibn Muhammad from all from 'Uthman ibn 'Isa from Sama'ah who has said the following:

"Abu 'Abd Allah, *'Alayhi al-Salam*, has said, 'It is desirable for the Imam who delivers sermons for the people on Friday to wear turban in winter and a Yamaniy or 'Adaniy gown. He must deliver the sermon in a standing position. In it he praises Allah and speaks of His glory, then advises people to observe piety (taqwa') before Allah, reads a small Surah (chapter) from al-Quran. He then sits down, then stands up and praises Allah, speaks of His glory and says Salawat, (O Allah, grant compensation to Muhammad and his family worthy of their services to Your cause). He prays for the Imam of the Muslims and asks forgiveness from Allah for the believers, male and female. When he completes the sermon the caller readies people for Salat (prayer) and the Imam performs Salat (prayer) of two Rak'at. In the first Rak'at he reads Surah (chapter) al-Jumu'ah after al-Fatihah, and in the second Rak'at Surah (chapter) al-Munafiqun after al-Fatihah.'"

H 5438, Ch. 71, h 2

Muhammad ibn Yahya has narrated from Ahmad ibn Muhammad from al-Husayn ibn Sa'id from Safwan ibn Yahya from al-'Ala' from Muhammad ibn Muslim who has said the following:

"Abu 'Abd Allah, *'Alayhi al-Salam*, has said, 'When the Imam delivers the sermon on Friday, it is not desirable for anyone to speak until he completes the sermon. When the Imam completes the sermons he can speak until Salat (prayer) begins, regardless of whether he hears the recitation or not; it is sufficient.'"

H 5439, Ch. 71, h 3

Al-Husayn ibn Muhammad has narrated from 'Abd Allah ibn 'Amir from Ali ibn Mahziyar from 'Uthman ibn 'Isa from abu Maryam who has said the following:

"I once asked abu Ja'far, *'Alayhi al-Salam*, about the sermon of the Messenger of Allah if it was before or after Salat (prayer). He (the Imam) said, 'The Messenger of Allah would first deliver sermons, then perform Salat (prayer).'"

H 5440, Ch. 71, h 4

Muhammad ibn Yahya has narrated from Muhammad ibn al-Husayn from 'Uthman ibn 'Isa from Sama'ah who has said the following:

"I once asked abu 'Abd Allah, *'Alayhi al-Salam*, about Salat (prayer) on Friday. He (the Imam) said, 'With Imam it is two Rak'at but if one performs it alone, it is four Rak'at like al-Zuhr Salat (prayer). If there is an Imam he delivers a speech but if the Imam who delivers a speech is not there, then it is four Rak'at even if performed in congregation.'"

H 5441, Ch. 71, h 5

Muhammad ibn Yahya has narrated from Muhammad ibn al-Husayn from Muhammad ibn Yahya al-Khazzaz from Hafs ibn al-Ghiyath who has said the following:

"Ja'far, abu 'Abd Allah, *'Alayhi al-Salam,* has said that his father, *'Alayhi al-Salam,* has said, 'A third Adhan on Friday is a heretical invention.'"

H 5442, Ch. 71, h 6

Muhammad ibn Yahya has narrated from Ahmad ibn Muhammad from al-Husayn ibn Sa'id from al-Nadr ibn al-Suwayd, from Yahya al-Halabiy from Burayd ibn Mu'awiyah from Muhammad ibn Muslim who has said the following:

"In the first sermon of Friday prayer, abu Ja'far, *'Alayhi al-Salam,* has said to say, 'All praise belongs to Allah. We praise Him, beg assistance from Him, ask Him for forgiveness, seek guidance from Him and seek protection with Him against the evil of our own selves and our own bad deeds. Whomever Allah guides, no one can mislead and whomever Allah causes to go astray, no one is able to guide.'

"I testify that no one, other than Allah, deserves worship. He (Allah) is one, He has no partner, and I testify that Muhammad is His servant and messenger. He chose him to serve as one with His Authority, made him a special person with His message and honored him with prophesy. He (Muhammad) is the trustee with Allah's unseen matters and is a mercy for all the worlds. O Allah, grant compensation to Muhammad and his family worthy of their services to Your cause. Servants of Allah, I advise you to observe piety before Allah and warn you of His punishment. Allah saves those who observe piety before Him to enjoy happiness. Thus, bad things cannot touch them and they do not feel sadness. Allah honors those who fear Him, protects against things from which they were afraid and allows them to experience affluence and joy. I encourage you to be interested in the grace of Allah, which is forever, I warn you of His punishment, which never ends, and there is no relief thereby for those who are subject to it. Thus, you must not allow worldly matters to deceive you and you should not rely on them; it is a dwelling of deception. Allah has deemed it and its dwellers to face destruction. Thus you must supply yourselves by the things with which Allah has honored you, in the form of observing piety and virtuous deeds; the good deeds of the servant of Allah do not receives acceptance before Allah unless they are pure and Allah does not accept (good deeds) from anyone other than the pious ones. Allah has informed you of the positions of those who believe in Him, do good deeds, and of the positions of the unbelievers of improper deeds saying, "That is the Day (of resurrection) where all people are gathered and that is the day of the presence of everyone. We delay it only for an appointed time. The day it comes not a single soul can speak without His permission. Thus, certain ones of the people are unfortunate and others are fortunate ones. The unfortunate ones are in the fire wherein they wail and cry. Therein they live forever as long as the skies and earth are there, except if your

Lord wishes otherwise. Your Lord certainly, does whatever He wants. Those who are fortunate, they are in paradise wherein they live forever as long as the skies and earth are there, unless your Lord wishes otherwise, such as granting unending gifts." (11:102-108). We pray to Allah who has brought us in this gathering to make our day a blessing and grant mercy to all of us; He has power over all things. The Book of Allah is the most truthful narration and has the best stories. Allah, the Most Majestic, the Most Glorious, has said, "When Quran is recited, listen to it and remain silent so that perhaps you receive mercy." (7:203) Thereafter recite a chapter from the Holy Quran and pray to your Lord and say, "Allahumma Salli 'Ala Muhammad wa 'Ali Muhammad (O Allah grant Muhammad and his family a compensation worthy of their serving Your cause)." Pray for the believing people, male and female. Then sit down for a short while and then say:

"All praise belongs to Allah. We praise Him, beg assistance from Him, and beg of Him to forgive us, seek guidance from Him, believe in Him, trust Him and seek protection with Him against the evil of our own selves and our own bad deeds. Whomever Allah guides, no one can mislead and whomever Allah causes to go astray no one is able to guide."

"I testify that no one, other than Allah, deserves worship. He (Allah) is one, He has no partner, and I testify that Muhammad is His servant and messenger. He sent him with guidance and true religion to make His religion stand supreme over all religions even though the pagans dislike, and He has made him to be a mercy for all the worlds, with glad news and warning that calls people to Allah by His permission and is a shining beacon. Whoever obeys Allah and His Messenger, finds the right guidance and whoever disobeys becomes lost.'

"Servants of Allah I advise you to observe piety before Allah. Those who obey Allah benefit thereby and those who disobey Him suffer losses. Allah is the One in whose presence you will all return. He is the One who will judge you (for your merits). Observing piety is Allah's advice for you and for those who lived before you. Allah, the Most Majestic, the Most Glorious, has said, "We advised those to whom heavenly book was given before you as well as yourselves to be pious before Allah but if you disbelieve all things in heavens and on earth belongs to Allah, Allah is self-sufficient and praiseworthy." (4:130).

"You must benefit from Allah's advice and hold fast to His book; it has most eloquent pieces of advice and the best of things in matters of consequences. Allah has established His arguments against people. He gives them the chance not to face destruction without enough opportunity to follow proper guidance, so if they face their own destruction they face it without any excuse and those who follow guidance and live can do so with valid proofs. The Messenger of Allah has already preached the message that he brought (from Allah). You must strictly follow his will and the matters that he has left among you, in the form of two heavy issues, the book of Allah and his family. Whoever follows them (the two issues) will never go astray and those who abandon them (the two issues) will never find any guidance.'

"Allahumma Salli 'Ala Muhammad (O Allah grant Muhammad, Your servant and messenger, the master of the messengers, the leader of the pious people, the messenger of the Lord of the worlds, and his family a compensation worthy of their serving Your cause." Then say, "O Allah grant Ali, Amir al-Mu'minin, the executor of the will of the messenger of the Lord of the worlds, a compensation worthy of his serving Your cause." Then mention all `A'immah one by one up to the twelfth Imam, *'Alayhim al-Salam*, and then say, "O Allah, please, grant him easy victory and support him with a mighty support. O Lord, make through him Your religion to stand supreme as well as the Sunnah (traditions) of Your prophet, so that nothing of the truth remains hidden for fear of any creature. O Lord, we wish to live under a graceful government in which You grant might to Islam and its followers, humiliate hypocrisy and hypocrite people. In such government, make us to be the preacher to following your laws and leaders to your path. Under such government, grant us the grace of this life as well as the life to come. O Lord, make us to know fully the truth that You have made us to bear and teach us to correct our shortcomings."

"He then should pray to Allah to condemn His enemies and pray for himself and his friends. They then should raise their hands and pray to Allah for all of their wishes until it is complete and then say, "O Lord, answer our prayers." At the end he should say, "Allah commands to practice justice and do good and to yield to the rights of relatives, and prohibits committing indecency, unlawful matters and to rebel against the truth. I give you good advice so you can be considerate." Then say, "O Lord, make us to be of those who are reminded and such reminders have benefited them." Then end the sermon.'"

H 5443, Ch. 71, h 7

Ali ibn Ibrahim has narrated from his father from Hammad ibn 'Isa from Hariz from Muhammad ibn Muslim who has said the following:

"I once asked him (the Imam), *'Alayhi al-Salam*, about Friday. He (the Imam) said, 'It has Adhan and 'Iqamah and the Imam comes out after Adhan, climbs the pulpit and delivers the sermon. People do not perform Salat (prayer) until the Imam is on the pulpit. He then sits on the pulpit for a time, which takes one to read Chapter 112. He then stands up and commences the sermon, then climbs down, then recites with them Surah (chapter) al-Jumu'ah (62) in the first Rak'at and Surah (chapter) al-Munafiqun (63) in the second Rak'at.'"

H 5444, Ch. 71, h 8

Muhammad ibn Yahya has narrated from Ahmad ibn Muhammad ibn 'Isa from al-Husayn ibn Sa'id from Fadalah ibn Ayyub from ibn Sinan who has said the following:

"About the words of Allah, most Majestic, most Glorious, 'spruce yourselves up near every Masjid,' (7:29) abu 'Abd Allah, *'Alayhi al-Salam*, has said, 'It is a reference to both 'Id and Friday.'"

H 5445, Ch. 71, h 9
Ali ibn Ibrahim has narrated from his father from al-Nawfaliy from al-Sakuniy who has said the following:
"Abu 'Abd Allah, *'Alayhi al-Salam*, has said, 'The Messenger of Allah has said, "All preachers are al-Qiblah, which means when the Imam delivers the sermon for the people on Friday it is appropriate for people to turn their faces to him."'"

(The following chapter is best explained in the form of fatwa.)

Chapter 72 - Recitations on Friday and Night

H 5446, Ch. 72, h 1
Muhammad ibn Yahya has narrated from Muhammad ibn al-Husayn from Safwan ibn Yahya from Mansur ibn Hazim who has said the following:
"Abu 'Abd Allah, *'Alayhi al-Salam*, has said, 'The recitation is not definite texts except on Friday in which there is Surah (chapter) al-Jumu'ah and al-Munafiqun.'"

H 5447, Ch. 72, h 2
Muhammad ibn Yahya has narrated from Ahmad ibn Muhammad from and Muhammad ibn al-Husayn from 'Uthman ibn 'Isa from Sama'ah from abu Basir who has said the following:
"Abu 'Abd Allah, *'Alayhi al-Salam*, has said, 'On Friday night recite Surah (chapter) al-Jumu'ah and Sabbih Isma Rabbika al-'A'la'. In Friday morning recite Surah (chapter) al-Jumu'ah and Chapter 112, and in Friday Salat (prayer) recite Surah (chapter) al-Jumu'ah and al-Munafiqun.'"

H 5448, Ch. 72, h 3
Al-Husayn ibn Muhammad has narrated from 'Abd Allah ibn 'Amir from Ali ibn Mahziyar from Fadalah ibn Ayyub from al-Husayn ibn abu Hamzah who has said the following:
"I once asked abu 'Abd Allah, *'Alayhi al-Salam*, 'What can I recite for the morning Salat (prayer) on Friday?' He (the Imam) said, 'In the first Rak'at recite Surah (chapter) al-Jumu'ah and in the second Rak'at recite Chapter 112 then read Qunut (supplication after recitation in second Rak'at) so both become equal.'"

H 5449, Ch. 72, h 4
Ali ibn Ibrahim has narrated from his father from 'Abd Allah ibn al-Mughirah from Jamil from Muhammad ibn Muslim who has said the following:
"Abu Ja'far, *'Alayhi al-Salam*, has said, 'Allah has granted honor to the believers by means of sending (Surah (chapter) of al-Jumu'ah). The Messenger of Allah established it a Sunnah (noble tradition) and good news for them. He sent al-Munafiqun to reprimand the hypocrites. It is not proper to omit it. Salat (prayer) of one who willfully omits it is not valid.'"

H 5450, Ch. 72, h 5
Ali ibn Ibrahim has narrated from his father from ibn abu 'Umayr from Hammad from al-Halabiy who has said the following:
"I once asked abu 'Abd Allah, *'Alayhi al-Salam*, about recitation on Friday when I perform Salat (prayer) alone of four Rak'at. Can I recite aloud? He (the

Imam) said, 'Yes, you can recite aloud.' He (the Imam) said, 'Recite Surah (chapter) al-Jumu'ah and al-Munafiqun on Friday.'"

H 5451, Ch. 72, h 6

Muhammad ibn Yahya has narrated from Ahmad ibn Muhammad from Ali ibn al-Hakam from fro al-'Ala' from Muhammad ibn Muslim who has said the following:

"I once asked one of the two Imam, *'Alayhim al-Salam*, about a man who intends to recite Surah (chapter) al-Jumu'ah on Friday but he recites Qul Huwa Allahu Ahad (Chapter 112). He (the Imam) said, 'He can go back to Surah (chapter) al-Jumu'ah.' It is also narrated that one completes it in two Rak'at, then performs it again."

H 5452, Ch. 72, h 7

Ali ibn Ibrahim has narrated from his father from ibn abu 'Umayr from Mu'awiyah ibn 'Ammar from 'Umar ibn Yazid who has said the following:

"Abu 'Abd Allah, *'Alayhi al-Salam*, has said, 'If one performs Friday Salat (prayer) without reciting Surah (chapter) al-Jumu'ah and al-Munafiqun, he is required to perform his Salat (prayer) again, on a journey or at home.' It is narrated that it is not an offense to recite Qul Huwa Allahu Ahad, Chapter 112 on a journey."

Chapter 73 - Qunut (Supplication after Recitation in Second Rak'at) in Friday Salat (Prayer)

H 5453, Ch. 73, h 1

Muhammad ibn Yahya has narrated from Ahmad ibn Muhammad from al-Husayn ibn Sa'id from certain persons of our people from Sama'ah from abu Basir who has said the following:

"Abu 'Abd Allah, *'Alayhi al-Salam*, has said, 'Qunut (supplication after recitation) on Friday is in the first Rak'at after recitation in which you can read, "No one deserves to be worshipped besides Allah, the Forbearing, the Honorable. No one deserves to be worshipped besides Allah, most High, most Great. No one deserves to be worshipped besides Allah who is the Lord of seven heavens, the seven earths, all that is in them and between them and the Lord of the great throne. All praise belongs to Allah, Cherisher of the worlds. O Allah, grant compensation to Muhammad and his family worthy of their services to Your cause as You have guided us through him. O Allah, grant compensation to Muhammad and his family worthy of their services to Your cause as You have granted us honor through him. O Lord, make us of those You have chosen for Your religion and have created for Your paradise. O Allah, do not allow our hearts to deviate from Your guidance and grant us mercy; You are the most Awarding One.'"

H 5454, Ch. 73, h 2

Al-Husayn ibn Muhammad has narrated from 'Abd Allah ibn 'Amir from Ali ibn Mahziyar from Fadalah ibn Ayyub from Mu'awiyah ibn 'Ammar who has said the following:

"I heard abu 'Abd Allah, *'Alayhi al-Salam*, say, 'Qunut (supplication after recitation) for Friday Salat (prayer), when himself being the Imam, is in the first

Rak'at. If it is performed four Rak'at then Qunut (supplication after recitation) is in the second Rak'at before Ruku' (bowing down on one's knees)."

H 5455, Ch. 73, h 3
Ali ibn Ibrahim has narrated from Muhammad ibn 'Isa from Yunus from Aban from 'Isma'il al-Ju'fiy from 'Umar ibn Hanzalah who has said the following:
"I once asked abu 'Abd Allah, *'Alayhi al-Salam*, about Qunut (supplication after recitation) on Friday. He (the Imam) said, 'You are my messenger to them in this matter. When performing in congregation, it is in the first Rak'at, but when performing alone, it is in the second Rak'at before Ruku' (bowing down on one's knees).'"

Chapter 74 - One Who Misses Friday Salat (Prayer) With Imam

H 5456, Ch. 74, h 1
Ali ibn Ibrahim has narrated from his father from ibn abu 'Umayr from Hammad ibn 'Uthaman from al-Halabiy who has said the following:
"I once asked abu 'Abd Allah, *'Alayhi al-Salam*, about a man who misses to attend the sermon of Friday. He (the Imam) said, 'He can perform the two Rak'at, but if he misses Salat (prayer), he performs four Rak'at.' He (the Imam) said, 'If you join the Imam before the Ruku' (bowing down on one's knees) for the last Rak'at, you have attended Salat (prayer), but if you join the Imam after Ruku' (bowing down on one's knees) of the last Rak'at, then it is al-Zuhr and four Rak'at.'"

Chapter 75 - Optional Salat (Prayer) On Friday

H 5457, Ch. 75, h 1
Ali ibn Muhammad and others have narrated from Sahl ibn Ziyad from Ahmad ibn Muhammad from ibn abu Nasr who has said the following:
"Abu al-Hassan, *'Alayhi al-Salam*, has said, 'Optional Salat (prayer) on Friday is six Rak'at very early, six Rak'at in midday, two Rak'at at Zawal (declining of the sun toward the west at noontime), then perform obligatory Salat (prayer), then perform six Rak'at thereafter.'"

H 5458, Ch. 75, h 2
A group has narrated from Ahmad ibn Muhammad ibn 'Isa from al-Husayn ibn Sa'id from Hammad ibn 'Isa from al-Husayn ibn al-Mukhtar from Ali ibn 'Abd al-'Aziz from Murad ibn Kharijah who has said the following:
"Abu 'Abd Allah, *'Alayhi al-Salam*, has said, 'On Friday morning, when the distance from the sun to the east becomes like the distance from the sun to the west at the time of al-'Asr, I perform six Rak'at. When it (morning) is wider, I perform six Rak'at, when it is Zawal (declining of the sun toward the west at noontime), I perform two Rak'at, then perform al-Zuhr, then I perform six Rak'at thereafter.'"

H 5459, Ch. 75, h 3

A group has narrated from Ahmad ibn Muhammad from al-Husayn ibn Sa'id from Fadalah or Muhammad ibn Sinan from ibn Muskan from 'Abd Allah ibn 'Ajalan who has said the following:

"Abu Ja'far, *'Alayhi al-Salam*, has said, 'If you have doubts about Zawal (declining of the sun toward the west at noontime), perform two Rak'at. When you become certain of Zawal, then begin performing obligatory Salat (prayer).'"

Chapter 76 - The Rare Ahadith about Friday

H 5460, Ch. 76, h 1

Al-Husayn ibn Muhammad has narrated from 'Abd Allah ibn 'Amir from Ali ibn Mahziyar from al-Nadr ibn al-Suwayd from 'Abd Allah ibn Sinan who has said the following:

"Abu 'Abd Allah, *'Alayhi al-Salam*, has said that on Friday night after optional Salat (prayer), after Maghrib (soon after sunset) Salat (prayer) one should say, 'O Lord, I appeal to You through Your gracious face and great name. "Allahumma Salli 'Ala Muhammad wa 'Ali Muhammad (O Allah grant Muhammad and his family a compensation worthy of their serving Your cause)" Forgive my great sin'- seven times."

H 5461, Ch. 76, h 2

Ali ibn Muhammad and Muhammad ibn al-Hassan have narrated from Sahl ibn Ziyad from Ja'far ibn Muhammad al-Ash'ariy from al-Qaddah who has said the following:

"Abu 'Abd Allah, *'Alayhi al-Salam*, has said that the Messenger of Allah has said, 'Say a great number of times, "Allahumma Salli 'Ala Muhammad wa 'Ali Muhammad (O Allah, please, grant Muhammad and his family a compensation worthy of their serving Your cause)" on the brilliant day and blossoming night of Friday.' He was asked about the meaning of great number of times and he (the Imam) replied, 'It is up to one hundred times and above this is excellent.'"

H 5462, Ch. 76, h 3

Muhammad ibn abu 'Abd Allah has narrated from Muhammad ibn Hassan from al-Hassan ibn al-Husayn from Ali ibn 'Abd Allah from Yazid ibn Ishaq from Harun ibn Kharijah from al-Mufaddal who has said the following:

"Abu Ja'far, *'Alayhi al-Salam*, has said, 'On Friday no other form of obedience to Allah is more beloved to me than saying, "Allahumma Salli 'Ala Muhammad wa 'Ali Muhammad (O Allah grant Muhammad and his family compensation worthy of their serving Your cause.)"'"

H 5463, Ch. 76, h 4

Ali ibn Muhammad has narrated from Sahl ibn Ziyad in a marfu' manner (from the Imam) who has said the following:

"After completing Friday Salat (prayer) say, 'Allahumma Salli 'Ala Muhammad wa 'Ali Muhammad. . . (O Allah grant Muhammad and his family a compensation worthy of their serving Your cause, the well accepted executors of his will, with most preferred compensations and grant them blessings of the best form of your blessings, he and they all are *'Alayhim al-Salam*, mercy and blessings).' Whoever says this after the afternoon Salat (prayer), Allah writes for him one hundred thousand good deeds, deletes his one hundred thousand bad deeds, makes his one hundred thousand wishes come true and raises his position by one hundred thousand degrees.'"

H 5464, Ch. 76, h 5

The narrator of the previous Hadith has narrated that if one says the expression stated in the previous Hadith seven times, Allah in return grants him one good from every servant. On that day his deeds are accepted and on the Day of Judgment he will come with a light between his eyes."

H 5465, Ch. 76, h 6

Al-Husayn ibn Muhammad has narrated from 'Abd Allah ibn 'Amir from Ali ibn Mahziyar from Muhammad ibn Yahya from Hammad ibn 'Uthman who has said the following:

"I heard abu 'Abd Allah, *'Alayhi al-Salam*, saying, 'It is preferable to recite Chapter 55 of the Holy Quran after the morning Salat (prayer) on Friday morning and after reciting the verse that says, "Which of the bounties of your Lord do you then deny?" say, 'I do not deny anyone of the bounties of my Lord.'"

H 5466, Ch. 76, h 7

It is narrated through the same chain of narrators as that of the previous Hadith from Ali ibn Mahziyar from Ayyub ibn Nuh from Muhammad ibn abu Hamzah who has said the following:

"Abu 'Abd Allah, *'Alayhi al-Salam*, has said, 'If one recites chapter 18 of the Holy Quran every Friday night, it serves as an expiation for the matters from this to the next Friday.'"

"The narrator of the Hadith has said that people other than him also have narrated about reciting this Chapter after the afternoon Salat (prayer) on Friday."

H 5467, Ch. 76, h 8

Abu Ali al-Ash'ariy has narrated from Muhammad ibn Salim from Ahmad ibn al-Nadr from 'Amr ibn Shimr from Jabir who has said the following:

"Abu Ja'far, *'Alayhi al-Salam*, would go to Masjid early Friday morning after sunrise when the sun would rise by about one spear's length (above the horizon). In the month of Ramadan he would do so earlier and say, 'The Fridays of the month of Ramadan have extra excellence over the Fridays of other months, just as the month of Ramadan has extra excellence over the other months.'"

H 5468, Ch. 76, h 9

Ali ibn Ibrahim has narrated from his father from and Ali ibn Muhammad al-Qasaniy from al-Qasim ibn Muhammad from Sulayman ibn Dawud al-Minqariy from Hafs ibn al-Ghiyath who has said the following:

"I once heard abu 'Abd Allah, *'Alayhi al-Salam*, say, 'If a man attends Friday in a dense crowd when the Imam says Takbir (Allah is great beyond description) and performs Ruku' (bowing down on one's knees), this man also performs Ruku' but cannot perform Sajdah (prostration). The Imam and the people stand up for the second Rak'at and he also stands up with them, then the Imam performs Ruku', but he cannot perform Ruku' in the second Rak'at because of crowd but he performs Sajdah (prostration). What is he required to perform?'Abu 'Abd Allah, *'Alayhi al-Salam*, said that the first Rak'at is complete in Ruku‘. He did not perform Sajdah (prostration) until the second Rak‘at, this he has missed. He has performed Sajdah (prostration) in the second Rak‘at; if he intended it to be the Sajdah (prostration) for the first Rak‘at, the first Rak‘at becomes complete for him, and when the Imam says Salam (the phrase of offering greeting of peace), he stands up to performs one Rak‘at. Then performs Sajdah (prostration), then Tashahhud (testimonies of belief) and Salam (the phrase of offering greeting of peace) to end his Salat (prayer). It would not suffice for the first Rak‘at or for the second Rak‘at if he did not have the intention for that Sajdah (prostration) to be for the first Rak‘at.’”

(Hadith 9 is best explained in the form of fatwa.)

H 5469, Ch. 76, h 10
Ali ibn Ibrahim has narrated from Ahmad ibn abu ‘Abd Allah in a marfu‘ manner saying:
“Someone said to abu ‘Abd Allah, *‘Alayhi al-Salam*, ‘Certain people consider applying Nurah (lime as hair cleaner) on Friday as undesirable.’ The Imam said, ‘It is not as they say. No other cleaner is a better cleaner on Friday than Nurah.’”

(The following chapters are best explained by fatwa.)

Chapters on the Rules of a Journey

Chapter 77 - Times of Salat (Prayer) on a Journey and Performing Two Salat (prayer) Soon one after the Other

H 5470, Ch. 77, h 1
Muhammad ibn Yahya has narrated from Ahmad ibn Muhammad from ibn abu Nasr from Safwan al-Jammal who has said the following:
“Once I performed Salat (prayer) behind abu ‘Abd Allah, *‘Alayhi al-Salam*, at the time of Zawal (declining of the sun toward the west at noontime) and I asked, saying, ‘I pray to Allah to keep my soul in service for your cause, when is it time for al-‘Asr Salat (prayer)?’ He (the Imam) said, ‘It is when you release your camel.’ I then asked, ‘When it (time of al-‘Asr) is when I am not on a journey?’ He (the Imam) said, ‘It is time for al-‘Asr when it (the shadow of an object) is less than a step or it is two-thirds of a step.’”

H 5471, Ch. 77, h 2
Ali ibn Muhammad has narrated from Sahl ibn Ziyad from Muhammad ibn al-Hassan ibn Shammun from ‘Abd Allah ibn al-Qasim from Misma’ abu Sayyar who has said the following:
“I once asked abu ‘Abd Allah, *‘Alayhi al-Salam*, about the time for Salat (prayer) of al-Zuhr on Friday on a journey. He (the Imam) said, ‘It is at Zawal (declining of the sun toward the west at noontime) which is its time on Friday when one is not on a journey.’”

H 5472, Ch. 77, h 3
Ali ibn Ibrahim has narrated from his father from ibn abu ‘Umayr from Hammad from al-Halabiy who has said the following:

"This is a Hadith that abu 'Abd Allah, *'Alayhi al-Salam*, has pronounced. 'The Messenger of Allah, when on a journey or being in need for something, would perform al-Zuhr and al-'Asr Salat (prayer) together soon one after the other, as well as al-Maghrib and al-'Isha' Salat (prayer).' He (the narrator) has said that abu 'Abd Allah, *'Alayhi al-Salam*, has said, 'It is not harmful to perform al-'Isha' al-Akhirah earlier on a journey and before the disappearance of brightness in the western horizon.'"

H 5473, Ch. 77, h 4

Muhammad ibn Yahya has narrated from Ahmad ibn Muhammad from ibn Faddal from ibn Bukayr from 'Ubayd ibn Zurarah who has said the following:

"Once a few persons of our people and I were in a company, among them was Muyassir, between Makkah and al-Madinah. As we traveled, we were in doubt about the time of Zawal (declining of the sun toward the west at noontime). Certain ones among us said that we must walk for a while until we are certain about Zawal, then perform Salat (prayer). Thus, we did so and we had walked only a little that the caravan of abu 'Abd Allah, *'Alayhi al-Salam*, appeared. I said, 'The caravan has come.' I saw Muhammad ibn 'Isma'il and asked him, 'Have you performed Salat (prayer) yet?' He replied, 'My grandfather instructed us so we performed Salat (prayer) al-Zuhr and al-'Asr all together.' We then left and I went to inform our people about it.'"

H 5474, Ch. 77, h 5

Al-Husayn ibn Muhammad has narrated from 'Abd Allah ibn 'Amir from Ali ibn Mahziyar from Fadalah ibn Ayyub from Aban from 'Umar ibn Yazid who has said the following:

"Abu 'Abd Allah, *'Alayhi al-Salam*, has said, 'The time for al-Maghrib on a journey is up to one-third of the night.' It is also narrated that it is up to midnight."

Chapter 78 - Required Length of Distance of a Journey for Shortened Salat (Prayer)

H 5475, Ch. 78 h 1

Ali ibn Ibrahim has narrated from his father from ibn abu 'Umayr from Jamil from Zurarah who has said the following:

"Abu Ja'far, *'Alayhi al-Salam*, has said, 'Salat (prayer) is reduced after traveling a distance of one barid and one barid is four farasikh (which is twelve miles).'"

H 5476, Ch. 78, h 2

It is a narration from him (narrator of previous Hadith) by his father from ibn abu 'Umayr from abu Ayyub who has said the following:

"I once asked abu 'Abd Allah, *'Alayhi al-Salam*, about the minimum distance after the traveling of which a traveler reduces his Salat (prayer). He (the Imam) said, 'It is one barid.'"

H 5477, Ch. 78, h 3

Muhammad ibn Yahya has narrated from Muhammad ibn al-Husayn from Muhammad ibn Yahya al-Khazzaz from certain persons of our people who has said the following:

"Abu 'Abd Allah, *'Alayhi al-Salam*, has said, 'Once we were sitting and my father was with the governor of banu 'Umayyah over the people of al-Madinah. My father came back and sat down and said, "I was in the court of this (governor) a little while ago and people asked about Taqsir (reducing Salat (prayer) on a journey after traveling a certain distance). Someone said that it is at three. Another one said that it is after traveling one day and one night. Yet another said that it is one rawhah. He (the Governor) then asked me and I said, 'When Jibril came with Taqsir (reducing Salat (prayer) on a journey after traveling a certain distance) to the Messenger of Allah, the Holy prophet asked him, "At what distance is this?" He (Jibril) said, "It is at one barid." He (the Messenger of Allah) asked, "What is that?" Jibril replied, "It is between the shadow of 'Ayr (a certain mountain) to the shadow of O'Ayr."" He (the Imam) said that time passed, then it was seen that banu 'Umayyah had placed marks on the road and mentioned what Abu Ja'far, *'Alayhi al-Salam*, had spoken of. They placed signs on the shadow of 'Ayr and the outline of O'Ayr. They then divided it into twelve miles and it was three thousand and five hundred yards for each mile. They had placed signs on them. When banu Hashim appeared they changed the affairs of banu 'Umayyah in a certain way because Hadith is from banu Hashim, thus they placed a sign next to each sign.'" (the Arabic word for yard is Dhira' (from the elbow to the tip of the fingers which is about eighteen inches)).

H 5478, Ch. 78, h 4

Ali ibn Ibrahim has narrated from his father from ibn abu 'Umayr from certain persons of our people who has said the following:

"Abu 'Abd Allah, *'Alayhi al-Salam*, was asked about the limit of the miles which is involved in Taqsir (reducing Salat (prayer) on a journey after traveling a certain distance). Abu 'Abd Allah, *'Alayhi al-Salam*, said, 'The Messenger of Allah had determined the limits of such mile to be from the shadow of 'Ayr to the shadow of O'Ayr and they are two mountains in al-Madinah. On sunrise the shadow of 'Ayr falls on the shadow of O'Ayr and that is the mile that the Messenger of Allah had set up for Taqsir (reducing Salat (prayer) on a journey after traveling a certain distance).'"

H 5479, Ch. 78, h 5

A number of our people have narrated from Ahmad ibn Muhammad from al-Barqiy, from Muhammad ibn Aslam al-Jabaliy from Sabbah al-Hadhdha' from Ishaq ibn 'Ammar who has said the following:

"I once asked abu al-Hassan, *'Alayhi al-Salam*, about the case of a people who are on a journey. When they arrived at the place where they were required to perform their Salat (prayer) in a reduced form, they reduced their Salat (prayer). After traveling two, three, or four farsakh, one of them without whom their journey could not be done remained behind. They waited for his arrival. Without him their journey was not possible. They stayed there for many days without knowing to go forward or return. Are they required to perform their Salat (prayer) complete or reduce it?' He (the Imam) said, 'If they have traveled four farsakh they reduce their Salat (prayer), regardless, they stay there or return. If they have traveled less than four farsakh, they perform their Salat (prayer) complete, regardless, they stay there or return.'"

Chapter 79 - Where to Apply Rules about Salat (Prayer) on a Journey

H 5480, Ch. 79, h 1

Muhammad ibn Yahya has narrated from Muhammad ibn al-Husayn, from Safwan ibn Yahya from al-'Ala' ibn Razin from Muhammad ibn Muslim who has said the following:

"I once asked abu 'Abd Allah, *'Alayhi al-Salam*, about a man who wants to travel. Where is he required to apply the rules about journey? He (the Imam) said, 'He must apply them where houses become invisible to him.' I then asked, 'A man begins his journey on Zawal (declining of the sun toward the west at noontime). What is he required to do?' He (the Imam) said, 'When you come out perform two Rak'at Salat prayers).' Also al-Husayn ibn Sa'id has narrated from, Safwan and Fadalah from al-'Ala' a similar Hadith."

H 5481, Ch. 79, h 2

Al-Husayn ibn Muhammad has narrated from al-'Ala' ibn Muhammad from al-Hassan ibn Ali al-Washsha' who has said the following:

"I once heard al-Rida', *'Alayhi al-Salam*, say, 'At Zawal (declining of the sun toward the west at noontime) if you are in a city and want to travel, if you go out after Zawal perform al-'Asr Salat in the reduced form.'"

H 5482, Ch. 79, h 3

Muhammad ibn Yahya has narrated from Ahmad ibn Muhammad from ibn Faddal from Dawud ibn Farqad from Bashir al-Nabbal who has said the following:

"Once abu 'Abd Allah, *'Alayhi al-Salam*, and I traveled until we were at al-Shajarah. Abu 'Abd Allah, *'Alayhi al-Salam*, said to me, 'O Nabbal.' I replied, 'Yes Imam, I am here.' He (the Imam) said, 'In this group no one other than you and I, are required to perform our Salat (prayer) in four Rak'at because it became the time for Salat (prayer), thereafter we came out.'"

H 5483, Ch. 79, h 4

Ali ibn Ibrahim has narrated from his father from Hammad, from Hariz from Muhammad ibn Muslim who has said the following:

"I once asked abu 'Abd Allah, *'Alayhi al-Salam*, about a man who returns from his journey when it has become the time for a Salat (prayer). He (the Imam) said, 'He is required to perform his Salat (prayer) as two Rak'at and if he goes out on a journey when it has become the time for Salat (prayer) he is required to perform his Salat (prayer) as four Rak'at.'"

H 5484, Ch. 79, h 5

Ahmad ibn Idris has narrated from Muhammad ibn 'Abd al-Jabbar and Muhammad ibn 'Isma'il from al-Fadl ibn Shadhan all from Safwan ibn Yahya from Ishaq ibn 'Ammar who has said the following:

I once asked abu Ibrahim, *'Alayhi al-Salam*, about a man who is on a journey, returns and arrives among the houses of al-Kufah. Is he required to perform his Salat (prayer) complete or as reduced until he comes to his family? He (the

Imam) said, 'He is required to perform his Salat (prayer) as reduced until he comes to his family.'"

H 5485, Ch. 79, h 6

Muhammad ibn Yahya has narrated from Muhammad ibn al-Husayn from Safwan from 'Is ibn al-Qasim who has said the following:

"I once asked abu 'Abd Allah, *'Alayhi al-Salam*, about a man who on a journey performs Salat (prayer) in complete form. He (the Imam) said, 'If there is time for it he is required to perform his Salat (prayer) again, otherwise, it is passed.'"

H 5486, Ch. 79, h 7

Ali ibn Ibrahim has narrated from his father from Hammad from Hariz from Zurarah who has said the following:

"I once asked him (the Imam), *'Alayhi al-Salam*, about a man who misses a Salat (prayer) while on a journey and remembers it when he is at home. He (the Imam) said, 'He performs Qada' (compensatory prayer) for it just as it was missed, if missed on a journey the compensatory prayer for it at home is as reduced and if it is missed at home the compensatory prayer for it, if performed on a journey, is complete.'"

H 5487, Ch. 79, h 8

Ali ibn Ibrahim has narrated from his father from ibn abu 'Umayr from Ali ibn Yaqtin who has said the following:

"I once asked abu al-Hassan, *'Alayhi al-Salam*, about a man who is on a journey and during performing a Salat (prayer) he decides to stay there for ten days. He (the Imam) said, 'If he decides to stay for ten days, he is required to perform his Salat (prayer) complete.'"

(The following chapter is best explained in the form of fatwa.)

Chapter 80 - How a Home Coming Traveler Applies Applicable Rules

H 5488, Ch. 80, h 1

Ali ibn Ibrahim has narrated from his father and Muhammad ibn Yahya has narrated from Ahmad ibn Muhammad ibn 'Isa and Muhammad ibn 'Isma'il from al-Fadl ibn Shadhan all from Hammad ibn 'Isa from Hariz ibn 'Abd Allah from Zurarah who has said the following:

"I once asked abu Ja'far, *'Alayhi al-Salam*, about a man who returns home from a journey. To what time is he required to perform his Salat (prayer) as reduced, and when is he required to perform his Salat (prayer) as complete? He (the Imam) said, 'If you enter a land and you become certain of staying there for ten days, then perform your Salat (prayer) as complete. If you do not know for how long you stay there and think that you may leave it tomorrow or the next day, then perform your Salat (prayer) as reduced up to a month. When a month passes in such condition, then perform your Salat (prayer) as complete even if you decide to leave at that hour.'"

H 5489, Ch. 80, h 2

Muhammad ibn Yahya has narrated from Ahmad ibn Muhammad ibn 'Isa from ibn Faddal from 'Abd Allah ibn Bukayr who has said the following:

"I once asked abu 'Abd Allah, *'Alayhi al-Salam*, about a man who is in al-Basra and he is from al-Kufah. He has a house there and he passes by al-Kufah just as a passer-by without an intention to stay there except for picking up supplies within one or two days. He (the Imam) said, 'He is required to stay in one side of the city and perform his Salat (prayer) as reduced.' I then asked, 'What is he required to do if he visits his family?' He (the Imam) said, 'He is required to perform his Salat (prayer) complete.'"

H 5490, Ch. 80, h 3

Ali ibn Ibrahim has narrated from his father from ibn abu 'Umayr from abu Ayyub who has said the following:

"Muhammad ibn Muslim once asked abu 'Abd Allah, *'Alayhi al-Salam*, when I was listening, about a traveler who thinks to stay for ten days. He (the Imam) said, 'He is required to perform his Salat (prayer) as complete. If he does not know for how long he will stay, like for one or more, he can count to thirty days, then perform his Salat (prayer) as complete even if thereafter he stays for one day or one Salat (prayer).' Muhammad ibn Muslim then said, 'I am told that you have said it is five.' He (the Imam) said, 'Yes, I had said that.' Abu Ayyub has said that he said, 'I pray to Allah to keep my soul in service for your cause, can it be less than five?' He (the Imam) said, 'No, it cannot be less than five.'"

Chapter 81 - Rules about Sailors and People Traveling Very often

H 5491, Ch. 81, h 1

Ali ibn Ibrahim has narrated from his father and Muhammad ibn Yahya has narrated from Ahmad ibn Muhammad ibn 'Isa from Muhammad ibn 'Isma'il from al-Fadl ibn Shadhan all from Hammad ibn 'Isa from Hariz from Zurarah who has said the following:

"Abu Ja'far, *'Alayhi al-Salam*, has said, 'Four kinds of people are required to perform their Salat (prayer) as complete on a journey or when at home. Of such people are muleteers, al-kariy (workers of muleteers), shepherds and mailmen, because it is their work.'"

"In another Hadith it is said that a muleteer performs his Salat (prayer) as reduced if his journey becomes condensed which means, completing two days, journey in one day."

H 5492, Ch. 81, h 2

Muhammad ibn Yahya has narrated from Muhammad ibn al-Husayn from Safwan ibn Yahya from al-'Ala' from Muhammad ibn Muslim who has said the following:

"One of the two Imam, *'Alayhi al-Salam*, has said, 'Sailors when in their vessel are not required to perform their Salat (prayer) as reduced as well as muleteers and camel drivers.' In another Hadith it is said that muleteers perform their Salat (prayer) as reduced when the journey becomes condensed, like walking two days of journey in one day.'"

H 5493, Ch. 81, h 3

Muhammad ibn al-Hassan and others have narrated from Sahl ibn Ziyad from Ahmad ibn Muhammad from ibn abu Nasr who has said the following:

"I once asked al-Rida', *'Alayhi al-Salam*, about a man who has a country estate where he goes and stays for one, two or three days. Is he required to perform his Salat (prayer) complete or reduced? He (the Imam) said, 'He is required to perform his Salat (prayer) complete whenever he is there.'"

H 5494, Ch. 81, h 4

Muhammad ibn al-Hassan has narrated from Sahl ibn Ziyad from Ali ibn Asbat from ibn Bukayr who has said the following:

"I once asked abu 'Abd Allah, *'Alayhi al-Salam*, about a man who goes hunting for one, two or three days. Is he required to perform his Salat (prayer) as reduced? He (the Imam) said, 'No, he cannot perform as reduced. However if one escorts one's brother in belief, then it is permissible to do so. Hunting is a way of falsehood and Salat (prayer) is not performed as reduced.' He (the Imam) said, 'When you escort your brother in religion you can perform your Salat (prayer) as reduced.'"

"A number of our people have narrated from Ahmad ibn Muhammad from al-Barqiy from certain persons of his people from Ali ibn Asbat a similar Hadith.

H 5495, Ch. 81, h 5

A number of our people have narrated from Ahmad ibn Muhammad from ibn Khalid from his father from Sulayman ibn Ja'far al-Ja'fariy from those whom he has mentioned who has said the following:

"Abu 'Abd Allah, *'Alayhi al-Salam*, has said, 'Arabs (desert dwellers) do not perform their Salat (prayer) as reduced because their homes are with them.'"

H 5496, Ch. 81, h 6

Muhammad ibn 'Isma'il has narrated from al-Fadl ibn Shadhan, from Muhammad ibn abu 'Umayr, from 'Abd al-Rahman ibn al-Hajjaj who has said the following:

"I once asked abu 'Abd Allah, *'Alayhi al-Salam*, about a man who has certain country estates which are near each other to which he goes and stays. Is he required to perform his Salat (prayer) as complete or reduced? He (the Imam) said, 'He is required to perform his Salat (prayer) as complete.'"

H 5497, Ch. 81, h 7

Al-Husayn ibn Muhammad has narrated from Mu'alla' ibn Muhammad from al-Washsha' from Hammad ibn 'Uthaman who has said the following:

"About the words of Allah, most Majestic, most Glorious, '. . . one who is compelled and who is not a rebel or transgressor. . .'(2:168) abu 'Abd Allah, *'Alayhi al-Salam*, has said, 'This rebel is a rebel to hunt. The transgressor is a thief and they do have permission to eat dead animals when they are compelled; it is unlawful for them. It is not for them as it is for the Muslims and they must not perform their Salat (prayer) as reduced (when hunting or stealing)'"

H 5498, Ch. 81 h 8

Muhammad ibn Yahya has narrated from Ahmad ibn Muhammad from ibn Faddal from ibn Bukayr from 'Ubayd ibn Zurarah who has said the following:

"I once asked abu 'Abd Allah, *'Alayhi al-Salam*, about a man who goes for hunting. Can he perform his Salat (prayer) as reduced? He (the Imam) said, 'He is required to perform his Salat (prayer) as complete, because it is not a journey in the way of truth.'"

H 5499, Ch. 81, h 9

Ali ibn Ibrahim has narrated from Muhammad ibn 'Isa from Yunus from Ishaq ibn 'Ammar who has said the following:

"I once asked him (the Imam), *'Alayhi al-Salam*, about the case of sailors and desert dwelling Arabs. Can they perform their Salat (prayer) as reduced? He (the Imam) said, 'No, they cannot do so because their homes are with them.'"

H 5500, Ch. 81, h 10

A number of our people have narrated from Ahmad ibn Muhammad from 'Imran ibn Muhammad from 'Imran al-Qummiy from certain persons of our people who has said the following:

"I once asked him (the Imam), *'Alayhi al-Salam*, about a man who goes hunting to a place which is one or two day's journey away. Is he required to perform his Salat (prayer) as complete or reduced? He (the Imam) said, 'If he goes to provide for his family, he is not required to fast, and performs his Salat (prayer) as reduced. If he goes in search for useless reasons then he cannot perform his Salat (prayer) as reduced and it is not honorable.'"

H 5501, Ch. 81, h 11

Muhammad ibn Yahya has narrated from 'Abd Allah ibn Ja'far from Muhammad ibn Jazzak who has said the following:

"I once wrote to him (the Imam), *'Alayhi al-Salam*, 'I pray to Allah to keep my soul in service for your cause. I have a few camels and I have a caretaker for them. At certain times I go to them on the way to Makkah because of desire for Hajj or for al-Nadrah (rarely) in certain places. Is it necessary to perform my Salat (prayer) as complete and fast, or as reduced? He (the Imam) wrote in answer, 'If you are not always with them and do not go on the journey with them all the time except the journey to Makkah, you must perform your Salat (prayer) as reduced and do not fast.'"

Chapter 82 - Salat (Prayer) of a Traveler Person behind a Non-Traveler

H 5502, Ch. 82, h 1

Ali ibn Ibrahim has narrated from his father from ibn abu 'Umayr from Hammad from al-Halabiy who has said the following:

"I once asked abu 'Abd Allah, *'Alayhi al-Salam*, about a traveler if he can perform Salat (prayer) behind a non-traveler. He (the Imam) said, 'After performing two Rak'at, he then can move away whenever he wants.'"

H 5503, Ch. 82, h 2

Al-Husayn ibn Muhammad has narrated from Mu'alla' ibn Muhammad, from al-Washsha' from Aban ibn 'Uthman, from 'Umar ibn Yazid who has said the following:

"I once asked abu 'Abd Allah, *'Alayhi al-Salam*, about a traveler who performs Salat (prayer) behind an Imam and joins only for two Rak'at, is it sufficient? He (the Imam) said, 'Yes, it is sufficient.'"

Chapter 83 - Performing Optional Salat (Prayer) on a Journey

H 5504, Ch. 83, h 1

Al-Husayn ibn Muhammad has narrated from 'Abd Allah ibn 'Amir from Ali ibn Mahziyar from al-Husayn ibn Sa'id from Zur'ah ibn Muhammad from Sama'ah who has said the following:

"I once asked him (the Imam), *'Alayhi al-Salam*, about Salat (prayer) on a journey. He (the Imam) said, 'It is a two Rak'at without anything before or thereafter, except that it is appropriate for a traveler to perform four Rak'at after al-Maghrib and optional Salat (prayer) during the night as much as he wants, if a traveler on foot; but if riding he can perform Salat (prayer) on his stumper. His Salat (prayer) is in the form of making gestures and bowing down his head for Sujud (prostrations) lower than that for Ruku' (bowing down on one's knees).'"

H 5505, Ch. 83, h 2

Muhammad ibn Yahya has narrated from Ahmad ibn Muhammad from al-Husayn ibn Sa'id from al-Nadr ibn Suwayd from Yahya al-Halabiy from al-Harith ibn al-Mughirah who has said the following:

"Abu 'Abd Allah, *'Alayhi al-Salam*, has said, 'There are four Rak'at after al-Maghrib. You must not omit them, regardless of being on a journey or while at home.'"

H 5506, Ch. 83, h 3

Ali ibn Ibrahim has narrated from Muhammad ibn 'Isa ibn 'Ubayd from Yunus ibn 'Abd al-Rahman from ibn Muskan from abu Basir who has said the following:

"Abu 'Abd Allah, *'Alayhi al-Salam*, has said, 'Salat (prayer) on a journey is of two Rak'at and there is nothing before or thereafter except al-Maghrib after which there are four Rak'at which you must not omit on a journey or while at home. You are not required to perform the compensatory Salat (prayer) during the day but you should perform the compensatory prayer, those missed during the night (optional Salat (prayer).'"

H 5507, Ch. 83, h 4

Muhammad ibn Yahya has narrated from Muhammad ibn al-Husayn from Safwan ibn Yahya from Dharih who has said the following:

"I once asked abu 'Abd Allah, *'Alayhi al-Salam*, about nightly optional Salat (prayer) which are missed. Can I perform the compensatory prayer for them during the day? He (the Imam) said, 'Yes, you can do so, if you are able to bear it.'"

H 5508, Ch. 83, h 5

Muhammad ibn Yahya has narrated from Ahmad ibn Muhammad from Muhammad ibn Sinan from ibn Muskan from al-Halabiy who has said the following:

"I once asked abu 'Abd Allah, *'Alayhi al-Salam*, about performing optional Salat (prayer) on the back of camel or stumper. He (the Imam) said, 'Yes, you can do so as your face is.' I then asked, 'Am I required to face al-Qiblah (al-

Ka'bah) when saying Takbir (Allah is great beyond description)? He (the Imam) said, 'No, you are not required but say Takbir (Allah is great beyond description) as your face is and that is how the Messenger of Allah of had done.'"

H 5509, Ch. 83, h 6

Muhammad ibn 'Isma'il has narrated from al-Fadl ibn Shadhan from Safwan ibn Yahya from Mansur ibn Hazim from Aban ibn Taghlib who has said the following:

"Once abu 'Abd Allah, *'Alayhi al-Salam*, and I journeyed between Makkah and al-Madinah and he would say, 'You, however, are young people, thus you delay. I am old so I hurry up.' He (the Imam) would perform the nightly optional Salat (prayer) in the beginning of the night."

H 5510, Ch. 83, h 7

Muhammad ibn Yahya has narrated from Muhammad ibn al-Husayn from Safwan ibn Yahya from Ya'qub ibn Shu'ayb who has said the following:

"I once asked abu 'Abd Allah, *'Alayhi al-Salam*, about a man who performs Salat (prayer) on his stumper. He (the Imam) said, 'He makes gestures for Sujud (prostrations) lower than the gesture for Ruku' (bowing down on one's knees).' I then asked, 'Can he perform Salat (prayer) while walking? He (the Imam) said, 'Yes, but in the form of gestures and make the one for Sujud (prostrations) lower than that for Ruku'.'"

H 5511, Ch. 83, h 8

Ali ibn Ibrahim has narrated from his father from ibn abu 'Umayr from 'Abd al-Rahman ibn al-Hajjaj who has said the following:

"I once asked abu 'Abd Allah, *'Alayhi al-Salam*, about a man who performs optional Salat (prayer) in the cities while on the stumper and to whatever direction it faces. He (the Imam) said, 'Yes, it is not harmful.'"

H 5512, Ch. 83, h 9

Ali ibn Ibrahim has narrated from his father from Hammad from Hariz from those whom he has mentioned who has said the following:

"Abu Ja'far, *'Alayhi al-Salam*, did not consider it harmful to perform Salat (prayer) while walking, but he must not be driving a camel."

H 5513, Ch. 93, h 10

Muhammad ibn Yahya has narrated from Ahmad ibn Muhammad from Muhammad ibn Sinan from ibn Muskan from al-Halabiy who has said the following:

"I once asked abu 'Abd Allah, *'Alayhi al-Salam*, about nightly Salat (prayer) and al-Witr in the beginning of the night on a journey if one is afraid of cold or not feeling well. He (the Imam) said, 'It is not harmful and I do it so.'"

H 5514, Ch. 83, h 11

Muhammad ibn Yahya has narrated from Ahmad ibn Sulayman from Sa'd ibn Sa'd from Muqatil ibn Muqatil from abu al-Harith who has said the following:

"I once asked him (Imam al-Rida'), *'Alayhi al-Salam*, about the four Rak'at after al-Maghrib on a journey, because camel man is in hurry and I am not able to perform on the ground. Can I perform Salat (prayer) in the carriage on the camel's back? He (the Imam) said, 'Yes, you can perform it in the carriage.'"

H 5515, Ch. 83, h 12
Muhammad ibn Yahya has narrated from Ahmad ibn Muhammad from ibn abu Najran from Safwan who has said the following:
"Al-Rida', *'Alayhi al-Salam*, has said, 'You can perform the two morning Rak'at in the carriage."

Chapter 84 - Salat (Prayer) on a Ship

H 5516, Ch. 84, h 1
Ali ibn Ibrahim has narrated from his father from Hammad ibn 'Isa who has said the following:
"I once heard abu 'Abd Allah, *'Alayhi al-Salam*, being asked about Salat (prayer) in the ship. He (the Imam) said, 'If you can come out to hard ground, you must do so; but if you cannot do so, then perform Salat (prayer) standing, if you cannot do so, then perform Salat (prayer) while sitting and try to make it toward al-Qiblah (al-Ka'bah).'"

H 5517, Ch. 84, h 2
Ali has narrated from his father and Muhammad ibn Yahya from Ahmad ibn Muhammad all from ibn abu 'Umayr from Hammad ibn 'Uthaman who has said the following:
"Abu 'Abd Allah, *'Alayhi al-Salam*, was asked about performing Salat (prayer) in ships. He (the Imam) said, 'One must face al-Qiblah (al-Ka'bah) and when it makes a turn, if one is able to face al-Qiblah (al-Ka'bah) one must do so, otherwise, it is whichever direction it faces.' He (the Imam) said, 'If one can perform in a standing position, it must be done so, otherwise, one can sit down to perform his Salat (prayer).'"

H 5518, Ch. 84, h 3
Ali has narrated from 'Abd Allah ibn al-Mughirah from certain persons of his people who has said the following:
"I once asked abu 'Abd Allah, *'Alayhi al-Salam*, about a man who is in a ship and does not know the direction of al-Qiblah (al-Ka'bah). He (the Imam) said, 'He must make an effort to find the direction al-Qiblah (al-Ka'bah) and if he cannot find it, performs Salat (prayer) facing toward where its head is.'"

H 5519, Ch. 84, h 4
Muhammad ibn Yahya has narrated from Muhammad ibn al-Husayn from Yazid ibn Ishaq from Harun ibn Hamzah al-Ghanawiy who has said the following:
"I once asked abu 'Abd Allah, *'Alayhi al-Salam*, about the case of Salat (prayer) in the ship. He (the Imam) said, 'If it is heavily loaded and when you stand up it does not shake, perform Salat (prayer) in a standing position, but if it is light that can turn upside down, then perform Salat (prayer) in a sitting position.'"

H 5520, Ch. 84, h 5
Ali ibn Muhammad has narrated from Sahl ibn Ziyad from abu Hashim al-Ja'fariy who has said the following:
"One abu al-Hassan, *'Alayhi al-Salam*, and I were in a ship on the Tigris. It became time for Salat (prayer) and I said, 'I pray to Allah to keep my soul in service for your cause, can we perform Salat (prayer) in congregation? He (the Imam) said, 'No, we perform Salat (prayer) in the valley in congregation.'"

Chapter 85 - The Optional Salat (prayer)

H 5521, Ch. 85, h 1

Muhammad ibn Yahya has narrated from Ahmad ibn Muhammad from ibn Faddal from ibn Bukayr from Zurarah who has said the following:

"I went to visit abu Ja'far, *'Alayhi al-Salam*. I was a young person. The Imam described for me optional Salawat (prayers) and fasting and he noticed from my face that I considered it heavy. He then said to me, 'This is not like obligatory Salawat (prayers), so that on neglecting, one is destroyed. It is optional and if you cannot do on time, you can do compensatory prayer for it. They disliked that their deeds are taken up one day complete and one day incomplete. Allah, the Most Majestic, the Most Glorious, says, "Those who perform their Salat (prayer) all the time" (71:23). They (true Muslims) disliked continuing Salat (prayer) until sun declines on midday to the west; the doors of heaven open on such time."'" (The meaning of 'all the time', is not performing Salat (prayer) without any intervals).

H 5522, Ch. 85, h 2

Ali ibn Ibrahim has narrated from his father from ibn abu 'Umayr from ibn 'Udhaynah from ibn Faddal ibn Yasar who has said the following:

"Abu 'Abd Allah, *'Alayhi al-Salam*, has said, 'Obligatory and optional Salat (prayer) are fifty-one Rak'at, of which there are two Rak'at after al-'Atmah in a sitting position which are counted as one Rak'at in a standing position. Obligatory Salat (prayer) are seventeen Rak'at and optional Salat (prayer) are thirty-four Rak'at.'"

H 5523, Ch. 85, h 3

Ali ibn Ibrahim has narrated from his father from ibn abu 'Umayr from ibn 'Udhaynah from ibn Fudayl ibn Yasar and al-Fadl ibn 'Abd al-Malik and Bukayr who have said the following:

"We heard abu 'Abd Allah, *'Alayhi al-Salam*, saying that the Messenger of Allah would perform of optional Salat (prayer) twice as much as obligatory Salat (prayer), and fast of optional fast twice as much as the obligatory one."

H 5524, Ch. 85, h 4

Muhammad ibn Yahya has narrated from Ahmad ibn Muhammad from Muhammad ibn Sinan from ibn Muskan from Muhammad ibn abu 'Umayr who has said the following:

"I once asked abu 'Abd Allah, *'Alayhi al-Salam*, about the most excellent item in the Sunnah of Salat (prayer). He (the Imam) said, 'It is the complete, all fifty (Rak'at).'"

"Al-Husayn ibn Sa'id has narrated from Muhammad ibn Sinan a similar Hadith.

H 5525, Ch. 85, h 5

Muhammad has narrated from Muhammad ibn al-Husayn from Muhammad ibn 'Isma'il ibn Bazi' from Hanan who has said the following:

"Once, when I was present, 'Arm ibn Hurayth asked abu 'Abd Allah, *'Alayhi al-Salam*, saying, 'I pray to Allah to keep my soul in service for your cause, tell me about Salat (prayer) of the Messenger of Allah.' He (the Imam) said, 'The Holy prophet performed eight Rak'at of Zawal (declining of the sun toward the west at noontime). He (the Messenger of Allah) performed the first four, then eight thereafter, then four of al-'Al-'Asr. He performed three of al-Maghrib, four after al-Maghrib, four of al-'Isha' al-Akhirah, eight of nightly Salat (prayer), three of al-Witr, two Rak'at at dawn and the morning Salat (prayer) of two Rak'at.' I then said, 'I pray to Allah to keep my soul in service for your cause, if I can do more than this, will Allah punish me because of a great deal of Salat (prayer)?' He (the Imam) said, 'No, however, He punishes because of omitting Sunnah.'"

H 5526, Ch. 85, h 6

Ali ibn Ibrahim has narrated from his father from ibn abu 'Umayr from Hammad from al-Halabiy who has said the following:

"I once asked abu 'Abd Allah, *'Alayhi al-Salam*, 'Is there anything before or after al-'Isha' al-Akhirah?' He (the Imam) said, 'No, except that I perform two Rak'at thereafter and I do not count it as part of nightly Salat (prayer).'"

H 5527, Ch. 85, h 7

Muhammad ibn Yahya has narrated from Salmah ibn al-Khattab from al-Husayn ibn Sayf from Muhammad ibn Yahya from Hajjaj al-Khashshab from abu al-Fawaris who has said the following:

"Abu 'Abd Allah, *'Alayhi al-Salam*, prohibited me from speaking between the four Rak'at after al-Maghrib."

H 5528, Ch. 85, h 8

Muhammad ibn al-Hassan has narrated from Sahl from Ahmad ibn Muhammad from ibn abu Nasr who has said the following:

"I once said to abu al-Hassan, *'Alayhi al-Salam*, that our people have differences about optional Salat (prayer). Certain ones among them say it is forty-four and others perform fifty. Please tell me about what you perform and how is it, so I can do similarly. He (the Imam) said, 'I perform fifty-one Rak'at.' He (the Imam) then said, 'Hold on to it.' He (the Imam) counted with his hand saying, 'Zawal (declining of the sun toward the west at noontime) is eight. There are four after al-Zuhr, four before al-'Asr, two after al-Maghrib, two before al-'Isha', two after al-'Isha' in a sitting position which are counted as one Rak'at in a standing position. There are eight Rak'at of nightly Salat (prayer), three of al-witr and two at dawn. Obligatory Salat (prayer) is seventeen Rak'at and this becomes fifty-one Rak'at.'"

H 5529, Ch. 85, h 9

Al-Husayn ibn Muhammad al-Ash'ariy has narrated from 'Abd Allah ibn 'Amir from Ali ibn Mahziyar from Fadalah ibn Ayyub from Hammad ibn 'Uthaman who has said the following:

"I once asked him (the Imam), *'Alayhi al-Salam*, about optional Salat (prayer) during the day. He (the Imam) said, 'He performs eight Rak'at before al-Zuhr and eight after al-Zuhr.'"

H 5530, Ch. 85, h 10

It is a narration from him (narrator of previous Hadith) by Mu'alla' ibn Muhammad from al-Hassan ibn Ali al-Washsha' from Aban ibn 'Uthman from Yahya' ibn abu al-'Ala' who has said the following:

"Abu 'Abd Allah, *'Alayhi al-Salam*, has said, "Amir al-Mu'minin, *'Alayhi al-Salam*, has said, "Salat (prayer) at noontime is Salat (prayer) of repenting people.""""

H 5531, Ch. 85, h 11

Ali ibn Ibrahim has narrated from his father from Hammad ibn 'Isa from Hariz from Zurarah who has said the following:

"I once asked abu Ja'far, *'Alayhi al-Salam*, about the words of Allah, '. . . during the night in Sajdah (prostration) and in standing position fearful of the next life and hopeful of the mercy of his Lord. . . .' (20:130). He (the Imam) said, 'It is a reference to the nightly optional Salat (prayer).' I then said, ' . . . and in both ends of the day perhaps you will become happy. . .' (20:130). He (the Imam) said, 'It is a reference to optional Salat (prayer) during the day.' I then said, '. . . when the stars go back. . . .' (52:49). He (the Imam) said, 'It is a reference to the two Rak'at before the morning Salat (prayer).' I then said, '. . . after Sujud (prostrations) . . .'(52:40) He (the Imam) said, 'It is a reference to the two Rak'at after al-Maghrib.'"

H 5532, Ch. 85, h 12

Ali ibn Ibrahim has narrated from his father from Hammad from Hariz from Zurarah who has said the following:

"Abu Ja'far, *'Alayhi al-Salam*, has said, 'At the time you wake up, at night for prayer (Tahajjud) then say, "All praise belongs to Allah who has returned my spirit so I can praise and worship Him." When you hear the rooster crow say, "He is free of all defects. He is most holy. He is the Lord of angels and the spirit. His mercy comes before His anger. No one, other than You (Allah), deserves worship. You do not have any partner. I have done bad deeds and have done injustice to my own soul, so forgive and grant me mercy; no one, other than You, is able to forgive sins." When you get up look to the sky and say, "O Lord, the dark night cannot curtain You, nor the sky with its constellations, or the vast expanse of earth, or the darkness one over the other, or the ocean with its giant waves that curtain Your creatures from each other. You know whatever eyes steal or the chests hide. The stars have disappeared, eyes have gone to sleep, You are the living guardian whom sleep and slumber cannot overtake. Free from all defect is the Cherisher of the worlds, Lord of the messengers and all praise belongs to Allah, The Cherisher of the worlds." Then read five verses from Chapter Three: "The creation of the heavens and the earth and the alternation of the day and the night are evidence (of the existence of Allah) for people of reason (3:190). It is these who commemorate Allah while standing, sitting, or resting on their sides and who think about the creation of the heavens and the earth and say, 'Lord, you have not created all this without reason. Glory be to You. Lord, save us from the torment of the fire.' (3:191). Our Lord, those whom You consign to the fire are certainly disgraced. There is no helper for the unjust. (3:192)

"Lord, we have heard the person calling to the faith and have accepted his call. Forgive our sins, expiate our bad deeds, and allow us to die with the righteous ones. (3:193) Lord, grant us the victory that You have promised Your

Messenger and do not disgrace us on the Day of Judgment; You are the One who never ignores His promise." (3:194)

"Thereafter brush your teeth; and make Wudu'. When placing your hand in water say, "(I begin) by the name of Allah, and with the power of Allah. O Lord, make me of the repenting ones and of those who purify themselves." When you complete Wudu' say, "All praise belongs to Allah, Cherisher of the worlds." When you stand up for Salat (prayer) say, "(I begin) in the name of Allah, with (the power of) Allah, to Allah, from Allah and with the will of Allah and there is no means or power except the power and means of Allah. O Lord, make me of the visitors of Your house and of the builders of Masjids, please open for me the door to repent before You and close to me the door of disobedience to You and all sins. All praise belongs to Allah who has made me of those who speak to Him. O Lord, turn to me with Your face, the majestic in praise." Then begin your Salat (prayer) with the first Takbir.'"

(Ahadith 2-12 can best be explained by fatwa.)

H 5533, Ch. 85, h 13

Ali ibn Ibrahim has narrated from his father from ibn abu 'Umayr from Hammad from al-Halabiy who has said the following:

"Abu 'Abd Allah, *'Alayhi al-Salam*, has said, 'The Messenger of Allah, after performing 'Isha' al-Akhirah (the late evening Salat (prayer)) would ask that water for his Wudu' and toothbrush be placed near his pillow under a cover. He then would sleep as long as Allah willed then he would wake up, brush, make Wudu' and perform four Rak'at Salat (prayer). He thereafter he would sleep, then wake up, brush, make Wudu' and perform four Rak'at Salat (prayer), then sleep until about dawn then he would get up for witr, then perform two Rak'at Salat (prayer).' The Imam then said, 'The Messenger of Allah was a good lesson for you.' I (the narrator) asked, 'What time would he wake up?' The Imam replied, 'He would wake up after one-third of the night.' In another Hadith he has said, 'He would wake up after midnight.' Yet in another Hadith it is stated that his waking up, Ruku' and sajdah were of the same proportion. Each time, after waking up, he would brush and read verses 190 -194 of Chapter Three."

H 5534, Ch. 85, h 14

Muhammad ibn Yahya has narrated from Ahmad ibn Muhammad ibn 'Isa from ibn Faddal from ibn Bukayr from Zurarah who has said the following:

"Abu Ja'far, *'Alayhi al-Salam*, has said that the Messenger of Allah would perform thirteen Rak'at at night of which one Rak'at was al-Witr and two Rak'at of the morning whether on a journey or at home.'"

H 5535, Ch. 85, h 15

Muhammad ibn Yahya has narrated from Ahmad ibn Muhammad from Ali ibn Hadid from Ali ibn al-Nu'man from al-Harith ibn al-Mughirah al-Nasriy who has said the following:

"I heard abu 'Abd Allah, saying, 'During the day there are sixteen Rak'ats Salat (prayer). There are eight after the sun declines to the west at noon, eight after Zuhr Salat (prayer), four Rak'at after Maghrib (soon after sunset) – O Harith do not miss them at home or on a journey- and two Rak'at after the 'Isha' al-Akhirah (late evening Salat (prayer)). My father would perform these two Rak'at in a sitting position. I perform them in a standing position. The Messenger of Allah would perform thirteen Rak'at Salat (prayer) during the night.'"

H 5536, Ch. 85, h 16

Ali ibn Ibrahim has narrated from Muhammad ibn 'Isa from Yunus who has said that narrated to him 'Isma'il ibn Sa'd al-Ahwas who has said the following:

"I asked al-Rida, *'Alayhi al-Salam*, 'Of how many Rak'at does Salat (prayer) consist?' He replied, 'There are fifty-one Rak'at (every day).'"

Muhammad ibn Ahmad ibn Yahya has narrated from Muhammad ibn 'Isa a similar Hadith.

H 5537, Ch. 85, h 17

Muhammad ibn Yahya has narrated from Ahmad ibn Muhammad from ibn abu 'Umayr from Hisham ibn Salim who has said the following:

"About the words of Allah, the Most Majestic, the Most Glorious, 'nightly initiation is of strong impression and of strongest words' (73:7) abu 'Abd Allah, *'Alayhi al-Salam*, has said, '"strongest words" means a man's getting up from his bed just for the sake of Allah and for no other considerations.'"

H 5538, Ch. 85, h 18

Ali ibn Ibrahim has narrated from his father from ibn abu 'Umayr from Ayyub al-Khazzaz from Muhammad ibn Muslim who has said the following:

"I heard abu 'Abd Allah, *'Alayhi al-Salam*, saying, 'A servant (of Allah) wakes up three times at night and if he still is not up (for Salat (prayer)) Satan comes and urinates in his ears.' I then asked about the words of Allah, the Most Majestic, the Most Glorious, 'They would sleep very little at night'. (51:18) The Imam replied, 'There were few nights in which they would miss getting up for Salat (prayer)).'"

H 5539, Ch. 85, h 19

It is a narration from him (narrator of previous Hadith) by his father from ibn abu 'Umayr from 'Umar ibn 'Udhaynah from 'Umar ibn Yazid say the following:

"I heard abu 'Abd Allah, *'Alayhi al-Salam*, say, 'In the night there is an hour in which if a Muslim performs Salat (prayer) and appeals before Allah for a wish; his prayer is answered every night. I (the narrator) then asked saying, 'I pray to Allah to keep you well, which hour is it?' The Imam replied, 'It is in the first one-sixth of the second half of the night.'"

H 5540, Ch. 85, h 20

A number of our people have narrated from Ahmad ibn Muhammad from al-Husayn ibn Sa'id from Hammad ibn 'Isa from Mu'awiyah ibn Wahab who has said the following:

"I once said to abu 'Abd Allah, *'Alayhi al-Salam*, 'A man of your followers, of their virtuous ones complained before me against sleep. He said that he wants to get up for the nightly optional Salat (prayer) but sleep overcomes him until it is morning. Sometimes he performs the compensatory prayer for a whole month of missed Salat (prayer) or two months and bears with its heaviness.' He (the Imam) said, 'It is the delight for his eyes, by Allah.' He (the narrator) has said that he (the Imam) did not give him permission to perform his nightly optional Salat (prayer) in the beginning of the night, saying, 'To do compensatory prayer for them during the day is better.' I (the narrator) then said, 'Of our virgin girls there are those who love good and people of goodness. They try to perform Salat (prayer) but sleep overcomes them, and perhaps they may perform the compensatory prayer for what is missed and perhaps face weakness in performing the compensatory prayer for what is missed, but she is able to perform in the beginning of the night. He (the Imam) granted them permission to perform Salat (prayer) in the beginning of the night if they feel weakness and lose performing the compensatory prayer for what is missed.'"

H 5541, Ch. 85, h 21

Ahmad ibn Idris has narrated from Muhammad ibn 'Abd al-Jabbar from Safwan from ibn Bukayr who has said the following:

"Abu 'Abd Allah, *'Alayhi al-Salam*, has said, 'A man who gets up in the end of the night to perform his nightly optional Salat (prayer), all of them at one time and goes away to sleep, is not very praiseworthy."

H 5542, Ch. 85, h 22

Ali ibn Ibrahim has narrated from his father from 'Abd Allah ibn al-Mughirah from ibn Muskan from al-Hassan al-Sayqal who has said the following:

"I once said to abu 'Abd Allah, *'Alayhi al-Salam*, about a man who performs two Rak'at of al-Witr, then stands up and forgets saying Tashahhud (testimonies of belief) until he performs Ruku' (bowing down on one's knees), then remembers when he is in Ruku'. He (the Imam) said, 'He is required to sit down from Ruku', say Tashahhud, then stand up and complete.' He (the narrator) has said that he asked, 'Have you not said that in obligatory Salat (prayer) if one remembers after Ruku', one continues, then performs two Sajdah (prostration) because of mistake after ending Salat (prayer) in which one says Tashahhud (testimonies of belief)?' He (the Imam) said, 'Optional Salat (prayer) is not like obligatory one.'"

H 5543, Ch. 85, h 23

Al-Husayn ibn Muhammad al-Ash'ariy has narrated from 'Abd Allah ibn 'Amir Ali ibn Mahziyar from Fadalah ibn Ayyub and Hammad ibn 'Isa from Mu'awiyah ibn Wahab who has said the following:

"I once asked abu 'Abd Allah, *'Alayhi al-Salam*, about the most excellent time for al-Witr. He (the Imam) said, 'Dawn is the beginning of it.''

H 5544, Ch. 85, h 24

Muhammad ibn Yahya has narrated from Al-Husayn ibn abu 'Umayr from 'Isma'il ibn abu Sarah from Aban ibn Taghlib who has said the following:

"I once asked abu 'Abd Allah, *'Alayhi al-Salam*, 'What time did the Messenger of Allah perform al-Witr?' He (the Imam) said, 'Within a time like from sunset to al-Maghrib Salat (prayer).'"

H 5545, Ch. 85, h 25

Ali ibn Ibrahim has narrated from his father from ibn abu 'Umayr from ibn 'Udhaynah from Zurarah who has said the following:

"I once asked abu Ja'far, *'Alayhi al-Salam*, about the two Rak'at before the morning, 'When is the time for them?' He (the Imam) said, 'It is before dawn. When it is dawn, it becomes time for the morning.'"

H 5546, Ch. 85, h 26

Ali ibn Muhammad has narrated from Sahl ibn Ziyad from ibn Asbat from Ibrahim ibn abu al-Balad who has said the following:

"I performed my Salat (prayer), in Masjid al-Haram. Al-Rida' *'Alayhi al-Salam*, led the Salat (prayer). It was Salat (prayer) of night. When he (the Imam) completed, he (the Imam) made his sleep (instead of sleeping after Salat (prayer)) into a Sajdah (prostration)."

H 5547, Ch. 85, h 27

It is a narration from him (narrator of previous Hadith) by Muhammad ibn al-Husayn from al-Hajjal from 'Abd Allah ibn al-Walid al-Kindiy from 'Isma'il ibn Jabir or 'Abd Allah ibn Sinan who has said the following:

"I once said to abu 'Abd Allah, *'Alayhi al-Salam*, 'I get up in the end of the night and I fear (of the coming of dawn before completing).' He (the Imam) said, 'Recite just al-Fatihah, and make it faster and faster.'"

H 5548, Ch. 85, h 28

Al-Husayn ibn Muhammad has narrated from 'Abd Allah ibn 'Amir from Ali ibn Mahziyar from Fadalah ibn Ayyub from al-Qasim ibn Yazid from Muhammad ibn Muslim who has said the following:

"I once asked abu Ja'far, *'Alayhi al-Salam*, about a man who gets up in the end of the night and he is afraid of coming of dawn (before completing). Should he begin with al-Witr or perform Salat (prayer) as normal so that al-Witr becomes the last item?' He (the Imam) said, 'He begins with al-Witr.' He (the Imam) said, 'I have done so.'"

H 5549, Ch. 85, h 29

Ahmad ibn Idris has narrated from Ahmad ibn Muhammad from ibn Mahbub from abu Wallad Hafs ibn Salim who has said the following:

"I once asked abu 'Abd Allah, *'Alayhi al-Salam*, about Salam (the phrase of offering greeting of peace) in the two Rak'at of al-Witr. He (the Imam) said, 'Yes, if you may need something, you can go out and when you are prepared, then come back to perform one Rak'at.'"

H 5550, Ch. 85, h 30

Ali ibn Ibrahim has narrated from Muhammad ibn 'Isa from Yunus from ibn Sinan who has said the following:

"I once asked abu 'Abd Allah, *'Alayhi al-Salam*, about al-Witr and what is recited in them all. He (the Imam) said, 'Qul Huwa Allahu Ahad is recited.' I then asked, 'Is it read in all three of them?' He (the Imam) said, 'Yes, it is read in all three of them.'"

H 5551, Ch. 85, h 31

Ali has narrated from ibn abu 'Umayr from Hammad from al-Halabiy who has said the following:

"Abu 'Abd Allah, *'Alayhi al-Salam*, was asked about Qunut (supplication after recitation) in al-Witr: if there is a definite reading for it which is followed and recited. He (the Imam) said, 'No, there is no definite reading for it. Praise Allah, most Majestic, most Glorious, and say, 'O Allah, grant compensation to Muhammad and his family worthy of their services to Your cause, and ask Allah to forgive your great sins.' He (the Imam) then said, 'Every sin is great.'"

H 5552, Ch. 85, h 32

Al-Husayn ibn Muhammad has narrated from al-'Ala' ibn Muhammad from Aban from 'Abd al-Rahman ibn abu 'Abd Allah who has said the following:

"Abu 'Abd Allah, *'Alayhi al-Salam*, has said, 'Qunut (supplication after recitation) in al-Witr is asking for forgiveness and in obligatory Salat (prayer) it is to ask for your wishes.'"

H 5553, Ch. 85, h 33

Muhammad ibn 'Isma'il has narrated from al-Fadl ibn Shadhan from Safwan ibn Yahya from Mansur ibn Hazim who has said the following:

"Abu 'Abd Allah, *'Alayhi al-Salam*, has said that in al-Witr, ask forgiveness from Allah seventy times."

(Ahadith 20-34 are best explained in the form of fatwa.)

H 5554, Ch. 85, h 34

Muhammad ibn Yahya has narrated from 'Imran ibn Musa from al-Hassan ibn Ali ibn al-Nu'man from his father from certain individuals of his people who has said the following:

"A man came to Amir al-Mu'minin Ali, ibn abu Talib, *'Alayhi al-Salam*, and said, 'O Amir al-Mu'minin, I am deprived of Salat (prayer) at night.' Amir al-Mu'minin said, 'Your sins have tied you down.'"

H 5555, Ch. 85, h 35

Ali ibn Muhammad has narrated from Sahl ibn Ziyad from Ali ibn Mahziyar from who has said the following:

"I have read in a letter of a man to abu 'Abd Allah, *'Alayhi al-Salam*, and it says, 'Are the two Rak'at before Salat (prayer) of dawn of Salat (prayer) during the night? Or it is of Salat (prayer) during the day and when should I perform them?' With his handwriting he (the Imam) had written, 'Fill them in Salat (prayer) of night a complete filling.'"

(Hadith 35 and the following chapter are best explained by fatwa.)

Chapter 86 - Performing Optional Salat (Prayer) before or after, Compensatory prayer for them and Salat (prayer) of al-Duha'

H 5556, Ch. 86, h 1
Al-Husayn ibn Muhammad has narrated from 'Abd Allah ibn 'Amir from Ali ibn Mahziyar from al-Husayn ibn Sa'id from Hammad ibn 'Isa from Burayd Damrah al-Laythiy from Muhammad ibn Muslim who has said the following:
"I once asked abu Ja'far, *'Alayhi al-Salam*, about a man who becomes busy at noontime; can he perform in the beginning of the day? He (the Imam) said, 'Yes, he can do so if he knows that he becomes busy, thus he can do them all early on.'"

H 5557, Ch. 86, h 2
Ali ibn Ibrahim has narrated from Muhammad ibn 'Isa from Yunus ibn 'Abd al-Rahman from Mu'awiyah ibn Wahab who has said the following:
"On the day of conquest of Makkah a black tent, made of wool, was pitched for the Messenger of Allah in al-Abtah. Water from a bowl was poured on it to remove marks of dough. The direction of al-Qiblah (al-Ka'bah) was marked in midday. The Messenger of Allah performed eight Rak'at which he never thereafter or before had done.''

H 5558, Ch. 86, h 3
Ali ibn Ibrahim has narrated from his father from ibn abu 'Umayr from Mu'awiyah ibn 'Ammar who has said the following:
"Abu 'Abd Allah, *'Alayhi al-Salam*, has said, 'Perform the compensatory prayer for whatever of Salat (prayer) is missed during the day in day time and what is missed during the night in night time.' I then asked, 'Can I perform the compensatory prayer for two al-Witr in one night?' He (the Imam) said, 'Yes, perform the compensatory prayer for al-Witr all the time.'"

H 5559, Ch. 86, h 4
Ali ibn Ibrahim has narrated from his father from ibn abu 'Umayr from Murazim who has said the following:
"'Isma'il ibn Jabir once asked abu 'Abd Allah, *'Alayhi al-Salam*, saying, 'I pray to Allah to keep you well, there is a great deal of optional Salat (prayer) upon me. What should I do?' He (the Imam) said, 'Perform the compensatory prayer for them.' He said, 'They are of a great number.' He (the Imam) said, 'Perform the compensatory prayer for them.' He said, 'I cannot count them.' He (the Imam) said, 'Try to perform them.' Murazim has said, 'I fell ill for four months in which I could not perform optional Salat (prayer). I said, 'I pray to Allah to keep you well, I pray to Allah to keep my soul in service for your cause, I fell ill for four months and I could not perform any optional Salat (prayer).' He (the Imam) said, 'There is no compensatory prayer for them upon you; one suffering from illness is not like one in good health. Whoever is overpowered by Allah, for him Allah is the first to pardon.'"

H 5560, Ch. 86, h 5

Muhammad ibn Yahya has narrated from 'Abd Allah ibn Muhammad from Ali ibn al-Hakam from Aban ibn 'Uthman from `Isma'il al-Al-Ju'fiy who has said the following:

"Abu Ja'far, *'Alayhi al-Salam*, has said, 'The best compensatory prayer for a Salat (prayer) missed is the compensatory prayer during the night for what is missed during the night and what is missed during the day is made during the day.' I then said, 'So there will be two al-Witr in one night.' He (the Imam) said, 'No, there will not be two al-Witr.' I then said, 'Why then do you instruct me to perform two al-Witr in one night?' He (the Imam) said, 'One of them is a compensatory prayer for what is missed.'"

H 5561, Ch. 86, h 6

Ali ibn Ibrahim has narrated from his father from ibn abu 'Umayr from Hammad from al-Halabiy who has said the following:

"Abu 'Abd Allah, *'Alayhi al-Salam*, once was asked about a man who has missed performing Salat (prayer) during the day. When is he required to perform the compensatory prayer for such Salat (prayer)? He (the Imam) said, 'He can do whenever he wants. He can perform them after al-Maghrib or after al-'Isha'.'"

H 5562, Ch. 86, h 7

Muhammad ibn Yahya has narrated from Muhammad ibn al-Husayn from Safwan ibn Yahya from al-'Ala' from Muhammad ibn Muslim who has said the following:

"I once asked abu 'Abd Allah, *'Alayhi al-Salam*, about a man who misses Salat (prayer) to be performed during the day. He (the Imam) said, 'He can perform them whenever he wants. He can perform them after al-Maghrib or after al-'Isha'.'"

H 5563, Ch. 86, h 8

Muhammad ibn Yahya has narrated from Muhammad ibn `Isma'il al-Qummiy from Ali ibn al-Hakam from Sayf ibn 'Amirah in a marfu' manner who has said the following:

"`Amir al-Mu'minin once passed by a man who was performing al-Duha' (optional Salat (prayer) at noontime before Zawal (declining of the sun toward the west at noontime) in Masjid of al-Kufah. He (`Amir al-Mu'minin) poked his side with his whip (handle) and said, 'You cut the throat of the Salat (prayer) of repenting people, may Allah cut your throat.' He asked, 'Must I omit it? He (the Imam) said that 'Amir al-Mu'minin said, "Have you seen the one who forbids a servant who performs Salat (prayer)" (96:9,10) he added.' Abu 'Abd Allah, *'Alayhi al-Salam*, then said, 'The denial of Amir al-Mu'minin is sufficient prohibition to perform such Salat (prayer).'"

('Amir al-Mu'minin meant that it is not permissible to prohibit Salat (prayer) but Salat (prayer) of a prescribed time performed before its time is not a Salat (prayer). (It seems the man performed the optional Salat (prayer) soon after Zawal (declining of the sun toward the west at noontime) before its due time).

H 5564, Ch. 86, h 9

Ali ibn Ibrahim has narrated from his father from Hammad ibn 'Isa from Hariz from Zurarah and al-Fudayl who has said the following:

"Abu Ja'far, and abu 'Abd Allah, *'Alayhim al-Salam*, have said that the Messenger of Allah has said, 'Salat (prayer) of al-Duha' (optional Salat (prayer) at noontime before Zawal (declining of the sun toward the west at noontime) is heresy."

H 5565, Ch. 86, h 10

Al-Husayn ibn Muhammad has narrated from Mu'alla' ibn Muhammad from al-Hassan ibn Ali al-Washsha' from Aban from Sulayman ibn Khalid who has said the following:

"I once asked abu 'Abd Allah, *'Alayhi al-Salam*, about Qada' (compensatory prayer for) al-Witr after al-Zuhr. He (the Imam) said, 'Perform Qada' (compensatory prayer for) al-Witr all the time just as it is missed.' I then asked, 'Can there be two al-Witr in one night?' He (the Imam) said, 'Yes, is not one of them a Qada' (compensatory prayer)?'"

H 5566, Ch. 86, h 11

Ali has narrated from his father from ibn al-Mughirah from abu Jarir al-Qummiy who has said the following:

"Abu 'Abd Allah, *'Alayhi al-Salam*, has said, 'Abu Ja'far would perform the Qada' (compensatory prayer) twenty al-Witr in one night.'"

H 5567, Ch. 86, h 12

It is a narration from him (narrator of previous Hadith) by his father from Hammad ibn 'Isa from Hariz from Zurarah who has said the following:

"Abu Ja'far, *'Alayhi al-Salam*, has said, 'If there, upon you, is Qada' (compensatory prayer for) two al-Witr or more, perform them as they were missed with an interval of a Salat (prayer) between each two al-Witr. It is because al-Witr is the last. You cannot perform something before its beginning. The first is what commences first, when you perform Qada' (compensatory prayer for) Salat (prayer) of the current night then is al-Witr.' He (the narrator) has said that abu Ja'far, *'Alayhi al-Salam*, said, 'Two al-Witr cannot be performed in one night except that one is a Qada' (compensatory prayer for) what is missed.' Abu Ja'far, *'Alayhi al-Salam*, said, 'If you perform al-Witr in the beginning of night and get up in the end of the night, then your first al-Witr is a Qada' (compensatory prayer for) what is missed. All Salat (prayer) that you perform in a given night must be intended to be Qada' (compensatory prayer for) what is missed. The last Salat (prayer) in a given night is Salat (prayer) for that night and not a Qada' (compensatory prayer for) what is missed. In the same way the last al-Witr that you perform in a given night is al-Witr for that night and not a Qada' (compensatory prayer for) what is missed.'"

H 5568, Ch. 86, h 13

Ali ibn Ibrahim has narrated from his father from 'Amr ibn 'Uthman from Ali ibn 'Abd Allah from 'Abd Allah ibn Sinan who has said the following:

"I once asked abu 'Abd Allah, *'Alayhi al-Salam*, about a man on whom there is Qada' (compensatory prayer for) optional Salat (prayer), so much that he does not know how many because of its great number. What is he required to do?' He (the Imam) said, 'He performs so many that cannot say how many is performed. In this way he has performed Qada' (compensatory prayer for) what is missed according to his knowledge.' I then said, 'He is not able to perform all the Qada' (compensatory prayer for) what is missed because of his business.' He (the Imam) said, 'If his business is for his living which is necessary or it is for the needs of his brother in belief, then he is not obligated for anything in this matter. If his business is for the worldly matters which keeps him away from his Salat (prayer), then it is necessary for him to perform the Qada' (compensatory prayer), otherwise, he will meet Allah as one considered neglectful, humiliated and destroying the Sunnah of the Messenger of Allah.' I then said, 'He is not able to perform the Qada' (compensatory prayer). Can he pay charity?' He (the Imam) remained quiet for a while then said, 'Yes, he can give charity.' I then asked, 'How much charity he must pay?' He (the Imam) said, 'As much as he can afford. The minimum is one handful of food to a destitute for every Salat (prayer).' I then asked, 'For how many Salat (prayer) one handful of food to a destitute is sufficient?' He (the Imam) said, 'It is for every two Rak'at of nightly Salat (prayer) and every two Rak'at of Salat (prayer) during the day.' I then said, 'He is not able to do so.' He (the Imam) said, 'It is one handful for four Rak'at.' I said, 'He cannot give that much.' He (the Imam) said, 'It is one handful for Salat (prayer) of every night and one handful for Salat (prayer) of every day but Salat (prayer) is better, Salat (prayer) is better.'"

H 5569, Ch. 86, h 14

Ali ibn Muhammad has narrated from Sahl ibn Ziyad from 'Amr ibn 'Uthman from Muhammad ibn 'Adhafir from 'Umar ibn Yazid who has said the following:

"Abu 'Abd Allah, *'Alayhi al-Salam*, has said, 'Optional Salat (prayer) is like present; whenever given is accepted.'"

H 5570, Ch. 86, h 15

Al-Husayn ibn Muhammad has narrated from Mu'alla' ibn Muhammad from Ali ibn Asbat from A number of our people who has said the following:

"Abu al-Hassan, the first, *'Alayhi al-Salam*, whenever distressed would not perform optional Salat (prayer)."

H 5571, Ch. 86, h 16

It is a narration from him (narrator of previous Hadith) by ibn Ma'bad or someone other than him who has said the following:

"One of the two Imam, *'Alayhim al-Salam*, has said that the Holy prophet has said, 'Hearts work with interest or with abhorrence. When they are interested, perform optional Salat (prayer) but when they have abhorrence then hold to obligatory Salat (prayer).'"

H 5572, Ch. 86, h 17

Muhammad ibn Yahya has narrated from Muhammad ibn al-Husayn from Muhammad ibn Yahya ibn Habib who has said the following:

"I once wrote to abu al-Hassan, al-Rida', *'Alayhi al-Salam*, asking, 'There is optional Salat (prayer) on me, when should I perform Qada' (compensatory prayer for) such missed Salat (prayer)?' He (the Imam) wrote to me in answer, 'You can perform them whenever you like, during the day or night.'"

H 5573, Ch. 86, h 18

Through the same chain of narrators as that of the previous Hadith it is narrated from Muhammad ibn al-Husayn from al-Hakam ibn Miskin from 'Abd Allah ibn Ali al-Sarrad who has said the following:

"Once, abu Kahmas asked abu 'Abd Allah, *'Alayhi al-Salam*, 'Should a man perform his optional Salat (prayer) in one or in different places?' He (the Imam) said, 'No, one should perform them here and there because they testify in one's favor on the Day of Judgment.'"

H 5574, Ch. 86, h 19

Ali ibn Muhammad has narrated from Sahl ibn Ziyad from Muhammad ibn all-Rayyan who has said the following:

"I once, wrote to abu Ja'far, *'Alayhi al-Salam*, and asked about a man who performs Qada' (compensatory prayer for) certain Salat (prayer). It is of the fifty Rak'at and he performs it in Masjid al-Haram or Masjid of the Messenger of Allah or Masjid of al-Kufah. Are such Salat (prayer) counted in multiples as is narrated from your ancestors, *'Alayhim al-Salam*? Because of being performed in these Masjids, are they counted to compensate for what is on him like the ten thousand Rak'at as reward, for which he can perform only one hundred Rak'at, in these Masjids, or less or more and how it works for him?' He (the Imam) (wrote) with his signature, 'It is counted in his favor in multiples. However, the case of reduced Salat (prayer) and its condition toward increase is more than toward decrease.'"

H 5575, Ch. 86, h 20

Ahmad ibn 'Abd Allah has narrated from Ahmad ibn abu 'Abd Allah from his father from 'Abd Allah ibn al-fadl al-Nawfaliy from Ali ibn abu Hamzah who has said the following:

"I once asked abu al-Hassan, *'Alayhi al-Salam*, about a man who is in a hurry. What is sufficient for him in optional Salat (prayer) for recitation?' He (the Imam) said, 'Three Tasbih (Allah is free of all defects) for recitation, one for Ruku' (bowing down on one's knees), and one for Sujud (prostrations).'"

Chapter 87 - Performing Salat (Prayer) in Dangerous Conditions

H 5576, Ch. 87, h 1

Ali ibn Ibrahim has narrated from his father from ibn abu 'Umayr from Hammad from al-Halabiy who has said the following:

"I once asked abu 'Abd Allah, *'Alayhi al-Salam*, about performing Salat (prayer) in fearful conditions. He (the Imam) said, 'The Imam stands up and one group of his people comes and stands up behind him. The other group faces the enemy. The Imam performs one Rak'at, then stands up and they also stand up. He remains standing but they perform the second Rak'at, then say Salam (the phrase of offering greeting of peace) to each other and end their Salat (prayer). They then stand up in place of the other group facing the enemy. Now this group comes and stands up behind the Imam who performs the second Rak'at with them. The Imam then sits down and they stand up to perform another Rak'at. He then says Salam (the phrase of offering greeting of peace) and they also end their Salat (prayer) with his saying Salam.' He (the Imam) said, 'In al-Maghrib they do similarly. The Imam stands up and one group stands up behind him. He then performs one Rak'at with them, then stands up and they also stand up. The Imam remains standing but they complete the two Rak'at, say Tashahhud (testimonies of belief), Salam (the phrase of offering greeting of peace) to each other and end their Salat (prayer). They then stand guard in place of the other group who joins the Imam for Salat (prayer). He performs with them a Rak'at with recitation, then sits down and says Tashahhud (testimonies of belief). He then stands up and they also stand up with him. He performs one more Rak'at with them, then sits down but they stand up to complete another Rak'at, then he says Salam (the phrase of offering greeting of peace) to them to end.'"

H 5577, Ch. 87, h 2

Muhammad ibn Yahya has narrated from 'Abd Allah ibn Muhammad ibn 'Isa from Ali ibn al-Hakam from Aban from 'Abd al-Rahman ibn abu 'Abd Allah who has said the following:

"Abu 'Abd Allah, *'Alayhi al-Salam*, has said that the Messenger of Allah performed Salat (prayer) with his followers during the armed expedition at Dhat al-Riqa' in a fearful condition. The Messenger of Allah divided his companions in two groups. One group was made to stand up facing the enemy and the other group behind him for Salat (prayer). He said Takbir (Allah is great beyond description) and they also did so. He recited and they remained silent. He performed Ruku' (bowing down on one's knees) and they also did so. He performed Sajdah (prostration), and they also did so. The Messenger of Allah in order to complete remained standing but they performed one Rak'at for themselves, then they said Salam (the phrase of offering greeting of peace) to each other. They then went to stand guard in place of the group facing the enemy. This group stood behind the Messenger of Allah who performed one Rak'at with them, then said Tashahhud (testimonies of belief) and Salam (the phrase of offering greeting of peace) to them. They then stood up to perform one Rak'at for themselves, then said Salam (the phrase of offering greeting of peace) to each other.'"

H 5578, Ch. 87, h 3

Al-Husayn ibn Muhammad has narrated from Mu'alla' ibn Muhammad from al-Hassan ibn Ali al-Washsha' from Hammad ibn 'Uthaman from abu Basir who has said the following:

"I once heard abu 'Abd Allah, *'Alayhi al-Salam*, say, 'If you are in a land where you are afraid of thieves or beasts, perform Salat (prayer) on your stumper.'"

H 5579, Ch. 87, h 4

A number of our people have narrated from Ahmad ibn Muhammad from ibn Khalid from his father from Zur'ah from Sama'ah who has said the following:

"I once asked abu 'Abd Allah, *'Alayhi al-Salam*, about a man who is a captive of the pagans. It becomes time for Salat (prayer) and they do not allow him to perform Salat (prayer). He (the Imam) said, 'He makes gestures as gestures are made.'"

H 5580, Ch. 87, h 5

Muhammad ibn Yahya has narrated from Ahmad ibn Muhammad from Muhammad ibn 'Isma'il who has said the following:

"I once asked him (the Imam), *'Alayhi al-Salam*, about my traveling between Makkah and al-Madinah and in the time of Salat (prayer), we disembark where Arabs are found. Can we perform the obligatory Salat (prayer) on the ground and recite just al-Fatihah, or perform it when riding and recite al-Fatihah al-Kitab and Surah (chapter) as well? He (the Imam) said, 'If you are afraid, then perform the obligatory Salat (prayer) and other Salat (prayer) on your stumper. If you recite al-Hamd and Surah (chapter) it is more beloved to me and I do not see anything harmful in what you have done.'"

H 5581, Ch. 87, h 6

Ahmad ibn Muhammad has narrated from Ali ibn al-Hakam from Aban from 'Abd al-Rahman ibn abu 'Abd Allah who has said the following:

"I once asked abu 'Abd Allah, *'Alayhi al-Salam*, about the words of Allah, most Majestic, most Glorious, '. . . if you are afraid then it is on foot or riding. . . .'(2:240), 'How is this Salat (prayer) performed and what do you say if one is afraid of beasts or thieves?' He (the Imam) said, 'He says Takbir (Allah is great beyond description) and makes gestures with his head as gestures are made.'"

Chapter 88 - Performing Salat (Prayer) in Battlefield

H 5582, Ch. 88, h 1

Ali ibn Ibrahim ibn Hashim al-Qummiy has narrated from his father from 'Amr ibn 'Uthman from Muhammad ibn 'Adhafir who has said the following:

"Abu 'Abd Allah, *'Alayhi al-Salam*, has said, 'When horses roam and swords shake, two Takbir (Allah is great beyond description) are sufficient for him and this is another reduction.'"

H 5583, Ch. 88, h 2

Ali ibn Ibrahim has narrated from his father from ibn abu 'Umayr from ibn 'Udhaynah from Zurarah and Fudayl and Muhammad ibn Muslim who has said the following:

"Abu Ja'far, *'Alayhi al-Salam*, about performing Salat (prayer) in frightening conditions during pursuits and the skirmishes, has said, 'Every one of them perform Salat (prayer) by making gestures to whatever direction they face, even if swords work neck and neck and the fight goes on in a hand-to-hand manner. 'Amir al-Mu'minin, *'Alayhi al-Salam*, performed Salat (prayer) during the night of Siffin which is called Lilatu al-Harir. Their Salat (prayer) of al-Zuhr, al-'Asr, al-Maghrib and al-'Isha' were only Takbir (Allah is great beyond description), Tahlil, (no one deserves worship except Allah), Tasbih (Allah is free of all defects), Tahmid (all praise belongs to Allah) and supplications. It was their Salat (prayer) and they were not commanded to perform Salat (prayer) again.'"

H 5584, Ch. 88, h 3

It is a narration from him (narrator of previous Hadith) by 'Abd Allah ibn al-Mughirah who has said the following:

"I have heard from certain persons of our people saying that the minimum recitation when swords are at work is two Takbir (Allah is great beyond description) for every Salat (prayer) except that there are three Takbir (Allah is great beyond description) for al-Maghrib."

H 5585, Ch. 88, h 4

Ali ibn Ibrahim has narrated from his father from and Ahmad ibn Idris Ahmad ibn Muhammad from Muhammad ibn Yahya from Ahmad ibn Muhammad from all from Hammad ibn 'Isa from Hariz who has said the following:

"About the word of Allah, most Majestic, most Glorious, 'It is permissible for you to reduce of Salat (prayer) if you fear that the unbelievers may create mischief for you,' (4:101), abu 'Abd Allah, *'Alayhi al-Salam*, has said, 'Two Rak'at becomes one Rak'at.'"

H 5586, Ch. 88, h 5

Muhammad ibn Yahya has narrated from Ahmad ibn Muhammad from 'Uthman ibn 'Isa from Sama'ah who has said the following:

"I once asked him (the Imam), *'Alayhi al-Salam*, about Salat (prayer) during fighting. He (the Imam) said, 'If they meet (the armies) and kill each other, then Salat (prayer) in such time is Takbir (Allah is great beyond description), but if they are standing and are not able to overpower the group, then it is in the form of gestures.'"

H 5587, Ch. 88, h 6

Muhammad has narrated from Ahmad from Hammad from Hariz from Zurarah who has said the following:

"Once, I asked abu Ja'far, *'Alayhi al-Salam*, about the case of a soldier who does not have Wudu' and what is he required to do when he is not able to dismount? He (the Imam) said, 'He can make Tayammum on his pad, saddle or mane of his stumper over which dust accumulates. He then performs Salat (prayer), makes Sujud (prostrations) lower than Ruku' (bowing down on one's knees) and does not turn to al-Qiblah (al-Ka'bah) but turns his face wherever his stumper goes, except that he turns to al-Qiblah (al-Ka'bah) when saying the first Takbir (Allah is great beyond description) when paying attention.'"

H 5588, Ch. 88, h 7

Muhammad ibn Yahya has narrated from al-'Amrakiy ibn Ali from Ali ibn Ja'far who has said the following:

"I once asked my brother, abu al-Hassan, *'Alayhi al-Salam*, about one who faces a beast and it is time for Salat (prayer). He is not able to walk, because of fear from the beast. If he stands up he fears to perform Ruku' (bowing down on one's knees) or Sujud (prostrations) with the beast in front of him in a direction other than that of al-Qiblah (al-Ka'bah). If he turns to al-Qiblah (al-Ka'bah), he fears the lion's attack. What is he required to do in such case? He (the Imam) said, 'He faces the lion and performs his Salat (prayer) with gestures in a standing position, if the lion is in a direction other than that for al-Qiblah (al-Ka'bah).'"

Chapter 89 - Salat (Prayer) of Both 'Id and the Sermon for it

H 5589, Ch. 89, h 1

Ali ibn Ibrahim has narrated from his father from ibn abu 'Umayr from 'Umar ibn 'Udhaynah from Zurarah who has said the following:

"Abu Ja'far, *'Alayhi al-Salam*, has said, 'There Adhan or 'Iqamah is not for the day of al-Fitr and al-Adha'. Adhan for it is sunrise. When it is sunrise, they go out. There is not any Salat (prayer) before or after it. If one does not perform Salat (prayer) with an Imam in congregation, there is not any Salat (prayer) for him and performing Qada' (compensatory prayer) also is not necessary for him.'"

H 5590, Ch. 89, h 2

Al-Husayn ibn Muhammad has narrated from Mu'alla' ibn Muhammad from al-Washsha' from Hammad ibn 'Uthaman from Ma'mar ibn Yahya who has said the following:

"Abu Ja'far, *'Alayhi al-Salam*, has said, 'There is not any Salat (prayer) on the day of al-Fitr or al-Adha' except with Imam.'"

H 5591, Ch. 89, h 3

Ali ibn Muhammad has narrated from Muhammad ibn 'Isa from Yunus from Mu'awiyah who has said the following:

"I once asked him (the Imam), *'Alayhi al-Salam*, about Salat (prayer) of both 'Id. He (the Imam) said, 'It is a two Rak'at and there is not anything before or after them. Adhan or 'Iqamah is not required. There are twelve Takbir (Allah is great beyond description). When Takbir is said and Salat (prayer) is commenced, he then recites al-Fatihah al-Kitab, then wa al-Shams and Duha'ha' (Chapter 91), then says five Takbir. After saying Takbir (Allah is great beyond description) he performs Ruku' (bowing down on one's knees), so he performs Ruku' after the seventh Takbir. He then performs two Sajdah (prostration), then stands up and recites al-Fatihah al-Kitab and Hal Ataka Hadith al-Ghashiyah (chapter 88), then says four Takbir, performs two Sajdah (prostration), says Tashahhud (testimonies of belief) and Salam (the phrase of offering greeting of peace). He (the Imam) said, 'This is how the Messenger of Allah did. The sermon is after Salat (prayer). 'Uthman was the one who initiated it before Salat (prayer). When the Imam delivers the sermon he sits down between the two sermons for a short time. It is proper for the Imam to wear burd (a certain kind of gown) on both 'Id days and a shatiy turban or Qa'iz (certain kinds of fabrics). He goes out in the open so he can see the horizons of the sky. He does not perform Salat (prayer) on a mat or Sajdah (prostration) on it. The Messenger of Allah would go to al-Baqi' and perform Salat (prayer) with people.'"

H 5592, Ch. 89, h 4

Muhammad ibn Yahya has narrated from Ahmad ibn Muhammad from ibn Faddal from al-Mufaddal ibn Salih from Layth al-Muradiy who has said the following:

"Abu 'Abd Allah, *'Alayhi al-Salam*, has said that once it was said to the Messenger of Allah, 'Would that you perform Salat (prayer) on al-Fitr or al-Adha' days in your Masjid!' The Messenger of Allah said, 'I love to come out for the horizons of the sky.'"

H 5593, Ch. 89, h 5

Ali ibn Ibrahim has narrated from Muhammad ibn 'Isa from Yunus from Ali ibn abu Hamzah who has said the following:

"Abu 'Abd Allah, *'Alayhi al-Salam*, has said that Salat (prayer) of both 'Id commences with Takbir (Allah is great beyond description). There is then the recitation, then five Takbir, and there is Qunut (supplication) between each two Takbir. Then is the seventh Takbir, then Ruku' (bowing down on one's knees), then Sajdah (prostration), then he (the Imam) stands up for the second Rak'at. He recites, then says four Takbir with Qunut (supplication) between every two Takbir, then says Takbir and performs Ruku' (bowing down on one's knees).'"

H 5594, Ch. 89, h 6

Ali ibn Muhammad has narrated from Sahl ibn Ziyad from al-Nawfaliy from al-Sakuniy who has said the following:

"Ja'far has narrated from his father, *'Alayhi al-Salam*, who has said that the Messenger of Allah prohibited taking out arms on both days of 'Id unless enemy was present.'"

H 5595, Ch. 89, h 7

Muhammad ibn `Isma'il has narrated from al-Fadl ibn Shadhan from Hammad ibn 'Isa from Rib'iy ibn 'Abd Allah from al-Fadl ibn Yasar who has said the following:

"Abu 'Abd Allah, *'Alayhi al-Salam*, has said, 'On the day of al-Fitr al-Khumrah (mat) was brought for my father but he commanded to return it and then said, "This is a day on which the Messenger of Allah loved to look at the horizons of the sky and place his face on earth."'"

H 5596, Ch. 89, h 8

Al-Husayn ibn Muhammad has narrated from Mu'alla' ibn Muhammad from al-Washsha' from Aban ibn 'Uthman from Salamah who has said the following:

"Abu 'Abd Allah, *'Alayhi al-Salam*, has said, 'During the time of `Amir al-Mu'minin two 'Id happened on one day. `Amir al-Mu'minin, *'Alayhi al-Salam*, delivered a sermon and said, "This is a day in which two 'Id have taken place. Those who love can join us and those who do not want to join us, they have permission to do so", meaning those who keep aside.'"

H 5597, Ch. 89 h 9

Ali ibn Ibrahim has narrated from Muhammad ibn 'Isa from Yunus from al-'Ala' ibn Razin from Muhammad ibn Muslim who has said the following:

"I once asked him (the Imam), *'Alayhi al-Salam*, about a man who has missed one Rak'at of Salat (prayer) with Imam on the days of al-Tashriq (11,12 and 13 of Dhul Hajj). He (the Imam) said, 'He must complete Salat (prayer) and say Takbir (Allah is great beyond description).'"

H 5598, Ch. 89, h 10

Muhammad ibn Yahya in a marfu' manner has narrated from the following:

"Abu 'Abd Allah, *'Alayhi al-Salam*, has said, 'It is of Sunnah for the people of the cities to go out in the open on both 'Id days except people of Makkah; they perform Salat (prayer) in Masjid al-Haram.'"

H 5599, Ch. 89, h 11

Muhammad ibn al-Hassan ibn Ali ibn 'Abd Allah has narrated from al-'Abbas ibn 'Amir from Aban from Muhammad ibn al-Fadl al-Hashimiy who has said the following:

"Abu 'Abd Allah, *'Alayhi al-Salam*, has said, 'There are two Rak'at Salat (prayer) which are of Sunnah but they are not performed anywhere else except in a certain place of al-Madinah.' He (the Imam) said, 'It is performed in Masjid of the Messenger of Allah on 'Id before going out to the place for Salat (prayer). It is not done anywhere else except al-Madinah; the Messenger of Allah did so.'"

Chapter 90 - Salat (prayer) for Rain

H 5600, Ch. 90, h 1

Ali ibn Ibrahim has narrated from Muhammad ibn 'Isa from Yunus from Muhammad ibn Muslim and al-Husayn ibn Muhammad from 'Abd Allah ibn 'Amir from Ali ibn Mahziyar from Fadalah ibn Ayyub from Ahmad ibn Sulayman all from Murrah Mawla' Muhammad ibn Khalid who has said the following:

"People of al-Madinah cried before Muhammad ibn Khalid about Salat (prayer) for rain. He said to me, 'Go to abu 'Abd Allah, *'Alayhi al-Salam*, and ask him what is his opinion. These people cry before me.' I went to him (the Imam) and conveyed to him (the Imam) the message. He (the Imam) told me to tell him (Muhammad ibn Khalid) to go out (for Salat (prayer) for rain). I then asked, 'I pray to Allah to keep my soul in service for your cause, when he should go out?' He (the Imam) said, 'He should go out on Monday.' I then asked, 'What should he do?' He (the Imam) said, 'He takes out the pulpit, then he goes out and walks as it is done on both 'Id days with those calling Adhan in front of him with their staff in their hands, until they are in the place for Salat (prayer). He performs, with people, two Rak'at without Adhan and 'Iqamah, then he climbs on the pulpit with his gown turned upside down by wearing its right shoulder (sleeve) on his left shoulder (arm) and its left sleeve on his right shoulder. He then faces al-Qiblah (al-Ka'bah) and says Takbir (Allah is great beyond description) one hundred times, raising his voice. He then turns to people on his right side and says Tasbih (Allah is free of all defects) one hundred times, raising his voice. He then turns to the people on his left side and says Tahlil, (no one deserves worship except Allah) one hundred times, raising his voice. He then turns to the people and says Tahmid, (all praise belongs to Allah) one hundred times, raising his voice. He then raises his hand and pleads. They also plead. I hope they will not be deprived.' He (the narrator) has said that he followed the instruction and when we returned rain came and they said, 'It is of the instruction of Ja'far (*'Alayhi al-Salam*).'"

"In the narration of Yunus it is said, 'We had not returned yet that rain came.'"

(Hadith 1 is best explained by fatwa.)

H 5601, Ch. 90, h 2

Ali ibn Ibrahim has narrated from his father from ibn abu 'Umayr from Hisham ibn al-Hakam who has said the following:

"I asked abu 'Abd Allah, *'Alayhi al-Salam*, about Salat (prayer) for rain. The Imam said, 'It is like Salat (prayer) of 'Idayn (Salat (prayer) for two 'Sa'id) in which there is Takbir (saying Allah is great) just like in 'Idayn. The Imam (prayer leader) comes out to a clean place with serenity, dignity, humbleness and a feeling of desperation. People also come with him, they then praise Allah, glorify Him, admire Him and strive to plead before Him. Say a great deal of Tasbih (Allah is free of all defects), Tahlil, (no one deserves worship except Allah), and Takbir (Allah is great beyond description) and perform Salat (prayer) just as in 'Idayn which has two Rak'at with supplications and striving. When Salat (prayer) ends with Imam's saying, "I pray to Allah to grant you peace," he then wears his gown upside down, places the right shoulder in place of the left shoulder and vice versa; the Holy Prophet would do so.'"

H 5602, Ch. 90, h 3
Muhammad ibn Yahya in a marfu' manner has narrated the following:
"I once asked abu 'Abd Allah, *'Alayhi al-Salam*, about how the Holy prophet turned his gown upside down when pleading before Allah for rain. He (the Imam), *'Alayhi al-Salam*, said, 'It is a sign between him and his companions that turns aridity to fertility.'"

H 5603, Ch. 90, h 4
It is in the narration of ibn al-Mughirah that Takbir (Allah is great beyond description) in Salat (prayer) for rain is said in the same way as on the day of 'Id, seven times in the first Rak'at and five times in the second Rak'at. He (the Imam) performs Salat (prayer) before the sermon; recites aloud and pleads for rain when he is sitting .

(Ahadith 3-4 and the following chapter are best by fatwa.)

Chapter 91 - Salat (Prayer) For Eclipses

H 5604, Ch. 91, h 1
Ali ibn Ibrahim has narrated from his father from 'Amr ibn 'Uthman from Ali ibn 'Abd Allah who has said the following:
"I heard abu al-Hassan Musa, *'Alayhi al-Salam*, saying, 'When Ibrahim son of the Messenger of Allah passed away three traditions were established. One tradition is that on that day a sun eclipse took place and people said that it is because of the death of the son of the Messenger of Allah. The Messenger of Allah went on the pulpit, praised Allah and glorified Him, then said, "O people, the sun and the moon are two signs of the signs of Allah which move because of His command and in obedience to Him. Their eclipse is not because of the death or life of anyone. If one or both of them eclipse perform Salat (prayer) for eclipse." He climbed down the pulpit and performed Salat (prayer) because of eclipse with the people.'"

H 5605, Ch. 91, h 2
Ali has narrated from his father and Muhammad ibn 'Isma'il from al-Fadl ibn Shadhan all from Hammad ibn 'Isa from Hariz from Zurarah from Muhammad ibn Muslim who has said the following:
"We once asked abu Ja'far, *'Alayhi al-Salam*, about Salat (prayer) because of eclipse. How many Rak'at has it and how we perform it? He (the Imam) said, 'It has ten Ruku' (bowing down on one's knees) and four Sajadat (prostrations). Salat (prayer) commences with Takbir (Allah is great beyond description),

Ruku' is performed with Takbir and you raise your head with Takbir, except the fifth Takbir, after which you perform Sajdah (prostration), and say Allah hears those who praise Him. Say Qunut (supplication after recitation in second Rak'at) in every two Rak'at before Ruku' and prolong Qunut and Ruku' equal to the time for recitation, Ruku' and Sajdah (prostration). If you finish before it (sun or moon) is cleared, sit down and pray before Allah, most Majestic, most Glorious, until it is cleared. If it clears before you finish Salat (prayer), complete the remaining. Make the recitation loud.' I then asked, 'How is recitation in this Salat (prayer)?' He (the Imam) said, 'If you recite Surah (a chapter) in every Rak'at, recite al-Fatihah al-Kitab, but if you reduce from Surah (chapter) something, then recite from where you left and do not recite al-Fatihah al-Kitab.' He (the Imam) said, 'It is desirable to recite al-Kahf (Chapter 18) and al-Hijr (Chapter 15), unless one is the Imam and is afraid of causing difficulties for people behind him. Your Salat (prayer) should be in the open, without being covered by a house, if you can do so. Salat (prayer) because of sun eclipse should be given more time than that because of moon eclipse, but Salat (prayer) because of both is equal in Ruku' and Sajdah.'"

H 5606, Ch. 91, h 3

Hammad has narrated from Hariz from Zurarah and Muhammad ibn Muslim who has said the following:

"We once asked abu Ja'far, *'Alayhi al-Salam*, about the wind and darkness that at certain times come, is there any Salat (prayer) because of it? He (the Imam) said, 'When anything frightening from the sky in the form of darkness, wind or noise takes place, perform Salat (prayer) like that of eclipse until it clears out.'"

H 5607, Ch. 91, h 4

Muhammad ibn Yahya has narrated from Ahmad ibn Muhammad from ibn abu 'Umayr from Jamil ibn Darraj who has said the following:

"I once asked abu 'Abd Allah, *'Alayhi al-Salam*, about the time of Salat (prayer) because of eclipse at sunrise and sunset if it can be performed at such time. Abu 'Abd Allah, *'Alayhi al-Salam*, said, 'It is obligatory.'"

H 5608, Ch. 91, h 5

It is a narration from him (narrator of previous Hadith) by Muhammad ibn al-Husayn from Safwan ibn Yahya from al-'Ala' ibn Razin from Muhammad ibn Muslim who has said the following:

"I once asked one of the two Imam, *'Alayhim al-Salam*, about performing Salat (prayer) because of eclipse at the time of obligatory Salat (prayer). He (the Imam) said, 'Begin with obligatory Salat (prayer).' He (the Imam) was asked, 'Can it be performed in the time of nightly optional Salat (prayer)?' He (the Imam) said, 'Perform Salat (prayer) because of eclipse before nightly optional Salat (prayer).'"

H 5609, Ch. 91, h 6

It is narrated from him (narrator of previous Hadith) Ahmad ibn Muhammad from Hammad from Hariz from Zurarah and Muhammad ibn Muslim who has said the following:

"Abu 'Abd Allah, *'Alayhi al-Salam*, has said, 'When a total sun eclipse takes place but you do not notice it and come to know about it later, you must perform

Qada' (compensatory prayer for) such Salat (prayer), but if it is not a total eclipse, you are not required to perform anything.'"

H 5610, Ch. 91, h 7

Muhammad ibn Yahya has narrated from 'Imran ibn Musa from Muhammad ibn 'Abd al-Majid from Ali ibn al-Fadl al-Wasitiy who has said the following:

"I once wrote to him (the Imam), *'Alayhi al-Salam*, asking, 'If a sun or moon eclipse takes place and I am riding and unable to dismount what must I do?' He (the Imam) wrote to me, 'Perform Salat (prayer) on your stumper which you ride.'"

Chapter 92 - Salat (prayer) with Tasbih

H 5611, Ch. 92, h 1

Ali ibn Ibrahim has narrated from his father from ibn abu 'Umayr from Yahya al-Halabiy from Harun ibn Kharijah from abu Basir who has said the following:

"Abu 'Abd Allah, *'Alayhi al-Salam*, has said that the Messenger of Allah once said to Ja'far: 'O Ja'far, should I grant you and give an award to you or a gift?' Ja'far then said, 'Yes, O Messenger of Allah, please do so.' The narrator has said that people thought the Messenger of Allah might give him gold or silver. People remained anticipating. The Messenger of Allah said, 'I give you something and if you practice every day, it will be better for you than the whole world and all that it contains. If you practice it every two days, Allah forgives you during the time in between. For your practicing it every Friday or every month or every year, Allah grants you forgiveness during the time in between. Perform four Rak'at Salat (prayer). Begin the Salat (prayer), complete the recitations and then say, "Allah is free of all defects, all praise belongs to Allah, no one, other than Allah, deserves worship and Allah is great" fifteen times. In Ruku' position, say it ten times. After Ruku' (bowing down on one's knees)', when standing, say it ten times. In the first sajdah say it ten times. When sitting between the two sajdah say it ten times. In the second sajdah say it ten times. After the second sajdah before standing up for the second Rak'at say it ten times. This amounts to seventy-five Tasbihah, which makes it three hundred Tasbihah in one Rak'at and in four Rak'at Salat (prayer) it becomes one thousand two hundred Tasbihah, Tahlilah, Tahmidah and Takbirah. You may perform this Salat (prayer) during the day or night as you wish.'

"It is in a Hadith (narration) from Ibrahim ibn 'Abd al-Hamid that abu al-Hassan, *'Alayhi al-Salam*, has said the following. 'In the first Rak'at after the first Chapter of the Holy Quran recite Chapter 99. In the second Rak'at you should recite Chapter 100, in the third Rak'at recite Chapter 110 and in the fourth Rak'at read Chapter 112 of the Holy Quran.' I then asked, 'What is the reward for this Salat (prayer)?' The Imam replied, 'If his sins are as many as grains of sand in a pile, Allah forgives him.' He then looked at me and said, 'This is for you and your people only.'"

H 5612, Ch. 92, h 2

It is narrated from ibn abu 'Umayr from Yahya ibn 'Imran al-Halabiy from Dharih who has said the following:

"Abu 'Abd Allah, *'Alayhi al-Salam*, has said, 'You can perform this Salat (prayer) during the night and on a journey, during the night or day, and if you like, you can make it part of your optional Salat (prayer).'"

H 5613, Ch. 92, h 3

Ali ibn Ibrahim has narrated from his father from Muhsin ibn Ahmad from Aban who has said the following:

"I heard abu 'Abd Allah, *'Alayhi al-Salam*, saying, 'One who is in a hurry may perform Salat (prayer) of Ja'far without Tasbihat, then perform Qada' (compensatory prayer for) them when walking (or working) for his needs.'"

H 5614, Ch. 92, h 4

Ahmad ibn Idris has narrated from Muhammad ibn Ahmad from Ali ibn Sulayman who has said the following:

"I wrote to the man (Imam), *'Alayhi al-Salam*, 'What do you say about reading Salat (prayer) of Tasbih while sitting in a carriage on the back of camel?' He wrote back, 'If you are on a journey you can perform it (in such carriage).'"

H 5615, Ch. 92, h 5

Ali ibn Muhammad has narrated from certain individuals of our people from ibn Mahbub in a marfu' manner that the Imam said:

"In the last Rak'at (sajdah of last Rak'at), in Salat (prayer) of Ja'far, you should say this. 'O the One, Who has dressed up in majesty and dignity, who is kind with glory and is gracious with glory, You are the One, besides whom no one deserves Tasbih (glorification). (You are) the One whose knowledge has encompassed all things, the bountiful and generous, the One who does favors with additional generosity and the powerful and gracious. I appeal to You through the majestic qualities of Your Throne and the limits of mercy from Your book and through Your great, the most High name and perfect words. Allahumma Salli 'Ala Muhammad wa 'Ali Muhammad (O Allah grant Muhammad and his family a compensation worthy of their serving Your cause). Please make my such and such wishes come true.'"

H 5616, Ch. 92, h 6

Muhammad ibn Yahya has narrated from Ahmad ibn Muhammad from 'Abd Allah ibn abu al-Qasim who has narrated from those who narrated to him from abu Sa'id al-Mada'iniy who has said the following:

"Abu 'Abd Allah, *'Alayhi al-Salam*, said, 'Should I teach you something to say after Salat (prayer) of Ja'far?' I replied, 'Yes, please do so.' The Imam said, 'In the last sajdah of the fourth Rak'at after Tasbihat (plural of Tasbih) say this. "O the One who has dressed up in majesty and dignity, (You are the one) who is kind with glory and is gracious with glory. (You are), the One, besides whom no one deserves Tasbih (glorification). (You are) the One whose knowledge has encompassed all things, the bountiful and generous, the One who does favors with additional generosity, the powerful and gracious. I appeal to You through the majestic qualities of Your Throne and the limits of mercy from Your book and through Your great, the most High name and perfect words in all truth and justice. Allahumma Salli 'Ala Muhammad wa 'Ali Muhammad (O Allah grant Muhammad and his family a compensation worthy of their serving Your cause)', please make my such and such wishes come true.''''

H 5617, Ch. 92, h 7

Muhammad ibn al-Hassan has narrated from Sahl ibn Ziyad from Ali ibn Asbat from al-Hakam ibn Miskin from Ishaq ibn 'Ammar who has said the following:

"I asked abu 'Abd Allah, *'Alayhi al-Salam*, 'If one performs Salat (prayer) of Ja'far, does Allah, the Most Majestic, the Most Glorious, grant him a reward like that which the Messenger of Allah mentioned for Ja'far?' The Imam said, 'Yes, by Allah, He does so.'"

Chapter 93 - Salat (prayer) of Fatimah al-Zahra', *'Alayha al-Salam*, and other Salawat (prayers) to build up Interests

H 5618, Ch. 93, h 1

Ali ibn Muhammad and others have narrated from Sahl ibn Ziyad from Ali ibn al-Hakam from Muthanna al-Hannat from abu Basir who has said the following:

"I heard abu 'Abd Allah, *'Alayhi al-Salam*, saying, 'One who performs, four Rak'at Salat (prayer) and reads two hundred times Chapter 112 of the Holy Quran, fifty times in each Rak'at, does not move away with any of his sins before Allah without being forgiven.'"

H 5619, Ch. 93, h 2

A number of our people have narrated from Ahmad ibn Muhammad from al-Barqiy from Sa'dan from 'Abd Allah ibn Sinan who has said the following:

"He has narrated from abu 'Abd Allah, *'Alayhi al-Salam*, a Hadith with the text which is the same as that of the previous Hadith."

H 5620, Ch. 93, h 3

Muhammad ibn Yahya has narrated from through the chain of his narrators in a marfu' manner who has said the following:

"Abu 'Abd Allah, *'Alayhi al-Salam*, has said that the text is the same as the previous Hadith except that it says, 'Read Chapter 112 of the Holy Quran sixty times in each Rak'at.'"

H 5621, Ch. 93, h 4

Ali ibn Muhammad has narrated from certain individuals of our people who have said the following:

"Abu al-Hassan al-Rida, *'Alayhi al-Salam*, has said, 'If one after performing Maghrib (Salat (prayer) soon after sunset), the four Rak'at and before speaking to anyone performs ten Rak'at Salat (prayer), recites al-Fatihah and Chapter 112 of the Holy Quran it is equal in reward to setting free of ten slaves."

H 5622, Ch. 93, h 5

A number of our people have narrated from Ahmad ibn Muhammad ibn 'Isa from ibn abu 'Umayr from Muhammad ibn Kurdus who has said the following:

"Abu 'Abd Allah, *'Alayhi al-Salam*, has said, 'If one cleanses himself (takes Wudu' or bath), then goes to bed for the night, his bed is considered a Masjid. If he wakes up during the night and speaks of Allah, his sins scatter away from him. One who may get up toward the end of the night, cleanse himself (take Wudu' or bath), perform two Rak'at Salat (prayer), praise Allah and speak of His glory. If then says, "Allahumma Salli 'Ala Muhammad wa 'Ali Muhammad (O Allah grant Muhammad and his family compensation worthy of their serving Your cause)." The wishes he asks for are given to him in substance or are saved for him in a better form.'"

H 5623, Ch. 93, h 6

Ali ibn Muhammad has narrated from through his chain of narrators who has said the following:

"One of the `A'immah about the words of Allah, 'An initiation (for Salat (prayer) is of a stronger impression' (73:6), the Imam has said, 'It is the two Rak'at Salat (prayer) after Maghrib (Salat (prayer) soon after sunset). In the first Rak'at read al-Fatihah and ten verses from the beginning of Chapter 2, verse 54 of Chapter 7, verses 153-154 of Chapter 2 and 15 times Chapter 112. In the second Rak'at after al-Fatihah read verses 255- 257, then verses 284 – 286 of Chapter 2 and 15 times Chapter 112 of the Holy Quran. Then ask for your wishes as you like. If one maintains this practice a reward of six hundred thousand Hajj will be given to him.'"

H 5624, Ch. 93, h 7

Ali ibn Muhammad has narrated in a marfu' manner who has said the following:

"Abu 'Abd Allah, *'Alayhi al-Salam*, has said that on the night of the middle of the month of Sha'ban perform four Rak'at Salat (prayer). In every Rak'at read al-Fatihah and Chapter 112 one hundred times. After completing say, 'O Lord, I am needy to You. I seek protection with You and I am afraid of Your (anger). I plead before You for your protection. O Lord, do not replace my name and do not change my body. O my Lord, do not make my trial extremely hard. I seek your protection with Your pardon against Your punishment, I seek protection with Your pleasure against Your anger, I seek protection with Your mercy against Your punishment, I seek protection with You from You. Your praise is exalted. You are just as You have said You are and beyond what others say.' The narrator has said that abu 'Abd Allah, *'Alayhi al-Salam*, then said this, 'On the twenty-seventh of the month of Rajab the Messenger of Allah gave people this information. It said, "One can perform a Salat (prayer), any time he wants, of twelve Rak'at. In each Rak'at he can recite al-Fatihah and another chapter from the Holy Quran. After completing and Salam, sits in his place, then reads al-Fatihah four times, chapters 112, 113 and 114 four times each. After completing while still in his place says four times, 'No one, other than Allah, deserves worship, Allah is great, all praise belongs to Allah, Allah is free of all defects and there is no means and power other than the power and means of Allah.' Then says four times, 'O Allah, (be a witness that) Allah is my Lord. I do not consider anyone as His partner.' Then he may ask for his wishes. His wishes will be made to come true about everything except for the destruction of a people or the destruction of good relations with relatives.'""

Chapter 94 - Salat (prayer) for Istikharah (asking Allah to Choose for One What Is Good)

H 5625, Ch. 94, h 1

Muhammad ibn Yahya has narrated from Ahmad ibn Muhammad from Muhammad ibn Khalid from al-Nadr ibn al-Suwayd from Yahya al-Halabiy from 'Amr ibn Hurayth who has said the following:

"Abu 'Abd Allah, *'Alayhi al-Salam*, has said, 'Perform two Rak'at Salat (prayer) and ask Allah to chose for you what is good. By Allah, if a Muslim asks Allah to choose for him what is good, He certainly chooses for him as such.'"

H 5626, Ch. 94, h 2

Ali ibn Ibrahim has narrated from his father from 'Uthman ibn 'Isa from 'Amr ibn Shimr from Jabir who has said the following:

"Abu Ja'far, *'Alayhi al-Salam*, has said, 'Whenever Ali ibn al-Husayn, *'Alayhi al-Salam*, would think of performing Hajj, 'Umrah or buying, selling or setting free a slave, he would first cleanse himself (take Wudu' or bath), then perform two Rak'at Salat (prayer) for Istikharah in which he read chapters 55 and 59. After completing Salat (prayer) he would read chapters 113, 114 and 112 while still in a sitting position. He then say, 'O Lord, if such and such thing is good for me in this world and for my religion, immediately or later, Allahumma Salli 'Ala Muhammad wa 'Ali Muhammad, (O Allah grant Muhammad and his family a compensation worthy of their serving Your cause), please make it easy for me in the best manner and make it come beautiful. O Lord, if such and such thing is bad for my religion and my worldly matters immediately or later, Allahumma Salli 'Ala Muhammad wa 'Ali Muhammad, (O Allah grant Muhammad and his family a compensation worthy of their serving Your cause), please keep it away from me. O Lord, Allahumma Salli 'Ala Muhammad wa 'Ali Muhammad, (O Allah grant Muhammad and his family a compensation worthy of their serving your cause), please grant me determination with guidance even if I dislike it and my soul refuses.'"

H 5627, Ch. 94, h 3

More than one person has narrated from Sahl ibn Ziyad from Ahmad ibn Muhammad al-Basriy from al-Qasim ibn 'Abd al-Rahman al-Hashimiy from Harun ibn Kharijah who has said the following:

"Abu 'Abd Allah, *'Alayhi al-Salam*, has said that when you think of doing something, take six pieces of paper and write on three of them, 'In the name of Allah, the Beneficent, the Merciful. It is to ask from Allah, the Majestic, the Wise, what is good for so and so son of so and so, "do it."' On the other, three write, 'In the name of Allah, the Beneficent, the Merciful. It is to ask from Allah, the Majestic, the Wise, what is good for so and so son of so and so, "do not do it."' Keep them under your prayer rug and perform two Rak'at Salat (prayer). After completing Salat (prayer), make a sajdah and say one hundred times, 'I ask Allah, through His mercy, to choose what is good and safe.' Then sit straight and say, 'O Lord, pick and choose for me in all matters with ease and safety.' Then mix the pieces and take out one. If three times, consecutively it comes 'do it', then you may do what you wanted to do. If three times consecutively it comes 'do not do it,' then do not do what you wanted to do. If one comes 'do it' and the other comes 'do not do it' continue taking out up to five pieces, then see which side is more then follow the side which is more and ignore the sixth piece.'"

H 5628, Ch. 94, h 4
Muhammad ibn Yahya has narrated from Ahmad ibn Muhammad from ibn Faddal who has said the following:
"Al-Hassan ibn Jahm asked abu al-Hassan, *'Alayhi al-Salam*, for ibn Asbat; ibn Asbat and we all were present. 'Should he travel by land or by sea to Egypt? Please tell him about the best road by land.' The Imam said, 'By land, but go to the Masjid in a time other than that for obligatory Salat (prayer). Perform two Rak'at Salat (prayer) and ask Allah, one hundred times, to choose for you the best. Then see what comes in your mind, then act accordingly.' Al-Hassan then said, 'By land is what I like for him.' The Imam said, 'I also like for him by land.'"

H 5629, Ch. 94, h 5
Ali ibn Ibrahim has narrated from his father from ibn Asbat and Muhammad ibn Ahmad from Musa ibn al-Qasim al-Bajaliy from Ali ibn Asbat who has said the following:
"I said to abu al-Hassan al-Rida, *'Alayhi al-Salam*, 'I pray to Allah to keep my soul in service for your cause. Do you advise if I travel by land or by sea? Our road is very dangerous and frightening.' The Imam said, 'Travel by land but there is no offense, if you go to the Masjid of the Messenger of Allah; perform two Rak'at Salat (prayer) in a time other than that for obligatory Salat (prayer). Thereafter ask Allah, one hundred times, to choose for you the best, then see what comes in your mind. If Allah has decided for you by sea, then say the words of Allah, the Most Majestic, the Most Glorious, "He said, 'Go onboard in the name of Allah who sets it afloat and anchors it down. My Lord is forgiving and merciful'" (11:41). If you find the sea turbulent then lean on your right side and say, "In the name of Allah, calm down with the serenity of Allah, rest by the dignity of Allah and quiet down by the permission of Allah. There is no means and power without help from Allah."'

"We then asked him, 'What is al-Sakinah (serenity)?' The Imam said, 'It is a wind that comes out of paradise and has a face like the face of man and it has a fine fragrance. It is this wind that descended down to Ibrahim (Abraham) and circled around al-Bayt (Ka'bah) when he was placing the pillars.' It was asked: 'Is it of that which Allah, the Most Majestic, the most Glorious, speaks, "In it there is Sakinah from your Lord, and remainder of that which people of Moses left and so did people of Harun (Aaron)"'(2:246). The Imam said, 'That al-Sakinah was in the Ark (chest) in which there was a tray wherein the hearts of prophets had been washed. And the Ark circled among the children of Israel with the prophets and then it came to us.' He asked, 'What is your Ark?' We said, 'It is the armaments.' He then said, 'You are right. That is your Ark.' The Imam said, 'If you travel by land, then say what Allah, the Most Majestic, the Most Glorious, has said, "Free of all defects is the One who has made it subservient to us, otherwise, we could not reach it (our destination). To our Lord we all return." (42:13-14) If any servant (of Allah) says it during his riding he will not, by the permission of Allah, fall off his camel or horse or get hurt.' He then said, 'When you come out of your home say, "In the name of Allah, I believe in Allah, I assign Allah as my attorney, there is no means and power without the help of Allah." The angels strike the face of Satans and say to them, 'He has spoken the name of Allah, believed in Allah and has assigned Allah as his attorney and has said, "There is no means and power without the help of Allah."'""

H 5630, Ch. 94, h 6

Muhammad ibn Yahya has narrated from Ahmad ibn Muhammad from Ali ibn Hadid from Murazim who has said the following:

"Abu 'Abd Allah, *'Alayhi al-Salam*, said to me, 'If one of you may think of doing something, he should perform two Rak'at Salat (prayer), then praise Allah, speak of His greatness and say, "Allahumma Salli 'Ala Muhammad wa 'Ali Muhammad (O Allah grant Muhammad and his family a compensation worthy of their serving Your cause)." Thereafter say, "O Lord, if this matter is good for my religion and worldly matters, please make it possible for me with ease; and if it is otherwise, keep it away from me."' I then asked, 'What should I read in the two Rak'at Salat (prayer)?' The Imam replied, 'You may read whatever you like. You can read Chapter 112 or 109.'"

H 5631, Ch. 94, h 7

Ali ibn Muhammad has narrated from Sahl ibn Ziyad from Muhammad ibn 'Isa from 'Amr ibn Ibrahim from Khalaf ibn Hammad from Ishaq ibn 'Ammar who has said the following:

"I said to abu 'Abd Allah, *'Alayhi al-Salam*, 'Sometimes I may get two different opinions: one for and the other against what I think to do, what then I should do?' The Imam said, 'If such is the case, then perform two Rak'at Salat (prayer) and ask Allah, one hundred and one times, to choose for you what is best. Thereafter choose the matter for which your determination is stronger; the choice is for it, by the will of Allah. Your choice should be based on what is safe; sometimes it is better for a man to see his hand cut off, or his son die or his property gone.'"

H 5632, Ch. 94, h 8

Ali ibn Muhammad has narrated in a marfu' manner from one of `A'immah who has said the following:

"The Imam, *'Alayhi al-Salam*, said to one of his companions who had asked about an issue that he wanted to do but did not find any one to consult with. The Imam said, 'Consult your Lord.' He then asked, 'How should I do so?' The Imam replied, 'Keep in your mind what you wish to do, then write two pieces of paper, "yes" on one and "no" on the other. Place them inside two balls of clay, perform two Rak'at Salat (prayer) and place them under your furnishing and say, "O Allah, I consult You in this matter and You are the best consultant and advisor. Grant me a sign about that which is beneficial and is of good consequences," then take out one of the papers; if it is "yes", then do what you wanted and if it is "no" then do not do it. This is how you consult your Lord.'"

Chapter 95 - Salat (prayer) when Asking for Increase in One's Sustenance

H 5633, Ch. 95, h 1

Muhammad ibn 'Isma'il has narrated from al-Fadl ibn Shadhan from Safwan ibn Yahya from ibn Muskan from Muhammad ibn Ali al-Halabiy who has said the following:

"A man complained before abu 'Abd Allah, *'Alayhi al-Salam,* against his poverty and deprivation in business after being affluent and that in whatever way he moves to make a living, he faces difficulties. Abu 'Abd Allah, *'Alayhi al-Salam,* commanded him to go to the special place of the Messenger of Allah which is between his grave and pulpit. 'Perform two Rak'at Salat (prayer) there and say, one hundred times, 'O Lord, I appeal to You through Your power, Your determination, Your majesty and through whatever Your knowledge has encompassed, please facilitate my business and increase it for my sustenance in a way that is better and of good consequences.' The man has said that thereafter in whichever way I moved for business Allah granted me benefits."

H 5634, Ch. 95, h 2

A number of our people have narrated from Ahmad ibn Muhammad ibn 'Isa from Ahmad ibn abu Dawud from abu Hamzah who has said the following:

"Abu Ja'far, *'Alayhi al-Salam,* has said that a man came to the Holy Prophet and said, 'O Messenger of Allah, I am a man with (a large) family, indebted; and my condition has become difficult. Please teach me a prayer through which Allah will provide me enough to pay my debts and help my family.' The Messenger of Allah said, 'Take Wudu' properly, then perform two Rak'at Salat (prayer) with complete Ruku' and sajdah in both Rak'at. Thereafter say, "O owner of glory, O the only One, O gracious, I turn to You through Muhammad, Your prophet, the prophet of mercy. O Muhammad, O Messenger of Allah, I have turned through you to Allah, your Lord and the Lord of all things. Allahumma Salli 'Ala Muhammad wa 'Ali Muhammad (O Allah grant Muhammad and his family a compensation worthy of their serving Your cause). I appeal to You for relief from that with which You grant relief, an easy success and vast sustenance with which I can overcome my difficulties, pay my debts and help my family.""""

H 5635, Ch. 95, h 3

A number of our people have narrated from Ahmad ibn Muhammad from ibn abu Najran from Sabah al-Hadhdha' from ibn al-Tayyar who has said the following:

"I said to abu 'Abd Allah, 'I had some property which now has scattered away and I am under severe constraint.' The Imam asked, 'Do you have a shop in the market place?' I replied, 'Yes, but I have abandoned it.' The Imam said, 'When you go back to Kufah, attend your shop and broom clean it. When you want to go to your market place, perform two Rak'at Salat (prayer) or four Rak'at and at the end say, "I have decided to go to work and it is without any power and means from myself but (O Lord), it is by Your power and means. I disassociate myself from all powers and means except for your power and means. You are my power and means. O Lord, grant me, with your generosity vast sustenance, plentiful and fine, so I become affluent in good health by Your help. No one owns it (good health) except You."' The narrator has said, 'I followed the instruction but I became afraid of tax collector due to my inability to pay the rent and that I might lose the shop for this reason and I did not have anything to pay. One day a merchant came to me and asked me to rent out to him half of my house. I then rented out one half for the rent of the whole house. He tried to sell his merchandise but did not get the price he wanted, thus he did not sell it. I then asked him if he could allow me to sell a certain amount of his merchandise in my shop; if sold I shall give him his purchase price and keep the extra. He said, "How can that happen?" I said, "Trust me before Allah." He agreed that I take a bundle. I took it. The weather became very cold. I was able to sell the merchandise the same day. I gave him his purchase price and kept the extra. I continued selling his merchandise, gave back his capital and kept the extra until I was able to buy horses, slaves and a house.'"

H 5636, Ch. 95, h 4

Ali ibn Ibrahim has narrated from Ahmad ibn Muhammad from Ali ibn al-Hakam from ibn al-Walid ibn Sabih from his father who has said the following:

"Abu 'Abd Allah, *'Alayhi al-Salam*, asked me, 'Where is your shop in relation to the Masjid?' I replied, 'It is near the door of the Masjid.' He then said, 'When you want to go to your shop, first go to the Masjid, perform two or four Rak'at Salat (prayer) and at the end say, "I have attended this morning by the means and power of Allah, but not by my own means and power, in fact it is by Your means and power O Lord. O Allah, I am Your servant and I appeal to You to grant me (wealth) through Your generosity, as You have commanded me to pray to You and appeal. Make this possible for me with ease, so I can be affluent and in good health by Your help."'"

H 5637, Ch. 95, h 5

A number of our people have narrated from al-Barqiy from his father from Safwan ibn Yahya from Muhammad ibn al-Hassan al-'Attar from a man from our people who has said the following:

"Abu 'Abd Allah, *'Alayhi al-Salam*, asked me, 'O so and so, do you sometimes need something? Do you visit the great Masjid near you in Kufah?' I replied, 'Yes, I do.' He said, 'Perform four Rak'at Salat (prayer) there and say, "I have attended this morning by the means and power of Allah, not by my own means and power, but with Your means and power, O Lord. I appeal before You for the blessings of this day and the blessing of the people of this day and I appeal before You to grant me through Your generosity lawful and fine sustenance which You will send to me through Your means and power so I can live affluently in good health by Your help."'"

H 5638, Ch. 95, h 6

Ali ibn Muhammad has narrated from 'Abd Allah from Ibrahim ibn Ishaq from 'Abd Allah ibn Ahmad from al-Hassan ibn 'Urwah son of the sister of Shu'ayb al-'Aqarqufiy from his maternal uncle, Shu'ayb who has said the following:

"Abu 'Abd Allah, *'Alayhi al-Salam*, said to me, 'If one feels hungry he should take Wudu' and perform two Rak'at Salat (prayer), then say, "O my Lord, I am hungry. Please feed me." He will be fed within the same hour.'"

H 5639, Ch. 95, h 7

Ali ibn Ibrahim has narrated from his father, from 'Abd Allah ibn al-Mughirah from al-Walid ibn Sabih who has said the following:

"Abu 'Abd Allah, *'Alayhi al-Salam*, has said that when you in the morning after Salat (prayer) want to go to work, perform two Rak'at Salat (prayer). After saying the testimonies say, 'O Lord, I have attended this morning and I seek favor through Your generosity, as You have commanded, in the form of lawful and fine sustenance with which You will grant me good health.' Say it three times. Then perform another two Rak'at Salat (prayer). At the end of testimonies say, 'By the power and means of Allah, I attend this morning not by my own power and means, but by Your power and means, O Lord, and I disassociate from all powers and means. O Lord, I appeal to You for the blessings of this day and the blessings of the people of this day. I appeal before You to grant me through Your generosity vast, fine and lawful sustenance which You will send to me by Your means and power so I can live affluently in good health.' Say it three times."

Chapter 96 - Salat (prayer) for one's Needs

H 5640, Ch. 96, h 1

Ali ibn Ibrahim has narrated from Ahmad ibn Muhammad from abu 'Abd Allah from Ziyad al-Qandiy from 'Abd al-Rahim al-Qasir who has said the following:

"I visited abu 'Abd Allah, *'Alayhi al-Salam*, and said, 'I pray to Allah to keep my soul in service for your cause; I have invented a prayer.' He said, 'Keep your invention away from me. When you face a difficult condition, seek asylum with the Messenger of Allah, perform two Rak'at Salat (prayer), as a present to the Messenger of Allah.' I then asked, 'How should I do it?' He said, 'Take a bath, perform two Rak'at Salat (prayer), begin just as you do in obligatory Salat (prayer) and read the testimonies just as you do in obligatory Salat (prayer). At the end of testimony and Salam say, "O Lord, You are Salam (peace or safety), from You comes safety, to You returns safety, Allahumma Salli 'Ala Muhammad wa 'Ali Muhammad (O Allah grant Muhammad and his family a compensation worthy of their serving Your cause). Deliver my salutation to Muhammad and the spirits of truthful `A'immah, *'Alayhim al-Salam*, and to me Salam from them and the blessings of Allah. O Allah, these two (Rak'at Salat (prayer)) are my gift to the Messenger of Allah. Please grant to me the reward that I wished and about which I placed my hopes before You and Your Messenger, O Guardian of the believers." Then make sajdah and say, "O the Living One, the Guardian, the Living who never dies, O the Living One, no one other than You, deserves worship, O the owner of glory, and grace, O merciful above all merciful ones"- forty times. Then place the right side of your face on the ground and say the above forty times. Then place the left side of your face on the ground and say the same forty times. Raise thereafter your head, stretch your hands and say the above forty times. Then hold your beard with your left hand, weep or make a weeping face and say, "O Muhammad, the Messenger of Allah, I complain before Allah and before you about my needs as well as before your Ahl al-Bayt (members of your family), the right guides about my needs, through you I turn to Allah about my needs." Then make sajdah and say, "O Allah, O Allah," for a full breath, Allahumma Salli 'Ala Muhammad wa 'Ali Muhammad (O Allah grant Muhammad and his family a compensation worthy of their serving Your cause).' Please grant my wishes and needs.'"

"Abu 'Abd Allah, *'Alayhi al-Salam,* has said, 'I guarantee from Allah, the Most Majestic, the Most Glorious, that He will not leave your needs and wishes without being met and fulfilled.'"

H 5641, Ch. 96, h 2

Ali ibn Ibrahim has narrated from his father from certain individuals of our people in a marfu' manner who has said the following:

"Abu 'Abd Allah, *'Alayhi al-Salam,* has said that if a man is sad and depressed about something or because of an unfulfilled wish, he should perform two Rak'at Salat (prayer). In one he should recite Chapter 112 of the Holy Quran one thousand times and in the second Rak'at once, then ask for his wish."

H 5642, Ch. 96, h 3

Muhammad ibn Yahya has narrated from Ahmad ibn Muhammad from Ali ibn Duwayl from Muqatil ibn Muqatil who has said the following:

"I said to al-Rida, *'Alayhi al-Salam,* 'I pray to Allah to keep my soul in service for your cause, teach me a prayer for help in my needs.' The Imam said, 'When you need something and want Allah, the Most Majestic, the Most Glorious, to help you, take a bath and dress up in your cleanest dress, use perfume, go under the open sky and perform two Rak'at Salat (prayer). Begin Salat (prayer) and recite al-Fatihah and then Chapter 112 of the Holy Quran fifteen times. Then kneel down for Ruku' and recite chapter 112 of the Holy Quran fifteen times. Thereafter complete this prayer like the Salat (prayer) of Tasbih discussed in Chapter 96 above, except that recitation in this Salat (prayer) is fifteen times. After Salam read Chapter 112 of the Holy Quran fifteen times. Thereafter bow down for sajdah to say, "O Lord, everything, other than You, from Your Throne down to earth if worshipped is false. You are Allah in all truth and clarity. Please grant me such and such wish that I need, in this hour." Strive to express your prayer as best as you can.'"

H 5643, Ch. 96, h 4

A number of our people have narrated from Ahmad ibn Muhammad from al-Husayn ibn Sa'id from abu Ali al-Khazzaz who has said the following:

"I visited abu 'Abd Allah, *'Alayhi al-Salam,* and a man also came to him saying, 'I pray to Allah to keep my soul in service for your cause, my brother suffers from something that I feel embarrassed to mention.' The Imam said, 'Do not mention it and tell him to fast on Wednesday, Thursday and Friday. When the sun declines to the west at noontime, he should go out somewhere so no one can see him while dressed in two pieces of his new or just washed clothes, and perform two Rak'at Salat (prayer), then expose his knees, place his palms and forehead on the ground. In his Salat (prayer), he should recite al-Fatihah al-Kitab ten times. Thereafter he should recite Chapter 112 of the Holy Quran ten times, in Ruku' fifteen times, in sajdah ten times, between the two sajdah when sitting twenty times. He should perform four Rak'at Salat (prayer) in this way. After completing Tashahhud (the two testimonies) he should say, "O the One who is known for His granting favor, O the First of all first ones, O the Last of all last ones, O the One who has strong power, O the One who grants sustenance to the destitute, O the most Merciful of all merciful ones. I have purchased myself from You with one-third of what I own. (With such payment) I pray to You, remove from me the evil of what I suffer from. You have power over all things."'''

H 5644, Ch. 96, h 5

Through the same chain of narrators as the previous Hadith, it is narrated from Ahmad ibn Muhammad from ibn Mahbub from al-Hassan ibn Salih who has said the following:

"I heard abu 'Abd Allah, say this. 'One, for coming true of his wish, may take a proper Wudu', perform two Rak'at Salat (prayer) with complete Ruku' and sajdah. He then can sit and praises Allah, the Most Majestic, the Most Glorious. He then can say, "Allahumma Salli 'Ala Muhammad wa 'Ali Muhammad (O Allah grant Muhammad and his family a compensation worthy of their serving Your cause)." Thereafter ask Allah for his needs, he has asked Him for needs in a time of a good chance for acceptance, in which case one is not deprived of coming true of his wish.'"

H 5645, Ch. 96, h 6

Muhammad ibn Yahya has narrated from Ahmad ibn Muhammad from Muhammad ibn Isma'il from 'Abd Allah ibn 'Uthman from abu Isma'il al-Sarraj from 'Abd Allah ibn Waddah and Ali ibn abu Hamzah from Isma'il ibn al-Arqat and his mother 'Umm Salamah sister of abu 'Abd Allah *'Alayhi al-Salam*, who has said the following:

"I became seriously ill in the month of Ramadan. I was not able to get up. Banu Hashim gathered at night for burial, seeing me about to die. My mother was restless. Abu 'Abd Allah, *'Alayhi al-Salam*, told her, 'My aunt, climb on the house, expose your head under the sky, perform two Rak'at Salat (prayer) and after Salam say, "O Allah, You give him to me as a gift. He was not anything. O Allah, I pray to You to give him to me as a gift on my own initiation so allow me to borrow him from You."' She did as she was told and I regained consciousness and sat up straight. They called everyone for food (so they can fast the next day). It was Harisah (mashed meat and grain). They ate and I ate with them.'"

H 5646, Ch. 96, h 7

Through the same chain of narrators as the previous Hadith, it is narrated from abu Isma'il al-Sarraj from ibn Muskan from Sharahbil al-Kindiy who has said the following:

"Abu Ja'far, *'Alayhi al-Salam*, has said that if you want to ask your Lord for something, take Wudu' properly, perform two Rak'at Salat (prayer), speak of the greatness of Allah. Say, 'Allahumma Salli 'Ala Muhammad wa 'Ali Muhammad (O Allah grant Muhammad and his family a compensation worthy of their serving Your cause).' After Salam say, 'O Allah, I appeal before You, You are the Owner and the King and have power over all things. You are dominant and whatever You want it comes into existence. O Allah I turn to You through Your prophet, Muhammad, the prophet of mercy. O Muhammad, O

Messenger of Allah, I turn to you before Allah, Your Cherisher and my Cherisher so that He makes my wish to come true. O Allah, through Your prophet, Muhammad, make my wish come true.' Then ask for your needs."

H 5647, Ch. 96, h 8

A number of our people have narrated from Ahmad ibn Muhammad and abu Dawud from al-Husayn ibn Sa'id from Fadalah ibn Ayyub from Mu'awiyah ibn Wahab from Zurarah who has said the following:

"Abu 'Abd Allah, *'Alayhi al-Salam*, has said that one who wishes that his Lord make his wish come true should feed sixty destitute people as an act of charity, one sa' (three kilograms), by the sa' of the Holy Prophet, of food per person. At night during the last third of the night, take a shower and dress in minimum form, except that it must have a loincloth. Then he should perform two Rak'at Salat (prayer). When placing his forehead on the ground in the last sajdah of the last Rak'at, he should say that no one, other than Allah, deserves worship, speak of His greatness, His Holiness, His glory and then remember his sins and confess, as much as he remembers, name them (one by one), committing them then raise his head. When he places his forehead on the ground for the second sajdah, he should ask Allah, one hundred times, to choose for him the best, saying, 'O Allah, I ask You to choose for me the best.' Then pray to Allah for whatever he wants. Whenever in sajdah he should expose his knees to touch the ground and secure the loincloth from behind between his legs."

H 5648, Ch. 96, h 9

Al-Husayn ibn Muhammad has narrated from Mu'alla' ibn Muhammad from al-Washsha' from Aban from al-Harith ibn al-Mughirah who has said the following:

"Abu 'Abd Allah, *'Alayhi al-Salam*, has said, 'If you need something, take Wudu', perform two Rak'at Salat (prayer) and then praise Allah, speak of His greatness and read of verses (of Quran), then ask for your needs, your prayer will be answered.'"

H 5649, Ch. 96, h 10

A number of our people have narrated from Ahmad ibn Muhammad from ibn Faddal from Tha'labah ibn Maymun from al-Harith ibn al-Mughirah who has said the following:

"Abu 'Abd Allah, *'Alayhi al-Salam*, has said, 'If you need something, perform two Rak'at Salat (prayer) and say, "Allahumma Salli 'Ala Muhammad wa 'Ali Muhammad (O Allah grant Muhammad and his family a compensation worthy of their serving Your cause)." Ask for your needs. They will be fulfilled.'"

H 5650, Ch. 96, h 11

Muhammad ibn Yahya has narrated from Ahmad ibn Muhammad from 'Umar ibn 'Abd al-'Aziz from Jamil who has said the following:

"I was in the presence of abu 'Abd Allah, *'Alayhi al-Salam*, when a woman came to him saying, 'I left my son dead; I had thrown a comforter on his face.' The Imam said to her, 'Perhaps he is not dead. Go back to your home, take a shower, perform two Rak'at Salat (prayer), pray and say, "O the One who gave him to me as a gift when he was not anything, please renew Your gift for me," then move him and do not tell anyone about it.' She has said, 'I followed the instruction and moved him and he began to cry.'"

Chapter 97 - Salat (prayer) of One Who Is Afraid

H 5651, Ch. 97, h 1

Muhammad ibn Isma'il has narrated from al-Fadl ibn Shadhan from Hammad ibn 'Isa from Shu'ayb al-'Aqarqufiy from abu Basir from abu 'Abd Allah, who has said the following:

"If something dismayed Imam Ali, *'Alayhi al-Salam*, he would feel restless for Salat (prayer). The Imam then read this, 'Seek help from exercising patience and performing Salat (prayer).'"

H 5652, Ch. 97, h 2

Al-Husayn ibn Muhammad has narrated from Mu'alla' ibn Muhammad from al-Washsha' from Aban from Hariz who has said the following:

"Abu 'Abd Allah, *'Alayhi al-Salam*, has said to assign a place in your home as Masjid. If something frightens you, dress in two pieces of your roughest clothes and perform Salat (prayer) with them. Thereafter rise on your knees and call for help, scream before Allah, ask Him for paradise, beg Him for protection against whatever has frightened you. Beware of having Allah to hear from you rebellious words even though You may feel very proud of yourself or your tribe."

Chapter 98 - Salat (prayer) of One Who Likes to Travel

H 5653, Ch. 98, h 1

Ali ibn Ibrahim has narrated from his father from al-Nawfaliy, from al-Sakuniy who has said the following:

"Abu 'Abd Allah, *'Alayhi al-Salam*, has said that the Messenger of Allah has said, 'A servant (of Allah) is not able to leave a successor among his people in his absence better than two Rak'at Salat (prayer). It is a Salat (prayer) that he performs when leaving for a journey. He should say, "O Allah, I leave myself, my family, my properties, my religion, my worldly affairs, the affairs of my next life, my trust and the consequences of my deeds in your trust." He (Allah) grants him what he has asked.'"

Chapter 99 - Salat (prayer) for Thanksgiving

H 5654, Ch. 99, h 1

Muhammad ibn Yahya has narrated from Ahmad ibn Muhammad from Muhammad ibn Isma'il from abu Isma'il al-Sarraj from Harun ibn Kharijah who has said the following:

"Abu 'Abd Allah, *'Alayhi al-Salam*, has said that when Allah grants you a bounty, you should perform two Rak'at Salat (prayer). In the first Rak'at recite al-Fatihah al-Kitab and Chapter 112 of the Holy Quran. In the second Rak'at recite al-Fatihah al-Kitab and Chapter 109 of the Holy Quran. In Ruku' and sajdah of the first Rak'at say, 'All praise belongs to Allah, with thanks, a great deal of thanks and praise.' In Ruku' and sajdah of the second Rak'at say, 'All praise belongs to Allah who answers my prayers and grants my wishes.'"

Chapter 100 - Salat (prayer) of One who Wants to Get Married or Go to Bed with His Wife

H 5655, Ch. 100, h 1

A number of our people have narrated from Ahmad ibn Muhammad from ibn Mahbub from Jamil ibn Salih from abu Basir who has said the following:

"I heard a man saying to abu Ja'far, *'Alayhi al-Salam*, 'I pray to Allah to keep my soul in service for your cause, I am an aged man. I have married a virgin young woman. I have not gone to bed with her yet. I am afraid in bed that on finding me of such age and the dye on my beard she may dislike me.' Abu Ja'far, *'Alayhi al-Salam*, said, 'When you are there, ask her before approaching you to take Wudu'. You also, should not approach her before taking Wudu' and performing two Rak'at Salat (prayer). Thereafter, speak of glory of Allah and say, "Allahumma Salli 'Ala Muhammad wa 'Ali Muhammad (O Allah grant Muhammad and his family a compensation worthy of their serving Your cause)." Thereafter ask her and others present with her to say A'min (O Allah grant his wishes). Thereafter say, "O Lord, provide her enough reasons to be kind to me, love me and be happy with me and grant me enough reason to be happy with her, bring us together in the best form of gathering, and the happiest kindness; You love lawfulness and dislike unlawfulness."' The Imam then said, 'You must bear in mind that kindness comes from Allah and hate comes from Satan so that people dislike what Allah has made lawful.'"

H 5656, Ch. 100, h 2

Through the same chain of narrators as that of the previous Hadith from Ahmad ibn Muhammad from al-Qasim ibn Yahya from his grandfather, al-Hassan ibn Rashid from abu Basir who has said the following:

"Abu 'Abd Allah, *'Alayhi al-Salam*, once said to me, 'When anyone of you likes to get married, what does he need to do?' I replied, 'I do not know.' The Imam then said, 'When one of you has such intention, he should first perform two Rak'at Salat (prayer) and praise Allah. Thereafter, say, "O Allah, I like to become married. Determine for me of women the most protective of her privacy, the most chaste in conjugal matters, protective of myself and my property and of a vast share of sustenance, of the greatest in blessing, and determine for me a fine son who will succeed me as a virtuous one in my lifetime and when I die."'"

H 5657, Ch. 100, h 3

Muhammad ibn Yahya has narrated from Ahmad ibn Muhammad from Ali ibn al-Hakam from a man from Muhammad ibn Muslim who has said the following:

"Abu Ja'far, *'Alayhi al-Salam*, has said, 'If one wants that his wife become pregnant, he should perform two Rak'at Salat (prayer) after Friday Salat (prayer). In this Salat (prayer) he should prolong his Ruku' and sajdah and then say, "O Allah, I ask You just what Zachariah asked You for, O my Lord, (rabbi) do not leave me lonely (childless) while You are the best heir. O Allah, grant me virtuous offspring. You hear (all prayers and appeals). O Allah through Your name she has become lawful for me and as Your trust, I have taken her as my wife. If You will decree a child in her womb, please make the child to be a righteous (honorable one, an intelligent) son and do not allow Satan to have a part or share in him.'"

Chapter 101 - The Rare Ahadith

H 5658, Ch. 101, h 1

Ali ibn Ibrahim has narrated from his father from ibn abu 'Umayr from ibn `Udhaynah who has said the following:

"Abu 'Abd Allah, *'Alayhi al-Salam,* asked me, 'What does the enemy narrate?' I then asked, 'I pray to Allah to keep my soul in service for your cause, what kind of narration do you mean?' He said, 'It is about their Adhan, Ruku', and sajdah?' I then said, 'They say, "Ubay ibn Ka'b has seen them in a dream."' The Imam said, 'They have spoken a lie. The religion of Allah, the Most Majestic, the Most Glorious, is by far more exalted than being seen in a dream.' The narrator has said that Sadir al-Sayrafiy then said, 'I pray to Allah to keep my soul in service for your cause, please enlighten us about it.' Abu 'Abd Allah, *'Alayhi al-Salam,* then said, 'When Allah, the most Majestic, the most Glorious, took His prophet for a journey to His seven heavens, in the first heaven He granted him blessing and in the second one He taught him his obligations. Allah sent down a carriage that was made of light with forty kinds of the kinds of light therein, surrounded by the Throne of Allah that covers the eyesight of the on-lookers. One of those lights is yellow from which yellowness is yellow. Another one is red because of which redness is red, yet another one is white because of which whiteness is white. The rest of them are like the number of the creatures in the form of light and colors. In that carriage, there are rings and chains of silver. Thereafter He took him up in the heaven. The angels moved in all directions of the heaven and fell down in prostration saying, "He is free of all defects and Most Holy. How similar is this light to the light of our Lord!"' Jibril (Gabriel) then said, 'Allah is greater than can be described, Allah is greater than can be described.' Then the doors of the heaven opened, the angels gathered and saluted to the Holy Prophet in large groups saying, "O Muhammad, how is your brother? When you go back to earth tell that we salute him." The Holy Prophet asked them, "Do you know him?" They replied, "How can we forget him. We were made (by Allah) to establish a covenant and commitment to (follow and) support him; support you and his followers until the Day of Judgment. We look on the faces of his followers five times every day – meaning thereby during the five times Salat (prayer). We say, 'Allahumma Salli 'Ala Muhammad wa 'Ali Muhammad (O Allah grant Muhammad and his family a compensation worthy of their serving Your cause).'" The Messenger of Allah thereafter has said, "Then my Lord granted me forty kinds of kinds of light of which no one resembled the ones given to me before. He gave me more rings and chains and took me to the second heaven. When I arrived near the second heaven's door, the angels moved to all directions of the heaven and fell down in prostration saying, 'Free of all defects and Most Holy is the Lord of the angels and the spirit. How similar is this light to the light of our Lord!' Jibril then said, 'I testify that no one, other than Allah, deserves to be worshipped.' The angels then gathered asking, 'O Jibril, who is this with you?' He replied, 'This is

Muhammad.' They then asked, 'Is he already commissioned to serve as the Messenger of Allah?' He replied, 'Yes, he is commissioned.'" The Holy Prophet has said that they then came to me, welcoming with salutations and saying, "Tell your brother we salute him." I asked them, "Do you know him?" They replied, "How can we forget him? We were made (by Allah) to establish a covenant and commitment to (follow and) support him; support you and his followers until the Day of Judgment. We look on the faces of his followers five times every day" – meaning thereby during the five times Salat (prayer).

"The Messenger of Allah has said, "My Lord then gave me another forty kinds of the kinds of light of which no one was similar to the light given to me before, and increased the number of rings and chains. Then He took me up to the second heaven. The angels moved to all directions in the heaven and fell down in prostration saying, 'Free of all defects and Most Holy is the Lord of the angels and the spirit. What is this light that is so similar to the light of our Lord?' Jibril then said twice, 'I testify that only Allah deserves worship. The angels gathered and said, 'O Jibril, who is he with you?' He (Jibril) replied, 'He is Muhammad.' They asked, 'Is he commissioned (as messenger of Allah)?' Jibril answered, 'Yes, he is commissioned.'" The Holy prophet, has said, "They (angels) came to me as if wanting to hold me in their arms and saluted me and said, 'Convey our salutations to you brother.' I asked, 'Do you know him?' They replied, 'Why we would not know him? We are made to establish a solemn covenant of support in your favor, in his favor and in favor of his followers until the Day of Judgment. We look at the faces of his followers five times every day and night.' They meant thereby the times of each of five daily Salat (prayer)."

The Messenger of Allah has said, "My Lord then gave me another forty kinds of the kinds of light of which no one was similar to the light given to me before. Then He took me up to the third heaven. The angels moved to all directions in the heaven and fell down in prostration saying, 'Free of all defects and Most Holy is the Lord of the angels and the spirit. What is this light that is so similar to the light of our Lord?' Jibril then said twice, 'I testify that Muhammad is the Messenger of Allah.' The angels all gathered and said, 'Welcome, we greet you, O the first. Welcome, O the last, welcome, O the one who brings about resurrection and welcome the one who brings about distribution (distributor of heavens and hell (one of the title of Imam Ali)), Muhammad is the best of the prophets and Ali is the best of the executors of the wills of the prophets of Allah.'"

"The Holy Prophet has said, "They then saluted me and asked about my brother and I said, 'He is on earth. Do you know him?' They replied, 'How can we forget him? We every year perform Hajj of Bayt al-Ma'mur where there is a white board on which there are the names of Muhammad, Ali, al-Hassan, al-Husayn, all A'immah and their followers till the Day of Judgment. We congratulate them every day and night five times' – meaning thereby the five times Salat (prayer) – 'and they wipe their heads with their hands.'" The Holy Prophet has said, "My Lord then increased the number of the kinds of lights for me by another forty kinds of light of which no one resembled the ones given to me before. He then took me higher until I reached the fourth heaven where the angels did not say anything. I heard a low intensity sound as if vibrating inside the chests. The angels then gathered, the doors of the heaven opened and they came to welcome me. Jibril then said, 'Come for Salat (prayer), come for Salat (prayer). Come to wellbeing, come to wellbeing.' The angels then said, 'They are two very familiar sounds.' Jibril then said, 'Salat (prayer) is about to be performed, Salat (prayer) is about to be performed.' The angels said, 'It is for his followers until the Day of Judgment.' The angels then gathered and asked, 'How is your brother?' I replied, 'Do you know him?' They replied, 'We know him and his followers. They are lights around the Throne of Allah and in al-Bayt al-Ma'mur, there is a board of light [on which there is a writing of light] and in this writing there are the names of Muhammad, Ali, al-Hassan, al-Husayn, all 'A'immah and their followers until the Day of Judgment from whom not even one man is increased or decreased. This (written document) is our covenant and a document of commitment which is read to us every Friday.' Thereafter it was said to me, 'Raise your head, O Muhammad.' I raised my head, I saw the levels of the heaven opened up, and the curtains rose. I then was told, 'Look downward.' I looked downward and I saw a house like your house, this one, a sacred precinct like this holy precinct. If I were to drop something down from my hand, it would only fall on this house but not on another place. It then was said to me, 'O Muhammad, this is the holy place and you are the Holy person; for every similitude there is something similar.' Allah then sent Wahy to me, 'O Muhammad go near the S'ad (a fountain at the foot of the Throne) wash the parts of your body that are used during sajdah, cleanse them and perform Salat (prayer) for the sake of your Lord.'" The Messenger of Allah then went near the S'ad, water that flows at the right foot of the Throne. The Messenger of Allah touched the water with his right hand and for this reason Wudu' is with the right hand. Allah, the Most Majestic, the Most Glorious, then sent Wahy to him (Muhammad), "Wash your face; you look to My greatness, then wash your right arm and then your left arm; you receive My words (book) in your hand. Thereafter wipe your head with your hand while still moist with the water of Wudu' and your feet up to your ankles; I like to bless you and allow you to step where no one, other than you, has ever stepped." This is the reason for Adhan and Wudu'. Then Allah, the Most Majestic, the Most Glorious, sent Wahy to him, "O Muhammad, face the direction of the black-stone and speak of My greatness an equal number of times as the number of My curtains." For this reason, the number of Takbir is seven, equal to the number of seven curtains. At the end of the curtains, he commenced Salat (prayer) and for this reason, commencement became a Sunnah (a noble tradition). The curtains are of parallel levels and in between every two level, there are oceans of light. This is the light, which Allah sent to Muhammad, O Allah grant compensation to Muhammad and his family worthy of their services to Your cause. For this reason, the number of (Takbir for) commencement is three because of the opening of the curtains three times. The number of Takbir, (altogether before commencement), are seven and the number of commencement three times. When he completed all

Takbir and (takbir of) commencement, Allah sent him Wahy to call Him by His name and for this reason, the phrase "In the name of Allah, the Beneficent, the Merciful" is placed before every Chapter of the Holy Quran. Then Allah sent him Wahy to praise Him. When he said, "All praise belongs to Allah, Lord of the worlds," the Holy Prophet to himself said, "My thanks (to Allah)." Allah, the Most Majestic, the Most Glorious, sent him Wahy saying, "You just discontinued My praise. Call Me by My name." For this reason the phrase "most Beneficent, most Merciful" has come twice in al-Hamd (Chapter 1 of the Quran). When the Holy Prophet reached the last word in al-Hamd' he said, "All praise belongs to Allah, Lord of the worlds and all thanks." Allah then sent him Wahy, "You discontinued speaking of Me. Call Me by My name." For this reason, at the beginning of every Chapter there is the phrase, "In the name of Allah, the Beneficent, the Merciful." Thereafter Allah, the Most Majestic, the Most Glorious, sent him Wahy, "O Muhammad, read about the relationship of your Lord, the most Holy, the most High.

"(I begin) in the Name of Allah, the Beneficent, the Merciful. (112:1)

(O Muhammad,) you must say, "He is Allah, Who is one only (112:2). Allah is Absolute (112:3). He does not have any child nor is He a child of others (112:4). There is no one equal to Him. (112:5)."

"Then Wahy was held back from him and the Messenger of Allah said, "One the only One who is self-sufficient." Allah then sent him Wahy, "He does not have any child nor is He a child of others (112:4). There is no one equal to Him. (112:5)." Then Wahy was held back from him and the Messenger of Allah said, "Thus is Allah. Thus is Allah, our Lord." When he said this Allah sent him Wahy, "Kneel down for Ruku‘ for the sake of your Lord, O Muhammad." He knelt down for Ruku‘. Allah then sent Wahy, while he was in Ruku‘ position, to say, "My Lord, the great, is free of all defects." He said this three times, Then Allah sent him Wahy, "Raise your head, O Muhammad." The Messenger of Allah did as he was told to do and stood up straight. Allah, the Most Majestic, the Most Glorious, sent Wahy, "Bow down in prostration for the sake of your Lord, O Muhammad." The Messenger of Allah bowed down in prostration, then Allah, the Most Majestic, the Most Glorious, sent Wahy, say, "My Lord, the most High, is free of all defects." He said it three times. Then Allah sent Wahy, "Sit upright, O Muhammad." He did as he was told. When he sat upright he looked at (signs of) His greatness that appeared to him, then, on his own he bowed down in prostration without anyone's command. He said three times, "Allah is free of all defects." Allah then sent Wahy that said, "Stand up straight." He obeyed but he did not see (of the signs) of greatness that had seen before and for this reason in Salat (prayer) every Rak‘at has one Ruku‘ and two sajdah. Allah, the Most Majestic, the Most Glorious, then sent Wahy, "Read All praise belong to Allah, Cherisher of the worlds" (the first Chapter of the Holy Quran) and he read as he had done before. Allah, the Most Majestic, the Most Glorious, then sent Wahy, "Read Chapter 97 of the Holy Quran; this Chapter speaks, of your relationship and the relationship of your family, until the Day of

Judgment." In Ruku' he did just as he had done before, then he did one sajdah. When he raised his head (signs of) greatness appeared to him, he then bowed down in prostration by his own choice, without anyone's command and again he said, "Allah is free of all defects." Allah sent Wahy, "Raise your head, O Muhammad, your Lord has made you steadfast." When he wanted to stand up, he was told, "Sit down in your place, O Muhammad." He then sat down. Allah sent Wahy, "O Muhammad, when I grant you a favor, you should call Me by My name." He was inspired to say, "In the name of Allah, with (the help of) Allah, no one, other than Allah, deserves to be worshipped, and all beautiful names belong to Allah." Then Allah sent Wahy, "O Muhammad, ask compensation for yourself and say, 'Allahumma Salli 'Ala Muhammad wa 'Ali Muhammad (O Allah grant Muhammad and his family a compensation worthy of their serving Your cause),'" which he did as he was told. He then noticed rows of angels and messenger and prophets of Allah and it was said to him, "O Muhammad, salute them." He then said, "I pray to Allah to grant you peace, mercy and blessings." Allah then sent Wahy, "You and your descendents are the peace, salutations, mercy and blessing." Allah then sent Wahy, "Do not pay any attention to the left." The first verse that he heard after Chapter 112 and 97 of the Holy Quran was the verse about the people of the right hand and people of the left hand. For this reason one salutation is toward the direction of Qiblah and for this reason there is Shukr (expression of thanks) in sajdah for Takbir and his saying, "Allah listens to all those who praise Him" because the Holy Prophet heard a great deal of voices of angels saying al-Tasbih, al-Tahmid and al-Tahlil. For this reason he said, "Allah listens to all of those who praise Him." For this reason, in the first and second Rak'at if something invalidating Wudu' takes place, one needs to perform them all over again. This is the first obligation in the prayer at noontime, that is, Salat (prayer) at noontime.'"

H 5659, Ch. 101, h 2

Ali ibn Muhammad has narrated from certain individuals of our people from Ali ibn al-Hakam from Rabi' ibn Muhammad al-Musliy from 'Abd Allah ibn Sulayman al-'Amiriy who has said the following:

"Abu Ja'far, *'Alayhi al-Salam*, has said, 'When the Messenger of Allah was taken up (to heavens) he was commanded to perform Salat (prayer) and he returned with ten Rak'at Salat (prayer) for every day. Each Salat (prayer) consisted of two Rak'at. When al-Hassan and al-Husayn, *'Alayhim al-Salam*, were born, the Messenger of Allah increased seven more Rak'at in thanksgiving to Allah and Allah granted him permission to do so. He did not increase anything to the Morning Salat (prayer) due to the short duration of its time in which time the angels of the night and day also attend it. When Allah commanded him to shorten Salat (prayer) while on a journey, he decreased six Rak'at and did not decrease anything from Maghrib (soon after sunset) Salat (prayer). The rules of how to deal with mistakes in Salat (prayer) apply to the Rak'at that was increased by the Messenger of Allah. Thus, if one faces doubts during the first and second Rak'at, he has to redo his Salat (prayer) from the beginning."

H 5660, Ch. 101, h 3

Ali ibn Ibrahim has narrated from his father from ibn abu 'Umayr from Jamil ibn Darraj from al-'Ai'dh al-Ahmasiy who has said the following:

"Once I visited abu 'Abd Allah, and I wanted to ask him a question about Salat (prayer) during the night and I said, 'You are a *'Alayhi al-Salam*, O son of the Messenger of Allah.' The Imam said, 'Wa 'Alayka al-Salam, yes, by Allah, we are his sons, not of his other relatives.' He said it three times. Then without any initiation from me he said, 'If you come in the presence of Allah with five daily obligatory Salat (prayer), He will not ask you about anything other than these.'"

H 5661, Ch. 101, h 4

Muhammad ibn Yahya has narrated from Ahmad ibn Muhammad from Muhammad ibn Isma'il from abu Isma'il al-Sarraj from Harun ibn Kharijah who has said the following:

"Once I spoke before abu 'Abd Allah, *'Alayhi al-Salam*, about a man of our people and I praised him well. The Imam asked, 'How is his Salat (prayer)?'"

H 5662, Ch. 101, h 5

Muhammad ibn Yahya has narrated from Muhammad ibn Ahmad from al-Sayyariy from al-Fadl ibn abu Qurrah in a in a marfu' manner who has said the following:

"Abu 'Abd Allah, *'Alayhi al-Salam*, was asked about fifty-one Rak'at Salat (prayer) daily. He replied, 'There are twelve hours in the day and twelve in the night. There is one hour between dawn and sunrise. From sunset to disappearing of western brightness is darkness. For every hour there are two Rak'at and one Rak'at for darkness.'"

H 5663, Ch. 101, h 6

Ali ibn Muhammad has narrated in a marfu' manner the following:

"Abu 'Abd Allah, *'Alayhi al-Salam*, was asked this question: 'Why is man told to incline toward the left when facing the direction of Qiblah?' He replied, 'Ka'bah has six limits, four on the left and two on the right; for this reason inclination is toward the left.'"

H 5664, Ch. 101, h 7

Ali ibn Ibrahim has narrated from his father who has narrated from al-Nawfaliy from al-Sakuniy who has said the following:

"Abu 'Abd Allah, *'Alayhi al-Salam*, has said that whoever performs five hundred Rak'at optional Salat (prayer) from one Friday to the next Friday, he can ask Allah whatever he wants except a wish for unlawful matters."

H 5665, Ch. 101, h 8

A number of our people have narrated from Ahmad ibn Muhammad from ibn abu Najran from 'Abd Allah ibn Sinan who has said the following:

"Abu 'Abd Allah, *'Alayhi al-Salam*, has said that a servant of Allah may rise to perform Qada' (compensatory prayer for) an optional Salat (prayer) that was missed in its proper time. The Lord then expresses surprise before the angels saying, 'My angels, look at My servant who makes up for the optional Salat (prayer) missed in time, when I have not even made it obligatory for him.'"

H 5666, Ch. 101, h 9

Muhammad ibn Yahya has narrated from Ahmad ibn Ishaq from Sa'dan ibn Muslim from 'Abd Allah ibn Sinan who has said the following:

"Abu 'Abd Allah, *'Alayhi al-Salam*, has said that nobility of a man is in his Salat (prayer) during the night and his honor is in his keeping away from unsettling people's confidentiality."

H 5667, Ch. 101, h 10

Abu Ali al-Ash'ariy has narrated from Muhammad ibn 'Abd al-Jabbar from Safwan ibn Yahya from Harun ibn Kharijah who has said the following:

"Abu 'Abd Allah, *'Alayhi al-Salam*, has said that for Salat (prayer) an angel is assigned and he has no other task to perform. When one completes a Salat (prayer), the angel takes it and ascends to heaven. If it is of the kind that is accepted, it then is accepted, but if it is of unacceptable kind, it then is said to him, 'Return it to My servant.' He then descends down with that Salat (prayer) and strikes it against his face saying, "Woe is upon you. You continue to have such deeds that make me tired."""

H 5668, Ch. 101, h 11

Muhammad ibn al-Hassan has narrated from Sahl ibn Ziyad from Ja'far ibn Muhammad al-Ash'ariy from al-Qaddah who has said the following:

"Abu 'Abd Allah, *'Alayhi al-Salam*, has said that a man came to the Holy Prophet asking, 'O Messenger of Allah, give me a good advice.' He said, 'You must not give up Salat (prayer) intentionally; the community of Islam is free from all obligations toward one who gives up Salat (prayer) intentionally.'"

H 5669, Ch. 101, h 12

Muhammad ibn Yahya has narrated from Muhammad ibn al-Husayn from Ali ibn Asbat from Muhammad ibn Ali ibn abu 'Abd Allah from abu al-Hassan, *'Alayhi al-Salam*, who has said the following:

"About the words of Allah, the Most Majestic, the Most Glorious, 'They invented monkish manners, even though We had not made it obligatory on them, except to seek the pleasure of Allah' (57: 26), the Imam said that it (pleasure of Allah) is a reference to Salat (prayer) during the night."

H 5670, Ch. 101, h 13

Ali ibn Muhammad has narrated from Sahl ibn Ziyad from Muhammad ibn al-Husayn from certain individuals of Talibiyin, also called R'as al-Madariy who has said the following:

"I heard abu al-Hassan al-Rida, *'Alayhi al-Salam*, say, 'The best place for the feet, during Salat (prayer) is one's shoes (clean Arabic shoes).'"

H 5671, Ch. 101, h 14

A number of our people have narrated from Ahmad ibn Muhammad from ibn abu 'Umayr from Jabir who has said the following:

"Abu Ja'far, *'Alayhi al-Salam*, has said, 'The Messenger of Allah asked Jibril (Gabriel), "Which places are more beloved to Allah, the Most Majestic, the Most Glorious?" He replied, "It is Masjids and most beloved to Allah of its people are those who enter them first and leave last."'"

H 5672, Ch. 101, h 15

Ali ibn Muhammad has narrated from Sahl ibn Ziyad from Muhammad ibn al-Hassan ibn Shammun from 'Abd Allah ibn 'Abd al-Rahman from abu Basir who has said the following:

"Abu 'Abd Allah, *'Alayhi al-Salam*, has said that even on cloudy days when the time for noon Salat (prayer) may remain obscure to people, the Imam knows about the sun. (He (the Imam) knows) what is unseen to people, so he always has the proof which town's people pay attention to the timing of Salat (prayer) and which town's people ignore it."

Chapter 102 - The Masjids in Kufa

H 5673, Ch. 102, h 1

Ali ibn Ibrahim has narrated from his father from 'Amr ibn 'Uthman from Muhammad ibn 'Adhafir from abu Hamzah or from Muhammad ibn Muslim who has said the following:

"In Kufa there are condemned Masjids and blessed Masjids. One of the blessed Masjids is the Masjid of Ghany. By Allah, the direction of Qiblah thereof is balanced and just and its soil is blessed. A believing man established it and before the end of the world, two fountains will gush forth there-from with two gardens nearby. However, the people around it are condemned and the Masjid is taken away from them. Banu Zafar's, al-Sahlah Masjid, is another such Masjid. Another Masjid is in al-Khumrah and yet another one is Al-Ju'fiy Masjid and today it is not their Masjid. He said, 'It is destroyed.'

"Other condemned Masjid are Saqif, al-Ash'ath and Jarir Masjids. There is also Sammak Masjid in al-Khumrah which is built on the grave of a pharaoh of the pharaohs."

H 5674, Ch. 102, h 2

Muhammad ibn Yahya has narrated from al-Hassan ibn Ali ibn 'Abd Allah from 'Ubays ibn Hisham from Salim who has said the following:

"Abu Ja'far, *'Alayhi al-Salam*, has said, 'Four Masjids were rebuilt in Kufa to express happiness for the killing of al-Husayn, *'Alayhi al-Salam*: Al-Ash'ath and Jarir Masjids, Sammak and Shabath ibn Rib'iy's Masjids."

H 5675, Ch. 102, h 3

Muhammad ibn Yahya has narrated from al-Husayn ibn Safwan ibn Yahya from certain individuals of our people who has said the following:

"Abu 'Abd Allah, *'Alayhi al-Salam*, has said that 'Amir al-Mu'minin, *'Alayhi al-Salam*, prohibited performing Salat (prayer) in five Masjids in Kufah, such as al-Ash'ath ibn Qays' Masjid, Jarir ibn 'Abd Allah al-Bajaliy's Masjid, Sammak ibn Makhruma's Masjid, Shabath ibn Rib'iy's Masjid and al-Taym's Masjid."

According to a Hadith from abu Basir, one such Masjid is banu al-Sayyid Masjid, banu 'Abd Allah ibn Darime Masjid, Ghany Masjid, Sammak' Masjid, Thaqif's Masjid and al-Ash'ath's Masjid."

Chapter 103 - Excellence of the Great Masjid of Kufah, Excellence of Performing Salat (prayer) and the Loveable places Therein

H 5676, Ch. 103, h 1

Muhammad ibn al-Hassan and Ali ibn Muhammad have narrated from Sahl ibn Ziyad from 'Amr ibn 'Uthman from Muhammad ibn 'Abd Allah al-Khazzaz from Harun ibn Kharijah who has said the following:

"Once abu 'Abd Allah, *'Alayhi al-Salam*, asked me, 'O Harun ibn Kharijah, how far away do you live from the Masjid of Kufah? Is it one mile?' I replied, 'No, it is less than a mile.' He then asked, 'Do you perform all Salat (prayers) there?' I replied, 'No, I do not perform all Salat (prayers) there.' He then said, 'If I were nearby I hope I would not miss performing any Salat (prayer) therein. Do you know what is the excellence of Salat (prayer) performed therein? There is no believer of good deeds or prophet who has not performed Salat (prayer) in the Masjid of Kufah. Even when the Messenger of Allah was on his night journey, Jibril asked him, "Do you know where your are, O Messenger of Allah? At this hour you are across the Masjid of Kufah." He said, "Ask my Lord for permission so I can go there and perform two Rak'at Salat (prayer) therein." He asked Allah, the Most Majestic, the Most Glorious, for permission, which was granted. On the right side of this Masjid, there is a garden of the gardens of paradise, in the middle of it, there is a garden of the gardens of paradise and behind it, there is a garden of the gardens of paradise. Performing one obligatory Salat (prayer) in it is equal to one thousand Salat (prayer). One optional Salat (prayer) in it is equal to five hundred Salat (prayer). Sitting in it without performing any Salat (prayer) or speaking of Allah is worshipping. Had people known its excellence they would go to it even crawling.' Sahl has said that narrators other than 'Amr have said that performing obligatory Salat (prayer) in it is equal to performing Hajj and performing optional Salat (prayer) is equal to 'Umrah."

H 5677, Ch. 103, h 2

A number of our people have narrated from Ahmad ibn Muhammad from Yusuf ibn Ya'qub ibn 'Abd Allah from the sons of abu Fatimah from Isma'il ibn Zayd, Mawla 'Abd Allah ibn al-Kahiliy who has said the following:

"Once, a man came to 'Amir al-Mu'minin, when he was in the Masjid of Kufah. He said, 'You are a *'Alayhi al-Salam*, His mercy and blessing, O 'Amir al-Mu'minin.' 'Amir al-Mu'minin responded to his salutation. The man then said, 'I pray to Allah to keep my soul in service for your cause, I want to visit al-Aqsa' Masjid so I have come to say farewell to you.' The Imam asked, 'What do you think you will receive from your visit?' He replied, 'I pray to Allah to keep my soul in service for your cause, I expect to receive excellence.' The Imam then said, 'Sell your horse, use your supplies and perform Salat (prayer) in this Masjid; performing one obligatory Salat (prayer) in it is equal to one accepted Hajj. Performing one optional Salat (prayer) in it is equal to performing one accepted 'Umrah. The goodness from there reaches up to twelve miles. Its right side houses goodness but its left side lodges wickedness. At its center, there is a fountain of oil, a fountain of milk, a fountain of water for believers to drink and a fountain of purifying water for believing people. From there the Ark of Noah set sail. Also, (unfortunately) Nasr, Yaghuth and Ya'uq were placed there. Seventy prophets and seventy successors of prophets, of whom one is myself [he pointed to his own chest], performed Salat (prayer) there. Every person, suffering from hardship, appealing for his wish to come true has found Allah make his wishes come true and remove his hardships.'"

H 5678, Ch. 103, h 3

Muhammad ibn Yahya has narrated from certain individuals of our people from al-Hassan ibn Ali from ibn abu Hamzah from abu Basir who have said the following:

"I heard abu 'Abd Allah, *'Alayhi al-Salam*, saying, 'The Masjid of Kufah is a very good Masjid. One thousand prophets and one thousand executors of the wills of the prophets have performed Salat (prayer) in it. The oven (of Noah) was there wherefrom water gushed forth and the Ark was carved there-from. Its right side houses the matters of the pleasure of Allah, its center houses a garden of the gardens of paradise and its left side lodges evil planners.' I (the narrator) asked abu Basir, 'What is meant by evil-planning?' He replied, 'It is a reference to the houses of the sultans (kings). 'Amir al-Mu'minin, would stand at the door of the Masjid then throw an arrow, which would reach the places of the sellers of dates and then say, "That is part of the Masjid." He would also say, "What is reduced from the basis of the Masjid is like what is reduced from its square."'"

H 5679, Ch. 103, h 4

Ali ibn Muhammad has narrated from Sahl ibn Ziyad from Ali ibn Asbat from Ali ibn Shajarah from certain individuals of sons of Mitham who has said the following:

"'Amir al-Mu'minin, *'Alayhi al-Salam*, would perform Salat (prayer) toward the seventh pillar which is before al-Kindah door with a remaining distance of the size of a goat between him and that pillar."

H 5680, Ch. 103, h 5

Ali ibn Muhammad has narrated from Sahl ibn Ziyad from ibn Asbat who has said that someone other than the narrator of the above Hadith narrated to me the following:

"He (the Imam), *'Alayhi al-Salam*, has said, 'Every night sixty thousand angels descend down to the seventh pillar to perform Salat (prayer), of which no one up to the Day of Judgment returns again."

H 5681, Ch. 103, h 6

Muhammad ibn Yahya has narrated from Muhammad ibn Isma'il and Ahmad ibn Muhammad from Ali ibn al-Hakam from Sufyan al-Simt who has said the following:

"Abu 'Abd Allah, *'Alayhi al-Salam*, has said, 'When you enter the Masjid through the second door on the right of the Masjid, count five pillars, two in shadow and three in the open compound, near the third is the station of Ibrahim, Allah has granted him peace. It is the fifth from the wall.' He (narrator) has said, 'During the rule of abu al-'Abbas, abu 'Abd Allah, entered through al-fil door, bore to the left on entering the door and performed Salat (prayer) near the fourth pillar which is opposite to the fifth pillar.' I then asked, 'Is this the pillar of Ibrahim?' He replied, 'Yes, it is.'"

H 5682, Ch. 103, h 7
Ali ibn Muhammad has narrated from Sahl from ibn Asbat in a marfu' manner who has said the following:
"Abu 'Abd Allah, *'Alayhi al-Salam,* has said that the seventh pillar counting from Kindah doors in the compound is the station of Ibrahim and the fifth is the station of Jibril (Gabriel), Allah has granted him peace."

H 5683, Ch. 103, h 8
Muhammad ibn Yahya has narrated from Muhammad ibn al-Husayn from Muhammad ibn Isma'il ibn Bazi'a from abu Isma'il al-Sarraj who has said the following:
"Mu'awiyah ibn Wahab, holding my hand, said to me, 'Abu Hamzah holding my hand said to me, "Asbagh ibn Nubatah holding my hand showed me the seventh pillar and said, 'This is the station of `Amir al-Mu'minin, *'Alayhi al-Salam.*'"' He (the narrator) has said, 'Al-Hassan ibn Ali, *'Alayhi al-Salam,* would perform Salat (prayer) near the fifth pillar. When `Amir al-Mu'minin passed away, al-Hassan, *'Alayhi al-Salam,* performed Salat (prayer) at that place and it is from the side of Kindah door.'"

H 5684, Ch. 103, h 9
Ali ibn Ibrahim has narrated from Salih al-Sindiy from Ja'far ibn Bashir from abu 'Abd al-Rahman al-Hadhdha' from abu 'Usamah from abu 'Ubaydah who has said the following:
"Abu Ja'far, *'Alayhi al-Salam,* has said, 'The Masjid of Kufah is a garden of the gardens of paradise. One thousand seventy prophets performed Salat (prayer) in it. Its right side houses blessing and its left side lodges wickedness. In it are the staff of Moses, the squash plant (mentioned in the holy Quran) and the ring of Sulayman (Solomon). The oven of Noah from which water gushed forth was there and the Ark was carved there from. It is the center of Babylon and the gathering place of prophets."

Chapter 104 - Al-Sahlah Masjid

H 5685, Ch. 104, h 1
A number of our people have narrated from Ahmad ibn Muhammad from Ahmad ibn abu Dawud from 'Abd Allah ibn Aban who has said the following:
"Once, we visited abu 'Abd Allah, *'Alayhi al-Salam,* and he asked us, 'Does anyone of you have anything of the knowledge of my uncle, Zayd ibn Ali?' A man from the group said, 'I have something of the knowledge of your uncle. Once, we were in the presence of Imam one night in the house of Mu'awiyah ibn Ishaq al-Ansariy when he said, "Allow us to visit al-Sahlah Masjid to perform Salat (prayer)."' Abu 'Abd Allah, *'Alayhi al-Salam,* then asked, 'Did he do so?' He (the man) replied, 'Something came up that prevented him from visiting al-Sahlah Masjid.' The Imam then said, 'By Allah, had he sought refuge with Allah therein for a year he would have given him such refuge. You should take notice that it is the house of prophet Idris. Therein he did his sewing works. From this place Ibrahim started his journey to Yemen, where al-'Amaliqah people has settled down. Dawud began his move against Jalut (Goliath) from this place. In it, there is the green stone on which every prophet's picture exists. From under this stone the clay of every prophet was taken and it is the place

where the rider disembarks for rest.' It was asked, 'Who is the rider?' The Imam replied, 'He is al-Khadir.'"

H 5686, Ch. 104, h 2

Muhammad ibn Yahya has narrated from Ali ibn al-Hassan ibn Ali from 'Uthman from Salih ibn abu al-Aswad who has said the following:

"Abu 'Abd Allah, *'Alayhi al-Salam*, when al-Sahlah Masjid was mentioned, said, 'It is the dwelling of our companion when he rises (with Divine Authority).'"

H 5687, Ch. 104, h 3

It is a narration from him (narrator of previous Hadith) by 'Amr ibn 'Uthman from Hassan ibn Bakr from 'Abd al-Rahman ibn Sa'id al-Khazzaz who has said the following:

"Abu 'Abd Allah, *'Alayhi al-Salam*, has said that in al-Kufah there is a Masjid called al-Sahlah Masjid. 'Had my uncle, Zayd, visited it to perform Salat (prayer) and asked Allah to grant him refuge, He would have granted him refuge for twenty years. In it is the place where the rider disembarks for rest and the house of prophet Idris. There has never been anyone suffering hardships who visited this, performed two Rak'at Salat (prayer) between the two Salat (prayer) after sunset and appealed to Allah for help whose wishes Allah did not make to come true and remove his hardships.'"

"It is narrated that the limits of al-Sahlah Masjid extend up to al-Rawha."

The end of the Book of al-Salat of al-Kafiy compiled by abu Ja'far Muhammad ibn Ya'qub al-Kulayniy (rh) followed by the Book of al-Zakat

In the Name of Allah, the Beneficient, the Merciful

Part Five: The Book of al-Zakat

Chapter 1 - The Obligation of al-Zakat (charity) and Necessary Payments from Properties

H 5688, Ch. 1, h 1

Ali ibn Ibrahim has narrated from his father from Hammad ibn 'Isa from Hariz from Zurarah and Muhammad ibn Muslim who has said the following:

"Once we both asked abu 'Abd Allah, *'Alayhi al-Salam*, about the words of Allah, most Majestic, most Glorious, in the following verse of the Holy Quran. 'Charity funds (zakat) are only for the poor, the destitute, and the tax collectors. (It is also for the) people whose hearts are inclined (toward Islam), the slaves, those who cannot pay their debts, for the cause of Allah, and for those who have become needy on a journey. Paying zakat is an obligation that Allah has decreed. Allah is All-knowing and All-wise.'(9:60) 'Can all the people and cases mentioned in this verse receive zakat even though they may not believe (in Divine Authority of `A'immah)?' He replied, 'The Imam gives charity to all of them; they announce their obedience to him.' I (the narrator) then asked, 'Even if they do not acknowledge (his Divine Authority)?' He then said, 'O Zurarah, were he to give charity only to those who acknowledge (his Divine Authority) and not to others, there would remain no one or cases as recipient of (zakat) charity. He gives charity to those who do not acknowledge (his divine authority) so they incline to religion to become strong (in faith). However, today you and your friends give zakat only to those who acknowledge (our Divine Authority) if you find one who believes (in our Divine Authority).' He then said, 'The share of those who show interest in Islam and the share of slaves to be emancipated are of general nature and other shares in a charity are for certain people but not for everyone.' I (the narrator) then asked, 'What happens if there is no recipient of zakat?' He replied, 'Allah, the Most Majestic, the Most Glorious, has not made any charity compulsory without any recipient.' I (the narrator) then asked, 'What happens if charity is not enough?' He replied, 'The amount of compulsory charity Allah has sanctioned in the properties of affluent people for the poor ones is enough. If He knew that it is not enough, He would sanction a greater amount. Shortages do not come from the amount Allah has made compulsory but it comes from non-payment. There are those who do not pay what belongs to the needy, thus, shortages are not due to the degree of Allah's sanctioned charity for the needy. Had people paid the rights of the needy, they would have lived happy.'"

H 5689, Ch. 1, h 2

A number of our people have narrated from Sahl ibn Ziyad and Ahmad ibn Muhammad all from ibn Mahbub from 'Abd Allah ibn Sinan who has said the following:

"Abu 'Abd Allah, has said that once this verse of the Holy Quran was revealed to the Messenger of Allah. 'Collect religious tax (zakat) from them to purify and cleanse them . . .' (9:103) It was revealed in the month of Ramadan, the Messenger of Allah commanded his announcer to announce among people that Allah has made it compulsory on you to pay zakat (charity) just as He has made obligatory upon you to perform Salat (prayer). Allah, the Most Majestic, the Most Glorious, has made it compulsory to pay zakat on gold and silver; and on cattle: camel, cows, sheep; and on grains: wheat, barley, dates and raisins. The announcer announced it in the month of Ramadan. He exempted them from payment of zakat on other forms of properties.' The Imam then said, 'Besides, He did not make it compulsory to pay zakat on their properties before the end of the year. They completed fasting. He then commanded his announcer to announce among the Muslims, "O Muslims, pay zakat on your properties; your Salat (prayer) will be accepted."' He said, 'Then he (the Messenger of Allah) sent his land assessor and tax collectors among people to collect zakat.'"

H 5690, Ch. 1, h 3

A number of our people have narrated from Sahl ibn Ziyad from Ahmad ibn Muhammad ibn abu Nasr from Hammad ibn 'Uthman from Rifa'ah ibn Musa who has said the following:

"I heard abu 'Abd Allah, *'Alayhi al-Salam*, say, 'No other obligation that Allah has made compulsory upon this nation is of more intensity than zakat. In the matter of zakat most of them face their destruction."

H 5691, Ch. 1, h 4

Ali ibn Ibrahim has narrated from his father from 'Abd Allah ibn al-Mughirah from ibn Muskan and more than one person who have said the following:

"Abu 'Abd Allah, *'Alayhi al-Salam*, has said that Allah, the Most Majestic, the Most Glorious, has assigned in properties of affluent people a share for the needy that is sufficient to meet their need; otherwise, He would have increased such share. Shortages come from non-payment of those who do not pay."

H 5692, Ch. 1, h 5

Ali ibn Ibrahim has narrated from his father from Hammad ibn 'Isa from Hariz from Muhammad ibn Muslim and abu Basir, Burayd and Fudayl who have said the following:

"Abu Ja'far and abu 'Abd Allah, *'Alayhim al-Salam*, have said that Allah has made zakat obligatory along with Salat (prayer)."

H 5693, Ch. 1, h 6

Ali ibn Ibrahim has narrated from his father from Isma'il ibn Marrar from Mubarak al-'Aqarqufiy who has said the following:

"Abu al-Hassan, *'Alayhi al-Salam*, has said, 'Allah, the Most Majestic, the Most Glorious, has made zakat as means of living for the needy and to increase your properties.'"

H 5694, Ch. 1, h 7

A number of our people have narrated from Ahmad ibn Muhammad from al-Husayn ibn Sa'id from al-Nadr ibn al-Suwayd from 'Abd Allah ibn Sinan who has said the following:

"Abu 'Abd Allah, *'Alayhi al-Salam*, has said that Allah, the Most Majestic, the Most Glorious, has made paying zakat compulsory as He has made performing of Salat (prayer) obligatory. If a man pays zakat publicly, it is not a blamable thing to do. It is because Allah, the Most Majestic, the Most Glorious, has assigned a share in the properties of affluent people for the needy enough to meet their needs. If it were in His knowledge that such share is not enough for them, He would have increased it. What the needy people face is because of withholding payment of zakat which is denying the rights of the needy, not because of the degree of the amount made compulsory."

H 5695, Ch. 1, h 8

Muhammad ibn Yahya has narrated from Ahmad ibn Muhammad from 'Uthman ibn 'Isa from Sama'ah ibn Mehran who has said the following:

"Abu 'Abd Allah, *'Alayhi al-Salam*, has said that Allah, the Most Majestic, the Most Glorious, has made it compulsory on affluent people to pay the share of the needy people from their properties and the affluent people will not be praised unless they pay the share of needy people. This share is zakat. Paying zakat protects their lives and because of paying zakat, they are called Muslims. However, Allah, the Most Majestic, the Most Glorious, has assigned other shares in the properties of the affluent people, which are other than zakat. This is what a man considers necessary to pay from his property as Allah, the Most Majestic, the Most Glorious, has mentioned in His book: 'They are those who assign a certain share of their property (70:24) for the needy and the deprived (70:25).' The 'certain share' is something other than zakat. It is what one considers necessary to pay to the needy. He must, however, do so according to his financial abilities and then pay what he has considered necessary. He may pay every day, every Friday or every month. Allah, the Most Majestic, the Most Glorious, has also said, 'The charitable men and women who give a virtuous loan to Allah will receive double from Him in addition to their honorable reward.' (57:18) This also is something other than zakat. Allah, the Most Majestic, the Most Glorious, has said again, '. . . My believing servants . . . spend for the cause of their Lord, both in private and in public, out of what We have given them. . . .' (14:31) Assistance is a form of loan, borrowing a certain item or lending a helping hand are also of matters Allah, the Most Majestic, the Most Glorious, has made necessary and they are other than zakat. Allah, the Most Majestic, the Most Glorious, has said, 'Those who fulfill their promise to and covenant with Allah (13:20), who maintain all the proper relations that Allah has commanded them to maintain, who have fear of their Lord and the hardships of the Day of Judgment' (13:21). Those who pay what Allah has made compulsory have fulfilled their duties and have paid thanks to Allah for His bounties in his properties. In this way he has thanked Allah for what Allah has granted him and has given him preference over others as wealthier than others and has given him the opportunity to fulfill his duty toward Allah, the Most Majestic, the Most Glorious, and has helped him to do so."

H 5696, Ch. 1, h 9

Ali ibn Ibrahim has narrated from his father from al-Husayn ibn Sa'id from Fadalah ibn Ayyub from abu al-Maghra' from abu Basir who has said the following:

"Once we were in the presence of abu 'Abd Allah, *'Alayhi al-Salam*. With us, there were certain wealthier persons. People spoke about zakat. Abu 'Abd Allah,

'Alayhi al-Salam, said, 'One does not become very much praiseworthy for paying zakat, although it is something purifying. Obviously, he has only protected his life and because of such payment is called a Muslim. Were he not to pay zakat his Salat (prayer) would not receive acceptance. However, on your properties, payments other than zakat are also due.' I (the narrator) than asked, 'I pray to Allah to keep you well, what other payments, besides zakat, are due on our properties?' He replied, 'Allah is free of all defects. Have you not heard the words of Allah, the Most Majestic, the Most Glorious, in His book, "They are those who assign a certain share of their property (70:24) for the needy and the deprived." (70:25) I (the narrator) then asked, 'What is the "certain share," in our properties, due on us?' He replied, 'It is the amount that one pays from his property every day, or every Friday or every month in small amounts or large amounts and continues doing so. It also is mentioned in the words of Allah, the Most Majestic, the Most Glorious, ". . . and refuse to help the needy." (107:7) This kind of help is what one considers necessary to pay as a loan, or a favor or household items borrowed and of this kind is zakat.' I then said, 'We have such neighbors that on lending things to them they may break or destroy them. Is it alright if we deny them such things?' He replied, 'In such case you are not blamed.' I then asked about the words of Allah, 'They feed the destitute, orphans, and captives for the love of Allah. . .' (76:8) He said, 'That is not of zakat.' I then asked about the words of Allah, Allah, most Majestic, most Glorious, '. . . they spent their property during the night and day, publicly or privately' (2:273) He said, 'It is not of zakat.' I then asked about the words of Allah, Allah, most Majestic, most Glorious, 'It is alright if you pay charity publicly but if you pay to the needy privately it is better for you.' (2:270) The Imam said, 'It is not of zakat. Keeping good relations with your relatives is not of zakat.'"

H 5697, Ch. 1, h 10

Ali ibn Muhammad has narrated from Ahmad ibn Muhammad from ibn Khalid from 'Uthman from ibn 'Isa from Isma'il ibn Jabir who has said the following:

"In the following words of Allah, the Most Majestic, the Most Glorious, there is the expression, 'certain share': 'They are those who assign a certain share of their property (70:24) for the needy and the deprived.' (70:25) Whether 'certain share' stands for zakat or something else, the Imam said, 'It is the property that Allah gives to an affluent person who pays a thousand or two or three or less or more to keep good relations with relatives or relieve the burdens of his people.'"

H 5698, Ch. 1, h 11

It is a narration from him (narrator of previous Hadith) by Ahmad ibn Muhammad from al-Hassan ibn Mahbub from 'Abd al-Rahman ibn al-Hajjaj from al-Qasim ibn 'Abd al-Rahman al-Ansariy who has said the following:

"I heard abu Ja'far, *'Alayhi al-Salam*, say, 'Once a man came to my father, Ali ibn al-Husayn, *'Alayhi al-Salam*, and said, "Please tell me about the expression 'certain share'. The words of Allah, the Most Majestic, the Most Glorious, say, 'They are those who assign a certain share of their property (70:24) for the needy and the deprived.' (70:25) What is this 'certain share'?"' Ali ibn al-Husayn, *'Alayhi al-Salam*, said to him, 'The 'certain share' is what a man pays from his property. It is not zakat or obligatory charity.' He then asked, 'If it is not of zakat or obligatory charity, then what is it?' The Imam replied, 'It is what a person pays from his property in small or larger amounts according to his ability.' The man then asked, 'What does he do with it?' The Imam replied, 'He thereby keeps good relation with relatives, entertains guest, relieves a burden, keeps good relations with a brother in faith, for the sake of Allah or fends off thereby a misfortune.' The man then said, 'Allah knows best where to keep (whom to entrust with) His message.'"

H 5699, Ch. 1, h 12

It is a narration from him (narrator of previous Hadith) by ibn Faddal from Safwan al-Jammal who has said the following:

"In the following words of Allah there is the expression 'deprived': 'They are those who assign a certain share of their property (70:24) for the needy and the deprived.' (70:25) Abu 'Abd Allah, *'Alayhi al-Salam,* has said, '"Deprived" is a professional who no longer is able to benefit from the labor of his hands in business transactions.'"

"In another Hadith it is narrated from abu Ja'far and abu 'Abd Allah, *'Alayhim al-Salam,* who have said, 'Deprived is a person who has no problem in his understanding but is very tight in means of living.'"

H 5700, Ch. 1, h 13

Ali ibn Muhammad has narrated from those whom he has mentioned (in his book) from Muhammad ibn Khalid from Muhammad ibn Sinan from al-Mufaddal who has said the following:

"Once I was in the presence of abu 'Abd Allah, *'Alayhi al-Salam,* when a man asked him, 'For how much property is it compulsory to pay zakat?' The Imam asked him, 'Do you mean thereby the apparent or unapparent zakat?' He replied, 'I mean both kinds.' The Imam said, 'The apparent kind is twenty-five due upon every one thousand. The unapparent kind is what you should not spare from your brother what he needs more than you do.'"

H 5701, Ch. 1, h 14

A number of our people have narrated from Ahmad ibn abu 'Abd Allah from al-Hassan ibn Mahbub from Malik ibn 'Atiyyah from 'Amir ibn Juza'ah who has said the following:

"Once a man came in the presence of abu 'Abd Allah, *'Alayhi al-Salam,* and appealed, 'O abu 'Abd Allah, grant me a loan until I am able to pay back.' Abu 'Abd Allah, *'Alayhi al-Salam,* asked, 'Do you want to borrow until the time you harvest your plantation?' The man answered, 'No, by Allah, (I do not have any plantation).' The Imam then asked, 'Do you want until you make a business gain?' He replied 'No, by Allah, (I do not have any business).' The Imam then asked, 'Do you want to borrow until you receive profit from a contract you have made?' He replied, 'No, by Allah, (I do not have any such contract)' Abu 'Abd Allah, *'Alayhi al-Salam,* then said, 'You then are of those for whom Allah has set a share in our properties.' He then asked to bring for him a bag with dirhams in it. He then picked up a handful of money there-from and gave it to him saying, 'Observe piety before Allah. Do not spend it extravagantly or miserly but spend it in a balanced manner. Spending in a wasteful manner is extravagance and Allah, the Most Majestic, the Most Glorious, forbids it, "Do not squander your belongings wastefully. . . (17:27)'"

"Al-Hassan ibn Mahbub has narrated from Sa'dan ibn Muslim from abu 'Abd Allah, *'Alayhi al-Salam,* a similar Hadith."

H 5702, Ch. 1, h 15

Ahmad ibn Muhammad ibn 'Abd Allah and others have narrated from Ahmad ibn abu 'Abd Allah from his father from 'Abd Allah ibn al-Qasim from a man of the people of Sabat who has said the following:

"Abu 'Abd Allah, *'Alayhi al-Salam,* once said to 'Ammar al-Sabatiy, 'O 'Ammar, do you own a great wealth?' He replied, 'Yes, I pray to Allah to keep my soul in service for your cause.' The Imam then asked, 'Do you pay what Allah has made compulsory in the form of zakat?' He replied, 'Yes, I pay.' The Imam then asked, 'Do you pay "certain share" out of your wealth?' He replied, 'Yes, I pay.' The Imam then asked, 'Do you maintain good relations with your relatives?' He replied, 'Yes, I do so.' The Imam asked, 'Do you keep good relations with your brothers in faith?' He replied, 'Yes, I do so.' The Imam then said, 'O 'Ammar, wealth goes away, bodies become old but deeds remain. The One who rewards for good deeds lives forever and never dies. O 'Ammar, what you save as good deeds do not leave you behind and what you postponed never come to join you.'"

H 5703, Ch. 1, h 16

Ali ibn Ibrahim has narrated from Ahmad ibn Muhammad from Muhammad ibn Khalid from 'Abd Allah ibn Yahya from 'Abd Allah ibn Muskan from abu Basir who has said the following:

"I asked abu 'Abd Allah, *'Alayhi al-Salam,* about the words of Allah, the Most Majestic, the Most Glorious, 'Charities are for the poor and the destitute. . .' (9:60) The Imam said, 'Poor is one who does not ask people for help, destitute is one of a worse condition, and hopeless is even of a worse condition. Paying, what Allah, the Most Majestic, the Most Glorious, has made compulsory upon you, publicly is better than paying privately. It is better to pay privately what is paid voluntarily. A person's carrying zakat that he must pay, on his shoulders that he then distributes in public is just fine and beautiful.'"

H 5704, Ch. 1, h 17

Ali ibn Ibrahim has narrated from his father from ibn abu 'Umayr from Ishaq ibn 'Ammar who has said the following:

"Abu 'Abd Allah, *'Alayhi al-Salam,* about the words of Allah, the Most Majestic, the Most Glorious, '. . . If you pay it privately to the needy, it is better for you. . . .' (2:273), has said, 'This payment is a payment other than compulsory zakat which is paid publicly and not privately.'"

H 5705, Ch. 1, h 18

Muhammad ibn Yahya has narrated from Muhammad ibn al-Hassan from Safwan ibn Yahya from al-'Ala' ibn Razin from Muhammad ibn Muslim from one of them (the two Imam):

"Someone asked the Imam, *'Alayhi al-Salam,* about poor and destitute. He replied, 'Poor is one who does not ask for help. Destitute is of a worse condition and he asks for help.'"

H 5706, Ch. 1, h 19

A number of our people have narrated from Ahmad ibn Muhammad ibn 'Isa from Ahmad ibn Muhammad ibn abu Nasr who has said the following:

"I mentioned something before al-Rida, *'Alayhi al-Salam*, and he said, 'Exercise patience. I hope Allah will do something good for you if He so wills.' He then said, 'By Allah, He does not delay anything from a believer of the worldly things unless it is better for him than to do it for him quickly.' He then belittled worldly things and said, 'It is worthless.' He then said, 'An affluent person faces the danger of owing compulsory payments of the rights of Allah. By Allah, I may receive bounties from Allah, most Majestic, most Glorious, and I continue to be afraid' – moving his hand- 'until I pay off what Allah has made compulsory upon me to pay.' I then said, 'I pray to Allah to keep my soul in service for your cause, why you fear with such a prominent position before Allah?' He replied, 'Yes, I do and I am thankful to Allah for what He has granted me.'"

Chapter 2 - Refusal to Pay Zakat

H 5707, Ch. 2, h 1

Ali ibn Ibrahim has narrated from his father from ibn abu 'Umayr from 'Abd Allah ibn Muskan from Muhammad ibn Muslim who has said the following:

"Once I asked abu 'Abd Allah, *'Alayhi al-Salam*, about the following words of Allah, most Majestic, most Glorious, '. . . whatever they are avaricious about will be tied to their necks on the Day of Judgment. . .' (3:180) The Imam said, 'O abu Muhammad, if one refuses to pay zakat Allah, the Most Majestic, the Most Glorious, on the Day of Judgment will make a serpent of fire to curl around his neck and bite his flesh until He completes His judging all people.' He then said, 'The words of Allah, most Majestic, most Glorious, "Whatever they are avaricious about will be tied to their necks" is a reference to their avarice in paying zakat.'"

H 5708, Ch. 2, h 2

Ali ibn Ibrahim has narrated from his father from Isma'il ibn Marrar from Yunus from ibn Muskan in a marfu' manner from a man who has said the following:

"Abu Ja'far, *'Alayhi al-Salam*, has said, 'Once, when, in the Masjid, the Messenger of Allah asked several people to stand up. They numbered five people and then he asked them, 'Leave our Masjid. Do not perform Salat (prayer) here; you do not pay zakat.'"

H 5709, Ch. 2, h 3

Yunus has narrated from Ali ibn abu Hamzah from abu Basir who has said the following:

"Abu 'Abd Allah, *'Alayhi al-Salam*, has said that if one refuses to pay even a Qirat of zakat, he is not a believer or a Muslim and this is mentioned in the words of Allah, most Majestic, most Glorious, as follows: '. . . Lord, allow me to go back so I can do good deeds in what I have left. . . .'(23:99-100)"

"In another Hadith it is said, 'His Salat (prayer) is not accepted.'"

H 5710, Ch. 2, h 4

Yunus has narrated from 'Abd Allah ibn Sinan who has said the following:

"Abu 'Abd Allah, *'Alayhi al-Salam*, has said that the Messenger of Allah has said, 'Whoever refuses to pay zakat due on any produce of his palm trees, plantations or vineyard, Allah makes that land up to seven levels to hang from his neck until the Day of Judgment.'"

H 5711, Ch. 2, h 5

A number of our people have narrated from Sahl ibn Ziyad from Muhammad ibn al-Hassan ibn Shammun from 'Abd Allah ibn 'Abd al-Rahman from Malik ibn 'Attiyyah from Aban ibn Taghlib who has said the following:

"Abu 'Abd Allah, *'Alayhi al-Salam*, said to me, 'Allah has made it lawful, in Islam, to destroy two kinds of lives. No one can issue judgment about it until the rise of a person from our Ahl al-Bayt. When Allah, the Most Majestic, the Most Glorious, allows this person from our Ahl al-Bayt, he then judges them according to the laws of Allah without calling any witness to testify. One such life is the life of an already married fornicator who is stoned to death and one who refuses to pay zakat due on him who is beheaded (for this crime).'"

"A number of our people have narrated from Ahmad ibn Muhammad ibn Khalid from Muhammad ibn Ali from Musa ibn Sa'dan from 'Abd Allah ibn al-Qasim from Malik ibn 'Atiyyah from Aban ibn Taghlib from abu 'Abd Allah, *'Alayhi al-Salam* a similar Hadith."

H 5712, Ch. 2, h 6

Humayd ibn Ziyad has narrated from al-Khashshab from ibn Baqqah from Mu'adh ibn Thabit from 'Amr ibn Jumay' who has said the following:

"Abu 'Abd Allah, *'Alayhi al-Salam*, has said that there is no one who pays his zakat who then experiences any decrease in his wealth. Also no increase takes place in the wealth of one who refuses to pay zakat which is due on him."

H 5713, Ch. 2, h 7

Ali ibn Ibrahim has narrated from his father from Hammad ibn 'Isa from Hariz from 'Ubayd ibn Zurarah who has said the following:

"I heard abu 'Abd Allah, *'Alayhi al-Salam*, say, 'If one dirham of rights of a person is denied it can cause double of this much to be spent elsewhere. If anyone refuses to pay a right which is due on his wealth, Allah, the Most Majestic, the Most Glorious, because of this will cause a serpent of fire to curl around him on the Day of Judgment.'"

H 5714, Ch. 2, h 8

Ali ibn Ibrahim has narrated from his father from ibn abu 'Umayr from abu Ayyub from abu Basir who has said the following:

"Abu 'Abd Allah, *'Alayhi al-Salam*, has said that the Messenger of Allah has said, 'Condemned and condemned indeed is one who refuses to pay zakat.'"

H 5715, Ch. 2, h 9

Ali ibn Ibrahim has narrated from his father from ibn Faddal from Ali ibn 'Uqbah from abu al-Hassan, the first, *'Alayhi al-Salam*, who has said the following:

"If one pays, completely, the amount of zakat which is due on his wealth to the proper recipient, he is not asked how he has earned his wealth."

H 5716, Ch. 2, h 10

Muhammad ibn Yahya has narrated from Ahmad ibn Muhammad ibn 'Isa from ibn Mehran from ibn Muskan from Muhammad ibn Muslim who has said the following:

"I asked abu Ja'far, *'Alayhi al-Salam,* about the words of Allah, the Most Majestic, the Most Glorious, '. . . whatever they are avaricious about will be tied to their necks on the Day of Judgment. . .' (3:180). The Imam said, 'O abu Muhammad, if one refuses to pay zakat, Allah, the Most Majestic, the Most Glorious, on the Day of Judgment will make a serpent of fire to curl around his neck and bite his flesh until He completes His judging all people.' He then said, 'The words of Allah, "Whatever they are avaricious about will be tied to their necks" are a reference to their avarice in paying zakat.'""

H 5717, Ch. 2, h 11

Ahmad ibn Muhammad has narrated from Ali ibn al-Husayn from Wahab ibn Hafs from abu Basir who has said the following:

"I heard abu 'Abd Allah, *'Alayhi al-Salam,* say, 'One who refuses to pay zakat, on the time of his death asks to be returned to life again and this is referred to in the words of Allah, the Most Majestic, the Most Glorious, ". . . Lord, allow me to go back so I can do good deeds in what I have left. . ."'" (23:99-100)

H 5718, Ch. 2, h 12

A number of our people have narrated from Sahl ibn Ziyad from Ali ibn Hassa'n from certain individuals of his people who have said the following:

"Abu 'Abd Allah, *'Alayhi al-Salam,* has said that performing an obligatory Salat (prayer) is more excellent than twenty Hajj and one Hajj is more excellent than giving as charity one houseful of gold.' The narrator has said that the Imam then said, 'There is no salvation for one who loses twenty housefuls of gold for only (because of not paying) twenty-five dirham.' I (the narrator) then asked, 'What is the meaning of twenty-five dirham?' The Imam replied, 'One who fails to pay zakat his Salat (prayer) is withheld until he pays zakat which is due on his wealth.'"

H 5719, Ch. 2, h 13

Ali ibn Ibrahim has narrated from Harun ibn Muslim from Mas'adah ibn Sadaqah who has said the following:

"Abu 'Abd Allah, *'Alayhi al-Salam,* has said that condemned, and condemned indeed is (a property or) one who does not pay zakat."

H 5720, Ch. 2, h 14

Abu Ali al-Ash'ariy has narrated from those whom he has mentioned from Hafs ibn 'Umar from Salim from abu Basir who has said the following:

"Abu 'Abd Allah, *'Alayhi al-Salam,* has said that one (Muslim) who does not pay zakat dies as a Jew or a Christian; (he is given the chance to choose)."

H 5721, Ch. 2, h 15

Ahmad ibn Muhammad has narrated from Ali ibn al-Hassan from Ali ibn al-Nu'man from Ishaq who has said the following:

"Narrated to me one who had heard abu 'Abd Allah, *'Alayhi al-Salam*, saying, 'A property is not lost, on land or in the sea, unless payment of its zakat is withheld. A bird does not become victim of hunting unless it forgets glorifying Allah.'"

H 5722, Ch. 2, h 16

Muhammad ibn Yahya has narrated from Ahmad ibn Muhammad from ibn Faddal from Ali ibn 'Uqbah from Ayyub ibn Rashid who has said the following:

"I heard abu 'Abd Allah, *'Alayhi al-Salam*, say, 'One who refuses to pay zakat will have a bald serpent curled around him. It will feed on his brain. This is mentioned in the words of Allah, the Most Majestic, the Most Glorious, ". . . whatever they are avaricious about will be tied to their necks on the Day of Judgment. . ."'" (3:180)

H 5723, Ch. 2, h 17

Muhammad ibn Yahya has narrated from Ahmad ibn Muhammad ibn 'Isa from al-Hassan ibn Mahbub from Malik ibn 'Atiyyah from abu Hamzah who has said the following:

"Abu Ja'far, *'Alayhi al-Salam*, has said, 'We have found in the book of Ali, *'Alayhi al-Salam*, that the Messenger of Allah said, 'When paying zakat is refused, the land withholds her blessings.'"

H 5724, Ch. 2, h 18

Abu 'Abd Allah al-'Asemiy has narrated from Ali ibn al-Hassan al-Mithamiy from Ali ibn Asbat from his father, Asbat ibn Salim from Salim Mawla Aban who has said the following:

"I heard abu 'Abd Allah, *'Alayhi al-Salam*, say, 'A bird does not become victim of hunting unless it forgets Tasbih (glorifying Allah). A property is not lost unless zakat which is due on it is withheld.'"

H 5725, Ch. 2, h 19

Ali ibn Ibrahim has narrated from his father from Muhammad ibn Khalid from Khalaf ibn Hammad from Hariz who has said the following:

"Abu 'Abd Allah, *'Alayhi al-Salam*, has said, 'Any wealthy person owning gold and silver who refuses to pay zakat, Allah, the Most Majestic, the Most Glorious, on the Day of Judgment will keep him in captivity in a flat land. He (Allah) will send a bald serpent who will chase him and he will flee until he finds it impossible to escape. He (the person) will then allow the serpent to get his hand and it will bite it like a turnip. It will then curl around his neck. This is referred to in the words of Allah, the Most Majestic, the Most Glorious, ". . . whatever they are avaricious about will be tied to their necks on the Day of Judgment . . ." (3:180) Every owner of camels, sheep or cows who refuses to pay zakat will be held in Allah's captivity on the Day of Judgment, in a flat land where every hooved-animal will walk on him and every sharp-toothed animal will bite him. Every owner of palm trees, vineyards or plantation who refuses to pay zakat will be made by Allah to have that land up to seven levels tied around his neck up to the Day of Judgment.'"

H 5726, Ch. 2, h 20

Ali ibn Ibrahim has narrated from his father, from al-Nawfaliy from al-Sakuniy from abu 'Abd Allah from his father, *'Alayhim al-Salam*, who has said the following:

"The Messenger of Allah has said, 'If a person withholds payment of zakat due on his wealth, his wealth does not increase.'"

H 5727, Ch. 2, h 21

Ali ibn Ibrahim has narrated from his father from ibn abu 'Umayr from Hisham ibn al-Hakam from who has said the following:

"Abu 'Abd Allah, *'Alayhi al-Salam*, has said that one who refuses to pay the right of Allah, most Majestic, most Glorious, spends double as much for falsehood."

H 5728, Ch. 2, h 22

A number of our people have narrated from Ahmad ibn Muhammad from Ayyub ibn Nuh from ibn Sinan from abu al-Jarud who has said the following:

"Abu Ja'far, *'Alayhi al-Salam*, has said, 'Allah, the most Holy, the most High, will raise a people from their graves, on the Day of Judgment, their hands tied up to their necks and they will not be able to take anything even from a distance of one finger. Angels along with them censure them severely and say, "These were the ones who withheld a small amount of good, which could gain for them a great deal of good. These are those who refused to pay the right of Allah from their wealth."'"

H 5729, Ch. 2, h 23

Ali ibn Muhammad has narrated from ibn Jumhur from his father from Ali ibn Hadid from 'Uthman from ibn Rashid from Ma'ruf ibn Kharrabuz who has said the following:

"Abu Ja'far, *'Alayhi al-Salam*, has said, 'Allah, the Most Majestic, the Most Glorious, has joined zakat with Salat (prayer), saying, "Maintain Salat (prayer) and pay zakat." Thus, if one does not pay zakat, he has not performed Salat (prayer).'"

Chapter 3 - The Reason for Amount of Zakat Levied without the Need to Increase or Decrease

H 5730, Ch. 3, h 1

Muhammad ibn Yahya has narrated from Ahmad ibn Muhammad from al-Hassan ibn Ali al-Washsha' from abu al-Hassan al-Rida', *'Alayhi al-Salam*, who has said the following:

"Once, a person asked abu 'Abd Allah, *'Alayhi al-Salam*, 'The amount of zakat Allah has levied is twenty-five for every one thousand. Why it is not thirty?' The Imam replied, 'Allah, the Most Majestic, the Most Glorious, has made it twenty-five to be paid from the wealth of affluent people. This much is enough to meet the needs of needy people. If people pay this much no one, in the society, remains needy.'"

H 5731, Ch. 3, h 2

Ali ibn Ibrahim has narrated from Salmah ibn al-Khattab, from al-Hassan ibn Rashid from Ali ibn Isma'il al-Mithamiy from Habib al-Khath'amiy who has said the following:

"Abu Ja'far al-Mansur once wrote to Muhammad ibn Khalid, his governor of al-Madinah, to ask people of al-Madinah about the amount of zakat that was five for every two hundred and how it has become seven for every two hundred which was not as such in the time of the Messenger of Allah. He commanded him to include 'Abd Allah ibn al-Hassan and Ja'far ibn Muhammad, *'Alayhi al-Salam*, among the people asked. He (the narrator) has said, 'He asked people of al-Madinah about it and they replied, "It is because people before us did so."' He sent someone to ask 'Abd Allah ibn al-Hassan about it. His answer was just like the answers of other people of al-Madinah. He then asked, 'What do you say about it, O abu 'Abd Allah?' He (the Imam) replied, 'The Messenger of Allah had levied one Awqiyyah on every forty. If you calculate, it becomes equal to seven. The weight was six and dirham was five Dawaniq each.' He (the narrator) has said, 'We calculate it and it was just as he (the Imam) had said.' 'Abd Allah ibn al-Hassan then came to the Imam and asked, 'On the basis of what source have you come up with this calculation?' He (the Imam) replied, 'I read it in the book of your mother, Fatimah, *'Alayha al-Salam*.' He (the narrator) has said, 'He then returned. Muhammad ibn Khalid then sent his people to the Imam asking for the book of Fatimah, *'Alayha al-Salam*.' Abu 'Abd Allah, *'Alayhi al-Salam*, then sent the answer, 'I only informed you about my reading it in the book of Fatimah, *'Alayha al-Salam*. I did not say that I have the book of Fatimah, *'Alayha al-Salam*, with me.' Habib has said, 'Muhammad ibn Khalid would say, "I have never seen anything like this."'"

H 5732, Ch. 3, h 3

Ahmad ibn Idris and others have narrated from Muhammad ibn Ahmad from Ibrahim ibn Muhammad from Muhammad ibn Hafs from Sabah al-Hadhdha' from Quthama who has said the following:

"I once said to abu 'Abd Allah, *'Alayhi al-Salam*, 'I pray to Allah to keep my soul in service for your cause, why the amount of zakat on every one thousand is twenty-five and not less or more and what is the reason?' He (the Imam) replied, 'Allah, the Most Majestic, the Most Glorious, created all people, small, large, wealthy and poor. He made twenty-five destitute ones in every one thousand. If this much did not suffice, He would have levied more; He is their Creator and He knows more about them than they do.'"

H 5733, Ch. 3, h 4

Ali ibn Ibrahim has narrated from his father from Muhammad ibn 'Isa ibn 'Ubayd from Yunus from abu Ja'far al-Ahwal who has said the following:

"Once an atheist asked me, 'Why is the amount of zakat twenty-five on every one thousand?' I replied, 'It is because Salat (prayer) is of two, three and four Rak'at.' He (the narrator) has said, 'He agreed with me. I then visited abu 'Abd Allah, *'Alayhi al-Salam*, and asked him about it.' He (the Imam) replied, 'Allah, the Most Majestic, the Most Glorious, calculated wealthy and destitute people. He found that twenty-five on every one thousand is enough. If this much did not suffice, He would have increased it.' I went to the atheist and informed him about it. He said, 'This answer has come from Hijaz on the back of camel.' He then said, 'Were I to obey anyone I would obey the author of this statement.'"

Chapter 4 - Amount of Zakat the Messenger of Allah Levied on the Properties of His Family Members

H 5734, Ch. 4, h 1

Ali ibn Ibrahim has narrated from his father from Hammad from Hariz Zurarah and Muhammad, abu Basir, Burayd ibn Mu'awiyah al-'Ijliy and Fudayl ibn Yasar who has said the following:

"Abu Ja'far, and abu 'Abd Allah, *'Alayhim al-Salam*, have said, 'Allah made Zakat, just as Salat (prayer) is, obligatory on wealth and the Messenger of Allah established it as a Sunnah (noble tradition) on six categories of wealth. The Messenger of Allah exempted the rest of the categories of wealth from Zakat. It is due on gold, silver, camel, cow, sheep, wheat, barley, dates and raisins. Other categories of wealth are exempt.'"

H 5735, Ch. 4, h 2

Ali ibn Ibrahim has narrated from his father from 'Isma'il ibn Marrar from Yunus from 'Abd Allah ibn Muskan from abu Bakr al-Hadramiy who has said the following:

"Abu 'Abd Allah, *'Alayhi al-Salam*, has said, 'The Messenger of Allah made Zakat obligatory on nine categories of wealth wheat, barley, dates, raisins, gold, silver, camel, cows and sheep. Other kinds of wealth are exempt.'" "Yunus has said that the meaning of his words 'Zakat is on nine things and other kinds are exempt,' was applicable at the time of the beginning of his prophetic mission like Salat (prayer) which was of two Rak'at in the beginning of his mission. Then the Messenger of Allah increased in it seven more Rak'at. So also is Zakat. In the beginning of his mission it was due on nine things, then he made it due on all kinds of grains."

Chapter 5 - Grains Subject to Zakat

H 5736, Ch. 5, h 1

Ali ibn Ibrahim has narrated from his father from Hammad ibn 'Isa from Hariz from Muhammad ibn Muslim who has said the following:

"I once asked him (the Imam), *'Alayhi al-Salam*, about grains which are subject to Zakat. He (the Imam) said, 'Zakat is due on wheat, barley, corn, millet, rice, sult (something similar to wheat and barley), lentil and sesame all are subject to Zakat as well as the like.'"

H 5737, Ch. 5, h 2

Hariz has narrated from Zurarah who has narrated a similar Hadith from abu 'Abd Allah, *'Alayhi al-Salam* who has said that whatever is measured with al-Sa' and it amounts to al-Awsaq (a certain unit of measurement) then it becomes subject to Zakat.' He (the Imam) said, 'The Messenger of Allah made charity (Zakat) obligatory on everything that earth grows except vegetable, legumes and things that perish on the same day.'"

H 5738, Ch. 5, h 3

Muhammad ibn Yahya has narrated from Ahmad ibn Muhammad ibn 'Isa from al-'Abbas ibn Ma'ruf from Ali ibn Mahziyar from who has said the following:

"I have read in the book (letter) of 'Abd Allah ibn Muhammad to abu al-Hassan, *'Alayhi al-Salam,* in which he has said, 'I pray to Allah to keep my soul in service for your cause. It is narrated from abu 'Abd Allah, *'Alayhi al-Salam,* who has said that the Messenger of Allah made Zakat obligatory on nine things which are wheat, barley, dates, raisins, gold, silver, sheep, cows and camels. The Messenger of Allah exempted other things from Zakat. A certain one then said, 'We have many other things of greater amount.' He (the Imam) asked, 'What are they?' He said, 'It is rice.' Abu 'Abd Allah, *'Alayhi al-Salam,* said, 'I say that the Messenger of Allah made Zakat obligatory on nine things. He (the Messenger of Allah) exempted all other things. You say that we have rice and corn. There was corn at the time of the Messenger of Allah.' He (the Imam), *'Alayhi al-Salam,* said, 'So also there is Zakat on everything that is measured by al-Sa'.' 'Abd Allah wrote and others besides this man have narrated from abu 'Abd Allah, *'Alayhi al-Salam,* that he (the Imam) was asked about grains and he (the Imam) asked, 'What is it?' He replied, 'It is sesame, rice, millet and all of these are grains like wheat and barley.' Abu 'Abd Allah, *'Alayhi al-Salam,* said, 'All grains are subject to Zakat.'"

H 5739, Ch. 5, h 4

It is also narrated that abu 'Abd Allah, *'Alayhi al-Salam,* has said, 'Everything that is measured by al-Qafiz are dealt with like wheat, barley, dates and raisins. He then asked saying, 'I pray to Allah to keep my soul in service for your cause, is there Zakat on rice and similar things like beans and lintel?' He (the Imam) *'Alayhi al-Salam,* signed, 'Pay charity from everything that is measured.'"

H 5740, Ch. 5, h 5

It is narrated from him (narrator of previous Hadith) Ahmad ibn Muhammad from Muhammad ibn 'Isma'il who has said the following:

"I once asked abu al-Hassan, *'Alayhi al-Salam,* 'We have fresh dates and rice. So what we owe for it?' He (the Imam) said, 'You do not owe anything because of fresh dates. If rice is watered by rains from the sky one out of ten is Zakat but if it is watered with buckets then one out of twenty is Zakat on whatever you measure by al-Sa' or that he (the Imam) said, 'Whatever is measured by measuring devices.'"

H 5741, Ch. 5, h 6

Humayd ibn Ziyad has narrated from Ahmad ibn Sama'ah from those whom he has mentioned from Aban from abu Maryam who has said the following:

"I once asked abu 'Abd Allah, *'Alayhi al-Salam,* about plantation and what is subject to Zakat from it. He (the Imam) said, 'There is Zakat on wheat, barley, corn, rice, al-sult, and lintels and all of these are subject to Zakat.' He (the Imam) said, 'Everything that is measured by al-Sa' and amounts to al-Awsaq are subject to Zakat.'"

Chapter 6 - What Is not Subject to Zakat of Plantation and so Forth

H 5742, Ch. 6, h 1

Muhammad ibn Yahya has narrated from Ahmad ibn Muhammad from 'Uthman ibn 'Isa from Sama'ah who has said the following:

"Abu 'Abd Allah, *'Alayhi al-Salam*, has said, 'Zakat is not due on legumes, melons and similar things except that if anything of grain accumulated with you remains for one year.'"

H 5743, Ch. 6, h 2

Muhammad ibn Yahya has narrated from Muhammad ibn al-Husayn, from Safwan ibn Yahya from al-'Ala' ibn Razin from Muhammad ibn Muslim who has said the following:

"Abu Ja'far, *'Alayhi al-Salam*, was once asked about vegetables if there is Zakat on it, if sold in exchange for a great wealth. He (the Imam) said, 'No, Zakat is not due on it (such wealth) unless it remains with one for one year (in store).'"

H 5744, Ch. 6, h 3

Ali ibn Ibrahim has narrated from his father from ibn abu 'Umayr from Hammad from al-Halabiy who has said the following:

"I once asked abu 'Abd Allah, *'Alayhi al-Salam*, 'How much Zakat is on vegetables. He (the Imam) asked, 'What is it?' I replied, 'Edible herbs, melons and similar things of legumes.' He (the Imam) said, 'Zakat is not due on it unless it is sold in exchange for another kind of wealth and it remains with him for one year; then there is charity on it.' I then asked if there is Zakat on fresh plum and similar things. He (the Imam) said, 'No, Zakat is not due on it.' I then asked if there is Zakat on what is received from the sale of such items. He (the Imam) said, 'If it remains with one for one year, then there is Zakat on it.'"

H 5745, Ch. 6, h 4

Ali ibn Ibrahim has narrated from his father from ill ibn Marrar and others from Yunus who has said the following:

"I once asked abu al-Hassan, *'Alayhi al-Salam*, if there is Zakat on saltwort. He (the Imam) said, 'No, Zakat is not due on it.'"

H 5746, Ch. 6, h 5

Muhammad ibn Yahya has narrated from Ahmad ibn Muhammad from Ali ibn Mahziyar from 'Abd 'Aziz ibn al-Muhtadiy who has said the following:

"I once asked abu al-Hassan, *'Alayhi al-Salam*, about cotton and saffron if there is Zakat on it. He (the Imam) said, 'No, Zakat is not due on it.'"

H 5747, Ch. 6, h 6

Ali ibn Ibrahim has narrated from his father from Hammad ibn 'Isa from Hariz from Muhammad ibn Muslim who has said the following:

"I asked abu Ja'far and abu 'Abd Allah, *'Alayhim al-Salam*, about a garden which has fruits that if sold becomes wealth and if there is Zakat on it. He (the Imam) said, 'No, Zakat is not due on it.'"

Chapter 7 - Minimum Zakat on Plantation Produce

H 5748, Ch. 7, h 1

Abu Ali al-Ash'ariy has narrated from Ahmad ibn Muhammad from 'Uthman ibn 'Isa from Sama'ah who has said the following:

"I once asked him (the Imam), *'Alayhi al-Salam*, about Zakat on raisins and dates. He (the Imam) said, 'On every five awsaq (a certain measurement) there is one wasq. One wasq is sixty Sa'. The amount of Zakat on both items is of the same amount. Of food items what is watered by rain from the sky Zakat is one out of ten, but if it is watered with use of energy and buckets Zakat on it is one of twenty.'"

H 5749, Ch. 7, h 2

A number of our people have narrated from Ahmad ibn Muhammad ibn 'Isa from Ali ibn Ahmad ibn 'Ushaym from Safwan ibn Yahya and Ahmad ibn Muhammad from ibn abu Nasr who has said the following:

"Once we spoke to him (the Imam) about al-Kufah and of taxes levied and where his family has moved. He (the Imam) said, 'Those who willingly accepted Islam their land was left in their hands. One out of ten is received from them for what is watered from the sky and canals. There is one out of twenty for what is watered by means of drawing water of what they have revived. What is not revived is under the authority of Imam who contracts with those who revive it. The share of the Muslims on the contractors is one out of ten or one out of twenty and Zakat is not due on what is less than twenty Awsaq. Whatever land is taken by the sword (Armed forces), it belong to the Imam who contracts it with whomever he deems proper, just as the Messenger of Allah did with the land of Khaybar and its black and white, its land and gardens. People would say land and palm trees are not proper for contract. The Messenger of Allah contracted the land of Khaybar and the contractors were to pay one out of ten or one out of twenty.' He (the Imam) said, 'People of Ta'if accepted Islam and they were to pay one out of ten or one out of twenty. There is the case of people of Makkah, where the Messenger of Allah entered by force, who became his captives, he set them free. Saying, "Go, you are set free."'"

H 5750, Ch. 7, h 3

Ali ibn Ibrahim has narrated from his father from and Muhammad ibn Yahya has narrated from Ahmad ibn Muhammad ibn 'Isa all from ibn abu 'Umayr from Hammad from al-Halabiy who has said the following:

"Abu 'Abd Allah, *'Alayhi al-Salam*, has said, 'Zakat on what is watered by canals or rain from the sky, is one out of ten and on what is watered by means of scoops and buckets and what trickles thereby is one out of twenty.'"

H 5751, Ch. 7, h 4

Ali ibn Ibrahim has narrated from his father from Hammad ibn 'Isa from Hariz from abu Basir and Muhammad ibn Muslim who has said the following:

"The two of them asked abu Ja'far, *'Alayhi al-Salam*, about the land cultivated by the people. He (the Imam) said, 'If you contract such land from government then out of what Allah makes it grow, comes your share according to the terms of the contract. One out of ten is not payable from its gross harvest. One out of ten is due on your net dividend.'"

H 5752, Ch. 7, h 5

A number of our people have narrated from Ahmad ibn Muhammad from al-Barqiy from Sa'd ibn Sa'd al-Ash'ariy who has said the following:

"I once asked abu al-Hassan, *'Alayhi al-Salam*, about the minimum Zakat due on wheat, barley, dates and raisins. He (the Imam) said, 'It is one wasaq out of five Awsaq of wasq of the Holy prophet.' I then asked, 'How much is wasaq?' He (the Imam) said, 'It is sixty Sa'.' I then asked, 'Is there Zakat on grapes or that there is Zakat on it only when it is turned into raisins. He (the Imam) said, 'Yes, when he estimates it then pays its Zakat.'"

H 5753, Ch. 7, h 6

Ali ibn Ibrahim has narrated from his father from ibn abu 'Umayr from Mu'awiyah ibn Shurayh who has said the following:

"Abu 'Abd Allah, *'Alayhi al-Salam*, has said, 'Zakat is one out of ten on what is watered from canals or rain from the sky and it is one out of twenty on what is watered by means of scoops and buckets.' I then said that we have a certain piece of land, which is watered, by means of buckets, then water increases and it then is watered from canals. He (the Imam) asked, 'Is it how it is with you?' I replied, 'Yes, that is how it is.' He (the Imam) said, 'It then is half and half. Zakat on one half is one out of ten and on the other half it is one out of twenty.' I then said, 'There is a piece of land which is watered by means of buckets and then water increases, it then is watered once or twice from canals.' He (the Imam) asked, 'Within what time once or twice watering takes place?' I replied, 'It happens within thirty or forty nights and before it a period of six or seven months has passed. He (the Imam) said, 'It (Zakat) is one out of twenty.'"

H 5754, Ch. 7, h 7

Ali ibn Ibrahim has narrated from his father from Hammad ibn 'Isa from Hariz from Muhammad ibn Muslim who has said the following:

"I once asked abu 'Abd Allah, *'Alayhi al-Salam*, about dates and raisins and the minimum amount on which Zakat is due. He (the Imam) said, 'It is five Awsaq. Zakat is not due on Mi'afarah and 'Umm al-Ja'rur (two undesirable kinds of dates) even if it is of a large quantity. One or two tree is left for the guard who looks after them and he leaves it for his family."

Chapter 8 - Dates Are Subject to Zakat Only Once

H 5755, Ch. 8, h 1

Ali ibn Ibrahim has narrated from his father from Hammad ibn 'Isa from Hariz from Zurarah and 'Ubayd ibn Zurarah who has said the following:

"Abu 'Abd Allah, *'Alayhi al-Salam*, has said, 'If one has plantations and dates for which charity (Zakat) is paid, thereafter no other Zakat is due on it. Zakat is not due even if it remains in one's possession for a whole year unless one changes it into another kind of wealth. After the change it remains in one's possession for a whole year in which case one is required to pay Zakat, otherwise, Zakat not is due on it even if it remains in one's possession for a thousand years in the same substance. Zakat is only one out of ten and once it is paid there is not anything else to pay until it is changed into another form of wealth and it remains in one's possession for a whole year.'"

Chapter 9 - Zakat on Gold and Silver

H 5756, Ch. 9, h 1

Muhammad ibn Yahya has narrated from Ahmad ibn Muhammad from 'Uthman ibn 'Isa from Sama'ah who has said the following:

"Abu 'Abd Allah, *'Alayhi al-Salam*, has said, 'On every two hundred dirham of silver Zakat is five dirham, and on less than two hundred Zakat is not due. On every twenty Dinar of gold half dinar is Zakat and on less than this Zakat is not due.'"

H 5757, Ch. 9, h 2

Ali ibn Ibrahim has narrated from his father from ibn abu 'Umayr from Rifa'ah al-Nakhkhas who has said the following:

"Once, a man asked abu 'Abd Allah, *'Alayhi al-Salam*, saying, 'I am a jeweler and I make jewelry with my own hands. Five or ten accumulates with me. Is Zakat due on it?' He (the Imam) said, 'If two hundred accumulates and it remains in your possession for one year then Zakat is due.'"

H 5758, Ch 9, h 3

A number of our people have narrated from Ahmad ibn Muhammad ibn 'Isa from ibn Faddal from Ali ibn 'Uqbah and A number of our people have narrated from who has said the following:

"Abu Ja'far, and abu 'Abd Allah, *'Alayhim al-Salam*, have said, 'Zakat is not due on what is less than twenty Mithqal of gold. If it is a complete twenty Mithqal, half Mithqal is Zakat thereof. Once it becomes complete twenty-four, then three-fifth of a dinar is Zakat thereof up until it is twenty-eight. Thereafter on the increase of every four, three-fifth of a dinar is Zakat thereof.'"

H 5759, Ch. 9, h 4

A number of our people have narrated from Sahl ibn Ziyad Ahmad ibn Muhammad ibn abu Nasr from ibn 'Uyaynah who has said the following:

"Abu 'Abd Allah, *'Alayhi al-Salam*, has said, 'Once the amount of gold becomes more than twenty dinar then on every four dinar Zakat is one out of ten dinar.'"

H 5760, Ch. 9, h 5

Ali ibn Ibrahim has narrated from his father from Hammad, from Hariz from Muhammad ibn Muslim who has said the following:

"I once asked abu 'Abd Allah, *'Alayhi al-Salam*, about gold and the amount of its Zakat. He (the Imam) said, 'Once its value amounts up to two hundred dirham then Zakat is payable.'"

H 5761, Ch. 9, h 6

Muhammad ibn Yahya has narrated from Ahmad ibn Muhammad ibn 'Isa from al-Husayn ibn Sa'id from al-Husayn ibn Bashshar who has said the following:

"I once asked abu al-Hassan, *'Alayhi al-Salam*, 'How much Zakat, the Messenger of Allah has levied? He (the Imam) said, 'It is five dirham on every two hundred and if it is less, then Zakat is not due. On every twenty dinar of gold Zakat is half dinar and Zakat is not due on less than twenty dinar.'"

H 5762, Ch. 9, h 7

Ali ibn Ibrahim has narrated from his father from and Muhammad ibn Yahya has narrated from Ahmad ibn Muhammad ibn 'Isa all from ibn abu 'Umayr from Hammad from al-Halabiy who has said the following:

"Abu 'Abd Allah, *'Alayhi al-Salam,* was once asked about the minimum Zakat on gold and silver. He (the Imam) said, 'The minimum is two hundred and the equivalent of it of gold.' I then asked about fifteen and change. He (the Imam) said, 'Zakat is not due on it until it becomes forty, then for every forty Zakat is one dirham.'"

H 5763, Ch. 9, h 8

Ali ibn Ibrahim has narrated from his father from 'Isma'il ibn Marrar from Yunus from Ishaq ibn 'Ammar who has said the following:

"I once said to abu Ibrahim, *'Alayhi al-Salam,* 'There is one hundred ninety dirham and nineteen dinar. Is there Zakat on it? He (the Imam) said, 'If gold and silver together amount to two hundred dirham, then there is Zakat payable, because dirham represents the value of wealth and items other than dirham like gold and goods are evaluated on the basis of dirham in matters of Zakat and compensations.'"

H 5764, Ch. 9, h 9

Muhammad ibn Yahya has narrated from Muhammad ibn al-Husayn from Muhammad ibn 'Abd Allah ibn Hilal from al-'Ala' ibn Razin from Zayd al-Sa'igh who has said the following:

"I once said to abu 'Abd Allah, *'Alayhi al-Salam,* that I have been in a town in Khurasan called Bukhara'. I saw dirhams used there had one-third of silver, one-third of copper and one-third of lead and it was lawful among them. I would use and spend them. Abu 'Abd Allah, *'Alayhi al-Salam,* said, 'There is no offence in it if it is lawful among them.' I then asked, 'If it remains with me for one year with other goods, is there Zakat on it? He (the Imam) said, 'Yes, there is Zakat on it; it is of your assets.' I then asked, 'If I take it to a town where they are not accepted and used and it remains with me for one whole year. Is there Zakat on it? He (the Imam) said, 'If you know that there is pure silver in it which amounts to a quantity subject to Zakat, then you must pay Zakat thereof for pure silver therein and leave the rest of dirt.' I then asked, 'If I do not know the amount of pure silver in it, however I know that the amount of silver existing is the amount which is subject to Zakat.' He (the Imam) said, 'Cast it until silver is pure and dirt is burned, then after passing of one year it becomes subject to Zakat.''

Chapter 10 - Jewelries, Ornaments Are Not Subject to Zakat

H 5765, Ch. 10, h 1

Muhammad ibn 'Isma'il has narrated from al-Fadl ibn Shadhan from Safwan ibn Yahya from ibn Muskan from Muhammad al-Halabiy who has said the following:

"I once asked abu 'Abd Allah, *'Alayhi al-Salam,* about Zakat and jewelry. He (the Imam) said, 'Zakat is not due on jewelries.'"

H 5766, Ch. 10, h 2

Muhammad ibn Yahya has narrated from Muhammad ibn al-Husayn from Safwan ibn Yahya from ibn Muskan from Muhammad al-Halabiy who has said the following:

"I once asked abu 'Abd Allah, *'Alayhi al-Salam*, about Zakat and jewelry. He (the Imam) said, 'Zakat is not due on jewelries.'"

H 5767, Ch. 10, h 3

Muhammad ibn Yahya has narrated from Muhammad ibn al-Husayn from Safwan ibn Yahya from Ya'qub ibn Shu'ayb who has said the following:

"I once asked abu 'Abd Allah, *'Alayhi al-Salam*, if there is Zakat on jewelries. He (the Imam) said, 'If so nothing will remain thereof.'"

H 5768, Ch. 10, h 4

Ali ibn Ibrahim has narrated from his father from ibn abu 'Umayr from Rifa'ah who has said the following:

"I once heard abu 'Abd Allah, *'Alayhi al-Salam*, say, when certain people asked him if there is Zakat on jewelries, 'Zakat is not due on jewelries even if it becomes a hundred thousand.'"

H 5769, Ch. 10, h 5

A number of our people have narrated from Ahmad ibn Muhammad ibn 'Isa from al-Hassan Ali ibn Yaqtin from his brother al-Husayn from Ali ibn Yaqtin who has said the following:

"I once asked abu al-Hassan, *'Alayhi al-Salam*, about goods which are not used or moved. He (the Imam) said, 'There is Zakat on it every year until it is used.''

H 5770, Ch. 10, h 6

Muhammad ibn Yahya has narrated from Ahmad ibn Muhammad from ibn abu 'Umayr from certain persons of our people who has said the following:

"Abu 'Abd Allah, *'Alayhi al-Salam*, has said, 'Zakat of jewelries is allowing others to borrow it.'"

H 5771, Ch. 10, h 7

Ali ibn Ibrahim has narrated from his father from Hammad ibn 'Isa from Hariz from Harun ibn Kharijah who has said the following:

"I once said to abu 'Abd Allah, *'Alayhi al-Salam*, that my brother, Yusuf accepts employment from these people from which he has earned great amounts of wealth and has turned them into jewelries to avoid Zakat. Is there Zakat on it? He (the Imam) said, 'Zakat is not due on jewelries; however, the loss that he has caused to himself in this way and depriving himself of the virtue of paying Zakat is greater than his fear of paying Zakat.''

H 5772, Ch. 10, h 8

Hammad ibn 'Isa has narrated from Hariz from Ali ibn Yaqtin who has said the following:

"I once said to abu Ibrahim, *'Alayhi al-Salam*, certain things accumulate with me and remain for about a year. Is there Zakat on it? He (the Imam) said, 'No, Zakat is not due on it. Use whatever is with you until one is passed, Zakat is not due on it and whatever is not rika`z you do not owe anything therefor.' I then asked, 'What is rika`z? He (the Imam) said, 'It is solid with designs on it.' He (the Imam) then said, 'If you like you can cast them because Zakat is not due on alloys of silver and gold.'"

H 5773, Ch. 10, h 9

Muhammad ibn Yahya has narrated from Ahmad ibn Muhammad from Ali ibn Hadid from Jamil from certain persons of our people who have said the following:

"Zakat is not due on gold. Zakat becomes due only on dinars and dirhams."

H 5774, Ch. 10, h 10

Ali ibn Ibrahim has narrated from his father from Hammad from ibn `Udhaynah from Zurarah Bukayr who has said the following:

"Abu Ja'far, *'Alayhi al-Salam*, has said, 'Zakat is not due on gems even if it becomes a large amount.'"

Chapter 11 - Zakat of Misplaced Wealth, Loans and Borrowed

H 5775, Ch. 11, h 1

Muhammad ibn Yahya has narrated from Ahmad ibn Muhammad ibn 'Isa from al-Hassan ibn Mahbub from al-'Ala' ibn Razin from Sadir al-Sayrafiy who has said the following:

"I once asked abu Ja'far, *'Alayhi al-Salam*, about a man who buries a certain amount of his wealth in a certain place and after one year goes to find out. He searches and digs around in the area but fails to find it. He then after three years goes to search again and finds the amount of wealth that was lost. He (the Imam) said, 'He pays only one year's Zakat because it was absent from him even though he had placed it in hold.'"

H 5776, Ch. 11, h 2

Ali ibn Ibrahim has narrated from his father from ibn abu 'Umayr from Rifa'ah ibn Musa who has said the following:

"I once asked abu 'Abd Allah, *'Alayhi al-Salam*, about a man whose wealth remains lost for five years. He then finds it and does not reject the capital. How much Zakat is he required to pay? He (the Imam) said, 'He pays one year's Zakat only.'"

H 5777, Ch. 11, h 3

Ali ibn Ibrahim has narrated from his father from `Isma'il ibn Marrar from Yunus from Durust from 'Umar ibn Yazid who has said the following:

"Abu 'Abd Allah, *'Alayhi al-Salam*, has said, 'Zakat is not due on loan unless the lender delays acceptance of payment. If he is not able to achieve payment, then Zakat is not due until payment is received.'"

H 5778, Ch. 11, h 4

Muhammad ibn Yahya has narrated from Ahmad ibn Muhammad ibn 'Isa from 'Uthman ibn 'Isa from Sama'ah who has said the following:

"I once asked him (the Imam), *'Alayhi al-Salam*, about a man to whom people owe loans and do not pay. Is there Zakat on such loans? He (the Imam) said, 'Zakat is not due until he receives payment. Once he receives payment, there is Zakat on him. If he does not receive payment and it remains for many years, still Zakat is not due on him until payment is received. Once payment is received he pays Zakat of that year. If he receives payment gradually, he pays Zakat of whatever is received by the order it comes. If his wealth, loan and goods are in business, then it is his business, which is at work, and in give and take, buying and selling, thus it is like the substance in his hand and he is required to pay Zakat. It is not proper for him to change the process if his case is as the case I just mentioned.'"

H 5779, Ch. 11, h 5

Muhammad ibn `Isma'il has narrated from al-Fadl ibn Shadhan from Safwan ibn Yahya from Mansur ibn Hazim who has said the following:

"I once asked abu 'Abd Allah, *'Alayhi al-Salam*, about a man who borrows a certain amount of wealth and it remains with him for one year. He (the Imam) said, 'If the person from whom he has borrowed pays Zakat for such wealth then Zakat is not due on the borrower but if the lender does not pay then he (the borrower) pays Zakat for such wealth.'"

H 5780, Ch. 11, h 6

Ali ibn Ibrahim has narrated from his father from Hammad from Hariz from Zurarah who has said the following:

"I once asked abu 'Abd Allah, *'Alayhi al-Salam*, about a man who gives a certain amount of asset to another person as loan with the condition that Zakat is on lender or borrower. He (the Imam) said, 'No, Zakat is due on borrower if it remains with him for one year.' He (the Imam) said, 'Zakat is not paid twice for the same thing in one year. Zakat is not due on lender because it is not in his hands. The asset is in the hands of the borrower. Whoever has the asset in his hand pays Zakat.' I then asked is he required to pay Zakat of the asset that belongs to someone else? He (the Imam) said, 'O Zurarah, consider the position of that asset. In whose hand is it and who gets its profits and whose liability is it?' I (Zurarah) said, 'It is the borrower.' He (the Imam) said, 'He then is responsible for its increase and decrease. He can marry thereby and pay thereby for his food. Is he not supposed to pay its Zakat? In fact, he is required to pay its Zakat.'"

H 5781, Ch. 11, h 7

Humayd ibn Ziyad has narrated from al-Husayn ibn Muhammad from Sama'ah and from more than one person from Aban ibn 'Uthman from 'Abd al-Rahman ibn abu 'Abd Allah who has said the following:

"I once asked abu 'Abd Allah, *'Alayhi al-Salam*, about a man who owes a loan and in his hands is the assets of another person. Is he required to pay Zakat for the asset of other people? He (the Imam) said, 'If it is loan and it has remained in his hand for one year, he then is required to pay its Zakat.'"

H 5782, Ch. 11, h 8

Ahmad ibn Idris has narrated from Muhammad ibn 'Abd al-Jabbar from Safwan ibn Yahya from 'Abd al-Majid ibn Sa'd who has said the following:

"I once asked abu al-Hassan, *'Alayhi al-Salam*, about a man who buys something to pay for after three years from a man who trusts him in his right and asset. Is he required to pay its Zakat every year or he pays it because he has the asset in his hands? He (the Imam) said, 'He who has taken it pays its Zakat.' I then asked, 'For how long he pays it?' He (the Imam) said, 'He pays it for three years.'"

H 5783, Ch. 11, h 9

A number of our people have narrated from Ahmad ibn Muhammad from al-Husayn ibn Sa'id from Fadalah ibn Ayyub from Aban ibn 'Uthman from those who narrated to him who has said the following:

"I once asked one of the two the Imam, *'Alayhim al-Salam*, about a man who owes a loan and in his hand is an asset that is sufficient to pay the loan but it belongs to someone else. Is he required to pay Zakat? He (the Imam) said, 'If he has borrowed and one year has passed, then its Zakat is on him if there is anything extra.'"

H 5784, Ch. 11, h 10

Muhammad ibn Yahya has narrated from Ahmad ibn Muhammad from Ali ibn al-Hakam from Ali ibn abu Hamzah who has said the following:

"Abu 'Abd Allah, *'Alayhi al-Salam*, has said, 'If a certain asset is deposited with you and you are allowed to make it work its Zakat is on you but if you are not allowed to make it work then you do not owe anything.'"

H 5785, Ch. 11, h 11

More than one person of our people has narrated from Sahl ibn Ziyad from Ali ibn Mahziyar from who has said the following:

"I once wrote to him (the Imam), *'Alayhi al-Salam*, about a man who owes Mahr of his woman who does not ask for payment due to sympathy or shyness. It goes on for their lifetime. Is he required to pay Zakat for that Mahr? He (the Imam) wrote, 'Zakat is not due on him except for his assets.'"

H 5786, Ch. 11, h 12

A number of our people have narrated from Ahmad ibn Muhammad from al-Husayn ibn Sa'id from Ali ibn al-Nu'man from ibn al-Sabbah al-Kinaniy who has said the following:

"I once asked abu 'Abd Allah, *'Alayhi al-Salam*, about a man who does not collect what he has lent because of forgetfulness or the desire to help his borrowers so his assets continue to remain as loans. How must he deal with Zakat? He (the owner of the assets) not the borrower pays Zakat.'"

H 5787, Ch. 11, h 13

Ali ibn Ibrahim has narrated from his father from Hammad ibn 'Isa from Hariz from Zurarah from abu Ja'far and Durays who has said the following:

"Abu 'Abd Allah, *'Alayhi al-Salam*, has said that the two Imam, *'Alayhim al-Salam*, have said, 'Whoever has an asset that remains with him for one year, he is required to pay its Zakat even if he owes to others an equal amount of asset or more. He is required to pay Zakat for what is in his hand.'"

Chapter 12 - Times Zakat Is Due

H 5788, Ch. 12, h 1

Ahmad ibn Idris has narrated from Muhammad ibn 'Abd al-Jabbar and Muhammad ibn `Isma'il from al-Fadl ibn Shadhan all from Safwan ibn Yahya from Muhammad ibn Hakim from Khalid ibn al-Hajjaj al-Karkhiy who has said the following:

"I once asked abu 'Abd Allah, *'Alayhi al-Salam*, about Zakat. He (the Imam) said, 'You can choose one of the months of the year and decide to pay Zakat in that month. In that month you must find out what are your assets and pay Zakat thereof. After one year you must do the same thing again and you are not required to do anything more than this.'"

H 5789, Ch. 12, h 2

Muhammad ibn Yahya has narrated from Ahmad ibn Muhammad in a marfu' manner from abu Basir who has said the following:

"I once asked abu 'Abd Allah, *'Alayhi al-Salam*, Is there a definite time to pay Zakat? He (the Imam) said, 'That depends on one's earnings. However, the time for al-Fitrah is definite.'"

H 5790, Ch. 12, h 3

Muhammad ibn Yahya has narrated from Ahmad ibn Muhammad from al-Hassan ibn Ali from Yunus ibn Ya'qub who has said the following:

"I once said to abu 'Abd Allah, *'Alayhi al-Salam*, that there is a certain month in which I pay Zakat. Can I keep a certain amount separate for an emergency, in case, someone comes asking? He (the Imam) said, 'Once the year is complete, you must pay Zakat of your asset and you must not mix it with anything, and then give whatever you want.' I then asked, 'Can I write it down and keep a record to make it straight? He (the Imam) said, 'That is not harmful.'"

H 5791, Ch. 12, h 4

A number of our people have narrated from Ahmad ibn Muhammad from Muhammad ibn Khalid al-Barqiy from Sa'd ibn Sa'd al-Ash'ariy who has said the following:

"I once asked abu al-Hassan, al-Rida', *'Alayhi al-Salam*, about a man whose accounting time comes three times in a year. Can he delay to make them all at one time? He (the Imam) said, 'Whenever it comes he must pay Zakat.' I then asked, 'When it is the time to pay Zakat of wheat, barley, dates and raisins? He (the Imam) said, 'It is when he cuts and estimates.'"

H 5792, Ch. 12, h 5

It is narrated from him (narrator of previous Hadith) Muhammad ibn Hamzah from al-Asfahaniy who has said the following:

"I once said to abu 'Abd Allah, *'Alayhi al-Salam*, that if I collect what I have lent to someone when must I pay Zakat? He (the Imam) said, 'Pay when you collect it.' I then said, 'I collect a certain amount in a certain time of the year and another amount in another time of the year. He (the Imam) smiled and then said, 'How good is the deal in which you are involved!' He (the Imam) then said, 'What you collect in the first six months, pay its Zakat after a year and what you collect in the other six months, pay its Zakat in the coming year. So also is the case with your earning, which you gain in separate times during a whole year. What you earn in the first six months pay its Zakat in that year and what you earn thereafter pay its Zakat in the coming year.'"

H 5793, Ch. 12, h 6

Ahmad ibn Muhammad from Ali ibn al-Hakam from Muhammad ibn Yahya from abu Basir who has said the following:

"I once asked abu 'Abd Allah, *'Alayhi al-Salam*, about a man whose asset is half in substance and half as loan. The time of paying Zakat comes. He (the Imam) said, 'He is required to pay Zakat of the substance and leave the loan.' I then said that he receives payment after six months. He (the Imam) said, 'He is required to pay its Zakat when he receives payment.' I then said, 'The year is complete and the month of paying Zakat comes but one half of his asset has remained with him for one year and the other half for six months.' He (the Imam) said, 'He must pay Zakat for what has been with him for one year and leave the other half until one year is passed.' I then asked, 'Can he pay its Zakat if he wants?' He (the Imam) said, 'That is very good.'"

H 5794, Ch. 12, h 7

Ali ibn Ibrahim has narrated from his father from 'Abd Allah ibn al-Mughirah from 'Abd Allah ibn Sinan who has said the following:

"I once asked abu 'Abd Allah, *'Alayhi al-Salam*, about a man who pays his Zakat. He distributes a certain amount of it and keeps a certain amount to find proper recipient and this takes three months altogether. He (the Imam) said, 'It is not harmful.'"

H 5795, Ch. 12, h 8

Ali ibn Ibrahim has narrated from his father from Hammad ibn 'Isa from Hariz from 'Umar ibn Yazid who has said the following:

"I once asked abu 'Abd Allah, *'Alayhi al-Salam*, about a man who pays Zakat when half of the year passes. He (the Imam) said, 'No, he must allow one year to pass. Just as it is not permissible to perform Salat (prayer) before its time, so also is Zakat. No one can fast for the month of Ramadan in a month other than the month of Ramadan. Every obligation is fulfilled when it is time for such obligation.'"

H 5796, Ch. 12, h 9

Hammad ibn 'Isa has narrated from Hariz from Zurarah who has said the following:

"I once asked abu Ja'far, *'Alayhi al-Salam*, 'Can one pay Zakat after one-third of the year passes?' He (the Imam) said, 'No, can one perform al-Zuhr before Zawal (declining of the sun toward the west at noontime)?'"

"It is also narrated that it is permissible if deserving recipient is present and to pay to him before the time for Zakat, except that he is responsible for it if at the time of Zakat, the recipient becomes affluent or an apostate, in which case he must pay Zakat again."

Chapter 13 - (Without Title)

H 5797, Ch. 13, h 1

Ali ibn Ibrahim has narrated from his father from ibn abu 'Umayr from Hammad from al-Halabiy who has said the following:

"Abu 'Abd Allah, *'Alayhi al-Salam*, has said, 'My father purchased a piece of land from Sulayman ibn 'Abd al-Malik for a certain amount with a condition that he (Sulayman) will pay its Zakat for six years.'"

H 5798, Ch. 13, h 2

Muhammad ibn Yahya has narrated from Ahmad ibn Muhammad from al-Hassan ibn Mahbub from 'Abd Allah ibn Sinan who has said the following:

"I once heard abu 'Abd Allah, *'Alayhi al-Salam*, say, 'My father purchased a piece of land from Hisham ibn 'Abd al-Malik for such and such hundred thousand dinar with a condition that he will pay its Zakat for ten years. He did it as such because Hisham was the ruler.'"

Chapter 14 - Rules about the Wealth Owned For Less Than a Year

H 5799, Ch. 14, h 1

Muhammad ibn 'Isma'il has narrated from al-Fadl ibn Shadhan from Safwan ibn Yahya from Ishaq ibn 'Ammar who has said the following:

"I once asked abu Ibrahim, *'Alayhi al-Salam*, about a man who has a certain number of children, a certain one of them disappears and he does not know where he is. The man dies. How his legacy is dealt with? He (the Imam) said, 'His share is kept aside until he comes.' I then asked, 'Is there Zakat on his share?' He (the Imam) said, 'No, until he comes.' I then asked, 'Is he required to pay Zakat as soon as he comes?' He (the Imam) said, 'No, until one year passes with the asset in his hands.'"

H 5800, Ch. 14, h 2

Through the same chain of narrators as that of the previous Hadith it is narrated from Safwan from 'Abd Allah ibn Muskan from Muhammad al-Halabiy who has said the following:

"I once asked abu 'Abd Allah, *'Alayhi al-Salam*, about a man who earns a certain amount of wealth. He (the Imam) said, 'He does not pay its Zakat until one year passes.'"

H 5801, Ch. 14, h 3

Ali ibn Ibrahim has narrated from his father from 'Abd Allah ibn al-Mughirah 'Abd Allah ibn Sinan who has said the following:

"I once asked abu 'Abd Allah, *'Alayhi al-Salam*, about a man who has a certain amount of asset and it is about the end of the year when he spends it just before the year is complete. Is there Zakat on him? He (the Imam) said, 'No, he is not required to pay Zakat.'"

H 5802, Ch. 14, h 4

It is a narration from him (narrator of previous Hadith) by Hammad ibn 'Isa from Hariz ibn 'Abd Allah from Zurarah who has said the following:

"I once asked abu Ja'far, *'Alayhi al-Salam*, about a man who has two hundred dirham less one dirham for eleven months, then he gains one more dirham thereafter during the twelfth month to complete the two hundred. Is there Zakat on him? He (the Imam) said, 'No, Zakat is not due on him until a year passes and it is two hundred dirham. If it was one hundred fifty dirham and after one month he finds a fifty dirham, in this case also, Zakat is not due on him until one year passes with two hundred dirham.' I then asked, 'If one has two hundred dirham less one dirham and after several days and before passing of a month he finds one dirham and then one year passes with the rest of dirham with him, is there Zakat on him? He (the Imam) said, 'Yes, (there is Zakat on him). If all of it has not remained with him for one complete year Zakat is not obligatory.'

"Zurarah and Muhammad ibn Muslim have said that abu 'Abd Allah, *'Alayhi al-Salam*, has said, 'If one has a certain amount of asset which remains with him for one year, he is required to pay its Zakat.' I then asked him (the Imam), 'What happens if he gives it as gift to someone, one month before the passing of one year or one day? He (the Imam) said, 'Zakat is not due on him ever.' Zurarah has narrated from him (the Imam) that he (the Imam) said, 'This is like the case of one who in the month of Ramadan is at home and then travels in the end of the day intending to avoid the penalty which becomes obligatory on him.' He (the Imam) said, 'When he sees the crescent of the twelfth month Zakat becomes obligatory on him.' He (the Imam) has said, 'When he sees the crescent of the twelfth month Zakat is due but if he gives it as a gift earlier, it is permissible, and he is not obligated for anything in this matter like the case of one who travels and then discontinues his fast. He cannot refuse once the year passes, but he can refuse if one year is not passed. He cannot refuse to pay what belongs to others. It applies to the asset on which one year has passed.' Zurarah has said that he then asked, 'A man had two hundred dirham and he gives it as gift to his brothers or children or his family to avoid Zakat. He did it one month before a year is complete.' He (the Imam) said, 'Once the twelfth month comes one year is complete and Zakat is obligatory.' I (Zurarah) then asked, 'Can he use it (like giving as gift) before the year is complete?' He (the Imam) said, 'Yes, it is permissible for him.' I then said, 'He is avoiding Zakat.' He (the Imam) said, 'What he has allowed into his soul is greater than avoiding payment of Zakat.' I said, 'He can get it back (from the recipient of gift).' He (the Imam) said, 'How can you tell if he can get it back? It is out of his hand (possession) already.' I said, 'He can give it as conditional gift.' He (the Imam) said, 'Once he calls it a gift it becomes a lawful commitment, the condition falls (is invalid) and he is held responsible for Zakat.' I then asked, 'Why does the condition fall, the gift is approved and he is responsible for Zakat?' He (the Imam) said, 'This is an invalid condition, commitment for the gift is made and punishment of non-payment of Zakat is necessary.' He (the Imam) then said, 'It is for him if he purchases therewith a house or land or goods.' Zurarah has said that he then said, 'Your father said to me that if one by doing so avoids Zakat he must pay it.' He (the Imam) said, 'My father has spoken the truth. He must pay what is obligatory on him and he is not required to pay what is not obligatory up on him.' He (the Imam) said, 'Think about a man who faints for a day, then dies and his Salat (prayer) is missed. Is there any Salat (prayer) on him now that he is dead?' I replied, 'No, Salat (prayer) is not obligatory on him unless he gains consciousness on the same day.' He (the Imam) then said, 'If a man becomes ill in the month of Ramadan and dies in that month, will there be fasting on his behalf?' I replied, 'No, it is not necessary.' He (the Imam) said, 'In the same way, a man is not required to pay Zakat until a year is complete.'"

H 5803, Ch. 14, h 5

Ali ibn Ibrahim has narrated from his father from 'Isma'il ibn Marrar from Yunus from Ishaq ibn 'Ammar who has said the following:

"I once asked abu Ibrahim, *'Alayhi al-Salam*, about a man who is absent but has inherited a certain asset. Is there Zakat on him? He (the Imam) said, 'No, Zakat is not due on him until he comes.' I then asked, 'Is he required to pay Zakat as soon as he comes?' He (the Imam) said, 'No, until one year passes.'"

Chapter 15 - Rules about Profits after Paying Zakat

H 5804, Ch. 15, h 1

Muhammad ibn Yahya has narrated from Ahmad ibn Muhammad and al-Husayn ibn Muhammad has narrated from Mu'alla' ibn Muhammad all from al-Hassan ibn Ali al-Washsha' from Aban from Shu'ayb who has said the following:

"Abu 'Abd Allah, *'Alayhi al-Salam*, has said, 'Whatever you gain by means of assets, pay Zakat thereof and whatever you receive as inheritance or gift, pay Zakat thereof after a year passes.'"

H 5805, Ch. 15, h 2

Ali ibn Muhammad has narrated from ibn Jumhur from his father from Yunus from 'Abd al-Hamid ibn 'Awwad who has said the following:

"I once asked abu 'Abd Allah, *'Alayhi al-Salam*, about a man who has a certain asset which remains in his possession for one year, then he gains other assets before the passing of one year. He (the Imam) said, 'When one year passes with the first asset, pay Zakat for both assets.'"

Chapter 16 - Rules about Business Losses

H 5806, Ch. 16, h 1

Muhammad ibn 'Isma'il has narrated, from al-Fadl ibn Shadhan, from Safwan ibn Yahya, from Mansur ibn Hazim, from abu Rabi' al-Shamiy who has said the following:

"I once asked abu 'Abd Allah, *'Alayhi al-Salam*, about a man who purchases a certain kind of goods but its value falls. He had paid Zakat before purchasing such asset. Is there Zakat on him or Zakat becomes due when he sells it? He (the Imam) said, 'If he had held it to increase his capital, he is required to pay Zakat.'"

H 5807, Ch. 16, h 2

Ali ibn Ibrahim has narrated from his father from Hammad ibn 'Isa from Hariz from Muhammad ibn Muslim who has said the following:

"I once asked abu 'Abd Allah, *'Alayhi al-Salam*, about a man who purchases a certain kind of goods and its value falls. He had paid Zakat of the asset with which he paid for the goods. When is he required to pay Zakat? He (the Imam) said, 'If he is holding it to preserve his capital, Zakat is not due but if he holds it after getting back his capital, he then is required to pay Zakat, with a view to the fact that he holds it after getting back his capital.' I asked him (the Imam) about a man with whom assets are kept in deposit and he uses them in business. He (the Imam) said, 'If one year passes he is required to pay Zakat.'"

H 5808, Ch. 16, h 3

Muhammad ibn Yahya has narrated from Ahmad ibn Muhammad from 'Uthman ibn 'Isa from Sama'ah who has said the following:

"I once asked abu 'Abd Allah, *'Alayhi al-Salam*, about a man who has an asset in stock which remains with him for one year or more time. He (the Imam) said,

'It is not subject to Zakat until he sells it, unless he has paid for it from his capital and has kept it on hold expecting an increase. If that is the case then it is subject to Zakat. If he has not paid for it from his capital, it is not subject to Zakat until he sells it. If he has kept it in stock in substance when he sells it then he is required to pay Zakat of one year only.'"

H 5809, Ch. 16, h 4

Sama'ah has said the following:

"I once asked abu 'Abd Allah, *'Alayhi al-Salam*, about a man who has a certain asset for profit-sharing purposes. Is such asset subject to Zakat if used in business? He (the Imam) said, 'He must ask the shareholders to pay Zakat and if they said that they pay Zakat, he then is not required to do anything more than that. If they ask him to pay Zakat then he must pay.' I then said, 'What happens if they said that we pay but he knows that they do not pay?' He (the Imam) said, 'If they confirm that they pay, he then is not required to do anything more than that, but if they say that they do not pay Zakat, then it is proper for him not to accept the asset to work with it in business.'"

"In another Hadith from him (the Imam) it is said that if he out of his own choice and from his own share of profit pays Zakat he can do so. I then asked him (the Imam) about a man who gains five hundred dirham profit in one year. Six and seven hundred is its expenses and the capital for profit sharing. He (the Imam) said, 'Zakat is not due on profits.'"

H 5810, Ch. 16, h 5

Ali ibn Ibrahim has narrated from his father from 'Isma'il ibn Marrar from Yunus from al-'Ala' ibn Razin from Muhammad ibn Muslim who has said the following:

"He (the Imam), *'Alayhi al-Salam*, has said, 'Any asset with which you work is subject to Zakat when one year passes.' Yunus has said that the explanation for it is that whatever asset is used in business, animals or other assets, it is subject to Zakat."

H 5811, Ch. 16, h 6

A number of our people have narrated from Sahl ibn Ziyad from Ahmad ibn Muhammad from ibn abu Nasr from Hammad ibn 'Isa from Ishaq ibn 'Ammar who has said the following:

"I once asked abu Ibrahim, *'Alayhi al-Salam*, about a man who keeps a certain asset in stock expecting increase and he wants to sell it. Is what is paid for it subject to Zakat? He (the Imam) said, 'No, it is not subject to Zakat until he sells it and one year passes with the asset in his possession.'"

H 5812, Ch. 16, h 7

Ahmad ibn Idris has narrated from Muhammad ibn 'Abd al-Jabbar from Safwan ibn Yahya from Muhammad ibn Hakim from Khalid ibn al-Hajjaj al-Karkhiy who has said the following:

"I once asked abu 'Abd Allah, *'Alayhi al-Salam*, about Zakat. He (the Imam) said, 'Whatever asset you have for doing business which increases and there is no obstacle for you to sell, except expecting increase over increase, then you must pay Zakat. Whatever you have for business in which there are losses then it is a different issue.'"

H 5813, Ch. 16, h 8

Muhammad ibn Yahya has narrated from Ahmad ibn Muhammad ibn 'Isa from al-Husayn ibn Sa'id from al-Qasim ibn Muhammad from Ali ibn abu Hamzah from abu Basir who has said the following:

"Abu 'Abd Allah, *'Alayhi al-Salam*, has said, 'Do not accept an asset for profit-sharing business unless you pay its Zakat or the shareholder pays.' He (the Imam) said, 'If you have an asset in stock in your home for which you are offered payment for your capital but you ignored to receive it, you are required to pay its Zakat.'"

H 5814, Ch. 16, h 9

A number of our people have narrated from Ahmad ibn Muhammad from Ali ibn al-Hakam from `Isma'il ibn 'Abd al-Khaliq who has said the following:

"Once Sa'id al-`A'raj asked him (the Imam), *'Alayhi al-Salam*, when I was listening, 'We stock oil and ghee for business and it remains with us for one year or two years. Is there Zakat on it? He (the Imam) said, 'If you make profit or find your capital, you must pay Zakat, but if you are just waiting because you do not find other asset, then Zakat is not due on it until it is sold for gold or silver. When it becomes gold or silver, then pay Zakat of the year in which you did business.'"

Chapter 17 - Animals Subject to Zakat and Those Not Subject to Zakat

H 5815, Ch. 17, h 1

Ali ibn Ibrahim has narrated from his father from Hammad ibn 'Isa from Hariz from Muhammad ibn Muslim and Zurarah who has said the following:

"The two Imam, *'Alayhim al-Salam*, have said that `Amir al-Mu'minin, levied two dinar of Zakat on every Arabian horse every year and one dinar of Zakat on non-Arabian horse."

H 5816, Ch. 17, h 2

Hammad ibn 'Isa has narrated from Hariz from Zurarah who has said the following:

"I once asked abu 'Abd Allah, *'Alayhi al-Salam*, if there is Zakat on mules. He (the Imam) said, 'No, Zakat is not due on it.' I then said, 'How is it that there is Zakat on horses but not on mules?' He (the Imam) said, 'It is because mules do not reproduce but mares do so and Zakat is not due on horses.' I then asked are donkeys subject to Zakat?' He (the Imam) said, 'It is not subject to Zakat.' I then asked, 'Are horses and camels that one uses for riding subject to Zakat?' He (the Imam) said, 'No, Zakat is not due on whatever one feeds. Only that which is left in pastures land to graze for one year is subject to Zakat, while in one's possession. Other than this is not subject to Zakat.'"

H 5817, Ch. 17, h 3

Muhammad ibn Yahya has narrated from Ahmad ibn Muhammad from 'Uthman ibn 'Isa from Sama'ah who has said the following:

"Abu 'Abd Allah, *'Alayhi al-Salam*, has said, 'Slaves are not subject to Zakat unless they are for business purposes, because they are from assets that are subject to Zakat.''

H 5818, Ch. 17, h 4

Ali ibn Ibrahim has narrated from his father from Hammad ibn 'Isa from Hariz from Zurarah and Muhammad ibn Muslim who has said the following:

"They asked abu Ja'far and abu 'Abd Allah, *'Alayhim al-Salam*, about slaves. They (the two Imam), *'Alayhim al-Salam*, said, 'Zakat which is more than one Sa' of date is not due per-head, when one year passes. There is nothing on what is paid as his price unless he has remained in one's possession for one year.'"

H 5819, Ch. 17, h 5

Hammad ibn 'Isa has narrated from Hariz from 'Abd al-Rahman ibn abu 'Abd Allah who has said the following:

"I once asked abu 'Abd Allah, *'Alayhi al-Salam*, about a man who has not paid Zakat for his camel or sheep for two years then sells to another man who, as part of the deal, is asked to pay its Zakat. He (the Imam) said, 'Yes, Zakat is collected from him and the seller pursues him for payment or himself pays its Zakat.'"

H 5820, Ch. 17, h 6

Ali ibn Ibrahim has narrated from his father from ibn abu 'Umayr from certain persons of our people who has said the following:

"I once asked abu 'Abd Allah, *'Alayhi al-Salam*, about a man who has a camel or cow or sheep or other assets. One year passes and the camel, cow or sheep dies and the asset is destroyed because of fire. He (the Imam) said, 'He does not owe anything.'"

H 5821, Ch. 17, h 7

Ali ibn Ibrahim has narrated from his father from ibn abu 'Umayr from who has said the following:

"'Amir al-Mu'minin, Ali, *'Alayhi al-Salam*, would not demand Zakat for small camels until one year passed as well as for working camels. It seems as if Zakat is not due on male (camels) because it is used to carry loads."

Chapter 18 - Zakat of Camels

H 5822, Ch. 18, h 1

Ali ibn Ibrahim has narrated from his father from Hammad ibn 'Isa from Hariz from Zurarah, Muhammad ibn Muslim, abu Basir, Burayd al-'Ijliy and al-Fudayl who has said the following:

"Abu Ja'far, and abu 'Abd Allah, *'Alayhim al-Salam*, have said that the amount of Zakat on camel is one sheep for every five camels, until they number twenty-five in which case it is one Ibnatu Makhad. Thereafter there is no increase in Zakat until the number reaches thirty-five, in which case Zakat is one Ibnatu Labun. Thereafter there is no increase in Zakat until the number reaches forty-five, in which case Zakat is one Hiqqah Taruqah al-Fahl. Thereafter there is no increase in Zakat until the number reaches sixty, in which case Zakat is one Jadha'ah. Thereafter there is no increase in Zakat until the number reaches seventy-five, in which case Zakat is Ibnata Labun. Thereafter there is no increase in Zakat until the number reaches ninety, in which case Zakat is Hiqqatan Taruqat al-Fahl. Thereafter there is no increase in Zakat until the number reaches one hundred twenty, in which case Zakat is Hiqqatan Taruqata al-Fahl. If one more camel increases, thereafter, on every fifty, Zakat is one

Hiqqah and on every forty, Zakat is one Ibnatu Labun. All additional camels from this point on are calculated according to the numbers already mentioned. Zakat is not due on what is between two numbers as well as on fractions, or working camels. Only camels that graze in pastures are subject to Zakat. He (the narrator) has said that he then asked, 'Is non-Arabic camel which grazes subject to Zakat?' He (the Imam) said, 'It is just like Arabic camels.'"

H 5823, Ch. 18, h 2

Ali ibn Ibrahim has narrated from his father and Muhammad ibn 'Isma'il from al-Fadl ibn Shadhan all from ibn abu 'Umayr from 'Abd al-Rahman ibn al-Hajjaj who has said the following:

"Abu 'Abd Allah, *'Alayhi al-Salam*, has said, 'On five Qala'is (young she camel) Zakat is one sheep and Zakat is not due on less than five camels. On ten Zakat is two sheep, on fifteen Zakat is three sheep, on twenty Zakat is four sheep, on twenty-five Zakat is five sheep and on twenty-six Zakat is one Bintu Makhad up to thirty-five.' 'Abd al-Rahman has said that this is the difference between us and the people. If one is increased Zakat is one Bintu Labun up to forty-five. With the increase of one more camel Zakat is one Hiqqah up to sixty, thereafter if one more camel is increased Zakat is one Jadha'ah up to seventy-five, thereafter if one more camel is increased Zakat is Binta Labun up to ninety. When camels become many, then for every fifty Zakat is one Hiqqah."

H 5824, Ch. 18, h 3

Ali ibn Ibrahim has narrated from his father from ibn abu 'Umayr from 'Umar ibn 'Udhaynah from Zurarah who has said the following:

"Abu Ja'far, *'Alayhi al-Salam*, has said, 'Zakat is not due on camel's young until one year passes from the day they are born.'"

(The following chapter seems to be the words of the compiler (rh))

Chapter 19 - (Without Title)

The ages of camels are calculated as follows: From the day a camel is born, up to one year it is called Huwar. When it enters the second year, it is called ibnu Makhad because the mother becomes pregnant. When it enters in the third year, it is called Ibna Labun because the mother has given birth and she has milk now. When it enters the fourth year, if a he-camel it is called Hiqqa and if it is a she-camel it is called Hiqqah because it has become able to carry a load. When it enters the fifth year, it is called Jadha'a. When it enters the sixth year, it is called Thaniyah because it has made its thaniyah (front teeth) to fall. When it enters the seventh year, it allows its ruba'iyah to fall and it is called Ruba'i. When it enters the eighth year, it allows its teeth which is after Ruba'iyah to fall and it is called Sadis. When it enters the ninth year, its canine tooth falls and it is called bazil. When it enters the tenth year, it is called Mukhlif and thereafter there is no name for it. The ages of camels mentioned and counted in Zakat are from bintu Makhad to al-Jadha'.

Chapter 20 - Zakat of Cows

H 5825, Ch. 20, h 1

Ali ibn Ibrahim has narrated from his father from Hammad ibn 'Isa from Hariz from Zurarah, Muhammad ibn Muslim, abu Basir, Burayd al-'Ijliy and al-Fudayl who have said the following:

"Abu Ja'far, and abu 'Abd Allah, *'Alayhim al-Salam*, have said, 'The amount of Zakat on cows is one Tabi' (a one year old cow) Hawliy for every thirty cows. Zakat is not due on less than this number of cows. Zakat on forty cows is one Musinnah (a young cow that is just growing teeth) Baqarah. Zakat is not due on what is between forty up to sixty. When it becomes sixty, Zakat is two Tabi' up to seventy. When it becomes seventy, Zakat is one Tabi' and one Musinnah up to eighty, in which case Zakat on every forty, is one Musinnah up to ninety in which case Zakat is three Tabi' Hawliy. When it becomes one hundred twenty, Zakat on every forty is one Musinnah; and thereafter the cows are counted according to their ages. Zakat is not due on what is between two numbers. (It is like the case of camels) Zakat is not due on fractions or working cows. Zakat is obligatory only on grazing cows, which are not fed by the owner. Zakat is not due for cows on which one year has not passed. When one year passes, then Zakat is obligatory.'"

H 5826, Ch. 20, h 2

It is narrated from Zurarah who has said the following:

"I once asked abu Ja'far, *'Alayhi al-Salam*, about buffalos if there is Zakat for it. He (the Imam) said, 'It is like cows.'"

Chapter 21 - Zakat of Sheep

H 5827, Ch. 21, h 1

Ali ibn Ibrahim has narrated from his father from Hammad ibn 'Isa from Hariz from Zurarah, Muhammad ibn Muslim, abu Basir, Burayd and al-Fudayl who have said the following:

"Abu Ja'far, and abu 'Abd Allah, *'Alayhim al-Salam*, have said, 'The amount of Zakat for sheep is one sheep for every forty sheep. There is not anything on what is less than forty. Thereafter there is no increase in Zakat up until it is one hundred twenty. Once it is more than one hundred twenty by one sheep, Zakat is two sheep; and Zakat is no more than two sheep until its number is two hundred. When it is more than two hundred by one sheep, then Zakat is three sheep. Thereafter there is no increase until it is three hundred and one sheep; in which case Zakat is four sheep. There is no increase until it is four hundred. When it is four hundred, then on every one hundred Zakat is one sheep and this supersedes the previous calculations. Thereafter Zakat is not due on what is less than one hundred or what is between the two taxable consecutive numbers.' The two Imam have said, 'Zakat is not due on whatever has not remained in the possession of its owner for one complete year. Once one year is complete, Zakat is obligatory.'"

H 5828, Ch. 21, h 2
Muhammad ibn 'Isma'il has narrated from al-Fadl ibn Shadhan and Ali ibn Ibrahim has narrated from his father from all from ibn abu 'Umayr from 'Abd al-Rahman ibn al-Hajjaj who has said the following:
"Abu 'Abd Allah, *'Alayhi al-Salam*, has said, 'Zakat is not due on what is fed at home (as opposed to grazing) or that which feeds others and that which is kept for its milk or ram kept for breeding.'"

H 5829, Ch. 21, h 3
Muhammad ibn Yahya has narrated from Ahmad ibn Muhammad from Muhammad ibn 'Uthman ibn 'Isa from Sama'ah who has said the following:
"Abu 'Abd Allah, *'Alayhi al-Salam*, has said, 'Akulah is not accepted. It is the great ewe among sheep, or the one that gives birth to it, as well as its breeder.'"

H 5830, Ch. 21, h 4
Ahmad ibn Idris has narrated from Muhammad ibn 'Abd al-Jabbar from Safwan ibn Yahya from Ishaq ibn 'Ammar who has said the following:
"I once asked abu 'Abd Allah, *'Alayhi al-Salam*, about lamb when Zakat is obligatory for it. He (the Imam) said, 'Zakat is obligatory when it becomes Jadha' (one year old).

Chapter 22 - Disciplines for Zakat Collector

H 5831, Ch. 22, h 1
Ali ibn Ibrahim has narrated from his father from Hammad ibn 'Isa from Hariz from Burayd ibn Mu'awiyah who has said the following:
"I heard abu 'Abd Allah, *'Alayhi al-Salam*, say, ''Amir al-Mu'minin, *'Alayhi al-Salam*, gave the following disciplinary instructions to a zakat collector. He (the Imam) then sent him to the suburbs of the city of al-Kufah. "O servant of Allah, set out for this task: but you must be pious before Allah who is one and has no partner. You must not give preference to your worldly matters over the matters of the next life. You must be protective of what I have entrusted you with and pay proper attention to the rights of Allah. When you arrive in the community of so and so tribe, disembark at the place, which is the source of their water. Do not mingle among their houses. Thereafter go in a dignified and honorable manner to meet them until you stand among them and say to them the expression of greeting, then say to them, 'O servants of Allah, the person who possesses Divine Authority has sent me to ask you to pay the rights of Allah which are due on your wealth and I collect them. Is there anything of the rights of Allah due on your wealth that you must pay to the person who possesses Divine Authority?' If anyone says, 'No, (there is not anything due on my wealth).' You must not ask him again. If anyone among them answered you positively, then follow him without frightening him or promising him anything but good. When you reach the location of his wealth, do not enter that place without his permission; he owns most of the wealth. Then say to him, 'O servant of Allah, do you allow me to enter the location of your wealth?' If he allows you, then do not enter in a dominant or rough manner. Make two sections of the wealth, then allow him to choose one section and do not interfere with the section that he chooses. Thereafter make the remaining section into two sections and again allow him to

choose whichever section he chooses. You must not interfere with his choice. Continue this process until you arrive at the remaining section that is the portion of zakat, the right of Allah, the most Holy, the most High. Take possession of the portion that is the right of Allah in his wealth. If he asks you to cancel the process, you should do so. Mix and start the process all over again until you can take possession of the right of Allah from his wealth. When you take possession, then do not mishandle it. You must remain helpful, kind, trustworthy and protective of the property you have received. You must not handle anything thereof roughly. Thereafter, dispatch promptly your collection of every community to us and we will handle it according to the commandments of Allah, the Most Majestic, the Most Glorious. If you dispatch it through a messenger, advise him not to block or separate a camel from her young, and do not over-milk the camel to harm her young. He must not tire the camel by riding excessively. He must follow rules of justice toward them. He must allow them to drink from every source of water on the way. In the hours, which are for their grazing and rest, he must not drive them on the plain road. He must be kind and caring to them so they can reach us, by the permission of Allah in good health and condition, not tired or overworked. We then, by the permission of Allah, distribute them according to the book of Allah and the Sunnah of the Messenger of Allah among the friends of Allah. Following these instructions will allow you to have greater reward and it is closer to the dictate of your reason. Allah looks upon you and these properties, and upon your hard work, good advice to your commander who has commissioned you for the task. The Messenger of Allah has said, 'Whoever, for the sake of Allah, pays attention to his guardian, works hard obediently and gives good advice to him (guardian) and to his Imam, in the company of the high position, he will join our company.'"" He (narrator) has said, 'Abu 'Abd Allah, *'Alayhi al-Salam*, wept and said, "O Burayd, by Allah, all respectable matters of Allah have already been disregarded. The book of Allah and the Sunnah of the Messenger of Allah are not followed in this world any more. Nothing of the laws of justice is maintained in this world after the passing away of Amir al-Mu'minin, *'Alayhi al-Salam*. Nothing of the laws of truth has ever since been followed." He then said, "I swear by Allah, days and night will not end until Allah will give life to the dead, cause the living to die, return the truth to the people of truth, and establish His religion which He has chosen for Himself and for His prophet. It is glad news for you. It indeed is glad news for you. Without any doubt, it is glad news for you. I swear by Allah, Truth does not exist anywhere in any place except in your hands.""'"

H 5832, Ch. 22, h 2

Hammad ibn 'Isa has narrated from Hariz from Muhammad ibn Muslim who has said the following:
"Abu 'Abd Allah, *'Alayhi al-Salam*, was asked, 'Does Zakat collector call people in one place or he comes to where people are? He (the Imam) said, 'No, he comes to their places and collects their charity (Zakat).'"

H 5833, Ch. 22, h 3

Muhammad ibn Yahya has narrated from Ahmad ibn Muhammad from Muhammad ibn Yahya from Ghiyath ibn Ibrahim who has said the following:

"Ja'far (abu 'Abd Allah), *'Alayhi al-Salam*, has narrated from his father from Ali, *'Alayhi al-Salam*, who has said, 'Charity (Zakat) is not sold before it is received (collected).'"

H 5834, Ch. 22, h 4

A number of our people have narrated from Ahmad ibn Muhammad ibn 'Isa from Muhammad ibn Yahya from Ghiyath ibn Ibrahim who has said the following:

"Ja'far, (abu 'Abd Allah), *'Alayhi al-Salam*, has narrated from his father who has that when Ali, *'Alayhi al-Salam*, would send a Zakat collector for his task and say to him, 'When you go to Zakat payer, say to him, "Give charity, may Allah grant you blessings, out of what Allah has granted you." If he turns away from you, then you must not go to him again.'"

H 5835, Ch. 22, h 5

Ali ibn Ibrahim has narrated from his father from ibn abu 'Umayr from 'Abd al-Rahman ibn al-Hajjaj from Muhammad ibn Khalid who has said the following:

"I once asked abu 'Abd Allah, *'Alayhi al-Salam*, about charity (Zakat). He (the Imam) said, 'It is not accepted from you.' He (the narrator) then said, 'I take it from my own assets.' Abu 'Abd Allah, *'Alayhi al-Salam*, said to him, 'Instruct your Zakat collector not to move from house to house, bring together what is apart and separate what is together. When he approaches people's assets he should make the sheep stand in two groups, then allow the owner to choose one of the two groups and allow him to have what he chooses. If the owner desires to have one, two or three sheep from the other group, allow him to have it. Thereafter receive his charity (Zakat). When charity (Zakat) is received, distribute it among those whom he (the owner of assets) wants. If something in exchange for the items received as Zakat is offered, then Zakat payer has the priority over others to have it, but if he does not want, it then can be sold (to others).'"

H 5836, Ch. 22, h 6

A number of our people have narrated from Ahmad ibn Muhammad from al-Hassan ibn Ali ibn Yaqtin from his brother Al-Husayn from Ali ibn Yaqtin who has said the following:

"I once asked abu al-Hassan, *'Alayhi al-Salam*, about Zakat which is of the rate of one out of ten and one who distributes it among those who are not harmful. He (the Imam) said, 'If he is trustworthy, instruct him to deliver it where it should be delivered; but if you cannot trust him, then take it from him and deliver where it should be delivered.'"

H 5837, Ch. 22, h 7

Ali ibn Ibrahim has narrated from his father from Muhammad ibn 'Isa from Yunus from Muhammad ibn Muqarrin ibn 'Abd Allah ibn Zam'ah ibn Subay' from his father from his grandfather from grandfather of his father who has said the following:

"Amir al-Mu'minin, *'Alayhi al-Salam*, wrote to him in the letter that he wrote to him with his own hand writing when he sent him to receive charity (Zakat). 'Those who owe Jadha'ah as Zakat for camels but do not have Jadha'ah but have Hiqqah, it is accepted from them, but they must give two sheep along with it or twenty dirham. Those who owe one Hiqqah as Zakat but do not have it, but have Jadha'ah, it is accepted from them and Zakat collector gives them two sheep or twenty dirham. Those who owe Hiqqah as Zakat but do not have Hiqqah but have Ibnata Labun, it is accepted from them with two sheep or twenty dirham. Those who owe Ibnata Labun as Zakat but do not have it, but they have Hiqqah, it is accepted from them and Zakat collector gives them two sheep or twenty dirham. Those who owe Ibnata Labun as Zakat but do not have it but they have Ibnata Makhad, it is accepted from them along with two sheep or twenty dirham. Those who owe Ibnata Makhad as Zakat but do not have it but they have Ibnata Labun, it is accepted from them and Zakat collector gives them two sheep or twenty dirham. Those who do not have Ibnata Makhad as it is but they have a male Ibnata Labun it is accepted from them without anything extra. Those who do not have anything other than four camels and have no other assets, there is not anything on them unless the owner desires (otherwise). If one's asset is five camels, then its Zakat is one sheep.'"

(Ahadith 2-7 are best explained in the form of fatwa.)

H 5838, Ch. 22, h 8
A number of our people have narrated from Sahl ibn Ziyad from Ali ibn al-Asbat from Ahmad ibn Mu'ammar who has said that narrated to me abu al-Hassan al-'Uraniy from Isma'il ibn Ibrahim from Muhajir from a man from Thaqif who has said the following:
"Ali ibn abu Talib, *'Alayhi al-Salam*, commissioned me as collector of zakat (charity) for Ban Qiya (al-Qadisiyah today) and suburbs of al-Kufah. In the presence of people he said to me, 'Take good care of taxes and do not disregard even one dirham.' However, see me before you leave for your work.' He (the narrator) has said, 'I went to see him and he said to me, "Whatever you heard me say to you was for protective measures only. Never ever beat up a Muslim, a Jew, or a Christian taxpayer for a dirham of tax or buy an animal for work for a dirham. We only receive taxes in ease."'"

(The following chapters are best explained by fatwa.)

Chapter 23 - Zakat on Wealth of Orphans

H 5839, Ch. 23, h 1
Ali ibn Ibrahim has narrated from his father and Muhammad ibn Yahya has narrated from Ahmad ibn Muhammad all from ibn abu 'Umayr from Hammad ibn 'Uthman from al-Halabiy who has said the following:
"I once asked abu 'Abd Allah, *'Alayhi al-Salam*, about the assets of the orphans if there is Zakat on it. He (the Imam) said, 'If it (asset) is not active (not used in business) Zakat is not due on it. If you use it in business, then you are responsible for it and its profit belongs to the orphan.'"

H 5840, Ch. 23 h 2
Muhammad ibn 'Isma'il has narrated from al-Fadl ibn Shadhan and Ahmad ibn Idris from Muhammad ibn 'Abd al-Jabbar all from Safwan ibn Yahya from Ishaq ibn 'Ammar from abu al-'Attar al-Khayyat who has said the following:
"I once asked abu 'Abd Allah, *'Alayhi al-Salam*, about the assets of orphans which are with me and I use it in business. He (the Imam) said, 'If you move it,

its Zakat is up on you.' I then said, 'I move it for eight months and leave it for four months.' He (the Imam) said, 'Zakat due on it is on you.'"

H 5841, Ch. 23, h 3

Ali ibn Ibrahim has narrated from his father from Hammad ibn 'Isa from Hariz from Muhammad ibn Muslim who has said the following:

"I once asked abu 'Abd Allah, *'Alayhi al-Salam*, if there is Zakat on orphan's assets. He (the Imam) said, 'No, Zakat is not due unless it is used in business or is made to work.'"

H 5842, Ch. 23, h 4

Hammad ibn 'Isa has narrated from Hariz from abu Basir who has said the following:

"I once heard abu 'Abd Allah, *'Alayhi al-Salam*, say, 'Zakat is not due on orphans' assets even when they become adults; they are not liable for Zakat of the previous years or of the remaining time, but when they become adults, they are required to pay Zakat. They are held responsible as others are held responsible.'"

H 5843, Ch. 23, h 5

Hammad ibn 'Isa has narrated from Hariz from Zurarah and Muhammad ibn Muslim who has said the following:

"Zakat is not due on loans people owe to orphans' as well as on the orphans immoveable assets; however, it is obligatory to pay Zakat for the orphans' grains.'"

H 5844, Ch. 23, h 6

Ali ibn Ibrahim has narrated from his father from 'Isma'il ibn Marrar from Yunus from Sa'id al-Samman who has said the following:

"I once heard abu 'Abd Allah, *'Alayhi al-Salam*, say, 'Zakat is not due on the assets of orphans unless it is used in business, in which case the profit belongs to the orphans' and if it (using it in business) is assigned to someone, then Zakat is upon the one who uses it in business.'"

H 5845, Ch. 23, h 7

Ahmad ibn Idris has narrated from Muhammad ibn 'Abd al-Jabbar from Safwan ibn Yahya from Yunus ibn Ya'qub who has said the following:

"I once sent (a letter) to abu 'Abd Allah, *'Alayhi al-Salam*, to find out when Zakat becomes obligatory for the assets of my small brothers. He (the Imam) said, 'When Salat (prayer) becomes obligatory up on them, Zakat also become obligatory; however, in the case of those of them on whom Salat (prayer) is not obligatory but their asset is used in business, you must pay Zakat for such assets.'"

H 5846, Ch. 23, h 8

Muhammad ibn Yahya has narrated from Muhammad ibn al-Husayn from Muhammad ibn al-Qasim ibn al-Fudayl who has said the following:

"I once wrote to abu al-Hassan, al-Rida', *'Alayhi al-Salam*, and asked about the executor of the will if it is obligatory on him to pay Zakat of al-Fitrah for the orphans if they have assets. He (the Imam) wrote to me, 'Zakat is not due on orphans.'"

Chapter 24 - Zakat on Wealth of Slaves, al-Mukatib and the Insane People

H 5847, Ch. 24, h 1

Ali ibn Ibrahim has narrated from his father from ibn abu 'Umayr from 'Abd Allah ibn Sinan who has said the following:

"Abu 'Abd Allah, *'Alayhi al-Salam*, has said, 'Zakat is not due on the asset of slaves even if it amounts to a million; but they cannot receive Zakat if they become needy.'"

H 5848, Ch. 24, h 2

Muhammad ibn 'Isma'il has narrated from al-Fadl ibn Shadhan, from ibn abu 'Umayr from 'Abd al-Rahman ibn al-Hajjaj who has said the following:

"I once asked abu 'Abd Allah, *'Alayhi al-Salam*, about the case of one of our women who is mixed (with insanity) if she is required to pay Zakat. He (the Imam) said, 'If her assets are made to work, then Zakat is obligatory on her, but if it is not made to work, Zakat is not obligatory.'"

H 5849, Ch. 24, h 3

Muhammad ibn Yahya has narrated from Ahmad ibn Muhammad from Muhammad from al-'Abbas ibn Ma'ruf from Ali ibn Mahziyar from al-Husayn ibn Sa'id from Muhammad ibn al-Fudayl from Musa ibn Bakr who has said the following:

"I once asked abu al-Hassan, *'Alayhi al-Salam*, about a woman who is affected mentally and she has an asset which is in the hands of her brother, if there is Zakat on it. He (the Imam) said, 'If her brother does business with it Zakat is obligatory.'"

"A number of our people have narrated from Sahl ibn Ziyad from Ahmad ibn Muhammad from ibn abu Nasr from Muhammad ibn Sama'ah from Musa ibn Bakr from Salih a similar Hadith."

H 5850, Ch. 24, h 4

Muhammad ibn Yahya has narrated from Ahmad ibn Muhammad ibn Khalid from abu ibn al-Bakhtariy who has said the following:

"Abu 'Abd Allah, *'Alayhi al-Salam*, has said, 'Zakat is not due on the assets of al-Mukatib (a slave who has contracted his freedom in exchange for a certain amount of payment to his owner).'"

H 5851, Ch. 24, h 5

Muhammad ibn Yahya has narrated from Ahmad ibn al-Khashshab from Ali ibn al-Husayn from Muhammad ibn abu Hamzah from 'Abd Allah ibn Sinan who has said the following:

"I once asked abu 'Abd Allah, *'Alayhi al-Salam*, about the case of a slave who has an asset; if there is Zakat on it. He (the Imam) said, 'No, Zakat is not due on it.' I then asked, 'Is his owner required to pay Zakat?' He (the Imam) said, 'No, because it (asset) cannot go to his owner and it is not for the slave.'"

Chapter 25 - Rules about Sultan's Taxes on Taxpayers

H 5852, Ch. 25, h 1

Ali ibn Ibrahim has narrated from his father from ibn abu 'Umayr from 'Abd al-Rahman ibn al-Hajjaj from Sulayman ibn Khalid who has said the following:

"I once heard abu 'Abd Allah, *'Alayhi al-Salam*, say, 'Once companions of my father came to him and asked about the money that al-Sultan (the ruler) makes them to pay. My father sympathized with them, knowing that receiving Zakat is not lawful unless one is a proper beneficiary, he instructed them to count such payment as Zakat. I, by Allah, thought about them and then said to my father, "Father, if they hear it, no one, thereafter, will pay Zakat (to proper beneficiaries)." My father said, "Son, it is a truth that Allah loves to be expressed."'"

H 5853, Ch. 25, h 2

Muhammad ibn Yahya has narrated from Muhammad ibn al-Husayn from Safwan ibn Yahya from Ya'qub ibn Shu'ayb who has said the following:

"I once asked abu 'Abd Allah, *'Alayhi al-Salam*, about a man who is made (by the ruler) to pay one out of ten if he can count it as Zakat. He (the Imam) said, 'Yes, he can do so if he wants.'"

H 5854, Ch. 25, h 3

A number of our people have narrated from Sahl ibn Ziyad from Ahmad ibn Muhammad from ibn abu Nasr from Rifa'ah ibn Musa who has said the following:

"I once asked abu 'Abd Allah, *'Alayhi al-Salam*, about a man who inherits a piece of land or buys it then pays its taxes to al-Sultan (the ruler), is he required to pay one out of ten (as Zakat)? He (the Imam) said, 'No, he is not required to pay.'"

H 5855, Ch. 25, h 4

Muhammad ibn 'Isma'il has narrated from al-Fadl ibn Shadhan from Safwan ibn Yahya from 'Is ibn al-Qasim who has said the following:

"Abu 'Abd Allah, *'Alayhi al-Salam*, has said, 'Whatever banu 'Umayyah make you to pay, count it (as Zakat) and do not give anything to them if you can; no assets will be left if you pay twice.'"

H 5856, Ch. 25, h 5

Muhammad ibn Yahya has narrated from Ahmad ibn Muhammad from 'Abd Allah ibn Malik from abu Qatadah from Sahl ibn al-Yasa' who after establishing Sahl Abad asked abu al-Hassan Musa, *'Alayhi al-Salam*, the following:

"Sahl once asked abu al-Hassan, Musa, *'Alayhi al-Salam*, about what he pays to al-Sultan (the ruler). He (the Imam) said, 'If al-Sultan (the ruler) receives its Kharaj (taxes) there is not anything on you; but if al-Sultan (the ruler) does not receive anything, then you pay one out of ten of whatever is due.'"

H 5857, Ch. 25, h 6

Ali ibn Ibrahim has narrated from al-Nawfaliy from al-Sakuniy who has said the following:

"Abu Ja'far, *'Alayhi al-Salam*, has narrated from his ancestor, *'Alayhim al-Salam*, this Hadith. 'Whatever the collector of one out of ten (Zakat collector) charges you and deposits it in the mug (the safe), it is your Zakat. If he does not do so then do not count it as your Zakat.'"

Chapter 26 - Rules about Leftovers of Household Expenses

H 5858, Ch. 26, h 1

Ahmad ibn Idris has narrated from Muhammad ibn 'Abd al-Jabbar from Safwan ibn Yahya from Ishaq ibn 'Ammar who has said the following:

"I once asked abu al-Hassan, who passed away, *'Alayhi al-Salam*, about the two thousand that one has left with his family for two years' expenses is there Zakat on it? He (the Imam) said, 'If he is present, there is Zakat due but if he is not present Zakat is not due on it.'"

H 5859, Ch. 26, h 2

A number of our people have narrated from Ahmad ibn Muhammad from ibn abu 'Umayr from certain persons of our people who has said the following:

"He once asked abu 'Abd Allah, *'Alayhi al-Salam*, about a man who leaves one thousand dirham for the expenses of his family and it remains with them for one complete year is there Zakat on it? He (the Imam) said, 'If he stays Zakat is due, but if he is absent, Zakat is not due on it.'"

H 5860, Ch. 26, h 3

Ali ibn Ibrahim has narrated from his father from 'Isma'il ibn Marrar from Yunus from Sama'ah from abu Basir who has said the following:

"I once asked abu 'Abd Allah, *'Alayhi al-Salam*, about a man who leaves with his family three thousand dirham for the expenses of two years is there Zakat on it? He (the Imam) said, 'If he is present, Zakat is due, but if he is absent, Zakat is not due.'"

Chapter 27 - Zakat Paid to One Who is Found not to Be a Needy Person

H 5861, Ch. 27, h 1

A number of our people have narrated from Ahmad ibn Muhammad from ibn abu 'Umayr from al-Husayn ibn 'Uthman from the one whom he has mentioned who has said the following:

"I once asked abu 'Abd Allah, *'Alayhi al-Salam*, about a man who pays Zakat to a person whom as he sees is a needy person, but later finds out to be affluent. He (the Imam) said, 'Such payment is not sufficient for Zakat.'"

H 5862, Ch. 27, h 2

Ali ibn Ibrahim has narrated from his father from Ahmad ibn Muhammad from Muhammad ibn 'Isma'il has narrated from al-Fadl ibn Shadhan from all from ibn abu 'Umayr from al-Ahwal who has said the following:

"About a man who pays his Zakat before due time then the recipient becomes affluent before due time (end of the year), abu 'Abd Allah, *'Alayhi al-Salam*, has said, 'Zakat payer must pay again.'"

H 5863, Ch. 27, h 3

Muhammad ibn Yahya has narrated from Muhammad ibn al-Husayn from 'Uthman ibn 'Isa from abu al-Maghra' who has said the following:

"Abu 'Abd Allah, *'Alayhi al-Salam*, has said, 'Allah, most Blessed, most High, has made the affluent to share their wealth with the needy people; thus, they must not share it with others (affluent ones).'"

Chapter 28 - Zakat Paid To Those Who Do Not Believe in the Divine Authority of `A'immah

H 5864, Ch. 28, h 1

Ali ibn Ibrahim has narrated from his father from ibn abu 'Umayr from 'Umar ibn `Udhaynah from Zurarah, Bukayr, al-Fudayl, Muhammad ibn Muslim and Burayd al-'Ijliy who have said the following:

"Abu Ja'far, and abu 'Abd Allah, *'Alayhim al-Salam*, were asked about the case of one who follows such opinions as al-Harawriyah, al-Murji'ah, al-'Uthmaniyah and al-Qadriyah. He then repents and recognizes this issue (the Divine Authority of `A'immah) and corrects his opinion, is he required to perform the Qada' (compensatory prayer for) all of his Salat (prayer), fasting, payment of Zakat and Hajj; or is he not required to do them again? He (the Imam) said, 'He is not required to do any of these things again, except Zakat which is necessary to be paid because he has placed it improperly. The proper place for it is people of al-Wilayah (people who acknowledge Divine Authority of `A'immah, *'Alayhim al-Salam*).'"

H 5865, Ch. 28, h 2

Ali ibn Ibrahim has narrated from his father from Hammad from Hariz from 'Ubayd ibn Zurarah who has said the following:

"I once heard abu 'Abd Allah, *'Alayhi al-Salam*, say, 'Whoever withholds one dirham of right, he ends up spending two dirhams for the cause of falsehood. If one denies payment of one dirham of right on his wealth, Allah makes a snake of fire to curl around him on the Day of Judgment.' He (the narrator) has said that he asked about a man who is knowledgeable, but has paid his Zakat to undeserving people at a certain time has he to pay it again to the deserving people if he knows them? He (the Imam) said, 'Yes, he is required to do so.' I then asked, 'What should he do if he does not find any deserving people? Thus he did not pay, or he did not know if he owes anything or not, but later finds out that he owes.' He (the Imam) said, 'He is required to pay to the deserving people for the past.' I then asked, 'What is he required to do if he does not find the deserving people and pays to undeserving people although he had done his best and then found out bad things that he had done.' He (the Imam) said, 'He is not required to pay it one more time.'" Zurarah has narrated a similar Hadith, except that if he does his best he becomes free of his responsibility, but if he has fallen short in doing his best to find out proper beneficiary, then he is not free of his responsibility."

H 5866, Ch. 28, h 3

Hammad ibn 'Isa has narrated from Hariz from Zurarah and Muhammad ibn Muslim who has said the following:

"Abu 'Abd Allah, *'Alayhi al-Salam*, has said, 'Zakat cannot be given as a gift to relatives or be denied to non-relatives.'"

H 5867, Ch. 28, h 4

Ali ibn Ibrahim has narrated from his father from ibn abu 'Umayr from Jamil ibn Darraj formal-Walid ibn Sabih who has said the following:

"Shihab ibn "Abd Rabbihi once asked me to convey his Salam (greeting of peace) to abu 'Abd Allah, *'Alayhi al-Salam*, and that he becomes terrified in his sleep. I then said to abu 'Abd Allah, *'Alayhi al-Salam*, that Shihab has offered Salam (greeting of peace) and has said that he becomes terrified in his sleep. He (the Imam) said, 'Tell him to pay Zakat of his assets.' I then conveyed the message to Shihab and he asked me, 'Will you deliver to him (the Imam) a message?' I replied, 'Yes, I can do so.' He said, 'Tell him (the Imam) that even children, not to mention adults, know that I pay Zakat obligatory on my assets.' I (the narrator) then conveyed the message to him (the Imam) and abu 'Abd Allah, *'Alayhi al-Salam*, said, 'Say to him that he pays Zakat due on his assets but he does not give it to a proper beneficiary.'"

H 5868, Ch. 28, h 5

Ali ibn Ibrahim has narrated from his father from ibn abu 'Umayr from ibn `Udhaynah who has said the following:

"Abu 'Abd Allah, *'Alayhi al-Salam*, has stated this Hadith. 'Every deed that a Nasib (one hostile to `A'immah) does in his condition as such, then Allah grants him the favor of making him to acknowledge this issue (the Divine Authority of 'A'immah), He gives him the reward for all of his deeds except Zakat which he must pay again. It is because of his giving it to improper beneficiaries. The proper beneficiaries of Zakat are people who acknowledge al-Wilayah (the Divine Authority of 'A'immah). However, he is not required to perform Qada' (compensatory prayer for) his Salat (prayer) and fasting.'"

H 5869, Ch. 28, h 6

A number of our people have narrated from Ahmad ibn Muhammad from `Isma'il ibn Sa'd al-Ash'ariy who has said the following:

"I once asked al-Rida', *'Alayhi al-Salam*, if Zakat can be given to those who do not acknowledge this issue (the Divine Authority of 'A'immah). He (the Imam) said, 'No, not even al-Fitrah Zakat can be given to them.'"

Chapter 29 - Paying Zakat on Behalf of a Deceased

H 5870, Ch. 20, h 1

Muhammad ibn Yahya has narrated from Ahmad ibn Muhammad ibn 'Isa from al-Hassan ibn Mahbub from 'Abbad ibn Suhayb who has said the following:

"I once asked abu 'Abd Allah, *'Alayhi al-Salam*, about a man who misses paying Zakat of his assets during his life time. When he is about to die, he calculates all that he owes as Zakat and then in his will states that such and such amount must be paid as Zakat. Can such Zakat be paid to proper beneficiaries? He (the Imam) said, 'Yes, it is permissible and it is taken from all of the assets. It is like debts due on him. The heirs do not have any right in his legacy before payment of such Zakat about which he has made a will.'"

H 5871, Ch. 29, h 2

Ali ibn Ibrahim has narrated from his father from Hammad ibn 'Isa from Hariz from Zurarah who has said the following:

"I once asked abu Ja'far, *'Alayhi al-Salam*, about a man who does not pay Zakat until he is about to die. At such time if he pays Zakat in full is that acceptable? He (the Imam) said, 'Yes, it is acceptable.' I then asked, 'If he makes a will that from one-third of his legacy, Zakat which due on him must be paid, will that kind of will be considered sufficient for his Zakat?' He (the Imam) said, 'Yes, it is counted as his Zakat and it is not an optional good deed when there are obligatory matters up on him.'"

H 5872, Ch. 29, h 3

Ali ibn Ibrahim has narrated from his father and Muhammad ibn 'Isma'il has narrated from al-Fadl ibn Shadhan all from ibn abu 'Umayr from Shu'ayb who has said the following:

"I once asked abu 'Abd Allah, *'Alayhi al-Salam*, about the case of my brother who owes a large amount of Zakat, can I pay for him? He (the Imam) asked, 'Why do you pay it?' I replied, 'I do so out of precaution.' He (the Imam) said, 'Obviously, you provide him great relief.'"

H 5873, Ch. 28, h 4

Ali ibn Ibrahim has narrated from his father from ibn abu 'Umayr from Mu'awiyah ibn 'Ammar who has said the following:

"I once asked him (the Imam), *'Alayhi al-Salam*, about a man who at death owed five hundred dirham of Zakat and one Hajjatu al-Islam. His legacy is three hundred dirham. He has made a will about performing Hajjatu al-Islam for him as well as to pay his debt of Zakat. He (the Imam) said, 'Hajj must be performed for him from the closest distance (Makkah) and the rest is paid for his Zakat.'"

H 5874, Ch. 28, h 5

Ali ibn Ibrahim has narrated from his father from ibn abu 'Umayr from Ali ibn Yaqtin who has said the following:

"I once asked abu al-Hassan, al-Awwal, *'Alayhi al-Salam*, about a man who has died and he owes Zakat. He has made a will about payment of Zakat and his children are needy. If such payment is made it will harm them a great deal. He (the Imam) said, 'They take the amount of Zakat out of the legacy and pay it to themselves, except something out of it to pay to others.'"

Chapter 30 - Minimum and Maximum Amount of Zakat Payable to a Needy Person

H 5875, Ch. 30, h 1

Muhammad ibn Yahya has narrated from Ahmad ibn Muhammad from al-Hassan ibn Mahbub from abu Wallad al-Hannat who has said the following:

"I once heard abu 'Abd Allah, *'Alayhi al-Salam*, say, 'Less than five dirham of Zakat must not be given to anyone. This is the minimum that Allah, most Majestic, most Glorious, has made obligatory on the assets of the Muslims. Do not give anyone less than five dirham but give more and so on.'"

H 5876, Ch. 30, h 2

It is a narration from him (narrator of previous Hadith) by Ahmad from 'Abd al-Malik ibn 'Utaybah from Ishaq ibn 'Ammar who has said the following:

"I once asked abu al-Hassan, *'Alayhi al-Salam*, 'Can eighty dirham be given as Zakat to someone? He (the Imam) said, 'Yes, and increase it.' I then asked, 'Can one hundred dirham be given as Zakat to someone?' He (the Imam) said, 'Yes, you can make him rich if you can do so.'"

H 5877, Ch. 30, h 3

Ahmad ibn Idris has narrated from Muhammad ibn Ahmad from Ahmad ibn al-Hassan ibn Ali ibn Faddal from 'Amr ibn Sa'id from Musaddiq ibn Sadaqah from 'Ammar ibn Musa who has said the following:

"Abu 'Abd Allah, *'Alayhi al-Salam*, was once asked about how much Zakat can be given to one person. He (the Imam) said, that abu Ja'far, *'Alayhi al-Salam*, has said, 'When you pay make him rich.'"

H 5878, Ch. 30, h 4

Ali ibn Ibrahim has narrated from his father from ibn abu 'Umayr from Sa'id ibn Ghazwan who has said the following:

"Abu 'Abd Allah, *'Alayhi al-Salam*, has said, 'Pay from Zakat until you make him rich (sufficient for his one year's expenses).'"

Chapter 31 - Paying Zakat to Small Dependents of a Believer or Offset a Loan

H 5879, Ch. 31, h 1

Ali ibn Ibrahim has narrated from his father from Hammad ibn 'Isa from Hariz from abu Basir who has said the following:

"I once asked abu 'Abd Allah, *'Alayhi al-Salam*, about a man who dies and leaves behind dependents. Can Zakat be given to them? He (the Imam) said, 'Yes, until they grow up, become adults and ask (themselves) by what means could they live and survive if that Zakat was cut off from them.' I then said, 'They do not know.' He (the Imam) said, 'The memories of their dead must be preserved and the religion of their father must be made beloved to them, so that they pay attention to the religion of their father; and if they become adults and decide to go to others; then do not give them any Zakat.'"

H 5880, Ch. 31, h 2

Muhammad ibn 'Isma'il has narrated from al-Fadl ibn Shadhan and Muhammad ibn Yahya has narrated from Muhammad ibn al-Hassan all from Safwan ibn Yahya from 'Abd al-Rahman ibn al-Hajjaj who has said the following:

"I once asked abu al-Hassan, *'Alayhi al-Salam*, about a man of knowledge and excellence who dies owing a certain amount of debts. He was not corrupt, a spendthrift, or a known beggar; can his debts be paid from Zakat like one or two thousand? He (the Imam) said, 'Yes, it can be paid.'"

H 5881, Ch. 31, h 3

Al-Husayn ibn Muhammad has narrated from Mu'alla' ibn Muhammad from al-Hassan ibn Ali al-Washsha' from Ahmad ibn 'A'idh from abu Khadijah who has said the following:

"Abu 'Abd Allah, *'Alayhi al-Salam*, has said, 'Children of a Muslim man who dies can receive Zakat and al-Fitrah just as their father would receive, until they become adults and become knowledgeable of what their father was knowledgeable (believed in); they still can receive Zakat but if they become hostile, then Zakat is not given to them.'"

Chapter 32 - Preferences among the Recipients of Zakat

H 5882, Ch. 32, h 1

A number of our people have narrated from Sahl ibn Ziyad from Ahmad ibn Muhammad from ibn abu Nasr from 'Utaybah ibn 'Abd Allah ibn 'Ajlan al-Sakuniy who has said the following:

"I once asked abu Ja'far, *'Alayhi al-Salam*, about the case of my gifts, for keeping good relations, to my friends and how I should do it. He (the Imam) said, 'Give it to them on the basis of their migration to religion, intelligence and fiqh (proper understanding of Shari'ah).'"

H 5883, Ch. 32, h 2

Muhammad ibn 'Isma'il has narrated from al-Fadl ibn Shadhan from Safwan ibn Yahya and ibn abu 'Umayr all from 'Abd al-Rahman ibn al-Hajjaj who has said the following:

"I once asked abu al-Hassan, *'Alayhi al-Salam*, if in paying Zakat priorities, such as those asking and those not asking for help can be given preference among beneficiaries. He (the Imam) said, 'Yes, those beneficiaries who do not ask for help have priority over those who ask for help.'"

H 5884, Ch. 32, h 3

Ali ibn Muhammad has narrated from Ibrahim ibn Ishaq from Muhammad ibn Sulayman from 'Abd Allah ibn Sinan who has said the following:

"Abu 'Abd Allah, *'Alayhi al-Salam*, once said, 'Zakat for animals with hooves and Zakat of the cloven-footed ones are given to Muslims who maintain good-looking style but Zakat of gold, silver, and whatever is measured by measuring devices of what the earth produces is given to those who sit on dirt.' Ibn Sinan has said that he then asked, 'How has this become so? He (the Imam) said, 'It is because those who maintain beauty feel shy before people to ask, thus more beautiful of the two to people is given to them and the whole thing is charity (Zakat) (after all).'"

H 5885, Ch. 32, h 4

Ali ibn Ibrahim has narrated from his father from 'Isma'il ibn Marrar from Yunus from ibn abu 'Umayr from Ali ibn abu Hamzah who has said the following:

"I once asked abu Ibrahim, *'Alayhi al-Salam*, about a man who is required to pay Zakat in the amount of one thousand dirham. He distributes it and thinks to give a certain amount to a certain person but then for some reason he gives it to someone else. He (the Imam) said, 'It is not harmful.'"

H 5886, Ch. 32, h 5

Ali ibn Ibrahim has narrated from his father from certain persons of his people from 'Anbasah ibn Mus'ab who has said the following:

"I once heard abu 'Abd Allah, *'Alayhi al-Salam*, say, 'Once something was brought to the Holy prophet and he distributed it among the people of al-Suffah (the platform); but it was not enough and he gave it to special ones among them. The Holy prophet, was afraid of what might the others think. The Holy prophet came to them and said, 'I before Allah, most Majestic, most Glorious, apologize to you, O people of al-Suffah. Something was brought to us and we wanted to distribute it among you but it was not enough; so we gave it to special ones among you for fear of their impatience and dismay.'"

H 5887, Ch. 32, h 6

Ali ibn Ibrahim has narrated from his father from ibn abu 'Umayr from al-Husayn ibn 'Uthman from those whom he has mentioned who has said the following:

"Abu 'Abd Allah, or abu al-Hassan, *'Alayhim al-Salam*, about a man who keeps something for someone then for some reason gives it to someone else, has said, 'It is not harmful.'"

Chapter 33 - Preferences for Relatives and Those of Them to Whom Zakat Cannot Be Paid

H 5888, Ch. 33, h 1

A number of our people have narrated from Ahmad ibn Muhammad ibn 'Isa from Ali ibn al-Hakam from 'Abd al-Malik ibn 'Utbah from Ishaq ibn 'Ammar who has said the following:

"I once said to abu al-Hassan, Musa, *'Alayhi al-Salam*, that I pay Zakat to my relatives and give preference to certain ones among them over the others when it is time to pay Zakat. He (the Imam) asked, 'Are they deserving beneficiaries?' I replied, 'Yes, they deserve.' He (the Imam) said, 'They are better than others, you should give it to them.' I then asked, 'Who among them is the one to whom I must not pay as Zakat?' He (the Imam) said, 'They are your father and mother.' I then said, 'My father and mother!' He (the Imam) said, 'The parents and children.'"

H 5889, Ch. 33, h 2

Ahmad ibn Muhammad from has narrated from Ali ibn al-Hakam from Muthanna' from abu Basir who has said the following:

"Once someone asked him (the Imam) *'Alayhi al-Salam*, when I was hearing, saying, 'Can I pay Zakat to my relatives and they do not know (this belief)? He (the Imam) said, 'Do not pay Zakat to anyone who is not a Muslim, but give them from other things.' Abu 'Abd Allah, *'Alayhi al-Salam*, then said, 'Do you think that Allah has made just Zakat obligatory on one's assets? In fact, other things that Allah has made obligatory on one's assets are more than Zakat. You pay to relatives, to one who asks you and you pay as long as you do not know him to be hostile; but when you learn that he is hostile, then do not pay him anything unless you are afraid of his tongue, in which case you buy your religion and dignity from him.'"

H 5890, Ch. 33, h 3

A number of our people have narrated from Sahl ibn Ziyad from Ahmad ibn Muhammad ibn 'Isa from Ahmad ibn Muhammad from ibn abu Nasr who has said the following:

"I once asked al-Rida', *'Alayhi al-Salam*, about a man who has relatives, friends and followers who love `Amir al-Mu'minin, *'Alayhi al-Salam*, but they do not acknowledge the owner of this issue (one who possesses Divine Authority) if he can give Zakat to them. He (the Imam) said, 'No, he cannot give Zakat to them.'"

H 5891, Ch. 33, h 4

Muhammad ibn Yahya has narrated from Ahmad ibn Muhammad from al-Husayn ibn Sa'id from al-Nadr ibn Suwayd from Zur'ah ibn Muhammad from abu Basir who has said the following:

"I once asked abu 'Abd Allah, *'Alayhi al-Salam*, about a man who owes Zakat and has needy relatives who do not know (one who possesses Divine Authority). 'Can he give Zakat to them?' He (the Imam) said, 'No, he cannot give them and it is not an honor. He must not make Zakat to guard his assets. He can give them from his other assets if he likes.'"

H 5892, Ch. 33, h 5

Muhammad ibn Yahya has narrated from Muhammad ibn al-Husayn from Safwan ibn Yahya from 'Abd al-Rahman ibn al-Hajjaj who has said the following:

"Abu 'Abd Allah, *'Alayhi al-Salam*, has said, 'Zakat cannot be given to five kinds of people: father, mother, children, slaves, and one's wife, because they are one's dependents for whom one must provide sustenance.'"

H 5893, Ch. 33, h 6

Ahmad ibn Idris and others have narrated from Ahmad ibn Muhammad ibn Ahmad from Muhammad ibn 'Abd al-Hamid from abu Jamilah from Zayd al-Shahham who has said the following:

"Abu 'Abd Allah, *'Alayhi al-Salam*, has said, 'Zakat can be given to one's brother, sister, uncle, aunt (paternal and maternal); but it cannot be given to grandfather and grandmother.'"

H 5894, Ch. 33, h 7

Muhammad ibn Yahya and Muhammad ibn 'Abd Allah have narrated from 'Abd Allah ibn Ja'far from Ahmad ibn Hamzah who has said the following:

"I once asked abu al-Hassan, *'Alayhi al-Salam*, about a man who is one of your followers whose relatives all speak of you and he owes Zakat; can he pay all of his Zakat to them. He (the Imam) said, 'Yes, he can do so.'"

H 5895, Ch. 33, h 8

Muhammad ibn abu 'Abd Allah has narrated from Sahl ibn Ziyad from Ali ibn Mahziyar from who has said the following:

"I once asked abu al-Hassan, *'Alayhi al-Salam*, about a man who pays all of his Zakat to his relatives who have accepted you as their Waliy (one who possesses Divine Authority). He (the Imam) said, 'Yes, he can do so.'"

H 5896, Ch. 33, h 9

Muhammad ibn Yahya has narrated from Ahmad ibn Muhammad from 'Imran ibn 'Isma'il ibn 'Imran al-Qummiy who has said the following:

"I once wrote to abu al-Hassan, the third, *'Alayhi al-Salam*, and asked, 'I have children, men and women. Can I pay from Zakat anything to them?' He (the Imam) wrote to me, 'It is permissible for you.'"

H 5897, Ch. 33, h 10

Ahmad ibn Idris and others have narrated from Ahmad ibn Muhammad from certain persons of our people from Muhammad ibn Jazzak who has said the following:

"I once asked al-Sadiq, abu 'Abd Allah, *'Alayhi al-Salam*, 'Can I give one out of ten of my asset to the children of my daughter? He (the Imam) said, 'Yes, it is not harmful.'"

Chapter 34 - Rare Ahadith

H 5898, Ch. 34, h 1

A number of our people have narrated from Ahmad ibn Muhammad from al-Hassan ibn Mahbub from abu Muhammad al-Wabishiy who has said the following:

"Certain persons of our people asked abu 'Abd Allah, *'Alayhi al-Salam*, about a man who has purchased with money from Zakat of his assets his own father. He (the Imam) said, 'He has purchased the best slave and it is not harmful.'"

H 5899, Ch. 34, h 2

Rid has narrated from Muhammad ibn 'Abd al-Jabbar from Safwan ibn Yahya from Ishaq ibn 'Ammar who has said the following:

"I once asked abu 'Abd Allah, *'Alayhi al-Salam*, about a man whose father is indebted and has certain expenses; if he can give his father from his Zakat to pay his debts. He (the Imam) said, 'Yes, who is more deserving than his own father.'"

H 5900, Ch. 34, h 3

Ali ibn Ibrahim has narrated from his father from Hammad ibn 'Isa from Hariz from Zurarah who has said the following:

"I once said to abu 'Abd Allah, *'Alayhi al-Salam*, that there is a man whose father has died and he is indebted. Can he pay the debts on his father from Zakat he owes when the son has a great wealth? He (the Imam) said, 'If his father has left a legacy for him and then it is found out that there are debts on his father that he did not know on that day, he pays the debts from the whole legacy, but he does not pay it from his Zakat. However, if he did not leave any legacy then no one is more deserving of his Zakat than the debts of his father. If he pays off the debts of his father in such case it is acceptable (as payment of Zakat).'"

Chapter 35 - Sending Zakat from one Place to Other Places . . .

H 5901, Ch. 35, h 1

Ali ibn Ibrahim has narrated from his father from Hammad ibn 'Isa from Hariz from Zurarah from Muhammad ibn Muslim who has said the following:

"I once asked abu 'Abd Allah, *'Alayhi al-Salam*, about a man who sends his Zakat for distribution but it is lost. Is he held responsible until it is distributed? He (the Imam) said, 'If he had found a proper beneficiary and did not pay, he is held responsible until he pays it; but if he did not find proper beneficiary thus, sent it for distribution, he is not held responsible because it was out of his hand. So also is the case of the executor of a will who is held responsible for what is given to him when he finds the one to whom he was told to deliver and if he does not find, it is not his responsibility.'"

H 5902, Ch. 35, h 2

Hammad ibn 'Isa has narrated from Hariz from abu Basir who has said the following:

"Abu Ja'far, *'Alayhi al-Salam*, has said, 'If one takes out his Zakat and assigns it to be paid to a people but it is lost, or he sends it to them and it is lost, he is not held responsible.'"

H 5903, Ch. 35, h 3

Hariz has narrated from 'Ubayd ibn Zurarah who has said the following:

"Abu 'Abd Allah, *'Alayhi al-Salam*, has said, 'If one takes away Zakat from his assets but does not name the beneficiary and it is lost, he is free from his obligation.'"

H 5904, Ch. 35, h 4

Hariz has narrated from Zurarah who has said the following:

"I once asked abu 'Abd Allah, *'Alayhi al-Salam*, about a man whose brother sends his Zakat to distribute among beneficiaries but it is lost. He (the Imam) said, 'The messenger is not responsible as well as the payer.' I then asked, 'If he does not find the beneficiary and it is spoiled or changed, is he responsible?' He (the Imam) said, 'No, he is not responsible. However, if he knows a beneficiary for it and it is destroyed or damaged, then he is responsible until he pays it off.'"

H 5905, Ch. 35, h 5

Muhammad ibn Yahya has narrated from Ahmad ibn Muhammad from al-Hassan ibn Mahbub from Jamil ibn Salih from Bukayr ibn `A'yan who has said the following:

"I once asked abu Ja'far, *'Alayhi al-Salam*, about a man who sends his Zakat but it is stolen or destroyed. He (the Imam) said, 'He does not owe anything.'"

H 5906, Ch. 35, h 6

Ali ibn Ibrahim has narrated from his father from ibn abu 'Umayr from the one who reported to him from Durust from a man who has said the following:

"I once asked abu 'Abd Allah, *'Alayhi al-Salam*, about a man who sends his Zakat from one town to another town. He (the Imam) said, 'It is not harmful to send one-third or one-fourth (uncertainty is from narrator).'"

H 5907, Ch. 35, h 7

Muhammad ibn `Isma'il has narrated from al-Fadl ibn Shadhan from and Ali ibn Ibrahim has narrated from his father all from ibn abu 'Umayr from Hisham ibn Hakam who has said the following:

"I once asked abu 'Abd Allah, *'Alayhi al-Salam*, about a man who gives Zakat for distribution, if he can take a certain amount to another place? He (the Imam) said, 'It is not harmful.''

H 5908, Ch. 35, h 8

Ali ibn Ibrahim has narrated from his father from ibn abu 'Umayr from 'Umar ibn `Udhaynah from Zurarah from 'Abd al-Karim ibn 'Utbah al-Hashimiy who has said the following:

"Abu 'Abd Allah, *'Alayhi al-Salam*, has said that the Messenger of Allah would distribute Zakat of the Bedouins among the Bedouins and Zakat of the town dwellers among the town dwellers. He would not distribute it among them in equal amounts, instead he would distribute it among those present without considering anything definite about it.'"

H 5909, Ch. 35, h 9

A number of our people have narrated from Ahmad ibn Muhammad from al-Hassan ibn Ali from Wuhayb ibn Hafs who has said the following:

"Once we were with abu Basir when 'Amr ibn 'Ilyas came to him and said, 'O abu Muhammad, my brother from Halab has sent to me a certain amount of goods of Zakat so I distribute in al-Kufah, but it was looted on the way. Do you have any Hadith about it?' He said, 'Yes, I once asked abu Ja'far, *'Alayhi al-Salam*, about this issue and I did not think anyone would ever ask me about it. I said to abu Ja'far, *'Alayhi al-Salam*, I pray to Allah to keep my soul in service for your cause, a man sends his Zakat from one land to another land and it is looted on the way. He (the Imam) said, 'It is sufficient (as payment for Zakat) but if it was up to me I would pay it again.'"

H 5910, Ch. 35, h 10

Abu Ali al-Ash'ariy has narrated from Muhammad ibn 'Abd al-Jabbar from Safwan ibn Yahya from 'Abd Allah ibn Muskan from al-Halabiy who has said the following:

"Abu 'Abd Allah, *'Alayhi al-Salam*, has said, 'Zakat of immigrants (converts to piety and religion) is not lawful for Arabs and the charity (Zakat) of Arabs is not lawful for immigrants.'"

H 5911, Ch. 35, h 11

Muhammad ibn Yahya has narrated from Ahmad ibn Muhammad from al-Husayn ibn Sa'id from al-Nadr ibn Suwayd from Yahya ibn 'Imran from ibn Muskan from Durays who has said the following:

"Once al-Mada'iniy asked abu Ja'far, *'Alayhi al-Salam*, and said, 'There is Zakat on our assets. To whom should we pay it? He (the Imam) said, 'Pay it to the people of your Wilayah, people who believe in (the Divine Authority of `A'immah).' He said, 'There is no one of your followers.' He (the Imam) said, 'Send it to where they are found. Do not give it to a people who will not accept your call if you will call them tomorrow. This by Allah is slaughter, (an expression of concern about enemies of `A'immah).''

Chapter 36 - Zakat for Distribution by a Needy Person who Himself is Needy

H 5912, Ch. 36, h 1

Muhammad ibn Yahya has narrated from Ahmad ibn Muhammad from Ali ibn al-Hakam from Aban ibn 'Uthman from Sa'id ibn Yasar who has said the following:

"I once asked abu 'Abd Allah, *'Alayhi al-Salam*, about a man to whom Zakat is given for distribution, if he can take a certain amount for himself. He (the Imam) said, 'Yes, can do so.'"

H 5913, Ch. 36, h 2

Ali ibn Ibrahim has narrated from his father from ibn abu 'Umayr from al-Husayn ibn 'Uthman who has said the following:

"I once asked abu Ibrahim, *'Alayhi al-Salam*, about a man to whom Zakat is given for distribution among deserving beneficiaries, if he can take a certain amount for himself even though not anything is assigned for him. He (the Imam) said, 'He can take for himself like what he gives to another person.'"

H 5914, Ch. 36, h 3

Ali ibn Ibrahim has narrated from Muhammad ibn 'Isa from Yunus ibn 'Abd al-Rahman ibn al-Hajjaj who has said the following:

"I once asked abu al-Hassan, *'Alayhi al-Salam*, about a man to whom dirhams are given for distribution among deserving people and himself is a deserving person, if he can take a certain amount for himself. He (the Imam) said, 'It is not harmful to take like what he gives to the other persons. However, it is not permissible for him to take for himself if he is instructed to give it to definite causes, unless with the permission of the donator.'"

Chapter 37 - Recipient Can Use Zakat as His Own Property

H 5915, Ch. 37, h 1

Muhammad ibn Yahya has narrated from Ahmad ibn Muhammad from 'Uthman ibn 'Isa from Sama'ah who has said the following:

"Abu 'Abd Allah, *'Alayhi al-Salam*, has said, 'When a person receives Zakat it is like his own property and one can use it as one likes.' He (the Imam) then said, 'Allah, most Majestic, most Glorious, has made a share in the wealth of the wealthy people obligatory for the needy. The affluent people are not appreciated until they pay it. That share is Zakat. Once it (Zakat) reaches in the hands of the needy, it then becomes like his own property and he uses it as he likes for marriage or Hajj. Yes, it is his property.' I then asked, 'Can a needy person who performs Hajj from Zakat receive the reward for Hajj as the wealthy person receives?' He (the Imam) said, 'Yes, the needy receive the same amount of reward.'"

H 5916, Ch. 37, h 2

A number of our people have narrated from Ahmad ibn Muhammad from al-Husayn ibn Sa'id from al-Nadr ibn Suwayd from 'Asem ibn Humayd from abu Basir who has said the following:

"I once said to abu 'Abd Allah, *'Alayhi al-Salam*, that among our people there is a shaykh, called 'Umar. He asked 'Isa ibn 'A'yan for help because he is needy. 'Isa ibn 'A'yan said to him, 'There is Zakat with me, but I cannot give to you.' He asked for reason. 'Isa replied, 'I saw you buying meat and dates.' He said, 'I had earned one dirham. With two daniq, I bought meat and with two daniq, I bought dates and I returned with two daniq for some other things that I needed.' Abu 'Abd Allah, *'Alayhi al-Salam*, placed his hand on his forehead for a while, then raised his head then said, 'Allah, most Blessed, most High, looked at the wealth of the wealthy, then He looked at the poor people. He then assigned a share for the needy in the wealth of the wealthy, which will be sufficient for their needs. Had it (Zakat) not been sufficient (for the needs of the needy) He would have increased it. They (needy) must receive from Zakat what is sufficient for them to eat, drink, dress, marry, give charity and perform Hajj.'"

H 5917, Ch. 37, h 3

Muhammad ibn Yahya has narrated from Ahmad ibn Muhammad from Ali ibn al-Hakam from al-'Ala' ibn Razin from Muhammad ibn Muslim who has said the following:

"Once, a man asked abu 'Abd Allah, *'Alayhi al-Salam*, when I was sitting, 'I receive Zakat. Can I save it so I perform Hajj therewith? He (the Imam) said, 'Yes, you can do so and Allah gives reward to one who gives you Zakat.'"

Chapter 38 - A Person's Performing Hajj and so on with Zakat He Has Received

H 5918, Ch. 38, h 1

A number of our people have narrated from Ahmad ibn Muhammad from ibn abu 'Umayr from Jamil ibn Darraj from 'Isma'il al-Ash'ariy from al-Hakam ibn 'Utaybah who has said the following:

"I once asked abu 'Abd Allah, *'Alayhi al-Salam*, about a man who gives Zakat to a man to perform Hajj. He (the Imam) said, 'It is Zakat money and he performs Hajj!' I then said, 'It is a Muslim man who gives Zakat to a Muslim man.' He (the Imam) said, 'If he is needy, Zakat must be given to him for his needs and poverty, and one must not say to him to perform Hajj. It is up to him to use as he likes.'"

H 5919, Ch. 38, h 2

Ahmad ibn Muhammad from has narrated from Ali ibn al-Hakam from 'Amr from abu Basir who has said the following:

"I once asked abu 'Abd Allah, *'Alayhi al-Salam*, about a man who saves from Zakat five hundred or six hundred to buy a slave and set him free. He (the Imam) said, 'So he does injustice to another group of people.' He (the Imam) remained quiet for a while, then said, 'However, if the slave is a Muslim in great need, then he can buy and set him free.'"

H 5920, Ch. 38, h 3

Ali ibn Ibrahim has narrated from his father from ibn Faddal, from Marwan ibn Muslim from ibn Bukayr from 'Ubayd ibn Zurarah who has said the following:

"I once asked abu 'Abd Allah, *'Alayhi al-Salam*, about a man who wants to pay Zakat of his asset which is one thousand dirham but cannot find a deserving beneficiary. He then sees a slave for sale, buys him with those thousand dirhams, and sets him free. Was his act permissible? He (the Imam) said, 'Yes, it is permissible and it is not harmful.' I then said that when the slave is free he works in business and earns a great wealth; then he dies without anyone to inherit legally his legacy. Who will inherit his legacy? He (the Imam) said, 'The poor believers who are deserving beneficiaries of Zakat inherit him, because he was bought with their asset.'"

Chapter 39 - Loan Is Protection for Zakat

H 5921, Ch. 39, h 1

A number of our people have narrated from Ahmad ibn Muhammad from ibn Faddal and al-Hajjal from Tha'labah ibn Maymun from Ibrahim al-Sindiy from Yunus ibn 'Ammar who has said the following:

"I once heard abu 'Abd Allah, *'Alayhi al-Salam*, say, 'Lending a loan to a believer is a great gain which hastens reward. If he earns, he pays you back; but if he dies before paying, you can count it as payment of Zakat.'"

H 5922, Ch. 39, h 2

Ahmad ibn Muhammad from has narrated from Muhammad ibn Ali from Muhammad ibn Fudayl from Musa ibn Bakr who has said the following:

"Abu al-Hassan, *'Alayhi al-Salam*, has said that 'Amir al-Mu'minin Ali, *'Alayhi al-Salam*, would say, 'Lending a loan is protection for Zakat.'"

H 5923, Ch. 39, h 3

Ahmad ibn Muhammad from has narrated from his father from Ahmad ibn al-Nadr from 'Amr ibn Shimr from Jabir who has said the following:

"If one lends a loan to a man until he becomes able to pay back, his (lender's) money is in Zakat and he is in Salat (prayer) with the angels until the loan is paid back.'"

Chapter 40 - Offsetting Loan for Zakat

H 5924, Ch. 40, h 1

Muhammad ibn Yahya has narrated from Muhammad ibn al-Husayn Ahmad ibn Muhammad from Muhammad ibn 'Isma'il has narrated from al-Fadl ibn Shadhan from all from Safwan ibn Yahya from 'Abd al-Rahman ibn al-Hajjaj who has said the following:

"I once asked abu al-Hassan, the first, *'Alayhi al-Salam*, about the case of my loan on a people, who have delayed payment for a long time. They are not able to pay and they are deserving beneficiaries of Zakat. Can I count it as payment of my Zakat? He (the Imam) said, 'Yes, you can do so.'"

H 5925, Ch. 40, h 2

A number of our people have narrated from Ahmad ibn Muhammad from al-Husayn ibn Sa'id from his brother al-Hassan from Zur'ah ibn Muhammad from Sama'ah who has said the following:

"I once asked abu 'Abd Allah, *'Alayhi al-Salam*, about a man to whom another man owes a certain amount of loan who is poor to whom he wants to pay Zakat. He (the Imam) said, 'The poor may have something in his possession or potentials, which is equal in value to the amount of loan, such as certain effects like a house, household effects or a certain work that he performs. He (the lender) can offset the amount of Zakat that he owes against the loan that the poor person owes to him. It is not harmful. However, the poor person may not have any of the things mentioned like a house, household effects or a certain work for which he receives payment. He (the lender) cannot offset the amount of Zakat that he owes against the loan that the poor person owes to him; instead the lender must pay Zakat to him and not offset anything.'"

Chapter 41 - If One Runs Away With Zakat

H 5926, Ch. 41, h 1

Ali ibn Ibrahim has narrated from his father from Hammad from Hariz from 'Umar ibn Yazid who has said the following:

"I once asked abu 'Abd Allah, *'Alayhi al-Salam*, about a man who runs away from paying Zakat by means of buying a piece of land or a house, if he still owes any Zakat. He (the Imam) said, 'No, he does not owe any Zakat even if he turns his asset into jewelries and silver; there is not anything on him. However, what he has denied his soul by the virtue of paying Zakat is much more than what he has saved by means of holding back the right of Allah that could have existed in his asset.'"

Chapter 42 - Payment of Zakat from Properties not Subject to Zakat

H 5927, Ch. 42, h 1

Muhammad ibn Yahya has narrated from Ahmad ibn Muhammad ibn Khalid al-Barqiy who has said the following:

"I once wrote to abu al-Hassan, al-Thaniy, *'Alayhi al-Salam*, and asked him (the Imam) if it is permissible to pay Zakat which is due on grains, like wheat and barley and on gold by means of dirham in equal value or is it necessary to pay from the same substance on which Zakat is due? He (the Imam) answered, 'Whichever is available can be paid as Zakat.'"

H 5928, Ch. 42, h 2

Muhammad ibn Yahya has narrated from al-'Amrakiy ibn Ali from ibn Ja'far who has said the following:

"I once asked abu al-Hassan, *'Alayhi al-Salam*, about a man who pays Zakat due on dirham with dinar and Zakat which is due on dinar with dirham. He (the Imam) said, 'It is not harmful.'"

H 5929, Ch. 42, h 3

Muhammad ibn abu 'Abd Allah has narrated from Sahl ibn Ziyad from Ahmad ibn Muhammad from ibn abu Nasr from Sa'id ibn 'Amr who has said the following:

"I once asked abu 'Abd Allah, *'Alayhi al-Salam*, if a man with Zakat (that he owes) can buy clothes, al-Sawiq (prepared food), flour, melons and grapes and distribute it among the deserving people. He (the Imam) said, 'No, he cannot pay except by dirham which Allah, most Blessed, most High, has commanded.'"

Chapter 43 - Who Can Lawfully Receive Zakat and Who Cannot

H 5930, Ch. 43, h 1

Ali ibn Ibrahim has narrated from his father from Hammad ibn 'Isa from Hariz from abu Basir who has said the following:

"I once heard abu 'Abd Allah, *'Alayhi al-Salam*, say, 'One who has seven hundred has permission to receive Zakat if no one other than him can be found.' I then asked, 'Does the one who owns seven hundred owe Zakat? He (the Imam) said, 'His Zakat is charity for his dependents and he must not receive charity (Zakat) except if he depends on seven hundred and it finishes before the end of the year, in which case he can accept charity (Zakat). Zakat is not lawful for one who has a profession or something on which Zakat is due.'"

H 5931, Ch. 43, h 2

Hammad ibn 'Isa has narrated from Hariz ibn 'Abd Allah from Zurarah ibn `A'yan who has said the following:

"I once heard abu Ja'far, *'Alayhi al-Salam*, saying, 'Charity (Zakat) is not lawful for those who have an established profession or a resourceful one who is capable and strong, so keep yourselves clean from receiving charity (Zakat).'"

H 5932, Ch. 43, h 3

Ali ibn Ibrahim has narrated from his father from Bakr ibn Salih from al-Hassan ibn Ali from 'Isma'il ibn 'Abd al-'Aziz from his father from abu Basir who has said the following:

"I once asked abu 'Abd Allah, *'Alayhi al-Salam*, about the case of a certain person of our people who has eight hundred dirham, works with pumice, and has a large family to feed, if he can receive Zakat. He (the Imam) asked, 'O abu Muhammad, can he earn with his dirham the expenses of his family with a certain amount of saving?' I replied, 'Yes, he does.' He (the Imam) then asked, 'How much does he save?' I replied, 'I do not know.' He (the Imam) said, 'If his saving amounts to half of his expenses, he cannot receive Zakat, but if it is less than half of his expenses, it is lawful for him to receive Zakat.' I then asked, 'Is there any Zakat on his assets?' He (the Imam) said, 'Yes, there is Zakat on his assets.' I then asked, 'How will he deal with it?' He (the Imam) said, 'With that he meets his expenses for his family, for their food, drink and clothes, and if anything remains he can give to others and what he receives from Zakat is to raise the standard of the living of his family.'"

H 5933, Ch. 43, h 4

A number of our people have narrated from Ahmad ibn Muhammad from al-Husayn ibn Sa'id from his brother al-Hassan from Zur'ah ibn Muhammad from Sama'ah who has said the following:

"I once asked abu 'Abd Allah, *'Alayhi al-Salam*, about Zakat if it can be paid to one who has a house and servants. He (the Imam) said, 'Yes, unless his house is income-producing from which he earns dirham which is enough for his expenses and the expenses of his family. If such income is not enough for his expenses and the expenses of his family like food, clothes and their other needs without excessiveness; then Zakat is lawful for him, but if the income from the house is sufficient for their expenses, then Zakat is not lawful for him.'"

H 5934, Ch. 43, h 5

Muhammad ibn Yahya has narrated from Muhammad ibn al-Husayn from Safwan ibn Yahya from 'Abd al-Rahman ibn al-Hajjaj who has said the following:

I once asked abu al-Hassan, the first, *'Alayhi al-Salam*, about a man whose father or uncle or brother provides his expenses, if he can receive Zakat to facilitate himself further, in case they do not provide enough facilities in all the things that he needs? He (the Imam) said, 'It is not harmful.'"

H 5935, Ch. 43, h 6

From Safwan ibn Yahya has narrated from Mu'awiyah ibn Wahab who has said the following:

"I once asked abu 'Abd Allah, *'Alayhi al-Salam*, about a man who has three hundred or four hundred dirham. He has a family to feed and has a profession that he practices but he cannot earn his expenses. Is he required to restrict himself within what he earns, and not to receive Zakat, or that he can receive Zakat also. He (the Imam) said, 'No, he must use the extra (profit from his dirham not the capital) for his expenses and his dependents and receive the deficit from Zakat, use dirham in business and must not spend it.'"

H 5936, Ch. 43, h 7

Ali ibn Ibrahim has narrated from his father from ibn abu 'Umayr from 'Umar ibn `Udhaynah from more than one person who has said the following:

"Abu Ja'far, and abu 'Abd Allah, *'Alayhim al-Salam*, were asked if a man who has a house and servant can receive Zakat. He (the Imam) said, 'Yes, he can receive Zakat, because house and servant are not wealth.'"

H 5937, Ch. 43, h 8

Ahmad ibn Idris has narrated from Muhammad ibn 'Abd al-Jabbar from Safwan ibn Yahya from Ishaq ibn 'Ammar who has said the following:

"I once asked abu 'Abd Allah, *'Alayhi al-Salam*, about a man who has eight hundred dirham, his son has two hundred dirham. He has ten dependents to feed. He lives with difficulty and does not have any profession. He only uses his dirham as capital to earn his living. It remains idle for months. He uses his savings for his expenses. Do you consider it proper his taking from Zakat that he owes to spend and facilitate his dependents? He (the Imam) said, 'Yes, he can do so, but he must take it in the form of dirham.'"

H 5938, Ch. 43, h 9

A number of our people have narrated from Ahmad ibn Muhammad from al-Husayn ibn Sa'id from his brother al-Hassan from Zur'ah from Sama'ah who has said the following:

"Abu 'Abd Allah, *'Alayhi al-Salam*, has said, 'Sometimes it is lawful for one who has seven hundred dirham to receive Zakat but it is unlawful for one who has fifty dirham.' I then asked, 'How can that happen?' He (the Imam) said, 'Sometimes the owner of seven hundred may have a large family to feed and it is not enough for them, so he can exempt himself and receive Zakat for his family. Zakat can become unlawful for the owner of fifty if he is alone and has a profession. He works and earns enough, by the will of Allah.'"

H 5939, Ch. 43, h 10

Ali ibn Ibrahim has narrated from his father from `Isma'il ibn 'Abd al-'Aziz from his father who has said the following:

"Once, abu Basir and I visited abu 'Abd Allah, *'Alayhi al-Salam*, and abu Basir said to him (the Imam), 'We have a friend and he is a truthful person. He follows Allah's religion as we do.' He (the Imam) asked, 'Who is he, O abu Basir, whom you admire?' Abu Basir, replied, 'He is al-'Abbas ibn al-Walid ibn Sabih.' He (the Imam) then said, 'May Allah grant mercy to al-Walid ibn Sabih! What has happened to him, O abu Muhammad?' Abu Basir said, 'I pray to Allah to keep my soul in service for your cause, he has a house which is valued at four thousand dirham. He has a slave-girl and slave servant who provides water every day for two to four dirham minus feed for the camel and he has a family. Can he receive Zakat?' He (the Imam) said, 'Yes, he can receive Zakat.' Abu Basir said, 'But he has all these assets.' He (the Imam) said, 'O abu Muhammad, do you command me to command him to sell his house which is for his dignity and the place of his birth? Alternatively, must he sell his slave-girl who protects him from hot and cold weather and protects him and his wife's dignity? On the other hand, must he sell his slave and his camel, which are means for his living and expenses? In fact, he must receive Zakat and it is lawful for him. He does not have to sell his house, his slave or his camel.'"

H 5940, Ch. 43, h 11

A number of our people have narrated from Ahmad ibn Muhammad from al-Husayn ibn Sa'id from his brother Zur'ah from Sama'ah who has said the following:

"I once asked abu 'Abd Allah, *'Alayhi al-Salam*, about a man who has a certain number of dirham which he uses in business, Zakat has become obligatory on him and his savings are enough for the expenses of his family, like food and clothes but not for cooking curry. It is only for their food and clothes. He (the Imam) said, 'He waits for the Zakat of his assets, pays from it to the deserving beneficiaries a certain amount. What is left, he spends on his family to buy with it gravy curry for them and what is for their well being and food without excessiveness but he himself must not eat from it; because sometimes poor people act more excessively than affluent ones.' I then asked, 'How can that happen?' He (the Imam) said, 'Affluent people spend from what they earn, but poor people spend without earning.'"

H 5941, Ch. 43, h 12

A number of our people have narrated from Ahmad ibn Muhammad from al-Hassan ibn Mahbub from Mu'awiyah ibn Wahab who has said the following:

"I once said to abu 'Abd Allah, *'Alayhi al-Salam*, 'They narrate from the Holy prophet, "Charity (Zakat) is not lawful for the rich people, or resourceful strong ones."' Abu 'Abd Allah, *'Alayhi al-Salam*, said, 'It is not proper for the rich people.'"

H 5942, Ch. 43, h 13

Ali ibn Ibrahim has narrated from his father from ibn abu 'Umayr from Hammad ibn 'Uthman from al-Halabiy who has said the following:

"I once asked abu 'Abd Allah, *'Alayhi al-Salam*, about how much is paid to Zakat collector. He (the Imam) said, 'It is whatever the Imam deems proper. There is nothing definite about it.'"

H 5943, Ch. 43, h 14

Muhammad ibn 'Isma'il has narrated from al-Fadl ibn Shadhan from Safwan ibn Yahya from 'Abd al-Rahman ibn al-Hajjaj who has said the following:

"I once asked abu al-Hassan, *'Alayhi al-Salam*, about a man who is a Muslim and a slave and his owner is a Muslim man and he has a certain amount of asset from which he pays Zakat. The slave has a small child who is free. Can the master pay Zakat to the child of his slave? He (the Imam) said, 'It is not harmful.'"

H 5944, Ch. 43, h 15

Ali ibn Ibrahim has narrated from Muhammad ibn 'Isa from Dawud al-Sarmiy who has said the following:

"I once asked him (the Imam), *'Alayhi al-Salam*, if Zakat can be given to one who consumes wine. He (the Imam) said, 'No, Zakat cannot be given to such person.''

Chapter 44 - A Qualified Recipient Who Refuses to Receive Zakat

H 5945, Ch. 44, h 1

Muhammad ibn Yahya has narrated from Ahmad ibn Muhammad ibn 'Isa from al-Haytham ibn abu Masruq from al-Hassan ibn Ali from Marwan ibn Muslim from 'Abd Allah ibn Hilal ibn Khaqan who has said the following:

"I once heard abu 'Abd Allah, *'Alayhi al-Salam*, say, 'One who refuses to receive Zakat, when it is obligatory on him to receive is like one who refuses to pay Zakat when it is obligatory on him to pay.'"

H 5946, Ch. 44, h 2

A number of our people have narrated from Ahmad ibn abu 'Abd Allah from 'Abd al-'Azim ibn 'Abd Allah al-'Alaviy from al-Husayn ibn Ali from certain persons of our people who has said the following:

"Abu 'Abd Allah, *'Alayhi al-Salam*, has said, 'One who refuses to receive Zakat, when it is obligatory on him to receive is like one who refuses to pay Zakat when it is obligatory up on him to pay.'"

H 5947, Ch. 44, h 3

A number of our people have narrated from Sahl ibn Ziyad from Ahmad ibn Muhammad from ibn abu Nasr from 'Asem from Humayd from abu Basir who has said the following:

"I once asked abu Ja'far, *'Alayhi al-Salam*, about a man of our people who is a deserving beneficiary of Zakat but feels shy to accept Zakat. Can I pay him Zakat without mentioning that it is Zakat?' He (the Imam) said, 'Pay him and do not mention and you must not humiliate the believer.'"

H 5948, Ch. 44, h 4

Ali ibn Ibrahim has narrated from his father from Hammad from Hariz, from Muhammad ibn Muslim who has said the following:

"I once asked abu Ja'far, *'Alayhi al-Salam*, about a man who is needy and I send him charity (Zakat) but he does not accept as charity (Zakat); it causes him to be protective, shy and depressed. Can I give without the aspect of charity (Zakat) when it is charity (Zakat) from us?' He (the Imam) said, 'If it is Zakat he must accept it and if he does not accept it with the aspect of Zakat, then do not give it to him. It is not proper for him to be shy about what Allah, most Majestic, most Glorious, has made obligatory. It is only obligatory from Allah for him and he must not feel shy about it.'"

Chapter 45 - Harvest Time

H 5949, Ch. 45, h 1

Ali ibn Ibrahim has narrated from his father from ibn abu 'Umayr from Mu'awiyah ibn Shurayh who has said the following:

"I once heard abu 'Abd Allah, *'Alayhi al-Salam*, say, 'On plantation there are two rights. One is that for which one is held responsible and the other is that which one must give.' I then asked, 'What is the right for which I am held responsible and what is that which I must give?' He (the Imam) said, 'The one for which you are held responsible is one out of ten or one out of twenty and the one which you must give is because of the words of Allah, most Majestic, most Glorious, 'On the day of harvest give his right. . . .' (6:142) meaning your harvesting something after something.' I think he said, 'bale after bale until the end.'"

H 5950, Ch. 45, h 2

Ali ibn Ibrahim has narrated from his father from Hammad ibn 'Isa from Hariz from Zurarah, Muhammad ibn Muslim and abu Basir who has said the following:

"About the words of Allah, most Majestic, most Glorious, 'Give His right on the day of its harvest . . .,' (6:142) all of them have said that abu Ja'far, *'Alayhi al-Salam*, has stated this Hadith. 'It is of charity (Zakat) that which is given to the destitute, a bunch after bunch and from fruits handful after handful until all fruits are picked up from trees. The guard has a definite right, which is left for him of the trees. Palm trees like Mi'afarah and 'Umm Ja'rur are left alone. One, two or three trees are left for the guard because of his guarding.'"

H 5951, Ch. 45, h 3

A number of our people have narrated from Ahmad ibn Muhammad from al-Hassan ibn Ali al-Washsha' from 'Abd Allah ibn Muskan from abu Basir who has said the following:

"Abu 'Abd Allah, *'Alayhi al-Salam*, has said, 'Do not harvest or pick-up fruits during the night, do not offer sacrifice during the night, and do not sow seeds during the night. If you did so there will be no al-Qani' or al-Mu'tar (those who ask only once and those who ask many times).' I then asked, 'What is al-Qani' and al-Mu'tar?' He (the Imam) said, 'Al-Qani' is one who is satisfied when you give him and al-Mu'tar is one who passes by and asks you. If you harvest during the night the one asking will not come. This is mentioned in the words of Allah, most, High. "Give His right on the day of its harvest," at the time of harvest, bunch by bunch when you harvest, and when it is out give a handful after handful so also at the time of cutting and at the time of sowing the seed give from seed just as you give from the harvest.'"

H 5952, Ch. 45, h 4

Al-Husayn ibn Muhammad has narrated from Mu'alla' ibn Muhammad from al-Hassan ibn Ali from Aban from abu Maryam who has said the following:

"About the words of Allah, most Majestic, most Glorious, '. . . give His right on the day of harvest . . .,' (6:142) abu 'Abd Allah, *'Alayhi al-Salam*, has said this. 'It requires one to give on the day of harvest in bunches, then during threshing, then when it is measured in Sa', it (charity (Zakat)) is one out of ten or one out of twenty.'"

H 5953, Ch. 45. h 5

Muhammad ibn Yahya has narrated Ahmad ibn Muhammad from Ali ibn Hadid from Murazim from Musadif who has said the following:

"I once was with abu 'Abd Allah, *'Alayhi al-Salam*, on his land where they were harvesting and someone asking for help came. I said, 'Allah gives you.' He (the Imam) said, 'Wait. You cannot say that until you give him three times. When you give him three times thereafter if you give, it is for you, and if you stop giving him is also for you.'"

H 5954, Ch. 45. h 6

Muhammad ibn Yahya has narrated from Ahmad ibn Muhammad from ibn abu Nasr who has said the following:

"I once asked abu 'Abd Allah, *'Alayhi al-Salam*, about the words of Allah, most Majestic, most Glorious, '. . . give His right on the day of harvest and do not be wasteful . . . ' (6:141). He (the Imam) said, 'My father would say that wastefulness in harvest and picking up fruits is giving the beggars with both hands. When people asking for help would come and if my father had seen the slaves give them charity with both hands, he called them and told them to give with one hand a handful after handful and a bunch after bunch of the ears of wheat.'"

Chapter 46 - Zakat of Tax Payers

H 5955, Ch. 46, h 1

Ali ibn Ibrahim has narrated from his father from Hammad ibn 'Isa from Hariz from Zurarah who has said the following:

"I once asked abu 'Abd Allah, *'Alayhi al-Salam*, about al-Jizyah (taxes paid by a non-Muslim taxpayer) of the people of the book. Is there anything definite, which does not change? He (the Imam) said, 'It is up to the Imam. He may receive from every one of them what he decides which they can afford in proportion to their assets. They have been spared their lives and from being exiled by their agreement to pay taxes; so al-Jizyah is received from them in proportion of their assets to the limit that they can afford to pay until they become Muslims. Allah, most Blessed, most High, has said, '. . . until they pay al-Jizyah with their hands with humbleness. How can they be humble if what they pay is negligible to them? Such payment must make them feel humiliated so that they accept Islam.' Ibn Muslim has said that I asked abu 'Abd Allah, *'Alayhi al-Salam*, about what they (rulers) receive as one-fifth from land of al-Jizyah, from the farmers per head. Is there anything in definite amounts?' He (the Imam) said, 'It was just that much which they had agreed to pay. Imam has no other choice but to receive al-Jizyah. He (the Imam) can assign it per head and not their assets or vice versa.' I then asked, 'What is the rule about this al-Khums (one-fifth)?' He (the Imam) said, 'This is how the Messenger of Allah had settled with them.''

H 5956, Ch. 46, h 2

Hariz has narrated from Muhammad ibn Muslim who has said the following:

"I once asked him (the Imam), *'Alayhi al-Salam*, about the case of non-Muslim taxpayers as to how much must they pay for the protection of their lives and properties. He (the Imam) said, 'It is al-Kharaj. If they pay al-Jizyah per head, then there is not anything on their land and if it is taken from their land, then there is not anything on them to pay per head.'"

H 5957, Ch. 46, h 3

Ali ibn Ibrahim has narrated from his father from and Muhammad ibn Yahya has narrated from Ahmad ibn Muhammad from Muhammad ibn Yahya all from 'Abd Allah ibn al-Mughirah from Talhah ibn Zayd who has said the following:

"Abu 'Abd Allah, *'Alayhi al-Salam*, has said, 'It is an established Sunnah that al-Jizyah is not received from those with physical or mental conditions.'"

H 5958, Ch. 46, h 4

Muhammad ibn Yahya has narrated from Ahmad ibn Muhammad from abu Yahya al-Wasitiy from certain persons of our people who has said the following:

"Once abu 'Abd Allah, *'Alayhi al-Salam*, was asked about the case of Zoroastrians if they had a prophet. He (the Imam) said, 'Yes, they had a prophet. Have you not heard about the letter of the Messenger of Allah to the people of Makkah? He asked them to accept Islam, otherwise, war is declared against you. They wrote back to the Messenger of Allah asking him to receive al-Jizyah and leave them to worship their idols. The Holy prophet wrote to them, 'I receive al-Jizyah only from the people of the book.' They then wrote to him (the Messenger of Allah) to rebut him, 'You think that you do not receive al-Jizyah except from the people of the book and then receive al-Jizyah from Majus (Zoroastrians) who have migrated.' The Holy prophet wrote to them, 'Majus had a prophet but they killed him. They had a book, which they burnt. Their prophet brought them a book on twelve thousand skins of bull.'

H 5959, Ch. 46, h 5

Ali ibn Ibrahim has narrated from his father from Hammad ibn 'Isa from Hariz from Muhammad ibn Muslim who has said the following:

"I once asked abu 'Abd Allah, *'Alayhi al-Salam*, about the case of al-Jizyah of taxpayers and what is received from them from their wine or flesh of pigs and dead animals. He (the Imam) said, 'They must pay al-Jizyah which is due on their assets from the flesh of pigs and the value of their wine. Whatever is received from them, its sin is upon them, and its value is lawful for the Muslims which they receive as al-Jizyah.'"

H 5960, Ch. 46, h 6

A number of our people have narrated from Sahl ibn Ziyad from Ahmad ibn Muhammad from ibn abu Nasr from ibn abu Ya'fur who has said the following:

"Abu 'Abd Allah, *'Alayhi al-Salam*, has said, 'al-Jizyah is not terminated (abolished) from lands subject to al-Jizyah. Al-Jizyah is a gift for the immigrants and charity (Zakat) is for its deserving beneficiaries whom Allah has named in His book. They do not have any share in al-Jizyah.' He (the Imam) then said, 'How vast is Allah's justice!' He (the Imam) then said, 'People will become rich if justice is practiced among them, the skies send their sustenance and the earth will produce its blessings by the permission of Allah, most High.'"

H 5961, Ch. 46, h 7

Muhammad ibn Yahya has narrated from Ahmad ibn Muhammad from al-Hassan ibn Mahbub from Muhammad ibn Muslim who has said the following:

"I once asked abu 'Abd Allah, *'Alayhi al-Salam*, about the case of people who pay al-Jizyah, if there is al-Jizyah on their assets and animal farms. He (the Imam) said, 'No, al-Jizyah is not due on them as such.'"

Chapter 47 - Rare Ahadith

H 5962, Ch. 47, h 1

Ali ibn Ibrahim has narrated from his father from `Isma'il ibn Marrar from Yunus from 'Abd Allah ibn Sinan who has said the following:

"Abu 'Abd Allah, *'Alayhi al-Salam*, has said, 'It is not harmful if a man passes by fruits and eats from them but does not destroy them. The Messenger of Allah prohibited building walls in al-Madinah because of people passing by.' He (the Imam) said, 'When dates ripened, he (the Messenger of Allah) would command to make openings in the walls for the people passing by.'"

"Muhammad ibn Yahya has narrated from Ahmad ibn Muhammad from al-Hassan ibn Mahbub from Khalid ibn Jarir from abu al-Rabi' al-Shamiy from abu 'Abd Allah, *'Alayhi al-Salam*, a similar Hadith except that he (the Imam) said, '. . . does not destroy and does not carry.'"

H 5963, Ch. 47, h 2

Ahmad ibn Idris and others has narrated from Muhammad ibn Ahmad from Ali ibn al-Rayyan from his father from Yunus or one other than him from those whom he has mentioned who has said the following:

"I once said to abu 'Abd Allah, *'Alayhi al-Salam*, 'I pray to Allah to keep my soul in service for your cause, I have heard that you had done certain things about the produce of the farm in 'Ayn Ziyad (name of a certain oasis) and I like to hear it from you.' He (the Imam) said, 'Yes, I would command at the time fruits ripened to open gaps in the walls so people could come in to eat. I would command every day to arrange ten platforms, on each of which ten people could sit. As soon as the ten finished eating, the other ten would come and every one received a handful (mud) a certain measurement, of dates. I would command the neighbors of the property, every one of them, old man, old woman, children, people suffering from illness, women and those who were not able to come; everyone may eat one mud (a certain measurement). When it was time to pick fruits I paid the guards, agents and men who were hired to carry what was left to al-Madinah. I distributed among the people of the houses and the deserving people two or three rahilah (camel-load) or less or more, proportionate to their deservingness. I earned four hundred dinar and its gross income was four thousand dinar.'"

H 5964, Ch. 47, h 3

Ali ibn Muhammad ibn 'Abd Allah has narrated from Ahmad ibn abu 'Abd Allah from Ali ibn Muhammad al-Qasaniy from those who narrated to him from 'Abd Allah ibn al-Qasim al-Ja'fariy from his father who has said the following:

"When fruits ripened the Holy prophet would command to open gaps in the walls (of the gardens for people passing by).'"

End of Volume three of al-Kafi according to this edition followed by Volume four that begins with chapters on charities

Printed in Great Britain
by Amazon

18120932R00302